Energy Policy

Timely Reports to Keep
Journalists, Scholars and the Public
Abreast of Developing Issues, Events and Trends

April 1979

CONGRESSIONAL QUARTERLY INC.
1414 22ND STREET, N.W., WASHINGTON, D.C. 20037

Congressional Quarterly Inc.

Congressional Quarterly Inc., an editorial research service and publishing company, serves clients in the fields of news, education, business and government. It combines specific coverage of Congress, government and politics by Congressional Quarterly with the more general subject range of an affiliated service, Editorial Research Reports.

Congressional Quarterly was founded in 1945 by Henrietta and Nelson Poynter. Its basic periodical publication was and still is the CQ *Weekly Report,* mailed to clients every Saturday. A cumulative index is published quarterly.

The CQ *Almanac,* a compendium of legislation for one session of Congress, is published every spring. *Congress and the Nation* is published every four years as a record of government for one presidential term.

Congressional Quarterly also publishes paperback books on public affairs. These include the twice-yearly *Guide to Current American Government* and such recent titles as *Urban America: Politics and Problems; Taxes, Jobs and Inflation* and *U.S. Defense Policy: Weapons, Strategy and Commitments.*

CQ Direct Research is a consulting service which performs contract research and maintains a reference library and query desk for the convenience of clients.

Editorial Research Reports covers subjects beyond the specialized scope of Congressional Quarterly. It publishes reference material on foreign affairs, business, education, cultural affairs, national security, science and other topics of news interest. Service to clients includes a 6,000-word report four times a month bound and indexed semiannually. Editorial Research Reports publishes paperback books in its fields of coverage. Founded in 1923, the service merged with Congressional Quarterly in 1965.

Editor: Margaret Thompson.
Major Contributors: Ann Pelham, Bob Rankin, Elder Witt. **Contributors:** Harrison H. Donnelly, Edna Frazier, Barry M. Hager, Carolyn Teague, James R. Wagner.
Indexer: Diane Huffman.
Art Director: Richard Pottern.
Production Manager: I. D. Fuller. **Assistant Production Manager:** Maceo Mayo.

Book Department Editor: Patricia Ann O'Connor.

Library of Congress Cataloging in Publication Data

Congressional Quarterly, Inc.
    Energy policy.

    Bibliography: p.
    Includes index.
    1. Energy Policy — United States.   2. Power resources — Law
and legislation — United States.
I. Title.
KF2120.C66 1979   343'.73'092   77-25243
ISBN 0-87187-122-X

Table of Contents

Appendix

Editor's Note

Six years after the Arab oil embargo of 1973-74 brought abut a world energy crisis, shortages and high prices still threatened to disrupt the economy of the United States and other nations.

Coping with the need to curtail America's huge energy appetite and its dependence on costly oil imports while seeking to increase the use of alternative sources of energy posed a major challenge to President Carter during his first term in office.

Energy Policy examines the response of the administration and Congress to the increasingly critical energy situation. The book includes chapters on the omnibus energy bill that cleared Congress in fall 1978 after a two-year effort; creation of a new Department of Energy; and passage of bills establishing regulations for offshore oil drilling and strip mining. Controversies surrounding oil imports and domestic oil pricing, utility rate reform, coal conversion and the nuclear licensing process are also discussed.

Other chapters focus on an examination of efforts to augment the Strategic Petroleum Reserve, a program to stockpile oil for use in emergencies established in 1975; concern about the safe disposal of nuclear and uranium wastes; and experimentation with the use of gasohol, a blend of gasoline and alcohol, in automobiles. The pros and cons of gas rationing and the potential for increasing natural gas supplies from Alaska as well as imports from Canada and Mexico are also included.

An appendix contains a chronology of major legislation in the energy field during the years 1973-78. There is also a selected bibliography.

Introduction

Three months after his inauguration, Jimmy Carter appeared on national television to make a dramatic appeal. "Tonight I want to have an unpleasant talk with you about a problem unprecedented in our history," he said. "With the exception of preventing war, this is the greatest challenge our country will face during our lifetimes. The energy crisis has not yet overwhelmed us, but it will if we do not act quickly. . . .

"Our decision about energy will test the character of the American people and the ability of the president and the Congress to govern this nation. This difficult effort will be the 'moral equivalent of war' — except that we will be uniting our efforts to build and not to destroy."

Two days later, on April 20, 1977, the new president unveiled his response to that challenge — a complex legislative package largely reliant upon tax measures to foster conservation of energy and an extensive shift from oil to coal and, to a lesser extent, other sources.

Carter made clear that he considered the energy program to be the cardinal proposal of his first year, if not of his entire presidential term. Its unveiling was followed by a media and lobbying blitz intended to gain rapid congressional approval, including a televised speech to a joint session of Congress on April 20 and a televised news conference on April 22.

Yet despite the administration's efforts, it took almost two years for Congress to pass an energy bill. And the legislation that finally cleared on the last day of the second session of the 95th Congress (Oct. 15, 1978) not only was drastically rewritten but promised to have little effect on the way Americans produced and consumed increasing quantities of energy.

Indeed, by 1979, the energy crisis loomed larger than it had when Carter assumed office. Energy consumption in the United States had continued to grow in 1978, increasing two percent over 1977 consumption. About half of that energy was provided by oil and about 45 percent of that was imported at increasingly high prices. To make matters worse, the civil war in Iran had brought that country's exports (about five million barrels a day to the noncommunist world; the United States had been importing 900,000 barrels a day from Iran, or about five percent of U.S. supplies) virtually to a halt in December 1978, and there was little chance that full production in the country could resume until late 1979.

Added to this problem was the December 1978 decision by the 13-member oil-producing cartel, the Organization of Petroleum Exporting Countries (OPEC), to increase prices by 14.49 percent in 1979, which would bring the price to $14.542 a barrel by the end of the year. However, in March 1979, OPEC members announced a further price hike of nine percent.

The ramifications for the U.S. economy of the impending (or existing, as some observers felt) energy crisis were widespread and unsettling. America's dependence on costly foreign oil imports — amounting to $42.7 billion in 1978 — fueled inflation and could lead to increased unemployment and a slower growth rate or even recession in the nation's economy. Oil imports accounted for a substantial share of the U.S. trade and balance of payments deficit and contributed significantly to the decline in the dollar's value with respect to other currencies.

All of these factors led Energy Secretary James R. Schlesinger to warn in February 1979 that the situation was "prospectively more serious" than the Arab oil embargo of 1973-74. However, other administration officials and some economists questioned the severity of the crisis, and there was skepticism among the general public as well.

Administration Options

U.S. energy officials estimated in early 1979 that the country's share of the international oil shortage — estimated at about 2 million barrels a day — could rise to 800,000 from 500,000 barrels a day by the end of the year. To cope with the anticipated shortage and increased prices of oil imports, the administration could take a number of measures. These included:

● Decontrolling the price of domestically-produced oil to encourage conservation and to bring up U.S. oil prices to the world level. Under the 1975 Energy Policy Act, the president would gain powers to raise oil prices without congressional approval on June 1, 1979. On April 5, Carter announced plans for gradual decontrol.

● Raising the price of gasoline. On March 2, 1979, the Energy Department announced it was putting into effect a regulation that would allow oil companies to increase gasoline prices. The impact, said Schlesinger Feb. 28, could mean that the price of unleaded gasoline could rise to $1 a gallon in a year.

● Instituting gasoline rationing and mandatory energy conservation measures. On Feb. 27, the administration requested congressional approval of emergency standby authority to ration gasoline, restrict weekend gas sales, ban decorative lighting and impose lower thermostat settings.

Congress had 60 days to accept or reject each plan. If accepted, either chamber would have 15 days to veto any move to put the plan into effect.

● Substituting natural gas for oil and seeking other sources of imported energy. In February, the United States and Mexico agreed to begin negotiations to increase the latter's oil and gas exports to the United States. In March, Canada also agreed to increase its natural gas exports to this country.

● Promoting the regional transfers of electricity, known as wheeling, to make better use of peak generation.

● Beefing up the Strategic Petroleum Reserve, a program to stockpile oil supplies in emergencies established by Congress in 1975.

● Revising laws governing the licensing of nuclear power plants to speed up the process, thereby increasing the use of nuclear power as an alternative energy source.

● Requiring oil-fueled power plants to shift to coal, where feasible.

● Relaxing environmental controls by allowing additives to gasoline, slowing the scheduled reduction of lead in gasoline, allowing the burning of higher-sulfur fuel oil and modifying restrictions on the strip mining of coal.

● Mandatory allocations of supplies of crude oil to refineries so that all would have an equitable share. The Energy Department Jan. 9, 1979, issued standby crude oil allocation rules, which were published in the *Federal Register* Jan. 16, 1979. The program, which had four phases, was designed to spread supplies among refiners.

● Mandatory allocations of gasoline and other products from oil companies to dealers. This program was published in the *Federal Register* Jan. 18, 1979.

● Increasing Alaskan oil and gas production. Alaska's North Slope contains some 26 trillion cubic feet of proven gas reserves. In addition to increasing gas production, Alaska's daily oil output could be increased to 2 million barrels from 1.2 million.

● More emphasis on alternative energy sources, including solar energy, conversion of coal to liquids or solids and promoting the use of gasohol — a blend of gasoline and alcohol — in automobiles.

● Reducing public and private demand for energy. On-going conservation efforts — such as the 55 mile-per-hour speed limit, car pooling and voluntary controls on thermostats — could be intensified.

Obstacles to Action

But most of these alternatives had their drawbacks and promoted considerable debate. An increase in domestic oil prices conflicted with the president's efforts to stem inflation and might not lead to the increased oil production that the administration predicted.

Gasoline rationing drew complaints from a wide variety of interest groups worried about the impact restrictions on gasoline use could have on their business. And many argued that a rationing program would be a costly bureaucratic nightmare to establish and run.

Nuclear licensing reform was bound up with concern over nuclear waste disposal, nuclear power plant safety and public doubt about the government's ability to store safely the toxic wastes created by nuclear plants.

Conversion from oil to coal was costly and fraught with environmental and health dangers. In addition, there was the question whether the industry could expand its output to meet an increased demand — particularly in view of labor problems as evidenced by numerous wildcat strikes and by the three-month long walkout by the United Mine Workers in the winter of 1977-78.

Environmentalists objected to relaxing strip mining controls as well as restrictions on automobile and industry pollution. They also were opposed to opening more federal lands in Alaska to oil and gas exploration. (Another difficulty in increasing Alaskan oil was that it could not be transported from pipelines on the West Coast to the East economically or easily.)

The administration's desire to beef up the Strategic Petroleum Reserve was questioned sharply by many in Congress. As of early 1979, the $25 billion program was more than a year behind schedule, with only about 70 million barrels of crude oil stored (the president had wanted 250 million barrels stored by the end of 1978) and with no pumps in place to extract the oil.

Other forms of alternative energy supplies were being held up by the high costs of development and skirmishes over the way the money would be distributed.

Finally, although the United States and Mexico agreed to begin negotiations on increasing the latter's oil and gas production and exports, negotiators had to tackle the touchy issue of agreeing on a price for Mexican natural gas. Moreover, Mexican President José López Portillo said that in order to avoid social and economic disruptions, his government would not permit Mexico's wells to pump more than 2.3 million barrels of oil and gas a day (in early 1979, Mexican production was 1.5 million daily) until at least 1982.

Although many energy experts have said that the world was not running out of oil, they have predicted that unless consumption were curtailed and other energy sources developed, nations could find themselves faced with the inability to obtain needed oil at affordable prices. And this could lead to a world depression.

Responding to the impending crisis, members of the International Energy Agency — composed of 20 leading Western industrial nations — agreed March 2, 1979, to cut back their oil imports by 2 million barrels a day, or about five percent of their current consumption. The decision was reached at a two-day meeting in Paris of the governing board of the agency, which was called into existence in the wake of the 1973-74 oil crisis. Assistant Secretary of State for Economic Affairs Richard Cooper said the United States would shoulder about half of the cutback, or about five percent of U.S. consumption, which was running almost 20 million barrels daily.

1978 Energy Bill

The administration's 1977 plan to confront the energy problem was massive and ambitious. It was designed to save energy by raising the price of fuel through taxes on crude oil, gas guzzling cars and business and industrial users of oil and natural gas. Other proposals included switching industrial oil or natural gas users to coal, raising federal price controls on natural gas and extending controls to intrastate gas.

Lobbyists and critics soon began dissecting the proposals, charging the administration had overestimated the plan's energy conservation, had failed to give producers incentives to find new energy supplies and had assured thousands would lose their jobs. Carter responded with statements decrying the special interests who were trying to dismantle his plan and leave the country without an energy policy.

The House cooperated with most of the administration plan, but the Senate in 1977 rejected most of it and proceeded to write its own plan, forcing a conference on two widely divergent methods of dealing with the energy crisis.

The five-part energy package that finally cleared Congress in October 1978 contained only remnants of Carter's original tough proposals. However, the president continued to fight for the watered-down plan, calling it his top legislative priority. When it was finally passed, Carter said, "We have declared to ourselves and the world our intent to control our use of energy and thereby to control our own destiny as a nation."

Mandatory Conservation Plans

But despite the president's statement hailing passage of the legislation, the measure could not quickly end the energy problems plaguing the nation. Faced with continuing oil and gasoline supply shortages, the administration in February 1979 sent to Congress a set of emergency energy contingency plans giving the president standby authority to impose mandatory thermostat settings, restrict weekend gas sales and advertising lighting, and institute a gas rationing plan. If Congress accepted the plans, they could remain active for only nine months. To extend them would require a new finding of a severe supply disruption.

With the exception of the gasoline rationing plan — which the Energy Department described as the last step to be taken "only in the event of a severe gasoline shortage" — the mandatory conservation measures were developed by the department's Economic Regulatory Administration on the basis of the following criteria:

● No plan could be based on the use of rationing, taxes, tariffs, user fees, pricing mechanisms for petroleum products or tax credits or deductions. This restriction was included in the Energy Policy and Conservation Act and eliminated use of a tax-rebate system, a tax on gasoline, an electricity bill surcharge or other similar measures.

● Plans had to be capable of rapid payoff. Two factors led to this requirement: the desire to respond quickly to an emergency and the requirement of the policy and conservation act that no contingency plan remain in effect more than nine months.

● Plans had to be enforceable by federal authorities, even though state and local officials would be asked to assist.

● There had to be significant potential for reducing energy demand.

● No measure could impose an undue hardship on any sector of the economy. This criterion was also a requirement of the act, which required that restrictions on energy use not impose "an unreasonably disproportionate share of such burden on any specific class of industry, business or commercial enterprise or any individual segment thereof."

● No plan could deal with more than one logically consistent subject matter, according to the 1975 law.

Carter April 5 Energy Message

In a nationally televised speech April 5, 1979, President Carter announced a gradual end to controls on domestic oil prices and asked Congress to tax the "huge and undeserved windfall profits" that oil companies would reap from the action. Lifting the controls, Carter said, was the best way to encourage energy conservation and production. "Each one of us will have to use less oil and pay more for it," he said, calling decontrol a "painful step."

The president proposed a variety of measures designed to reduce dependence on foreign oil. "Our national strength is dangerously dependent on a thin line of oil tankers stretching halfway around the earth" to the Persian Gulf, Carter warned. He called on Americans to drive less and support other conservation efforts, such as controls on thermostats. The nation's energy problem is "serious — and it's getting worse," Carter said. "There is no single answer. We must produce more. We must conserve more."

But his boldest move was the plan to let the price of oil rise. Decontrol would be phased in starting June 1, when existing law gave the president new authority over prices. That law automatically ends all controls in 1981.

The oil price decontrol proposal was coupled with an excess profits tax, the proceeds of which would go to low-income families to help with higher energy costs; to mass transit programs; and to a new "energy security fund" for research and development.

Carter also announced several moves to help make more energy supplies available. They included:

● Reduction of red tape delaying pipelines and other energy projects.

● Expedited approval of permits for the Standard Oil Company of Ohio (Sohio) pipeline from California to Texas. The administration would support federal preemption of state laws holding up the pipeline.

● Increased production from federal lands, including private exploration of the National Petroleum Reserve in Alaska, a move that required congressional approval.

● Removal of restrictions on the export of Alaskan oil to provide flexibility for securing energy supplies.

Other plans included: waiver of fees on crude oil imports, about 21 cents a barrel at the time; tightening of tax credits to oil companies drilling in foreign countries (legislation was required); and a one-year delay in a rule, scheduled to go into effect Oct. 1, 1979, which would require the lead content in gasoline to average less than .5 grams per gallon. The standard instead would be .8 grams a gallon. The administration said the delay would prevent loss of 350,000 barrels a day.

Legislative Outlook

In addition to considering the president's emergency energy contingency plans and his oil decontrol and tax measures — all of which were highly controversial — the 96th Congress would have to contend with other unpopular and complex issues that were unlikely to be resolved in one or two years. They included the problem of safely storing radioactive nuclear waste, the role of the government in developing new energy sources and the possibility of instituting mandatory rationing to conserve energy. One of the most volatile issues facing the nation in 1979 concerned the future of nuclear power. The March 28, 1979, accident at the Three Mile Island nuclear plant near Harrisburg, Pa., as well as the closing of five other plants earlier in the year, cast a broad shadow over public and congressional acceptance of a wider role for nuclear power in the nation's energy mix.

Margaret Thompson
April 1979

1978 Energy Bill: The End of an Odyssey

The determined Democratic leadership of the House, stubbornly wearing down opponents in the wee hours of the morning, presented President Carter with a five-part energy package on Sunday, Oct. 15, 1978.

The vote was held up by a 15-hour filibuster by Senate opponents. But at 7:30 a.m. sleepy House members cast the final vote on the five-part package and cleared it for the president. The vote was 231-168.

The legislation passed by Congress contained only remnants of the tough plan originally presented by Carter in April 1977, that would have raised gasoline taxes, increased the price of domestic crude oil through taxes and revamped electric rate-making. Carter wanted to force Americans to curb their profligate energy consumption, which required the United States to import about 8 million barrels of oil per day. That figure represented about 45 percent of the current consumption rate of 18.2 million barrels per day.

But Congress, worried about the political repercussions of higher prices and buffeted by intense lobbying from industry and other interest groups, chipped away at Carter's plan. The gasoline tax, for example, was dropped early, and the Senate defeated the key element — a tax on domestic crude oil to raise prices to world levels.

Generally, the legislators chose to encourage conservation rather than penalize waste.

The decision-making spawned some of the bitterest fights in years, with members allied or divided by region, by party, by ideology. An example of the depth of the split was the 207-206 House vote Oct. 13 by which members chose to keep the controversial natural gas pricing bill in a package with the four other more popular parts of the bill.

Although the plan had been watered down, Carter and Energy Secretary James R. Schlesinger continued to fight for it, learning new ways to persuade politicians in the process. When the bill was finally passed, 18 months after it was proposed, Carter said, "We have declared to ourselves and the world our intent to control our use of energy and thereby to control our own destiny as a nation."

Import Savings

Just exactly what effect the energy bill would have was the subject of some dispute. A primary goal of Carter's original plan was to cut oil imports, which the White House projected would be between 11.5 million and 16 million barrels per day by 1985, without new legislation. The plan was to use a combination of conservation, increased production and substitution of coal for oil and gas to keep 1985 imports at 4.5 million barrels less than projected.

But Congress rewrote the original proposal. The tax section, for example, which accounted for 43 percent of the savings projected by the White House, was substantially changed by Congress. Though Carter wanted to force industry to switch from oil and gas to coal, Congress provided only encouragement, but no punishment if industries chose not to comply. Carter also wanted stiff penalties for gas guzzling cars, but Congress weakened the penalties.

As those and other provisions were dropped or softened, the natural gas pricing section became the most controversial part of the bill. Carter had wanted to continue regulation, extending federal price controls to gas sold within producing states. The House agreed with Carter, but the Senate voted for deregulation of prices. The protracted conference between the two houses threatened the future of the entire energy package. But the administration and a few congressional negotiators finally came up with an agreement that doubled the price of newly discovered gas by 1985, when controls would be lifted.

The natural gas bill originally had not been counted on by Carter to contribute to savings of imported oil. But Department of Energy figures released after final passage predicted savings of from 1 million to 1.4 million barrels of oil per day from the natural gas provisions.

Total savings in imported oil from the legislation were estimated by the administration to range from 2.39 to 2.95 million barrels of oil per day by 1985.

Highlights of Energy Package

Natural Gas (HR 5289 — PL 95-621). Prices of newly discovered natural gas were allowed to rise about 10 percent a year until 1985, when the price controls would be lifted. Special pricing categories were set up to make industrial users pay the brunt of the higher prices until the cost reached a certain level, when residential users were to assume more of the burden. Some price controls were extended for the first time to gas produced and sold within the same state.

Carter originally had proposed that price controls be extended to the gas sold within producing states with the general philosophy that gas, an ideal residential fuel, be saved for that purpose by switching industrial and utility users to other fuels.

Coal Conversion (HR 5146 — PL 95-620). New industrial and utility plants were required to be built to use coal or a fuel other than oil or gas. Existing utility plants using oil or gas were to switch to other fuels by 1990, and the energy secretary could order some industries, on a case-by-case basis, to switch fuels. But he could also exempt utilities and companies from the requirements if certain conditions, such as an inadequate supply of coal, existed.

Carter had proposed a stiff tax on industrial use of oil and gas that would have given gas users an incentive to convert to coal, but Congress dropped that tax.

Utility Rates (HR 4018 — PL 95-617). State utility commissions and other regulatory agencies were required to consider the use of energy-saving methods, such as pricing electricity lower in off-peak hours to avoid heavy loads in the middle of the day and discontinuing discounts for large volume users. The energy secretary was authorized to intervene in the regulatory proceedings to argue for energy-saving measures.

Carter had wanted state agencies to be required to follow certain federal guidelines in rate-making in order to

ENERGY BOXSCORE

A chart detailing House and Senate action on key parts of President Carter's energy program follows.

The dates given for approval of the various pieces reflect final floor votes. The dates for rejection of programs are the days on which floor votes on the questions were taken or when committee reports were issued that did not contain those Carter proposals.

Carter Energy Proposal	House Action	Senate Action	Conference	Final Action
Tax credits for home insulation (HR 5263)	Approved August 5, 1977	Approved Oct. 31, 1977	Maximum $300 credit approved and conference report filed Oct. 12, 1978	Senate and House passed conference report Oct. 15, 1978
Boost in gasoline tax	Rejected Aug. 4, 1977	Rejected by Finance Committee Oct. 21, 1977		
Tax on "gas guzzling" cars (HR 5263)	Approved Aug. 5, 1977	Rejected; ban on their production approved instead Sept. 13, 1977, as part of HR 5037	Approved and conference report filed Oct. 12, 1978	Senate and House passed conference report Oct. 15, 1978
Rebate of "gas guzzler" tax to buyers of gas saving cars	Rejected by Ways and Means Committee June 9, 1977	Not considered		
Mandatory energy efficiency standards for home appliances (HR 5037)	Approved Aug. 5, 1977	Approved Sept. 13, 1977	Approved Oct. 31, 1977; conference report filed Oct. 10, 1978	Senate passed conference report Oct. 9, 1978; House passed conference report Oct. 15, 1978
Extention of natural gas price controls, with higher price ceiling (HR 5289)	Approved Aug. 5, 1977	Rejected; approved ending federal price controls for new gas Oct. 4, 1977	Agreement to end federal price controls on new natural gas by 1985, reached May 24, 1978; conference report filed Aug. 18	Senate passed conference report Sept. 27, 1978; House passed conference report Oct. 15, 1978
Tax on crude oil (HR 5263)	Approved Aug. 5, 1977	Rejected by Finance Committee Oct. 21, 1977	Killed by conference	
Tax on utility and industrial use of oil and natural gas (HR 5263)	Approved, weaker than Carter plan Aug. 5, 1977	Approved, but weaker than House or Carter plan Oct. 31, 1977	Killed by conference	
Authority to force utility, industrial conversion from oil, gas to coal (HR 5146)	Approved Aug. 5, 1977	Approved, but weaker than House version Sept. 8, 1977	Compromise reached Nov. 11, 1977; conference report filed July 14, 1978	Senate passed conference report July 18, 1978; House passed conference report Oct. 15, 1978
Reform of electric utility rates (HR 4018)	Approved Aug. 5, 1977	Rejected by Finance Committee Sept. 19, 1977	Compromise reached Dec. 1, 1977; conference report filed Oct. 6, 1978	Senate passed conference report Oct. 9, 1978; House passed conference report Oct. 15, 1978

save energy. But Congress, arguing that the states should continue to oversee the utilities, refused to make it mandatory to follow the guidelines.

Conservation (HR 5037 — PL 95-619). Utilities were required to give customers information about energy conservation devices such as insulation and storm windows. Though the utility could not sell the devices or install them, the utility could arrange for the installation and allow customers to pay for the improvements through utility bills. Direct loans from utilities to consumers of up to $300 were allowed.

Over the next three years, schools and hospitals were to receive $900 million to install energy-saving equipment. Grants and government-backed loans would be available to low-income families for home conservation investments. Mandatory efficiency standards were authorized for 13 major home appliances, including refrigerators, furnaces and water heaters, with the standards to take effect in the mid-1980s.

Carter's original proposal had called for a more aggressive role for utilities and mandatory conservation standards for new residential and commercial buildings. But, generally, this was the least controversial of the five parts and came through Congress relatively intact.

Taxes (HR 5263 — PL 95-618). Homeowners and businesses would get tax credits for installing energy-saving devices in their buildings. Homeowners were eligible for a credit of 15 percent on the first $2,000 spent on insulation or other devices, for a maximum of $300. Investment in solar, wind or geothermal energy equipment made the homeowner eligible for a tax credit of up to 30 percent on the first $2,000 and 20 percent on the next $8,000, for a total maximum credit of $2,200.

A 10 percent investment credit was made available to businesses that installed specified types of energy conservation equipment. The bill also provided tax incentives for companies that produced synthetic fuels from coal or other resources.

Cars that used fuel inefficiently, known as gas guzzlers, were to be taxed to discourage manufacture and purchase. Starting with 1980 models, new cars getting less than 15 miles per gallon (mpg) would be taxed $200. The tax and mileage standards would increase every year so that by 1986, cars getting less than 12.5 mpg would be taxed $3,850.

Taxes on 1986 models would apply to all cars getting less than 22.5 mpg.

The administration had wanted the gas guzzler tax to start on 1978 models averaging less than 18 miles per gallon, with the first year penalty ranging from $52 to $449. And by 1986, Carter wanted to be taxing heavily any car that got less than 27.5 miles per gallon.

Central to Carter's original energy proposal were taxes on industrial use of oil and gas, a wellhead tax on domestically produced crude oil to bring the price to world levels and authority to add a tax of five cents per gallon of gasoline each year through 1989 if gasoline consumption exceeded target levels. All of those proposals were dropped by Congress, which emphasized tax credits instead.

Major Provisions

NATURAL GAS PRICING

As cleared by Congress, HR 5289:

Title I — Wellhead Pricing

Price Controls. Established a scaled ceiling price for "new" gas starting at $1.75 per million British thermal units (MMBtu's) as of April 20, 1977 — the date Carter proposed his energy program.

● Provided that the initial price would rise monthly to cover inflation as measured by the gross national product (GNP), plus .2 percent, plus another 3.5 percent, until April 1981; and plus 4 percent thereafter, instead of 3.5 percent.

● Defined new natural gas found onshore to include gas from 1) new wells at least 2.5 miles from a "marker" well — one producing commercial quantities of gas between Jan. 1, 1970, and April 20, 1977; 2) a new well with a bottom depth 1,000 feet below the nearest and deepest well bottom within 2.5 miles; 3) a newly drilled onshore reservoir.

● Defined "new" offshore gas to include gas from new leases or from new reservoirs in old leases.

● Excluded from the "new" category 1) gas located "behind the pipe" — in an untapped reservoir adjacent to a well being drilled; 2) gas "withheld" from production; 3) gas from Alaska's Prudhoe Bay.

● Provided that new wells in old onshore reservoirs would draw a new ceiling price of $1.75 per MMBtu and would increase at a rate equal to inflation. Some of this gas would be deregulated by 1985.

● Provided that all other interstate gas would draw a ceiling price of $1.45 per MMBtu as of April 20, 1977, and that price would rise by the GNP inflation rate.

● Provided that gas sold under existing intrastate contracts would draw a new price equal to the contract price or the new gas ceiling price, whichever was lower.

● Directed that gas sold under an interstate contract that expired — a "rollover" contract — was eligible to draw the higher price between the applicable "just and reasonable" standard under existing law (the Natural Gas Act — PL 75-690), or $.54 per MMBtu.

● Provided that gas sales under expiring intrastate contracts would get the contract price or $1 per MMBtu, whichever was higher.

● Provided that all gas sold under rollover contracts would draw price increases equal to inflation.

● Specified that certain categories of "high cost" gas would be deregulated about one year after enactment.

● Included in that category gas 1) from wells deeper than 15,000 feet; 2) from geopressurized brine; 3) from coal seams; 4) from Devonian shale; and 5) produced under conditions determined by the Federal Energy Regulatory Commission (FERC) to pose unusual risks or costs.

● Provided that gas produced from "stripper" wells — those producing on average not more than 60 thousand cubic feet (Mcf) per day — would draw an initial ceiling price of $2.09 per MMBtu, which would rise according to a special monthly inflation formula.

● Specified that state severance taxes were not to be considered part of any ceiling prices set by the act.

Decontrol. Eliminated federal price controls as of Jan. 1, 1985, on 1) new natural gas; 2) deep new onshore wells; and 3) existing intrastate contracts over $1 per MMBtu as of Dec. 31, 1984.

● Provided that either the president or Congress could reimpose controls for one 18-month period.

● Specified that the authority to reimpose price controls existed only from July 1, 1985, until June 30, 1987.

● Provided that either the House or Senate could veto the president's decision to reimpose controls, but that both houses would have to act together to reimpose controls.

Title II — Incremental Pricing

● Required FERC to develop within 12 months of enactment an incremental pricing rule for industrial boiler fuel facilities. The rule would define which low priority gas consumers would bear the increased costs of gas disproportionately to ease the impact on high priority gas users.

● Directed FERC to develop a second incremental pricing rule within 18 months of enactment that would broaden the application to more low priority users.

● Specified that the second incremental pricing rule would be subject to veto by either house of Congress.

Energy Bill Imported Oil Savings

(Thousands of barrels of oil equivalent per day)

Legislation	Projected Savings by 1985
Conservation (HR 5037)	
Building improvements/appliance standards	410
Automobile, truck fuel efficiency standards*	265
Utility rate reform (HR 4018)	0 to 160
Natural gas pricing** (HR 5289)	1,000 to 1,400
Coal conversion (HR 5146)	300
Energy taxes (HR 5263)	
Residential credits for conservation	225
Crude oil tax (rejected by Congress)	0
Gasoline taxes (rejected by Congress)	0
Gas guzzler tax	80
Business credits for conservation	110
Total	***2,390 to 2,950

*Assumed that penalties set in the Energy and Policy Conservation Act for makers of gas guzzling cars would be raised to the maximum level of $10 for each tenth of a mile a car exceeded the national fleetwide average fuel consumption rate. By 1985 that standard would be 27.5 miles per gallon.

**The range depended on the degree to which increased use of natural gas displaced use of oil. Domestic natural gas, for example, could displace imported liquified natural gas, instead of oil.

***The administration projected that, without the legislation, oil imports in 1985 would range from 11.5 million to 16 million barrels of oil per day.

SOURCE: Department of Energy

• Directed that any costs that could be passed along to low priority users under the incremental pricing rules be placed in a special account. Incrementally priced users would have to pay the higher gas costs until their gas expenses equalled the cost of substitute fuels.

• Required FERC to determine what the competitive cost of substitute fuels would be, on a regional basis.

• Directed that once an incrementally priced industrial facility reached the price level for gas equal to that of an alternative fuel, the pass-through of higher gas costs to that facility would be limited to the amount necessary to keep it at the alternative fuel price.

• Required distributors to pass through the higher gas costs to incrementally priced industrial facilities instead of rolling the extra charges into all consumer rates.

• Exempted from incremental pricing 1) certain small industrial boiler fuel facilities; 2) specific agricultural uses; 3) residences; 4) small commercial uses; 5) schools; 6) hospitals and other institutions, and 7) electric utilities.

• Empowered FERC to provide other exemptions subject to congressional review.

• Provided that existing gas imports would be exempted from incremental pricing.

• Required distributors to roll Alaska's Prudhoe Bay gas into general consumer rates. (Conferees gave this subsidy to Alaskan gas development, the report explained, "because they believed that private financing of the pipeline [to be built to move the Alaskan gas] would not be available otherwise.")

Title III — Emergency Authority

• Authorized the president to declare natural gas emergencies.

• Authorized the president to authorize any interstate pipeline or local gas distributor to make emergency purchases of gas under short term contracts.

• Authorized the president in emergencies to allocate supplies to meet high priority needs.

• Provided that gas could not be allocated until the emergency sales option had been exhausted.

• Barred the president from taking gas from one class of users in one state to give to the same class of users in another state.

• Required compensation for allocated gas.

• Authorized FERC to allow interstate pipelines to move gas for intrastate pipelines or distributors, and vice versa.

Title IV — Curtailment

• Specified that in the event of gas curtailment, the last uses to be curtailed would be residences, small commercial uses, schools, hospitals and like institutions, and other uses when the energy secretary determined that curtailment to them would endanger life, health or property maintenance.

• Specified that certain agricultural uses would have priority after the uses spelled out above.

• Specified certain industrial processes or feedstock uses would hold the next curtailment priority.

Title V — Administration

• Provided FERC with general rule making authority.

• Authorized the state or federal agency with regulatory jurisdiction over gas production to determine the category for which a given well qualified.

• Authorized FERC to review agency decisions.

• Provided both civil and criminal penalties for violations of the act.

• Gave the energy secretary power to intervene in state proceedings concerning gas production.

• Provided judicial review authority modeled on that under the existing Natural Gas Act.

Title VI — Coordination with Existing Law

• Reserved to states the right to mandate lower price ceilings than provided by the act.

COAL CONVERSION

As cleared by Congress, HR 5146 had seven titles:

Title I — Goals, Definitions

The first title set forth the act's purpose and defined key terms.

Among its purposes was to cut oil imports and stimulate use of coal and other plentiful substitute fuels to save dwindling supplies of oil and gas. One key definition specified that regulatory orders in the measure applied to existing utility plants or major fuel burning installations only if they burned fuel at rates of at least 100 British thermal units (Btu's) per hour or more. A British thermal unit is the amount of heat required to raise the temperature of one pound of water by one degree Fahrenheit at or near 39.2 degrees Fahrenheit.

New utility power plants or major fuel burning facilities were defined as those on which construction began or which were acquired after April 20, 1977, the date Carter proposed his energy program. New plants were subject to different terms than existing ones in some sections of the proposed law.

Title II — New Facilities

Title II flatly barred new electric power plants and new major fuel burning installations from burning oil or natural gas as their primary energy source. It also directed that all new power plants be built with the capability to burn coal or another alternate fuel instead of oil or gas.

The title also gave the energy secretary power to issue rules prohibiting broad categories of new major fuel burning installations from burning oil or gas in uses other than boilers. The secretary further was empowered to prohibit on a case-by-case basis the burning of oil or gas for uses other than boilers in new major fuel burning installations.

Temporary Exemptions. Temporary exemptions of up to five years could be granted for use of gas or oil. The burden of proving worthiness for an exemption would be on the applicant. Temporary exemptions could be won if:

● The applicant demonstrated that coal or other substitute fuels would be inadequate or unreliable.

● The plant site were physically incapable of adjusting to use of alternate fuels.

● Environmental constraints required the continued use of oil or gas.

● The applicant could show he would be in compliance with the act at the end of the exemption period by using synthetic fuels.

● The secretary determined the exemption would be in the public interest.

Permanent Exemptions. Permanent exemptions could be granted if it were shown that:

● Coal or other alternative fuels would not be available throughout the useful life of the facility.

● The use of coal or other fuels would preclude the obtaining of capital.

● State or local laws precluded compliance, except those laws passed solely to allow the plant to escape the act.

● The facilities were to use cogeneration technology.

● Gas or oil were to be used in mixture with coal or other fuel substitutes.

● Gas or oil were required for emergency operation, with the secretary to define what constituted an emergency.

● A permanent exemption were necessary to assure reliable service.

● A new power plant were to be used as a "peakload" facility, i.e., used only when customer demand on the power system was at defined "peak" levels.

Permanent exemptions also could be won for new plants:

● To be used as "intermediate" load facilities for use of oil only, subject to specific conditions.

● For which the use of coal or other fuels would not be feasible technically due to special needs to ensure product quality.

● That required gas- or oil-fired units to cover their operations during specially scheduled equipment outages.

Condition on Exemptions. Section 213 of Title II required that before granting any temporary or permanent exemptions — except in the case of fuel mixture and peakload exemptions — the secretary had to find that use of a mixture of oil and coal or other fuels was not economically or technically feasible.

Title III — Existing Facilities

Existing electric power plants were prohibited from burning natural gas after Jan. 1, 1990, except under rigidly defined circumstances. Power plants that did not use gas as a primary fuel during 1977 were prohibited from converting to its use.

Existing electric power plants that burned gas were prohibited from consuming more of it than they burned on average between 1974 and 1976.

Existing electric power plants awaiting judgment on petitions for continued use of gas, which were filed prior to Jan. 1, 1990, could continue to use gas pending the outcome of their petitions.

The energy secretary was empowered to order oil or gas burning power plants or existing major plant facilities, which by design were capable of burning coal or other fuels, to cease burning oil or gas. But the burden of proof that the plants could burn substitute fuels would be on the government.

Exemptions. A full range of temporary and permanent exemptions, like those available for new power plants and industrial facilities, were available subject to conditions similar to those for existing plants.

In addition, temporary exemptions to prohibitions on oil or gas use were available to existing plants if the secretary were convinced the plant would later comply by use of innovative technologies, or if the plant were due to be retired within certain time restrictions.

Similarly, permanent exemptions were available under the same kinds of conditions as for new plants and if the plant were to use liquid natural gas and the appropriate federal or state environmental agency certified that coal use there would violate environmental laws.

Also, before any exemptions could be granted for existing plants, the secretary would have to be satisfied that fuel mixtures could not be used.

Title IV — Other Prohibitions, Authorities

The energy secretary was empowered to prohibit the use of natural gas in new or existing boilers used for space heating if the boiler consumed as much as 300,000 cubic feet of gas per day and could run on oil.

Decorative Lighting. The measure prohibited new outdoor decorative lights fueled by natural gas and empowered the secretary to prohibit gas pipeline and distribution companies from delivering gas to residential, commercial or industrial customers for such purposes. Existing residential and municipal outdoor gas lights had to comply by Jan. 1, 1982.

The gas lamp ban could be exempted for lights on memorials or in areas of historical significance upon petition to the secretary from appropriate federal, state, or local government agencies or historic associations.

Civil penalties for violations of the gas lamp ban would be assessed against the local gas distribution company up to $500 per lamp, and up to $500 per day to a maximum $5,000 for industrial violators.

Emergency Powers. The president was authorized to allocate coal, to order any plant to cease burning oil or gas and to suspend the terms of the law in time of severe energy supply emergencies, as defined in existing law or as he declared. Presidential orders under such emergency powers would be for the extent of the emergency or 90 days, whichever was less.

Title V — System Compliance Option

This title was designed to ease the transition from oil and gas dependence for utility systems, such as those in southwestern states, that were almost entirely dependent upon natural gas to fuel their plants.

Under Title V, such utilities would have the option of submitting compliance plans by Jan. 1, 1980, identifying their gas-dependent plants and outlining how they planned to comply with the mandatory phase-out of natural gas boiler fuel consumption by 1990. The plan would have to include commitment not to build new baseload capacity electric power plants that used oil or gas as their primary fuels. The utility also would have to pledge, in lieu of all other exemptions under the act, to phase all gas-fired power plants into only peak or intermediate load use by Jan. 1, 1995, and into peakload use only by the end of 1999. The secretary could extend the 1999 date five years under criteria for peakload or emergency exemptions.

Title VI — Financial Assistance

Title VI provided that when a governor declared an area of his state to be impacted because of development of coal or uranium, the federal government could provide cash grants to ease the impact, subject to conditions.

The governor would have to demonstrate to the energy secretary's satisfaction that:

● The development had increased employment directly over the past year by 8 percent or was projected to do so by at least that much annually for the next three years.

● The increase would require substantial public facilities such as schools and roads.

● State and local governments could not handle the financial burden.

Once an area was designated an energy impacted area, the secretary of agriculture could give 100 percent planning grants to affected states or localities to help plan how to cope with the development's impact. Land for public facilities or housing also could be acquired with such funds.

The legislation authorized $60 million for fiscal 1979 and $120 million for fiscal 1980 to cover program costs.

Pollution Control Loans. Section 602 authorized loans for existing power plants to finance the cost of installing pollution control devices required to burn coal under the act. The measure authorized $400 million for such purposes in both fiscal 1979 and 1980.

Title VII — Administration

Title VII dealt with promulgation of rules under the act, provided judicial review rights and listed enforcement provisions and penalties for violations. Penalties ranged up to one year in prison and a $50,000 fine for each criminal violation and up to $25,000 for each civil violation.

The act authorized $1.9 million for the program in fiscal 1978.

Title VIII — Miscellaneous Provisions

Title VIII combined a series of miscellaneous provisions. Among them was an authorization for $100 million for rehabilitation of branch line railroads to enable them to better carry coal. The money would go to the Railroad Rehabilitation and Improvement Fund.

UTILITY RATES

As cleared by Congress, HR 4018:

● Required that, within three years of enactment, each state utility commission or non-regulated electric company consider, with appropriate public hearings, implementation of the following federal standards for rate making on a utility-by-utility basis:

1) Setting of rates to reflect the actual cost of providing electric service to each class of consumers.

2) Prohibition of the use of "declining block rates" under which the cost of electricity decreased as consumption increased, unless the block rates reflected actual costs.

3) Use of "time-of-day" rates that reflected the cost of providing power at peak hours, when all power plants and back-up facilities were in use, versus the cost of power at off hours.

4) Use of "seasonal" rates when different seasons of the year affected the costs of providing electricity.

5) Use of "interruptible" rates when the cost of providing power was less when service could be interrupted.

6) Offering of other "load management techniques" to consumers when they would be practicable, cost effective, reliable and provide useful management advantages to the utility.

● Provided that if the state commissions did not comply voluntarily, the Department of Energy or any affected rate payer could request the commission to consider those standards. If intervention was denied, the department could seek an order for compliance from a federal court.

● Required each commission, within two years of enactment and to the extent deemed appropriate by each commission, to: 1) prohibit or restrict master metering, 2) adopt procedures to review automatic adjustment clauses, 3) adopt procedures to prohibit rate discrimination against solar, wind or other small power systems, 4) adopt procedures to provide consumer information, 5) prohibit charging rate payers for advertising and 6) adopt procedures to protect rate payers from abrupt termination of service.

● Required each state utility commission, within one year of enactment and annually thereafter, to report to the Department of Energy on its progress in considering and putting those standards into effect.

● Required the Department of Energy, within 18 months of enactment and annually thereafter, to report to the president and Congress its analysis of those commission reports and recommendations for further federal laws.

● Provided that if a consumer "substantially contributed" at "significant financial hardship" to a proceeding in which he prevailed, then the utility would have to compensate the consumer for reasonable costs incurred in the intervention.

● Provided that state commission actions on the standards would be subject to review in state courts only, not federal courts, except as existing federal law guaranteed the right to appeal to the U.S. Supreme Court.

● Authorized grants of $58 million each in fiscal 1979 and 1980 for states to use in implementing the rate reforms, with most funds to be spent on additional personnel.

● Authorized the Federal Energy Regulatory Commission (FERC) to order utilities to interconnect their facilities and to exchange energy supplies, subject to tests of reasonableness and judicial review.

● Authorized FERC to order a utility to "wheel" power from one supplier to another, subject to tests of reasonableness.

● Required FERC to review for up to one year the potential advantages of utility pooling of resources and to report to the president and Congress on its findings.

• Provided for disclosure of interlocking relationships between the top officials of public utilities and the top officials of banks, energy companies and related industries.

• Established an Office of Public Participation within FERC.

• Required that the energy secretary study and report on gas utility rate procedures within 18 months of enactment.

• Authorized the federal government to provide loans for up to 90 percent of the cost of feasibility studies for small hydroelectric projects on existing dams.

• Authorized government loans of up to 75 percent of the costs of such projects, subject to certain conditions.

• Required the interior secretary to expedite his review of and recommendations on crude oil transportation systems.

• Authorized the president, in emergency situations, to prohibit power plants from burning natural gas to generate electricity when the plant had the capability to burn petroleum products.

CONSERVATION

As cleared by Congress, HR 5037:

• Required that gas and electric utilities inform their customers of available energy-saving measures and offer to inspect homes to point out other energy saving steps.

• Required utilities to offer to arrange for financing and installation of home energy conservation improvements, such as insulation and storm windows, and allowed utilities to make direct loans of up to $300 for such improvements unless prohibited from doing so by state law.

• Allowed customer costs for insulation and other home energy conservation measures to be paid through utility bills, regardless of who installed them.

• Authorized the Department of Energy to spend up to $200 million in each of fiscal years 1979 and 1980 for weatherization grants to low-income families, with grants limited to $800 for the costs of materials for each home, except in certain cases. To qualify, a family's income could not exceed 125 percent of the national poverty level.

• Authorized the Government National Mortgage Association (GNMA) to purchase $3 billion in loans from commercial lenders to provide subsidized low interest loans for energy conservation improvements to families whose income was below the median income for their area.

• Authorized GNMA to purchase an additional $2 billion in loans, provided the energy secretary decided the purchase was necessary, to provide loans at market rates for energy conservation improvements by households with incomes above the poverty level.

• Authorized GNMA to purchase up to $100 million in loans to provide loans at market rates to homeowners for purchase and installation of solar energy systems.

• Authorized $295 million in fiscal 1979 and $400 million in fiscal 1980 for grants to schools and hospitals for energy conservation improvements. The grants would be distributed according to population, with consideration also given to such factors as area climate and costs of fuel. No single state could receive more than 10 percent, and each would receive at least 0.5 percent, of the total appropriated.

• Doubled the maximum penalty assessed an automaker whose fleet had an average fuel efficiency below the national standard set in the Energy Policy and Conservation Act of 1975 (PL 94-163). The penalties could be raised as high as $10, up from $5, per car for each tenth of a mile in excess of the average.

• Provided that the penalty could be increased if the transportation secretary found the increased fine would result in substantial energy savings in future auto production and would not increase unemployment, hurt competition or increase automobile imports.

• Required the Energy Department to set mandatory energy efficiency standards for 13 major home appliances, with the effective date not later than the mid-1980s. Appliances covered were refrigerators, furnaces, room and central air conditioners, water heaters, freezers, dishwashers, clothes washers and dryers, home space heaters, television sets, kitchen ranges and ovens, humidifiers and dehumidifiers.

• Authorized spending $100 million through fiscal year 1980 for demonstrations in federal buildings of solar heating and cooling technology.

• Authorized spending $98 million through fiscal year 1981 to acquire and operate photovoltaic solar electric systems to provide energy needs of federal agencies.

TAXES

As cleared by Congress, HR 5263:

Title I — Residential Credits

Insulation. Provided a nonrefundable income tax credit of 15 percent of the first $2,000 (maximum $300) spent by homeowners to install insulation and other specified energy-conserving improvements at their principal residence.

• Provided the credit would be available for expenditures made between April 20, 1977, and before Jan. 1, 1986.

• Provided that credits would carry over for two years, through Jan. 1, 1988, if the credit exceeded the amount of tax the homeowner owed.

• Specified that credits for expenditures made in 1977 would be claimed, along with 1978 credits, on 1978 tax returns and that the carryover would apply only to taxes owed in 1978.

• Provided that the credit would be available for expenditures made for insulation, furnace replacement burners for cutting fuel consumption, flue opening modifications, furnace ignition systems to replace gas pilot lights, storm or thermal windows or doors, automatic energy-saving setback thermostats, caulking or weather stripping, meters displaying the cost of energy usage or other items specified in regulations by the energy secretary.

Solar. Provided a nonrefundable credit of 30 percent of the first $2,000 and 20 percent of the next $8,000 — for a total maximum of $2,200 — for homeowners who installed solar, wind or geothermal energy equipment in their principal residences.

• Provided the credit would be available for expenditures made between April 20, 1977, and Dec. 31, 1985.

• Provided a credit carryover if the credit exceeded the amount of taxes owed by the homeowner and specified that the carryover would apply through taxable years ending before Jan. 1, 1988.

• Specified that credits for expenditures made in 1977 would be claimed, along with 1978 credits, on 1978 tax returns and that the carryover would apply only against taxes owed in 1978.

• Specified that the credit would apply to "passive" as well as "active" solar systems. "Passive" refers to building design while "active" means the use of mechanical devices, such as fans.

Title II — Transportation

Gas Guzzler Tax. Imposed a "gas guzzler tax" on the sale by the manufacturer of passenger cars — beginning with model year 1980 — that used fuel inefficiently, with certain exceptions for ambulances, police cars and other emergency vehicles.

• Set the taxes as follows:

1) For model year 1980, taxes ranged from $550 for cars that got less than 13 miles per gallon (mpg) to $200 for cars that got at least 14 mpg but less than 15 mpg.

2) For model year 1981, taxes ranged from $650 for cars that got less than 13 mpg to $200 for cars that got at least 16 mpg but less than 17 mpg.

3) For model year 1982, taxes ranged from $1,200 for cars that got less than 12.5 mpg to $200 for cars that got at least 17.5 mpg but less than 18.5 mpg.

4) For model year 1983, taxes ranged from $1,550 for cars that got less than 13 mpg to $350 for cars that got at least 18 mpg but less than 19 mpg.

5) For model year 1984, taxes ranged from $2,150 for cars that got less than 12.5 mpg to $450 for cars that got at least 18.5 mpg but less than 19.5 mpg.

6) For model year 1985, taxes ranged from $2,650 for cars that got less than 13 mpg to $500 for cars that got at least 20 mpg but less than 21 mpg.

7) For model year 1986, taxes ranged from $3,850 for cars that got less than 12.5 mpg to $500 for cars that got at least 21.5 mpg but less than 22.5 mpg.

Gasohol. Exempted from the federal excise tax on motor fuel, gasohol sold after Dec. 31, 1978, and before Oct. 1, 1984, if the gasohol was at least 10 percent alcohol. The exemption would apply only if the alcohol was made from products — such as grain or solid waste — other than petroleum, natural gas or coal. Gasohol is a blend of gasoline and alcohol.

• Directed the Treasury secretary to expedite applications for permits to distill ethanol for use in the production of gasohol. Directed the energy secretary to make annual reports to Congress on the use of alcohol in fuels from 1980 through 1984.

Excise Taxes. Repealed as of Dec. 31, 1978, the 2-cent-a-gallon reduction of the excise taxes on gasoline and special motor fuels and the refund of the 6-cent-a-gallon tax on lubricating oil for gasoline, special fuels and lubricating oil used for nonbusiness, non-highway purposes (such as lawn-mowers and snowmobiles) and for motorboats.

• Specified that there would be no change in the exemptions for commercial fishing vessels.

Buses. Repealed the 10 percent manufacturers excise tax imposed on the sale of buses over 10,000 pounds, which were sold on or after April 20, 1977.

• Repealed the 8 percent manufacturers excise tax on the sale of bus parts and accessories.

• Removed the excise taxes on highway tires, inner tubes, tread rubber, gasoline, other motor fuels and lubricating oil for private intercity, local and school bus operations.

Commuter Vehicles. Provided a full 10 percent investment tax credit for "commuter highway vehicles" used in van pooling if the vehicles could carry at least nine adults, were used at least 80 percent of the time for van pooling for transporting employees to and from work and were acquired after the date of enactment and placed in service before Jan. 1, 1986.

Title III — Business Credits

Alternate Energy Property. Provided a special 10 percent investment credit for businesses that installed specified equipment, limited to 100 percent of tax liability, but provided that the credit rate was 5 percent for property financed with tax exempt industrial development bonds.

• Provided that the credit would be available for property acquired and placed in service after Sept. 30, 1978 and before Jan. 2, 1983.

• Defined equipment eligible for the credit as equipment for producing synthetic fuel, geothermal energy and solar and wind energy if installed in connection with a new building. Hydroelectric and nuclear equipment and structures did not qualify; nor did "passive" solar equipment.

• Excluded from eligibility for the credit persons trading with educational, religious, charitable and scientific organizations, electric utility cooperatives, state and local governments and public utility property.

• Provided that the credits, except those for solar and wind energy equipment, were not refundable.

Specially Defined Energy Property. Provided a special 10 percent investment credit, which could be applied against 100 percent of tax liability, for eligible property placed in service after Sept. 30, 1978, and before Jan. 1, 1983.

• Included as eligible property recuperators, heat wheels, regenerators, heat exchangers, waste heat boilers, heat pipes, automatic energy control systems and other items specified by the energy secretary that reduced the amount of heat wasted or energy consumed in existing industrial processes.

Energy Property Tax Credit. Provided the special 10 percent tax credit, which could be applied against 100 percent of tax liability, for eligible property acquired or placed in service after Sept. 30, 1978, and before Jan. 1, 1983.

• Included as eligible property specified recycling equipment, shale oil equipment and equipment to produce natural gas from geopressured brine.

Denial of Credit. Provided that portable air conditioners, portable space heaters and boilers fueled by oil or gas and other specified equipment would not be eligible for the credit if it were placed in service after Sept. 30, 1978.

Depreciation. Provided special treatment for depreciation of a natural gas or oil fueled boiler replaced before it was no longer useful.

Geothermal. Provided a percentage depletion allowance for gas produced from geopressured brine of 22 percent for production in 1978-1980, 20 percent for 1981, 18 percent for 1982, 16 percent for 1983 and 15 percent for all years thereafter.

• Specified that geothermal provisions would take effect on Oct. 1, 1978, and would apply to taxable years ending on or after Oct. 1, 1978.

Geopressured Natural Gas Depletion. Provided that natural gas produced from geopressured brine would be eligible for special treatment under the Natural Gas Policy Act of 1978.

• Provided that the 10 percent depletion for natural gas produced from geopressured brine would be allowed only for wells drilled after Sept. 30, 1978 and before Jan. 1, 1984. Wells drilled within that period would continue to be entitled to percentage depletion for their entire producing lives. But wells drilled before and after those dates would be treated as natural gas wells as under existing law.

● Provided that the section would take effect Oct. 1, 1978, and would apply to taxable years ending on or after Oct. 1, 1978.

● **Drilling Costs.** Allowed a deduction of intangible drilling costs for geothermal wells, which would be separate from that from oil and gas wells. The provision did not affect wells producing natural gas from geopressured brine.

Title IV — Miscellaneous Provisions

● Exempted the sale of lubricating oil from the 6-cent per gallon manufacturers excise tax if the oil were sold for use in a mixture with previously used or waste lubricating oil that had been cleaned, renovated or rerefined.

● Specified that for the exemption to apply, the blend of old and new oil had to consist of 25 percent or more of waste or rerefined oil. All of the new oil in a mixture would be exempt from the tax if the blend contained 55 percent or less new oil. If the mixture contained more than 55 percent new oil, the excise tax exemption would apply only to the portion of the new oil that did not exceed 55 percent of the mixture.

THE PROCESS

The fate of the energy package, particularly the natural gas pricing and tax portions, remained in doubt until the last day of the session, Oct. 15, 1978.

All five pieces began the year in a conference committee and remained there for many months. Three parts of the bill — coal conversion, utility rate reform and conservation — had been generally agreed upon by conferees in late 1977, but not formally approved.

But further action on those relatively non-controversial sections of the bill was delayed by long-running disputes over natural gas pricing and energy taxes. The majority of the natural gas conferees refused to finish up the other sections until they had resolved the gas controversy. In the tax conference, Sen. Russell Long, D-La., chairman of the Finance Committee, led senators in their refusal to meet on taxes until an agreement had been reached on natural gas.

For most of the year, it looked as through the gas pricing section would fail, that compromise was impossible. Nearly every time conferees appeared close to agreement, some new difficulty seemed to present itself. The opposition was a powerful coalition of consumer advocates who felt prices would go up too fast and industry sympathizers who asserted that price controls would not be lifted fast enough. The deadlock on natural gas threatened the entire energy package.

The Strategies

The Senate chose to handle the energy bill as it had in 1977, when it chopped the Carter bill into five measures and voted on each separately. It did the same with the conference reports; each was voted on as it emerged from the conference committee.

In the House, however, Speaker Thomas P. O'Neill, Jr. D-Mass., insisted on keeping the package together and permitting only one up or down vote on energy. That way, he reasoned, members could not approve the popular parts of the package without facing the more politically difficult questions of gas pricing and taxes.

O'Neill had employed a similar strategy in 1977 when the energy package went through the House the first time as one bill (HR 8444). He wanted to treat the conference reports the same way, postponing House action until all the reports had been passed by the Senate. Then the House would be permitted one final vote on the whole package.

But O'Neill's strategy came very close to failing. On Oct. 13, opponents of the natural gas pricing portion came within one vote of splitting that section away from the more popular parts of the package.

But even that crucial House vote did not clear the way for the energy bill. The next day in the Senate, retiring James Abourezk, D-S.D., began a filibuster against the only part of the energy package still before the Senate — the conference report on energy taxes. Abourezk, a key opponent of the gas bill, opposed the tax report and instead wanted Congress to pass a Senate version (HR 112) with more generous credits for conservation and solar energy. He vowed to give up his filibuster only if the House passed that Senate bill separately.

But O'Neill refused to allow a House vote on the package until the fifth piece — the tax conference report — was sent over by the Senate. The House had a long wait. Abourezk and a few other senators talked and delayed for about 15 hours — from Saturday morning until 12:30 a.m. Sunday, when they finally gave up. Soon after, the Senate easily passed the conference report and sent it to the House. There, four hours later, at 7:30 a.m. Oct. 15, the House approved the whole package.

Natural Gas

The first meeting of the year for the gas conferees was delayed by the death of Sen. Lee Metcalf, D-Mont., who died in his sleep Jan. 11. All 18 members of the Senate Energy Committee were conferees and had split 9-9 on price deregulation. Metcalf had supported Carter on continuing federal price controls on natural gas sales.

Supporters of Carter's plan needed a sympathetic senator appointed to maintain that balance. But senators wanting to end price controls threatened a floor fight if Sen. Henry M. Jackson, D-Wash., chairman of the Energy Committee, tried to arrange the appointment of a pro-regulation senator to Metcalf's conference seat. Eventually, two senators were elected to the Energy Committee, but not to the conference committee.

On Feb. 23, the 17 Senate conferees resumed daily sessions behind closed doors.

Tentative Senate Compromise

Several weeks later, on March 7, nine Senate conferees announced they had formed a shaky coalition behind a compromise plan to end federal price controls on new natural gas by 1985. The coalition was so shaky that the three Republicans who were part of the nine-member majority — Pete V. Domenici, N.M.; James A. McClure, Idaho, and Mark O. Hatfield, Ore. — said they would back out if House conferees tried to alter the agreement significantly.

Initial reaction from leading House conferees was cautious. They praised the Senate for hard work and good faith and pledged to analyze the compromise in a spirit of reconciliation.

But John D. Dingell, D-Mich., who had led the fight against gas dergulation since coming to the House in 1955,

Gas Price Hike Upheld

The Supreme Court declined Feb. 27 to overturn a controversial 1976 Federal Power Commission (FPC) ruling that almost tripled natural gas prices.

Without dissent, the justices left standing a lower court decision upholding the FPC rate hike. Associate Justices Potter Stewart and Lewis F. Powell Jr. did not participate in the case.

A coalition of consumers and municipal gas systems, led by the American Public Gas Association, charged that the FPC decision had been based on inadequate evidence and that it would have a "devastating" impact on consumers.

The FPC approved the rate boost July 27, 1976, after a two-month study. The higher price levels were designed to cover gas producers' costs plus a 15 percent return on investment. *(Background, see Appendix, p. 71-A)*

Under the FPC's ruling, newly discovered gas sold in interstate commerce after Jan. 1, 1975, could draw prices of up to $1.42 per thousand cubic feet (mcf), up from the old rate of $.52 per mcf.

The ruling also allowed that ceiling price to rise by one penny per quarter, starting Oct. 1, 1976, as an inflation adjustment. Through that mechanism, the current ceiling price for new natural gas sold in interstate commerce was $1.48 per mcf, and was to rise one cent April 1.

The FPC ruling also set a new price ceiling of $1.01 per thousand cubic feet for gas produced in 1973-74.

said he found major portions of the compromise " quite troublesome." And, he said, if Senate Republican coalition members intended the compromise as a "take-it-or-leave-it" proposition, "I would be compelled to leave it."

Of the nine Senators who backed the compromise, four had been committed to backing Carter's plan to continue regulation, while five had favored deregulation.

Carter had proposed boosting the price ceiling for new natural gas from $1.48 per thousand cubic feet (mcf) to $1.75 per mcf, with the new price to rise as oil prices rose. Carter's plan also called for providing that gas produced and used in the same state would be subject to price controls and allocations for the first time.

The Carter supporters in the coalition were Jackson, Dale Bumpers, D-Ark., Frank Church, D-Idaho, and Spark M. Matsunaga, D-Hawaii. The five former deregulation supporters in the coalition were the three Republicans plus Democrats Wendell H. Ford, Ky., and J. Bennett Johnston, La.

The Terms

Under key terms of the compromise "tentative agreement in principle":
- Price controls for new natural gas would expire Jan. 1, 1985.
- The president or Congress could reimpose controls for a two-year period any time after June 30, 1985, if prices went too high.
- In the period before 1985, new gas prices would start at $1.75 per mcf and would rise annually at a rate equal to the rise in the consumer price index plus 3.5 percent through April 20, 1981; and plus 4 percent from then through 1984.

- New onshore gas was defined as gas from new wells at least 2.5 miles from the surface location of an old well or at least 1,000 feet deeper than any well within 2.5 miles. Also qualifying as new gas would be gas from reservoirs which had not been in commercial production before April 20, 1977. New offshore gas was defined as gas from a lease commissioned since April 20, 1977, or from a reservoir discovered since July 27, 1976.
- State severance taxes would not be included in terms specifying first sale prices.
- The president, after declaring a natural gas emergency, would have authority to allocate natural gas from low priority users to others for up to 120 days.
- Certain "high cost gas" would be freed from price regulation immediately after passage of the bill. That category would include gas produced from Devonian shale, geopressurized brine, new wells drilled to depths below 15,000 feet and occluded gas from coal seams.
- Gas from low-yield "stripper" wells producing up to 60 mcf per day would qualify for first sale prices of $2.09 per mcf, with annual price escalation rates the same as for new gas.
- Within 18 months of enactment, the Federal Energy Regulatory Commission would be required to issue a rule providing that major fuel burning installations would bear the increased costs for new high-priced gas until their fuel costs equalled the reasonable cost of other substitute fuels, such as oil.

March 22 Conference

On March 22, the House and Senate conferees held their first public session in three months. The results were inconclusive.

Senate conferees voted 10-7 to offer formally to the House their compromise plan to deregulate new natural gas by 1985.

House conferees did not vote directly on the Senate compromise. Instead, they voted 13-12 to accept it with an amendment. The amendment was their own substitute compromise.

Superficially, the House version was built on the same concepts as the sensitive Senate compromise. But close analysis revealed it would make extensive and fundamental changes in it.

Standing Room Only

The two-hour conference session took place before a standing room only crowd in an atmosphere of growing disorder, frustration, confusion and bad temper.

After the House conferees voted for their substitute, the Senate conferees mirrored their tactic. They voted 10-7 to accept the House version with an amendment. The amendment was the original Senate compromise that they had endorsed just an hour before.

"This is like the Mad Hatter's tea party," one veteran Capitol Hill reporter commented in an aside.

One Senate conferee asked Energy Chairman Jackson where that left the issue. Jackson said it left it where it was after the House conferees' vote, but admitted he was not sure what that meant.

"You can see why I have urged strongly that we engage in quiet diplomacy," Jackson said. "I think these public get-togethers before we get our ducks in a row create nothing but trouble."

Carter Statements on Gas Deregulation

President Carter startled many observers at a March 9 press conference by endorsing a phased-in end to government regulation of natural gas prices.

The surprise came because for almost a year Carter had fought hard to continue government price controls over natural gas. In that time, some of the harshest rhetoric he had employed as president was issued to denounce the oil and gas companies for trying to end such federal gas price regulation.

From the record, it was clearly true that Carter as a candidate for president called for phased-in deregulation. It was also true that in his April 20, 1977, speech on energy to a joint session of Congress that he pledged to "work carefully toward deregulation."

But his National Energy Plan clearly called for continuing federal price controls on natural gas. The controlled prices would be higher and the control system

would be different under Carter's plan. But the point was that gas would not be deregulated.

Most important, when it appeared that either house of Congress was about to vote to deregulate new natural gas, Carter strongly and publicly denounced the moves. At those times he seemed to argue that the oil and gas lobby was pushing for total deregulation of all natural gas, both newly discovered and that already flowing from old wells. But that was not the case.

The gas deregulation legislation which threatened Carter's program in the House in July and which triumphed in the Senate in October 1977, aimed only at deregulating new natural gas — although "new" gas was liberally defined. In arguing against those deregulation measures, Carter incorrectly implied they would end regulation over all gas. A representative compilation of Carter's statements on natural gas deregulation follows:

June 16, 1976

Presentation to the Democratic Platform Committee: "For natural gas, we should deregulate the price of only that natural gas not currently under existing contract (less than 5 percent) for a period of five years. At the end of the period of time, we should evaluate this program to see if it increases production and keeps gas-related products at prices the American people can afford."

Oct. 19, 1976

Letter to Texas Gov. Dolph Briscoe, D: "First, I will work with the Congress, as the Ford administration has been unable to do, to deregulate new natural gas."

April 20, 1977

Energy speech to joint session of Congress: "I want to work with the Congress to give gas producers an adequate incentive for exploration, working carefully toward deregulation of newly discovered natural gas as market conditions permit. I propose now that the price limit for all new gas sold anywhere in the country be set at the price of the equivalent energy value of domestic crude oil, beginning in 1978. This proposal will apply both to new gas and to expiring intrastate contracts. It would not affect existing contracts."

April 22, 1977

News conference: **Q:** "Mr. President, do you foresee a recommendation to eventually take the cap off of gas; that is, as long as there is a cap on it, it would seem to be regulated? . . .

A: "I think that would still have to remain for future analysis. I believe that . . . setting the natural gas price at its equivalent in oil is an adequate level of

deregulation. Others, of course, want complete deregulation of oil and gas.

"I don't think it's possible for us to do that in the immediate future. I think the adverse impact on consumers and on our economy would just be too severe. . . ."

Sept. 24, 1977

Campaign speech at Norfolk, Va.: "I put forward to the Congress a comprehensive energy package. Part of it calls for deregulation, over a period of time, of natural gas. . . . But the gas companies — very powerful in Washington as you well know — want to deregulate immediately and add tremendous costs to the American public, not only for new gas to be discovered in the future but for gas that already has been discovered and that will be coming to you in any case. . . .

"I hate to veto a bill that a Democratic Congress passes, but you can depend upon it: I'll protect your interests when the bill crosses my desk."

Sept. 26, 1977

White House remarks: "The Congress has been lobbied continuously by the oil and gas industry to deregulate the price of new natural gas. . . . There comes a time when we must ask how much is enough. . . . It's time for the public interest to prevail over special interest lobbyists."

Sept. 29, 1977

Press conference: "I do not support complete deregulation of natural gas prices which would provide windfall profits without increasing supply. Deregulation would cost consumers an extra $70 billion by 1985 but would increase supplies very little, if any."

Oct. 13, 1977

News conference: Carter denounced "potential war profiteering in the impending energy crisis. This could develop with the passing months as the biggest ripoff in history." . . .[T]he oil companies apparently want it all. . . . If we deregulate natural gas prices, then the price will go to 15 times more than natural gas prices were before the oil embargo."

Oct. 28, 1977

Question and answer session with visiting newspaper executives: "As I said in my campaign and also as I said to the Congress when I made my energy speech last April, we are working toward deregulation of natural gas."

Nov. 4, 1977

Question and answer session: "I don't believe that I've changed my position. I don't interpret it that way. My position was that I would work with Congress, as had President Ford, for deregulation of natural gas. . . . The difference is in the rapidity with which natural gas is deregulated. . . .

March 9, 1978

News conference: **Q:** "Mr. President, are you willing to accept energy legislation that in a few years would lead to the deregulation of natural gas?"

A: "Yes, I am. This was a campaign statement and commitment of mine — that I thought natural gas should be deregulated. In my speech to the Congress last April, I repeated this hope and I think a long phased-in deregulation process without any shock to our national economy would be acceptable."

The conference then adjourned for Easter recess with no new meeting date set.

The session had revealed several things.

Fragile Coalition. First, the fragile Senate coalition behind the compromise had been badly shaken by the extent of the changes called for by the House compromise.

Clear evidence of this came after the session broke up. Thomas L. Ashley, D-Ohio, Speaker O'Neill's personal coordinator on the energy conference approached an angry Sen. Domenici in an apparent peacemaking effort.

Domenici had made it clear that his support for the Senate compromise was tenuous and that he would back out if the House insisted on tampering much with its terms.

Domenici seethed as he talked to Ashley. "You prepared a whole new deal," he said, referring to the House plan. That was not his understanding of what had been tacitly agreed upon, he said. The Senate coalition had been assured that if it could strike a bargain, the House and the Carter administration would go along with little resistance. Instead, Domenici fumed, the House offering included at least "12 major changes."

Second, it also was apparent from vote splits on both sides that the coalitions behind the compromise plans were thin and insecure.

Conservative Republicans joined with consumer-oriented Democrats to oppose each compromise, although the alliances were formed for different reasons. The Republicans thought the plans achieved deregulation too slowly and insufficiently; the liberals thought even phased deregulation would rob consumers while handing undeserved windfall profits to the oil and gas industry.

Splitting the Bill. A third potentially significant development was that extensive support appeared to be growing among both House and Senate conferees to split the Carter energy program into separate bills. If progress toward agreement on natural gas pricing were to bog down again, as it had so often in the past, several leading conferees said, they would break loose the three non-controversial portions of the program already resolved in conference and pass them without resolving natural gas pricing and major energy taxes.

House-Senate Differences

Ironically, the compromise proposals put forward by House and Senate conferees showed the two sides were closer than ever before.

A majority of House conferees formally went on record for the first time in favor of phasing out federal price controls over new natural gas.

Controls would end Dec. 31, 1984, under the Senate plan and six months later under the House plan.

The House version would accept the Senate price structure in the interim, with one major change. The Senate plan would set new gas prices at $1.75 per thousand cubic feet (mcf) as of April 20, 1977, with annual boosts equal to the rate of inflation as measured by the Consumer Price Index plus 3.5 percent through April 20, 1981, and plus 4 percent thereafter.

The House version would tie the inflation adjustor to changes in the gross national product, which was more stable.

The most important changes called for by the House were in defining what gas would be "new" and hence would qualify for high prices and eventual deregulation. The Senate compromise terms were extremely broad, so that almost any newly drilled well — even into existing reser-

voirs currently producing — could draw the high prices. The House version would redraft several technical sections to cut back severely the amount of gas eligible for high prices.

In other major conflicts, the House plan would require a system of "incremental pricing" whereby industrial gas consumers would bear the burden of paying for new high priced gas disproportionately at first, while smaller gas consumers would indefinitely draw lower priced gas from wells still under controls. The Senate version required only that such pricing plans be drafted and submitted to Congress for separate approval.

The House version also would substantially redraw terms empowering the President to allocate gas supplies and a section allowing either the President or Congress to reimpose price controls.

The Votes

Voting with the majority in the Senate conferees' 10-7 split to endorse their compromise plan were Republicans Domenici, Hatfield and McClure, and Democrats Johnston, Ford, Jackson, Church, Bumpers, Matsunaga and Floyd K. Haskell, Colo. Haskell's vote came by proxy and was a surprise. Facing a hard re-election fight, he delivered a message through Jackson that his vote March 22 did not mean he would not support the plan later.

Opposing the Senate compromise were three Democrats — John A. Durkin, N.H.; James Abourezk, S.D., and Howard M. Metzenbaum, Ohio. They were joined by four Republicans — Clifford P. Hansen, Wyo.; Dewey F. Bartlett, Okla.; Paul Laxalt, Nev., and Lowell P. Weicker Jr., Conn.

Opposing the House compromise were Joe D. Waggonner Jr., D-La., an oil-state conservative, three consumer-state liberals — Toby Moffett, D-Conn., Charles A. Vanik, D-Ohio, and Charles B. Rangel, D-N.Y. — and all eight Republican House conferees: John B. Anderson, Ill.; Clarence J. Brown, Ohio; Frank Horton, N.Y.; John W. Wydler, N.Y.; Garry Brown, Mich.; William A. Steiger, Wis.; James M. Collins, Texas, and Bill Archer, Texas.

Carter Intervenes

Faced with a standstill on gas, President Carter intervened personally in the dispute April 11 by calling key conferees together for a series of White House meetings.

On April 12 Carter met separately with a group of House Republican conferees in an effort to soothe their anger at being shut out of the closed-door sessions that key conferees had been holding in the Capitol.

After the April 12 meeting, Clarence Brown of Ohio reported that Carter said "he would support, in effect, anything that came out of the conference."

All sides reported that Carter's intervention renewed their dedication to resolve their differences. But after three days of White House meetings, serious differences continued to divide the conferees.

One published report indicated that Senate conferees listed eight specific areas of disagreement as the April 13 meeting began and that the House side then added four more.

Protest Vote. Meanwhile, the House overwhelmingly went on record April 13 to protest the practice of key conferees meeting privately in informal meetings instead of in public as both chambers' rules required.

Toby Moffett, a key conference leader on behalf of those favoring continued federal controls on gas prices, forced a floor vote on the question. To finesse the parliamentary confusion of the issue, Moffett's motion had to be phrased as a formal instruction to close the conference. Moffett hoped it would be strongly voted down as a signal to conference leaders that the House wanted the meetings open. The House agreed with him, voting down the motion 6-371.

The April 21 Agreement

A major breakthrough in the gas debate came one year and one day after President Carter presented Congress with his omnibus energy program. On April 21 a small group of leading House and Senate conferees ended four months of stalemate by agreeing to end federal regulation of prices for new natural gas beginning Jan. 1, 1985.

But the agreement had been reached by fewer than a dozen of the 43 conferees involved.

Marathon Session

Most of the final agreement was reached during a marathon 13-hour session stretching until 3:30 a.m. April 21. With Energy Secretary Schlesinger pushing the small group each step of the way, the leading House and Senate conferees settled all but two technical points, according to key participants.

They reconvened for another tense two and a half hours April 21 at 11 a.m. in plush but cramped quarters in an obscure third floor room of the Capitol.

J. Bennett Johnston, D-La., created a deadline by insisting he had to catch a plane at 1:30 p.m.

As the Senate delegation and the House members caucused in different rooms about 100 paces apart, Schlesinger periodically emerged in shirtsleeves to shuttle messages back and forth. Each venture into the hall by any participant brought a crush of questions from about 100 reporters and technicians milling about outside.

In the end, Johnston left without agreeing.

But at 1:25 p.m. a burst of applause from inside the caucus room signaled the impasse had been broken.

"We have been able to merge our differences for the first time in 30 years [on the issue]," announced Henry Jackson.

And John Dingell, who had doggedly insisted on terms to protect consumers from too steeply rising gas bills, pledged: "I'm going back and I'm going to try to sell this proposal to my colleagues."

PROVISIONS

Following are the main points of the agreement reached April 21 by leading House and Senate conferees, according to a summary prepared by the Senate Energy Committee. The agreement:

Price Controls

- Imposed price controls on all categories of natural gas, both interstate and intrastate, effective between enactment of the legislation and Jan. 1, 1985.
- Mandated an end to federal price regulation, effective Jan. 1, 1985, of new natural gas, of most gas currently sold in intrastate commerce and of natural gas from new wells deeper than 5,000 feet located in old reservoirs.

- Specified that gas freed from price controls would remain free from those controls at least between Jan. 1, 1985, and July 1, 1985.
- Provided that either Congress or the president, subject to veto by both houses of Congress, could reimpose price controls at any time between July 1, 1985, and July 1, 1987.
- Provided that the level of reimposition would be set by statute and would vary by type of gas.
- Provided that reimposed controls last 18 months.
- Specified that authority to reimpose controls could be used only once.

New Gas Definitions

- Defined new onshore gas as gas from new wells 2.5 miles beyond an existing well or 1,000 feet deeper than an existing well, or gas from new wells into reservoirs that had not produced in commercial quantities before April 20, 1977.
- Excluded from the new gas definition gas which producers intentionally had withheld from the market.
- Defined new gas from the outer continental shelf as gas from leases issued after April 20, 1977.
- Defined as "special development incentive gas" gas from new wells in an old reservoir within 2.5 miles of an old well, provided the new well met spacing requirements.
- Provided that special development incentive price gas from wells shallower than 5,000 feet would be freed from federal price regulation on July 1, 1987, unless price controls had been reimposed. If controls had been reimposed, that gas would be freed from regulation at the end of the reimposition period.

Interim Price Scale

- Provided that in the interim period between enactment of the legislation and Jan. 1, 1985, new natural gas ceiling prices would increase at a level equal to inflation as measured by the Gross National Product (GNP) deflator plus 0.2 percent, plus 3.5 percent as an incentive to gas producers, through April 20, 1981. The 3.5 percent producer incentive would rise to 4 percent on April 20, 1981, effective to Dec. 31, 1984.
- Specified that the starting price for that interim pricing scale would be $1.75 per million British thermal units (MMBtu's) as of April 20, 1977, (which staff estimated equalled about $1.93 as of April 21, 1978).
- Provided that in the interim period prior to Jan. 1, 1985, gas qualifying as special incentive price gas would draw price increases equal to inflation as measured by the GNP deflator plus 0.2 percent. The base price would be $1.75 per MMBtu as of April 20, 1977, (an estimated $1.86 as of April 21, 1978).
- Provided that special development incentive price gas from wells shallower than 5,000 feet would draw prices from a scale splitting the difference between its old price increase rate and the new price increase standard.
- Specified that prices for old gas not under contract or under federal regulation would be allowed to increase at a rate equal to the inflation rate. The starting price was estimated to be $1.45 per MMBtu as of April 20, 1977, or $1.54 as of one year later.
- Provided that outer continental shelf gas from reservoirs discovered after July 27, 1976, in old leases would draw new gas prices, but would not be deregulated.

Rollover Contracts

● Provided that as contracts for interstate gas sales expired or "rolled over," the new ceiling price for that gas would be 54 cents per MMBtu if the original contract price were below that level. If higher, the new ceiling price would be limited to the old contract price.

● Provided that as contracts for intrastate gas expired, the new ceiling price for that gas would be $1 per MMBtu if the contract price were below that amount and would be limited to the contract price if higher.

● Provided that for intrastate gas contracts existing at the time of enactment of the legislation, price escalator clauses would apply until the contract price equalled the new gas price.

Allocation Powers

● Provided that in times of natural gas supply emergencies, the president would have powers to allocate gas supplies after voluntary emergency sales were exhausted.

● Limited the president's emergency allocation powers to a set of ordered priorities. First, he must allocate gas from boilers capable of being fired by coal, including those fed by either interstate or intrastate gas. Second, he could allocate gas used by other low priority users served by interstate pipelines only. Third, he could allocate gas owned by low priority end users.

Regulatory Powers

● Provided the Federal Energy Regulatory Commission (FERC) with authority to specify duration of gas contracts and specified that outer continental shelf contracts would be for a minimum of 15 years.

● Provided FERC with authority to provide a right of first refusal on interstate contracts.

● Empowered FERC to issue rules and regulations under the legislation.

High Cost Gas

● Provided that upon the effective date of the first FERC incremental pricing rule, gas from Devonian shale, methane gas from coal seams, gas from new wells drilled below 15,000 feet deep and gas derived from geopressurized brine would be deregulated immediately.

● Authorized FERC to establish price incentives to encourage investment in development of other kinds of high cost gas.

● Specified that the authority given FERC was to be exercised prior to the drilling of wells and that the authority was not to be "cost based;" i.e., limited to covering the costs of production.

Stripper Wells

● Provided that stripper wells were wells producing gas not associated with oil at a maximum efficient production rate of 60 thousand cubic feet (mcf) per day or less.

● Set a ceiling price of $2.09 per mcf for gas from stripper wells, with the price ceiling to rise at the same rate as for new gas.

● Specified that gas from stripper wells was not to be deregulated.

● Directed FERC to provide a rule allowing wells that qualified as stripper wells to increase production if the producer used recognized production enhancement techniques.

Incremental Pricing

● Directed FERC to devise within 12 months of enactment a rule mandating that industrial consumers of gas as boiler fuel should bear the disproportionate burden of paying higher costs for the higher-priced gas flowing under the act.

● Specified that schools, hospitals and other similar institutions and agricultural users would be exempt from this "incremental pricing" provision.

● Specified that those eligible industrial boiler fuel users would have to pay the increased costs of gas disproportionately until their gas costs reached the costs of buying substitute fuel; i.e., the cost of No. 2 fuel oil as determined regionally. No. 2 fuel oil was the grade of oil used in home heating.

● Directed FERC to develop a second incremental pricing rule within 18 months of enactment which would apply incremental pricing terms to other low priority gas consumers.

● Specified that the second incremental pricing rule would be subject to a one house veto by Congress.

● Specified that incremental pricing rules would apply only to users served by interstate pipelines.

● Specified that incremental pricing would apply to that portion of an interstate pipeline's cost of certain supply categories that exceeded $1.48 per MMBtu, adjusted for inflation.

● Spelled out those categories as new natural gas, rollover contract gas previously fed solely into the intrastate system and special development incentive price gas.

● Provided that incremental pricing also would be applied to deregulated high cost supplies if the price of those supplies exceeded the price of imported No. 2 fuel oil plus 30 percent.

● Provided that imports of liquid natural gas would be incrementally priced, but also provided that approved projects could qualify for a "grandfather" clause.

● Specified that liquid natural gas import projects pending before the Department of Energy and those determined by FERC to involve binding contractual and financial commitments would be priced under the existing Natural Gas Act.

● Provided that natural gas imports that exceeded the new natural gas ceiling price and were in excess of existing contract volumes also would be priced incrementally.

Squabbling Continues

By April 24, the optimism generated by the April 21 agreement was waning. On the 24th, conferees cancelled a public meeting scheduled for the 26th when it became apparent that a majority of the 25 House conferees would not support the compromise.

President Carter and House leaders, anxious for agreement, spent the week of the 24th trying to round up the last few votes needed. Reportedly, the pressure concentrated on two House conferees — Henry S. Reuss, D-Wis., and James C. Corman, D-Calif. — who voted for the March 22 compromise offer.

Both told reporters they believed the April 21 compromise was overly generous to the oil and gas industry. Reuss also said that he feared the gas compromise would pave the way for adoption of Carter's proposed crude oil equalization tax, which Reuss opposed.

Corman, conversely, insisted he would oppose the April 21 compromise at least until conferees on energy taxes

Carter on Natural Gas Compromise

Following is the White House transcript of President Carter's remarks at a news briefing Aug. 18 on the natural gas compromise. Energy Secretary James R. Schlesinger also took part in the briefing.

THE PRESIDENT: Good morning, everybody.

Last night the House and Senate conferees on the energy legislation reached agreement on one of the most difficult aspects of the entire energy package, and that is natural gas, ending a 30-year debate on this question.

Now the conference report will go to the House and Senate for further action.

This is a major step forward under the most difficult of circumstances and I and everyone in our country owe the House and Senate conferees a debt of gratitude for their assistance and tenacity and their willingness to accommodate their own deeply felt personal and sectional interests in the best interests of our country.

The legislation, when passed, will give us a new national market, making available new supplies of natural gas, which will be at a lower price than competitive foreign oil.

The bill is specially designed to protect home owners and small business leaders, small businesses.

It is also designed to give industry adequate supplies of natural gas at a good and competitive price. The bill encourages additional American production of natural gas, gives better prices in the future, and more sure prices in the future for those producers, at the same time protecting the interests of consumers.

We have been especially careful in natural gas legislation and the other elements of the overall energy package to protect the interests of the poor, the underprivileged and those who don't have the flexibility to accommodate changing prices.

The next step will be for the Senate to make a decision about the conference committee report.

My hope and expectation is that the individual Members of the Senate will show the same deep interest, a willingness to be flexible, a willingness to accommodate the needs of our Nation, as have the conferees themselves.

There is no doubt that this legislation, when passed, will protect the security interests of our country. It will protect the energy interests of our country. It will help us to assure continued prosperity and jobs for the American people, it will help us to control inflation, it will also help us to have a more stable economy and to protect the integrity of the dollar overseas.

All these benefits that will come from this legislation when and if it is passed, I am sure, will be an inspiration to the Members of the House and Senate to act expeditiously and positively on this very difficult and challenging but very important legislation.

Jim, are you prepared to answer questions?

SECRETARY SCHLESINGER: Yes, sir.

THE PRESIDENT: Secretary Schlesinger, who has done a superb job in bring together opinions and working very continuously with legislation that is perhaps as complex as any that has ever faced the Congress, will now answer questions that you might have.

QUESTION: Did you have to make any promises to [Reps. Charles B.] Rangel [D-N.Y.] and [James C.] Corman [D-Calif.] that we should know about to get them to sign?

THE PRESIDENT: That you need to know about?

QUESTION: That we should know about. (Laughter) Did you have to promise them something?

THE PRESIDENT: No. The only thing they were interested in was that I would repeat for the Congress and for the American public my interests along with theirs to protect the interests of the poor and the underprivileged, not only in this particular legislation, but in other aspects.

QUESTION: But no deals?

THE PRESIDENT: No.

---

reached an agreement that included a strong crude oil tax and a strong tax on utility and industrial use of oil and gas as Carter proposed and as the House approved in 1977. The energy tax conferees had not met since Dec. 7, 1977. *(Oil taxes, background, p. 44)*

THE MAY 4 SESSION

House and Senate conferees next met in public May 4, but spent most of the session quarreling about closed meetings.

No vote was taken on the April 21 compromise, apparently because House leaders lacked firm commitments for approval from a majority of their conferees. But conference Chairman Harley O. Staggers, D-W.Va., announced that a vote on the plan would be taken May 9.

The compromise pricing proposal, the result of an "intensive and emotional struggle," is the "best hope we have for resolution of this issue," Staggers said.

Senate Energy Chairman Jackson asserted that the compromise proposal was "neither left nor right ideologically, but clearly in the center."

Costs of Proposal

According to estimates by the House Commerce Energy Subcommittee, the compromise proposal was expected to provide by 1985 about $23 billion more in revenues to natural gas producers than the House-passed bill, which kept more controls on gas prices.

Compared to existing regulations, the compromise would give producers an extra $9 billion, the staff study said. The Senate-passed bill would have increased revenues to producers by $46 billion or more by 1985 over existing regulations, committee staff said.

Differences Flare Up

The inconclusive, raucous public meeting of the conferees came two days after the tenuous agreement among leading conferees threatened to come apart.

The problem was that the conferees disagreed about what they had agreed upon.

On May 2, House conferees met in closed session on one side of the Capitol with Energy Secretary Schlesinger while, on the other side of the building, Senate staff — and, from time to time, senators — waited for a scheduled 2 p.m. meeting of the two sides to begin.

Eventually, the two sides met together and, by 10 p.m. that night, had again worked out their differences.

Delays in Vote

Opponents of the compromise proposal, already upset because it had been worked out in closed session by a select group of conferees, also fussed at the May 4 meeting about not being able to vote on the compromise.

But Jackson, a leader of the small group that worked it out, asserted that, "we'd be charged with railroading" if the vote were held before members had a chance to read the document detailing the compromise.

But Jackson also noted, "The name of the game happens to be votes."

Sens. Weicker, Metzenbaum and other conferees tried to sidetrack the compromise proposal by raising points of order about the closed sessions and about new provisions in the compromise that were not in the Senate bill.

But Staggers and Jackson insisted that the group of conferees had not acted officially as conferees, but as individual members.

"The truth is," Jackson said, "we meet in members' offices all the time. . . . This was just the longest, most protracted discussion, meeting, 'getting together thing,' probably in congressional history, but that doesn't change the substance [that it was informal]."

DEADLOCK REMAINS

The May 9 date set by Staggers for a vote on gas came and went as House conferees continued their search for a majority.

Attention was focused on one man — Joe D. Waggonner, D-La., — thought by supporters to be the key to getting a majority of the 25 conferees. They could count as supporters 12 of the 13 votes they needed.

Waggonner, from a gas producing state where gas prices were not federally controlled, was concerned because the compromise would extend limited federal controls to the intrastate sale of gas.

Another representative from a gas producing state, Charles Wilson, D-Texas, also had problems with the provision on intrastate gas. But Wilson had won new language to benefit producers that would keep the government from holding prices down to the generally low levels set in contracts signed before the 1973 Arab oil embargo.

Waggonner and Wilson also eventually worked out a compromise with Bob Eckhardt, D-Texas, that after 1985 would raise the price ceiling for certain existing intrastate contracts under which the price per thousand cubic feet was more than $1.

On May 9, the seriousness of the stalemate prompted Speaker O'Neill to say for the first time that he was considering splitting up the five-part package. Such a move would dim substantially chances for passage of the crude oil equalization tax, an unpopular piece of the package, which Carter had described as its centerpiece.

Whatever O'Neill's announcement meant for the future of the tax, it apparently won Reuss' vote for the gas compromise. Reuss opposed the tax.

Two More Meetings

House conferees on natural gas held two more uneventful meetings on May 9 and 10. A third meeting scheduled for May 11 was cancelled when supporters of the compromise again didn't have the votes for a majority.

The conferees spent most of their time listening to staff explain the compromise and asking questions of each other about the proposal.

At one point, Toby Moffett, who opposed deregulation and the compromise, tried to end the proceedings. "I move

we dispense with this explanation," he said. "It's not serving any useful purpose [as evidenced] both by the [poor] attendance and by the fact that we have already heard this explanation."

But, one by one, supporters of the compromise spoke up. "I would hate to be deprived of this edification," said Richard Bolling, D-Mo.

"I yet find several areas of this very complicated question of what constitutes new natural gas" that are confusing said Eckhardt. "I still need an explanation of it."

Moffett's frustration was evident. Because supporters of the compromise weren't sure they had enough votes, "there is a great penchant for discussion, dialogue, reflection. It's rather obvious what's going on here," Moffett said.

His motion was ruled out of order by Staggers, chairman of the conference and a supporter of the compromise.

MAY 24: DEADLOCK BROKEN

The deadlock was finally broken May 24 when House and Senate conferees voted to accept a proposal for deregulation that even supporters said they did not like.

The final vote was far from dramatic as weary conferees cast their ballots, but the action represented the most significant move toward deregulation of natural gas since Congress had begun fighting over the issue 30 years before.

On May 23, House conferees who opposed the deregulation plan had tried unsuccessfully to derail the compromise with amendments. But in late afternoon, the final vote, as predicted, was 13-12.

The next day, Senate conferees also spent hours defeating crippling amendments and, about 6 p.m., finally approved the plan, 10-7.

President Carter praised the conferees' "historic agreement" and predicted it would cost consumers "no more than they would pay if today's inadequate regulatory system were to be maintained."

He predicted that new supplies of natural gas would move from intrastate markets, where prices were higher, into interstate markets, where prices were low but shortages had occurred.

Conference Action

At the meeting of House conferees May 23, Toby Moffett led the opposition to the compromise.

The proposal "lines [the] pockets" of the gas industry "without getting much in return for the public," Moffett said. The push to "get a bill" had led House conferees to go "against the will of the House" and agree to a proposal "crafted and agreed to in an atmosphere . . . of political hysteria," said Moffett, who did not participate in the closed-door sessions that led to the agreement.

His concern about the benefits of deregulation to producers was shared by Staggers, conference chairman, who took the industry to task at the meeting of the full conference May 24.

The bill is "generous to you," said Staggers, addressing the gas industry in general. He warned he would consider it "treason against the interests of America if you withhold gas from the marketplace in the future." Monopolistic actions or price fixing would bring "corrective legislation that would be unwelcome to you," Staggers said.

A leader of the Senate opposition to the agreement was James Abourezk, D-S.D., who called the deregulation a "rip-off" and "rape of the American consumer." The sole beneficiary of the proposal will be the "titans of the oil and gas industry, whose lust for profits has been unmatched in the annals of American business," he said.

FLOOR ACTION DELAYED

In the weeks after May 23, staff worked to translate the delicate gas agreement into legislative language and to write the report to go with the bill.

The task proved difficult. Conferees saw the final terms for the first time July 31. Some members who earlier had agreed to the compromise balked at signing the report, contending that the final language was not what they thought they had agreed upon. The disagreements held up floor action.

By mid-August the situation looked bleak for the bill's supporters. Three of the 13 House conferees who had agreed to the May 24 compromise — Reuss, Waggonner and Wilson — were refusing to sign. Of the 10 senators who had okayed the compromise, four were withholding support. They were Johnston and Republicans McClure, Hatfield and Domenici.

Basically, the defectors said the formal legislative language was not what they had agreed to in principle. But shifting political winds may have been just as reponsible for their change of heart.

Reuss, for instance, had been reluctant to go along with the agreement initially because he said it rewarded the gas industry at the expense of consumers. One of the reasons he yielded to heavy pressure to support the agreement was his announced concern that President Carter have evidence for world leaders that the United States was dealing with its energy problems.

Reuss' support came before Carter's attendance at a mid-July economic summit meeting in West Germany. The legislator's later refusal to sign the report came after the summit.

Industry's Objections

Wilson, Waggonner and the four Senate conferees pulling back were gas industry partisans who preferred immediate deregulation of new natural gas to the complex, phased system proposed under the agreement.

They argued that the compromise language meant prices would rise more slowly between 1978 and 1985 than they thought the May agreement had provided. They also objected to terms giving the president powers to allocate gas in intrastate markets. And other technical terms were different from those agreed on in May, they said.

But other pressures were at work, too. The two Louisianans, for instance — Sen. Johnston and Rep. Waggonner — reassessed their support for the gas compromise in part because of a case pending before the Federal Energy Regulatory Commission (FERC).

The case involved the United Gas Pipeline Co. of Shreveport, La., one of the nation's largest natural gas pipeline companies. A tentative FERC ruling blocked the company's plan to give preference to Louisiana gas customers when gas supplies were short, as they had been repeatedly in periods of high demand.

Johnston and Waggonner made personal pitches to the commission to overturn the preliminary judgment. Waggonner publicly linked the case to his vote on the gas

Cats and Dogs?

For those curious about how the Senate-House conferees on President Carter's energy bill continued to drone on without resolution, the events of June 7 may prove instructive.

What started out as debate on national energy policy quickly degenerated into a quixotic discussion of dog and cat food.

Although the basic principles of a natural gas pricing agreement had finally been agreed to May 24 after six months of hard, secret bargaining, several highly technical questions remained.

On June 7, conferees were presented with a staff-drawn definition of "essential agricultural user," which would have protected the use of gas in the production of, among other things, animal feed.

Sen. Howard M. Metzenbaum, D-Ohio, objected. He said dog and cat food production should not supercede the national interest in energy policy.

Staff explained the provision was intended for beef cattle farmers and other essential agricultural purposes, not dog and cat food production.

Metzenbaum insisted the staff language be amended to exclude dog and cat food.

Debate ensued.

Sen. John A. Durkin, D-N.H., wondered if Metzenbaum's dog and cat amendment shouldn't be altered to exempt food for Alaskan dogs, because they are essential to sled transportation.

Senatorial tongues were planted firmly against cheeks.

Sen. Clifford P. Hansen, R-Wyo., contributed the thought that sheep dogs, too, were important, and their food should be excluded.

Conference Chairman Rep. Harley O. Staggers, D-W.Va., told Metzenbaum he could not go along with the amendment because there were too many voting dog and cat owners in his district.

The audience howled.

Sen. Wendell H. Ford, D-Ky., wanted hunting dogs differentiated from Metzenbaum's dogs.

At length — roughly 30 minutes of much more of the same — Senate conferees adopted Ford's amendment to Metzenbaum's amendment by a show of hands, then quickly voted down Metzenbaum's amendment, as amended.

compromise, and Johnston made a telephone call to commission Chairman Charles Curtis stressing how important the case was to him.

Their interest stemmed from fears that the combination of the commission ruling and the deregulation compromise could leave Louisiana with severe gas shortages. The compromise would extend federal controls for the first time to gas sold in states where it was produced, like Louisiana. And it would free such gas for distribution to other states.

Meanwhile, the compromise also was drawing even heavier fire from a diverse range of interest groups. Among them were the U.S. Chamber of Commerce, the Independent Petroleum Association of America, the AFL-CIO, the Consumer Federation of America and the Americans for Democratic Action.

New Gas Ceiling Price Projections

| | Status Quo | | | | |
	Intra-state	Inter-state	House Bill	Senate Bill	Conference Agreement
1978	$1.82	$1.50	$1.87	$2.84	$1.99
1979	1.93	1.59	2.04	3.79	2.21
1980	2.04	1.69	2.24	4.73	2.42
1981	2.17	1.79	2.44	4.64	2.65
1982	2.30	1.89	2.65	4.58	2.91
1983	2.44	2.01	2.87	4.53	3.19
1984	2.58	2.13	3.11	4.50	3.50
1985	2.74	2.26	3.36	4.48	3.86

Price per million Btu's, as of midyear each year. Projection assumes 6 percent annual inflation,.

SOURCE: Conference Committee

Energy Department 1985 Natural Gas Retail Price Projections

(in million Btu's, 1978 dollars)

	Current Law	House Bill	Senate Bill	Conference Agreement
Residential	$3.22	$2.92	$2.97 to $3.62	$3.31
Commercial	3.02	3.46	3.70 to 3.19	3.25
Raw Material	2.38	2.77	2.98 to 2.67	2.55
Industrial	2.35	2.81	3.02 to 2.69	2.59

SOURCE: Department of Energy/Energy Information Administration

AUG. 17 AGREEMENT

The months of haggling seemed to be nearing an end on Aug. 18 when a majority of House and Senate conferees signed the conference report (S Rept 95-1126) and seemingly cleared the way for floor action on the embattled agreement.

In the House, James Corman and Charles Rangel did an unexpected about-face and signed the conference report after a personal appeal from Carter in a late-night White House session. Their decision came on the eve of a three-week House recess.

Corman and Rangel were needed to replace Waggonner and Reuss, the two House conferees who had given their verbal endorsement to the agreement in May, but then refused to sign the final report. They were the 11th and 12th House conferees to sign. The 13th signature, providing a majority, came from Charles Wilson.

Asked how he had persuaded the two reluctant House conferees, Carter told an Aug. 18 press conference that the two liberal Democrats had wanted reassurance that the gas agreement would protect "the poor, the underprivileged" from higher gas prices. Carter denied that any deals had been made to get the two signatures.

Also at the White House meeting were Domenici and McClure, but they said that factors other than presidential persuasion caused them to sign the report Aug. 17. They provided the needed majority of Senate conferees.

Heading for the Floor

As the beleaguered gas bill headed for the Senate floor, it seemed subject to attack from all sides.

Opponents, led by Sen. Abourezk, were threatening to filibuster the measure. But its chances of approval on a straight up or down vote did not look good either.

Recommittal Sought

On Aug. 23, a coalition of 18 senators representing both ends of the political spectrum announced they would not support the agreement. The group, including opponents and proponents of gas price deregulation, said the compromise would "lead to a situation worse than under the status quo."

The senators, representing both producing and consuming states, said they would move to send the conference report back to committee when the agreement reached the floor. By that time floor action had been postponed until after the Labor Day recess.

The senators said their motion also would require the conferees to finish action on the utility rate reform and conservation portions of the energy plan, which they asserted had been "held hostage to the gas bill."

The coalition of 11 Democrats and seven Republicans was glued together with opposing interests. Some of the senators opposed the gas provisions because they believed consumers would be badly hurt by higher prices. Others opposed the agreement because it did not decontrol the price of gas fast enough to suit the gas industry and encourage production.

All of the Republicans in the group supported deregulation when the Senate voted on the question Sept. 22, 1977. All but one of the Democrats voted against deregulation.

Democrats in the coalition were Metzenbaum, Abourezk, Durkin, Edward M. Kennedy, Mass.; William Proxmire, Wis.; George S. McGovern, S.D.; Birch Bayh, Ind.; Gaylord Nelson, Wis.; Donald W. Riegle Jr., Mich.; Muriel Humphrey, Minn., and Wendell R. Anderson, Minn. Muriel Humphrey had not been a member of the Senate when the deregulation vote was taken.

Republicans supporting the coalition were Hansen, Weicker, Dewey F. Bartlett, Okla.; John G. Tower, Texas; Henry Bellmon, Okla.; Richard G. Lugar, Ind., and Jake Garn, Utah.

In a "Dear Colleague" letter circulated Aug. 24, they asserted that the restrictions the compromise imposed on the intrastate market would reduce producer incentive and that it would mean higher prices for consumers without assuring additional supply.

Breeder Deal

Also complicating approval of the conference agreement was McClure's announcement Aug. 23 that the president had softened his opposition to breeder reactors in return for McClure's signature on the conference report. *(Breeder background, nuclear power chapter, p. 105)*

But by the next day there were signs that the agreement with McClure might have backfired. Senate Republican leader Howard H. Baker Jr., Tenn., said Aug. 24 that he would not try to stop the filibuster against the compromise. Baker feared the agreement with McClure could shift funding away from the Clinch River breeder reactor in his state to some other breeder project. Baker's announcement was significant, because without his help, supporters would have trouble getting enough votes for cloture.

Also waivering because of the concessions to McClure were two signers of the conference report — Republican Mark Hatfield and Democrat Dale Bumpers. Both opposed the Clinch River project and had fought hard in the Energy Committee for the administration position against it. Bumpers told Congressional Quarterly it was "unbelievable" that Carter would promise to spend $1.5 billion on a type of reactor Carter opposed.

McClure Compromise

Just what Carter and McClure had agreed on was the subject of some dispute.

According to Michael D. Hathaway, legislative assistant to McClure, the agreement postponed the decision to terminate or construct the breeder reactor at Clinch River, Tenn., until March, 1981. In the meantime, work would continue on design of Clinch River, and components for the project would continue to be purchased. At the same time, government researchers would try to come up with another, more modern type of breeder reactor that would not use plutonium or, if plutonium were the fuel, would be designed to prevent its diversion to nuclear weapons. One of the reasons Carter had opposed the Clinch River project was his fear that the plutonium would be used to make nuclear bombs.

Then, according to Hathaway, one of four options would be chosen in 1981: construction of Clinch River; cancellation of Clinch River and construction of the more modern breeder; construction of both projects or construction of neither.

COMPROMISE'S PROS AND CONS

As the date neared for a floor vote on the gas bill, it became clear that nobody really liked the compromise.

Even supporters had little enthusiasm for the complicated bill. Carter Perkins, a vice president of Shell Oil Co., said, "It's not a good bill, but if that's all we can get, it's better than the status quo."

Congressional authors of the compromise were just as lukewarm about the product. "It's the best we can hope for," Jackson said often.

Energy Secretary Schlesinger was somewhat more enthusiastic. "On balance, this bill is good for producers, it is good for consumers and, above all, it is good for the nation itself," he said.

Opponents were vociferous in their criticism. 'It's a mess, a disaster," said Talbott Smith, an associate manager of the U.S. Chamber of Commerce.

Only heavy lobbying by the Carter administration, which touted the agreement as the key to meaningful energy legislation for the 95th Congress, gave the conference report a chance of approval. And at that point, the chances of passage did not look good. *(Lobbying, box, next page)*

Uncertainties Spur Debate

Voting on the natural gas bill posed an "interesting Catch-22 situation" for senators, Dale Bumpers told his colleagues in a Senate floor speech Sept. 12.

"It does not make any difference how you vote," Bumpers said. "You are going to get it. Gas prices are going to go up if we defeat the bill, and they are going to go up if we pass the bill. You just book that."

Except for those higher prices, little else related to the gas compromise could be booked with certainty, either by supporters or opponents. But the difficulties of predicting the future did not stop either side from trying.

Depending on whom one believed, the bill would either increase gas production, or slow it down; aid the dollar, or harm it; curb inflation, or fan it; encourage industry to use more gas, or prompt switches to oil; be easier to administer than existing law, or spawn a regulatory nightmare.

The crystal ball was even cloudier after Jan. 1, 1985, when price controls would expire. The predictions on the charts and diagrams did not extend beyond that date.

The Administration Line

The most elaborate arguments for the gas compromise were expounded by the Carter administration.

As lobbying for the bill intensified, administration officials emphasized the link between the gas bill and the ailing dollar.

"Unless Congress acts soon on a natural gas bill," President Carter wrote in an Aug. 31 letter to senators, "the world will remain convinced of our unwillingness to face the energy problem, with continuing uncertainties and pressures on the dollar in foreign exchange markets."

Energy Secretary Schlesinger repeatedly stressed the international aspects of the legislation. "It is a very important symbol, internationally, of America's ability to face up to its energy problems," he said in late August.

Two basic aspects of this international argument stood out: the psychological impact U.S. action on energy would have on the image of the United States abroad and the actual impact the predicted decrease in oil imports associated with the bill would have on the trade deficit.

At an economic summit in Bonn in July, Carter promised Chancellor Helmut Schmidt of West Germany, Prime Minister Takeo Fukuda of Japan and others that the United States would have in place, by the end of 1978, a plan to cut imports by 2.5 million barrels of oil per day by 1985. Left vague was how the reduction would be accomplished, but administration officials believed passage of the gas bill would be a step in that direction.

The picture of the United States taking direct action on energy was supposed to shore up the dollar in international money markets, which in turn would slow domestic inflation, according to the administration. "At present, every 1 percent decline in the dollar's value against the currencies of the countries from whom we import adds .1 percent to the consumer price index," Carter told senators in the letter.

But the validity of these claims of a psychological boost to the dollar were challenged by opponents of the compromise. "We might as well pass a blank sheet of paper and just write 'energy bill' across the top of the sheet of paper and hope to fool somebody," said Russell B. Long, D-La., chairman of the Senate Finance Committee and one of the bill's powerful opponents. "What good will it do us to pass such a bill in the hope of fooling some foreigner?"

But the brunt of the opponents' criticisms were against the second part of the administration's argument: that passage of the bill would cut oil imports.

White House Lobbyists Employ the Hard Sell . . .

On the afternoon of Aug. 28, two dozen executives from major paper, textile and glass companies crowded into the Roosevelt Room in the White House to hear the hard sell for the natural gas pricing bill.

Some of the executives were dead set against the bill. Others were ambivalent. Not one could be counted on as a solid supporter.

First, according to the notes taken by one man who was there, Energy Secretary James R. Schlesinger, using multi-colored charts and new figures on gas production developed by his department, described the substance of the legislation (HR 5289).

Next, G. William Miller, the ostensibly independent chairman of the Federal Reserve Board, argued that passage of the compromise bill — any bill, really — was essential to the stabilization of the value of the dollar against foreign currencies.

Finally, an hour or so into the meeting, the Carter administration's super salesman took the floor. It was a "time for candor," Robert S. Strauss, the president's all purpose adviser, told the businessmen, and he was not about to pretend that the compromise bill was first-rate legislation. But, he went on, "it no longer makes a difference whether the bill is a C-minus or an A-plus. Certainly, it is better than a zero, and it must pass."

Then, in the same folksy style he used to raise money for George McGovern in 1972 and to win votes for Jimmy Carter in 1976, in the same Texas drawl with which he spoke to Japanese negotiators on trade policy and labor leaders on inflation, Strauss made his pitch.

"This is close enough," he asserted, "so a half-dozen bankers I had in this morning and the people in this room could pass or defeat the bill."

At least some of the executives must have been impressed. Those from the glass and paper companies remained opposed to the bill, but their opposition seemed somewhat muted after the session at the White House. Some of those from the textile industry switched to active support for the administration's position.

That meeting was one of a dozen held in the White House with key industrial consumers of natural gas in the three weeks before the bill was brought up on the Senate floor Sept. 11.

There were similar sessions, for instance, with representatives of the insurance, steel, automobile, construction and aerospace industries. A group of bankers had lunch with President Carter in the family dining room. One hundred thirty of the most ardent industrial opponents of the bill were called to the East Room on Sept. 6.

The meetings were the cornerstone of the White House effort to win passage of the natural gas bill, the focus of the most extensive administration lobbying on a piece of domestic legislation since Carter took office.

By all accounts, the lobbying was effective. In late August, only a handful of important businessmen could be counted on to support the legislation. On Sept. 11, the Department of Energy supplied all senators with a list of 55 major industrial and financial corporations and 20 trade associations that were backing the bill.

Administration Strategy

The administration's basic problem was that the bill that came out of conference committee was the product of so many compromises that it had a wealth of natural opponents and no strong supporters. Therefore, according to administration officials, the strategy, designed primarily by Schlesinger, Strauss and Vice President Walter F. Mondale, was to mount a campaign to neutralize the opposition, while pleading for support on the grounds of national prestige and loyalty to the president.

The day-to-day tactics were planned by a group of ranking aides from the White House and the Department of Energy, who met every weekday morning from mid-August on in the White House office of Frank B. Moore, assistant to the president for congressional liaison.

The regulars at the 8:30 a.m. meetings were Hamilton Jordan, the president's chief political adviser; Anne Wexler, special assistant for political matters; Stuart E. Eizenstat, head of the domestic policy staff; Gerald Rafshoon, the president's media adviser; three top officials from the Department of Energy; one of Strauss's assistants, and two of Mondale's aides, William C. Smith and Gail L. Harrison. Danny C. Tate, the White House's chief Senate lobbyist, usually presided over the meetings and William H. Cable, the lobbyist assigned to the House, normally attended.

Participants at the meetings said that most of the time was spent deciding which senators should be approached by Strauss, which by Schlesinger, which by Mondale and which by the president himself.

Many uncommitted senators reported receiving repeated calls from each of them. "It's been Carter, Schlesinger, Strauss, Mondale and then they start all over again," said an aide to Sen. Patrick J. Leahy, D-Vt.

Sen. John C. Culver, D-Iowa, visited Alaska over Labor Day weekend and reportedly received a call from Carter on the natural gas issue at 5 a.m. Alaska time.

All told, a White House spokesman said, the president telephoned 26 senators that weekend. The following weekend, during breaks in the Middle East summit talks, he called several more from Camp David.

Once the bill hit the Senate floor, Mondale began to spend most of his time in the Capitol, buttonholing senators on the floor and calling them into his private office just off the Senate chamber. Mondale was given much of the credit for swinging Sen. Edmund S. Muskie, D-

The Department of Energy estimated that the gas bill would cut oil imports by 1.4 million barrels per day by 1985. This was based on the assumption that an additional 2 trillion cubic feet (tcf) of gas annually would be available in the lower 48 states, plus additional supplies from Alaska of about another .8 tcf annually. Roughly translated, each

1 tcf of gas would provide energy equivalent to that from about 500,000 barrels of oil per day, thus leading to the prediction of savings of 1.4 million barrels of imported oil per day.

Though it appeared straightforward, the equation was based on a long string of assumptions, each of which was at-

...To Win Senate Support for Natural Gas Bill

Maine, the influential chairman of the Budget Committee, to the administration's point of view.

"They don't talk about the merits of the bill," one senator said. "They tell you that the president needs a bill to pass to save face politically and that the country needs it for international prestige."

But, most of all, the administration's strategy was to seek support from special interest groups that could, in turn, put pressure on senators to back the bill. Wexler was in charge of finding out from senators the interest groups that were leaning most heavily on them, and it was representatives from those groups who were invited to the White House.

Entire industries were split. Some important oil companies, like the Atlantic-Richfield Corp., agreed to support the bill, and others, like Exxon, were persuaded to remain neutral. Some oil companies, like Amoco, continued to oppose the bill.

The steel industry and the automobile manufacturers were also divided, and many important financial institutions, including the Manufacturers Hanover Trust Co. and the Bank of America, came out for the president. The farm lobby was also split, with the American Farm Bureau Federation, for instance, opposing the bill, and the National Grange supporting it.

The divide-and-conquer tactics showed results. A ranking congressional staff member noted, for example, that Sen. Robert P. Griffin, R-Mich., could not support the bill as long as all the major automobile makers were in opposition, but once the Chrysler Corp. announced its support, Griffin, too, felt free to do so.

Opposition Strategy

Opponents of the bill were an unusual coalition of senators and interest groups. Some of them believed that the compromise bill would not lift price regulations on natural gas fast enough while others felt it would allow gas prices to rise too fast.

For example, Sen. Russell B. Long, D-La., one of the most ardent supporters of deregulation of gas prices, met regularly to plot strategy with Sens. James Abourezk, D-S.D., and Howard M. Metzenbaum, D-Ohio, who led a filibuster in 1977 against deregulation legislation.

Other senators who worked to round up votes against the bill included Edward M. Kennedy, D-Mass.; Howard H. Baker Jr., R-Tenn., the minority leader; John Tower, R-Texas, and Clifford P. Hansen, R-Wyo.

The interest groups working against the bill were equally unlikely bedfellows. Amoco officials, for instance, were working hand-in-glove with James Flug, director of Energy Action, an organization devoted to representing consumer interests against those of the oil companies.

Lobbyists for the Chamber of Commerce of the United States consulted regularly on tactics with representatives of the AFL-CIO and the United Auto Workers. George Meany, president of the AFL-CIO, and Douglas A. Fraser, president of the UAW, wrote all senators urging defeat of the bill, primarily on the ground that it would be too costly to consumers.

For the most part, those against the bill concentrated on maintaining their strength against administration forays. Republicans were urged not to extricate the president from his political dilemma, and efforts were made to persuade Democrats that the compromise measure was such bad legislation that they could not afford blind loyalty to the administration.

Trade-off Controversy

Throughout the late summer, reports surfaced that the administration had made improper political trade-offs to win the votes of crucial senators. All the reports were denied by administration officials.

On Aug. 23, Sen. James A. McClure, R-Idaho, said he had agreed to support the bill and left the impression that he had done so in exchange for administration support for a $417 million energy research project in his state. Carter denied any deal. *(Details, Clinch River breeder reactor, p. 113)*

On Sept. 2, *The Detroit News* reported that Sen. Paul Hatfield, D-Mont., had been offered a federal judgeship if he would vote for the natural gas bill. Hatfield and Jody Powell, the White House press secretary, said there was no truth to the report.

On Sept. 7, *The Washington Post* reported that the administration had promised tax relief, protection against imports and other aid to steel and textile manufacturers in order to obtain their support for the bill. The next day, the Post printed a letter from Strauss in which he called the allegation "so far from the truth as to do disservice not only to me but to the nation."

Rep. Clarence J. Brown, R-Ohio, ranking Republican on the House Subcommittee on Energy and Power, took note of alleged "threats, promises and warnings" in a letter he sent to more than 100 corporate officials. He urged the businessmen "not to be cajoled into silence or coerced into support by misinformation, threats of retaliation or untoward offers of reward."

Brown then charged in his letter that Schlesinger had warned industrial users of natural gas that they would lose their right to make emergency gas purchases from the intrastate market, which had to be approved by the independent Federal Energy Regulatory Commission, if the bill were defeated. Schlesinger said that he had not made such a threat.

tacked by the bill's opponents. The disputes spilled over into such predictions as how much domestic gas would be produced; what types of wells would provide it, which would determine price; what the average gas price would be; what the price of other fuels, such as oil and coal, would be.

Current Situation

Earlier legislation and court rulings going back to 1938 had created two separate markets for natural gas in the United States. Gas produced and sold within the same state was not federally regulated and was known as intrastate gas. Gas sold across state lines was federally regulated, by the Federal Energy Regulatory Commission, and was known as interstate gas.

Because producers had been able to get higher prices in the intrastate market, where the price was not regulated, they tended to sell the gas there. About 40 percent of domestic gas was sold on the intrastate market. This had led to plentiful and even surplus supplies in producing states such as Louisiana, and shortages in states such as North Carolina, which bought on the interstate market.

Both those favoring price regulation and those opposing it recognized the problem caused by a dual market. But the two sides favored different solutions.

One proposed solution had been to extend federal controls to the intrastate market, thus removing the advantage of selling within producing states. But producers resisted this concept, preferring a different solution. They favored removal of price controls from the interstate market so those buyers could compete equally for gas supplies with intrastate users.

The Carter administration initially took the first approach and proposed in the 1977 energy plan to extend federal controls to intrastate markets. The ceiling price would have been raised to equal the cost of domestic crude oil, estimated at $1.75 per thousand cubic feet (Mcf).

The House basically agreed with Carter. But the Senate took the opposite approach and voted to lift price controls from the interstate market within five years.

The conference agreement combined the two solutions.

Production and Supply

The art of predicting what supplies would be available if the bill were passed was so uncertain that analysts came up with no less than six estimates of 1985 supplies. They ranged from the Independent Gas Producers Committee's prediction of 5 trillion additional cubic feet annually, to the Energy Department's 2 tcf, to the more conservative Congressional Budget Office's estimate of .7 to .8 tcf in additional supplies.

The new gas from Alaska, which the administration estimated at 800 billion cubic feet annually, was counted in the total new gas from the bill because of price subsidies the bill provided for Alaska gas. The higher priced Alaska gas would be rolled into the price of all gas, forcing all users to share the cost burden.

The administration assumed that the intrastate market could provide an additional .7 to 1 tcf annually, without additional discoveries. In other words, the administration thought that much gas was being held back from the interstate market because the price was not high enough. As evidence, they noted the price of intrastate gas had dropped from an average of $1.85 per Mcf in early 1977 to $1.75 per Mcf in early 1978.

Another assumption by the Department of Energy and the administration was that the higher prices would spark new drilling and production, particularly of gas found below 15,000 feet. The price of gas from these deep reservoirs and other expensive, hard-to-reach areas would be deregulated by the bill within one year of enactment.

But opponents who preferred deregulation objected to these assumptions, arguing that:

• The amount of surplus gas in the intrastate market was vastly overestimated.

• Producers would be discouraged from drilling, not encouraged to drill by the new laws, because the price

through 1985 was not high enough, and complying with federal regulations would be costly. Besides, producers would not know when they started drilling what category of gas the government would decide their new wells fell into. That determined the price. The bill set up 17 categories of new gas.

• The ceiling price meant that interstate buyers would be limited in their ability to outbid intrastate buyers.

Consumer and labor groups that opposed the bill also questioned claims that it would increase supplies. Instead of encouraging use of gas, they said the jump in price of 250 percent by 1985 would cause users to switch from gas to oil. This would increase oil imports, not curb them, they argued.

Price

Consumer groups opposing the bill were sharply critical of the effect the higher gas prices would have on low-income families. The Carter administration believed that higher prices were an effective way to increase production and encourage conservation.

But groups such as the Consumer Federation of America disagreed. "Experience since 1970 demonstrates that even 100 percent price increases have failed to yield increased production," according to the federation. "For billions of dollars more, we get less."

The administration and congressional proponents of the gas compromise said they had cushioned residential users from higher prices by a provision called "incremental pricing." The highest price gas would be newly discovered gas, and certain industrial users, such as those using gas as boiler fuel, would bear this higher cost initially.

But consumers pointed out that residential users would still be paying higher prices for gas than would industry.

But administration charts also showed that the estimated cost of domestic gas would still be less in 1985 than the estimated cost of oil, liquified natural gas (LNG) and other substitutes. What would happen after 1985 was an open question.

The administration also pointed out that interstate gas users were paying for high-priced LNG and other substitutes because not enough domestic gas was available. With the additional domestic gas they said would be produced and brought onto the market, those higher priced fuels could be replaced with domestic gas.

All in all, the price, as Bumpers predicted, would certainly go up. The transfer of money from consumers to producers was expected to be about $29 billion more over the next six years than under existing law, according to the Department of Energy. Other predictions ranged from $9 billion to $50 billion.

Outlook for 1985

One of the things that worried opponents of the compromise the most was what might happen in 1985, when price controls in the bill were scheduled to expire.

Opponents favoring no regulation worried that Congress and the president might continue controls beyond 1985. The bill gave them authority to reinstitute controls for one 18-month period six months after they were lifted.

Senate Floor Action

Senate floor debate on the gas bill finally began Sept. 11. Supporters of the measure averted the threatened filibuster by agreeing not to vote until Sept. 19 on the motion to send the bill back to conference committee. Opponents thought the extra time could win more votes for the recommittal motion.

But heavy White House lobbying turned the extra days of debate into an advantage for the bill's supporters.

Metzenbaum Amendment

The recommittal motion sponsored by Metzenbaum was to instruct conferees to strike all provisions relating to gas pricing, except the section allowing some higher prices across-the-board to reflect the extra cost of Alaska gas. The measure would still contain authorization for the president to allocate gas in an emergency.

Though Metzenbaum and others argued recommittal would lead to an acceptable bill, Majority Leader Robert C. Byrd, D-W.Va., and Energy Chairman Jackson insisted it would kill any chance for major energy legislation in the 95th Congress or for some time to come.

"This motion . . . would sabotage the efforts of 17 months in this Congress, the best chance we have had in more than three decades of finding a solution to our natural gas pricing problem," Byrd told the Senate.

Besides, Jackson noted, House conferees had told him that even if the bill were recommitted, they would not meet again to consider it.

On Sept. 19, about half an hour before the scheduled 3 p.m. vote, the Senate turned away from debate on a Department of Education and back to natural gas.

Abourezk, arguing for recommittal, called the compromise "monstrosity legislation." Kennedy, sitting beside Abourezk, rose to add his voice against the compromise, also labeling it an "absolute monstrosity. Something better can be developed" in another conference, Kennedy said.

Metzenbaum also urged recommital of "a bill . . . that everyone has agreed is not a good bill . . . The only argument that has been made for it is that it is the only bill in town."

But those favoring the compromise — and opposing recommittal — were heading into the showdown with two new supporters picked up that morning — Majority Whip Alan Cranston, D-Calif., and Sen. Maryon Allen, D-Ala., The momentum, and the vote counts, were on their side as Vice President Walter F. Mondale, in the chair, directed the clerk to call the roll. The motion to recommit failed, 39-59.

Forty-four Democrats voted against the recommittal motion, along with 15 Republicans. Those voting to recommit included 21 Republicans and 18 Democrats.

THE LAST DAY

In the days between the Sept. 19 recommittal vote and Sept. 27, the date set for the final vote on the conference report, debate on gas droned on intermittently. But generally the Senate shifted to other business, putting the gas bill aside and waiting for the scheduled vote.

"I think it sort of begs the questions to imply that this subject needs more debate," Hansen told the Senate. "If there ever were any subject that has been debated, it has to be the natural gas bill."

On Sept. 26, led by Robert Dole, R-Kansas, opponents made a second try at sending the measure back to conference. Like the first recommittal vote, the motion was to instruct the conferees to approve presidential authority to allocate gas in emergencies and to delete all pricing provisions except those relating to Alaska gas. Dole also added a clause giving priority to agricultural users.

The Senate rejected the motion, 36-55.

The Final Vote

On Sept. 27, about half an hour before the scheduled 1 p.m. vote on the conference report, the Senate turned once again to debate on natural gas pricing.

Metzenbaum recited a litany of complaints against the bill and warned the Senate this would not be the final vote on gas pricing. "No senator should yield to the temptation to believe that after today, the natural gas issue will be a thing of the past," Metzenbaum said. "It will not be, not by any means. It is an issue that will come back time and again to this body."

But Charles H. Percy, R-Ill., repeated the argument that the pending gas bill was the best possible. "It is this compromise or nothing for several years," he said.

The vote began, with Vice President Mondale in the chair.

There were no real surprises as the senators generally repeated the votes they had cast on the two recommittal motions.

Schlesinger walked into the visitors' gallery above the Senate floor, his pipe in his mouth. A Senate guard scurried over to tell him no smoking was allowed.

The final tally was 57-42.

The vote brought to a head a months-long ordeal for Jackson, who once told the Senate he had given "the best of my life for the last more than 12 months on the energy program — and 90 percent of that on the gas bill, working into the midnight oil."

In Mondale's office, just off the floor, the victory call was placed to Carter. Later, the president praised the Senate leaders for pursuing "one of the most difficult pieces of legislation that the Congress has ever faced in the history of our country. . . .

"I think it proves to our nation and to the rest of the world that we in this government, particularly the Congress, can courageously deal with an issue and one that tests our national will and our ability."

The Last Lap

Even before the final Senate vote, Speaker O'Neill was marshaling his forces in the House to push the energy package through.

The Speaker appointed a 40-member task force to shepherd the measure, and named Rep. Phil Sharp, a 36-year-old Democrat from Indiana, to head the lobbying effort. The job of the task force was to provide rapid, accurate information about the energy bill.

Opponents of the gas bill in the House, as in the Senate, were an unlikely coalition of conservatives favoring an end to controls on gas prices and liberals supporting tight regulation.

For example, Minority Leader John J. Rhodes, R-Ariz., was working against the bill with the man who narrowly lost the 1977 race for majority leader, Phillip Burton, D-Calif. Clarence Brown of Ohio continued the alliance he formed on the conference committee with Connecticut Democrat Toby Moffett, even though Republican Brown wanted controls lifted and Moffett wanted regulation to continue.

THE FINAL HOURS

The last lap for the energy bill began the morning of Thursday, Oct. 12, when the Senate took up the conference report on energy taxes. Quick approval was expected so the tax report and the four other bills cleared by the Senate could be put before the House Rules Committees. Approval from Rules, which was meeting that morning on the other side of the Capitol, was needed before a final House floor vote.

But Abourezk had other ideas. Senate action on the tax bill gave Abourezk one last shot at the natural gas pricing bill. As long as the Senate vote was delayed, House leaders would have an incomplete version of the package they wanted to put before the House. That meant delays in the House vote on natural gas pricing, which might help opponents.

When someone made the routine request that the reading of the bill be dispensed with, Abourezk shouted, "I object." What followed was a one hour and 15 minute recitation by the clerk. Abourezk's efforts forced Majority Leader Byrd, anxious to vote on other bills, to withdraw the bill from the floor. Byrd also filed a cloture petition to limit debate, which was to be voted on Saturday. The Senate then went on to other business.

But over in the House Rules Committee room, that was a minor irritant compared to the major problem looming before those seeking a single vote on the five-part energy package. Opponents of the gas bill were pushing Rules to reject the packaged bill, believing they had a better chance to defeat the gas bill with a separate vote.

But after an all day session, neither side had won. A motion to keep the package intact and a motion to allow it to be split both failed on a 8-8 tie.

But the next day, Oct. 13, the panel voted 9-5 to approve the rule permitting only one vote.

Later in the afternoon of the 13th, in a dramatic 207-206 vote, the House agreed to consider the five parts as one package.

The victory for the president came only after several members voted late or switched their votes.

The Filibuster

But as the House cleared one obstacle to final passage, another skirmish was developing. A group of House members — Reps. Christopher J. Dodd, D-Conn., James M. Jeffords, R-Vt., Richard L. Ottinger, D-N.Y., and others — preferred a tax credit bill (HR 112) already passed by the Senate to the one reported by the energy tax conferees. HR 112 had no credits for business and provided bigger credits for homeowners. Dodd and company wanted the House to approve that bill and drop the conference version. *(Energy taxes, below)*

They found an ally in Abourezk. As long as he delayed the Senate vote on the tax conference report, the House could not vote on a five-part package. The House group hoped the House leadership would get impatient, agree to take up HR 112 and then vote on a four-part energy package.

Abourezk began his filibuster in mid-morning Oct. 14 — after the Senate voted 71-13 for cloture. He and a few other senators continued to tie up the proceedings by demanding quorum calls and using other stalling tactics.

By late afternoon, Dodd was shuttling back and forth, carrying the message to Speaker O'Neill that Abourezk would end the filibuster as soon as O'Neill agreed to take up

HR 112. But the Speaker, who had worked for months to keep the package together, wouldn't give in.

But neither would Abourezk. As evening wore on, House members clustered near the Senate floor to watch.

Majority Leader Byrd, becoming increasingly irritated, begged for an end to the filibuster. House leaders had assured him, Byrd said, his voice rising, "that in no event will they allow the House to be blackmailed into calling up HR 112 and acting on it. That bill is down the drain, dead — d-e-a-d."

O'Neill "gave me his word," Byrd said. "And the majority leader [Jim Wright, D-Texas] gave me his word."

A couple of hours later, about 12:30 a.m. Oct. 15, Abourezk finally wound down.

Calling the energy bill "extremely bad, noxious legislation," Abourezk said, "Whom it pleases I am not certain, but I know it will not please the people we are supposed to represent."

The 46-year-old senator apologized for inconveniencing his colleagues, but insisted, "I do not regret having made this effort."

Byrd thanked Abourezk "for myself and on behalf of the Senate."

The energy tax conference report was then passed, 60-17.

House Floor Debate

The House finally began to debate the energy bill about 2:45 a.m. Thomas Ashley, chairman of the Ad Hoc Energy Committee, led off. Only about two dozen members were on the floor. Most of them were sleeping elsewhere, having heard the arguments on the energy bill many times before.

"Millions of words have been exchanged. Millions of words have been printed.... Now is the time to declare," Ashley said, aware there was little left to say. "We have an energy bill which can be translated into a comprehensive national energy policy," he said. Later, he called it "an initial foundation for a national energy policy." "This is the best thing we could come up with," said conference chairman Staggers.

Opponents were harsh in their criticism of the natural gas section. The gas bill, charged John Anderson, became "merely a convenient vehicle for the president to prove his supposed new dynamism, macho and legislative competence....

"The bill is, indeed, a marvel of tangled regulations and bureaucracy at its worse."

Brown of Ohio accused the White House of unfair lobbying tactics. "In mid-August, the smart money was betting that Congress would vote down the natural gas legislation. But that was before the White House invited the chief executive officers of major U.S. corporations to Washington for a little straight talk about the realities of doing business in a federally regulated environment," he said. Brown charged that business leaders were "threatened, promised and cajoled into passive opposition, silence or grudging support of this legislation."

The arguments continued through the scheduled four hours of debate.

When the time for a vote came, the leadership asked for a quorum call first, giving the scattered members an extra 15 minutes to get to the floor. Finally, about 7:30 a.m., with Energy Secretary James R. Schlesinger looking on from the gallery, the House voted 231-168 for the five-part energy bill.

Energy Taxes

Progress on energy taxes was even slower than on the gas bill.

Tax conferees held no meetings between Dec. 7, 1977, and July 13, 1978, primarily because Russell Long, chairman of the Senate Finance Committee, insisted that the gas pricing controversy be resolved before the tax issues were settled. After that, the conferees did not meet again until Sept. 29.

Largely responsible for the tax hangup was the crude oil equalization tax, which Carter had dubbed the centerpiece of his program. The tax would raise the controlled price of American-produced oil to world levels over three years. Designed to stimulate energy conservation, the tax would drive up prices of all petroleum-related goods. Economists had estimated that it would boost gasoline prices by about seven cents a gallon.

Under Carter's proposal, revenue from the tax would be rebated to the public, though Long and other legislators argued that the money should be applied toward more energy production instead.

'Dead Horse'

Chances for passage of the tax had never looked very good and looked bleaker and bleaker as the year wore on.

In March, Long announced that the crude oil tax could not pass the Senate in 1978 "under any imaginable set of circumstances."

". . .[T]he White House is beating a dead horse when they are talking about that crude oil equalization tax," Long said. He said outraged public reaction to the stiff increases in Social Security taxes passed by Congress in 1977 made passage of the oil tax impossible in an election year.

Energy Chairman Jackson was not quite so negative at that stage when asked if he agreed with Long's assessment of the situation. "Clearly, the only honest answer I can give is that taxes at this stage of the election year are very difficult," Jackson said.

At the same time, Toby Moffett, generally a strong supporter of the president's tax program, was quoted as saying the crude oil tax was " dead as a door nail."

PREPARATION FOR THE SUMMIT

Despite the gloomy predictions from Capitol Hill about the crude oil tax's fate, the administration was reluctant to give it up.

The president was scheduled to go Bonn, West Germany, July 16 and 17 for an economic summit conference with other western leaders. He would have liked nothing better than to arrive with positive news on the oil tax.

Aware that leaders of other western nations were insisting that the president take action to cut heavy U.S. oil imports, congressional leaders tried to arrange things so Carter could at least claim to be making progress.

The July 12 remarks by French President Valery Giscard D'Estaing in the Paris newspaper *Le Monde* appeared typical of the attitude of western leaders.

"At the present time," Giscard said, "an important reduction in [U.S.] oil imports is the precondition for an improvement in the world economy . . . In my view, this is the most important single source of upheaval in the world-wide network of trade and payments."

Hoping to put on a good front for the summit, Senate and House energy tax conferees met July 13. The meeting was intended at least in part to show a skeptical world that Carter's plan was not dead.

But the session produced few signs of life for the taxes. No decisions were made, and there was no significant debate. Several conferees suggested the main Carter energy taxes were dead, especially in light of the nation's burgeoning "taxpayer's revolt."

INSULATION, SOLAR CREDITS

As the crude oil tax languished and debate on the gas bill droned on, proponents of the less controversial pieces of the energy tax bill grew increasingly concerned.

Included in the measure were tax credits for homeowners and businesses that installed solar energy collectors, insulation and other energy-saving devices. Proponents of those credits argued that they were being "held hostage" to the crude oil tax and that the impasse had disillusioned and created hardships for homeowners who had made improvements on the assumption that they would be eligible for the credits.

In an effort to liberate the solar credits, a group of senators, led by Gary Hart, D-Colo., moved in August to tack them onto a minor tax bill (HR 112). On Aug. 23, by voice vote, the Senate agreed.

In addition to creating hardships for homeowners, Hart argued, Congress' inaction had had a "devastating effect"on the solar industry. Business had dropped since the announcement of Carter's energy plan in April, 1977, because consumers were waiting for Congress to act before investing in expensive solar equipment.

He estimated that the amendment would cost $978 million a year.

Gravel's Maneuvers

Debate on the bill was prolonged because of an attempt by Mike Gravel, D-Alaska, to attach tax breaks for producers of energy to Hart's amendment.

The provisions in Gravel's amendment had been passed by the Senate in 1977 as part of the energy tax bill, as had the provisions Hart proposed. And they were stalled in conference along with the insulation and tax credits.

HR 112, the tax bill being used as the vehicle for the solar and insulation credits, had been reported from the Finance Subcommittee Gravel chaired. That bill, which passed the House Feb. 28 under suspension of the rules, reduced from 4 percent to 2 percent the excise tax on investment income of private foundations.

Hart moved to table Gravel's amendment. The motion was agreed to 53-43.

Gravel then reintroduced his amendment after adding to it provisions giving credits for gasohol production and small hydropower projects. That amendment was defeated, 42-54.

The Hart amendment and the bill then were passed by voice vote.

Provisions

The Hart amendment provided tax credits for installation in principal residences of conservation or solar or renewable source energy equipment.

A tax credit would be subtracted from the amount due the government after a tax had been computed. The credits would be applicable to equipment installed between April 20, 1977, the date of the president's energy message, and Dec. 31, 1985. Credits could not be refunded but could be carried forward for two years if they were not used in the year earned.

For solar and other renewable source energy equipment, the amendment allowed a maximum credit of $2,200. For up to $2,000 in expenses, a homeowner could take a 30 percent credit ($600 maximum), plus a 20 percent credit on expenses between $2,000 and $10,000 ($1,600 maximum).

Qualifying for the credit would be equipment for:
• Solar heating, cooling and hot water heating, including passive solar (building design);
• Wind energy for non-business residential purposes;
• Geothermal.

For residential energy-conserving improvements, a maximum $400 credit would be allowed. For up to $2,000 in expenses, a homeowner could take a 20 percent credit.

Improvements qualifying for the residential energy conservation credit were:
• Insulation;
• Replacement boilers or furnaces;
• Boilers or furnaces replaced to reduce fuel consumption;
• Devices to modify flue openings to increase efficiency;
• Electrical or mechanical furnace ignition systems to replace pilots;
• Storm or thermal windows or doors;
• Automatic energy-saving setback thermostats;
• Caulking or weatherstripping of doors or windows;
• Heat pumps to replace electric resistance heating systems;
• Meters that displayed the cost of energy use;
• Replacement fluorescent lighting systems;
• Evaporative cooling devices;
• Space heating devices, other than fireplaces, designed to burn wood or peat.

CONFERENCE ACTION

It was not until after the Sept. 27 Senate vote on gas that conferees again turned their attention to energy taxes. By then the crude oil tax was considered officially dead.

On Sept. 29, the conference met but reached no agreement.

Insulation, Solar Credits

After two long days of meetings Oct. 3 and 4, the conferees agreed on a tax credit for homeowners who insulated their houses and for homes and businesses that installed solar heating devices. The maximum credit agreed on was $300.

This was $100 less than approved earlier by both House and Senate and by the Senate as part of HR 112. However, the amount was not in dispute among the conferees who on their own decided to cut back in order to reduce the cost of the bill to the government. Critics of the credit had argued that homeowners should not receive a tax break for doing something they probably would do anyway.

The credit would be equal to 15 percent of the first $2,000 spent by homeowners on insulation, storm windows, caulking, weatherstripping and other specified energy-saving measures. It would be available for improvements made between April 20, 1977, and 1985.

Homeowners who installed solar, wind or geothermal energy equipment would be eligible for a maximum credit

of $2,200, also retroactive to April 20, 1977. For up to $2,000 in expenses, a homeowner could take a 30 percent credit, plus a 20 percent credit on expenses between $2,000 and $10,000.

Credits for improvements made in 1977 would be claimed on 1978 tax returns.

Conferees also agreed on a non-refundable 10 percent credit for businesses effective Oct. 1, 1978.

The credit would be available for boilers, burners for combustors other than boilers, geothermal power equipment, not including turbines or generators, equipment for producing synthetic gas, pollution control equipment required by regulation, solar or wind energy equipment and equipment for heat recovery, recycling, shale oil production and geopressurized methane production.

The conferees adjourned at 10 p.m. Oct. 4 after the House conferees adopted, 18-6, a package of provisions that eliminated an industrial use tax on oil and retained a gas guzzler tax that would begin with 1980 model cars that used excessive amounts of fuel.

On Oct. 12, the conferees finally completed their work and reported the bill (H Rept 95-1773). They agreed to drop the proposed tax on industrial use of oil and natural gas, but retained the gas guzzler tax.

FINAL ACTION

Senate floor action on the energy tax bill began Oct. 12, but was quickly cut short by Abourezk's filibuster attempt. Majority Leader Byrd pulled the bill from the floor, filed a cloture petition to be voted on Saturday, Oct. 14, and the Senate went on to other business. *(Details, p. 28)*

Cloture was voted early Saturday, but that did not stop Abourezk, who continued his stall into the early hours of Oct. 15 by spreading out his allotted debate time and using delaying tactics, such as quorum calls. When he finally quit, the tax bill was passed easily and was sent to the House for consideration with the rest of the energy package.

Conservation

Although generally noncontroversial, the energy conservation bill also ran into some snags. It was bogged down along with the other portions in the arguments over the gas bill. And it also had a controversial provision, approved by the Senate in 1977, that banned production of gas guzzling cars.

House and Senate conferees were in agreement that production of big cars that wasted gas should be discouraged, but they had considerable difficulty trying to decide how to do it.

The Senate wanted to ban by 1980 production of cars getting less than 16 miles to the gallon. But the House preferred President Carter's proposal to levy a tax on gas guzzlers.

The tax was conditionally approved in late 1977 by the energy tax conferees. Final agreement depended on a decision by the non-tax conferees not to endorse the Senate ban.

At a June 21 meeting of non-tax conferees, Senate members were reluctant to give up the ban when prospects were bleak at that point for congressional approval of the gas guzzler tax.

"The tax conferees have been sitting on this since last December," Energy Chairman Jackson lamented. "That tells me something. There's no real determination to do anything about the tax portion."

But House conferees, led by Thomas Ashley, argued that the Senate ban would not save gas and would penalize smaller automobile manufacturers. 'I am concerned about the major auto employer in my district," said Ashley, referring to an American Motors Co. plant in Toledo.

The impasse was fueled by the lack of firm information on how much gas either the tax or the ban would save. A Department of Energy study was inconclusive, the conferees complained.

When Sen. Howard Metzenbaum tried to use the department study to discredit the claim that the tax would save gas, John Durkin reminded Metzenbaum, "Yes, but it also says your [ban] would have zero [savings]."

In addition to the ban, the Senate wanted to change existing law to double penalties for automakers with cars that did not meet specific mileage standards.

The impasse continued until July 25, when Metzenbaum announced that he would give up his fight for the Senate terms banning production of gas guzzlers.

But that still left the question of tougher penalties.

CONFERENCE ACTION

The conferees met again on Sept. 28 and, after a full day of haggling, reached accord on tougher penalties for auto makers who produced fleets of gas guzzling cars.

The Senate conferees agreed to drop their ban on production of cars that did not meet minimum fuel consumption standards in return for an agreement by House conferees to increase penalties under an existing gas-mileage law if certain conditions were met.

The existing law, the Energy Policy and Conservation Act of 1975 (PL 94-163), penalized auto makers if their fleets had an average fuel consumption rate that exceeded the national standard. The existing standard was an average of 18 miles per gallon. It was to increase to 27.5 miles per gallon in 1985.

The Senate wanted to double the penalty for not meeting the standard to force compliance. For each tenth of a mile in excess of the average, an automaker would be charged $10, up from $5, per car. But the House insisted on, and won, a provision making higher penalties dependent on certain findings. They also authorized a range of penalties, from $5 up to $10.

Michigan Democrat John Dingell resisted the tougher penalties, worried they would lead to layoffs in his district. Energy Chairman Jackson at one point whispered to a colleague, "John's like a stone wall."

As the arguing began, Dingell insisted that the increased penalties be contingent on findings by the secretary of transportation that they definitely would lead to energy savings and would not harm the economy.

"The moral equivalent of war, and we just lost it," Metzenbaum said quietly after one of Dingell's aides recited a long list of procedures necessary to meet the requirement. The reference was to Carter's description of the energy crisis.

The difficulty of showing absolutely that the penalties would result in energy savings and would not harm the economy would "drag out the hearings, literally for years, and that's not achieving the objective, which is energy savings," Metzenbaum said.

Metzenbaum then tried to define more loosely what the secretary would have to prove. He suggested the secretary need show only that the penalties would "be likely to lead to" energy savings. Others offered other phrases.

FINAL ACTION

Although differences over the conservation bill had been resolved by the conference, its report (S Rept 95-1294) was not filed immediately. Conferees who opposed the gas bill withheld their signatures from the report, aware that a delay in final Senate action could foul up House plans to cast a single vote on the package.

The conferees eventually relented and the report was filed Oct. 6. The Senate then adopted the conference report Oct. 9, with an 86-3 vote, sending it on to the House for consideration with the rest of the package.

Coal Conversion

The first piece of Carter's energy program to emerge from the conference committee was the coal conversion measure, which was reported July 13. It was a watered-down version of the president's proposed regulatory scheme to force utilities and major industries to burn coal or other fuels instead of oil and natural gas. Multiple grounds for exemptions had been included by the conferees, weakening Carter's original proposals. In addition, the tax penalties for using oil and gas, designed to accompany the coal conversion scheme, were voted down by tax conferees.

Carter supporters, like Senate Energy Chairman Jackson, argued the measure would result in savings of slightly more than one million barrels of oil per day by 1985.

But Carter critics, like ranking Energy Committee Republican Hansen, claimed the bill would save no more than 250,000 barrels of oil per day by 1985.

Harsher critics, like Dewey Bartlett, insisted that the bill was unnecessary because, where possible, industry was switching to coal already because it made better economic sense than using oil or gas. Bartlett also asserted that the measure actually would increase U.S. dependence on foreign oil, because it directed some facilities to stop burning gas by 1990, and the only other fuel some of them could burn would be oil.

Senate and House conferees reached final agreement on basic compromise principles for the coal conversion bill on Nov. 11, 1977. But the hangup over natural gas pricing threw the entire package into a freeze until June.

The conference report (S Rept 95-988) on the coal conversion bill was drafted in a rush, and it was not until July 13 that a majority of conferees from each chamber signed it. Even then, the final language of the bill and report never was discussed in an open meeting, a fact that outraged House Republican conferees, all of whom refused to sign it.

The bill went to the Senate floor July 14. The Democratic leadership hoped to get quick Senate passage before Carter's economic summit conference July 16 in West Germany. The hope was to allay foreign fears that the United States was doing nothing to curb its massive oil imports, which had been blamed for a number of worldwide economic problems.

But Harrison Schmitt — one of six senators, all Republicans, who voted against the bill — forced a delay in the vote until July 19 by insisting upon time to ask extensive questions. Majority Leader Byrd called Carter in Bonn late July 14 to assure him the measure would pass the coming week.

The conference report was finally adopted July 18 by a lopsided 92-6 vote.

Utility Rate Reform

There was little debate in 1978 over the utility rate reform section of the energy plan because conferees had resolved most of the questions in 1977. All that remained was for staff to put the agreement into legislative language and to draft the conference report.

In November and December, 1977, House conferees on the bill gave in to Senate demands that the states retain the power to force electric utilities to reform the way they billed customers.

President Carter had proposed, and the House had passed, a series of minimal federal reforms revising utility billing practices, which the states would have been required to carry out. The reforms were designed to spread customer demand for electricity more evenly, avoiding the existing pattern of "peak" demand periods. It was hoped the change would result in energy savings and reduce the need for utility expansion.

But the Senate had argued that the proposed reforms were experimental and needed further tests of experience before they could be mandated. The Senate had also insisted that regulation of utility rates was properly a state function, not a federal one.

Although the conference agreement was softer than the House bill, its backers asserted that it was much stronger than the original Senate version. And it would guarantee, they said, that each state utility commission consider thoroughly a wide variety of innovative rate reforms.

It guaranteed that the Department of Energy could intervene before a state regulatory commission hearing on a proposed utility rate increase and made the case for rate reforms.

And it provided that, whenever consumer advocates succeeded in winning adoption of their proposed reforms, utilities would have to pick up the consumer group's expenses for making the case.

The conferees also reached the following agreements:

Wheeling. The Federal Energy Regulatory Commission (FERC) could order a utility to "wheel" power from one supplier to another, subject to tests of reasonableness.

Pooling. FERC had to review for up to one year the potential advantages of utility pooling of resources and report to the president and Congress on its findings.

Interconnection. FERC would be empowered to order utilities to interconnect their facilities and to exchange energy supplies, subject to tests of reasonableness and judicial review.

Lifeline Rates. A Senate provision was abandoned that required utilities to offer elderly persons 62 and over enough electricity to cover heating, lighting, cooking, refrigeration and other essential needs at rates no higher than that utility's lowest rate.

Final Action

Once the legislative language and the conference report were drafted, the utility rate bill ran into snags similar to those facing the conservation measure. Some conferees who opposed the natural gas pricing bill withheld their signatures from the utility rate measure, hoping to delay plans for a House vote on the whole package and possibly defeat the gas bill.

They eventually signed, however, and the report (S Rept 95-1292) was filed Oct. 6. It was passed by the Senate Oct. 9 with a 76-13 vote and then sent to the House for consideration with the rest of the energy bill. ∎

Background: Carter Proposals, 1977 Action

Jimmy Carter's crusade for a comprehensive national energy policy dominated Congress and public affairs more than any other domestic issue during his first year as President.

Both the new Democratic President and the Democratic congressional leaders made passage of a national energy policy their top legislative priority for 1977.

And yet, when the year ended, there was no comprehensive energy policy signed into law. Congress did not finish the job. Both the House and Senate passed versions of the program, but the Senate went far afield from the President's approach in two key areas—natural gas regulation and energy tax policy. Conference committees settled other issues but bogged down over gas and taxes. Conferees quit Dec. 22; they did not meet again until February 1978.

At his last 1977 press conference Dec. 15, Carter asserted that the inability to erect an energy policy was "the only major failure this year...." The story behind that failure tells a lot about Congress, President Carter and the formation of American public policy in 1977.

The Need. It had been painfully evident to policymakers since the Arab oil embargo of 1973-74 that America was in need of a national energy plan. That need was underscored as Jimmy Carter prepared to take the oath of office. An unprecedented cold wave caused such rapid depletion of the nation's declining natural gas supplies that many schools and factories were closed and workers went jobless. Special legislation was needed to divert supplies to gas-short areas.

Both the oil embargo and the gas crisis four years later provided vivid evidence that America no longer was producing enough fuel to power its growing economy. The difference was increasingly made up by expensive imports of foreign fuels. *(Background, Appendix, p. 3-A)*

With worldwide energy consumption growing faster than supply availability, the clear trend was that a devastating energy crisis loomed in the future. The Central Intelligence Agency (CIA) warned in an April 1977 study that such a crisis probably would occur by 1985 unless energy conservation measures were "greatly increased."

A month later a prestigious panel of international experts assembled by the Massachusetts Institute of Technology (MIT) warned that a worldwide shortage of oil would occur before the year 2000 and possibly as soon as 1981 unless extraordinary efforts were made to conserve energy.

Carter's Plan. Upon taking office, President Carter ordered a small team of energy planners to construct a comprehensive national energy program in 90 days; the deadline was met.

The primary goal of Carter's vaunted "National Energy Plan" was to cut America's appetite for oil and natural gas and to use energy more efficiently.

His answer was an exceedingly complex package of regulatory and tax measures. The Carter plan would have empowered the federal government: to require industries to make products meeting mandated standards of energy efficiency; to tell businesses to burn certain fuels but not others; to sponsor massive programs encouraging property owners to insulate their buildings; to levy stiff taxes against cars that guzzled too much gasoline, against businesses that burned oil or natural gas and against purchasers of domestically produced oil. The taxes were aimed at spurring energy conservation; their effect would be to drive energy prices higher.

By his own admission, Carter did not expect his program to be popular. But, he said, it was necessary.

Pushing It. Carter and the Democratic congressional leaders pushed hard to complete action on the program in 1977, before the next election year.

Carter spoke to the nation via evening television addresses only three times during his first year in Washington; each time the subject was energy. The first was a fireside chat about the natural gas crisis. The next two were to rally support for his energy program. The only speech Carter made to a joint session of Congress during his first year was also on the subject of his energy program.

When the going got tough on Capitol Hill against his plan, the President dispersed his Cabinet across the country to plug for the energy plan. Though his critics at times faulted Carter's tactics, it was clear that no other single domestic issue received so much presidential attention in 1977.

The same could be said of Congress. The first session of the 95th Congress could be said to have had two agendas: energy, and everything else. In the House, Speaker Thomas P. O'Neill Jr., D-Mass., used all the powers he could muster to strongarm the Carter program to passage in record time, passing it as one bill (HR 8444) Aug. 5, 244-177.

Next, Senate Majority Leader Robert C. Byrd, D-W.Va., cleared all other bills from the Senate agenda to give the energy program undivided attention. It was passed as five major bills between Sept. 28 and Oct. 31.

And yet, the Carter energy program did not make it through.

ANALYSIS

There was no single, simple answer why President Carter's energy program encountered so many difficulties in Congress. But there were a number of clearly identifiable contributing factors.

Five basic problems plagued the program from the beginning:

● It was a plan tackling inherently difficult political problems that was drafted virtually in secret by nonpolitical technicians without outside consultation. That alienated not only Capitol Hill, but also interest groups and even members of the Carter administration who held relevant expertise but were not consulted.

- Its drafting was rushed and consequently the plan suffered from technical flaws, which undermined confidence in it.
- It was the object of intense and negative lobbying by a broad range of powerful special interest groups.
- It was poorly sold to Congress by Carter's lobbyists.
- It lacked a constituency.

Despite those factors, the Carter energy program managed to pass the House virtually intact Aug. 5. Then it ran into the Senate, where it was butchered. In addition to the five basic problems listed above, which continued to plague the Carter plan in the Senate, at least four other problems were thrown on the scales, tilting the balance against the President:

- There was a complete loss of momentum between House passage and Senate consideration, caused principally by two things: the August recess and the troubles of Bert Lance, then Carter's budget director.
- The two Senate committees handling the Carter energy plan were dominated by a different predisposition toward energy policy than were their two counterpart committees in the House.
- The Senate was guided by a different style of leadership than was the House, due in part to the nature of the Senate and in part to the nature of Majority Leader Byrd.
- The administration misread the Senate almost to the end, hoping it would come through somehow for the President as had the House.

The Basic Problems

Drafting

From the outset of his term, President Carter vowed to present a comprehensive national energy program to the nation by April 20, 1977, exactly 90 days after he took office.

Later Carter abandoned his early habit of forcing arbitrary deadlines for completion of complicated policy proposals. But on energy, the deadline was met.

The challenge was handed to his energy adviser, James R. Schlesinger. The Harvard-trained economist and former Nixon-Ford Cabinet member gathered around him a small, close-knit team of fewer than two dozen economists, lawyers and Washington-wise administrators.

To beat the clock, they were forced to work almost in isolation. Though the plan came to rest largely on energy tax proposals, Treasury Department tax experts later complained they had not been consulted. Though the plan would need congressional approval to become law, key members of Congress were not invited to help shape the policy and they were miffed. Likewise, experts from private industry were left out, though the plan as conceived would touch every phase of American life.

The political consequence of such a policy formation process was that many who were left out felt little or no obligation to support the final product.

Tacitly recognizing that danger, the White House attempted to present an image of openness via an innovative public relations campaign featuring "mini-conferences" with industry leaders, citizen town meetings and 450,000 letters to citizens requesting energy policy suggestions.

White House protestations to the contrary, most observers were convinced these efforts were all show. They believed the real decisions on the new energy policy were being made in isolation by Schlesinger's small band in the second floor offices of the Old Executive Office Building next door to the White House.

But the deadline was met. And with it came one of the most complex legislative packages ever devised. The Schlesinger team had strung together 113 separate interlocking provisions that together would affect virtually every facet of American society.

Technical Flaws

"The legislation itself was written at white heat, and as a result there are serious technical problems."

That observation came in early May, 1977, from Frank M. Potter, staff director of the House Commerce Subcommittee on Energy and Power. That panel held jurisdiction over most non-tax aspects of the Carter energy plan.

The "technical problems" Potter mentioned began to show up soon after administration officials began defending the plan before congressional committees. The whole program was held together by numbers—estimates of how much energy this proposal would save, how much money that proposal would cost—and with embarrassing frequency, the administration's numbers conflicted with each other.

There were repeated examples of this in May testimony before the House Ways and Means Committee. Administration witnesses from Schlesinger's team provided different answers than Treasury Department tax experts to the same queries.

Doubts about the soundness of the Carter program were magnified during the summer as four comprehensive analyses of the plan performed by non-partisan Capitol Hill research units were unveiled. In each case, the four congressional agencies—the Congressional Budget Office, the General Accounting Office, the Library of Congress and the Office of Technology Assessment—concluded that Carter's program would fall far short of attaining its energy goals.

Lobbying

When things got tough for the White House during Congress' eight-month 1977 examination of the energy plan, the President's men would scream "lobbyists."

On June 9, a House Commerce subcommittee voted to decontrol new natural gas prices, contrary to Carter's plan. The House Ways and Means Committee the same day overwhelmingly rejected the President's proposed gasoline tax, tossed out a proposed rebate for buyers of fuel-efficient cars and weakened Carter's proposed tax on "gas guzzling" autos.

The next day Jody Powell, Carter's press secretary, howled "lobbyists." Gas decontrol, he said, was a "ripoff of the American consumer.... [Y]esterday, the oil companies, the auto companies and their lobbies won significant preliminary victories," Powell said.

At a news conference June 13, the President added his voice to that theme, decrying the "inordinate influence" of the oil and auto industries on Capitol Hill.

Later, the full Commerce Committee overturned its subcommittee vote on gas deregulation and Carter's position was muscled through the House. And though his gasoline tax never resurfaced, the President got most of what he wanted from Ways and Means as well. There was no more talk from the White House about lobbies until the energy bill reached the Senate.

On Oct. 13, the White House screamed louder than ever. The Senate Finance Committee recently had rejected all of the President's key energy tax proposals. At a televised news conference, Carter suggested the nation's oil companies were preparing for "war profiteering in the impending energy crisis.... [T]he oil companies apparently want it all," Carter said.

There is no doubt that the formidable oil and gas industry lobby was working overtime against Carter's program during most of 1977. Their efforts were concentrated on natural gas regulation, but many company representatives were also working to either defeat Carter's taxes or to ensure that the proceeds from the taxes went to the oil industry instead of to consumers, as Carter preferred.

The automobile industry was well represented, especially at sessions on Carter's proposed tax on gas guzzling cars. Union lobbyists, consumer groups and environmentalists all were heavily involved. The nation's major utilities were scrambling all over, opposing Carter's proposed utility rate reforms, his tax on utility use of oil and gas and his proposal to force utilities to burn coal instead of oil and gas.

And those were just the major actors. There were scores of narrowly focused lobbies. Small oil refiners worked their own angles. One lobbyist represented shopping center associations concerned about a possible ban against master utility meters.

In short, the Capitol was crawling with lobbyists of every shape, stripe and persuasion from the day Carter sent his energy package to Congress. But blaming lobbyists alone for Congress' failure to clear the bill is too simplistic. The House, which essentially adopted Carter's program, was no less besieged by pleaders for special interests than was the Senate, which rejected much of the President's program. Lobbyists were an ever-present factor, but hardly the only one.

Selling It

From April 29, the day the White House delivered the energy program to Congress in formal legislative language, complaints were raised on both sides of the Capitol about White House salesmanship.

Key energy legislators did not receive adequate individual attention from White House liaison, they said. They felt disregarded, left out, and most importantly, in the dark.

When they did receive personal attention and briefings, it came late; too often the administration pitchmen did not know the issues sufficiently well to be of much help, members said.

And, both Senate and House members added, there were too many administration aides trying to explain the various portions of the complex package. No one White House salesman save Energy Secretary Schlesinger could make sense of the whole program, some said.

"I don't think they had anyone who could fully explain the package," said Sen. Spark M. Matsunaga, D-Hawaii. "It was a truly awful mess." Matsunaga cast votes on both the Senate Energy and Finance Committees, which together ruled on every facet of Carter's energy program.

A partial exception to the criticism of the White House sales effort was President Carter himself, whose personal efforts were considered diligent and effective. He made telephone calls to round up wavering votes throughout. He held repeated White House meetings with select groups of energy legislators. His major personal slip-up was to not keep the public pressure on the Senate when it was gearing up to tackle the energy program.

No Constituency

In his speech to the nation April 18, 1977, explaining the need for his energy program, President Carter observed:

"I am sure each of you will find something you don't like about the specifics of our proposal.... We can be sure that all the special interest groups in the country will attack the part of this plan that affects them directly."

Six months later, Carter again tried to sell the public his energy program via television Nov. 8, and he noted: "I said six months ago that no one would be completely satisfied with this national energy plan. Unfortunately, that prediction has turned out to be right."

Gallup Polls throughout the year demonstrated one of the biggest obstacles Carter faced: About half the nation refused to take the energy crisis very seriously.

In mid-December, Gallup reported that 40 per cent of the nation's people believed that the U.S. energy situation was "very serious"; another 42 per cent viewed it as "fairly serious." Fifteen per cent, Gallup said, saw the problem as "not at all" serious.

Those figures had remained virtually unchanged since early April, before the President's plan was presented, Gallup said. "...[A]pproximately half of the public can be said to be relatively unconcerned about our energy problems," Gallup wrote in late June. Despite all the political fury in Washington, despite repeated presidential addresses and unceasing media attention, the American public's views on energy changed barely at all in 1977.

The absence of a strong body of public opinion behind Carter's program made it difficult to repel sophisticated lobbying campaigns against the plan waged by committed special interests. As Energy Secretary Schlesinger summed up Oct. 16 on CBS television's "Face the Nation:"

"...[T]he basic problem is that there is no constituency for an energy program. There are many constituencies opposed. But the basic constituency for the program is the future...."

Complicating Factors

As noted earlier, all those problems were present from the start, yet the House accepted the heart of the Carter plan, and the Senate did not. After House passage Aug. 5, new and critical factors came into play.

Momentum

The House, to the surprise of many—including a good number of its own members—managed to meet Speaker O'Neill's ambitious schedule and passed the Carter energy plan almost unchanged before the August recess.

Passage marked the high point of Carter's legislative year; afterwards Congress closed down for a month until Sept. 7. Carter never regained the momentum in 1977.

Having momentum, as every football coach knows, is like having an extra player on the team. The same is true in politics. Jimmy Carter still had some of the luster of political wizardry and a shiny new presidency about him going into the August recess. All that changed over the next few weeks.

Part of the explanation for the loss of momentum lies simply in the nature of the August recess. Washington tends to slow down and catch its breath. The heat is oppressive; people take their vacations while Congress is gone. Members of Congress go home, talk to people, do a little politicking. There is a collective taking of stock, looking back and looking forward. And then after Labor Day, Washington comes back and starts a new cycle.

It is hard to sustain a sense of momentum through such a break. But for Carter in August 1977 it was impossible. During that period the Carter administration had a few holes blown in its bow and was gasping for air by the time Congress returned in September.

The reason for the abrupt turn of events was the Bert Lance fiasco. The President's budget director, close friend and adviser got caught in a scandal stemming from his pre-Washington banking days. With Washington lacking in competing news during August, the Lance affair dominated the news media for weeks. In the end Lance resigned, on Sept. 21, 1977.

Lance's loss was a major blow to the young administration. Apart from the substance of the charges against him, the Lance case was also a very real power fight between the new Carter team and its established institutional opponents in Congress, the bureaucracy and the news media.

The President made it clear he did not want to yield, but in the end he was forced to. Carter looked very vulnerable once he announced Lance's resignation Sept. 21. While difficult to measure, there was no doubt that the Lance debacle contributed to a loss of influence by the Carter team that continued to weaken the President throughout 1977.

Committee Contrasts

The President's energy plan went to the House first, then to the Senate. In the House, though five committees reviewed portions of the bill, the large majority of the work fell to only two panels. Most non-tax proposals were handled by the Interstate and Foreign Commerce Committee, while all energy tax proposals went to Ways and Means.

In the Senate there were only two committees with jurisdiction. Non-tax concerns came under the new Energy and Natural Resources Committee; tax proposals went to the Finance Committee.

It was predictable that Carter's energy plan would receive a more favorable hearing before the two House panels than it did from their Senate counterparts. The House committees had compiled strong records of support for precisely the kinds of energy policies that Carter proposed. The Senate panels either had records of support for opposite kinds of policies, or no records at all.

Utility rate reform provided a good example. In 1976, House Commerce's Subcommittee on Energy and Power held eight days of thorough hearings on that complex subject. A massive record of expert testimony was compiled. The subcommittee chairman, John D. Dingell, D-Mich., sponsored a bill that year growing out of those hearings. Dingell's bill was distinctly pro-consumer.

One of the major sections of President Carter's energy plan dealt with utility rate reform, and his proposals bore a marked resemblance to Dingell's of the previous year. This was more than coincidence; one of Dingell's chief aides in drawing up his 1976 bill was committee counsel Robert Riggs Nordhaus. In early 1977, Nordhaus joined Carter's tem of energy planners.

Consequently, Carter's utility rate reform proposals sailed through the Commerce Committee, and later, the House. *(Utility rate reform, p. 97)*

It was a different story in the Senate. The Energy Committee was new in 1977. Built on the old Interior Committee, its members had never examined electric rate reform before.

In 1977, the panel's Subcommittee on Energy Conservation and Regulation held two days of hearings in late July and three more in September on Carter's rate reform proposals. By the subcommittee's own admission, its members did not know enough about that exceedingly complex field to legislate responsibly.

Also working against Carter on that topic was simply the dominant value position on the subcommittee. Unlike Dingell's panel, its Senate counterpart had not built a similar record of pro-consumer positions on energy issues. It seemed simply to be a more conservative forum.

Natural gas deregulation was another exemplary issue. In the House, Dingell failed narrowly to carry his subcommittee behind the Carter proposal. Carter wanted to continue federal regulation over natural gas prices.

But when the issue reached the full House Commerce Committee, its pro-consumer majority backed Carter and reversed the subcommittee.

The Senate Energy Committee was different. There was no pro-consumer majority. The issue went straight to the full committee and it deadlocked, 9-9. Later, in a major defeat for Carter, the full Senate voted 50-46 to end federal regulation over new gas sales.

The House and Senate committees handling energy taxes were distinctly different as well. The House Ways and Means Committee was large, with 37 members. Since its authoritarian chairman, Wilbur D. Mills, D-Ark. 1939-77, was deposed in 1975, it had been much more democratic in its deliberations and much more responsive to the House leadership. Its approval of an ill-fated, tough energy tax bill in 1975 demonstrated that under Chairman Al Ullman, D-Ore., it had built a record of support for the kind of energy initiatives Carter proposed. And like the Energy Committee in the Senate, the Finance Committee had not.

The Senate Finance Committee was a relatively small group with only 18 members. Unlike Ullman, who worked closely with his party's leadership, Senate Finance was headed by Russell B. Long, D-La., who tended to function as a kind of supreme leader apart from either party's official leadership on tax matters. Long, far more than Ullman, was a master of both the tax code and his committee.

And on matters of energy taxes, unlike Ullman, Long's philosophical bent was very different than President Carter's.

Long represented Louisiana, heartland of the nation's oil and gas industry. He looked out for that industry's interests. From the day Carter announced his energy plan in April, Long said he thought the plan did not provide adequate incentives to the industry for production.

Long's committee was no more sympathetic to Carter's energy taxes than its chairman; arguably less so. After rejecting virtually all of Carter's energy tax proposals, the Finance Committee in October wrote its own vastly different energy tax bill. Rather than trying to induce conservation through penalty taxes, the Finance Committee bill tried to induce additional energy production primarily through tax incentives to industry.

Different Leadership

It had become a commonplace in Washington by the end of 1977 that Jimmy Carter's best ally in the capital during his first year was House Speaker O'Neill. Certainly that was true on the energy bill.

O'Neill saw to it that the Carter energy program got through the House, fast. He made it clear that he saw the energy program as a test of Congress and a test of whether the Democratic Party could govern when it controlled both the executive and legislative branches.

The House Speaker saw the Carter energy plan as the Democrats' plan, and he made it the O'Neill plan as well. He went all out to pass it.

His first move was to create a special blue-ribbon select committee to coordinate House review of the program. To it he appointed 40 hand-picked members, with a majority top-heavy with senior Democrats favorably inclined toward the Carter plan.

Next he set strict short deadlines for the regular standing committees to meet in conducting hearings and mark-ups on the complex bill. He insisted that the deadline be honored and it was; the committees finished work in six weeks and sent the bill to the select committee.

His select committee rushed the bill through in three days, proposing a handful of strengthening amendments. Then the measure was sent to the House Rules Committee, stacked with O'Neill lieutenants who obeyed his directions to protect the bill by issuing a modified closed rule, limiting floor debate and amendments.

O'Neill kept abreast of the measure's progress at every point, and when the legislation appeared in trouble on the floor, he stepped in directly to help.

Delivering a thundering oration, the Speaker appealed to party unity and congressional responsibility and helped block a move to overturn Carter's policy on natural gas.

As with so many other things, leadership on the bill was quite different in the Senate.

On April 20, after Carter outlined his energy plan to Congress, the reaction of Senate Majority Leader Byrd was noticeably cooler than was O'Neill's: "...The President cannot expect every jot and tittle to be enacted as he proposed it," Byrd warned.

Byrd's commitment to the Carter energy plan was of quite a different kind than O'Neill's. The West Virginian's deepest commitment is not to party or President, or to legislative policy, but to the Senate. Though pledged to back the plan and evidently dedicated to working with Carter as smoothly as possible, Byrd stopped short of O'Neill-like efforts.

Byrd's strongest exertions were aimed at getting the energy bill through Congress in 1977, one way or the other. His commitment was, in a phrase he repeated time and again, to "let the Senate work its will" on the program, not necessarily to force the Senate to adopt it.

But even if Byrd had wanted, he would not have been able to manipulate the Senate as O'Neill did the House. Senate rules simply do not allow a leader such power.

"I don't know that anybody today could run this Senate" as strong majority leaders have in the past, observed Sen. Lloyd Bentsen, D-Texas, in an October interview.

Administration Misreading

If the Carter administration saw trouble coming in the Senate, it was slow to react.

There was little evidence that the White House was alarmed at all by initial votes against the plan in the Senate. President Carter himself conceded Oct. 13 that he

was perhaps remiss in not leaning more heavily on the Senate during August and September to pass his program.

But as late as Oct. 16 there was strong evidence that the administration still was expecting the Senate to somehow come through for the President, even though by that time the Senate had finished action on four of the five basic portions of the Carter plan and the fifth had been gutted in the Finance Committee.

On Oct. 16, in an appearance on CBS television's "Face the Nation" program, Energy Secretary Schlesinger downplayed the Senate's actions to date.

"When the original package went to the House," he recalled, "there were all these comments to the effect that the program was being gutted or riddled and so on. Then in August, when the House voted out virtually the entire package, everyone said it was a remarkable triumph. I would not be surprised if we went through the same cycle with regard to the Congress as a whole."

Conference Action

The White House and congressional leaders held out hope following completion of Senate action Oct. 31 that conference agreements on the Carter package could be reached and final action attained before the year's end.

But that was not to be. The reason, basically, was that there were such wide gulfs to be bridged between Senate and House that time simply ran out. A secondary reason was that conferees set a fairly relaxed pace in pursuing their negotiations.

Conferees took up the first of the five basic portions of the Carter energy package –general energy conservation—Oct. 18. They reached agreement on it Oct. 31, just under two weeks later. On Oct. 31, they started the second bill—coal conversion—and completed it Nov. 11, again in less than two weeks. On the third bill—utility rates—they reached their key agreement in four days, took a 10-day Thanksgiving recess and returned to finish the bill after five days more.

On each of those bills, the conferees seldom worked more than five hours a day and often took three-day weekends. Nevertheless, for such far-reaching and complex legislation, working out conference agreements between radically different bills in less than two weeks each cannot be considered unusually slow by normal standards.

It was when they reached natural gas regulation that the conference completely bogged down. That conference started Dec. 2. Battle lines on that question were rigid and there was little middle ground for compromise. Complicating negotiations immensely was the fact that Senate conferees were evenly split, 9-9, and could not agree among themselves on anything.

Completing the conference breakdown was the fact that negotiators on the complex energy tax proposals refused to do much of anything until the natural gas bill was worked out.

Because House Speaker O'Neill was insistent that the House would not vote on any conference agreement until all could be combined for a single up or down vote, none of the Carter energy plan could be sent to the floor for final congressional action until the conferees finished natural gas pricing and taxes.

Consequently, Congress adjourned Dec. 15 with three conference agreements on Carter's energy package on the shelf while two more were still caught in intense negotiations.

Background

During his campaign, Jimmy Carter emphasized the need for conservation as the foundation of the nation's effort to move into a stronger energy posture. Critical of the failure of the nation's leaders to convince the American people of the urgency of the energy problem, he promised to institute a comprehensive conservation program to cut back on energy waste. "Americans are willing to make sacrifices," he said, "if they understand the reason for them and if they believe the sacrifices are fairly distributed." Only the future would prove, however, whether Carter could be sufficiently convincing to the American people to overcome the inertia that had frustrated earlier conservation efforts.

After he became President, one of Carter's first imperatives was to succeed where his predecessors had failed in convincing the American people that the energy crisis was indeed real, and potentially severe. An April Gallup Poll showed that a majority of Americans thought the energy crisis was something less than "very serious." On April 18, Carter delivered what he termed "an unpleasant talk" to the nation via television in an effort to change America's mind. A White House aide was quoted as calling this speech "the-sky-is-falling" message.

"With the exception of preventing war, this is the greatest challenge our country will face during our lifetimes," he said. "The energy crisis has not yet overwhelmed us, but it will if we do not act quickly...."

The energy crisis is worse now, he said, than during the 1973 Arab oil embargo, worse than during the natural gas emergency which threatened the nation the past winter.

The President recited the facts, he said, that lay behind the problem. "The oil and natural gas we rely on for 75 per cent of our energy are running out.... [D]omestic production has been dropping steadily at about 6 per cent a year. Imports have doubled in the last five years. Our nation's independence...is becoming increasingly constrained...."

Carter said America suffered from bad energy habits. "Ours is the most wasteful nation on earth," he said. "We waste more energy than we import. With about the same standards of living we use twice as much energy per person as do other countries like Germany, Japan and Sweden."

If America does not mend its ways, he said, it can look forward to a virtual doomsday nightmare as its future reality. "Unless we act, we will spend more than $550-billion for imported oil by 1985—more than $2,500 for every man, woman and child in America.... [W]e will live constantly in fear of embargoes. We could endanger our freedom...to act in foreign affairs. Within 10 years, we would not be able to import enough oil...our factories will not be able to keep our people on the job...we will not be ready to keep our transportation system running."

Carter's Program

On April 20, 1977, Carter appeared again on nationwide television, this time to outline before a joint session of Congress what he proposed to do about the energy crisis.

As described by Carter and outlined by administration background briefings, the President's energy program featured the following key elements:

Oil, Gas, Coal

Oil Pricing. Oil price controls would be continued indefinitely on oil under current production. Carter asked Congress to apply a tax on all domestic oil production, increasing in three annual stages, to eventually bring the price of all domestic oil to world market price levels in 1980. Net funds collected under the tax would be rebated to the public. Administration spokesmen said the tax would cause each gallon to rise seven cents, and the rebate would theoretically amount to $75 per person per year.

Natural Gas Pricing. Congress was asked to require that new natural gas be sold at federally controlled prices, whether sold interstate or in the state where it was produced. (Under the existing system, intrastate gas was not subject to federal controls.) All new gas would be priced equal to the cost of an energy equivalent amount of oil, or approximately $1.75 per thousand cubic feet in 1978. Gas currently under production would continue under existing price controls, or under interstate market contracts. More expensive new gas would be allocated only to industrial customers; gas at old controlled cheaper prices would be reserved for residential and commercial users. The President also asked for emergency gas allocation authority for three more years.

Oil Stockpile. Carter proposed doubling the strategic oil reserve program to one billion barrels to provide enough oil to cover U.S. needs for 10 months. In addition, oil rationing contingency plans would be drafted.

Outer Continental Shelf. The administration announced its support for pending legislation to tighten leasing policies for oil and gas development on the Outer Continental Shelf.

Gasoline Decontrol. The administration said it hoped to eliminate federal price and allocation controls on gasoline by autumn 1977, reserving the right to reimpose controls if prices exceed a target level.

Coal. Carter asked for a legislative package taxing industries using oil or natural gas as boiler fuel at levels designed to encourage a switch to coal. The tax would take effect in 1979 for most industries and 1983 for utilities. A 10 per cent tax credit would apply to costs entailed in converting facilities to coal use. New industrial and utility boilers would be prohibited from being fueled by oil or gas. The administration reiterated its intent to insist on strong clean air and strip mine standards. Coal-fired plants would be required to install the best available pollution control technology. The administration also pledged to expand research on coal technologies that would reduce pollution associated with coal burning.

Transportation

Gas Guzzler Tax. Current law mandated that new car fleets must average 18 miles per gallon (mpg) in 1978, 19 mpg in 1979, 20 mpg in 1980, graduating to 27.5 mpg in 1985. Carter asked Congress to impose an excise tax beginning in model year 1978 on new cars and light trucks not meeting those standards. The tax rates would increase annually. The least efficient cars would be taxed the most.

Cars exceeding efficiency standards would earn manufacturers rebates. Total rebates would not exceed total revenue from the excise tax. Rebates for vehicles made overseas would be available after treaties or executive agreements were made. By 1985, the worst gas guzzlers would be taxed $2,488; the most efficient cars, including electric vehicles, would earn rebates of $493.

Standby Gasoline Tax. Beginning Jan. 15, 1979, if national gasoline consumption exceeded the previous year's target level, Carter asked Congress to levy a five-cent-per-gallon tax each year. The tax could total 50 cents after 10 years. Funds collected would be rebated to consumers under a mechanism not yet devised. Target consumption levels would allow limited increases in national gasoline consumption until 1980, and call for decreases thereafter, although mileage totals would increase due to improved efficiency.

Nuclear, Non-Conventional Power

Nuclear. The administration's indefinite deferment of programs for nuclear fuel reprocessing, use of plutonium for fuel and construction of a demonstration breeder reactor were reaffirmed.

Legislation was requested to guarantee sale of enriched uranium to countries agreeing to conditions concerning nuclear non-proliferation. Plans were announced to increase domestic uranium enrichment capacity and build a more efficient centrifuge enrichment technology plant. Safety and inspection standards for conventional nuclear power plants would be strengthened and the licensing process sped up.

Solar, Geothermal Energy. A tax credit of 40 per cent for the first $1,000 and 25 per cent for the next $6,400 would be extended for installation costs of solar equipment by homeowners. The credit would decline over time and be applicable through 1984.

Carter proposed tax deductions to stimulate geothermal drilling and increased funding for research on non-conventional energy technologies.

Buildings

Homeowners Tax Credit. Congress was asked to give homeowners a tax credit of 25 per cent of the first $800 and 15 per cent of the next $1,400 spent on approved conservation home improvements. The credit would apply for improvements from April 20, 1977, to 1985.

Utility Insulation Program. Legislation was requested mandating utilities to offer home insulation financed by loans repaid through monthly utility bills.

Federal Loans. Carter asked Congress to cut red tape to improve access to loans for home energy conservation improvements through federal mortgage programs.

Weatherization. The Carter budget would increase federal funding for low-income weatherization programs to $130-million in fiscal 1978 and $200-million in fiscal 1979 and 1980. Also the Agriculture Department was directed to implement a rural home weatherization program.

Business Tax Credit. Congress was asked to enact a 10 per cent tax credit for approved conservation improvements by business.

Mandatory Standards. The Secretary of Housing and Urban Development was required to develop mandatory efficiency standards for new buildings by 1980 instead of 1981.

Other Aspects

Appliances. Congress was asked to make voluntary appliance efficiency standards mandatory for home appliances like air conditioners, furnaces and water heaters.

Industrial Conservation. Carter asked Congress to enact a five year, 10 per cent investment tax credit for industrial investment in approved equipment such as solar heaters, in addition to the current 10 per cent credit.

Cogeneration. In a new legislative proposal, Carter asked enactment of a special 10 per cent tax credit for industrial investment in cogeneration equipment, a process much used in Europe which utilizes industrial heat waste to generate energy.

Utility Rate Reform. Congress was asked to ban declining block rate structures that promote electricity consumption. Utilities would be required to offer peak use pricing rates to customers willing to pay meter costs.

Energy Information. In an administrative action, the proposed Department of Energy, once created, would take over audit and verification functions currently performed by the American Gas Association and the American Petroleum Institute. Oil and gas companies would be required to submit detailed data on their operations to the government.

HOUSE ACTION

Without fanfare, Majority Leader Jim Wright, D-Texas introduced President Carter's energy plan May 2. It was packaged in a single bill (HR 6831), entitled the National Energy Act. Various parts of the 283-page bill were referred to five different committees. The deadline for their work on the President's requests was set as July 13, 1977. Once that work was completed the sections were to be sent to a new House Ad Hoc Select Committee on Energy to be reassembled.

HR 6831 consisted of two titles: Title I dealt with non-tax matters, Title II contained all the tax-related requests. Title II, referred in its entirety to the Ways and Means Committee, included Carter's proposals for:

● A tax credit for homeowners who installed conservation or solar energy equipment in their residences.

● A "gas-guzzler" tax on inefficient cars and a rebate for more efficient cars.

● The standby gasoline tax of 5-cents-a-gallon imposed each year that gasoline consumption did not taper off, and provision for *per capita* rebates to consumers from these revenues.

● A new investment tax credit to encourage businesses to install energy-saving or solar energy or cogeneration equipment.

● The crude oil "equalization" tax to raise the cost of domestic oil to that of foreign oil and provision for *per capita* rebates to some consumers from these revenues.

● A tax on the industrial use of oil and gas, with provision for crediting against that tax the cost of the plant's conversion to the use of coal.

● The second largest portion of HR 6831 went to the Interstate and Foreign Commerce Committee whose Energy and Power Subcommittee was to begin hearings May 9. It received Carter's requests for:

● Revising the system of federal controls over the price of natural gas.

● Restructuring the ratemaking policies of the electric utility industry in line with the premise that the rates charged a consumer should reflect the cost of providing him service.

● Development of plans through which utilities would educate and assist consumers in making their homes more energy-efficient.

● Eestablishment of energy efficiency standards for major consumer products and disclosure of how such products comply or fail to comply with those standards.

● A federal grant program to encourage schools and hospitals to undertake energy conservation measures.

● A prohibition on the use of oil or natural gas by new fuel-burning plants and a new set of requirements for the conversion to other fuels of existing plants now burning oil and gas.

In addition, the portions of HR 6831 designed to encourage lending institutions to finance energy-related home improvements and to increase funding for weatherization of low-income homes and development of building energy standards were referred to the House Banking, Finance and Urban Affairs Committee.

The House Government Operations Committee received the provisions of the bill concerning the establishment of vanpooling arrangements for federal employees. And the House Public Works and Transportation Committee was given the provisions concerning the demonstration of solar energy heating and cooling equipment in federal buildings.

Standing Committees' Action

The House Ways and Means Committee finished nearly four weeks of marking up the crucial tax portions of the energy bill June 30. The administration appeared to win most of the key battles, seeing only the proposal for a standby gasoline tax rejected outright. But the committee also substantially watered down the taxes to force industries and utilities to convert from oil and gas to coal—primarily by excluding large categories of industries from having to pay.

While the Ways and Means Committee was marking up the tax portions of the energy bill, the Interstate and Foreign Commerce Committee was working on its sections of the bill. The action took place first in the Energy and Power Subcommittee and then in the full Commerce Committee. In both forums most of the action focused on the explosive gas regulation issue. The subcommittee and full committee gave almost uniform endorsement to the other aspects of the energy plan that came under their purview.

Of the three small parts of the energy plan referred to other committees, the House Government Operations Committee reported its provisions June 28, the Banking Committee July 11 and the Public Works Committee July 13.

The House Ways and Means Committee formally approved its sections of the bill July 13. The Commerce Committee finished July 14, a day late. At that point the portions of the bill were ready to be sent to the Ad Hoc Committee on Energy to be spliced together.

Ad Hoc Energy Committee

The Ad Hoc Energy Committee which received the energy bill from the five standing committees was the product of a careful compromise between House Speaker Thomas P. O'Neill Jr., D-Mass., and the chairmen of several House committees that traditionally held jurisdiction over energy legislation.

In late 1976, O'Neill pledged to work for creation of a new standing energy committee to speed development of a comprehensive energy policy. He criticized the existing House committee structure, saying responsibility over energy policy was split between too many panels.

O'Neill's plan met resistance from key House committee chairmen. After months of consultation they worked out an agreement that gave the Speaker much less than he originally wanted but turned out to be an effective tool for channeling Carter's energy plan to the House in the form he desired.

O'Neill explained the compromise to House members in a "Dear Colleague" letter April 20. A special ad hoc committee would be created to facilitate House consideration of President Carter's energy proposals. Legislation first would be parceled out to appropriate standing committees just as if no ad hoc committee existed. But they would have to finish their work within deadlines set by the Speaker. Then their marked-up versions of the legislation would be referred to the Speaker's committee, whose powers would be limited.

"The committee will not have authority to change the recommendations reported by the standing committees," the letter said. "It will have authority to recommend amendments for consideration on the floor."

O'Neill promised in the letter that he would recommend to the Rules Committee that the standing committees be allowed to manage those portions of the bill that fell within their jurisdictions when the legislation reached the floor.

Moreover, the Speaker wrote, "when the House finally goes to conference with the Senate on the energy legislation, primary responsibility will rest with representatives of each of the standing committees to settle differences relating to its portion of the bill."

On April 21, one day after President Carter's energy address to a joint session of Congress and one day after release of O'Neill's letter, the House by voice vote approved H Res 508 authorizing the committee's formation.

When HR 6831 was introduced and referred to the five standing committees, O'Neill directed the committees to complete their work and report the legislation to the ad hoc committee by July 13. The timetable was set to ensure House floor action on the bill before the summer recess.

In the meantime, the ad hoc committee members held a few general hearings amid a swirl of publicity, receiving testimony painting an overview of the nation's energy plight and the Carter energy plan. Once the regular standing committees began hearings and markup on the Carter legislation, the ad hoc panel retreated into the background. Its members kept up with what was happening in the standing committees through regular briefings from congressional and White House aides. Daily packets of updated information were circulated to the panel members as markup progressed.

Speaker O'Neill chose the new committee's members. He drew almost all of his selections from the standing committees holding jurisdiction over energy affairs.

The ad hoc panel had 40 members, 27 of them Democrats and 13 Republicans, reflecting the partisan alignment in the House. Of those 40, 11 were drawn from the Commerce Committee and 10 from Ways and Means. Five more were selected from the Banking Committee.

Rounding out the 40 members were representatives from Government Operations, Public Works, Interior and Insular Affairs, and Science and Technology. The latter two committees did not have a hand in review of the Carter package, but frequently were involved in energy policy.

Heading the collection of leaders was Thomas L. Ashley, 54, a well-respected Democrat from Toledo, Ohio, who never before had chaired a full committee despite 22 years in the House.

When the ad hoc committee received the energy program from the five standing committees Chairman Ashley July 20 introduced the compilation as a clean bill (HR 8444).

The committee hurried through the provisions of the bill in three days, July 20-22. During the consideration the committee functioned largely as a Democratic forum; GOP proposals were soundly defeated.

Democratic members on the panel, basically working as an arm of the party leadership that named them, established an unshakable majority to protect President Carter's energy program.

They operated principally through private caucuses they held the day before each committee meeting to agree among themselves on specific amendments they would allow the next day.

The pattern prevailed throughout with the agreed-upon amendments easily approved and others easily rejected—mostly along party lines. The actions produced howls of protest from Republicans who said they were being frozen out of decisions on national energy policy.

The committee did approve several important amendments. Under the terms by which the committee was set up the amendments were not automatically added to HR 8444, but were to be offered to the bill when it reached the floor.

Among the amendments approved by the committee were an additional federal gasoline tax of four cents a gallon and an expanded definition of newly discovered natural gas that could be sold at higher prices.

Gasoline Tax. The gasoline tax was proposed by Dan Rostenkowski, D-Ill., and was supported by the caucus. Rostenkowski's proposal would have levied a new two-cent tax per gallon of gasoline in 1978, and another two cents starting in 1979. Once in full effect, it was estimated that the extra tax would generate an estimated $4.8-billion annually in revenue.

Rostenkowski proposed putting all revenue in a special trust fund for three purposes. Two cents of every four would be allocated for energy research and for building the strategic oil reserve program; one and one-half cents would go toward car-pooling and mass transit programs; and one-half cent would go to state transportation programs.

Natural Gas. In another significant amendment, Eckhardt proposed expanding the Carter plan's definition of "new natural gas" to include more wells within the designation.

New gas discoveries under the Carter plan would be eligible for a ceiling price of $1.75 per thousand cubic feet starting in 1978. Old gas would be controlled at lower prices. The Carter plan was relatively stringent in specifying the conditions necessary for a well to qualify as "new" so it could draw the top controlled price.

Eckhardt's proposal allowed more potential gas reserves to receive that designation, and hence, allowed producers of wells from those properties the opportunity to make more money from gas production.

House Floor Action

The House passed HR 8444 Aug. 5, 244-177 after a week of debate.

The bill gave Carter much of what he wanted. But backers of the package suffered a momentary scare just before passage when a Republican motion to kill the crude oil equalization tax, a key part of the program, failed by only a 203-219 vote.

Of the key amendments developed by the Ad Hoc Energy Committee, the gas tax was overwhelmingly rejected but the natural gas compromise was adopted. The natural gas amendment was accepted after the administration forces beat back a deregulation proposal. The tense,

close natural gas battle was the highlight of the debate on the bill.

Natural Gas

The deregulation proposal was rejected by the House Aug. 3, 199-227, thanks to a carefully drawn compromise and the solid support of the House Democratic leadership.

Compromise Proposal. On Aug. 3 sponsors presented the natural gas compromise developed by the ad hoc committee designed to pull over enough votes from the deregulation forces to ensure passage for the Carter pricing system. It was approved by voice vote the same day.

The amendment was cosponsored by Bob Eckhardt, a Texas Democrat normally opposed to deregulation of natural gas, and Charles Wilson, a Texas Democrat normally in favor of deregulation.

Their proposal expanded the definition of "new" natural gas so that potentially much greater amounts of the fuel could draw the high ceiling price under the Carter pricing system. Under the Carter plan, "new gas" was limited to that found in new reservoirs at least two and one-half miles away from or 1,000 feet deeper than existing wells.

The Eckhardt-Wilson amendment changed the language to define all gas as "new" which was found beyond those limits, or in any new reservoirs within those limits. And their proposal gave states the right to determine if a reservoir was new, subject to FPC oversight.

Ashley, chairman of the ad hoc committee, said the amendment would provide incentives for natural gas production and at the same time would "protect the American consumer from unwarranted high prices...."

Gasoline Tax. Despite backing by President Carter and the House Democratic leadership, two amendments to raise the federal tax on gasoline never had a chance. Both were drowned in a deluge of negative votes Aug. 4.

A rare coalition — Democrats and Republicans, conservatives and liberals, rural representatives and defenders of the urban poor — united enthusiastically against the proposals.

SENATE ACTION

The Senate took a very different approach to the energy program, taking it up and passing it in the form of the following six bills: S 977 forcing new electric utility and major industrial plants to burn coal or other fuels instead of oil and natural gas; S 701, a minor measure authorizing matching grants for energy conservation in schools and hospitals; S 2057, containing wide-ranging energy conservation incentives; S 2104, deregulating natural gas; S 2114, relating to electric rates; and HR 5263, providing energy tax incentives.

Each Senate bill was added to a minor House-passed bill to speed the legislation in Congress. The move was made in committee on the energy tax bill; the other substitutions were made on the floor. S 977 was combined with S 701 and added to HR 5146; S 2057 became HR 5037; S 2104 became HR 5289; and S 2114 became HR 4018.

Coal Conversion

The Senate Energy and Natural Resources Committee July 25 reported S 977 (S Rept 95-361). The bill was designed to force electric utilities and major industrial plants to burn coal and other fuels instead of oil and natural gas. It was expected to save less oil and natural gas than the

Carter plan and House bill. It also contained the following major provisions not in those versions which:

• Authorized $1-billion in federal loans to help plants cover the cost of converting to coal and authorized $5-billion in federal guarantees to back conversion loans made by others.

• Authorized an additional $1.2-billion for federal aid to areas affected by "boomtown-like" development of coal.

• Authorized federal payments to companies whose plants could not be economically converted to coal. This provision was aimed at companies that would be eligible for an exemption from a coal conversion order because the changeover would be disproportionately expensive. Standards for granting an exemption were spelled out elsewhere in the legislation. The bill placed no limit on the amount of federal aid.

The committee report estimated that the bill would force up electric utility rates nationwide by an average of 2.5 per cent.

Prices of industrial goods would rise an average of 1.4 per cent to 2.1 per cent because of the measure, the report said. But some industries would be hit harder than others.

In the petrochemical industry, for instance, product prices would rise between 6.2 per cent and 9.3 per cent, the report said. Aluminum prices would go up between 4 and 7 per cent. And paper and steel both would rise as much as 2.6 per cent.

"These price changes are due to the coal program alone," the report said. Other energy proposals currently under review in Congress also would affect prices, it noted.

The Senate passed S 977 Sept. 8, 74-8. It then combined its provisions with those of S 701 (S Rept 95-351), passed by voice vote July 20, authorizing $900-million in federal matching grants for approved energy conservation expenses in schools and hospitals. Those provisions, along with the coal conversion provisions of HR 8444, the House energy bill, were added to a minor House-passed bill (HR 5146) in order to expedite consideration in conference.

Before passing the bill the Senate adopted an amendment by J. Bennett Johnston, D-La., further diminishing the amount of oil the bill would save. The Johnston amendment greatly expanded the number of new major industrial plants that would be allowed to burn oil—but not natural gas—instead of being forced to use coal.

With three important exceptions, the 29 amendments adopted by the Senate did not change the substance of the measure as reported from the Energy Committee.

The three exceptions were the Johnston amendment; two related amendments by Jacob K. Javits, R-N.Y., expanding terms allowing the FEA to make direct loans and to guarantee loans to help plants cover the costs of converting to coal; and an amendment by John A. Durkin, D-N.H., authorizing an additional $100-million for the rehabilitation of branch and spur rail lines to transport coal.

Energy Conservation

The Senate Committee on Energy and Natural Resources voted 14-4 Aug. 1 to report S 2057 with four Republicans — Clifford P. Hansen, Wyo., James A. McClure, Idaho, Dewey F. Bartlett, Okla., and Paul Laxalt, Nev. — in opposition. The report (S Rept 95-409) was filed Aug. 18.

As reported, the bill provided $1.022-billion in authorizations through fiscal 1982 for a broad range of energy conservation programs. It substituted a ban on new

cars that do not meet specified standards of fuel efficiency for the administration's proposed tax on "gas guzzlers."

The Senate passed S 2057 Sept. 13, 78-4. It then added its provisions and the equivalent provisions of the House energy bill to a House-passed private bill (HR 5037).

Debate on S 2057 took three days, during which the Senate adopted 33 largely noncontroversial amendments by voice vote.

Nine amendments were rejected including an attempts to kill the gas guzzler ban.

Several highly inflammatory proposals were among the rejected amendments, turned down by overwhelming margins.

Included in that category were proposals from Lowell P. Weicker Jr., R-Conn., to require each car to be kept off the roads one day a week and to close gasoline stations from Saturday evening until Monday mornings.

Equally incendiary proposals from Dale Bumpers, D-Ark., to ration gasoline and from Charles H. Percy, R-Ill., to make federal employees pay for parking spaces they now use for free were also rejected.

Natural Gas

Instead of marking up the administration proposal to continue and extend gas regulation with higher prices, a deadlocked Senate Energy Committee sent the proposal to the floor without recommendation. The report on the bill (S 2104—S Rept 95-436) was filed Sept. 15.

The key committee vote, Sept. 12, was a 9-9 tie on a bill (S 256) to phase out regulation of new gas within five years. Voting with Republicans for the measure were Democrats J. Bennett Johnston, La., and Wendell H. Ford, Ky.

Earlier, the committee had turned down, 6-12, a proposal (S 110) by Dewey F. Bartlett, R-Okla., to deregulate immediately the price of all natural gas except that under contract. Both bills were offered as substitutes to the administration plan.

The tie vote prompted the sponsor of S 256 in committee, Clifford P. Hansen, R-Wyo., to move that the panel release the President's plan without further action. Johnston and Ford cast the only dissenting votes, although Howard M. Metzenbaum, D-Ohio, and James Abourezk, D-S.D., were absent. The committee agreed to report the natural gas provisions of the Carter energy plan as a clean bill.

The Senate passed a substitute version of S 2104 Oct. 6 after 14 days of debate that included a nine-day filibuster by supporters of the administration bill. The filibuster was finally broken when Majority Leader Robert C. Byrd, D-W.Va., and Vice President Walter F. Mondale, despite their support for deregulation, decided that it was tying up the Senate futilely and joined forces to end it.

The end of the filibuster enabled a modified deregulation substitute offered by James B. Pearson, R-Kan., and Lloyd Bentsen, D-Texas, to come to a vote. It was adopted 50-46. The bill was then passed by voice vote. Its provisions were attached to a House-passed private bill (HR 5289) along with the House-passed gas regulation provisions.

As passed by the Senate, HR 5289:

• Ended federal price regulation for new natural gas found onshore.

• Specified that for two years after enactment, the price of deregulated new natural gas would not exceed $2.48 per thousand cubic feet (mcf).

• Specified that prices of gas produced offshore would continue to be regulated through Dec. 31, 1982.

Administration Faulted for Poor Energy Lobbying

While President Carter chided "special interests" and a potentially irresponsible Senate for his energy woes, the consensus on Capitol Hill appeared to be that the President and his team were themselves largely to blame for the plunder of his energy program in the Senate.

Despite Carter's April declaration that his energy package responded to the "moral equivalent of war," the widespread judgment was that his own administration waged a poorly timed, politically insensitive and error-plagued lobbying battle on behalf of his energy proposals. *(1978 Lobbying, p. 24)*

The major criticisms were that he drafted the program in haste, consulted too little with the key committee chairmen in Congress, paid inadequate attention to the program during the crucial months prior to September and either poorly defended or too easily abandoned major components of the legislation.

The various tax proposals in the bills were not thoroughly checked out with the administration's own Treasury Department officials or with Sen. Long's Finance Committee, a fact confirmed both by administration and congressional sources. Since the energy package was heavily reliant on tax incentives and disincentives, the failure to sign on members of the taxwriting Finance Committee contributed largely to that committee's hostility to several crucial pieces of the program, the crude oil equalization tax and the industrial energy users' tax.

Little Expertise

Some senators and aides were privately contemptuous of the level of expertise the administration group displayed in working the Hill. Aides and lobbyists friendly to the administration program complained that basic legwork—the briefing of staffs on substantive issues, the early and steady checking to meet the needs and doubts of legislators was done either too little or too late. Occasionally, substantive errors by the administration team proved costly.

Examples of such complaints were numerous. In the Senate, the administration was criticized for failing to defend its own gas-guzzler tax in the Finance Committee. Committee aides were not briefed or even called by the administration up to a week before the committee vote on the proposal.

One document relating to the tax was not given to staffers in time to be useful. The result on Sept. 20 was a strong committee vote to kill the tax, despite Chairman Long's support for it and widespread expectations that it would pass.

Before that, according to Sen. Howard M. Metzenbaum, D-Ohio, the administration also had failed to contact him or work with him in his successful effort to have the Energy Committee impose an outright ban on the biggest gas-guzzlers.

Likewise, Senate aides complained that the administration's utilities package was never adequately defended.

"It was disappointing in terms of the groundwork that they laid," said an aide to a liberal Democrat on the Energy Committee. "They really have not gone out of their way to explain the administration program." Again, the result, in conjunction with poor drafting, was the gutting of the proposal.

On the House side, one example cited by key energy aides was a substantive gaffe committed by the administration team on an amendment offered in the Ways and Means Committee to the proposed industrial user's tax.

The administration first approved the amendment, aiding its approval by Ways and Means. Belatedly, it discovered the amendment was damaging to the overall program and was forced to oppose it in the Ad Hoc Energy Committee, with only partial success.

Ways and Means Chairman Al Ullman, D-Ore., said that the administration lobbying had not "hampered" the committee's work, had on occasion proved helpful and had left no great impression, either positive or negative. The ranking minority member, Barber B. Conable Jr., R-N.Y., was less kind, contending that the administration lobbying effort was "nonexistent.... It's just remarkable that they don't care how I vote."

Carter's Personal Role

Conable offered some mild criticism of the President's own performance in wooing the committee last spring. At two breakfast meetings held at the White House, Carter offered what Conable viewed as inconsistent and less-than-effective arguments for his program.

The President's own lobbying role was criticized in other ways. A widespread criticism was that he had let the political ball drop for months between his dramatic April plea and a Sept. 24 speech at Norfolk attacking the near-victorious deregulation forces in the Senate.

Another fundamental criticism of the administration handling of its energy program was its failure to support initiatives from legislators considered friendly to the administration package. One example was the administration decision not to support the moves by Sen. Edward M. Kennedy, D-Mass., toward horizontal divestiture—keeping gas companies out of coal and uranium ownership.

According to James Flug of the Energy Action Committee, that decision was also a tactical as well as a political mistake. "If they needed anything once things started to unravel over here in the Senate, they needed a good strong showing," Flug said. "Even if they didn't win, which I think they might have done, they could have thrown a scare into the industry and dealt from a position of strength with the oil boys."

In the natural gas muddle that deadlocked the Senate for two weeks the administration posture appeared to be one not of strength but of professed willingness to compromise, again prompting criticism from some of its allies.

The Carter administration did not support or even communicate very well with the two filibustering senators working for the administration's original proposal—Metzenbaum and James Abourezk, D-S.D.

"They don't know what we're doing and we don't know what they're doing," Abourezk said on the morning of the Sept. 27-28 all-night session. "We've called them a few times, and they say they're working but we don't know at what."

● Defined new gas as that sold or delivered for the first time in interstate commerce after Jan. 1, 1977, subject to certain qualifications.

● Allowed the Federal Energy Regulatory Commission to determine if gas was ineligible for being considered "new" because it had been "wrongfully withheld" from the market previously.

● Provided a system of incremental pricing whereby old gas sold at lower regulated prices must be allocated to high priority consumers, such as residences, schools, hospitals and essential agricultural users, until the cost of new gas to other users equalled the reasonable cost of substitute fuel oil.

Utility Rates

On Sept. 19, the Senate Committee on Energy and Natural Resources voted 12-3 to report out a bill (S 2114 —S Rept 95-442) aimed at utility energy conservation, but the panel purposely dropped from the measure virtually all of Carter's far-reaching initiatives.

As reported, S 2114:

● Provided that the federal government could intervene in state rate-making procedures as an advocate, but with no other powers.

● Authorized a study of natural gas rate-making procedures.

● Required large non-regulated utilities to report to the federal government on their costs of servicing customers.

● Established federal guidelines and exemptions relating to cogenerators and small power producers.

● Authorized loans and studies of small hydroelectric projects.

● Provided for establishment of a research institute to aid state regulatory agencies.

When S 2114 reached the Senate floor Oct. 5, bill manager J. Bennett Johnston, D-La., explained why the Energy Committee had turned down the administration plan. Johnston said the administration bill "contemplated a radical extension of federal authority into the highly complex matter of the design of retail rates for electricity." He said the problem had traditionally been handled at the state level because of geographic, climatic and economic regional differences.

"The committee felt strongly and the committee record clearly showed," Johnston said, "that at present there is no clear justification for such an extension of federal authority. At a later time, after more study and experimentation with alternative rate structures, it is conceivable that a case for enforcement of some sort of federal standards could be made. But that case simply cannot be made based on the record available at the time."

Energy Committee Chairman Henry M. Jackson, D-Wash., agreed with Johnston. He also cautioned that there were no easy answers to the problem of rising utility costs: "Utility rates are going to continue to rise both because fuel prices will continue to rise and because national policy has been unable to bring down the rate of inflation."

The Senate attached the provisions of S 2114 to a minor House-passed bill (HR 4018) along with the electric rate provisions of HR 8444, the House-passed Carter energy bill, and passed the bill, 86-7.

Energy Taxes

The Senate Finance Committee took an entirely different approach to energy tax proposals than the Carter administration and the House. During markups it systematically rejected each of Carter's three key tax proposals—the equalization tax on crude oil, the tax on utility and industrial use of oil and gas and the tax on "gas guzzling" cars. Together these taxes accounted for roughly half of the Carter energy program. Finance Committee Chairman Russell B. Long, D-La., had supported the equalization tax, but only if the revenues were channeled toward production of more energy rather than consumer rebates, and the majority of his committee refused to go along even with that. Instead, the committee voted 13-5 Oct. 21 to report out HR 5263 (S Rept 95-529) rolling together a mixture of tax credits for energy production and conservation which, if enacted, would cost the federal Treasury an estimated $40-billion through fiscal 1985 and save an estimated 2.1 million barrels of oil per day.

The only revenue raiser in the Finance Committee bill was an extension of the current four cent per gallon tax on gasoline through 1985, estimated by the staff to bring in $20-billion, cutting the bill's negative budget impact in half.

The Senate Oct. 31 passed HR 5263, 52-35.

Passage came after six days of debate, during which 49 amendments were adopted and 15 rejected. Through it all Finance Committee Chairman Long was in firm control.

He bested Energy Committee Chairman Henry M. Jackson, D-Wash., in a direct head-to-head challenge over whether the Senate should allow Long the flexibility he sought to deal in conference. He persuaded Jackson, Budget Committee Chairman Edmund S. Muskie, D-Maine, and Banking Committee Chairman William Proxmire, D-Wis., to drop threatened challenges to his bill on grounds of jurisdictional disputes with their committees.

Long was successful also in defeating an attempt to recommit his bill to committee for redrafting. To win, he overcame a coalition broad enough to include conservatives like Robert Dole, R-Kan., and Jesse Helms, R-N.C., and liberals like Edward M. Kennedy, D-Mass., and Howard M. Metzenbaum, D-Ohio.

Time and again, amendments Long accepted were subsequently approved, while those he opposed were rejected.

Once, Long's motion to table a controversial amendment was narrowly rejected, apparently setting up the proposal's imminent victory. But then Long persuaded the amendment's sponsor, Dewey F. Bartlett, R-Okla., to withdraw his proposal to avoid setting off a filibuster by opponents.

On another occasion, the Appropriations Committee proposed an amendment to knock out some of Long's favored tax credits. Long moved to table the Appropriations Committee proposal, and lost. Then, however, on a motion to adopt the Appropriations Committee proposal, Long fought hard and the amendment was rejected.

Only twice was Long forced to swallow proposals he opposed, and even then his opposition was qualified.

In the first case, the Senate adopted a greatly scaled-back tax on industrial and utility use of oil and gas, despite Long's argument that adoption might hamper his ability to deal in conference. The tax was offered by Metzenbaum.

In the second, Kennedy succeeded in trimming back the major energy-saving tax break in the committee bill, cutting the credit for business investment in alternate energy equipment from 40 percent to 15 percent. Long agreed to accept that cut only after having failed to table Kennedy's original amendment, which would have cut the credit to 10 percent.

New Department Given Wide Energy Powers

President Carter's request for a new Cabinet-level Department of Energy, consolidating the vast array of federal energy programs in one agency, was approved with ease. He signed the bill into law (S 826 — PL 95-91) Aug. 4, 1977. James R. Schlesinger, Carter's chief energy adviser, was immediately nominated to head the department; the nomination was approved by a Senate voice vote Aug. 4.

Under the legislation, the new department was given all powers then held by the Federal Power Commission (FPC), the Federal Energy Administration (FEA), and the Energy Research and Development Administration (ERDA). Those three sprawling agencies were abolished.

The new department also gained control over programs that had been housed in five other federal agencies and was given a strong consulting role in at least two others.

The President got essentially what he wanted in the new department. However, Congress refused Carter's request to grant the Secretary the final say over energy prices. Congress vested that far-reaching power in an independent commission within the department. The Secretary could circumvent the commission on oil pricing if the President said a national emergency required quick action.

With that major exception, Congress strongly supported Carter's requests—as the passage votes in both chambers showed. The Senate passed its version of the bill May 18 by a 74-10 vote; the House approved its bill 310-20 on June 3.

The new department, the first since the Department of Transportation was created in 1966, was expected to employ an estimated 20,000 workers once it was launched and have a budget of about $10.6-billion for fiscal 1978, according to the White House's original proposal.

For the department's first full year of operation — fiscal 1979 — the president requested a $12.6 billion budget authorization, 22 percent more than the fiscal 1978 levels for all programs combined in the new department.

Energy Pricing Issue

The one critical area of disagreement between Carter and Congress concerned who should have the power to set prices and regulations for natural gas, oil and electricity.

Carter proposed creation of an Energy Regulatory Administration within the new department to administer those powers. A Board of Hearings and Appeals would provide the independent, quasi-judicial structural framework necessary to ensure the integrity of the regulatory process, he maintained, while ultimate price-setting authority would be vested in the department's Secretary.

Neither house of Congress bought that approach. Both insisted that sensitive economic decisions on pricing would be shielded better from political pressures if vested wholly in an independent collegial body within the department than if held by a single person serving at the President's pleasure.

Congressional insistence on that critical point constituted the only serious setback Carter sustained during

legislative review of his proposal. The agency's ultimate creation, despite that conflict, would have to be considered a major victory for the President.

By contrast, proposals from President Nixon in 1971 and 1973 to reorganize the federal energy bureaucracy went nowhere in Congress.

Provisions

As signed into law, S 826:

Title I—Findings and Purposes

Declared that energy problems present a serious threat to the United States which the government could respond to best through formation of a new Department of Energy.

Title II—Establishment of the Department

Created a Department of Energy headed by a Secretary appointed by the President subject to Senate approval.

Created within the department the following positions to be filled by presidential appointment subject to Senate confirmation: a deputy secretary, a general counsel, an under secretary and eight assistant secretaries.

Specified 11 broad areas of functional responsibility over which the assistant secretaries would hold primary management control, including: fuel supply and leasing procedures, research and development, environment, international energy policy, national security, intergovernmental relations, competition and consumer affairs, nuclear waste management, energy conservation, power marketing, and public and congressional relations.

Specified that upon appointment of each assistant secretary, the President shall identify which functions that individual would manage.

Created within the department a Federal Energy Regulatory Commission.

Created within the department an Energy Information Administration, to be headed by an administrator appointed by the President subject to Senate confirmation.

Directed the administrator to create a central unified energy data collection and analysis program, and assigned him the energy data gathering functions provided by the Energy Supply and Environmental Coordination Act of 1974 and the Federal Energy Administration Act of 1974.

Protected the administrator from having to obtain approval from departmental superiors in the collection or analysis of energy data.

Provided that the information administration would be subject to an annual professional audit.

Specified that the administration must provide promptly any information requested by any other office in the department.

Specified that information held by the administration must be released to the public promptly upon request, except for such information exempted by law from disclosure.

Directed the administrator to identify major energy companies in the United States and to prepare a financial report form for those companies to fill out at least annually.

Specified that the financial report form should be designed to allow the government to evaluate each company's revenues, profits, cash flow and costs resulting from each phase of its energy-related operations.

Directed that the form should be in use by the second full calendar year following enactment of this law and that the information gathered should be summarized for inclusion in the department's annual report.

Created within the department an Economic Regulatory Administration to be headed by an administrator appointed by the President subject to Senate confirmation.

Created within the department an Office of Inspector General headed by an Inspector General and a deputy appointed by the President subject to Senate approval.

Provided that the Inspector General and his deputy could be removed from office by the President, but required the President to explain the reasons for the removal to both houses of Congress.

Charged the Inspector General with responsibility for auditing and investigating department activities in an effort to promote efficiency and economy and to detect and prevent fraud and abuse.

Required the Inspector General to report on March 31 each year to the Secretary, to Congress and to the Federal Energy Regulatory Commission on problems in the department and his recommendations for correcting them.

Directed the Inspector General to report immediately to the Secretary and the Federal Energy Regulatory Commission, and within 30 days thereafter to appropriate congressional committees, upon discovery of any flagrant or serious problems.

Provided the Inspector General with authority to inspect all documents available to the department, and gave him subpoena power.

Created within the department an Office of Energy Research to be headed by a director appointed by the President subject to Senate approval.

Charged the Office of Energy Research with responsibility for monitoring the department's research and development programs and related activities and for advising the Secretary on those matters.

Created a Leasing Liaison Committee composed of an equal number of members appointed by the Secretary and the Secretary of the Interior.

Title III—Transfer of Functions

Transferred to the Secretary all functions held by the Federal Energy Administration (FEA) and the Energy Research and Development Administration (ERDA).

Transferred to the Secretary all functions held by the Federal Power Commission (FPC) except those reserved to the Federal Energy Regulatory Commission (FERC) under Title IV *(see below)*.

Transferred to the Secretary from the Department of the Interior authority over the Southeastern Power Administration, the Southwestern Power Administration, the Alaska Power Administration, the Bonneville Power Administration, and the power marketing functions of the Bureau of Reclamation and of the Falcon Dam and Amistad Dam on the Rio Grande.

Provided that the Southeastern, Southwestern, Bonneville and Alaska power administrations shall remain separate and distinct entities within the department.

Created a separate administration within the department to be headed by an administrator appointed by the Secretary to oversee functions transferred from the Bureau of Reclamation and the Falcon and Amistad Dams.

Transferred to the Secretary from the Department of the Interior the power to set economic terms over leases for energy development on public lands, including authority to set production rates and diligence requirements.

Transferred to the Secretary from the Department of the Interior's Bureau of Mines authorities to gather data on fuel supplies, and to conduct research on technology for the production of solid fuel minerals and on coal.

Reserved to the Secretary of the Interior all other authority over public lands leasing, including sole power to issue leases and to enforce their regulation.

Specified that the Secretary must consult with the Interior Secretary before setting down economic regulations over leases and must allow him at least 30 days for comment prior to the issuance of such regulations.

Specified that the Secretary would have 30 days prior to publication of final lease terms to veto any economic terms included in the lease.

Required that in the event of any veto of a lease term, the Secretary must explain his action in a detailed written statement to the Interior Secretary.

Transferred to the Secretary from the Department of Housing and Urban Development authority to set energy conservation standards for new buildings.

Provided that in setting automotive fuel efficiency standards, the Secretary of Transportation must consult with the Energy Secretary and allow him not less than 10 days for comment on standards before they are proposed.

Transferred to the Secretary from the Interstate Commerce Commission authority over oil pipelines.

Transferred to the Secretary from the Department of Defense authority over three naval oil reserves and three oil shale reserves.

Transferred to the Secretary from the Department of Commerce authority over industrial energy conservation programs.

Transferred to the Secretary from the Department of Defense authority over the Division of Naval Reactors and the Division of Military Applications.

Transferred to the Department of Transportation from the FEA authority over a van pooling and car pooling program.

Title IV—Federal Energy Regulatory Commission (FERC)

Created within the department an independent regulatory commission of five members appointed by the President subject to Senate approval.

Provided that the commission's members would serve staggered terms of four years and that not more than three could belong to the same political party.

Transferred to the commission from the Federal Power Commission power to set rates on the sale of natural gas and wholesale purchases of electricity.

Transferred to the commission from the Federal Power Commission power to regulate mergers and securities acquisitions under the Federal Power and Natural Gas Acts.

Transferred to the commission from the Interstate Commerce Commission authority to set rates for the trans-

James R. Schlesinger: First Energy Secretary

Immediately after signing the bill creating the Energy Department, Carter named James R. Schlesinger, his chief energy adviser, to be its first Secretary. Schlesinger had been serving as the nation's "energy czar" since Dec. 23, 1977, when President-elect Carter had named him coordinator of all federal energy programs.

Schlesinger was born in New York City Feb. 15, 1929. He is a *summa cum laude,* Phi Beta Kappa graduate of Harvard University (1950), where he also earned his masters (1952) and doctorate (1956) degrees, all in economics.

From 1955 through 1963 he taught at the University of Virginia and during those years also served as a consultant to the Naval War College and the Federal Reserve System's Board of Governors.

In 1960 he published *The Political Economy of National Security: A Study of the Economic Aspects of the Contemporary Power Struggle.* The book was "based on the contention that the East-West schism will stay unresolved and that this country's position in the western influence sphere must be held at any cost," according to a contemporary review by Library Journal.

Officials of the Rand Corporation, a national security think tank in Santa Monica, Calif., were impressed enough to invite Schlesinger in 1963 to become a senior staff member, and by 1967 he was Rand's director of strategic studies.

From 1965 to 1969 he doubled as a consultant to the federal Bureau of the Budget. He entered that agency as an assistant director in 1969 and became assistant director with responsibilities in the areas of national security and energy when the agency became the Office of Management and Budget (OMB).

In August 1971 Schlesinger was named chairman of the Atomic Energy Commission, where he stayed until he became director of the Central Intelligence Agency (CIA) in February 1973. Although only at CIA about three months, Schlesinger launched an ambitious reorganization of "the company." Most analysts credit him with firing about 10 percent of the total staff.

Richard Nixon saved the CIA from Schlesinger by making him Secretary of Defense. Schlesinger took over the Pentagon July 2, 1973, and it was there that he rose to his greatest fame.

Although he was widely credited with trimming $6 billion from the Pentagon's budget while at OMB, once in the top defense job he became an adamant and articulate advocate for beefing up America's defense.

He was vocally skeptical of detente and hostile to cuts in the defense budget. He warned that the Russians were building a huge military machine while America — under President Ford and Secretary of State Henry A. Kissinger — was having the wool of a false detente pulled over its eyes.

Schlesinger's carping proved too much for President Ford and he fired him in November 1975. His dismissal was seen a victory for Kissinger and as a reflection of Ford's discomfort with intellectuals. The act was applauded by few. Even foes of the military on Capitol Hill had respected Schlesinger, a man who "puts things into perspective," as Rep. Les Aspin (D Wis.), an outspoken defense critic, said.

After his curt dismissal Schlesinger served on an academic study project jointly funded by Johns Hopkins and Georgetown Universities, biding his time until he might return to government service.

Adjectives commonly used to describe Schlesinger include brilliant, tweedy, pipe-smoking, arrogant, rumpled, principled, philosophical, professorial, conservative and efficient.

portation of oil by pipelines and for setting the valuation of such pipelines.

Specified that the commission could claim jurisdiction over any proposal by the Secretary to alter oil price regulations under the Emergency Petroleum Allocation Act of 1973.

Provided that if the commission recommended either that the proposed oil pricing rule be changed or killed, the Secretary would have to either issue the rule as urged by the commission or not issue it at all.

Provided that the Secretary could issue oil pricing decisions without referring them to the commission if the President declared the existence of an emergency of overriding national importance. Oil pricing decisions under those circumstances would be subject to veto by either house of Congress within 15 days of their submission, as provided by the Energy Policy and Conservation Act of 1975 and the Emergency Petroleum Allocation Act of 1973.

Provided that the commission would hold jurisdiction over any other matter before the department required by law to be settled by on-the-record decision after an opportunity for a hearing.

Reserved to the Secretary jurisdiction over exports and imports of natural gas and electricity.

Specified that commission decisions on matters under its jurisdiction would be final agency actions.

Empowered the Secretary to propose rules for commission action, to intervene in any commission proceeding and to set reasonable time limits for commission actions.

Title V—Administrative Procedures, Judiciary Review

Made the Administrative Procedures Act applicable to department rules and orders.

Provided that any proposed rule must be posted for comment in the *Federal Register* at least 30 days before it becomes effective.

Allowed the Secretary to waive notice and comment provisions if he determines that no substantial issue is at stake and that the proposed rule would be unlikely to have a substantial impact on large numbers of people or businesses.

Provided that when previous law specified which courts held judicial review authority over functions assigned to the new department, review would occur as those laws required; otherwise, federal district courts would hold original jurisdiction for judicial review of the act.

Provided that a person charged by department administrators with violating the Emergency Petroleum Allocation Act of 1973 must be issued a written remedial order which would become effective in 30 days unless the person served notice he would contest the order.

Specified that contested remedial orders would be referred to the FERC for resolution.

Specified that the Secretary shall provide adjustments as necessary to any rule to prevent special hardships or inequities.

Provided that persons believing themselves unfairly denied a special adjustment to a rule may appeal to the FERC.

Directed the Secretary to report to Congress within one year after the act became effective on the department's experience with administrative procedures.

Title VI—Administrative Provisions

Prohibited departmental supervisory employees from knowingly receiving compensation or owning any interest in any energy concern.

Gave personnel transferred to the department six months to comply with that divestiture of energy interests requirement.

Allowed the Secretary to waive the divestiture of energy interests requirement where he determined it would result in exceptional hardship, and provided he published any such waiver in the *Federal Register.*

Required all employees of the department to disclose the extent of income from energy concerns which they or their dependents received in any year during their service in the department.

Required employees to disclose within 60 days of taking a supervisory job any payment over $2,500 which they had received from any energy concern within the past five years.

Prohibited supervisory employees from attempting to influence the department on any matter for one year after leaving the department.

Prohibited supervisory employees who were formerly with energy concerns from participating for one year in any department proceeding in which their former employers are substantially involved (other than in general rulemaking activities).

Provided criminal penalties up to one year in jail and fines up to $2,500 for persons who knowingly violated provisions governing disclosure of interests in an energy concern, and fines up to $10,000 for violations of other ethical standards under this title.

Authorized 689 "supergrade" Civil Service level positions for the department, 200 of which would be exempt from Civil Service laws and regulations.

Authorized the appointment by the Secretary of 14 additional executive level personnel.

Authorized the Secretary to provide various amenities for employees stationed in remote locations.

Directed the Secretaries of Defense, Commerce, Housing and Urban Development, Transportation, Agriculture, Interior, and the administrators of the U.S. Postal Service and the General Services Administration to designate one senior official as the agency's energy conservation officer.

Directed the Secretary to submit to the President, for later submission to Congress, an annual report as soon as possible after the end of each fiscal year.

Specified that such annual reports should include a statement of the Secretary's goals and plans and an assessment of progress toward their achievement.

Directed that the reports include projections on the nation's energy needs, estimates of domestic and foreign energy supplies, estimates on trends in energy pricing and use, a summary of energy research and conservation programs, and to the extent possible, a summary of activities in the United States by companies owned or controlled by foreign interests which own or control domestic energy supplies.

Directed the Secretary of the Interior to submit to Congress within one year after the measure's enactment a report on the government's leasing operations.

Title VII—Transitional and Other Provisions

Transferred to the Secretary all personnel, assets and liabilities that go along with functions transferred under this act.

Provided that personnel transferred to the department shall not be fired or reduced in pay scale for one year.

Directed the Civil Service Commission to report to Congress within one year on the effects of this department's creation on employees.

Title VIII—Energy Plan

Required the President to submit to Congress, beginning by April 1, 1979, a biennial energy plan outlining the nation's goals for energy production and conservation for the next five years and the next 10 years.

Required that the plan include estimates of energy supplies needed to meet goals listed.

Provided that the plan be referred to appropriate congressional committees, but omitted any obligation on them for action.

Title IX—Effective Date

Provided that the act shall take effect 120 days after the Secretary takes office, or sooner if the President so orders.

Provided that the President might appoint officers to positions requiring Senate confirmation on an interim basis until the positions can be filled as prescribed.

Title X—Sunset Provisions

Provided that not later than Jan. 15, 1982, the President shall submit to appropriate congressional committees a comprehensive review of each department program, outlining that program's goals, achievements and justification for continued funding.

Background

Efforts to reorganize the American government began in 1787 when the founding fathers sat down to tinker with the Articles of Confederation and wound up with the Constitution. Since then reorganization has been attempted far more often than achieved. Such plans inevitably spark political warfare because they mean someone will lose power or influence, and those endangered tend to fight to keep it.

President Nixon proposed reorganization of the energy bureaucracy in 1971. He urged creation of a new Department of Natural Resources, which would have been based upon the Department of the Interior. Also brought together under Nixon's scheme would have been the Forest Service and soil and water conservation programs from the Department of Agriculture; planning and funding for the civil functions of the Army Corps of Engineers; the civilian power functions of the Atomic Energy Commission; the interagency Water Resources Council; the oil and gas pipeline safety functions of the Department of Transportation; and the National Oceanic and Atmospheric Administration from the Department of Commerce.

Congress greeted Nixon's proposal with yawns, and it did not progress beyond hearings. In 1973, Nixon asked again, this time for a slightly stripped-down model. Once again, the proposal went nowhere.

As the energy crisis worsened in 1974, Congress responded to pressure from the Nixon administration by creating the temporary Federal Energy Administration (FEA), composed largely of the Federal Energy Office and several Interior Department offices. The FEA was empowered to deal with short-term fuel shortages, but Congress granted it far less power than Nixon had sought for it. Also created was a new Energy Research and Development Administration (ERDA) that consolidated energy research efforts. It brought together programs from the Atomic Energy Commission, Interior Department, National Science Foundation and Environmental Protection Agency.

As it became clear that efforts of the 94th Congress to deal with energy problems were less than successful, there were pressures from Democrats and Republicans for further consolidation of federal energy functions.

Ford Plan

One of President Ford's final official acts was to submit a detailed plan for reorganizing the energy bureaucracy into a new Department of Energy. Under the Energy Conservation and Policy Act (PL 94-385), which extended the life of the FEA through 1977, the President was directed to submit an energy reorganization proposal to Congress by Dec. 31, 1976.

Ford was 11 days late, but no one seemed to mind.

Ford's proposal called for consolidation of the FEA, ERDA and the FPC. Also added would have been the Bureau of Mines, and power marketing agencies from the Department of Interior, including such agencies as the Bonneville, Southeastern, Southwestern and Alaska Power Administrations. Also, the Rural Electrification Administration (REA) would have been taken from the Department of Agriculture, and a Cabinet-level Energy Resources Council created in 1974 would have been abolished.

Carter Plan

On March 1, President Carter unveiled his plan to reorganize the federal energy bureaucracy. It was his first step toward creation of a new national energy policy, and at the same time, his first attempt to live up to his oft-repeated campaign promise to streamline the entire federal government if elected.

"Nowhere is the need for reorganization and consolidation greater than in energy policy," Carter said in a message to Congress. "All but two of the executive branch's Cabinet departments now have some responsibility for energy policy, but no agency...has the broad authority needed to deal with our energy problems in a comprehensive way."

Carter's proposed Department of Energy called for consolidation of the following structures and functions:

● The FEA in its entirety, including authority over oil producing and allocation.

● The FPC in its entirety, including authority over natural gas regulation and wholesale sales of electricity.

● ERDA in its entirety, including research and development on energy resources and development of nuclear weapons.

● Power marketing functions from the Bureau of Reclamation and the Department of the Interior's four regional administrations (Bonneville, Alaska, Southwest and Southeast).

● Fuels data collection and research on coal technology from the Department of the Interior's Bureau of Mines.

● Authority to develop energy efficiency standards for new buildings from the Department of Housing and Urban Development, which would implement them.

● Industrial energy conservation program development from the Department of Commerce.

● Jurisdiction over the three naval petroleum reserves in California and Wyoming and over three naval oil shale reserves in Colorado and Utah, currently in the Defense Department.

● Authority currently vested in the Securities and Exchange Commission to regulate mergers in the electric utility industry.

● Authority currently held by the Interstate Commerce Commission to regulate oil and coal slurry pipelines.

In addition, the proposed department would have an advisory role to recommend goals for automobile efficiency standards to the Department of Transportation, and would hold prior approval authority over Rural Electrification Administration loans or loan guarantees for construction or operation of generating plants or transmission systems.

Finally, the new department would share control over leasing policy for public lands with the Department of the Interior, which then held sole authority over that function.

The Energy Resources Council, which consisted of the heads of several Cabinet departments who coordinated energy policy, would be abolished. Carter said he intended to establish by executive order an interdepartmental body to coordinate energy policy.

The Nuclear Regulatory Commission and the Environmental Protection Agency would remain separate and independent. "I believe that health, safety and environmental regulation relating to energy—unlike economic regulation—should not be brought into the new Energy Department," Carter explained in his message to Congress.

The consolidated programs were budgeted to receive $10.6-billion in fiscal 1978 outlays under Carter's proposed budget and employed 19,767 full-time workers at the time. None would lose their jobs, Carter pledged. Of those employees, 46 percent worked in ERDA, 25 percent in Interior, 20 percent in FEA, 7 percent for FPC and the remaining 2 percent in the other agencies.

Hearings

The Senate Governmental Affairs Committee and House Government Operations Committee held extensive hearings on the Carter proposal (S 826, HR 4263) in March and April. Two aspects of the plan—incorporation of the FPC and shared public lands leasing authority—came in for considerable criticism.

In testimony March 15 before the Senate Governmental Affairs Committee, two former Democratic FPC chairmen argued that the FPC should remain independent. Joseph C. Swidler, FPC chairman from 1961 to 1965, said of Carter's proposal: "The bill was framed in generalities without real understanding of how the...commission functions." His charges were echoed by Lee C. White, FPC chairman from 1966 to 1969.

Both said Carter's proposal did not delineate clearly which functions from the FPC would be held by which officers in the new energy department. Their concerns mirrored fears that the new department's policy makers would be able to influence the decisions of the regulators, whom many believed should be insulated from political pressures.

Their testimony ran counter to that of the current FPC chairman, Richard Dunham, who was appointed in 1975. Dunham endorsed Carter's plan March 9, saying the nation's independent regulatory agencies had gained such enormous economic powers that they had become "a virtual fourth branch of government" contrary to the intentions of the framers of the Constitution.

Spokesmen for most of the nation's local power systems and for state utility regulators urged Congress to leave the FPC separate and independent.

Two powerful chairmen of House Commerce subcommittees on energy, Rep. John D. Dingell (D Mich.) and John E. Moss (D Calif.), also expressed doubts about the wisdom of abolishing the FPC.

The FPC provision was not the only aspect of Carter's energy reorganization plan to catch flak.

Rep. Morris K. Udall (D Ariz.), chairman of the House Interior and Insular Affairs Committee, criticized the plan's proposal to split authority over leasing of public lands for energy development in March 29 testimony before the House Government Operations Committee.

Udall said he feared the emphasis was too strong on meeting energy supply needs, to the detriment of other important public lands functions. "At the risk of sounding like a doomsayer, I might add that great supplies of oil and gas won't help us if we cannot graze livestock, if watersheds are destroyed and topsoil washed away," Udall said.

The public lands leasing proposal also bothered Sen. Henry M. Jackson (D Wash.), chairman of the new Senate Committee on Energy and Natural Resources. Jackson, a cosponsor of S 826, termed the leasing of public lands "the most important aspect" of the legislation, in testimony March 7, and said he feared conflicts would occur between the Interior and Energy Departments under Carter's proposal.

Senate Committee Action

After 12 days of hearings in March and April, the Senate Committee on Governmental Affairs voted 14-0 May 9 to report S 826 as amended. The report (S Rept 95-164) was filed May 4, 1977.

The committee endorsed creation of a Cabinet-level Department of Energy basically along the lines requested by President Carter. The panel made a few significant revisions, however, and generally tightened definitions and nailed down specifics in more detail than had the administration.

Price-Setting. The most important change was a recommendation to cut back severely the authority proposed for the department Secretary to set prices for oil and natural gas.

Despite White House opposition, the Senate panel insisted on placing the price-setting powers in a three-member Energy Regulatory Board rather than with the Secretary. "...[I]mportant energy pricing decisions that must be made could significantly affect the prosperity and living habits of every American," the committee report said. "No single official should have sole responsibility for both proposing and setting such prices."

Under the committee version, the Secretary could propose prices and set deadlines for board action, but could not overrule the board. Board decisions would be made by majority vote. The President could veto key board pricing decisions within 10 days, in which case the board review would begin again. In addition, board decisions on oil pricing and allocation, but not on gas pricing, could be vetoed by either house of Congress within 15 days under terms of the 1975 Energy Policy and Conservation Act (PL 94-163). Board actions would be subject also to judicial review.

Leasing. The second most controversial aspect of Carter's proposal was his plan to split authority over leasing of public lands for energy development between the Interior Department and the new Energy Department. Environmentalists voiced fears that, in the stampede to develop energy resources, other important public land values might be sacrificed.

As reported, S 826, unlike the administration plan, spelled out specifically what leasing functions would be transferred. It made the Energy Secretary responsible for fostering competition for federal land leases, implementing alternative bidding systems for such leases, setting diligence requirements for federal lease operations, setting production rates from leased lands, and collection and distribution of revenues from federal leases.

All other federal land leasing responsibilities would be retained by the Secretary of the Interior, who also would hold sole responsibility for issuing leases and enforcing their terms. The Energy Secretary would have 30 days prior to publication of lease terms to review and veto any items falling under his areas of responsibility.

As reported, S 826 created a Leasing Liaison Committee composed of appointees from both departments to coordinate federal lease procedures. Carter's proposal called for a liaison committee composed only of Energy Department employees and intended only for information gathering.

Disputes between the two departments over leases would be referred to the President.

Planning and Information. In provisions added by the committee, S 826 launched the federal government into the process of delivering five-year and ten-year energy plans every two years to Congress. The plans would outline the nation's energy production and conservation goals in detail, and would have to be approved by Congress.

As President Carter had requested, an Energy Information Administration would be created within the new department. The information administration would consolidate the more than 100 energy data collection and analysis programs housed in agencies to be folded into the new department.

As reported, S 826 included terms designed to protect the data agency from political manipulation and to insure its credibility. One key function that the energy data administration would perform would be to systematically gather comprehensive information from major energy firms regarding their financial operations. Major firms would be required to file reports at least annually; smaller firms

Fiscal 1980 Budget Proposals in Energy Field

Stronger emphasis on solar energy, a commitment to solving the nuclear waste disposal problem and a reassessment of expensive demonstrations of new energy technologies were the major initiatives in the Carter administration's proposed fiscal 1980 budget.

These policy shifts were made within a Department of Energy budget that called for spending in fiscal 1980 at levels nearly identical to the previous year. This ended a pattern of large annual increases in energy spending that began after the 1973 Arab oil embargo.

Though Congress had been urging increased attention to solar energy and the radioactive waste problem, disputes were certain over these and other aspects of the budget.

Major budget proposals likely to be debated included:

● Reductions in programs to speed development and commercialization of synthetic fuels, such as gas or liquids made from coal. Debate about which demonstration plants to build were likely to take a decidedly local slant as legislators from Kentucky, West Virginia, Illinois and Ohio fight to save joint industry/government projects proposed for their states.

● Zero funding of the plutonium-powered nuclear breeder reactor at Clinch River, Tenn. Generous funding in the budget for research and development of other types of breeder reactors could aid Carter's attempt to win congressional approval for termination of the $2 billion demonstration plant. *(Details, nuclear power chapter)*

● Utilization of new funds for nuclear waste management. Tied to this were disputes over a Waste Isolation Pilot Plant planned for New Mexico; the future of an unfinished private plant in Barnwell, S.C., designed to reprocess spent fuel; the amount government should charge industry for storing spent fuel from reactors; the type of storage to be provided for the spent fuel and the direction of research on waste storage methods.

● Progress on the Strategic Petroleum Reserve, a program to store oil underground as insurance against future embargoes and shortages. Energy Secretary James R. Schlesinger admitted the program had been "mismanaged," and many congressional critics agreed. Only 70 million barrels had been stored, although the original goal was to have 250 million barrels stored by the end of 1978.

Programs were continued at generally the same levels as fiscal 1979 and reflected the administration's continuing belief that the government's "principal responsibility" was to smooth the transition to an era of less abundant, more expensive energy. But the Office of Management and Budget (OMB) emphasized in budget documents that the government should not do research and demonstration projects that the private sector could handle.

The Breakdown

Fiscal 1980 outlays for the Department of Energy were projected at about $10.2 billion, about $124 million above fiscal 1979 levels.

Because about $3 billion in budget authority was carried over from fiscal 1979, these spending levels could be maintained despite the administration's proposed 22 percent cut in budget authority for the agency. Budget authority proposed for fiscal 1980 was $8.4 billion, down from $10.8 billion in fiscal 1979.

The left over authority came from delays in scheduled spending for the Strategic Petroleum Reserve. Excluding the reserve, budget authority for the department increased by 8 percent over fiscal 1979 and outlays increased by 7 percent.

The delays in establishing the reserve put off a fight between OMB and the department over funding for the program, which was mandated by Congress in 1975 (PL 94-163). OMB has said the program is a possible "budget-buster."

In addition to the Energy Department funding, the government will forego another $4 billion in tax revenues to encourage energy production, conservation and use of solar energy. About $1 billion of that was for tax credits included in the energy tax bill passed in 1978.

The Highlights

Highlights of energy funding changes in the new budget were:

● A 17.5 percent increase — to about $844 million — in government-wide budget authority for solar energy over fiscal 1979 levels. Of that amount, $646 million went to the Energy Department.

● A 91 percent increase in budget authority for nuclear waste programs, to $924 million. The largest part of the increase — $300 million for storage of commercial spent fuel — would eventually be repaid by the nuclear industry, according to the Energy Department. Defense waste management received a 45 percent increase.

● A 13 percent increase in projected fiscal 1979 funding for atomic weapons activities. The increase was expected to prompt debate in the energy field similar to the dispute over higher defense spending. Defense-related activities accounted for more than a third of the budget authority proposed for the Energy Department in fiscal 1980.

● A winding down of government exploration for oil and gas in the federal Naval Petroleum Reserve in Alaska, with budget authority reduced to $69 million from the fiscal 1979 level of $120 million. Officials explained that enough data had been gathered to formulate recommendations to Congress. The House voted in 1978 to protect the 22.5-million acre area as a national wildlife refuge.

● An increase of $15 billion in the amount the Tennessee Valley Authority was allowed to borrow to continue construction of nuclear power plants and other power development programs.

would be sampled selectively. The goal would be to draw an "energy industry profile," that the government could use to evaluate energy industry profits, cash flow, investments, degree of competition, and costs for exploration, production and distribution.

Senate Floor Action

The Senate May 18 passed S 826, 74-10.

Senate passage was surprisingly easy, and quick. As early as April, Capitol Hill rumblings indicated widespread fears that Carter wanted too much power for the department. It appeared the proposal might get entangled with the President's controversial energy policy proposals and face indefinite delay.

But the bill was rushed through the Senate with less than a full day's debate, with Governmental Affairs Chairman Abraham Ribicoff (D Conn.) and Energy Committee Chairman Henry M. Jackson (D Wash.) leading the charge.

Ribicoff may have summed up the main reason for the rush in his introductory remarks. "Mr. President," he said, "there is universal agreement that a consolidation of functions and agencies in the energy area is necessary." But the swift and overwhelming approval also appeared to reflect a determination by Democratic congressional leaders to work with the President in tackling the nation's energy problems.

The debate was not only brief, but was for the most part quite narrowly focused. Most floor discussion centered on 17 proposed amendments that addressed relatively small issues. Of the amendments, 14 passed by voice vote without significant challenge. Three failed on roll calls. With few and fleeting exceptions, the broad sweep of the measure and its major policy controversies escaped the Senate without floor examination.

Sen. James A. McClure (R Idaho) complained of that at length near the debate's end. "I think the fact that the report was available yesterday and we are acting upon it today is, in itself, an indictment of the process under which we labor," he said. Such rushed consideration of "one of the most important single actions that this body will make this year" was, McClure said, "a grave disservice to the country."

Sen. Clifford P. Hansen (R Wyo.) echoed McClure. "I shall vote against the bill, not because I believe there is no energy emergency facing the nation, nor because I believe that action need not be taken, but rather because of the feeling I have that too many senators, including myself, do not understand many of the specifics contained in the bill."

Republicans did not complain alone. Sen. John A. Durkin (D N.H.) said: "This may be the finest bill this body has ever passed, or it may be the worst, but I estimate that 75 per cent of the membership does not know whether it is the best or the worst.... I realize...that this has been discussed in committee; but the committee system...is not supposed to supplant discussion on the floor."

House Committee Action

The House Government Operations Committee May 16 reported its version of the administration bill (HR 6804—H Rept 95-346 Part I). Part II, dealing with Civil Service provisions, was filed by the Post Office and Civil Service Committee May 24.

The House bill created the department from exactly the same building blocks as the Senate, but the two bills differed in several important ways.

The most critical difference was that the House measure allowed the department Secretary to set oil and natural gas prices, while the Senate bill vested such authority in a semi-independent, three-member board. The power to set fuel prices is fundamental to energy policy; the House version was in line with the administration request.

The two bills also differed on some mechanics of setting up the department internally. Both provided for a presidentially appointed Secretary at its head. The Senate bill then called for two under secretaries, which HR 6804 omitted. The Senate version called for eight assistant secretaries and did not assign them titles; the House measure called for nine, and specified their jobs.

One innovation inserted by the House panel created an Office of Inspector General to investigate fraud and program abuses within the department. The Senate measure and Carter proposal did not mention such an office.

The House bill did not contain several key sections added to the administration plan by the Senate committee. S 826 required extensive five-year and ten-year energy plans every two years; the House measure did not mention long-range plans. As Carter requested, both bills created an Energy Information Administration.

One key item on which both measures agreed substantially was the way the new department should share authority with the Interior Department over public lands leasing, an issue second only to fuel pricing powers as an item of controversy when the legislation was being drafted.

House Floor Action

The House June 3 passed the bill, 310-20, after substituting its provisions for S 826. Before passage it made one major change, eliminating the Secretary's authority to set the price of natural gas and make other economic decisions. Passage came after two days of debate that was more substantive than the Senate consideration.

Through most of the debate, one theme dominated: Did the bill give too much power to the head of the proposed department?

"I think there is a truly ominous aspect in concentrating as much power in the Secretary," as HR 6804 would do, said William L. Armstrong (R Colo.). Because energy issues are so pervasive and important, he said, "We're talking about putting in one person authority to say who gets to keep a job and who does not, which regions get fuel in time of shortage, and which do not...we're talking really about the life or death power over every farm, business and industry in this country."

"HR 6804 seeks to vest far too much power in a single individual," agreed John E. Moss (D Calif.).

Jack Brooks (D Texas), chairman of the Government Operations Committee and the measure's floor manager, tried to assuage such fears. "I believe, Mr. Chairman, that far from creating an energy czar who will have dictatorial power over our lives and our country's economy, we instead would be creating a balanced office," Brooks contended.

Pricing Debate. Debate on the issue of the power of the Secretary climaxed with an amendment from Moss that empowered the five-member Federal Energy Regulatory Commission within the department—rather than the

Secretary—to set the wellhead price of natural gas, and to issue rules of general applicability as issued now by the FPC. The rules govern such issues as "wheeling" of interstate electricity supplies, whether to allow utilities to include expenses for construction work in progress in their rate bases for interstate power sales, and other far-ranging policy decisions. In effect, according to the amendment's cosponsor, Clarence J. Brown (R Ohio), the Moss proposal would transfer whole into the Energy Department the FPC's key powers, and cut the Secretary out of the picture.

Backers of the Moss amendment said those critical powers would be better insulated from political pressures in a semi-independent regulatory agency than if vested in the Secretary alone. They warned too that if the Secretary held those authorities, decisions would be made "behind closed doors," but if held by the commission, decisions would be made in public under the "sunshine" act of 1976. (PL 94-409).

But the core of their argument was simply that no one person should wield so much power. The Moss amendment was adopted on a roll call vote, 236-119. Two earlier amendments of similar intent had been rejected.

Leasing. Getting into one of the other controversial areas of the bill, Morris K. Udall (D Ariz.), chairman of the Interior and Insular Affairs Committee, proposed strengthening the hand of the Secretary of the Interior over the leasing of public lands for energy development. HR 6804 as reported divided authority over public lands leasing between the Interior Secretary and the Energy Secretary. Udall proposed deleting language giving the Energy Secretary veto power over economic terms of leases, though he would have left intact the Energy Department's other powers over leasing. Udall's amendment was rejected, 170-180.

Congressional Veto. Elliott H. Levitas (D Ga.) proposed giving either house of Congress the power to review and reject all rules and regulations issued by the new department. Levitas argued that such rules carry the force of laws "and I think we should...establish once and for all that the Congress passes the laws." He said similar terms had been added to over 200 other public laws. The amendment was adopted, 200-125. A similar amendment had been defeated in the Senate.

Conference Action

Conferees were slow to get started and did not finish resolving their differences until July 22. The conference report (H Rept 95-539) was filed July 26.

Federal Energy Regulatory Commission. The most troublesome issue facing the conferees was the question of how to balance authority over pricing and regulation of natural gas, electricity and oil between the new department's Secretary and an independent regulatory commission, which both houses insisted upon creating within the department.

The Senate version placed price-setting powers in an independent three-member Energy Regulatory Board. The Secretary could propose prices and set deadlines for board action, but could not overrule the board. The President was given the power to veto board pricing decisions within 10 days, in which case board review would begin anew. In addition, board decisions on oil pricing and allocation, but not on gas or electricity, could be vetoed by either house of

Congress within 15 days under terms of the 1975 Energy Policy and Conservation Act (PL 94-163).

The House version called for creation of an independent five-member Federal Energy Regulatory Commission within the department.

It would receive sole powers to set prices for interstate sale of natural gas and electricity, cutting the department Secretary out of those decisions completely. In effect, the House version recreated the Federal Power Commission inside the new department. The House version did not provide for a presidential veto of commission decisions. Under the House version, however, the Secretary would receive power over oil pricing and allocation.

Conferees combined the two approaches. They agreed to create a five-member, independent Federal Energy Regulatory Commission (FERC) within the department. It was granted power to set oil, gas and electricity prices. The department Secretary was empowered to propose commission actions, to intervene in any commission proceeding and to set reasonable time limits for commission decisions.

Conferees further provided that the Secretary could circumvent the commission on oil pricing rules if the President declared the existence of a national emergency requiring quick action. In such cases, oil pricing decisions still would be subject to veto by either house of Congress within 15 days under the 1975 law.

Sunset. The House version provided that the department would be abolished by Dec. 31, 1982, unless Congress specifically renewed its authorities before then. The purpose of the "sunset" provision was to force Congress to make a careful evaluation of the department's activities. The Senate version contained no such provision.

Conferees cut back the sunset terms. Instead they provided that the President must submit to Congress by Jan. 15, 1982, a detailed comprehensive review of each program in the department.

Planning. The Senate version provided that, beginning in 1979, the President must present to Congress detailed five-year and 10-year energy plans every two years. The plans would outline the nation's energy goals and thoroughly review estimates of energy resources and government energy programs. Deadlines were specified for congressional action on the plans. The House did not include such a provision.

Conferees adopted most of what the Senate version provided on this point, but deleted the requirements for congressional action.

Inspector General. The House created an Office of Inspector General within the department to be responsible for auditing and investigating department activities in an effort to promote efficiency and economy, and to prevent fraud and abuse. The inspector general was required to report his findings annually to the Secretary, the Federal Energy Regulatory Commission and the Congress. Flagrant problems were to be reported immediately. The Senate did not provide for such an office.

Conferees adopted the House terms with one change. In the event of discovery of flagrant problems, the inspector general was to report immediately to the Secretary and the FERC, but did not have to report to Congress for 30 days. This was to allow department officials time to make comments on the report, conferees said.

Other. Conferees dropped House floor amendments giving either chamber the power to veto department rules and providing that all "supergrades" in the new department would be subject to normal Civil Service regulations. A House amendment giving authority over federal vanpooling to the Transportation Department was retained in the final version.

Final Action

The House adopted the conference report by a vote of 353-57 Aug. 2.

Final acceptance came after a motion by Thomas N. Kindness (R Ohio) to recommit the legislation to a conference committee failed, 157-257. The recommittal motion was made after several members had raised objections to the conference report. The objectors wanted three provisions restored to the bill as passed originally by the House: a "sunset" provision, whereby the department would expire Dec. 31, 1982; a provision under which either house of Congress could veto rules issued by the new department; and a provision subjecting all "supergrade" officials in the new department to normal Civil Service regulations.

S 826 was cleared for the President when the Senate adopted the conference report a few hours later, 76-14. ∎

Energy vs. Inflation: The High Cost of Oil

The Carter administration's goal of somehow raising domestic oil prices to world levels was jolted sharply by the 14.49 percent jump set for 1979 by the Organization of Petroleum Exporting Countries (OPEC).

The Dec. 17, 1978, decision widened the gap between controlled domestic prices and world prices and would make equalizing the two "more difficult," according to Energy Secretary James R. Schlesinger.

The goal of equal prices — part of President Carter's energy plan — was running into serious conflict with the administration's anti-inflation program even before OPEC acted. Alfred E. Kahn, Carter's chief inflation-fighter, said that trying to balance the energy and inflaton problems is "tearing us apart."

"We are on the horns of a terrible dilemma," Kahn told a House energy panel in December 1978.

The larger-than-expected OPEC price hike, which could add from .3 to .4 percentage point to the 1979 inflation rate, meant Carter would find it politically difficult to add further to inflation by raising domestic prices. Already by early 1979, world oil prices were exceeding the 14.49 percent increase announced by OPEC, with further hikes announced March 27. *(Box p. 57)*

The domestic controls, which keep about 35 percent of domestic oil at less than half the OPEC price, shield U.S. consumers from the higher world prices. Ending the controls immediately would cost consumers an extra $12 billion plus a year and could add .75 percentage point to the inflation rate, according to several economic analyses.

However, the administration, pushed by Schlesinger, has long supported raising domestic oil prices to world market levels as a way of curbing oil imports. In theory, the higher prices would force conservation and encourage shifts to other energy sources. President Carter April 5 announced a phased-in decontrol program, beginning June 1, when existing legislation provided him with broad new pricing powers. *(Box, p. 61)*

Spurring the effort to raise domestic prices was the promise Carter made to world leaders at a Bonn economic summit in July 1978. He said then he was "determined" that U.S. oil prices would equal world levels by the end of 1980. His hope was to stem further increases in the U.S. trade deficit by reducing oil imports. The estimated $42.7 billion that the United States paid for imported oil in 1978 was the major factor in the anticipated 1978 trade deficit of $34.9 billion.

In announcing the gradual end to controls on domestic oil prices, the president asked Congress to tax the "huge and undeserved windfall profits" that oil companies could reap. This would be done by imposing new taxes on oil to raise prices and then rebating the revenues to consumers. Some officials had wanted to avoid a difficult legislative fight over taxes, but raising prices without some sort of tax rebate would result in what the administration had criticized as a "massive transfer of wealth from consumers to the oil industry."

Yet, the 95th Congress flatly rejected Carter's request for a tax on crude oil, and congressional sources said getting the 96th Congress to pass a similar tax was just not politically feasible. A tax on the windfall profits of oil companies would be slightly more palatable, but still unpopular in the key committees — House Ways and Means and Senate Finance.

But ending price controls on oil without a tax and rebates would conflict with Carter's desire to avoid giving producers undeserved windfalls. It also could spur efforts by labor and consumer groups to extend mandatory price controls beyond June 1, 1979.

Arguments for Higher Prices

In the first half of 1978, U.S. refiners paid about $4 less for a barrel of domestically produced oil than they did for imported oil. The OPEC price increase for 1979 would widen that gap by at least $1, according to government officials. The less expensive domestic oil accounted for about 55 percent of the oil used by the United States and meant that U.S. refiners paid about $2 less per barrel than refiners elsewhere.

To the Carter administration, these lower oil prices paid by Americans encouraged consumption when conservation should be the goal. The philosophy guiding Carter's 1977 national energy plan was that the price of energy should equal the cost of replacing it, which meant that domestic oil should be priced at world levels. Otherwise, according to the theory, the use of oil is being subsidized by government policies that hold down domestic prices.

The administration believed the lower U.S. prices lead producers to hold back, thus fueling the trend of declining U.S. production. The lower U.S. prices also increase consumption, according to the administration, and oil imports are then needed to fill the gap between supply and demand. Imports doubled between 1970 and 1978.

This continued growth in energy demand, according to Schlesinger and others, will eventually run up against a limited world supply, creating a "gap" between supply and demand that will mean very high prices and possible shortages. A failure to make adjustments now to delay or get ready for that "gap" would mean "economic difficulties and political unsettlement," warned Schlesinger in a Nov. 29, 1978, speech.

Effects of Increase

If U.S. prices increase as planned, the administration has predicted:

● The growth in demand for oil will slow and with it the growth in oil imports.

● Domestic production of "hard-to-get" oil, such as that from very deep wells, will increase.

● Alternative energy systems, such as solar, will become competitive economically.

● The nation's capital stock — houses, factories, cars and other things that run on energy — much of it built when energy was inexpensive, will be more quickly adapted to use less of the expensive oil.

● Competition among oil companies will be enhanced, thus resulting in better supplies for consumers.

Another reason to begin ending controls was the complexity of the oil pricing system, administration officials have pointed out. A particularly intricate part of that system was its "entitlements" program, which forced refiners with access to cheaper domestic oil to share the benefits with refiners who had to rely on expensive imported oil. Department of Energy spokesman James Bishop Jr. labeled that program a "regulatory octopus."

Supporters of Control

Consumer groups and labor unions rejected the administration's list of benefits from higher prices and pointed instead to the economic dislocation they said price increases would cause. They were highly critical of the decontrol proposal.

If raising prices does work to discourage consumption, "it only works with the poor . . . and ends up being a very regressive way of cutting back" energy use, said Ellen Berman, executive director of the Consumer Energy Council, a coalition of labor unions and consumer groups.

"A lot of people do not have alternatives to the automobile," said Edwin Rothschild of Energy Action, a consumer-oriented lobby. "They have to drive to work, drive to get food. The demand for gasoline is 'inelastic.' It's one of those things we have to have."

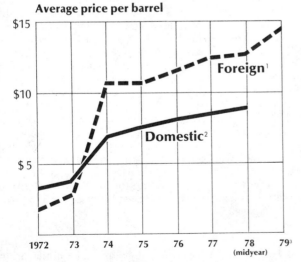

Domestic and Foreign Crude Oil Prices

Average price per barrel

[Line graph showing Foreign[1] and Domestic[2] crude oil prices from 1972 to 79[3], with price axis marked at $5, $10, and $15. Foreign prices rise from below $5 in 1972 to nearly $15 by 79. Domestic prices rise more gradually to about $9.]

1972 73 74 75 76 77 78 79[3]
(midyear)

[1] Official sales price of Arabian light (excludes transportation costs).

[2] U.S.-produced crude oil at the wellhead.

[3] OPEC ministers voted Dec. 17 to increase the official sales price by 14.49% in 1979. Domestic prices in 1979 depend on a variety of factors and cannot be firmly predicted.

SOURCES: Independent Petroleum Association of America, Petroleum Industry Research Foundation, Inc.

Another assumption made by the administration was that decontrol would enhance competition in the oil industry, resulting in better supplies to consumers. But critics said there was no competition in the oil industry because integrated companies, which handle production, refining and marketing, control the marketplace.

Ending controls on oil prices would "exchange one set of controls that is public for another that is private," said Rothschild, who argued for divestiture of the oil industry.

The President's Powers

In 1977, when President Carter sought to raise oil prices, he needed authority from Congress to carry out his plans. Congress refused to go along. But in 1979, the president could raise oil prices on his own, without any additional authority from Congress.

Carter would gain these new pricing powers June 1, 1979, when existing mandatory oil price controls become discretionary with the president. The powers are provided by the Energy Policy and Conservation Act of 1975 (EPCA) (PL 94-163). *(Legacy of laws, box, p. 61)*

The 1975 law established rules for the president to follow in setting oil prices and required compliance until June 1, 1979. For two and a half years after that date, the president would still have control over oil prices, but would not have to use the pricing system spelled out in the law. Then, on Oct. 1, 1981, all price controls are scheduled to expire.

The philosophy behind the 1975 law was that higher prices should be allowed to cover inflation and encourage production, not to provide windfall profits to producers of already-flowing oil. The average annual price increase was limited to 10 percent a year.

Carter's new authority gave him several options in setting oil prices. He could continue to apply the rules set by the 1975 law, modify them with new price controls or drop controls completely. In choosing gradual decontrol over a two-year period, it was expected that domestic oil prices would rise to world levels — the highest price the market would stand. At the same time, officials estimated the higher prices would bring oil savings of up to 110,000 barrels a day by 1981 and up to 250,000 barrels a day by 1985. It was unlikely that those in Congress who opposed higher oil prices would be able to stop Carter from increasing prices.

Extension of Controls

Though the 94th Congress turned down President Ford's efforts to lift controls on oil, those in the 95th Congress who advocated continued control of energy prices were not so successful. Their test case was the natural gas pricing bill — and they lost. Controls on the price of newly discovered gas will be gradually lifted until 1985, when they expire. *(Gas bill, p. 5)*

However, the pro-control legislators did win some concessions, as they probably would in a fight over oil pricing. But a proposal to extend existing mandatory controls over crude oil prices beyond the May 31, 1979, expiration date would have almost no chance of passing.

"We don't have the votes," Sen. Henry M. Jackson, D-Wash., chairman of the Energy Committee, said bluntly when asked in late 1978 about new controls.

OPEC Votes Oil Price Hike

Ending an 18-month freeze on its crude oil prices, the Organization of Petroleum Exporting Countries (OPEC) Dec. 17, 1978, announced a 14.49 percent price increase for 1979.

The increase would boost the price of Arabian light, the benchmark grade for the cartel, from $12.70 to $14.54 per 42-gallon barrel. *(Oil price graph, p. 56)*

However, on March 27, 1979, members of OPEC voted to raise the price of crude oil by an additional 9 percent and to give individual members permission to add surcharges. The surcharges meant prices could average as much as $4 above the new base price of $14.54. The new price hike had originally been scheduled for October.

The 13-member cartel was responsible for about half the oil produced in the world. The price hike was expected to spur similar increases by other producers, including U.S. producers of oil not restricted by federal price controls. Mexico, a potential U.S. supplier, already had announced a 10 to 12 percent increase for 1979.

However, U.S. consumers were shielded from the full brunt of the OPEC move by federal controls that kept the price of about 35 percent of domestically produced oil at less than $6 a barrel. Averaging the price of domestic oil with the OPEC hike means prices would increase at the gasoline pump by about 3 cents a gallon, instead of the full 4.4 cents they would if the OPEC increase applied to all oil consumed domestically.

The increase voted by OPEC in the price of Arabian light had initially been scheduled to be implemented in four stages, starting with a 5 percent increase on Jan. 1, 1979, which would bring the price to $13.335 a barrel. Then, on April 1, the price would be increased another 3.809 percent, to $13.843. That increase would be followed on July 1 by a 2.294 percent increase, bringing the price to $14.161. On Oct. 1, the scheduled increase of 2.691 percent would bring the price to $14.542 a barrel.

The official OPEC communiqué called the increase "an amount of 10 percent, on average, over the year 1979." A volume of oil bought from OPEC in 1978 would

cost 10 percent more in 1979 because the full price increase would not be in place until October. However, the total price increase for the year would be 14.49 percent.

The phased-in schedule means the U.S. would pay another $4 billion for foreign oil in 1979, according to Federal Reserve Board Chairman G. William Miller. In 1980, when the full increase would apply for the whole year, imports would cost an additional $7 billion. The U.S. bill for foreign oil could be as high as $50 billion in 1979, an estimate that factors in both the higher OPEC prices and an expected increase in consumption. That was a sharp increase over the estimated bill for 1978 of about $42.7 billion, a figure that contributed substantially to the 1978 trade deficit of about $34.9 billion.

In response to the OPEC decision, the White House Dec. 17, 1978, issued a statement asking for reconsideration of the increase. "We regret OPEC's decision and hope that it will be reconsidered before the next steps take effect," the statement said. "This large price hike will impede the programs to maintain world economic recovery and reduce inflation. Responsibility for the success of these programs is shared by the oil producing countries."

The OPEC oil ministers said the increase was designed to recoup some of the decline in OPEC purchasing power caused by inflation and the decline of the dollar. The dollar is the currency on which the OPEC pricing system is based. The increase ended a price freeze in effect since mid-1977. An oil surplus had prevented OPEC from raising prices during that time.

But 1978 political troubles in Iran disrupted oil production, reducing the surplus. Production from Iran dropped from normal output of six million barrels a day to as low as one million barrels a day. The reduction drove up prices.

The members of OPEC are Algeria, Iraq, Kuwait, Libya, Qatar, Saudi Arabia, the United Arab Emirates, Ecuador, Gabon, Indonesia, Iran, Nigeria and Venezuela.

In devising a plan to raise prices gradually, Carter could have asked Congress for the authority to control prices beyond Sept. 30, 1981. Then he would have had more time to spread out the price increases. Insiders working on oil pricing have called this solution "building a ramp" so that a graph of prices would show a gradual incline, not an abrupt jump. The extended authority could also be used if there were an emergency, such as an oil shortage, or to lessen the impact of a steep rise in foreign prices which, without controls, would mean a similar rise in domestic prices.

The natural gas pricing bill, reflecting such concern with abrupt price increases, gave Congress authority to reimpose controls for 18 months beyond the 1985 date set for lifting price constraints on newly discovered gas. But a similar clause in oil pricing legislation was strongly opposed by the oil industry.

If the option of continued mandatory controls was out, or at least very unlikely, that left two options — immediate

decontrol or presidential manipulation of price controls through Sept. 30, 1981, when the controls in existing law expire. Carter chose the latter.

Immediate or Phased Decontrol

From the outset, Carter had not been expected to propose an immediate end to all oil price controls. In addition to the inflationary pressures inherent in such a move, an Energy Department spokesman explained that it was "not an attractive option because of the transfer of dollars from consumers to producers." Consumer and labor groups were strongly opposed to any decontrol measures, as were several influential members of Congress.

An immediate end to controls would be a shock to the economy at a crucial stage of Carter's anti-inflation efforts. At a December 1978 hearing before the House Commerce Subcommittee on Energy and Power, Rep. W. Henson Moore, R-La., suggested to Alfred Kahn that waiting to

Congress, Carter Ponder Higher Gasoline Prices

New rules for gasoline pricing proposed by the Department of Energy would increase gasoline prices in 1979 almost as much as higher world oil prices.

The changes, which allow refiners to "pass through" more of their costs to buyers, would add about five cents to the gallon price in 1979.

That's in addition to the extra 3 to 4 cents a gallon consumers would pay by fall 1979 because of price increases voted by the Organization of Petroleum Exporting Countries (OPEC). Total increases in the price of gasoline could exceed 15 cents by 1980.

The revision in gasoline pricing rules was one of several regulatory changes made by the Energy Department in February and March 1979. Other proposals included lifting controls on jet fuel, marginal oil well prices and prices of newly discovered oil.

Congress has veto power over gasoline decontrol, and any decontrol proposal would be carefully scrutinized by the legislators. Senate Energy Chairman Henry M. Jackson, D-Wash., said in December 1978 that gasoline decontrol during "double-digit inflation . . . is something I don't think Congress is in the mood to accept at this time." His aides said later that the OPEC price hike decreased the chance that Congress would approve gasoline decontrol.

Prospects were good for additional increases in gasoline prices beyond the predicted jump of 7 to 8 cents a gallon. If the Carter administration went through with plans to begin gradually ending price controls on domestic crude oil, that could add another 3 cents to the gallon price of gasoline, bringing the total increase to a possible dime a gallon. Even without decontrol of crude oil, inflation, the growing demand for gasoline and higher domestic prices could further boost prices at the pump.

Department Opposes Controls

The Department of Energy wanted to end gasoline controls. The agency believed controls have discouraged refiners from investing in new capacity and from switching from production of leaded to unleaded fuel.

A "major contributing factor" to the shortages of premium unleaded gasoline and the prospect of future shortages has been the "present price and allocation controls on gasoline," Deputy Energy Secretary John O'Leary said in December 1978 hearings.

Existing regulations meant refiners could not recoup the full cost of adding capacity to their plants. The result of this has been that refineries were "reaching full capacity and no one is expanding," O'Leary said.

He noted that the restriction had particularly affected the production of unleaded gasoline. Unless investments were made to expand the capacity of plants that produced unleaded fuels, O'Leary predicted possible shortages after 1980.

In December 1978, shortages showed up in supplies of unleaded premium gasoline, a high octane fuel made by only three companies. Owners of new cars prefer the premium blend because it reduces engine "knock," according to oil industry spokesmen.

Officials from Shell Oil Co., which started rationing gasoline supplies to dealers in early December 1978, said

at congressional hearings that federal controls had kept its prices below the market price in early fall, which resulted in a 10 to 15 percent increase in demand over 1977 levels. The high demand led to shortages.

The demand for unleaded gas is increasing annually because it is required by the emission control systems of most new cars. About 35 percent of cars on the road needed unleaded fuel in 1978 and by 1982 that share will increase to 60 percent, according to estimates by the Environmental Protection Agency (EPA). EPA was counting on the less harmful exhaust from those cars to reduce air pollution.

O'Leary believed the changes in price control regulations, which would be in place in early 1979, would encourage the needed investment in refineries. But he believed the best solution was decontrolling gasoline prices.

Asked if the oil companies needed decontrol to get money for the new investments, O'Leary replied that the oil companies have "plenty of money." But instead of investing it in refineries, where controls keep the profit margin at 1973 levels, the oil companies were putting their money into real estate, petrochemicals and other businesses that provided a better return.

"There's no power in government [that allows us] to go to some of these admittedly rich companies and say, 'Take some of this wealth and put it into production of unleaded gasoline,' " O'Leary said. The answer is providing a more attractive profit margin, he told the House panel, and that requires gasoline decontrol.

But a plan to lift gasoline price controls must be submitted to Congress, where either house has 15 days to veto the proposal. Congress clearly had that authority through May 31, 1979, but there was some dispute among lawyers for the Energy Department and congressional committees about whether the veto authority extended beyond that date.

The oil industry supported gasoline decontrol, but ran into opposition at the Dec. 11, 1978, Senate hearing. "The oil industry is not just another business," said Jackson, predicting "more regulation unless you . . . have the ability to meet and keep pace with the requirements of the public."

The OPEC price hike decreased the chance of congressional appoval of a decontrol proposal, according to staff members of the Senate Energy Committee, because members did not want to share the blame if gasoline prices increased a dime a gallon in 1979.

Conflict with Clean Air

Further complicating the issue was concern about how decontrol would affect the operation of pollution-control devices on cars. The government estimated that decontrol would widen the gap between the gallon price of leaded and unleaded gasoline from 4.4 cents to about 7 cents.

EPA worried this would tempt drivers of cars requiring the more expensive unleaded fuel to switch to leaded gas. Such "fuel-switching" was practiced by 10 percent of drivers, and ruins emission control systems.

decontrol was a mistake because the time was "never right." But Kahn, reflecting the administration's concern with inflation, responded, "But this is an awful time."

Immediate Decontrol Ruled Out

If Carter were to have chosen the option of immediate decontrol, according to Rep. Bob Eckhardt, D-Texas, "I think that would be totally politically unacceptable." Allowing the oil industry such price increases would be "completely unfair" in a time of inflation when other industries and unions are being asked to keep prices down, said Eckhardt, who was a principal author of the 1975 law governing oil pricing.

Rep. Albert Gore, D-Tenn., agreed with Eckhardt. An effective anti-inflation program requires "the confidence of the people that all parts of society are making sacrifices that are roughly equal," Gore said in December 1978. If the energy industry was given an exemption from price controls, Gore continued, "I don't see how they are sharing in the anti-inflation program."

If those in Congress favoring decontrol tried to end price controls before the 1981 expiration date, Carter could veto the legislation to protect his own oil pricing plan. Supporters of decontrol probably could not get the support of the two-thirds of each house needed to override the veto.

Phased Increases

The most likely option that emerged, then, was presidential manipulation of oil price controls with the authority available to him June 1, 1979, and extending through Sept. 30, 1981. In choosing this option, Carter also asked Congress for new taxing authority to cushion consumers against the higher prices.

If Carter had decided to raise prices gradually without taxes, he would have been following the path endorsed by Congress in the 1975 law. The legislators set up a system that, even if not changed, meant continued increases in domestic oil prices.

The existing pricing system provided for two major categories of oil:

● "Old" — oil from wells producing as of mid-1973. Old (lower tier) oil was expected to cost $5.71 a barrel in January 1979.

● "New" — expanded production from "old" wells or oil from wells opened since mid-1973. New (upper tier) oil was priced close to the world price and was expected to cost $12.75 a barrel in January 1979. *(Chart of oil prices by category, p. 60)*

A third category, really a type of new oil, is called "stripper," and was decontrolled in 1976, which meant its price was at world levels. Stripper wells were defined as those producing less than 10 barrels a day.

The legislators programmed an end to controls by Oct. 1, 1981, thus tacitly endorsing higher prices at that time. But they also assured higher prices in two other principal ways:

● One, by setting the lowest prices for oil that is declining in volume. The amount of "old" oil declines naturally as old wells run dry. As the percentage of lower-priced oil drops, the average price of all domestic oil goes up. *(Domestic production graph, p. 60)*

● Two, by allowing an annual price increase of 10 percent in the average, or "composite," wellhead price. Part of that 10 percent was designed to cover the higher average cost

Some Facts About Oil

The United States was blessed with vast petroleum deposits that originated from organic matter sealed by layers of sediment more than 200 million years ago. The bulk of the deposits are in Texas, Louisiana, California and Oklahoma. Oil fields in the Gulf of Mexico have also been tapped, and development of the Outer Continental Shelf off the Eastern seaboard has been expanding.

These domestic sources, which supplied about 95 percent of oil used in the United States before World War II, by 1978 met only 55 percent of U.S. needs. Domestic production has been declining since 1970. The gap between demand and domestic supply has been filled by imports. The Organization of Petroleum Exporting Countries (OPEC) was the source for nearly 70 percent of the imported oil.

The United States in 1978 used more than 18 million 42-gallon barrels of oil a day. That represented about half the energy consumed in this country. Natural gas, also a hydrocarbon, supplied another quarter of demand. Most of the United States' other energy came from coal, hydroelectric power and nuclear power.

Though the United States had only 6 percent of the world's population, the nation consumed more than 30 percent of the world's energy.

Americans used oil primarily for transportation. More than half the oil consumed here fueled cars, trucks, airplanes and other vehicles. About 18 percent of the nation's oil was used by homes and businesses, primarily for heating. Industrial uses, including manufacturing and some heating, accounted for another 18 percent. The remaining 10 percent was used by utilities to generate electricity.

that results as higher-priced "new" oil replaces the declining volume of cheaper "old" oil.

Another segment of the 10 percent was expected to cover inflation.

The remainder of the 10 percent, if any was left, could be used by the executive branch to encourage production. For example, hard-to-get oil could be given even larger price increases than other types of oil to encourage producers to remove it from the ground.

But since September 1977, the Carter administration has allowed only price increases to cover inflation — not the price increases to encourage production. These "banked" increases were a bargaining tool for the administration in its efforts to win passage of the energy bill from Congress.

The "banked" increases meant the average domestic price at the wellhead was in 1978 about $1 less than it could be under existing law. John E. Swearingen, president of the American Petroleum Institute, has said these increases, not allowed "for purely political reasons," meant that, by the end of 1978, the Energy Department would have "withheld" from producers about $3.75 billion.

Carter's Steps to Decontrol

The administration's complicated schedule for phasing out controls was based in part on the 1975 law. Under Carter's scheduled increases, the definition of oil eligible for world prices would be broadened on June 1, 1979. Controls would be lifted on oil discovered after June 1; oil from marginal wells, which are deep and produce low volumes; and oil recovered by certain expensive techniques, called tertiary recovery.

Also on June 1, the volume of oil in the lower tier category would start to decline and would be gradually redefined as upper tier. The rate of decline between June 1 and Jan. 1, 1980, would be 1 percent to 1.5 percent a month. After Jan. 1, the decline rate would increase to 3 percent a month.

On Jan. 1, 1980, the price of upper tier oil would start to rise so that equal monthly increments would take it to the world levels by Oct. 1, 1981. Any remaining controls would be lifted then.

The administration expected that decontrol would spur additional production of 330,000 barrels a day in 1981 and up to 800,000 barrels a day in 1985. By spreading the price hike over a two-year period to avoid shocking the economy, administration officials said the decontrol steps would increase inflation by .2 percent in 1981 and again in 1982.

Industry Proposal

The oil industry had its own proposal for closing that gap.

Both the American Petroleum Institute and the Independent Petroleum Association of America offered plans for gradual decontrol of domestic prices based on the existing pricing system. The organizations, which generally reflect the position of the oil industry, opposed any new taxes. Institute members included a wide range of oil-related companies, while the association's membership consisted of about 5,000 independent producers.

Their proposals, which were very similar, would end controls June 1 on "new," higher-priced oil. Then, gradually, the price of old oil would be allowed to increase, with controls lifted by Sept. 30, 1981, when existing law expires.

Domestic Oil Prices at the Wellhead

	1974	1975	1976	1977	1978[5]
Old[1]	$ 5.03	$ 5.03	$ 5.13	$ 5.19	$ 5.38
New[2]	10.13	12.03	11.71	11.22	11.98
Stripper[3]	—	—	12.16	13.59	13.93
Alaskan North Slope	—	—	—	6.35	5.27
Domestic Average	**6.87**	**7.67**	**8.19**	**8.57**	**8.88**
Foreign Average[4]	10.77	10.72	11.51	12.40	12.70

1. Oil from wells producing as of May 15, 1973.
2. Oil in excess of a well's production as of May 15, 1973, or oil from wells not producing as of that date.
3. Oil from wells producing less than 10 barrels a day. Stripper oil was exempted from price controls Sept. 1, 1976.
4. Official sales price, FOB, of Arabian light (excluding transportation costs).
5. Average price through August.

Industry officials have long insisted that lifting controls would spur exploration and development of domestic resources. In order to drill now for future oil supplies, producers need a better cash flow, said Jack Allen of Texas, president of the association. "The five dollars [a barrel for old oil] won't do it."

As for the effect of higher prices on inflation, Allen referred to a study done by Data Resources Inc., a Lexington, Mass., consulting firm. Data Resources estimated that a decontrol plan similar to the industry proposals would add .1 percentage point to the inflation rate in 1979, .4 percentage point in 1980, and .5 percentage point in 1982. The inflation rate in 1978 was expected to exceed 9 percent, but administration officials hoped to hold the rate to 7 percent in 1979.

Petroleum Institute economists have estimated that immediate decontrol would have a one-time inflationary impact of .75 percent. Spread over three years, the institute study said, the annual impact would be about .25 percent.

To Allen, the benefits of decontrol in exchange for this impact on inflation made "a very good trade." It was not as inflationary to raise prices and provide revenues for production, he contended, "as it is to continue to import and rely on foreign oil," with corresponding increases in the trade deficit.

New Taxes

In 1977, President Carter, proposed a tax on crude oil to gradually bring domestic prices to world levels. Under the proposal, "new" oil would continue to be priced at or close to world levels. The tax on "old" oil, to be carried out in three stages, would bring that price to world levels. The tax was scheduled to expire Sept. 30, 1981, at which point the assumption was that all controls would be lifted.

The tax revenues, according to Carter's plan, would have been rebated to consumers in the form of a tax credit.

But Carter tried — and failed — to get the tax passed by the 95th Congress. The Senate Finance Committee rejected Carter's concept of rebates to consumers and eventually abandoned entirely the proposal for a tax on oil. The House Ways and Means Committee agreed to provide the rebates for one year only.

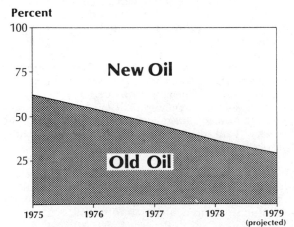

Domestic Production at the Wellhead

Percent

New Oil

Old Oil

The declining volume of "old" oil, which federal controls keep at less than $6 a barrel, is being replaced by "new" oil, which costs about $13 a barrel. More "new" oil means higher domestic prices.

SOURCE: U.S. Department of Energy, Energy Information Administration

Legacy of Oil Pricing Laws

The legislative history of oil pricing is almost as complicated as the options the Carter administration was facing in 1979. Three laws, called EPAA, EPCA and ECPA for short, govern oil pricing and provide new meanings for words like "old" and "stripper."

Domestic oil prices have been controlled since 1971, when President Nixon imposed general wage and price controls throughout the economy.

Congress continued the oil controls with the **Emergency Petroleum Allocation Act of 1973** (EPAA) (PL 93-159). Congress started work on the legislation because of fuel shortages in midwinter and inadequate gasoline supplies in summer. Action was concluded during the Arab oil embargo. The higher prices for foreign oil were shocking the economy, and government officials wanted to keep domestic oil prices from following that price spiral.

Ironically, in pre-embargo days, the situation was reversed, and domestic oil was more expensive than foreign. To prevent the cheaper foreign oil from undercutting U.S. producers, the United States in 1959 restricted the amount of oil that could be imported. The rationale for this policy was "national security." The quota system remained intact for the next decade. *(Pricing graph, p. 60)*

The first major effort to end the 1973 price controls came from President Ford, who announced in his 1975 State of the Union message that he would lift controls. He believed in "conservation-by-price" — allowing prices to rise to discourage consumption. With decontrol, refiners were expected to pay about $5 more per barrel for domestic oil, which was expected to rise to the price they paid for imported oil — $12.52 a barrel.

Congress Rejects Decontrol

But congressional opposition, which under existing law could have blocked Ford's action, forced him to propose a modified plan for a gradual end to price controls. For several months, Ford and Congress fought bitterly over oil pricing controls. The bill finally signed by Ford, over opposition from conservative Republicans and the oil industry, was the **Energy Policy and Conservation Act of 1975** (EPCA) (PL 94-163). *(1975 action, appendix p. 37-A)*

In addition to its provisions on oil pricing, the far-reaching 1975 law set fuel economy standards for automobiles, authorized a "strategic petroleum reserve" in the United States as insurance against future embargoes and included general calls for energy conservation.

In its most controversial section, the law also established an elaborate mechanism for holding down the price of oil already discovered and under production, called "old." But it allowed higher prices for "new" oil to encourage exploration and production. The law also set up a "composite" price, which was a weighted average of the old and new oil prices. An escalator was built in so prices could rise with inflation. But the combined inflation and production incentive increases were limited annually to 10 percent of the composite price.

In 1976, Congress adjusted the pricing system by exempting from controls "stripper" wells, so called because only oil that was difficult and expensive to extract, such as oil at the bottom of a well, remained to be "stripped" from the deposit. Regulations defined stripper wells as those producing less than 10 barrels per day. The stripper provision, designed to spur production from those wells, was included in the **Energy Conservation and Production Act** (ECPA) (PL 94-385).

On May 31, 1979, the mandatory price controls provided by these three laws expire. For the next two and a half years, the president could continue price controls, either by continuing to use the composite price or by devising new controls. He could also lift controls. On Sept. 30, 1981, the price ceilings would be automatically lifted.

Oil Refinery at Baytown, Tex.

Dispute Over Restrictions

To change the system that governs oil pricing, the president must change existing regulations. These changes would be subject to the government's formal rulemaking procedure, which includes public hearings, and to judicial review.

The president's actions would also have to be consistent with the goals of the oil pricing legislation. Various provisions in the pricing laws required that the president's actions not adversely affect supply, the economy or competition and not result in "inequitable" prices.

However, there was some dispute among lawyers for congressional committees and the Department of Energy about what restrictions on presidential action would still apply after May 31, 1979. Benjamin Cooper of the Senate Energy Committee staff said Congress would retain some limited review. If, for example, the president wanted to exempt a category of refined product, such as gasoline, from price controls, Congress would have 15 days to veto such a proposal — even after May 31, according to Cooper. But the administration questioned this interpretation, suggesting that the veto authority would expire May 31.

A similar tax proposal was expected to run into the same kinds of problems in the 96th Congress. Russell B. Long, D-La., Carter's most formidable opponent on the tax, again chaired the Senate Finance Committee. Long has insisted that any tax revenues from oil go back to the industry as production incentives.

The House Ways and Means Committee also had few enthusiastic supporters of a crude oil tax.

1979 Windfall Profits Proposal

Carter's April 1979 windfall profits tax plan had two parts. Under the first part, in effect until 1981, 50 percent of the price increase the oil industry would get for most already flowing oil would go to the government. Oil that at the time was expensive to produce or that was discovered in the future would not be taxed.

The second part of the plan called for an "OPEC tax" that would apply indefinitely to all oil once it was decontrolled. If the OPEC members raised prices again, thus boosting the market price of all oil, the tax would take 50 percent of the increased revenues U.S. companies would receive.

Without the tax, the administration estimated, oil company revenues from decontrol would be $26 billion to $31 billion through 1982, depending on OPEC action. With the tax, the oil companies would get an extra $12 billion to $13 billion through 1982.

Though Carter said the tax would "capture part of this money for the American people," only low-income families would benefit directly from the $11.4 billion expected from the tax through fiscal 1982. About 18 percent of what was collected would go to low-income families to help with higher energy costs. About 6 percent of the revenues, or $700 million through 1982, would be spent on mass transit programs.

But the bulk of the money collected would go to an "energy security fund," which Carter said would "put American genius to work solving our long-range energy problems." He mentioned new development of coal, solar, oil shale and hydroelectric power. The fund would get an estimated $900 million in fiscal 1980, $3 billion in 1981 and $4.7 billion in 1982. In 1979 the Department of Energy was spending more than $3.5 billion a year on similar energy research and development.

Reaction. In his speech, Carter fired the opening rounds in what promised to be a lengthy battle with Congress. "Every vote against [the tax] will be a vote for excessive oil company profits and for reliance on the whims of the foreign oil cartel," the president said in his televised announcement. "As surely as the sun will rise," the oil industry will "fight to keep the profits which they have not earned. Unless you speak out, they will have more influence on the Congress than you do."

Carter's plan was sent to the House Ways and Means and Senate Finance committees, and the cross fire began almost immediately. Six Ways and Means Republicans quickly proposed cutting the tax to 25 percent, instead of 50 percent, and making it temporary. Meanwhile, three liberal Democrats on the same committee wanted to raise the decontrol tax to 85 percent and make it permanent.

Some liberal members were expected to try to channel more of the funds to low-income and middle-class consumers. Others, notably Senate Finance Chairman Long, were opposed to the sort of energy fund Carter planned to set up. They argued that the oil industry, not the government, was best equipped to find new energy sources and probably would try to "plow back" more of the revenues to the industry. "If a windfall profits tax on oil company profits is necessary . . . then full credit should be given to oil companies for plowing back profits into the discovery and development of new energy sources," commented Sen. Charles H. Percy, R-Ill., who supported the phased decontrol plan. ∎

Oil Import Crisis Prompts Talk of Rationing

It would begin with long lines at the stations. Prices would jump 30 cents, 40 cents a gallon. Soon the order would come to close the stations on Sundays, then all weekend.

And then it would come — in the mail. A permit would arrive allowing the driver to pick up coupons at a bank, department store or other location. Free coupons would allow 50 gallons per month per car. Additional coupons would be available at a price of $1 each, meaning that gasoline beyond the basic ration would cost $1.80 to $2.00 a gallon — the price of the coupon plus the price of the gas. Gasoline rationing would have arrived.

This scenario, scripted by federal officials, came closer to reality in 1979 as the impact of the cutoff of Iranian oil became clearer.

Even if U.S. consumers found enough gasoline, they were certain to have to pay more for it. The tight supply of oil in the world market already by early 1979 had pushed prices to $20 a barrel for some high grades of oil, which was about $5 or more above average. These price increases would eventually show up at the gasoline pump and in heating bills.

Beyond urging voluntary conservation, no one was willing to predict when the supply crunch would become critical or what the best response to tight supplies might be. But Energy Secretary James R. Schlesinger said Feb. 7, 1979, that the loss of Iranian exports was "prospectively more serious" than the Arab oil embargo of 1973-74 because it could last much longer. Even if Iran started producing oil for export later in 1979, few experts expected production to reach the levels that once made that country the world's second leading oil exporter. Iran once provided 5 percent of the almost 20 million barrels used daily by the United States.

The Carter administration contended it would take more than the loss of Iranian imports to force mandatory conservation measures, such as Sunday closings of gasoline stations. Voluntary conservation by individuals, such as lowering thermostats, could make up for the reduction in supply, government officials said.

Rationing, called a "last resort," would not be considered unless supplies were more than 10 to 12 percent short of demand, according to Energy Department officials.

But the administration wanted to have contingency plans in place. Disruptions in other countries could cause chaos in the world oil market. In addition, under an international agreement designed to spread shortages equitably, the United States might be called on to share its supplies with 18 other Western nations and Japan.

"By April 1, at the latest, we should have firmly in mind, within this government, what we are prepared to do," Schlesinger told the Senate Energy Committee Feb. 7, 1979.

The contingency plans, required by a 1975 law, were due on Capitol Hill in June 1976. The administration reportedly was drawing up a series of executive actions that could be taken to help overcome the oil shortage. On Feb. 26, 1979, the administration sent Congress one of its plans, a proposal for standby emergency powers, including rationing. Before the plans could be valid, both the House and Senate must pass resolutions approving them. The Energy Policy and Conservation Act of 1975 (PL 94-163) gives Congress 60 days to act. If no action is taken, the plans are considered disapproved.

Schlesinger, who described world oil supplies as "stretched taut," conceded that other disruptions in supply — in addition to Iran — could trigger restrictions on energy use.

Although both the president and Schlesinger said that rationing would be used only as a last resort, it was included in the list of proposed standby emergency powers. The administration's rationing plan would limit gasoline supplies on the basis of registered vehicles rather than licensed drivers. It would allow from 40 to 45 gallons per vehicle per month — depending on the supply shortage.

The president also proposed mandatory conservation measures including a ban on Sunday gasoline sales and on decorative lighting and imposition of mandatory thermostat settings of 80 degrees during the summer and 65 degrees in the winter.

However, at a Feb. 28, 1979, news conference, Carter said "we don't have any present intention of implementing any of those measures." He went on to say, "I can't see at this point, not knowing the degree of shortage in the future of energy and particularly gasoline, what I would do. But I think those standby rights that I could exercise if necessary are important, and I'll just have to make a judgment when the time comes."

International Scene

Political upheaval in other major oil-producing countries could reduce world supplies. Diplomats were worried that the fall of the Shah Mohammad Reza Pahlavi in Iran could erode U.S. influence in the Persian Gulf. One worried senator, Dale Bumpers, D-Ark., noted that "a couple of well-aimed bullets" in less stable oil-producing countries could radically change their favorable posture towards the United States.

But Schlesinger, describing possible disruptions, was also referring to the chance that Saudi Arabia, which in early 1979 supplied one-third of exports to non-communist countries, could decide to reduce its higher-than-normal production levels.

Saudi Arabia, Kuwait and other producers have made up for roughly 3 million of the 5 million to 5.5 million barrels a day once exported by Iran to non-Communist countries. But the Saudis, who at times were exporting more than 10 million barrels a day in late 1978, had reportedly cut back to 9.5 million barrels a day in early 1979 and could decide to hold production even lower. In addition, a premium price was being charged for oil produced beyond the level of 8.5 million barrels a day.

In the United States, about 400,000 of the 900,000 barrels once supplied by Iran were covered by the higher production levels in Saudi Arabia and other countries in early 1979.

The Arab countries with rich oil deposits have developing economies that are able to absorb only so many revenues without risking disruption of traditional cultures and lifestyles. Caution about too rapid development, as well as the prospect that the oil in the ground would continue to increase in value, could lead to reductions in production.

The remaining loss of Iranian imports to the United States, not made up by this increased production, was about 500,000 barrels a day.

But the administration was concerned that the U.S. rate of consumption had not adjusted to this decrease. Instead, oil companies had borrowed from inventories, which were especially high because companies had been stocking up to beat 1979 price increases scheduled by the Organization of Petroleum Exporting Countries (OPEC).

But at some point, after any cushion of extra supply is used up, this practice of borrowing from inventories begins to squeeze future supplies.

In winter, companies usually have to use oil from inventories as well as from current production to meet higher demand. Then, in the spring and summer, inventories are built up again in anticipation of the next winter's demand.

"If Iranian curtailments continue much beyond this spring [1979], summer supplies will be particularly tight, and there will be little chance for rebuilding stocks during the fall in time to meet next winter's peak demand," Schlesinger told the congressional Joint Economic Committee Jan. 23, 1979. "Should stocks be insufficient to meet demand during next winter's heating season, prices could increase substantially."

Obligations to the World

Though the United States got only 5 percent of its oil from Iran, other countries were far more dependent on Iranian exports. Overall, Iran supplied about 10 percent of all the oil used by non-communist countries. Japan got an estimated 19 percent of its oil from Iran, and several Western European countries depended on Iran for 10 to 20 percent of their oil supplies.

Their losses could eventually affect the United States because of a 1975 international agreement that set up the International Energy Agency, now based in Paris.

Average U.S. Gasoline Consumption

(Barrels per day)

Year	Total	%Change
1972	6,376,000	+ 4.7
1973	6,674,000	− 2.1
1974	6,537,000	+ 2.1
1975	6,675,000	+ 4.5
1976	6,978,000	+ 2.8
1977	7,176,000	+ 3.0
1978	7,393,000*	+15.95

* Figure is an average of the daily consumption rates in January through November.

SOURCE: Energy Information Administration, U.S. Department of Energy

As of early 1979, an informal allocation system being used by the international oil companies was spreading around the shortage. But experts predicted squeeze would get tighter.

The international agreement essentially required that all countries represented by the International Energy Agency share any shortages on an equitable basis. The agency could reroute oil shipments to needy countries.

The two countries hardest hit by the Iranian cutoff — Israel and South Africa — were not members of the international agency. The new political leaders in Iran were not likely to sell oil to those countries in the future because of political differences.

The United States signed an agreement with Israel in 1975 that committed this country to sell some of its supplies to Israel if no other oil were available. Administration sources estimated that Israel could require 70,000 barrels a day. But, as of early 1979, Israel had not asked for assistance.

If the agreement were called into play, top Energy Department officials have suggested that Alaskan oil could meet Israel's needs. But that would require congressional action to loosen existing restrictions that bar export of oil from Alaska.

There was no similar U.S. agreement with South Africa, which received 90 percent of its oil from Iran.

Higher World Prices

The disruptions in the world oil supply had already begun to affect the price of oil on "spot markets," where oil not under long-term contract is bought and sold. Prices in 1979 were averaging as much as $4 to $5 higher a barrel than the price posted by the Organization of Petroleum Exporting Countries (OPEC). Some prices were as high as $24 a barrel, compared to the January 1979 price of $13.34 a barrel set by OPEC.

Some analysts predicted the higher spot market prices could encourage OPEC oil ministers to raise prices at a faster rate than planned at their December 1978 meeting. That meant OPEC could decide to start charging $14.54 a barrel in spring or summer 1979, instead of waiting until Oct.1, when that price was scheduled to take effect.

Under U.S. regulations controlling gasoline prices, oil companies were allowed to "pass through" higher oil prices to consumers. A study released Jan. 31, 1979, by the Department of Energy predicted that U.S. gasoline prices would increase about nine to 12 cents a gallon by the end of 1980, but a continued crisis in Iran could push those prices higher. *(Domestic oil pricing, p. 55)*

The tighter world oil market and resulting higher prices had forced almost to a halt the acquisition of oil for the Strategic Petroleum Reserve, a program to store oil underground as insurance against future shortages. Schlesinger said the government was not filling the reserve because the only oil available was priced at spot market levels, which he said the government did not want to pay. The cutback in oil purchases meant further delays in the program, which in 1979 was already a year behind schedule. *(Background, p. 71)*

Domestic Scene

Since the first day of 1979, the Carter administration urged the public to conserve energy because of the Iranian shutdown.

"I don't think there's any doubt we can cut back consumption of oil by 5 percent without seriously damaging our economy," Carter said at a Jan. 17, 1979, news conference. "And I would hope that all Americans who listen to my voice now would do everything possible within their own capabilities to cut down on the use of oil and the waste of all energy supplies."

Another government official reiterated this belief that voluntary cutbacks could make up for the reduction in supply. "There is a capacity to make minimal changes in lifestyle and consume a great deal less gasoline," said David J. Bardin, administrator of the Economic Regulatory Administration, at a February 1979 Senate hearing. His agency, part of the Department of Energy, was responsible for emergency energy planning.

Convincing the Public

But the exhortations to conserve seemed to have had little effect. The public was generally skeptical of past calls for conservation when the reasons for cutting back — and the rewards for doing so — had not been readily apparent.

Besides, Sen. John A. Durkin, D-N.H., told Bardin, people were already conserving. "We turned down the thermostat in New Hampshire and New England long ago," Durkin said. "It's there at 65 [degrees] and below already."

Sen. Paul E. Tsongas, D-Mass., suggested to Schlesinger that this skepticism made mandatory conservation measures necessary in order to convince the public of the severity of the energy problem.

The difficulty of convincing the public there was an oil supply problem was conceded by government officials. One source described oil supply problems as "not like the kind of crisis we had with Pearl Harbor, but more like a cancer that erodes the situation."

An Energy Department official said telling people inventories are being depleted "doesn't have the clarion call that it's time to hit the trenches."

Any government-imposed restrictions on energy use were certain to be very controversial and politically risky.

Though Bardin conceded the danger of moving too slowly to force conservation, he also noted it was "just as important not to move too fast." With rationing, "the government would be trying to tell millions of people how to manage their lives," he said. "I don't think we'd be very good at that."

In addition to pushing voluntary conservation, the administration was urging industry to switch from oil to natural gas in facilities that are capable of burning either fuel. Schlesinger said the existing surplus of 1 trillion cubic feet of natural gas could replace 500,000 barrels a day of oil. *(Gas background, p. 67)*

The administration also was encouraging use of nuclear energy and coal, instead of oil, to fuel power plants.

Another possibility mentioned by Schlesinger was "temporary suspension of selected environmental requirements," such as allowing plants to burn "dirty" oil with high sulfur content.

Only if these measures, combined with conservation, did not work would the government consider mandatory conservation measures, Schlesinger said.

Standby Measures

The first of these mandatory restrictions to be carried out would be a requirement that oil companies allocate supplies to refiners and retailers on an equitable basis. That would mean that those heavily dependent on im-

ported oil could get enough oil to stay in business. Some independent refiners were already cutting back on production because of the tighter world market, and several had already closed. Though oil may be available to these refiners on the spot market, the prices were so high that the products coming from the refineries would be too expensive to be competitive.

After the allocation systems were operating, the government could consider placing restrictions on how the general public uses energy. Once Congress gave the Energy Department authority for the standby conservation plans, the president could trigger them during an energy shortage.

The standby measures proposed Feb. 27 included:

● Restrictions on weekend gasoline sales. This could mean Sunday closings of stations or restrictions on the sale of gasoline during certain hours. Energy officials estimated this proposal could save 284,000 barrels a day.

● Limits on thermostats. Heating and cooling guidelines, as well as limits on hot water temperatures, would have to be followed by commercial and public building operators. Estimates of savings from this provision ranged from 200,000 to 350,000 barrels a day.

● Controls on lighted advertisements. Signs not needed to direct customers to businesses would have to be turned off.

Rationing

The government had in storage in Pueblo, Colo., about 4.8 billion coupons for gas rationing that were printed during the Arab oil embargo. The coupons, which cost $10 million to print, could be used in a rationing program "if we had nothing better," Bardin said. The problem with the coupons is that they have no serial numbers, which made them easy to counterfeit. Bardin said, "We would prefer to have them serialized . . . but we have no intention of throwing them away."

Rationing was "a possibility, but a remote possibility," in the early 1979 situation, according to Schlesinger. Rationing is "one of the last things you do," said Bardin, who called managing a rationing program "a very substantial challenge."

If the administration decided to impose rationing, the proposal would have to go to Congress, where either house could veto it within 15 days.

The plan offered by the administration was published in the *Federal Register* June 28, 1978. It would allocate rationing coupons on the basis of vehicle registrations, of which there were about 160 million. Every car owner would get a certain number of coupons, but could buy additional coupons or sell unneeded ones legally on an unregulated "white market."

Bardin estimated that a coupon for a gallon of gasoline would probably cost $1.25 on the white market if there were a 20 percent shortage of gasoline. Then, in addition, the coupon-holder would have to pay for the gasoline itself. Coupons would be less expensive if more gasoline were available.

Under the administration's plan the quarterly allotments of coupons would be mailed as checks, which would then have to be cashed at participating banks, businesses or post offices that had sufficient security measures. The coupons in turn would be required to purchase gasoline at a service station, with each coupon worth five gallons. Energy officials were reluctant to have gas stations accept and cash the checks.

But the American Banking Association disliked the idea that everyone would have to exchange his ration check for coupons — and probably would do so at participating banks. "That would mess up any bank lobby like crazy," said William A. Wood, an official with the association, which represented about 92 percent of the nation's 14,000 banks.

The bankers have argued that some coupons should be mailed directly to car owners to cut down on the check cashing. They also wanted gas stations to share more of the burden of the rationing program than they would under the draft Energy Department proposal.

After initial start-up costs, a rationing program would cost about $415 million every quarter, or more than $1.7 billion a year. In 1978, the Energy Department estimated operating costs at less than half that amount, but Bardin said the original estimate of $175 million per quarter did not include grants to states for operating their part of the program. States would make decisions about who qualified for extra coupons.

Bardin called rationing a "rough and ready equalizer" that would depend on the white market to allocate supplies to those with special needs. "It is not designed for social equity."

Opposition to Administration Plan

Even before the administration announced its standby plan, critics were lining up against rationing and proposals to restrict weekend gas sales, prohibit some lighted outdoor advertising and control thermostats in commercial and industrial buildings.

The rationing plan drew complaints from a broad spectrum of interest groups worried about the impact restrictions on gasoline use could have on their business.

The National Automobile Dealers Association, for example, started an extensive national advertising campaign late in 1978 with the theme, "Help us protect your freedom to drive." The campaign was financed by the association, Chrysler, Ford, General Motors and others who have contributed to a new corporation, called The Automobile Fund.

"Don't take your wheels for granted," stated one advertisement that appeared in February 1979 issues of national magazines. "There are people, in government and others, whose only answer to our environmental and energy problems is to restrict use of the automobile. . . . Join with us. . . . Because, if you don't speak up today, your freedom to drive may be restricted tomorrow."

The proposal to restrict weekend gas sales was strongly opposed by the tourism industry. Weekend station closings would "single us out unfairly," said Albert L. McDermott, Washington representative for the American Hotel and Motel Association. During the 1973-74 Arab oil embargo, when many stations were closed on Sunday, the tourism industry lost $717 million in revenues, McDermott said.

In a telegram to President Carter, the association noted that hotels and motels "do not object to doing our fair share" to conserve energy. "But if we are, for all intents and purposes, to go without business for one or two days of the week, then a similar sacrifice should be borne by others," said the statement.

Criticism from GAO

Since the 1973-74 Arab oil embargo, the General Accounting Office (GAO) has done several studies of government plans to handle similar emergencies and to curb overall energy consumption.

In a Feb. 13, 1979, letter to chairmen of energy-related panels in the House and Senate, GAO officials noted that the delays in developing emergency standby rationing and conservation plans "provide convincing evidence that since the 1973 oil embargo, the government has not significantly improved its ability to deal with a crude oil supply disruption. This problem is particularly relevant in view of the current Iranian oil situation."

The GAO report summarized three major problems its studies showed reduced the effectiveness of existing federal plans for handling emergencies and for decreasing energy consumption. The problems were:

● Lack of planning that clearly identified what contribution energy conservation is to make in the overall national energy plan.

● Lack of an aggressive, coordinated effort to conserve energy in federal operations and facilities.

● Failure of the administration to develop in a timely fashion, and have approved by Congress, emergency energy conservation plans.

But concern about being prepared has been matched by worries about overreacting. Administration officials have said publicly that they were concerned that government action could make problems worse.

A study by the American Enterprise Institute of the Arab embargo found that government efforts to allocate gasoline exacerbated shortages rather than eased them. The February 1975 report, called "Performance of the Federal Energy Office," was written by Richard B. Mancke, and done as part of the institute's National Energy Project.

Edward J. Mitchell, director of the project, carried that argument a step further. "It is more correct to say that the problem was created almost out of nothing," said Mitchell, a professor of business economics at the University of Michigan, in an interview. "I would have argued that the lines and all that were almost entirely the creation [of government rules]."

Lines at gas stations "didn't exist anywhere else in the world," he noted. Other countries affected by the oil embargo "just let the price [of oil and gasoline] go [up]," and Mitchell recommended that the United States do the same thing.

Mitchell's argument that price be allowed to play a larger role in allocating scarce supplies would probably be made several times by witnesses and members of Congress as the plans were considered. Many critics thought government intervention, even in minor ways, should be avoided if at all possible. In their view, the marketplace is a far more efficient and satisfactory mechanism for distributing scarce supplies than government regulations.

Use of New Natural Gas Supplies Encouraged

Supplies of natural gas — once so erratic they provoked winter shortages and wholesale industrial switches to other fuels — were in early 1979 in temporary surplus, according to statements by Energy Secretary James R. Schlesinger.

In addition, the promise of future supplies — from increased production in the lower 48 states, the North Slope of Alaska and new finds in Canada and Mexico — would make possible continued use of natural gas by industry and others. The new supplies could cut oil imports and decrease the need for future imports.

"Overall, supplies are prospectively adequate," Schlesinger told a group of petroleum investment analysts in New York Jan. 9, 1979. The speech was a major policy statement on natural gas. "Indeed, over the next 20 or 30 years gas usage may well rise here in the United States," the secretary said.

This was a marked change from 1977, when the Carter administration's national energy plan described clean-burning gas as a "premium fuel in short supply" and discouraged its use by industry.

Though Schlesinger insisted Jan. 9 that administration policy still called for new facilities to use coal, he asked that existing plants burn gas instead of oil if they have the ability. He estimated that a "bubble" of 1 trillion cubic feet of gas in excess of demand was available.

New Sources

That the government must step in to encourage the use of gas was evidence of the remarkable changes in the natural gas supply situation between 1976 and 1979.

Demand, which skyrocketed during the 1973-74 oil embargo, began to taper off as shortages and the prospect of continued uncertainties of supply led many industrial users to switch to other fuels. Homeowners, because of higher prices and government programs, also began to conserve. In many states, there was a moratorium on the hook-up of new gas customers, the assumption being that existing users should have priority access to the limited supplies.

This declining demand was compatible with declining production. But supply, or at least the prospect of supply, dramatically improved. Instead of having to turn to expensive imports of liquefied natural gas (LNG) to meet demand, gas suppliers were finding new gas supplies available on this continent, via pipeline — a far more efficient and cheaper method of transportation.

Canada. New finds in Canada, which exported 1 trillion cubic feet a year to the United States, meant that its National Energy Board was likely to approve additional exports. In February 1979, the board gave the go-ahead to a 28 percent increase in exports to the United States.

Mexico. Mexico, which has been recognized as harboring vast reserves of oil, also has abundant supplies of gas. Much of it is "associated" with oil, which means that, unless tapped as the oil is drilled, the gas must be flared — burned off. Mexico, according to Schlesinger, was flaring 500 million cubic feet a day. The United States uses 53.5 billion cubic feet daily. President Carter discussed U.S. purchase of Mexican oil and gas during a February 1979 visit to Mexico.

Domestic. More gas also was expected from domestic producers. Incentive pricing, which gives higher prices to new discoveries and production from deep wells, was included for domestic producers in the 1978 Natural Gas Policy Act (PL 95-621). These pricing incentives were eventually expected to "insure a high rate of drilling activity," according to Schlesinger. He predicted that by 1985 the new law would result in production in the continental United States of at least 2 trillion cubic feet more that would otherwise be expected.

Alaska. Alaska's North Slope contains some 26 trillion cubic feet of proven gas reserves. In 1976, Congress, giving as its rationale that "a natural gas supply shortage exists," voted to expedite government approval of a privately financed gas pipeline through Canada from Alaska. The pipeline also received a boost from the gas pricing act, which allows the Alaskan gas, higher-priced because of transportation costs, to be "rolled-in" with other gas so that all users, not just direct users, share the burden of the higher price. Final action on the pipeline by the Federal Energy Regulatory Commission was expected in mid-1979. Then the pipeline's developers will escalate their search for financial backing.

The combination of declining demand and increased supply meant that, in economic terms, the gas market was "soft." Unless some industrial users signed up, the United States could find it has more gas available than it could use.

Usually, in a free market, a "soft" market means that the price of a commodity will fall, drawing in more users who will eventually soak up the excess supply. Then, as demand and supply adjust, the price might go up again.

The Priorities

But the natural gas market is controlled. Schlesinger, by listing priorities for development of gas sources, indicated that the Carter administration would like to retain that control.

"Over the next 20 or 30 years [natural] gas usage may well rise here in the United States."

—James R. Schlesinger, Secretary of Energy

"Alternative supplies of gas should neither endanger nor discourage base production from the lower 48 states," Schlesinger said Jan. 9.

Following domestically produced gas on Schlesinger's list of priorities is Alaskan gas, followed by Mexican and Canadian, then by short-haul liquefied natural gas, then domestically produced synthetic gas (from coal) and finally "long-haul, high-cost, possibly insecure LNG."

He elaborated on the reasons for giving a lower priority to Mexican and Canadian gas:

"We would welcome such additional supplies [from Canada and Mexico] — to the extent that they are reasonably reliable, are priced sufficiently attractively to maintain a market in the United States and do not force the shutting-in of domestic production. This last is a vital but frequently ignored aspect of the problem. We should be reluctant to contract for supplies, even from our neighbors, on a take-or-pay basis, if that should be at the expense of American producers — resulting in the shutting-in of domestic capacity or diminishing the domestic incentives for drilling."

By favoring some gas supplies over others, Schlesinger supported continued government interference in the natural gas market. But the improved outlook for gas supplies prompted such ardent supporters of gas regulation as Sen. Edward M. Kennedy, D-Mass., to reconsider their positions.

By adding Mexican and additional Canadian gas to the United States supply, Kennedy said, competition could be restored to the gas industry. Instead of regulations, the resulting free market could then control the price. "Our objective should be to introduce competition into the United States market with gas from Mexico and Canada," Kennedy told a group of broadcasters in Boston Jan. 9, 1979, the same day Schlesinger was outlining the administration's natural gas policy in New York. "Our goal should be the creation of a continent-wide natural gas market in which gas flows freely with minimum government interference," Kennedy said.

On Jan. 10, Kennedy sharply criticized the policy outlined by Schlesinger, calling it "a policy for protecting domestic gas from competition" that was designed to "clear out the gas glut, which embarrasses domestic producers."

Schlesinger gave a strong endorsement to the $12 billion gas pipeline from Alaska, urging the petroleum investment analysts in New York to "remain sympathetic on this critical issue until the significant regulatory decisions expected over the next several months are complete."

Even though Alaskan gas would initially cost $4 per thousand cubic feet (Mcf), or as much as $6 by some estimates, Schlesinger argued that the price would go down as the pipeline is paid for, making Alaskan gas "a bargain for U.S. consumers."

This stated preference for domestic gas could affect the imports of gas from Canada and Mexico if demand does not catch up with supply. Though Schlesinger told the Senate Energy Committee Jan. 17 that the administration would welcome both Mexican and Canadian gas, his strong endorsement of the Alaska pipeline was read by many as dampening the chance of a gas purchase agreement with Mexico.

The Mexican Question

One of Schlesinger's chief arguments for giving Alaska and other domestic gas priority over Mexico and Canada was the lower price.

Under the terms of a 1977 sales agreement between Petroleos Mexicanos (Pemex), the state-run oil company, and six American companies, led by Tenneco Inc., the Mexican gas price was to be tied to the cost of heating oil arriving in New York harbor, which at the time meant a gas price of $2.60 per thousand cubic feet.

But the price, when compared to domestic prices of less than $2 per Mcf and the Canadian price of $2.16 per Mcf, was considered too high by the administration. Schlesinger vetoed the sales agreement.

The impasse over price angered the Mexicans, who said they would burn off the gas or use it domestically rather than sell it to the United States at this lower price. That issue was discussed during Carter's February visit to Mexico, following which the two governments agreed to begin negotiations on oil and gas prices.

Some analysts questioned the argument that this price was too high. They argued for short-term contracts with Mexico, which the 1977 agreement called for, that would allow a renegotiation of prices should an oversupply of gas cause prices to drop. In the meantime, they noted, Mexican gas would be much cheaper than Alaskan gas.

But the primary argument used against Schlesinger's emphasis on price and his preference for domestic production was that U.S. purchase of Mexican gas should be considered within the context of overall U.S.-Mexican relations, including U.S. access to Mexican oil.

Some presidential advisers have endorsed this view, urging that relations with Mexico be given a special status and that oil and gas purchases be considered in that context, along with immigration and trade.

But President Carter, at a Jan. 17, 1979, news conference, indicated he shared Schlesinger's view that Mexican gas purchases should not be isolated from the "surplus of natural gas in our own country [at this moment]" or from the "problem of using efficiently gas produced in the 48 states of our country and in the future [bringing] the natural gas that is available from Alaska down through Canada to our nation."

"It's a very complicated thing," Carter said, noting there is "no urgency about acquiring Mexican natural gas."

But some senators have publicly disagreed with the administration's position. Sen. Alan Cranston, D-Calif., noting that California could be a primary user of Mexican gas, called Schlesinger's list of priorities "unacceptable" and urged that the United States pursue an agreement to buy natural gas from Mexico. Purchase of natural gas would be a valuable aid in helping Mexico develop "industrially and agriculturally," Cranston said in a Jan. 12, 1979, speech in California.

Sen. Lloyd Bentsen, D-Texas, also criticized what he called the "either-or" posture of the administration. Instead of choosing to develop domestic gas instead of foreign sources, Bentsen said Jan. 10, the United States "must pursue twin goals" of developing domestic reserves and reliable foreign supplies. He endorsed a policy of assisting Mexico in developing its oil and gas reserves.

When Schlesinger testified Jan. 17 before the Senate Energy Committee, Sen. Frank Church, D-Idaho, a member of the Energy panel and chairman of the Senate Foreign Relations Committee, reminded Schlesinger of the benefits of gas contracts with Mexico.

The balance of payments would be "relatively unaffected," Church said, because Mexico already spends more in the United States than the United States spends there. There are advantages of having supplies close by, Church continued, and Schlesinger agreed. The availability of oil from Mexico could be enhanced by purchase of gas, Church noted, and Schlesinger replied, "It could have that effect."

"If we could work out a kind of package, addressed to the various problems [between the United States and Mexico], including oil and gas, it would greatly serve our relations," Church told Schlesinger. Energy Chairman Henry M. Jackson, D-Wash., agreed. "The arrangement would be different than a customer on a straight buyer-seller basis," Jackson said, urging "cooperation in social and economic improvement" and consideration of gas purchases "in that broader context."

But Schlesinger argued that the United States would "do no favor to Mexico" by buying gas "at a high price that destroys the possibility of a substantial American market." He also said Mexican officials were very sensitive about the "the perception of the United States moving in to grab their resources."

Schlesinger said the senators should recognize that, by buying Mexican gas despite its high price, they would also be agreeing to have the U.S. government subsidize the price of the Mexican gas on the U.S. market.

Though he did not elaborate, such subsidies could presumably include regulatory policies, similar to those applied to Alaskan gas, for example, that allow the higher priced gas to be averaged in with lower priced gas.

U.S.-Mexican Talks Planned

Even though the United States and Mexico agreed in February to hold energy talks, the two countries were far apart on the touchy question of how much U.S. customers would pay for Mexican natural gas.

Resolution of that dispute would substantially boost U.S. chances of signing up for some of the 40 billion plus barrels of proven oil reserves that Mexico was starting to tap.

In turn, failure to agree on a price range for natural gas would be a serious setback to overall energy negotiations.

The negotiations, which could start in March or April 1979, would renew the discussions that had been broken off in December 1977 when Schlesinger had vetoed the sales agreement between Pemex and six U.S. companies.

The ill will that dispute raised between the two countries was apparently smoothed during President Carter's visit to Mexico. In a joint communiqué issued Feb. 16, Carter and Mexican President José López Portillo agreed to try again to break the impasse over gas pricing.

The government negotiations will set the "outer limits of price," explained one State Department official, and those parameters would then guide the discussion of specific contracts between Pemex and U.S. companies. Purchase of natural gas would be a two-step process. If the governments could reach agreement, company-to-company negotiations would follow, the official said.

Representing the United States will be a team of officials from the Energy Department, the State Department and the National Security Council. Their progress would be followed by several members of Congress who had criticized the Carter administration for taking a hard line on the price of natural gas, rather than considering gas purchases a prelude to future oil purchases and improved relations with Mexico.

The negotiators would be guided by the wishes of Carter and López Portillo as expressed in a joint communiqué.

"The two presidents decided," stated the communiqué, "to start immediately the design of plans to collaborate in the field of energy, with a strict observance of their respective national policies, and to initiate or expand, whatever might be the case, trade in hydrocarbon products, electricity and other energy resources."

Mexico has been firm about setting its own pace for development of its vast reserves and has resented any implication that it should speed its efforts just to meet U.S. needs. Mexico's energy resources have greatly enhanced its position in negotiations with the United States on a variety of issues, including illegal immigration and drug traffic.

"It is the first time we have been in a position of strength in dealing with this country," said Florenncio Acosta, minister counselor for economic affairs at the Mexican Embassy in Washington, D.C. "We have something the United States wants and needs. It helps."

Carter, in a Feb. 16 address to a joint session of the Mexican Congress, clarified his view of Mexico's policy:

"The petroleum reserves of Mexico are the national patrimony of the Mexican people, to be developed and used as Mexico sees fit. We respect the imperative that Mexico will produce at a rate suited to your development objectives. As a good customer, we are prepared to pay a fair and just price for the gas and oil you wish to sell."

Mexico's Resources

Mexico's oil and gas reserves became known only in the last few years. The government estimates proven reserves at 40.1 billion barrels and possible reserves at 200 billion barrels, although others have suggested that estimate was very low. One reason for optimism was that Mexican officials said about 70 percent of the one million square miles in Mexico have geological formations where oil is likely to be found. "Only 10 percent [of that area] has yet been explored," said Acosta, the Mexican Embassy official.

Mexico in 1979 was producing more than 1.5 million barrels of oil a day. Of the 500,000 barrels a day that are exported, 400,000 barrels, or 80 percent, were sent to the United States. Pemex wanted to produce 2.25 million barrels a day by 1980, according to Mexican officials.

Natural gas and oil are found together in the Mexican fields, so that gas extracted along with the oil must be piped out or burned off. Mexican industry was using much of the gas, since the country had no liquefaction facilities that could make export possible. But 500 million cubic feet were being flared each day. Because gas moves most efficiently through pipelines, the United States would be the ideal customer for gas not used by Mexican industry.

Mexico has carefully planned how it will develop its energy resources and use the revenues. Oil income goes into a special fund for investment in Mexico.

"There's enough experience on somebody else's hands to know what's in store for us," if we develop too rapidly, said Acosta. "Oil can be a bad thing, like going to the races and winning — money comes in without too much effort."

Instead, Acosta said, "we will be creating jobs — in petrochemicals, . . . in synthetics, with textiles . . . We may finance [agricultural] industries." Then, when the oil is gone, Mexico would still have a strong economy, he said.

"We do not want to be exporters of capital, having money around without being able to invest it in Mexico," Acosta said. "We want balanced growth with the earnings [from oil and gas sales]. Otherwise we could get into great problems."

Oil Storage Program Poses Costly Problems

When Congress voted in 1975 to store oil in salt caverns as insurance against shortages, nobody really worried much about cost.

Sen. Edmund S. Muskie, D-Maine, chairman of the Budget Committee, did warn his colleagues that the "Strategic Petroleum Reserve" could cost "well over $6 billion over its life." But there was no other discussion, and no limit placed on appropriations. *(Energy policy act, appendix, p. 37-A)*

But by early 1979, the oil reserve was expected to cost more than $25 billion.

This cost — along with a Pentagon analyst's prediction that the reserve could become "a giant fiscal disaster" — prompted new questions about the plan to store 1 billion barrels of oil "insurance" by 1985.

A major target of critics was the Department of Energy's management of the program.

"Clearly the failures in the [reserve] program are management failures," said Rep. John D. Dingell, D-Mich., at December 1978 hearings before his Commerce Subcommittee on Energy and Power.

Energy Secretary James R. Schlesinger admitted the program once suffered from "bad management," but pointed to improvement. A new director — Deputy Under Secretary Joseph Deluca, a retired Air Force general — became the program's third manager in July 1978.

In addition to these complaints about management, some presidential advisers have questioned the need for a billion-barrel reserve, suggesting that 750 million barrels would be adequate. Scaling down the program would save $6 billion, according to Office of Management and Budget estimates.

Congress authorized a billion-barrel reserve in 1975 (PL 94-163) after it was proposed by the Ford administration. Ford set a goal of 500 million barrels in the ground by 1985. In May 1978, President Carter doubled the goal, calling for storage of the full billion barrels by 1985. However, the Senate unilaterally rejected the plan that year.

Problems Plague Reserve

In addition to cost overruns, the program in early 1979 was about a year behind schedule. President Carter had wanted 250 million barrels in storage by the end of 1978. But by year's end, only 70 million barrels — a little more than the United States imports in a week — were in place.

Should those supplies be needed, they would not be available because no pumping mechanism had been installed to extract the oil from storage. Energy Department officials said the pumps would be working by the end of the summer of 1979.

The pumps had been given a lower priority earlier in the program, Deluca explained, because the project was governed by the idea that "the earlier the oil is acquired and stored, the lower the real cost to the United States."

Other problems have plagued the agency in its efforts to store oil and construct a system to extract and transport the oil in an emergency. The mishaps included:

●A fire at one storage site. While a contractor was repairing equipment at West Hackberry, La., too much

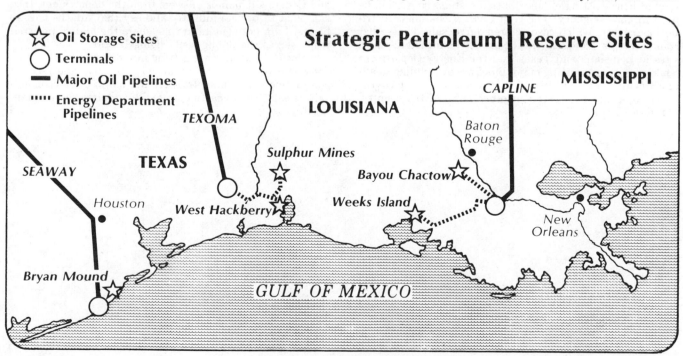

pressure built up and there was an explosion. The oil spewing from the storage site caught fire.

● Several storage caverns that turned out to be smaller than expected. As a result, the government paid an extra $8 million to the owners of oil tankers that had to wait in the Gulf of Mexico because not enough storage space was available to hold the oil.

● Underground wells that could not "swallow" salty water displaced from the caverns as fast as planners had predicted, which caused delays in the program. The agency had drilled the wells into sand, which could absorb the

---

"Clearly the failures in the program are management failures."

—Rep. John D. Dingell, D-Mich.

---

brine. The Energy Department now has a permit to dispose of some brine in the Gulf of Mexico. "Five months ago I did not know what the hell brine was," Deluca told the Commerce panel. "Now I live with it."

In addition, storage costs originally estimated at less than $1 a barrel, had risen to $3.50 a barrel by early 1979. The price of crude oil purchased for the reserve averaged about $13 a barrel.

The Process

The concept of storing oil in the ground seems fairly straightforward and has, in fact, been done before. West Germany, for example, has a petroleum reserve. But, in reality, a working system of buying, storing and distributing the oil is complicated, as Energy Department officials have been finding out. And no one had tried it before on such a large scale or with such an ambitious timetable.

The Energy Department wanted to store the oil underground near existing oil distribution systems so it could be used in an emergency. The Gulf Coast was a major distribution center, which also offered large salt domes that could serve as storage sites. The agency identified five such sites in Louisiana and Texas that the Energy Department could connect to existing major pipelines by building smaller connector lines. Additional sites, needed to complete the program, could be located in other parts of the country. *(Map of sites p. 71)*

For example, the department had to build a 67-mile, $78 million pipeline in Louisiana between a storage site at Weeks Island and the St. James tanker terminal. The terminal feeds into the Capline pipeline, a major commercial artery that goes to Illinois. The department's pipeline is used to put oil into storage and also would be used to take it out in an emergency.

The Weeks Island storage is in caverns created by the Morton salt company as it mined rock salt, which is used to melt ice from roads and for making ice cream at home.

Though the Weeks Island site was ready to accept the oil, other salt caverns were not because they had been used as storage sites by chemical companies. Unlike Morton, those companies were not interested in dry salt, but wanted salty water — brine — that they used in chemical processes. These firms, such as Dow Chemical Co., which owned Bryan Mound in Texas, pumped water into the dome, where it mixed with salt to become brine. The brine was then pumped out and tranferred to chemical plants. But not all the brine was removed from the caverns and, as oil is pumped in, the brine is displaced. As that salty sludge comes out of the caverns, the Energy Department has to find ways to dispose of it.

Contracting with Industry

The complexities of the oil storage program prompted the Department of Energy to ask industry to estimate what its costs would be for storing and planning for distribution of 250 million barrels of oil not yet stored. Those proposals from oil companies and others, solicited in August 1978, were being received by the agency.

However, Dingell and others were critical of the plan to involve private industry in the reserve program.

"Now that the costs of the program have skyrocketed and the program is delayed, the solution of the agency to its problems is to shift responsibility," Dingell said at his December 1978 hearing.

"Then next year, when the program is still bedeviled and Congress demands answers from the department, they can point to private industry and say they are the ones to blame. I am not convinced this 'share the blame' proposal really serves the public well," Dingell said.

But Deluca said that getting input from private industry would be useful and promised "objective analysis." If contracting out to industry were not found to be economical, he said, the department would complete the program itself. ∎

New Rules for Offshore Oil Search Enacted

In an effort to reconcile the need to step up the search for new energy sources with the need to protect the environment, Congress in 1978 enacted legislation providing new regulations for offshore oil and gas drilling.

The bill (S 9 — PL 95-372) — the first overhaul of oil and gas leasing laws on the Outer Continental Shelf in 25 years — was signed by President Carter Sept. 18, 1978. The long-sought changes had been given final approval by the House Aug. 17 on a 338-18 vote, and by the Senate Aug. 22, on an 82-7 vote.

The bill was designed to foster competition for leases and increase state participation in federal leasing decisions. Restrictions on drilling and production were tightened to protect the environment.

Congress had been struggling for almost four years to reach agreement on the controversial legislation, which had been bitterly opposed by the oil industry. However, the latest compromise was generally accepted by most major oil companies, environmentalists and the Carter administration.

The congressional action came within days of the first commercial discovery of oil and gas deposits off the Atlantic coast. Texaco Inc. announced Aug. 14 it had struck gas about 100 miles from Atlantic City, N.J.

It was this coming expansion of offshore drilling to the Atlantic from the Gulf of Mexico that prompted the push for reform of the Outer Continental Shelf Lands Act of 1953. Most OCS activity already underway was in the Gulf of Mexico, primarily off the Louisiana coast.

The East Coast states, protective of their healthy resort and fishing industries, sought, and won in the new law, more control over potentially harmful offshore activities.

Enactment of the new rules governing Outer Continental Shelf (OCS) exploration was expected to spur development on the Atlantic shelf, which was an extension of the continent that stretches up to 200 miles from shore. *(Map, p. 74)*

In particular, leasing of tracts off the coast of New England, in an area known as Georges Bank, was likely to go forward. The state of Massachusetts and a conservation group had held up scheduled 1978 leasing with successful court suits, arguing that the new law should be in place before additional drilling was allowed.

The U.S. Geological Survey had estimated that potential recoverable resources of from 10 to 49 billion barrels of crude oil and from 42 to 81 trillion cubic feet of natural gas were located on the OCS of the United States.

OCS lands began three miles from the shoreline, where state jurisdiction ended.

The federally held lands had been under the jurisdiction of the Department of Interior. However, some authority for offshore energy development was transferred by the new law to the year-old Department of Energy. The energy secretary was to write many of the rules the interior secretary would have to follow in administering the legislation.

Provisions

As cleared by Congress, S 9 amended and modified the Outer Continental Shelf Lands Act of 1953 (PL 83-212).

Exploration and Development

Title I called for more aggressive management of the Outer Continental Shelf, submission of plans by lessees for active exploration and development of OCS tracts and more involvement of coastal states in OCS activities.

New provisions were added to the 1953 law to:

● Require the appropriate Cabinet secretary to develop a comprehensive five-year program for OCS leasing that was to consist of a schedule of proposed sales indicating the size, timing and location of activities. Considerations in developing the program were to include the relative environmental sensitivity and marine productivity of different areas and the return of a "fair market value" for the public lands leased.

● Direct the secretary to solicit recommendations regarding the leasing program from the governors of affected states and from interested federal agencies. If the recommendations were rejected, the secretary was to explain the reasons for doing so.

● Require an environmental study of each general area proposed for leasing.

● Provide for a study, review and, if necessary, revision of safety regulations to ensure safe operations on the Outer Continental Shelf.

● Provide that the interior secretary and the secretary responsible for the U.S. Coast Guard enforce the regulations, along with any other "applicable federal officials."

● Permit "any person having an interest which is or may be adversely affected" to file a suit against any person, including a government agency, for alleged violation of the act or of a lease, or against the secretary for alleged failure to perform a non-discretionary act or duty.

● Set civil penalties of up to $10,000 per day for failure to comply with the act; set criminal penalties of up to $100,000 (per day for some violations) and 10 years in prison or both for deliberate violation of the act or regulations issued under it.

● Require submission of a development and production plan for all future leases and all existing leases where no oil or gas had yet been discovered, except for leases in the Gulf of Mexico.

● Provide that the interior secretary review and approve or disapprove the plan. If a plan were not submitted or complied with, the secretary could cancel the lease.

● Provide that the plan set forth a description of the specific work to be performed; a description of all facilities and operations located on the OCS; the environmental safeguards to be implemented; all safety standards to be met; an expected rate of development and production and a time schedule for performance and any other relevant information required by the secretary.

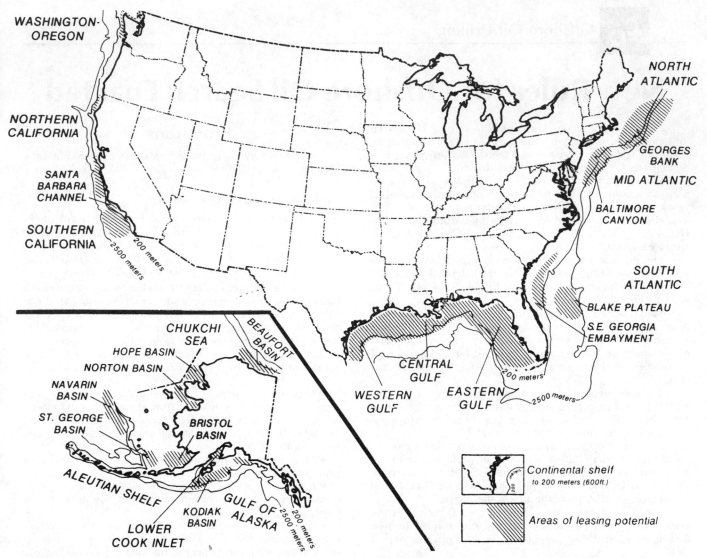

WASHINGTON-OREGON

NORTHERN CALIFORNIA

SANTA BARBARA CHANNEL

SOUTHERN CALIFORNIA

200 meters

2500 meters

NORTH ATLANTIC

GEORGES BANK

MID ATLANTIC

BALTIMORE CANYON

SOUTH ATLANTIC

BLAKE PLATEAU

S.E. GEORGIA EMBAYMENT

CENTRAL GULF

WESTERN GULF

EASTERN GULF

200 meters

2500 meters

CHUKCHI SEA

BEAUFORT BASIN

HOPE BASIN

NORTON BASIN

NAVARIN BASIN

ST. GEORGE BASIN

BRISTOL BASIN

ALEUTIAN SHELF

KODIAK BASIN

GULF OF ALASKA

LOWER COOK INLET

200 meters

2500 meters

Continental shelf to 200 meters (600ft.)

Areas of leasing potential

• Required a lessee to give the secretary access to all data and information relating to OCS activities.

• Provide that the secretary share the information, except for proprietary information, with the affected states.

Existing provisions were amended to:

• Transfer to the energy secretary functions of the interior secretary relating to:

(1) Fostering of competition for federal leases including, but not limited to, prohibition on bidding for development rights by certain types of joint ventures.

(2) Implementation of alternative bidding systems authorized for the award of federal leases.

(3) Establishment of diligence requirements for operations conducted on federal leases including, but not limited to, procedures relating to the granting or ordering by the interior secretary of suspension of operations or production as they related to such requirements.

(4) Setting rates of production for federal leases.

(5) Specifying procedures, terms and conditions for acquisition and disposition of federal royalty interests taken in kind.

(The interior secretary retained responsibility for conducting lease sales, for monitoring the effect of exploration and development on the environment and for generally enforcing the OCS law. The interior secretary also retained authority to suspend or cancel a lease.)

• Establish a liaison committee of top Energy and Interior officials to coordinate administration of the act.

• Provide that a lease be suspended or canceled, after suspension, if there was threat of harm or damage to life (including fish or other aquatic life), to property, to any mineral deposits, to the national security or to the marine, coastal or human environments.

• Provide that a lease be suspended or canceled if the lessee failed to comply with the terms of the lease or act.

• Provide new bidding procedures to be used in addition to cash bonus bids with a royalty of at least 12.5 percent, including variable royalty, variable net profit, fixed net profit and work commitment bidding procedures. The secretary was authorized to use other, unspecified systems if, after 30 days, neither house of Congress had passed a resolution disapproving the alternative system.

• Mandate that new bidding systems be used in at least 20 percent and not more than 60 percent of the tracts offered for leasing in all OCS areas during each of the next five years.

• Allow leases, currently set for five-year terms, to have

a term of 10 years where the secretary found the longer period to be necessary in areas with "unusually deep water or other unusually adverse conditions."

● Require that lessees offer for purchase at least 20 percent of OCS-recovered crude oil or natural gas to small refiners.

● Permit the attorney general, in consultation with the Federal Trade Commission, to conduct a review of lease sales and make recommendations as to whether the sales indicated a situation inconsistent with antitrust laws. If the secretary rejected the attorney general's recommendations, the secretary would have to notify the lessee and the attorney general of the reasons for his decision.

● Retain language in the 1953 law which provided that: "Any agency of the United States and any person authorized by the secretary may conduct geological and geophysical explorations in the Outer Continental Shelf, which do not interfere with or endanger actual operations under any lease maintained or granted pursuant to this act, and which are not unduly harmful to aquatic life in such area."

● Require that a lessee submit to the secretary a plan for exploring a leased OCS tract that included a schedule of anticipated exploration activities; a description of equipment to be used; the general location of each well to be drilled and other information deemed pertinent by the secretary.

Offshore Oil Pollution Fund

To deal with spills from offshore production and transportation of oil, a new Title III was added to:

● Establish an Offshore Oil Pollution Compensation Fund of up to $200 million, funded by a three-cent per barrel fee on oil produced on the OCS.

● Provide that owners and operators of offshore facilities and vessels have unlimited liability for cleanup of oil spills and a liability for damages of up to $35 million for offshore facilities and of $300 per gross ton, up to $25,000, for vessels.

● Authorized the president to clean up an oil spill, using money from the fund, if the owner or operator responsible would not clean up or had not been identified.

● Provide that damaged parties can make claims to the fund and be paid by the fund, with the fund subsequently acquiring the claimant's rights to sue the spiller.

Fisherman's Contingency Fund

To aid commercial fishermen whose livelihood was jeopardized because of OCS activity, primarily damage to equipment, Title IV was added to:

● Establish a Fishermen's Contingency Fund of up to $1 million, with area accounts established therein of up to $100,000.

● Require each lessee to pay into the fund up to $5,000 per calendar year per lease, permit, easement or right of way.

Amendments to the Coastal Zone Management Act

Contained in Title V were amendments to the Coastal Zone Management Act of 1976 (PL 94-370) to:

● Modify the formula used to distribute OCS formula grants to base allocation of funds on new acreage leased adjacent to a coastal state (50 percent); oil and gas produced adjacent to a coastal state (25 percent); and oil and gas first landed in the coastal state (25 percent).

● Ensure that no state eligible under the existing formula would receive less than 2 percent of the total appropriation. States not eligible under the formula, but which were in the region of affected coastal states, would be entitled to receive 2 percent of the total if the secretary of commerce determined that the state was affected by OCS activity and could use the money as required by the coastal zone act.

● Provide that no state could receive more than 37.5 percent of the total.

● Authorize appropriation of $130 million annually for the OCS formula grants.

● Authorize appropriations of $5 million annually to help states carry out their responsibilities under the OCS act.

Background

Interest in the Outer Continental Shelf and the vast resources thought to lie there accelerated in the early 1970s as the Nixon administration pushed the Interior Department to step up the pace of OCS leasing, moving particularly into frontier OCS areas never before developed. It is estimated that as much as 49 billion barrels of oil and 81 trillion cubic feet of natural gas is recoverable from these offshore lands out to a water depth of 200 meters. The OCS is the underwater margin of the North American continent, extending 150 to 200 miles out to sea.

In 1973 President Nixon proposed that the government triple the acreage leased offshore in a year, from one million acres to three million acres. In 1974 he again tripled the goal, to 10 million acres a year. At that time, less than 10 million acres had been leased in the entire history of OCS development. The 10-million acre annual goal was later quietly abandoned by the Interior Department.

Until the mid-1970s, the only offshore oil and gas development in the United States was in the Gulf of Mexico, primarily off the shores of Louisiana and Texas, and off the southern California coast in the Santa Barbara Channel. The proposed move into frontier OCS areas off New England and other portions of the Atlantic Coast, off the Pacific Coast and the Alaskan Coast, suddenly enlarged the constituency of people and governments concerned about OCS development and policy.

In 1974 the Senate passed a bill (S 3221) setting new guidelines for OCS development and creating a grant program to help coastal states cope with the impact of such activity. The House did not act on the measure in the 93rd Congress.

In 1975 the Senate passed two OCS bills, one (S 586) containing primarily the aid provisions, the other (S 521) revising the OCS policy guidelines. The House approved both measures in 1976. The aid measure was enacted as the Coastal Zone Management Act Amendments of 1976, but the policy measure was killed in late September 1976 when the House voted, 198-194, to send it back to conference.

The oil and gas industry had opposed any change in the 1953 law that governed Interior Department leasing of lands on the Outer Continental Shelf. The industry argued that the new requirements proposed by Congress to safeguard the public interest, states' rights and environmental values, would cause unnecessary delay in leasing and exploiting OCS resources.

The Ford administration had adopted these arguments and opposed the bill which the House killed in September 1976.

However, the change of administrations in early 1977 brought a reversal of the White House position on the proposed OCS Act amendments. Interior Secretary Cecil D. Andrus worked closely with the House and Senate committees to develop new legislation.

The effect of administration support was clear in Senate passage in July of a strong version of an OCS leasing bill (S 9). Every major industry-backed amendment to the bill was rejected. Moreover, the Senate adopted a floor amendment that was particularly unpopular with industry authorizing the government to contract for exploratory drilling in underdeveloped areas of the OCS before putting those areas up for bids from private industry.

A companion measure (HR 1614) reported by the House Ad Hoc Select Committee on the Outer Continental Shelf did not contain that Senate floor amendment but was still strongly opposed by industry.

Industry lobbying in the House was concentrated in the Rules Committee rather than the ad hoc committee where approval had been a foregone conclusion. The Rules Committee had bottled up a similar bill for weeks in 1976. The 1977 oil industry lobbying effort proved successful: the Rules Committee voted 10-5 on Oct. 25 to defer approval of a rule for HR 1614 until 1978.

The Rules Committee decision temporarily shifted the stage for the continuing battle over the development of offshore oil and gas reserves from Congress to the Department of Interior. Interior Secretary Andrus, a staunch supporter of the legislation, had already moved to implement as much of it as possible through promulgating numerous parallel regulations.

1978 House Action

After accepting a hodgepodge of amendments that calmed many critics, the House Feb. 2 voted 291-91 to approve HR 1614.

The House Rules Committee, which had prevented the bill from reaching the House floor in fall 1977, voted 8-6 on Jan. 23 to clear the bill for floor action.

HR 1614, as passed, would increase environmental controls, provide for more state participation in federal leasing of offshore tracts, share federal revenues from lease sales with coastal states and broaden competition for leases by changing bidding procedures.

Even though the House had defeated 187-211 an industry-backed substitute on Jan. 26, adoption of the various amendments during the four days of floor debate gained the support of key opponents for final passage.

The House-passed bill was "the Breaux substitute by another name," said Rep. John B. Breaux, D-La., who had originally pushed an industry version of the legislation. "I'm very pleased," he said of the final bill.

A turning point in the House floor debate came on Jan. 31 when the chief sponsors accepted changes in the two provisions that had sparked most criticisms.

First, OCS Committee Chairman John M. Murphy, D-N.Y., and committee members did not challenge an amendment by Rep. David C. Treen, R-La., to strike the bill's separation of leases for exploration from leases for production, a procedure known as dual leasing.

Industry officials had charged that this provision, sought by the administration to open up the leasing process, would reduce incentives and cause delays in production. Treen also criticized the partnership of the federal government and private companies during the exploration stage that was called for in the bill.

After Treen's amendment was accepted by voice vote, Rep. Gerry E. Studds, D-Mass., a key supporter of the committee version of HR 1614, proposed an amendment to weaken government authority to conduct pre-lease drilling in order to discover a tract's potential. His move was an effort to defuse criticism by opponents. *(Box, next page)*

"My amendment removes the only remaining language in the bill which has been construed by some as authorizing federal exploratory drilling," Studds told the House, which accepted his amendment 328-77.

Though his amendment was modified by Treen, the effect was to return to 1953 language, which authorized the government to permit or contract for pre-lease exploration. The Studds amendment clarified that the government could not do the exploration itself, an authority implied in the 1953 act.

Studds later explained his action. "You can go down in flames like we did two years ago, or you can try to get a bill that has some very good things in it," he said.

Alternative Bidding Systems

In addition to criticizing dual leasing and federal drilling, the industry and its supporters in the House had focused their attention on the bill's proposed changes in bidding procedures for OCS leases.

"We have finally got to the hub of why the major oil companies are opposed to HR 1614," Rep. William J. Hughes, D-N.J., told the House when it took up bidding changes. "It is because we are tampering with the bonus bid system. It is as simple as that. All the other is window dressing."

Under the bidding system currently used most of the time, an up-front, cash-bonus payment was required before a lease was granted. Critics said this system favored major oil companies and kept out smaller companies that could compete if the lease were based on royalties from future production instead of the early cash payment.

The committee bill had mandated the use of such alternative bidding systems at least half the time, while Breaux had sought to mandate continued use of the bonus system at least half the time.

The House eventually agreed to an amendment by Rep. David F. Emery, R-Maine, that would require use of alternatives in at least 20 percent and up to half the sales. The amendment was a substitute for an amendment by Treen that would have simply eliminated the 50 percent bidding requirement.

Though the 219-188 vote appeared to be a defeat for the administration and the committee, Rep. George Miller, D-Calif., a leader in the debate, had another idea. "We have the acceptance, with a Republican author, of a mandate on alternative bidding systems," Miller said later. "We never had that before."

The House had previously rejected, 196-207, a substitute proposed by Rep. Clarence J. Brown, R-Ohio, to apply alternative bidding systems to at least 10 percent and no more than 30 percent of the lease sales.

The House later strengthened its support of alternative bidding by accepting a Miller amendment that would allow the secretary of interior to decide on which tracts to use alternative systems. The amendment killed language in the committee bill that had required that the tracts be selected

OCS Bill: Effective Lobbying on Both Sides

The red capital letters in the full-page newspaper advertisement were two inches high: "If dependence on foreign oil is what you want, HR 1614 will get it for you."

The National Ocean Industries Association (NOIA) wanted to be sure the House knew that NOIA's 345 members opposed pending Outer Continental Shelf (OCS) legislation, even if it cost them more than $11,000.

"Propaganda," bill supporter Rep. Gerry E. Studds, D-Mass., called the various ads. "Red herrings," he labeled their claims that the bill would lead to an imaginary outfit dubbed FOGCO, a federally operated oil and gas company.

To a House aide trying to garner support for the very complicated bill, the ads were one more headache. "You've got full-page ads, with screaming headlines, saying 'We're industry, we know this bill is going to be an unmitigated disaster,'" said the aide. "It's got to have an effect. How do you counter that sort of rhetoric?"

The members of the House Ad Hoc Select Committee on the Outer Continental Shelf eventually countered it by agreeing to take out offending sections on dual leasing and federal exploratory drilling. This defensive effort by the bill's supporters was evidence that their opponents were having some effect.

"It was a full-court press," said James Flug of Energy Action, a consumer and environmental organization, when asked about the oil and gas industry efforts against the committee bill.

Letter Writing Campaign. In addition to dramatic, full-page newspaper ads, individual companies and associations that represented them used some fairly sophisticated techniques to generate interest in the bill in districts far removed from the coast.

For example, Exxon Corporation, which refused to support even a watered down substitute proposal endorsed by most companies, sent letters to each of its stockholders explaining its opposition to HR 1614 and suggesting that letters be written to Congress. Many responded.

NOIA, with a membership that included producing companies, diving contractors, caterers, makers of drilling rigs and other support services for OCS activity, tried to capitalize on its diversity with the same sort of "grass roots" lobbying.

"This bill is so complicated," said Charlie Matthews, NOIA president. "The average member of Congress...who's not associated with the coast, not associated with this issue, well, he has so many demands, he can't know the details. I have tried to get my [member] companies to write and say, 'I'm in Oshkosh and I manufacture widgets that they use in Houston on drilling rigs. I oppose this bill.'"

Matthews also coordinated the placement of ads in a Washington newspaper by other groups, such as the Association of Diving Contractors, which also belonged to NOIA. The divers wanted to keep the Occupational Safety and Health Administration from getting jurisdiction over OCS activity, and they succeeded.

United Business Community. When the South Carolina banking community started calling Rep. John W. Jenrette Jr., D-S.C. about HR 1614, he was a little confused about why they should be interested.

"I started asking questions about dual leasing and revenue sharing, and the guy finally had to admit he was returning a favor for a fellow in Texas," said Jenrette, who voted against the position of the banking community and oil and gas interests.

"They're trying to work some trades" with votes on other bills, such as labor law, said another southern Democrat who had been contacted by local members of a national business community that was apparently united against the OCS bill.

Various segments of the energy industry had already been working together on the energy legislation before Congress. "There's a real need to be together," said Talbott Smith, associate manager of the resources and environment division of the Chamber of Commerce.

Breaux as Lobbyist. The old coalition of Republicans and southern Democrats, boosted by the solidarity of the Louisiana and Texas delegations, was operating on the OCS issue.

One of the reasons the coalition hung together on most votes was Rep. John B. Breaux, D-La. "When the issue is this complex, many members take their cues from the neighboring delegation," explained one committee aide.

"Breaux has been very effective," admitted a Carter administration lobbyist.

Administration Efforts. With the rash of votes on amendments and substitutes, both sides could claim some victories, and the administration was credited with the initial defeat of the weaker Breaux substitute, as well as with getting the bill through the reluctant Rules Committee.

"They made the difference," said a House aide, and Breaux agreed.

In 1976, when the conference report on similar OCS legislation was recommitted in the waning days of the 94th Congress, the Ford administration had been working hard against passage.

The Carter administration came through quickly with separate letters from Energy Secretary James R. Schlesinger and Interior Secretary Cecil D. Andrus renewing their endorsement of the committee bill after Republicans on the House floor raised the specter of a divided administration.

Deputy Under Secretary of Interior Barbara Heller, who formerly lobbied for the Environmental Policy Center on the same issue, spent hours nursing the legislation through the House. Liaison staff from Interior and Energy, operating out of a room near the House chamber, kept a close watch on the progress.

The major criticism of the administration effort was the arrival on the Hill just before Rules action of some 50 primarily technical amendments that the administration wanted in the bill. Members of the Rules Committee who sought to delay floor action seized on the amendments as another reason for postponing debate.

randomly. Under the Miller change, a secretary such as Andrus who wanted to increase the impact of alternative bidding could apply the new systems to the choice tracts. The amendment was adopted 225-174.

Conference Action

House and Senate conferees haggled off and on for months, starting in March and ending in July, before finally filing their conference report (S Rept 95-1091) Aug. 10.

Though the basic outlines of the two bills were similar, there were some substantive and numerous technical differences that had to be worked out. Many of the same conferees had met on OCS legislation in 1976, but the House recommitted that conference report late in the 94th Congress.

Federal Exploration

The most controversial provision — one that had doomed the bill in the past — was a Senate mandate that the federal government determine what oil and gas was deposited offshore before leasing the public land.

The House had refused to require federal exploration, but did retain language in the 1953 act authorizing the interior secretary to conduct "geological and geophysical explorations."

The compromise worked out by the conferees retained the exact 1953 language, dropping a House modification. Although Interior Secretary Cecil D. Andrus claimed the language gave him authority to conduct explorations, any use of the authority was almost certain to be challenged in court. The conferees did not interpret the law in their report, and the resulting ambiguity was a major reason the compromise was acceptable to some House conferees.

Bidding Procedures

Both the House and Senate modified bidding procedures in hopes of encouraging smaller, independent companies to bid on OCS leases. Critics of the current system said big, wealthy oil companies were favored by the existing requirement that bidders pay large sums in advance in order to get a lease.

Alternative bidding systems would allow a leaseholder to pay the government royalties as the oil or gas was produced from the tract, instead of paying the up-front, "cash bonus."

The House wanted such alternative systems to be used in at least 20 percent and not more than 50 percent of all lease sales during each of the next five years. The Senate wanted to mandate that alternative procedures be used in at least 50 percent of the leases offered in previously undeveloped areas.

The compromise required that alternative bidding systems be used in at least 20 percent and not more than 60 percent of the tracts offered for leasing in all OCS areas during each of the next five years.

The conferees dropped a Senate provision, added on the floor by Sen. J. Bennett Johnston, D-La., that would have required the secretary to select randomly the areas for which alternative bidding procedures would be used. Without a requirement for random selection, a secretary who favored alternative bidding could pick out the choicest tracts for alternative procedures.

The conferees also dropped a Senate provision that called for use of a dual leasing system off the coast of Alaska. Dual leasing was a new system that provided separate leases for exploration and then for development, thus giving the secretary more information before leasing for development.

Other Issues

Among other compromises, the conferees also:

● Modified a House requirement that OCS activities comply with national air quality standards. The conferees agreed that air pollution from OCS activities should be regulated when it "significantly affects the air quality of a state." The conferees said they did not intend that the air mass above the OCS meet the standards, but that it be controlled to prevent harmful effects on the air above an adjacent shoreline.

● Modified a House provision that allowed local governments, as well as states, to submit recommendations to the secretary. Local governments could still make proposals, but their comments would have to be forwarded to the secretary by the governor of the state.

● Dropped a House provision that earmarked 20 percent of federal OCS revenues for the Coastal Energy Impact Fund, a revolving fund that had given loans and bond guarantees to states providing services and facilities to support coastal energy activity. The conference report contained a standard authorization of $130 million annually for the fund, which would also provide OCS formula grants. ▮

Strip Mining Control: Energy vs. Environment

The five-year effort to impose federal regulation on the strip mining of coal ended Aug. 3, 1977, when President Carter signed the Surface Mining Control and Reclamation Act into law (HR 2 — PL 95-87). HR 2 was among the relatively few bills that genuinely deserved to be called "landmark legislation."

Until 1977, environmentalists and others who supported the legislation had been thwarted. The House approved a bill in 1972 but the Senate did not act. President Ford pocket-vetoed a bill in 1974 after the 93rd Congress had adjourned. In May 1975 Ford vetoed another bill, and the House failed to override by only three votes. Twice in 1976, with a veto still certain, the House Rules Committee prevented strip mining bills from reaching the floor.

Although it was clear from the beginning that HR 2 would be signed, the bill was slightly weaker than the versions of earlier Congresses that had been tailored in the vain hope of avoiding a veto. Coal companies, facing the inevitability of strip mining legislation at last, lobbied hard for certain exemptions and simplified procedures and, in some cases, they won. They were particularly successful in the Senate, where leadership for a strong strip mining bill was not as effective as it was in the House. Conferees roughly split the difference between the weaker Senate bill and the House version. House language allowing surface owners to veto mining of federally-owned coal beneath their land—a particularly tough issue—was retained.

But as finally approved in 1977, HR 2 pleased environmental lobbyists for the most part. Coal mining representatives who had opposed all such legislation were unhappy with the bill, but relieved that certain exemptions and variances had been allowed. Senate and House conferees generally felt they had reached a good compromise. Rep. Morris K. Udall (D Ariz.), a principal advocate of strip mining control, said through a spokesman that he felt "personal satisfaction" that the long struggle was over.

Focus on Coal

The legislation was directed primarily at strip mining for coal. Other types of strip mining were largely untouched by the bill.

Environmentalists acknowledged that this was a substantial omission and noted that early versions of the legislation drafted several years before covered all strip mining. This universal coverage was dropped when it became clear that opposition from copper and other mining interests plus coal companies probably would have permanently doomed any legislation.

But even as it eventually was written, the strip mining bill dealt with an enormous problem and became all the more crucial as President Carter made increased use of coal a key element in his energy program.

Earlier in 1977, the Senate Energy and Natural Resources Committee reported that coal strip mining disturbs 1,000 acres of land each week. Of four million acres

Highlights of Bill

As cleared by Congress, HR 2 contained the following major provisions:

● Set performance standards for environmental protection to be met at all major surface mining operations for coal.

● Provided for joint responsibility and enforcement by the states and the federal government.

● Established a self-supporting Abandoned Mine Reclamation Fund to restore lands ravaged by uncontrolled mining operations in the past.

● Protected certain lands regarded as unsuitable for surface mining.

● Established mining and mineral resource institutes, and provided funds for coal research laboratories and energy graduate fellowships.

already disturbed by surface mining of all sorts, 43 per cent were damaged by coal extraction.

Moreover, the coal strip mining problem—unlike that of other mining efforts—was nationwide. The legislation recognized that.

In the East, much of the damage to land had already been done. Only half of the 1.3 million acres of strip-mined land in eastern coalfields had been reclaimed. HR 2 established a special fund to help pay for reclamation.

In the West, vast deposits of coal exist to be claimed, principally by strip mining. The recent record of strip mining suggested that extraction of that coal would increase dramatically: In 1970, almost 44 per cent of U.S. coal production came from surface mines; for 1976 it was estimated this figure would jump to 56 per cent. Carter's emphasis on coal made this increase likely, coal experts agreed. In recognition of this, much of HR 2 was directed at controlling the conditions under which strip mining would occur.

The Congressional Budget Office (CBO) estimated that the federal government's five-year net cost of HR 2 would be $360-million for fiscal 1978-1982. Larger amounts were expected to be collected and spent through the Abandoned Mine Reclamation Fund, supported through fees on mined coal.

Implementing Legislation

In late July 1978, Congress cleared legislation authorizing $100 million in fiscal 1979-80 to carry out the 1977 strip mining law.

The bill (S 2463 — PL 95-343) increased the amounts originally provided under the act for federal enforcement and state inspection programs and for aid to operators of small mines who were required to conduct various hydrologic and geologic tests.

Provisions

As signed into law, HR 2, the Surface Mining Control and Reclamation Act of 1977:

Title I—Findings and Policy

● Found that surface mining operations adversely affect commerce and the public welfare by diminishing or destroying land use, polluting water, damaging natural beauty and habitats, and creating hazards to life and property.

● Found that expanded coal mining to meet the nation's energy needs required establishment of protective standards.

● Found that the primary responsibility for developing and enforcing regulations for surface mining and reclamation should rest with the states because of the diversity of terrain and other physical conditions.

● Recognized the need for national standards in order to eliminate competitive advantages or disadvantages in interstate commerce among sellers of coal.

● Called for reclamation of mined areas left unreclaimed before enactment of the act.

Title II—Office of Surface Mining

● Established an Office of Surface Mining Reclamation and Enforcement in the Interior Department; provided that its director be subject to Senate confirmation.

● Identified the specific duties of the office, including administering the act's regulatory and reclamation programs, approving and disapproving state programs, and providing grants and technical assistance to the states.

● Stipulated that there was to be no use of coal mine inspectors hired under the Federal Coal Mine Health and Safety Act of 1969 for strip mining inspection unless the director published a finding in the *Federal Register* that such activities would not interfere with inspections under the 1969 act.

● Directed the office to develop and maintain an Information and Data Center on Surface Coal Mining, Reclamation and Surface Impacts of Underground Mining to provide information to the public and other government agencies.

● Prohibited any federal employees who performed functions under the act from having a direct or indirect financial interest in coal mining operations and made violators subject to fines of up to $2,500, imprisonment of up to one year, or both.

Title III—State Mining Institutes

● Authorized each state to establish, or continue to support, a state mining and mineral resources research institute at a public or private college that would conduct research and train mineral engineers and scientists.

● Authorized for each participating state $200,000 in fiscal 1978, $300,000 in fiscal 1979, and $400,000 for each fiscal year thereafter for five years, to be matched by non-federal funds, to support the institutes.

● Authorized an additional $15-million in fiscal 1978, to be increased by $2-million in each fiscal year for six years, for specific mineral research and demonstration projects of industry-wide application at the mining institutes.

● Specified that the use of federal funds for the institutes did not authorize federal control or direction of education at any college or university.

● Established a center in the Interior Department for cataloging current and projected research on mining and mineral resources.

● Established an Advisory Committee on Mining and Mineral Research composed of representatives from the Bureau of Mines, National Science Foundation, National Academy of Sciences, National Academy of Engineering, U.S. Geological Survey and four other persons knowledgeable in the field, at least one of whom represented working coal miners.

Title IV—Abandoned Mine Reclamation

● Established within the U.S. Treasury a trust fund called the Abandoned Mine Reclamation Fund consisting primarily of amounts derived from the sale, lease or use of reclaimed land and from a reclamation fee of 35 cents per ton of surface mined coal and 15 cents per ton of underground mined coal (or 10 per cent of the value of coal at the mine, whichever was less), except that fees for lignite or brown coal were set at 2 per cent of the value of the coal or 10 cents per ton, whichever was less. Such fees were to be paid by 30 days after each calendar quarter ended.

● Provided that the fund be used to acquire and reclaim abandoned surface mines and deep mines, including sealing off tunnels and shafts. However, up to one-fifth of the fund would be transferred to the Agriculture Secretary for a rural lands reclamation program; up to 10 per cent, but not more than $10-million annually, was to be used for hydrologic planning and core drilling assistance on behalf of small mine operators.

● Provided that up to 50 per cent of the fees collected annually in any state or Indian reservation were to be allocated to that state or reservation for abandoned mine reclamation. But after reclamation was completed, the Secretary could allow use of the remainder of the 50 per cent for construction of public facilities in communities impacted by coal development—if certain specified federal payments were inadequate to meet the needs.

● Provided that the balance of reclamation funds could be spent in any state at the discretion of the Secretary for mine reclamation.

● Required the Secretary to set rules and regulations for state reclamation programs within 180 days of enactment. States having approved regulatory programs could submit reclamation plans for funding, including grants of up to 90 per cent for the cost of acquiring lands to be reclaimed.

● Authorized the Secretary of Agriculture to enter into agreements with small rural landowners of abandoned mines for land stabilization, erosion and sediment control, and reclamation. Landowners were to furnish conservation and development plans, and agree to effect the land uses and treatment outlined in the plans. Federal grants to carry out the plans were not to exceed 80 per cent of costs on not more than 120 acres, or lower amounts on up to 320 acres in certain instances, unless justified to enhance off-site water quality or to enable a landowner of limited income to participate.

● Gave the Interior Secretary and the states broad authority to study reclamation sites, acquire lands not already owned by the public, reclaim the land according to a cost-benefit analysis for each project, and determine use of the land after reclamation. For work done on private lands, the Secretary and the states were directed to establish a lien on the property after reclamation to the extent that the market value of the land was enhanced. Restored land could be sold by competitive bidding or added to the public lands.

• Authorized the Interior Secretary to construct public facilities necessary to a reclamation project that created public outdoor recreation areas.

• Provided for the filling of voids and the sealing of abandoned tunnels, shafts and entryways, and reclamation of other surface impacts of mining—not limited to coal mine impacts.

• Gave the Secretary power to use the fund for emergency abatement or prevention of adverse coal mining practices and gave him access to land where any such emergency existed.

• Authorized the transfer of abandoned mine reclamation funds to other federal agencies in order to carry out reclamation activities.

Title V—Environmental Control of Surface Mining

• Required the Interior Secretary to issue interim regulations for environmental standards within 90 days of enactment, and waived provisions of the National Environmental Policy Act of 1969. Permanent regulations were to be issued one year after enactment.

• Required approval of the administrator of the Environmental Protection Agency for regulations concerning air and water quality standards.

• Required all new mines within six months of enactment and all existing mines within nine months to comply with the interim standards. However, an exception was made for operators whose surface and underground mines combined produced no more than 100,000 tons per year; they were given until Jan. 1, 1979, to comply.

• Established a federal enforcement program within six months of enactment, to include at least one inspection for every mining site every six months.

• Set interim standards requiring surface mine operators to keep waste materials off steep slopes, return mined lands to their approximate original contour, preserve topsoil for reclamation, stabilize and revegetate waste piles, minimize disturbances to water tables, notify the public about blasting schedules and take certain prescribed safety precautions.

• Provided that within two months after approval of a state regulatory plan, or after implementation of a federal regulatory plan, all mine operators within a state had to apply for a permit to mine lands they expected to be working on eight months later. The state regulatory authority or the Secretary had to grant or deny a permit within eight months.

• Directed states that wished to assume jurisdiction over surface mining to submit state regulatory programs to the Secretary within 18 months of enactment, demonstrating that they had the legal, financial and administrative ability to carry out the act. Among other requirements, the state program was to provide sanctions for violations of state laws and establish a process for the designation of areas as unsuitable for surface mining.

• Directed the Secretary to approve or disapprove a state program. States were allowed 60 days to submit a new program if their first attempts were unsuccessful; the Secretary was required to rule on the resubmitted program in 60 days.

• Authorized the Secretary to implement a federal strip mining regulation program in any state that failed to submit a program within 18 months, or failed to resubmit an acceptable program within 60 days of federal disapproval, or otherwise failed to implement, enforce and maintain an approved program. Federal programs were to be im-

plemented no more than 34 months after enactment, and following a public hearing in each affected state. A state could apply for approval of a new state program any time after implementation of a federal program.

• Allowed state programs to include more stringent environmental protection regulations than required by the act.

• Required surface mine operators to obtain a permit no more than eight months after approval of a state program or implementation of a federal program. Permits were to be issued for a period of five years, but could be extended if necessary for an operator to obtain financing. If mining operations did not begin within three years, under normal circumstances, the permit expired.

• Required that permit applications be accompanied by fees as determined by the regulatory authority.

• Required mine operators to submit detailed information with their applications, including the following: identification of all officials and corporations involved; history of the applicant's experience with past mining permits; a demonstration of compliance with public notice requirements; maps of the proposed mining area and land to be affected; description of the mining methods; starting and termination dates of each phase of the mining operation; schedules and methods for compliance with environmental standards; description of the hydrologic consequences of mining and reclamation; results of test borings; soil surveys if the mine might include prime farmlands; a blasting plan.

• Provided, for mining operations not expected to exceed 100,000 tons annually, free hydrologic studies and test boring analyses performed by qualified public or private laboratories designated and paid by the regulatory authority.

• Required proof of public liability insurance, or evidence of other state or federal self-insurance requirements, as part of a permit application.

• Required operators to submit a reclamation plan as part of their permit application.

• Required that reclamation plans submitted with permit applications must include the following information: identification of the area to be mined or affected; condition of the land prior to mining, including a description of the uses, topography and vegetation; the use to be made of the land following reclamation and how that use is to be achieved; description of the steps taken to minimize effects on renewable resources; engineering techniques for both mining and reclamation; consideration given to maximum recovery of coal to avoid reopening the mine later; estimated timetable for each reclamation step; measures to be taken to protect surface and ground water systems, and the rights of water users; confidential results of test boring.

• Prescribed the requirements for obtaining a performance bond of at least $10,000 covering the area to be mined within the term of the permit. Bonds, payable to federal or state authority, had to cover the full cost of reclamation. States were permitted to establish alternative systems in lieu of bonding programs, subject to federal approval.

• Provided that a mining permit could not be approved unless the regulatory authority found that all requirements of the act would be met, reclamation could be accomplished, damage to the hydrologic balance would be prevented, and the area to be mined was not one designated as unsuitable for mining—unless the operator showed that substantial legal and financial commitments were made before Jan. 1, 1977.

• Required findings that mining operations would not interrupt, discontinue or preclude farming on alluvial valley floors west of the 100th meridian, nor materially damage the quality or quantity of underground or surface water there. Exempted undeveloped rangeland and farmland of small acreage where mining would not adversely affect agricultural production. Also provided that the requirement did not apply to mines in commercial production or for which state permits had been granted during the year preceding enactment.

• Authorized the Secretary to lease other federal coal deposits in exchange to operators who had made "substantial financial and legal commitments" before Jan. 1, 1977, to alluvial valley mining outlawed under the act.

• Required, in cases where the private surface ownership and private mineral ownership were separate, the written consent of the surface owner for strip mining the property, or a conveyance that expressly granted the right. Disputes were to be settled under state law and in state courts.

• Permitted the mining of prime farmlands, as defined in the act, if the regulatory authority finds in writing that the mine operator has the technological capability to restore the area within a reasonable time to equal or higher farm productivity.

• Set terms for revision of permits when there was to be significant alteration in the permit plan.

• Prescribed standards for coal exploration, including reclamation requirements, and restricted exploration operations to removing 250 tons of coal.

• Established procedures for public notice and hearing of an applicant's intention to mine. Required the regulatory authority to hold public hearings if operators requested them or if serious objections were filed.

• Required the regulatory authority to rule on a permit application within 60 days if a public hearing is held, or "within a reasonable time" under other circumstances. Set procedures for appeals.

• Established in section 515 the performance standards for environmental protection, to apply to all surface coal mining and reclamation.

• Required operators to regrade mining sites to their approximate original contour in most instances and to eliminate highwalls, spoil piles and depressions. Regraded slopes had to assure mass stability and prevent surface erosion and water pollution.

• Directed operators to preserve, segregate and reuse topsoil taken from the mine site, protecting it from erosion and contamination. If prime agricultural areas were mined, operators had to provide in the regraded soil a root zone of comparable depth and quality to that of the natural soil.

• Allowed water impoundments as a part of reclamation if they met certain water quality and dam safety standards and if embankments were graded properly.

• Required operators to minimize disturbances to the hydrologic balance and to the quality and quantity of surface and underground water by avoiding acid and toxic mine drainage, preventing suspended solids from entering the stream flow, cleaning out and removing temporary settling and siltation ponds, preserving hydrologic functions of alluvial valley floor in arid regions, and avoiding channel enlargement in operations having a water discharge.

• Permitted permanent disposal of surplus spoil in areas other than mine workings (but within the permit area) if certain standards were met to stabilize the spoil mass, control surface erosion, provide internal drainage and take other precautions.

• Required operators to revegetate mined lands with cover native to the area, and to assume responsibility for revegetation for five years after the last seeding or planting. In areas having less than 26 inches of annual precipitation, the responsibility period was extended to 10 years.

• Prohibited surface mining within 500 feet of active or abandoned underground mining to protect the health or safety of miners. However, variances could be permitted if the mining efforts were coordinated and if they improved resource recovery.

• Prescribed conditions and standards for blasting, including advance notice of schedules.

• Permitted the mining practice known as mountaintop removal without regrading to its approximate original contour—although no highwalls were permitted—in certain cases when the proposed post-mining use of the land was an equal or better economic use, or when the applicant presented specific plans for the post-mining use.

• Required complete backfilling of all highwalls, but permitted a variance for certain operations that left a very wide and stable bench for post-mining land uses.

• Set standards for mining on slopes steeper than 20 degrees, including a prohibition against placing any spoil or other mining debris on the downslope below the bench (mining cut), and a requirement that highwalls be covered completely by backfilling and the land be returned to its approximate original contour.

• Set minimum environmental standards to control the surface impacts of underground mining operations. These included protection of surface land uses from subsidence hazards and protection of surface waters from mine discharges and drainage from mine waste piles. Required coordination in this effort between the Interior Secretary and the Administrator of the Mining Enforcement and Safety Administration.

• Required inspections of each surface mining operation, without prior notice, to occur on the average of at least one partial inspection a month and one complete inspection every three months. Provided for rotation of inspectors and public availability of inspection reports.

• Established environmental monitoring procedures, with special procedures for operations that remove or disturb strata that serve as aquifers affecting the hydrologic balance either on or off the mining site.

• Placed tight restrictions on the financial interests any employee of a regulatory authority performing functions under the act might have in coal operations.

• Set civil penalties of up to $5,000 for each violation under Title V, and provided that each day of continuing violation could be deemed a separate violation for purposes of penalty assessments.

• Provided that any person who knowingly violates a condition of a permit, or makes a false statement on an application, could be fined up to $10,000 or imprisoned for one year, or both.

• Provided that civil and criminal provisions of state programs be no less stringent than such provisions in the act.

• Established procedures for the release of performance bonds.

• Set forth the standing and procedural rules to be applied to lawsuits brought under the act. Allowed citizens to bring suit against the United States or other government instrumentalities under the act, or against any person for violations of rules, regulations, orders or permits issued under the act—including violations that resulted in injury.

● Gave primary responsibility for enforcing state programs to the states, but allowed the Interior Secretary to reinforce that authority with federal action following public hearings.

● Gave the Secretary authority to stop a mining operation immediately if it posed an imminent danger to public health or safety or might cause irreparable damage to the environment.

● Required states to establish plans for designating lands unsuitable for surface mining. The designation was required if land could not be reclaimed under requirements of the act. All other designations were discretionary with the regulatory authority, but lands could be deemed unsuitable if: strip mining would be incompatible with government objectives; the lands are fragile or historic; the site is a natural hazard area where development could endanger life or property; the area contains renewable resources where development would result in a loss of long-range productive capacity.

● Exempted unsuitable lands on which surface mining operations were being conducted on the date of enactment, or where substantial legal and financial commitments in such operations were made prior to Jan. 4, 1977.

● Directed the Secretary to review federal lands to determine which were unsuitable for surface mining. Existing operations on federal lands were allowed to continue until completion of the review.

● Prohibited strip mining operations in the National Park System, National Wildlife Refuge System, National System of Trails, National Wilderness Preservation System, Wild and Scenic Rivers System, or Custer National Forest.

● Permitted surface mining in other national forests if the Secretary found there were no significant recreational, timber, economic or other values that might be incompatible with such operations, and where surface operations were incident to underground mines and where the Agriculture Secretary determined that surface mining in areas west of the 100th meridian having sparse forest cover would be in compliance with existing law.

● Required the Interior Secretary to promulgate a program for federal lands within one year of enactment, incorporating all requirements of the act.

● Authorized the Secretary to enter into a cooperative agreement with a state for state regulation of strip mining on federal lands, provided that the Secretary retained authority to approve or disapprove mining plans and to designate federal lands as unsuitable for surface coal mining.

● Required all public agencies, public utilities and public corporations to comply with the environmental protection standards of Title V.

● Provided for judicial review in the appropriate U.S. District Courts of the Secretary's decisions regarding approval or disapproval of state programs.

● Authorized separate regulations for bituminous coal mines in the West which were in production prior to Jan. 1, 1972, and which met special criteria.

● Authorized the Secretary to issue separate regulations for anthracite coal surface mines if such mines were regulated by environmental protection standards of the state.

Title VI—Lands Unsuitable for Non-Coal Mining

● Permitted the Secretary of Interior, if requested by a state governor, to review any federal land within a state to assess whether it was unsuitable for mining for minerals other than coal.

● Authorized designation of any area as unsuitable if it were predominantly urban or suburban or if a mining operation would have an adverse impact on lands used primarily for residential purposes. The provision would not apply to any lands already being mined.

● Permitted any person with an interest which might be adversely affected to petition for exclusion of such an area from mining activities.

Title VII—Miscellaneous Provisions

● Defined technical terms and descriptions used throughout the act.

● Exempted coal owned by the Tennessee Valley Authority from the surface owner and federal lessee protection requirements applicable to other federal coal, but authorized the Secretary to set guidelines for mining TVA-owned coal.

● Made it unlawful to discharge or discriminate against an employee for filing suit or testifying under provisions of the act.

● Made it a criminal violation to resist or impede investigations carried out by a regulatory authority under the act.

● Authorized the Secretary to make grants to the states to develop and implement state regulatory programs. Grants could be up to 80 per cent the first year, 60 per cent the second year, and 50 per cent each year thereafter.

● Required the Secretary to report annually to the President and Congress on activities under the act.

● Authorized the Secretary to modify application of environmental protection provisions of the act to Alaskan surface mines for up to three years if he decided that was necessary to continue operation of the mines. Required the Secretary to make a study of strip mining conditions in Alaska and report to Congress within two years and authorized $250,000 for the study.

● Mandated a study within 18 months of enactment concerning surface and open pit mining and reclamation technologies for minerals other than coal, with emphasis on oil shale and tar sands deposits in western states. Authorized $500,000 for the study.

● Required a special study of surface mining regulation on Indian lands, and authorized $700,000 to assist the Indian tribes in the study.

● Permitted departures from environmental performance standards for mining and reclamation on an experimental basis, in order to allow post-mining land use for industrial commercial, residential or public use, including recreation.

● Authorized $10-million a year for fiscal 1978 through fiscal 1980 for initial regulatory procedures and administration of the program; $10-million each year for 15 years beginning in fiscal 1978 for hydrologic studies and test borings for small mine operations; $20-million in fiscal 1978 and $30-million each in fiscal 1979 and 1980 for grants to the states in preparing their regulatory plans. It also authorized up to $2-million in fiscal 1977 for the Secretary to begin implementing the act.

● Provided that surface owners, as defined by the act, must give their written consent before the Secretary could lease federally owned coal beneath the land they lived and worked on.

● Provided, in cases where the surface above federally owned coal was subject to a federal lease or permit, that there must be either written consent of the lessee or permittee, or evidence of bonding for payment of damages to the lessee or permittee.

Title VIII—University Coal Research Laboratories

● Authorized the Administrator of the Energy Research and Development Administration to designate 10 institutions of higher education for establishing university coal research laboratories.

● Authorized the administrator to make grants of up to $6-million for initial costs, and up to $1.5-million annually for operating expenses for each institution.

● Established an 11-member Advisory Council on Coal Research to help administer the title.

● Authorized appropriations of $30-million for fiscal 1979, and $7.5-million annually for fiscal years 1980-1983.

Title IX—Energy Resource Graduate Fellowships

● Authorized the Administrator of the Energy Research and Development Administration to award up to 1,000 graduate fellowships annually in fiscal years 1979-1984 for study and research in applied science and engineering related to the production, conservation and use of fuels and energy.

● Set terms and conditions of the fellowships.

● Authorized appropriations of $11-million for each of the six fiscal years.

● Authorized the Interior Secretary to conduct and promote research and demonstration projects of alternative coal mining technologies.

● Authorized annual appropriations of $35-million for fiscal years 1979-1983.

House Committee Action

The House Interior and Insular Affairs Committee April 22, 1977, reported HR 2 (H Rept 95-218). Markup had been completed in five days.

The House bill set minimum environmental standards that the states would be required to follow in controlling strip mining of coal. If a state program failed to meet those standards, a federal program would take effect. In the future, land that could not be reclaimed could not be stripped. HR 2 also established a reclamation program for land that had already been stripped and abandoned, financed by fees on new production of surface and deep-mined coal. Other key provisions provided for citizens' suits for enforcement and for protections for the rights of surface owners whose land lay on top of federally-owned coal.

As reported, HR 2 did not include administration-backed amendments banning mining on prime agricultural lands and providing more protection for alluvial valley floors in the West. The bill also permitted mountaintop removal under certain circumstances—a procedure opposed by environmentalists.

In reporting its fifth strip mining bill since 1972 the committee found that the environmental and social costs of coal extraction had not been reduced with the passage of time. Yet the energy crisis necessitated expansion of coal production. Coal represents over 90 per cent of the nation's total hydrocarbon energy reserves, but in 1974 it contributed only 18 per cent of the energy supply, the committee said.

The committee noted that increasingly coal was being

extracted through surface mining operations. In 1970, 43.8 per cent of U.S. coal production came from surface mines. In 1971 the share jumped to 50 per cent. For 1976 it was estimated that 55.9 per cent of the 671 million tons of coal produced was from surface mines.

The strongest dissent was signed by six Republicans who wrote: "This misguided legislation tramples states' rights, destroys small business, invites endless litigation, increases federal bureaucratic power many times over, increases consumer costs and lastly, will cause a major reduction—yes, a reduction—in our annual output of coal."

The Republicans who filed the dissent were Robert E. Bauman (Md.), Keith G. Sebelius (Kan.), Steven D. Symms (Idaho), Mickey Edwards (Okla.), Eldon Rudd (Ariz.) and Manuel Lujan Jr. (N.M.). All but Lujan voted against reporting the bill. Four Democrats had also voted against reporting the bill: Abraham Kazen Jr. (Texas), Dawson Mathis (Ga.), Ted Risenhoover (Okla.) and Harold Runnels (N.M.).

House Floor Action

The House April 29 passed HR 2, 241-64. Passage came after two days of debate. Most of the substantive action occurred on the second day when several amendments were adopted strengthening key environmental protections in the bill.

APRIL 28 DEBATE

Debate got underway April 28 with bill manager Morris K. Udall (D Ariz.) asking his colleagues to "put this one piece of our energy mosaic in place and...put this bill on the books where it should have been long ago." He said the bill was essentially the same as the legislation passed by the House in earlier years although regulations had been simplified to ease the burden on industry and reclamation requirements had been tightened.

In floor action April 28 the House adopted five amendments, none of which were major, and rejected four. There were no recorded votes. The bulk of the amendments related to Title IV, which established a system for reclamation of abandoned mines.

One of the amendments accepted, offered by Dan Marriott (R Utah) and adopted on a 15-3 standing vote, directed the Interior Secretary to return 50 per cent of the federal reclamation fee on mined coal to the state where the coal was mined; the bill gave him discretionary authority to do so. By voice votes the House adopted amendments allowing reclamation funds to be used to prevent acid water damage and making Indian reservations eligible to use reclamation funds in the same manner as states.

In other action on the reclamation provisions, the House rejected an amendment by Robert E. Bauman (R Md.) on behalf of Joe Skubitz (R Kan.) specifying that reclamation funds could be used only to reclaim coal mines; the bill permitted their use to repair devastation from other kinds of mining. Also rejected, on a 22-32 standing vote, was an amendment by Joseph M. McDade (R Pa.) that would have altered the method of financing reclamation by substituting Outer Continental Shelf leasing fees for the reclamation fee on mined coal.

At the end of the debate April 28 the House began consideration of the most controversial part of the bill—Title V, setting forth environmental standards. On a 16-42 standing vote it rejected an administration amendment, offered by James M. Jeffords (R Vt.), that would have imposed a five-year moratorium on strip mining on prime agricultural lands and required a study of farmland reclamation techniques.

APRIL 29 DEBATE

Supporters of the Carter administration fought hard on the House floor to strengthen environmental provisions of HR 2. They won with two amendments out of three and made an unusual second effort for the alluvial valley amendment that failed April 28.

Environmental Amendments

On a 170-149 recorded vote April 29 the most important administration-backed amendment was adopted, restricting mining on western alluvial valley floors. It was offered by Max Baucus (D Mont.), who had talked with both Secretary of the Interior Cecil D. Andrus and presidential energy adviser James R. Schlesinger. Interior and Insular Affairs Committee Chairman Udall said the administration considered it "the single important remaining environmental issue to be resolved."

Identical to provisions approved by the House in 1974 and 1975, the Baucus amendment permitted surface mining in alluvial valleys west of the 100th meridian only if permits were issued before Jan. 4, 1977, or if mines were in commercial production in the year prior to enactment of the bill. The committee bill had a much broader "grandfather clause," permitting mining where "substantial financial and legal commitments" had been made.

There was almost no debate on the second successful administration-backed amendment, offered by John F. Seiberling (D Ohio). It specified that only a minimal amount of spoil could be taken from mountaintops during the mining operation known as mountaintop removal. Udall said that mountaintop removal was "one of the major concessions we [the committee] made to the coal industry" and that the amendment clarified "on the environmental side" that the technique should involve rearranging as much spoil as possible on top.

Richard Nolan (D Minn.) offered a revised version of the administration's prime farmlands amendment that was rejected the day before. Udall supported it reluctantly. "I had limited enthusiasm for it yesterday and I must say I have less today," he said. "Since then the administration and others have made such a fuss about this [amendment] and they will not quit."

The Interior Department, which had sought the amendment offered the previous day by Jeffords, did not engineer the second attempt. But the Agriculture Department wanted it, and administration supporters also hoped to get a roll-call vote on the provision.

Nolan's amendment was rejected on a 9-41 standing vote. Nolan then asked for a recorded vote, but not enough members supported his request.

After consultation with Udall, the administration decided not to seek an amendment to ban surface coal mining in all national forests. Udall felt the committee bill, which would allow some such mining, was a necessary compromise.

The Interior Department maintained the national forests should be off-limits to strip mining.

Senate Committee Action

The Senate Energy and Natural Resources Committee May 10, 1977, reported S 7 (S Rept 95-128), its version of the strip mining bill. The committee had approved the legislation May 2 by a 15-3 vote.

The Senate committee bill was close to the House-passed version, and resembled legislation vetoed by President Ford in 1975. But S 7 as reported allowed more mining of alluvial valley floors in the West, and gave a 30-month reprieve to mining operations that produce less than 200,000 tons of coal annually.

HR 2 included some provisions not in S7, as reported: a separate title providing broad support for state mining and mineral research institutes; authority for the Interior Secretary to declare some federal lands unsuitable for non-coal mining; special provisions for anthracite coal; and a study of surface mining in Alaska.

The committee reported that the strip mining provisions in S 7 were necessary "to assure that surface coal mining operations—including exploration activities and the surface effects of underground mining—are conducted so as to prevent or minimize degradation to the environment."

The report said coal strip mining disturbs 1,000 additional acres of land each week. Of four million acres already disturbed by surface mining of all sorts, 43 per cent were damaged by coal extraction. Only half of the 1.3 million acres of strip-mined land in eastern coalfields have been reclaimed.

Committee members recalled that Congress had considered strip mining control bills for six years, and they blamed delays on the coal industry for having opposed "far less stringent measures than the legislation before Congress today."

The majority report refuted the industry argument that S 7, if enacted, would cut coal production while the energy crisis became more serious. "It is ridiculous to talk about a diminution in production at present prices, much less those anticipated in the future," the report said, "and it is even more ridiculous, given the massive amount of our coal reserves, to refuse to assume the relocation of mining operations, for example, to areas which can be prudently mined."

Not all members agreed with the committee's support for a tough bill. Three western Republicans—Dewey F. Bartlett (Okla.), Pete V. Domenici (N.M.) and Paul Laxalt (Nev.)—published minority views saying, "It is unthinkable to us that the Congress in its first response to the call for greater coal utilization would enact a measure which would accomplish the very opposite result."

Senate Floor Action

The Senate May 20 approved HR 2 after substituting the provisions of S 7. The final vote was 57-8.

Passage came after two days of debate during which numerous amendments were considered. Debate, particularly on May 20, went to the heart of many of the key controversies over the bill.

The Senate May 20 made significant changes in the committee-reported language limiting mining in alluvial valley floors in the West, requiring surface owners' consent for mining of federally-owned coal, exempting small miners from the interim environmental standards set by the bill, and allowing some variance from the requirement that the land be restored to its approximate original contour after mining.

Environmental groups and the Carter administration generally considered the Senate version of HR 2 somewhat less satisfactory than the House version.

May 19 Amendments

During the May 19 debate the Senate rejected three amendments on roll-call votes and accepted three others by voice vote.

Senators argued for 2½ hours before defeating, 25-67, an amendment offered by J. Bennett Johnston (D La.) to change the bill's "surface owner consent" provision which in effect allowed surface owners to veto mining of federally-owned coal beneath their property. The position was reversed the next day.

Johnston, who had voted against reporting S 7 because of the provision, said it would allow a "ripoff of the tax-payers." His amendment sought to eliminate a requirement for written consent before mining could occur and established procedures by which owners would be compensated for the mining of federal coal under their land.

The amendment was opposed by some western senators, especially Clifford P. Hansen (R Wyo.) and John Melcher (D Mont.), who argued that U.S. coal reserves were enormous and ranchers should not be forced against their will to cede their land.

Johnston also lost on a "state's rights" amendment that permitted states to retain exclusive jurisdiction over mining on their lands if the Interior Secretary determined that a state's environmental protection standards were as strong as the federal standards in S 7. Bill manager Lee Metcalf (D Mont.) argued in opposition that the timing set forth in the amendment would enable states to avoid imposing strict standards for up to eight years. The amendment was rejected on a vote of 39-51.

Before rejecting the amendment the Senate defeated a modification by Malcolm Wallop (R Wyo.) allowing the states to retain jurisdiction if their enforcement procedures, as well as their environmental standards, were as strong as the federal standards in S 7. It was rejected, 22-68.

With almost no discussion and by voice vote the Senate adopted an amendment by H. John Heinz III (R Pa.) to establish mining research institutes in qualified states. It added to the Senate bill a title similar to one in HR 2.

On two other voice votes the Senate quickly approved amendments to authorize the Interior Secretary to issue special regulations for coal mining in Alaska's permafrost areas, and to coordinate inspections under S 7 with existing mine safety and health laws.

Alluvial Valley Mining

Much of May 20 debate was dominated by discussion over language in the bill barring most mining in the alluvial valley floors of the West. The House bill (HR 2) allowed mining there only if permits were issued before Jan. 4, 1977, or if mines were in commercial production in the year before enactment of HR 2. The Senate committee bill (S 7) would have allowed mining in those areas under those two circumstances or if substantial financial and legal commitments had been made to mining operations.

The Senate May 20 rejected, 37-45, an administration-backed amendment proposed by Gary Hart (D Colo.) that would have substituted language identical to that in the House version.

The Senate then adopted three amendments to this portion of S 7:

● It replaced the committee language on alluvial valley mines with language of a 1976 strip mining measure. Described by its sponsor, John Melcher (D Mont.), as a "middle ground," it allowed strip mining in these valleys if it would not disrupt farming there or adversely affect the water supply. It did not protect these valleys if they were simply undeveloped rangeland and it would allow mining there if the mines were in commercial operation or had been granted a permit by the state in the year before enactment of HR 2. The Senate adopted this amendment, 58-13.

● It restored, by voice vote, the 1976 language defining an alluvial valley floor.

● And it adopted an amendment proposed by Malcolm Wallop (R Wyo.) to provide for compensatory treatment of coal mine operators foreclosed by this ban from mining areas in which they had already made a financial commitment.

Surface Owners' Rights

The Senate May 20 also returned to the surface owner consent issue that had dominated debate May 19.

In a turnaround, the Senate May 20 voted to allow development of this coal without the surface owner's consent, establishing a method for paying the surface owner twice the amount of the change in the value of his land due to the mining and for reimbursing him for the cost to him, in lost income and other expenses, of the mining. This amendment, proposed by Dale Bumpers (D Ark.), was adopted, 44-32.

After the amendment was adopted, the Senate continued to debate the matter at length. Clifford P. Hansen (R Wyo.), one of the critics of this change, proposed to restore the consent requirement in all cases except those in which the President found that the national need for coal could not be satisfied unless such deposits were mined without surface owners' consent—and then the Bumpers provision would apply.

The issue was finally settled when Bumpers proposed, and the Senate by voice vote adopted, a substitute for the Hansen amendment. This required surface owners' consent for such mining unless the Secretary of Interior found it necessary in the national interest that the coal be strip mined. In that case the Bumpers provision approved earlier would take effect, providing some compensation for the unhappy surface owner.

Exemptions and Variances

As reported from committee, S 7 exempted small mining operations from compliance with its interim environmental standards 30 months after enactment. They were defined as those producing 200,000 tons of coal a year or less. This exemption would ease the financial burden that compliance would impose on these small operators, its advocates said.

The exemption was strongly opposed by environmentalists. Pointing out that it would exempt 93 per cent of the nation's mine operators who produce 33 per cent of its coal, Howard M. Metzenbaum (D Ohio) proposed an amendment May 20 to eliminate it.

Under pressure from Wendell H. Ford (D Ky.) and other senators from Appalachia—where most mine operators are small operators—Metzenbaum revised his amendment to narrow the exemption to operators producing

100,000 tons per year or less and to shorten the time of the exemption to 24 months. The Senate adopted this by voice vote. This exemption, Metzenbaum said, would affect 86 per cent of the coal operators who produce 23 per cent of the nation's coal.

To the dismay of environmentalists, Ford won an easy victory May 20 when the Senate by voice vote adopted his amendment allowing some variance from the requirement that strip-mined land be returned to its approximate original contour. Arguing that there was a scarcity of flat land in his state, Ford urged that this change be made to allow some "highwalls"—clifflike cuts in hills resulting from strip mining—to remain in order that the flat land beneath them, known as "benches," might be put to some desirable public use.

In other action May 20, the Senate approved, 45-41, an amendment that allowed states that had a surplus of reclamation fund revenues after reclaiming all the strip-mined lands to use those funds for constructing public facilities in communities affected by coal development.

The Senate also adopted an amendment that required mine operators, before strip mining any land that contained as much as 10 per cent prime agricultural land, to demonstrate that they can restore the land to a condition at least fully capable of supporting its original agricultural use. The Carter administration had proposed a flat five-year ban on strip mining on prime agricultural land, but neither chamber chose to go that far.

Conference Action

The conference report on HR 2 was filed July 12 (H Rept 95-493, S Rept 95-337). Conferees noted that it was the third report in the last three Congresses on strip mining legislation. They said that the five years of legislative experience had resulted in substantially similar House and Senate bills. The few key differences were resolved as follows:

Surface Owner Consent. The House required the written consent of surface owners before federally-owned coal beneath their lands could be strip mined. The Senate bill was similar, but a floor amendment gave the Interior Secretary the right to override the surface owner if leasing was in the national interest. The conference agreed to the House language.

Modifying House language on disputes arising when both the surface and mineral estates were in separate private ownership, conferees decided that the disputes should be settled by state law and state courts.

Alluvial Valley Floors. The House had banned mining on alluvial valley floors in the West unless permits had been obtained before enactment, and specified that mines were not to damage water systems that supplied valley floors. The Senate only restricted such mining, prohibiting it on most farmland but allowing it on undeveloped rangelands or small farmland if it would have a negligible impact on agricultural production. It also authorized the Interior Secretary to lease other federal coal deposits to coal operators who had made a substantial financial commitment to mine coal in alluvial valleys where mining would now be prohibited under the law.

The conference basically adopted the Senate provision, permitting mining of the valley floors if it did "not interrupt, discontinue or preclude farming," and authorized the coal exchange program.

Prime Farmlands. Before a strip mining permit could be issued, the Senate required demonstration that prime farmlands, as defined by the legislation, would be restored to full productivity. The House bill had no such provision. Conferees stipulated that permits could be granted if the applicant has "the technological capability to restore such mined area" to equivalent or higher productivity, and set soil reconstruction standards.

"Small Operators" Exemption. The Senate bill gave "small operators"—those producing 100,000 tons or less per year—an exemption from most environmental standards for 24 months after enactment of the legislation. The House allowed no similar exemption. Conferees shortened the exemption deadline to Jan. 1, 1979, and made sure the 100,000-ton limit applied per operator (not per mine) for both surface and underground coal.

Highwalls. In provisions on steep slope mining, the Senate had provided that spoil from the first cut could be placed below the strip bench. The House had no such provision and Senate conferees agreed to drop theirs. The Senate bill also allowed variances from requirements that highwalls be backfilled and the land be returned to approximate original contours. Conferees required that highwalls be backfilled but allowed a variance of the approximate original contours to permit a broad range of post-mining uses for lands left with very wide and stable benches.

Mountaintop Mining. Conferees melded provisions concerning the mining method called mountaintop removal. They permitted it, provided spoil disposal standards are met, if it provided for a better post-mining land use or if applicants submitted specific plans for post-mining land use.

Lobbyist Reaction. A coal lobbyist who sat through the conference, Carter Manasco of the National Coal Association, was not pleased with the results. "Every day they want more and more coal production, then they put more and more roadblocks," Manasco said.

Karl Englund, an environmentalist who followed the legislation all through the 95th Congress for the Northern Plains Resource Council, was happy with the conference agreements on prime farmlands, elimination of highwalls and return to approximate original contours. But he was unhappy that small coal operators got a partial exemption.

Final Action

Before the conference report could be adopted, HR 2 had to clear one last hurdle in the Senate July 20. Dale Bumpers (D Ark.), a member of the conference committee, moved to recommit the report. He wanted to instruct the Senate conferees to reconsider the issue of surface owner protection and insist on restoring the language of his amendment adopted on the Senate floor.

Bumpers said the provision in HR 2 meant: "If anybody owns the surface over the coal the United States owns, we just cannot mine it, no matter how badly we may want it." He argued that the federal government had retained mineral rights many years ago in order to have the reserves when they were needed. Bumpers said the provision in HR 2 applied almost entirely to four states — Montana, Wyoming, South Dakota and North Dakota — where about half the federal coal is under privately owned land.

Bumpers' motion to recommit was rejected, 43-53. The conference report was then promptly adopted, 85-8.

HR 2 was cleared for the President when the House approved the conference report by a 325-68 vote July 21. ∎

Carter Energy Plan Stressed Coal Conversion

Coal was one of the focal points of the energy program that Carter proposed in April 1977. The administration had considered legislation to force utilities and industries to burn coal instead of oil and natural gas as central to the success of its energy plan. Carter had originally proposed a stiff tax on industrial use of oil and gas that would have given gas users a clear economic incentive to convert to coal, but the tax was dropped by Congress in the final 1978 version of the energy package (HR 5146 — PL 95-620). *(Details, see energy bill chapter, p. 5)*

The purpose of the Carter energy program was to reduce American dependence on oil and gas. The White House said the entire program would save the nation 4.5 million barrels of oil a day; more than half of the total savings would come from coal conversion alone.

In 1975, 25 percent of all the oil consumed in the United States was burned by utilities and industries; they consumed 60 percent of all the natural gas. The Carter plan would have substituted coal and saved the oil and gas for uses like heating homes.

The White House argued that there simply was not enough oil and gas available, whereas coal supplies were bountiful. Oil and gas make up only 7 percent of America's total energy reserve, the administration said, but coal constitutes 90 percent.

Beyond any doubt, there is plenty of coal. The U.S. Geological Survey said it was certain there are 1.8 trillion tons of coal beneath American soil; it projected there may be as much as 4 trillion tons.

Of that staggering amount, only 437 billion tons are located where existing technology can dig it out. And since about half of the coal in an underground mine and about 15 percent of the coal in a surface mine cannot be removed, the bottom line figure on how much coal America could

produce — given existing technological and economic constraints — is about 266.5 billion tons, according to the Interior Department's Bureau of Mines.

That is still a lot of coal. And as technology improves, more can be retrieved.

But experts questioned whether Carter's short-term goals could be achieved. There was no certainty that the coal industry, habitually crippled by labor problems and short on capital, could meet the president's goal of almost doubling output in less than 10 years.

This problem was underscored by the three-month-long coal strike that began Dec. 6, 1977, and ended March 27, 1978, when striking members of the United Mine Workers (UMW) union ratified a new three-year contract calling for a 39 percent increase in wages and fringe benefits by 1980. The final contract had been negotiated under pressure from the White House, which had obtained a temporary restraining order from a federal judge March 9 directing the miners to return to work. The order was widely ignored, however, and the judge refused to grant an extension.

In addition to problems within the industry, analysts also doubted that the nation's transportation system — especially the troubled railroads — could haul the coal even if it were produced.

Industries and utilities said converting their plants was a lot easier said than done. They said it would cost too much, that Carter's timetable was too fast, and that even if they switched their facilities to coal, environmental laws would prohibit them from burning it.

Environmentalists worried that increased burning of coal would poison the nation's air and that rapid energy development would cause a host of problems for the West.

Following is a description of the original Carter coal conversion proposal and the issues it raised — ranging from coal production to its transportation and actual use.

Carter 1977 Proposal

President Carter's original coal conversion proposals were a complex package of tax and regulatory measures aimed at getting large industries and utilities to switch from oil or gas to coal. Under the proposed regulations:

• No new industry or utility boiler would be allowed to burn oil or gas, with limited exceptions for extreme environmental or economic circumstances;

• All new facilities, even those designed to burn low-polluting coal, would be required to install the best available technology to control pollution;

• Industrial firms also could be prohibited from burning gas or oil in other new combustors, such as furnaces and kilns, by case by case decisions or through class of use orders;

• Existing facilities capable of burning coal could be ordered when feasible not to burn oil or gas;

• Virtually no utility would be allowed to burn natural gas after 1990;

A barge being loaded with coal on the Ohio River.

• Virtually no major industrial facility would be allowed to burn natural gas after an unspecified future date.

Tax Proposals. The Carter plan also included tax penalties and credits designed to encourage voluntary switches to coal. Those proposals:

• Taxed consumption of natural gas starting in 1979 for large industries and in 1983 for utilities. The tax would have made the cost of burning gas equal to the cost of burning an equivalent amount of distillage fuel oil. The tax started low but built to full impact by 1985.

• Taxed industrial use of oil for boiler fuel at $.90 per barrel beginning in 1979; the tax would have risen to $3.00 per barrel by 1985. Utilities using petroleum would have paid $1.50 per barrel starting in 1983. *(Figures do not include inflation adjustment; see box, p. 95)*

The oil and gas consumption tax applied only to large consumers burning more than one-half trillion Btu's (British thermal units) per year. That included only 2,000 industrial firms out of 100,000 in the country, according to Federal Energy Administrator John O'Leary, but those 2,000 firms were responsible for about 90 percent of all industrial oil and gas consumption, he said.

Rebates. Industries and utilities could avoid paying the oil and gas consumption taxes by voluntarily converting to coal. Costs of conversion — such as buying coal-fired boilers — could be offset against the consumption tax as a rebate. In effect, such investment substituted for tax payment, although the amount of investment eligible to receive tax credit in any given year could not exceed the amount of conversion taxes imposed in that year. Investment in excess of that year's consumption tax could be carried over for application to the next year's tax. Industry had an alternate option: An extra 10 percent investment tax credit could be available, in addition to the existing 10 percent investment credit.

O'Leary explained the administration's rationale for the tax and rebate package in May 1977 testimony before the House Commerce Subcommittee on Energy and Power: "[T]he decision-making process in board rooms would be changed from whether to invest in coal facilities or not, to a new decision of whether to pay the federal government taxes, or use these funds to invest in facilities to reduce or eliminate the use of oil and gas."

The oil and gas consumption taxes would result in a cumulative revenue gain by 1985 of $40.9 billion after rebates of $44.2-billion for conversion investment, according to May 1977 testimony before the same panel by Laurence N. Woodworth, assistant Treasury secretary for tax policy.

FEA Program. The FEA since 1974 held authority to order utilities to burn coal instead of oil and gas; in 1975, the power was expanded to cover major industrial plants. (In 1977, FEA powers were transferred to the new Energy Department.)

But even the FEA conceded in 1977 that the program had been a flop. FEA head O'Leary contended in 1977 congressional testimony that the program was hampered by restrictions built into the authorizing laws. The program was created by the 1974 Energy Supply and Environmental Coordination Act. It was extended and expanded by the 1975 Energy Policy and Conservation Act.

Those laws required the FEA to proceed on a case by case basis, with the burden of proof falling on the FEA to demonstrate feasibility before final conversion could be ordered. Numerous procedural roadblocks frustrated decisive action.

An investigation of the program by the House Energy and Power Subcommittee staff concluded that bureaucratic infighting and lack of management coordination within FEA were to blame for the program's ineffectiveness.

Coal Production Issues

The Carter program called for expansion of coal production by 1985 by at least 400 million tons above 1976 levels; the president's upper end production goal was 565 million tons above the 1976 level. Meeting either target would have required an unprecedented effort by the coal industry.

In 1976, the industry mined 665 million tons of bituminous and lignite coal and an additional 6.2 million tons of anthracite, according to the National Coal Association (NCA). The total production of 671.2 million tons was a record high.

Some experts said the industry was incapable of meeting Carter's goals. Dr. Hans H. Landsberg, an economist and coal authority with Resources for the Future, a Washington research center, was among them.

In a May 1977 essay, Landsberg noted that 1976 was a record coal production year. "Now every added ton produced sets a new record," he said. "Consequently not only must mining companies grow, but all facilities associated with coal, including, prominently, transportation and manpower, must grow apace. State/federal conflicts must be resolved, the aspirations of Indian tribes controlling large amounts of western coal have to be reconciled, land-use and restoration practices must be established.

"That in this context the coal industry can raise output by an annual average of 60 million tons is highly unlikely, if not outright impossible," Landsberg concluded.

Coal Industry Views. The coal industry said it could meet the challenge if government would only untie its hands.

"The goal of increasing coal production and use by at least 400 million tons by 1985 is modest because plans for even larger amounts are well along," claimed NCA President Carl E. Bagge in May 1977 testimony before the Energy and Power Subcommittee.

Bagge based his claim on the following points:

• An August 1976 survey by the NCA revealed plans for new mine expansions and additions by 1985 that would produce about 500 million tons;

• Electric utilities had reported to the Federal Power Commission (FPC) plans to bring on line voluntarily 250 new coal-fired plants by 1985 which would require about 390 million tons of coal;

• A November 1976 FPC study of 211 of the 250 planned new electric plants found that 68 percent of the coal they required already was under contract;

• Industrial use of coal was 19 percent higher in January 1977 than one year before, according to the Bureau of Mines;

• Electric utilities planned no new gas-fired baseload units after 1979 and no new oil-fired baseload plants after 1982.

Those trends showed, Bagge said, that utilities and industry already were committed to coal for their future without the Carter program, and that the coal industry was gearing up to meet the increased demand.

The coal industry liked Carter's goal of increased coal use, Bagge said, but opposed his program to reach that goal. Opposition rested on five arguments.

• Forced conversion orders were unnecessary given existing trends;

• The existing FEA conversion program demonstrated the ineffectiveness of such regulatory approaches;

• Converting old facilities tied up manpower and money better spent on larger, new facilities that could then replace older, smaller or more inefficient gas and oil-fired plants;

• The Carter plan required more unwanted bureaucracy to manage the regulatory program;

• A mandatory conversion program would be likely to lead to government allocation and price controls over coal.

Constraints. The coal industry's proclamations of confidence were hedged by warnings that several "constraints . . . could make it difficult" to meet 1985 production goals.

Among those constraints were: state and federal air pollution control laws that discouraged coal burning; federal price regulations that held oil and gas prices competitively low with coal; state prohibitions against allowing power companies to charge costs of converting to coal to customers while construction was under way; a federal moratorium on leasing public lands for coal development; proposed mine safety requirements; wildcat strikes and labor problems. The industry said Carter's program should be redirected toward easing those constraints.

Costs. The FEA estimated that the industry needed $23 billion by 1984 to meet its expansion goals; that was almost four times as much as the $6.5 billion the industry spent between 1965 and 1974.

"If the market is there, the capital will flow," Bagge said in April 1977 testimony before a Senate subcommittee.

Bagge also defended the recent trend of major oil companies buying into the coal industry. The oil companies provided necessary money and expertise, he said.

Labor. Meeting coal production goals required more men as well as more money. To produce one billion tons of coal per year required a jump in the number of miners from 191,000 in 1977 to 308,200, according to testimony before the Energy and Power Subcommittee by Dr. John F. Finklea of the National Institute for Occupational Safety and Health.

New miners, including those to replace retirees, might have to total 152,000 in the next 10 years, according to Robert E. Barrett, head of the Mining Enforcement and Safety Administration (MESA). ". . .[A] huge training program would be required to get the job done," Barrett added. "Not just anybody can mine coal. . . . Educating and training miners is a primary concern to the industry. Certified mine foremen are in critically short supply. . . ."

Building up the needed manpower would not be easy; mining is without question one of the most dangerous occupations. In 1976, according to MESA, 141 miners were killed on the job. Another 13,944 suffered disabling injuries.

UMW Problems. Also clouding the outlook for coal production was the political war under way in the mines.

Three out of every four miners belonged to the United Mine Workers (UMW) union, which had been wracked by internal strife since at least 1969. Reformers toppled the old-guard union leadership in 1972 but have failed in the years since to weld the union together. As a result, the miners have lacked coherent leadership and have forced a growing series of crippling wildcat strikes.

According to the NCA, 500,000 man-days were lost to the industry in 1969 due to wildcat strikes; by 1976, the lost time amounted to more than 2 million man-days.

Productivity has been declining as well. According to the NCA, underground mines produced 16.5 tons per man in 1969, but only 8.5 tons per man in 1976. Industry management complained that more stringent health and safety standards for mines proposed by the Interior Department would cut productivity further.

Transportation

Even if the industry can dig up enough coal, questions remained about the ability of America's transportation system to move it where it's needed.

Currently, about two-thirds of all coal shipments move by train; the rest is hauled by barge or truck, or converted to energy by plants at mine mouths. Bidding to compete with the railroads' share of the coal-hauling market were several companies proposing to pulverize coal into fine particles and mix it with fluid into a "slurry," which would be pumped through pipelines from mine to user. The call for more coal presented each of these transportation systems with new opportunities, and new problems.

Railroads. In 1976, coal shipments gave the nation's railroads 29 percent of their tonnage and 14 percent of their gross freight revenues, according to the Association of American Railroads (AAR).

The train systems welcomed the chance to move more coal, according to William H. Dempsey, AAR president, and they were quite capable of moving that extra load, he said.

Dempsey told the Energy and Power subcommittee that the railroads would have to acquire between 9,700 and 13,400 new coal cars each year to handle the increase in coal traffic. The variance reflects uncertainty as to how much of the load can be carried by "unit" trains, which run continuously between fixed points like a conveyor belt on rails.

"In recent years," Dempsey said, "deliveries of new open top hoppers have averaged 20,000 annually, three-fourths of which were destined for coal service." Builders of railroad cars are capable of producing as many as 72,000 coal cars annually if needed, he said. A car shortage therefore appeared unlikely. He also said there would be no problem in supplying needed locomotives.

The industry would need to invest between $4.3 billion and $5.9 billion over the next eight years for cars and engines, Dempsey said. "These amounts are clearly manageable."

Further, Dempsey contended, "It is all but inconceivable that the railroads can be caught unprepared by a surge in coal production." He said railroad cars and locomotives were delivered within three to five months after order, and that track could be shipped in 90 days. By contrast, new strip mines took two years to develop, and new underground mines took twice that time. Lead times for power plants took even longer.

Where the railroads faced problems was in their deteriorating roadbeds, Dempsey said.

"Most of the nation's mainlines outside the Northeast are in top-flight condition," he testified. "Other mainlines in the Northeast, some areas of the Midwest and secondary rail lines throughout the nation are not presently in a physical condition" to meet increased demand, he conceded. Those lines could be prepared, however, before "any actual surge in coal traffic — there is no question," Dempsey insisted.

DOT View. The government apparently shared Dempsey's optimism that the railroads could handle the job. In May 1977 testimony before the Energy and Power

Subcommittee, Transportation Secretary Brock Adams echoed Dempsey's analysis. Rail cars and engines should be no problem, he indicated.

"To the extent that contraints on the shipment of coal by rail do emerge, they are likely to involve the ability of financially marginal railroads to secure the financing required," Adams said.

". . .[T]he bulk of investment in question would be for improved signalling systems, rolling stock and lengthened sidings, or intermittent double tracking. We are not likely to be faced with the need to construct whole new rail routes."

A 1977 FPC analysis of new coal-fired utility plants planned for operation by 1985 concluded that 358 million tons would be used by the plants annually, of which 221 million tons would be moved by rail. Less than one half of that total coal supply had any assured means of transport as of October 1976, the report said, and only one-third of the projected rail shipments were under contract.

Nevertheless, the report said, most utilities did not appear worried about the railroads' ability to bring them coal when they needed it. The exceptions were utilities in Texas, Arkansas, Louisiana and Oklahoma. Utilities there were unwilling to meet railroad demands for 20-years or longer transport contracts, the report said, and were hoping slurry pipelines would bring their coal.

Barges. Slightly more than 10 percent of all coal shipments are hauled via the nation's inland waterways, primarily the Ohio and Mississippi river systems. According to May 1977 testimony by H. J. Bobzien Jr., president of the American Commercial Barge Line Co., the barge industry could easily handle its share of the increased coal load.

Bobzien said building yards could expand the barge fleet 20 percent per year if necessary.

The only problems Bobzien foresaw centered on the continuing complaints by barge operators that certain waterways were impeded by inadequate lock and dam structures.

Trucks. Adams noted too that trucks played an essential coal transport role, especially in the Appalachian region. Trucks there move coal short distances from mines to washing plants and to rail and barge loading facilities.

Those trucks often were too heavy for the small roads they traveled, Adams said. This burdened state highway maintenance programs. Also, Adams said, increased western coal development in particular would require "numerous railroad/highway grade crossing separations and line relocations" there.

Adams mentioned other possible negative side effects of increased coal traffic. Small town streets in the route of coal movement could get clogged. Settlements in the path of unit train operations could be severely disrupted by repeated intrusion of the trains 20 to 30 times a day, he said.

Coal Slurry. Another transportation issue in the coal controversy concerned development of coal slurry pipelines that would pump a mixture of pulverized coal and water from mines to coal users like utilities. Five major pipelines had been on the drawing boards for years, but they would cross lands owned by railroads. The railroads, anxious to block competition in the lucrative coal hauling business, had thwarted pipeline development by refusing to grant rights of way. As a result of an intense lobbying campaign by the railroads, the House July 19, 1978, defeated a bill (HR 1609) that would have given the Department of the Interior authority to grant pipeline developers federal powers of eminent domain, subject to certain restrictions. *(Details, appendix, p. 97-A)*

Impact of Conversion

Utility Opposition

The nation's electric utilities mounted four basic arguments against President Carter's proposed coal conversion program:

(1) No new baseload plants had been planned to be fueled by oil or gas, so Carter's conversion proposals for new utility plants were superfluous;

(2) Forced conversion of existing plants to coal within a time frame as short as Carter proposed would cost an exorbitant amount of money, cause consumer bills to skyrocket and jeopardize already shaky utility credit ratings; in addition, mass conversion efforts would endanger the reliability of electric service;

(3) Many existing boilers could not be converted but in fact would require complete replacement; in many cases an entire plant would have to be replaced because existing plants lacked sufficient space for coal boilers and related facilities;

(4) The Clean Air Act and related air quality plans would prohibit coal burning in many areas.

Some plants were relatively lucky because they either once burned coal or were designed to be able to in the future. For example, the New England Power Co. operated six such Massachusetts plants.

In the late 1960s, all six were converted from coal to oil to save money on fuel and to reduce pollution. On April 25, 1977, the FEA issued a preliminary order to the company to convert the six units back to coal. The utility said it was willing to convert three units voluntarily, but contended converting the other three, at Salem Harbor, would be prohibitively expensive.

According to 1977 House testimony by Donald G. Allen, a company vice president: "FEA predicts capital costs of $119.3 million and net annual savings (for fuel) of $19.8 million. Our estimates predict capital costs of $340.8 million and net increased costs to our customers of $138 million." The only thing FEA and the utility agreed on, Allen said, was that it would be "uneconomic" to convert the Salem Harbor units.

Allen said that if his system were forced to convert to coal anyway, customers' bills would rise between 10 and 15 percent.

Such a jump in electric bills would be modest compared to the amount utilities said Texas and Mississippi consumers would pay if they were forced to switch to coal.

"We feel that the price of electricity will increase at least three to five times," said George W. Oprea Jr., executive vice president of Houston Light and Power Co.

"We'd just about triple the bill to our customers," said Donald C. Lutken, president of Mississippi Power & Light Co. Both men's comments came in May 1977 House testimony.

Unlike New England Power Co., the Houston and Mississippi systems' plants never were designed with coal capacity. They burned natural gas exclusively, as did most utilities in gas-producing states in the South and Southwest. Other utilities, especially those on the East and West coasts, were equipped to burn oil only.

According to Edison Electric Institute, the nation's total 1976 electric generating capacity included 152,000 megawatts fired by oil and gas boilers; of that amount, "only 22,000 megawatts are convertible to coal without major reconstruction."

In some if not most cases, "major reconstruction" meant essentially rebuilding the entire power plant, perhaps at a new location. This would be necessary because coal-fired boilers are usually about twice as large as gas or oil boilers; they simply cannot fit into many plants' current space.

Industry Problems

Similar problems beset industry. "[C]onversion is the wrong word," maintained Cornell C. Maier, president of Kaiser Aluminum & Chemical Corp. before the Joint Economic Committee's Energy Subcommittee in May 1977. "None of our plants are convertible to coal. They must be completely rebuilt and the existing plants scrapped. In several instances the new power plants cannot even be constructed at the same site. Physical space won't permit it. The new plants will have to be constructed miles away from where the power will be used. This means time-consuming new construction." Maier said his firm would need at least seven years to convert to coal. "Eight years is probably more realistic."

The experience of the Celanese Corp. efforts to convert its Pampa, Texas, chemical plant to coal was instructive as to what private companies were up against.

"When this complex project is completed we will have spent in excess of $70 million to convert from gas to coal and we will not have increased our production capacity," said Daniel F. Twomey, a Celanese official, in House testimony May 27, 1977.

"Of this total amount, approximately $20 million will be for coal handling facilities and approximately $4 million will be for coal hopper cars," Twomey said. He explained that railroads sometimes required the shipper or receiver to buy the necessary cars.

The company also would have to pay either to build its own facility to maintain the coal cars in good condition or to contract with someone else to do it, Twomey said. At the time, there were no such services available between the spot where the coal would be mined in Colorado and the plant in Texas, he said.

Finally, he said, Celanese Corp. was having difficulty reaching a contract agreement with the railroads for hauling the coal. He said that since the railroads had no competition, they were holding out for unfairly high freight rates now that their services were in growing demand. He noted several complaints before the Interstate Commerce Commission making that allegation.

Conflicting Analysis

The Congressional Budget Office in May 1977 released a comprehensive review of the whole Carter energy program. The analysis disagreed with the administration's estimate on the extent of industrial conversion to coal by 1985.

The White House said the Carter program would result in conversion to coal by about 10 percent of existing industrial facilities and that about 44 percent of new industrial facilities would use coal. The report said the 44 percent figure was more likely to be 33 percent, which would mean 50 million tons less in industrial coal consumption.

A miner operates a modern continuous mining machine in an underground mine.

Environmental Issues

Digging coal and burning it present obvious inherent threats to the environment. Yet the administration insisted that when it comes to coal, America can have its cake and eat it too — that the nation could almost double coal production and consumption by 1985 without sacrificing environmental standards.

Douglas M. Costle, head of the Environmental Protection Agency (EPA), explained the administration's reasoning on that point in a series of May 1977 appearances before congressional committees.

"While coal conversion would tend to increase emissions, the administration's energy plan also encourages energy conservation. Together with the administration's proposed changes in the Clean Air Act," Costle said, "these conservation measures would result in compensating decreases in emission."

Costle said that utilities would use about the same amount of coal by 1985 whether or not Carter's plan was adopted, but that the plan would cause reduced utility use of oil and gas, and hence reduced overall emissions.

For industry, Costle said, the plan would cause about 200,000 more tons of coal per year to be burned than otherwise, and he conceded that would produce "increased emissions in the industrial sector." He argued that those emissions "can be substantially but not entirely offset by installing the best available control technology on all new industrial sources burning coal."

Even those increased industrial emissions would be offset by the net decrease in emissions from utilities, Costle maintained. "The net result is that the total of industrial and utility emissions are expected to be about the same under the president's plan in 1985 as they would be without the plan."

For those results, Costle said, several steps must be taken: all new facilities must install the best available pollution control technology; all existing facilities must install pollution control equipment as needed to meet current emission limits as defined in state and federal laws; the equipment must be taken proper care of.

Carter's policy would allow exemptions for units which could not meet environmental standards and for which costs of conversion would be excessive, Costle said.

A coal unit train that runs continuously between fixed points.

Costle agreed with Sen. Edmund S. Muskie, D-Maine, that the program would require extensive revision of state clean air plans, which Muskie predicted would trigger "confrontations all across the country."

Under questioning from the House Commerce Energy and Power Subcommittee, Costle admitted that EPA's estimates on the program's air pollution impact were only that — estimates. And the estimates were national projections, while pollution varies greatly from region to region. "The plain answer is . . . that you cannot know precisely [what the regional pollution impact will be]," Costle said, ". . .but we think these are reasonable estimates."

General Criticism. Rep. Toby Moffett, D-Conn., found Costle's assurances less than convincing. He questioned skeptically how EPA could be sure the Carter plan's conservation features would compensate for increased pollution as Costle claimed, when conservation initiatives were mainly voluntary, and hence, unpredictable.

"We won't know . . . with absolute precision," Costle conceded, until site-by-site analysis was undertaken.

"Maybe I'm missing something," Moffett said, "but I don't understand how all this being done afterwards makes any sense. . . . Very little analysis has been done about the impact on my region, and I'm being asked to go into mark-up on this legislation very soon.

"I'm troubled by this. It's becoming extremely difficult to keep our enthusiasm to respond to various portions of the plan," Moffett said.

The strongest criticism of the plan's environmental effects came from Richard E. Ayres, a lawyer with the Natural Resources Defense Council Inc., in May 1977 testimony before the House subcommittee.

The coal conversion program, he said, "will result in increased death and disease from additional pollution. . . .The air quality standards in the president's program . . . simply are not adequate. . . ."

Ayres said a small industrial boiler with a 50 million Btu per hour capacity produced 0.0006 pounds per million Btu of sulfur oxide pollution when gas was used as fuel. If coal of 1 percent sulfur content were burned — a relatively low sulfur content — that converted boiler would produce 1.8 pounds of sulfur oxide per million Btu, Ayres said.

"This is over 3,000 times greater than the gas-fired emission rate. Even if the 1 percent coal were scrubbed by 90 percent, the coal emission rate would be 300 times greater than the gas emission rate," Ayres contended.

He said that for metropolitan areas where FEA had proposed forced conversion to coal emission projections "will jump precipitously." He said sulfur oxide pollution would increase by 108 percent in the the Hartford-Springfield-New Haven region, by 387 percent in Boston and by 271 percent in greater New York. Particulates would soar too, Ayres said, by 499 percent in the Hartford region, 7,513 percent in Boston and 870 percent in New York.

The environmentalist leveled one other blast at the Carter plan. The United States still produces about half its own crude oil supply, he observed, and "an irreducible portion — about 20 percent — of that crude remains as residual oil after refining, suitable only for fueling large boilers.

"Eliminating the use of this and other heavy oils which are still usually cleaner than coal, will not reduce oil imports by a barrel, but it will dirty the air."

Scrubber Costs. One of the key environmental issues in the coal controversy was the cost of "scrubbers" or flue gas desulfurization equipment. When the EPA spoke of "best available control technology," scrubbers were what it meant. There were other pollution control systems being developed, but they would not be in wide use for at least a decade.

Scrubbers cleanse coal smoke of sulfur oxides, which are dangerous to human respiratory systems. They are about 90-95 percent effective, EPA said. Scrubbers utilize a mixture of water spray and lime, limestone or other agents to filter sulfur oxides from smoke.

EPA estimated that pollution control equipment would add about $5 billion to the cost of new power plants by 1985, increasing utility capital costs by about 2 percent between 1975 and 1985. That would result in average rate increases to consumers of about 1 percent, Costle said, with higher hikes in some places. Costle estimated that about $4 billion would be spent on scrubbers by other industrial facilities by 1985 under the Carter plan.

Business and industry disliked scrubbers. Testimony on behalf of the National Association of Manufacturers April 5, 1977, before a Senate Energy subcommittee illustrated why.

Matthew Gould, a Georgia Pacific Corp. executive, spoke for NAM and told of a utility's 1970 decision to install a lime scrubbing system. The system took a year and a half to install; it broke down after three months for five months of repairs; it generated excess sludge and was plagued by operating problems. A 1975 company review of the system concluded that more than $30 million had been spent on the equipment in less than five years and the plant's operating costs had increased "approximately 35 percent due to the operation of the scrubbers," Gould said.

Other Environmental Hazards. Sen. Gary Hart, D-Colo., charged in a May 1977 press conference that the coal conversion program would produce dangerous amounts of nitrous oxide air pollution. Nitrous oxide has been linked to lung cancer and causes eye and respiratory irritation.

Hart quoted a preliminary study by the Energy Research and Development Administration (ERDA) that said the coal conversion program would increase nitrous oxide emissions by about 2.2 million tons annually, or about 30 percent, even with "stringent control techniques."

Greenhouse Effect. Some experts said the coal program could pose a longer-term threat to the entire earth's environment, the phenomenon commonly called "the greenhouse effect." Some scientists, among them Dr. Wallace S. Broecker of Columbia University, contended that heavy coal burning would produce so much carbon dioxide that the earth's cloud cover would grow excessively dense, trapping heat inside the atmosphere that slowly would raise the temperature of the whole planet.

Dr. Broecker said in May 1977 that within 50 years the earth's temperature could rise an average of four degrees, eventually melting the polar ice caps.

Air now has about 330 parts of carbon dioxide (CO) per million parts of air (PPM), according to Dr. James L. Liverman of the Energy Research and Development Administration (ERDA). When the industrial revolution took hold in the mid-1880s, he testified in June 1977, the air had about 290 PPM of CO. The level was increased by 15 PPM since 1958 alone, he said.

President Carter in 1977 requested nearly $3-million to study the long-term effects on the atmosphere of carbon dioxide build-up from burning coal and other hydrocarbons.

Acid Rain. Yet another nasty byproduct of burning coal is the phenomenon of "acid rain." Not much is known about what dangers acid rain might pose, but it is known that sulfur and nitrous oxides can create it, and that burning coal creates them. According to Dr. James M. Galloway of the University of Virginia, more than 2,000 Scandinavian lakes have been contaminated by acid rain, as have between 100 and 200 lakes in the New York State Adirondack Mountain region. Fish cannot reproduce in those lakes, Dr. Galloway said.

Western Impact. Slightly more than half of the nation's recoverable coal is in the American West. Most western coal is in seams near the earth's surface and is best extracted through strip mining. Western coal also has relatively little sulfur in it, which means it produces less pollution when burned than does eastern coal.

About 26 percent of the nation's 1976 coal production came from the West; that figure will grow in the future, because coal mining is booming there.

Gov. Arthur A. Link, D-N.D., spoke of westerners' fears of crash energy development on behalf of 16 western states before a House Interior subcommittee in June 1977. The states of Colorado, Montana, New Mexico, North Dakota and Wyoming "will probably experience great pressures to perhaps quadruple coal production by the end of the century," he said.

While such development will bring economic benefits, Gov. Link said, it also presents "enormous financial, environmental, and socio-economic burdens and impacts. There are dangers that the West, with its great natural beauty, agricultural assets, fragile ecology, and limited water supplies, could become . . . a 'national sacrifice area' or 'energy colony' for the rest of the nation."

Coal production had already created a boomtown impact in some western communities, Gov. Link testified, citing Craig, Colo., and Rock Springs, Wyo., as examples. Rapid coal development there has brought a host of problems, he said. "Trailer towns" have sprung up to house construction workers and their families. Schools were overcrowded. Crime rates were up. Virtually all goods and services were in short supply, all facilities inadequate. *(Energy boomtowns, appendix, p. 108-A)*

Link also cited farmers' and ranchers' fears that energy developers might outbid them for rights to scarce water

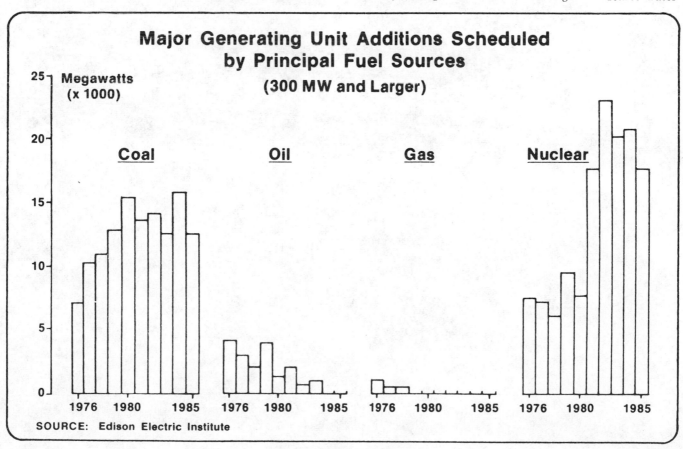

Major Generating Unit Additions Scheduled by Principal Fuel Sources
(300 MW and Larger)

SOURCE: Edison Electric Institute

supplies. He cited studies showing that energy developments in 11 western states will require between 2 million and 3 million acre feet of water by the year 2000.

Two aspects of the Carter plan would help ease the impact of the coal rush on western states. First, the White House supported strict strip mine controls and reclamation standards designed to protect fragile western ecology. The bill cleared Congress in 1977. *(Strip mining, p. 79)*

Second, the administration would require all new plants to install the best available pollution control technology. There had been fears that plants in the East would attempt to burn only low sulfur western coal to minimize pollution and thus avoid having to buy pollution control equipment. The Carter plans' requirement that all new plants must install pollution control devices was designed to eliminate that competitive advantage enjoyed by western coal. Since the coal's sulfur content becomes largely irrelevant to plant managers' decisions, the reasoning goes, eastern plants will contract for eastern coal to minimize transportation costs.

Fears that the West would be raped to produce coal for the East appeared to have been exaggerated, however. The FPC study of new power plants' coal needs through 1985 concluded that "about 94 percent of the incremental coal produced in the West will be used by new units in the West."

Electric Rate Reform: A Tricky Issue

There are, of course, the economic horror stories: people with electric heat and big rooms in a cold winter whose monthly electric bills total hundreds of dollars.

And there are other horror stories: people who do not use very much electricity, but who have little money. Sometimes they find their power shut off for non-payment of utility bills, like Eugene Kuhn, 74, of Mansfield, Ohio. Kuhn froze to death in January 1977 after the Ohio Edison Co. turned off his electricity because he failed to pay an $18.38 bill.

Cases like those illustrate the extremes of the problem, but the problem in its less extreme forms touches almost everyone. The problem is the price of electricity. After decades of cheap, easy availability, in the last several years the cost of electricity has risen astronomically.

Nationwide, the average price consumers paid for electricity rose 70 per cent between 1970 and 1976, according to the Federal Energy Administration (FEA).

Rep. John D. Dingell, D-Mich., chairman of a House subcommittee that examined the problem extensively, offered even more dramatic statistics. "Electric rates . . . after decreasing for a decade at an annual rate of almost 1 per cent, in 1970 began a rapid increase resulting in an almost 90 per cent increase in average rate per kilowatt hour by 1975," Dingell said.

The average residential bill for 500 kilowatt hours — a use level close to the average monthly residential consumption — rose about 7.4 per cent in 1975 to $19.26, according to the Federal Power Commission (FPC). The average bill for 1974 had been $17.93.

Families earning under $6,000 in 1975 on the average spent 5 per cent of their income on electricity, according to the Washington Center for Metropolitan Studies. *(Chart, p. 99)*

The figures have varied slightly from agency to agency, depending upon what data they used and how it was analyzed. But the statistics agreed on what it meant: Electricity was no longer cheap, and it was getting more expensive all the time.

Those central facts lead to two basic questions: (1) Why?, and (2) What can be done about it?

The basic answer to the first question was simple — the price of electricity rose dramatically because the costs of producing it have skyrocketed. That incontrovertible fact has transformed the entire economic structure of the utility industry.

The second question was as complex as a Zen riddle, and the solution was less satisfying. There is no easy answer, but there have been many suggestions. Most proposals called for revision of the economic formulas by which costs borne by utilities in making electricity are apportioned among consumers through billing rates. There was dissatisfaction with all of them because, regardless of how electric billing rates are revised, electricity still would cost a lot to produce and consumers still would have to pay a lot to consume it.

Even dedicated consumer lobbyists in Washington have faced up to that.

"We see that rates are going up sharply, and undoubtedly there is adequate justification for some of those increases," Lee C. White, then chairman of the Consumer Federation of America's Energy Policy Task Force, said in 1976 congressional testimony.

"I do not advocate, and I don't know how many consumer people who do believe, that we are about to see any drastic backward movement to those days of cheaper energy.

"Something might happen, there might be some breakthroughs, but I think we had better steel ourselves for high prices and for all I know, even higher prices," White said.

While experts were resigned to high costs, there has been general agreement on a need to revise electric rate structures, and proposals abound. Some promised no more than to hold future electricity price hikes below what they otherwise would be. Some were designed to help bill-payers and at the same time to meet the national need for energy conservation. Some, like the well-publicized "lifeline" concept, would guarantee a minimum amount of electricity to the impoverished at a price they could afford.

All were controversial, all were complex and all were grounded in the murky technicalities of utility industry economics.

And despite passage of the 1978 energy bill, the problems persisted. The Carter administration's April 1977 energy proposal had addressed the problems of revising utility rate structures. Carter wanted state agencies to be required to follow certain federal guidelines in rate-making in order to save energy. Congress was asked to ban declining block rate structures that promote electricity consumption and to require that utilities offer peak use pricing rates to customers willing to pay meter costs.

Although the House generally went along with the Carter utility rate revision proposals, the Senate version of the energy bill dropped virtually all of Carter's major innovations on the grounds that at the time there was no justification for extending federal authority into the complex matter of utility rates. The final 1978 version of the bill represented a compromise between the House and Senate

Electric generating station, Chalk Point, Md.

positions, requiring that state utility commissions only consider thoroughly a wide variety of rate reforms.

Background

Congressional Action

Various bills designed to reform electric utility rates were the subject of eight days of hearings in 1976 before the House Interstate and Foreign Commerce Subcommittee on Energy and Power, chaired by Rep. Dingell. Similar proposals were reviewed in two days of hearings by the Senate Commerce Committee.

That was as far as electric utility rate reform got in the 94th Congress; neither committee reported out a bill.

Congress served notice that it would take up the issue again in 1977, however, by adding provisions to legislation (HR 12169—PL 94-385) that extended the life of the FEA through 1977. The relevant provisions directed the FEA to develop proposals for improving utility rate design and to submit them to Congress by mid-February 1977. (The FEA subsequently was absorbed into the Energy Department created in October 1977 — *see p. 45*)

It was early March before FEA delivered its mandated report to Congress. The report, 276 pages long with four appendices, contained no policy recommendations. It was, in effect, a lengthy background discussion of the issue.

Industry Profile

To understand the controversies surrounding electric rates, it is first necessary to understand some basic facts about the electric industry.

The industry is dominated by the roughly 250 privately owned utility companies that provide about 80 per cent of the nation's electric power. Another 10 per cent of the nation's power comes from federally owned electric generation plants, half of which are under the Tennessee Valley Authority (TVA). State and local utility companies and cooperatives comprise the other 10 per cent.

Electric power systems are frighteningly expensive to build and maintain. The cliché is that the industry is the most "capital intensive" industry there is. What that means, according to the FEA, is that $3.47 must be invested to produce every annual dollar that sale of electric power produces. By contrast, the nation's automobile industry invests only $.67 per dollar of annual sales.

Because it is so enormously expensive, electric utilities have been granted local monopolies to avoid duplication and needless expense. Government theoretically protects the consumer from abuse by this monopoly economic power through regulating the industry. The FPC has regulated wholesale interstate sales of electric power, but the primary regulators are state utility commissions.

Setting Rates

Regulators set the price of sale of electricity, which means they set rates. In setting rates, the regulator must analyze a utility's costs and then set billing rates that will guarantee that the utility will get back enough cash to cover its expenses. For investor-owned utilities (the industry's backbone), the rate-makers also must allow rates high enough to generate enough profit to give the utility's stockholders a fair return on their investment.

The heart of the argument over how to fairly set rates lies in disputes over how to fairly determine a utility's costs. The two elements—rates and costs—are inextricably intertwined.

One of the concepts fundamental to the debate is determining what costs are eligible to be included within a utility's rate base. The rate base is the total value of assets and costs borne by the utility upon which a regulatory authority allows a rate of return.

Another key concept—and one subject to varying interpretation—involves determination of the costs borne in serving customers. Under the cost of service concept, ideally, a customer's bill reflects the costs borne by the utility in bringing him electricity. Both reformers and defenders of the status quo wave the flag of "cost-of-service" billing when justifying their approach to rate-making.

There are three basic customer classes—residential, commercial and industrial. Approximately 34 per cent of the nation's electricity is consumed by residential customers, about 24 per cent by commercial customers and about 38 per cent by industry. (The remaining 4 per cent is used primarily for street lighting and mass transit, according to the FPC.)

Each customer class imposes differing costs on the utility. Residential and commercial class customers require an extensive and expensive distribution system to convert high voltage power to low voltage and carry it to each final user. Industrial users, on the other hand, often can handle power straight from transmission lines at full strength high voltage. Industrial users also consume power in steadier, more dependable time patterns, imposing a more stable—if larger—drain on the power generation system over a 24-hour period.

Declining Block Rates. Because of those kinds of factors, the traditional approach to electricity pricing has been based on the principle of "declining block rates." Under that structure, which is in general use throughout the nation, the price charged a customer per unit of electricity drops as his consumption increases. This structure is based on the premise that the utility company's costs of serving each customer decline with increased consumption because the utility's fixed costs are spread further.

The declining block rate structure applies to all classes of customers. What it means in practice is that if the first block of electricity used—say 100 kilowatt hours—were priced at four cents per kilowatt hour, the next 100 would be priced at three cents, and succeeding blocks at successively lower prices.

The end result under that system is that large volume users end up paying less per unit of electricity than do small volume users.

In the industry's early days, the utilities sought to promote electricity consumption through such pricing practices. Their aim was to stimulate enough consumption to create a need for plant expansion, which would lead to economies of scale and lower average costs for all.

But now changing economic realities have fueled a movement to revamp the traditional declining block rate structure.

Soaring Costs

Basically what happened was the the cost of building new power plant capacity inflated so much over the past 15 years that economies of scale became impossible to achieve. According to the FEA, the cost per kilowatt of new plant capacity increased by 34 per cent between 1960 and 1970.

The cost increased another 68 per cent between 1970 and 1975. Building new plants no longer produces economies of scale, and reformers contend that means the rationale behind the declining block rate structure is no longer valid.

Inflation drove up utilities' costs for everything, but they were hit hardest in paying for fuel. According to the FEA, "fuel expenses are the largest production expenses for utilities.... Between 1970 and 1975, the price of oil, gas and coal used by utilities increased 403 per cent, 176 per cent, and 177 per cent respectively."

Those are the fuels that most electric power plants burn to generate electricity. Electric utilities in 1975 consumed 28 per cent of all energy burned in the nation, according to the FEA.

Roughly 44 per cent of the nation's power plants are coal-fired, the FEA said, and about 30 percent are powered by oil and gas. Roughly 16 per cent are hydroelectric, and the remaining 10 per cent are nuclear-powered.

The costs of electricity production vary according to what fuel a plant uses. Plants powered by fossil fuels—coal, residual oil, natural gas—are cheaper to build and safer than nuclear or hydroelectric plants.

But the rub there is that plants fired by fossil fuels are wasteful of energy resources in short supply and more expensive to operate once built, due mainly to high fuel costs. *(Chart, p. 100)*

The least expensive plants to build are those designed for use only when customer demand exceeds normal limits and becomes "peak" demand. Such facilities are designed to be thrown quickly into action and usually are powered by gas turbines and internal combustion engines. While comparatively cheap to build, their fuel costs and energy waste are enormous.

Soaring fuel costs led most regulatory authorities to permit utilities to pass their increased fuel expenses directly to their consumers through "fuel adjustment clauses." In 1975 all but seven states allowed some kind of fuel adjustment clause, according to the FEA.

In 1975 alone, according to a Library of Congress study for Sens. Edmund S. Muskie, D-Maine, and Lee Metcalf, D-Mont., private electric utilities earned $9.2 billion in new rates, and $5.9 billion of that was derived purely from fuel adjustment clauses.

"The massive and rising fuel adjustment charges are often automatic and therefore escape regulatory challenge," the two senators said.

Their displeasure mirrored consumer outrage at budget-breaking electric bills. Throughout the nation, state and local citizens' groups have fought utility rate increases and worked for revised rate structures for years.

All these trends leave electric utilities caught between soaring costs and outraged citizens. That combination threatens the economic structure of the entire industry. "These higher bills have caused tremendous resistance, by utility commissioners and by consumers, to additional rate increases that might be needed to maintain the overall financial health of the utility sector or to finance new plants," said Eric R. Zausner, deputy administrator of FEA, in 1976 testimony before the Senate Commerce Committee.

As political pressure against higher rates built, regulatory decisions lagged behind utility requests for higher rates and more money. As that happened, at the same time lead times for new plants stretched out to as long as 10 years. Environmental restrictions added to utilities' costs as well. As earnings declined relative to costs, outside

Average Annual Household Expenditures for Electricity
by Income Groups, May 1973-May 1975

Figures in parentheses are expenditures as a per cent of average income

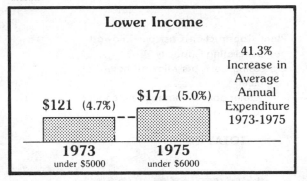

Lower Income

$121 (4.7%) 1973 under $5000 — $171 (5.0%) 1975 under $6000

41.3% Increase in Average Annual Expenditure 1973-1975

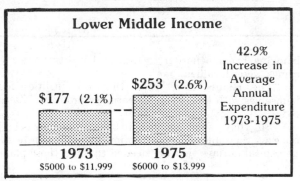

Lower Middle Income

$177 (2.1%) 1973 $5000 to $11,999 — $253 (2.6%) 1975 $6000 to $13,999

42.9% Increase in Average Annual Expenditure 1973-1975

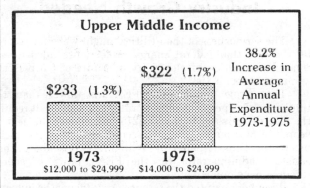

Upper Middle Income

$233 (1.3%) 1973 $12,000 to $24,999 — $322 (1.7%) 1975 $14,000 to $24,999

38.2% Increase in Average Annual Expenditure 1973-1975

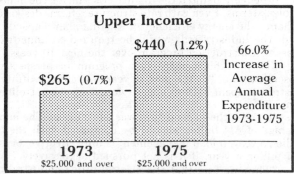

Upper Income

$265 (0.7%) 1973 $25,000 and over — $440 (1.2%) 1975 $25,000 and over

66.0% Increase in Average Annual Expenditure 1973-1975

SOURCE: Washington Center for Metropolitan Studies, 1973 and 1976

Power Production Costs by Privately-Owned Electric Utilities by Type of Generation, 1974

	Fossil-Fired Steam Power Production[1]	Nuclear Power Production	Hydroelectric Power Production	Other Power Production[2]
Plant Construction Cost per Kilowatt of Generating Capacity	$ 136	$ 230	$ 196	$ 91
Operating Costs per Kilowatt-hour				
Fuel	$ 9.050	$ 2.389	$——	$20.535
Other operation and maintenance	1.341	2.065	1.239	4.067
Carrying cost of plant	4.148	8.454	6.193	11.751
TOTAL COST	$14.539	$12.908	$7.432	$36.353

[1] Includes coal, residual fuel oil, and some natural gas.
[2] Primarily gas turbines and internal combustion engines.

SOURCE: Federal Power Commission

financing became harder to find and utility bond credit ratings were devalued.

"The results have been that the utilities found themselves with a very serious earnings problem," Zausner said.

"So they were caught in the classic cash flow squeeze...they allowed construction plans to slip to avoid the capital outlays that are needed to build those plants."

Industry Growth Needed

The seriousness of the utilities' plight was underscored by the fact that federal energy projections called for increased production of electricity at a rate of 5.5 per cent annually through 1985.

That projection by the FEA was lower than the traditional 7.5 per cent annual rate, but still "will require the electric industry to invest $275-billion over the next 10 years" in new plant capacity, according to 1976 testimony before the Dingell panel by William G. Rosenberg, then assistant administrator for the FEA's office of energy resource development.

Rosenberg painted the finance crisis facing the industry in bleak terms. Even with rate structure reforms designed to enhance the energy efficiency of existing plant capacity, he said, the industry still would be required to undertake a massive construction program over the next 10 years.

"To put this construction program in perspective," Rosenberg said, "in the past 10 years the electric utility industry has spent $110-billion, or an average of $11-billion a year.

"In 1975 the expenditure was $15-billion. The annual average of $11-billion should be compared with the $21-billion a year, if load management is fully effective, or up to $27-billion a year, if it is not pursued aggressively."

"Thus we find that the electric utility industry must face a doubling of its capital requirements at a time when it has suffered what is perceived by most observers a substantial weakening of its financial condition."

Load Management Proposals

Most experts agreed that massive expansion by the utility industry would be necessary over the next few years. But some experts argued that the extent of expansion required could be reduced through effective "load management."

The concept of "load" refers to the amount of demand placed by customers on a utility's generating capacity. Demand varies by time; it fluctuates by season, by days of the week, by hours of the day. A utility is obligated to have available sufficient production capacity to meet the heaviest, or "peak," demand. When demand is less than peak, then a portion of the utility's capacity lies idle.

The measurement index for determining how much of a utility's capacity is actually used is called the "load factor," which is the ratio of average utility load to peak load.

Between 1965 and 1975, the average annual load factors for the nation's electric industry declined from 65 per cent to 61 per cent, according to the FEA. That meant that a growing proportion of plant capacity was lying idle more often, which hurts utilities economically.

According to 1976 testimony before the Dingell subcommittee by Roger W. Sant, then FEA's assistant administrator for energy conservation and environment, the lower load factor trend "can be traced to the growth of temperature sensitive loads, i.e., loads that are at their greatest during the hottest days of the summer and the coldest days of the winter. This growth can be traced in turn to the general rise in American living standards..." which allowed electric heating and air conditioning of homes, as well as an endless supply of electric-powered gadgets.

Sant said that when utilities run low load factors—when a lot of their plant capacity is not in use—there are several unfortunate consequences. His reasoning was based on the fact that most utilities employ less efficient generating equipment when they gear up to meet peak loads. The consequences, Sant said, are that utilities must bear the fixed costs for those facilities 24 hours a day even though they are not producing or returning revenue much of the time; that facilities used to meet peak demand burn more fuel to produce a given amount of power than do baseload plants, which means their inefficiency and operating costs are higher; and that use of those peak load facilities, because they "depend almost completely on oil or natural gas," is inconsistent with national energy goals to reduce consumption of those fuels.

"For those reasons," Sant said, "FEA is committed to a policy of promoting load management."

The aim of load management is to raise load factors, to spread demand more evenly. If successful, load management would result in baseload plants—which are more efficient handling a greater portion of overall system load. It also would reduce the need to build expensive new capacity, which even if efficient, is still painfully expensive.

Sant said implementation of load management policies could "save at least $60-billion in cumulative capital costs by 1985. For consumers, this level of savings translates into an 8 per cent drop in the real price of electricity, or savings of approximately $7-billion in electric bills every year.

"Moreover," Sant continued, "customers of all classes can reduce their electric bills by the order of 15 or 20 per cent if their present consumption patterns tend to be off-peak, or if they can shift a portion of their electricity usage away from peak periods."

To achieve those results, load factors would have to be raised to an annual average of 69 per cent, Sant said.

Time-of-Use Pricing

The key to load management involves revising the way electric rates are structured so that customers are billed at rates that vary according to the time they use electricity. Electricity consumed during peak periods would cost more per kilowatt hour than electricity consumed off-peak. This kind of rate design is usually termed "peak load" pricing or "time-of-use" pricing.

Peaks occur on extremely hot or cold days. But daily peaks occur at regular periods too, such as the first two hours after workers get home, or the hours when meals are cooked. Peak periods vary from utility to utility, due to economic and cultural differences of service areas.

The idea behind peak load pricing is that consumers will alter their consumption pattern if it saves them money, or especially, if it costs them penalizing amounts of cash to continue using electricity during peak hours.

But that is only part of the overall "load management" concept. Proponents recognize that even with a heavy price incentive, there still could be times when consumers would pay any price to satisfy a yearning for the benefits of electricity. One of those times, theoretically, might be the fourth or fifth day of a sweltering summer heat wave, when air conditioners would be turned to "max" no matter what the costs. Such a situation is termed a "needle peak." Even if rare, the problem is that a utility must have sufficient capacity to cope with such demand.

Therefore, for time-of-use pricing to be effective, proponents urge combining that approach with other load management techniques to reduce utility load factors. Sant told the Dingell panel that FEA backed time-of-use pricing combined with two other practices: (1) interruptible rates, which give large industrial consumers reduced rates in exchange for agreement that their service can be shut off on short notice, and (2) mechanical load control systems, which allow selective reduction of electricity flow for short periods of time.

Load Management Devices

There are a wide variety of load management devices, according to the FEA's 1977 study. With some, the utility would control power flow interruptions, such as with:

● Circuit breakers, which would automatically cut power off to certain circuits when switched on;
● Time switches, which are clocklike devices which cut power to certain circuits at pre-set times;
● Cycling regulators, which cycle power to certain circuits, such as air conditioners, on and off in regulated spurts, such as each 15 minutes;
● Instruments that would regulate which of several competing loads would get power when several were turned on simultaneously, perhaps allowing power to flow to an electric range while cutting power to an electric water heater;
● "Ripple" or radio control systems which allow the utility to send short bursts of high voltage current, or radio signals, to automatically cut power to selected appliances;
● Utility storage systems, with which electricity generated during off-peak hours could be converted to another energy form, such as heat, and stored for later reconversion and use during peak hours.

There are a number of similar devices that would be at the control of the customer. Among those are hybrid heat systems, which would be fueled by electricity during off-peak hours and by another fuel during peak periods; warning devices to alert a consumer when a peak period was current; and customer storage devices like special batteries.

Marginal Cost Pricing

Proponents of load management were convinced that a new method of pricing was necessary because the traditional declining block approach did not fairly apportion the costs of utility service.

"Electric rate structures generally in effect in the United States fail to reflect the marginal costs of supplying electricity," FEA's Sant declared.

The theory of marginal costs, most simply defined, holds that the price of one extra unit of any commodity should equal the cost of producing that additional unit. Proponents of marginal cost pricing for electricity pointed out that the costs of producing it vary by time. Conventional electric rates do not reflect that variance, however.

"As a result," Sant explained, "on the one hand, peak period electricity is priced below its marginal costs, and is, consequently oversold. On the other hand, electricity consumed during off-peak periods is priced above its marginal costs, and is consequently undersold."

The concept of marginal costs in conjunction with time of use pricing, or other rate reform proposals, has made some people uncomfortable, especially representatives of large industries.

Basically, they feared that such a system would make industrial customers bear a high and unfair level of utility costs. Their fears were based on the fact that large industrial users exert a much steadier drain on a utility over 24 hours than do most residential users, and consequently, the large user's load is not so variable by time. Stiff peak hour prices would hit them less hard because they are less able to alter their demand patterns.

Ronald S. Wishart, executive director of a trade association of 10 large industrial users called the Electricity Consumers Resource Council (ELCON), spoke of industry's concerns before the Dingell panel.

"[D]eclining block rates reflect the realities of a utility's incurred costs," he said. "Distribution costs are markedly less for large users.... Those who do contend that industrial users get a free ride or preferential treatment at the cost of residential consumers have simply not considered these realities of costs."

There are other objections. Rep. Clarence J. Brown, R-Ohio, noted during the Dingell hearings that if industries tried to shift their working schedules to off-peak hours, plantworkers might have disrupted lifestyles. He also noted skeptically that attempts to shift the timing of electricity demand might run counter to "the fact that a lot of people like to watch television in prime time...(and) the fact that in New York it gets dark now in the afternoon and people have to start cooking dinner for their husbands who get home at that time."

Brown also voiced another concern widely held: "...I think marginal cost pricing can have about five definitions," he said. Depending upon how one defines the application of the principle, Brown suggested, marginal cost pricing "is kind of like the blessing of childbirth. There are certain circumstances in which it is not as much of a blessing as in others."

European Experience. Despite fears and uncertainty, proponents of rate reforms based on marginal costs theory argued that such systems have worked elsewhere. Specifically, they noted that Western European nations, which have not had the history of cheap energy that America has had, have used such approaches successfully for years. For example, Switzerland maintained annual load for factors of around 70 per cent, according to the FEA.

The experience of Great Britain may give pause, however. The 1977 FEA study noted that although residential consumption patterns shifted significantly to off-peak hour use under time-of-use pricing, and although load factors improved considerably, "the costs of metering completely eliminated the financial gains of the individual consumer."

Few meters in America are equipped to measure time of use. Cost estimates vary, but the lowest figure for a residential meter is about $71. High costs for meter installation could cancel out price benefits to American consumers. The FEA study said it was impossible to determine whether meter costs would have that effect.

Control panel, Chalk Point generating station

Other Reform Proposals

Other rate reform proposals have been widely circulated. Among them were:

Lifeline Rates

Under this concept, a certain minimum level of electricity is guaranteed to certain residential class customers at a low price. The amount of electricity guaranteed varies with proposals, but usually is in the range of 300 to 500 kilowatt hours per month. The proposals vary in application as well: some are limited to people over 65, some to poor families within specified income levels, and some are subject to other limitations.

Another variation among lifeline proposals is found in prescribed methods of making up the money lost in giving lifeline recipients a break on their electricity prices. Some lifeline proposals would spread the extra costs only to other residential class customers. Other proposals would spread the extra costs among all consumer classes.

Advocates of lifeline rates asserted that a minimum amount of electricity — usually defined as enough to provide lighting and food refrigeration — should be available to the poor as a "basic human right."

The utility industry has opposed lifeline rates. Such an approach "would mark a drastic departure from cost-based ratemaking," maintained W. Donham Crawford, president of Edison Electric Institute, an association of most privately owned utilities, in congressional testimony. Crawford said lifeline proposals are based on a premise that low income homes use less electricity, which he said was not necessarily true. He added that if government wants to provide relief to the poor for high electric bills, it should do so directly through programs like energy stamps instead of making utilities into social welfare agencies.

The 1977 FEA study concluded that: "Lifeline rates are not likely to affect significantly the overall cost of supplying electricity or aggregate consumption, although they are likely to redistribute consumption within the residential sector.

"These rates make cost allocation less fair in the traditional cost-of-service sense, since larger customers will explicitly subsidize those customers with lifeline rates."

Some form of lifeline rates were in effect in parts of California, Maine, Ohio, Pennsylvania and Vermont, the FEA study said.

Flat Rates

Under this formula, each kilwatt hour would be priced the same to all users in all classes. Advocates said traditional declining block rates were unfair and argued that costs of serving large customers like industries are not significantly different from costs of serving small ones, like residences. Further, they argued that flat rates would give small consumers a break and discourage waste at the same time.

The FEA study concluded that flat rates would decrease electricity consumption and probably force large electricity users to switch to other fuels. Flat rates, the FEA said, "do not accurately reflect utility costs...."

Inverted Rates

This structure would invert the existing declining block rate structure by pricing successive blocks of electricity higher. Proponents said this would give small consumers a break and reduce the need for constructing new power plants by encouraging conservation.

The FEA study concluded that the same problems besetting flat rate proposals also plague inverted rates.

"Construction In Progress"

There are still other proposals advanced in any comprehensive discussion of reforming electric rates. One of the most controversial concerns whether rate-making authorities should allow a utility's costs for "construction work in progress (CWIP)" to be included in the utility's rate base.

Industry spokesmen have said allowance of construction work in progress in the rate base was an essential element in meeting the capital needs associated with growing electricity requirements." But consumer advocates feared that allowing utilities to charge customers for construction costs before the new facilities were operating would encourage utilities to build even when new facilities might not be needed.

Richard Morgan of Environmental Action Foundation, a clearinghouse on rate reform for numerous consumer and environmental groups, testified in House hearings that such allowances were "similar to a landlord requiring his tenants to pay rent five years in advance." He quoted estimates that allowance of construction work in progress costs in rate bases would raise consumer bills between 11 and 17 percent.

Carter Proposals

In announcing hs energy plan April 20, 1977, Carter asked Congress to ban declining block rate structures and to require utilities to offer either daily off-peak rates to each customer who was willing to pay metering costs, or provide a direct load management system. Under the Carter plan, utilities would be required to offer lower rates to customers who were willing to have their power interrupted at times of highest demand. Master metering would generally be prohibited in new structures. Legislation was also requested mandating utilities to offer home insulation financed by loads repaid through monthly utility bills.

The 1977 House-passed version of the energy bill generally followed Carter's proposals. Provisions of the bill would establish, for the first time, minimum national standards for states to follow in setting electric rates. Declining block rate structures would be prohibited except where they could be proven to reflect costs of service, and utilities were required to use "time of use" and seasonal rates.

However, most of Carter's far-reaching initiatives did not survive Senate action. When the bill reached the Senate floor, manager J. Bennett Johnston, D-La., explained why the Senate Energy Committee had turned down the administration plan. Johnston said the administration bill "contemplated a radical extension of federal authority into the highly complex matter of the design of retail rates for electricity." He said the problem had traditionally been handled at the state level because of geographic, climatic and economic regional differences.

The utility rate provisions of the bill agreed to by conferees in late 1977 and cleared by Congress in 1978 were stronger than the Senate bill but weaker than the original House version. The bill would require each state utility commission to consider thoroughly a wide range of reforms as well as placing a prohibition on the use of "declining block rates." *(Details, energy bill, p. 5)*

Nuclear Industry Pushes Licensing Reform

At 4 a.m. on March 28, 1979, the cooling system at the Three Mile Island nuclear power plant near Harrisburg, Pa., broke down, causing the worst accident ever at a commercial nuclear plant. The accident occurred despite redundant safety features that engineers described as "defense in depth."

The crisis left the public with a series of graphic images, among them: top level government officials debating evacuation of a half million people; the state capital at Harrisburg temporarily reduced to a veritable ghost town as residents stayed inside; and the Pentagon flying in tons of lead bricks to assist a team of government officials in bringing the overheated reactor under control. The net result appeared to have been increasing confusion among average citizens about nuclear power safety and new questions about the industry's future.

Less than 10 years ago, America's energy planners looked to nuclear power as the fuel of the future. But in recent years that vision has looked increasingly like a fading dream. There have been but a handful of new reactors ordered by electric utilities between 1973 and 1978. The cost of constructing nuclear plants has skyrocketed throughout the 1970s, far beyond the normal inflation rate.

With future electricity demand uncertain, with it taking 10 years or longer to bring new nuclear plants into operation, utilities have found the economic risks too great. They have cancelled more than 30 earlier decisions to build new nuclear reactors, and have deferred indefinitely construction plans on scores more.

One of the obstacles to increased use of nuclear power has been the lengthy licensing process. As of early 1979, 10 to 12 years passed between the time a utility decided to build a nuclear power plant and the time that plant was licensed.

Carter Proposal

Responding to this problem, the Carter administration March 17, 1978, unveiled its proposal to streamline the licensing of nuclear power plants. The action came after 11 months of bureaucratic infighting.

"We believe at the present time that the nuclear option is barely alive," Energy Secretary James R. Schlesinger told a news conference. The proposed bill, a department release said, was "intended to assure that nuclear power will remain a viable option." Schlesinger said the proposed bill would cut the licensing time lag to about 6.5 years.

But because it would take several years before the proposal could be implemented, he said, "It will be a decade approximately before we begin to see the effects of these new procedures."

President Carter had called for streamlining the licensing process April 20, 1977, in his energy policy speech to Congress. The Energy Department had prepared a draft bill by August, but objections to it from other agencies and environmental and public interest groups led to months of internal administration debate and redrafting.

In the end, however, it apeared Schlesinger had won the bureaucratic war; the bill as submitted was strikingly similar to what his department had proposed originally.

The proposed legislation was introduced into both chambers of Congress March 21, 1978 (S 2775, HR 1704). However, the bill failed to clear Congress that year.

The last hope for even limited action by the 95th Congress was in a House Energy panel chaired by Morris K. Udall, D-Ariz. But Udall abandoned his plan for an "informal" markup Aug. 14 when he ran into resistance from members of his Interior Subcommittee on Energy.

Neither the House Commerce Committee, which shared jurisdiction, nor the Senate Environment Committee reported a licensing reform bill in 1978.

"We should give guidance [to the Carter administration] before we fold our tents for the year," Udall told the panel. But James Weaver, D-Ore., who opposed the administration bill, said it would be "going into the snake pit for no purpose" to hold a markup where there was no hope of further action.

Bob Carr, D-Mich., agreed with Weaver. He complained that the administration had devised changes to end delays in nuclear licensing without first pinpointing what caused the delays.

Jonathan B. Bingham, D-N.Y., argued that a markup would be useful because the panel could "crystallize" its thinking and "be further along when we come back next year."

When a motion by Carr to end the markup appeared about to fail, Carr noted the absence of a quorum. The eight members present were one shy of the required number. After a brief attempt to find another member, Udall gave up trying to meet on licensing reform in 1978.

Reaction

Initial reactions served warning that the proposal faced a rocky road.

The Atomic Industrial Forum, the nuclear industry's trade association, welcomed the bill but said it "needs substantial improvement."

Environmentalists and public interest groups said the bill gave short shrift to environmental concerns, unfairly restricted public access to the licensing process, ignored the real reasons behind nuclear power's development problems, failed to remedy existing problems associated with nuclear plants, such as where to store nuclear wastes, and proposed ineffective reforms which existing law already provided.

"It's a badly conceived, badly drafted and badly motivated piece of legislation," said Anthony Z. Roisman, a lawyer with the Natural Resources Defense Council. "[The bill] represents the final corruption of the president's moral and political courage on the nuclear issue. . . . The president has chosen to pay the price of losing his environmental constituency in exchange for a legislative proposal that will not win him a new constituency. This is curious politics for an election year."

Background

As recently as 1972, the government was forecasting that nuclear power by the year 2000 would provide 1,200 gigawats (GWe) of electricity. (A gigawatt equals a million kilowatts.) In 1975, the government had cut that forecast by a third, to 800 GWe. In 1977, the Carter administration projected a nuclear capacity in the year 2000 of only 380 GWe, less than half the 1975 expectation and less than a third of 1972. *(Projections, box, p. 110)*

Industry Worried

Even the industry's leaders conceded the future looked bleak. Unless new reactor orders come soon, said Craig Hosmer, president of the American Nuclear Energy Council, in an Oct. 13, 1977, letter to a senior White House aide, "the U.S. nuclear industry will move quickly to extinction."

But the nuclear industry was not quite ready to die. In fact, its spokesmen said, if it could just hold on a few years, the future might yet turn its way.

Electric utilities remain central to the American economy, and figure to remain so for a long time. Electric power plants run on steam, which turns turbines, which power generators, which produce electricity.

The steam is produced by intense heat. And the heat is produced in two ways: either by burning immense quantities of fossil fuels or by a nuclear fission reaction.

With oil and natural gas supplies insecure, and with their prices skyrocketing, there were not many realistic options left to utility executives contemplating plant expansion.

Even though Jimmy Carter stressed while campaigning that he viewed nuclear power "as a last resort," the nuclear industry pressed his administration for help. And in 1978 it drew support from sources unaccustomed to being nuclear's allies.

On Feb. 27, 1978, Carter was presented with a three-page statement from a majority of the nation's governors calling for "a more positive commitment to nuclear energy by the administration.... The President must take the lead and rally public support...." The governors' stand followed by about a month a policy statement from the NAACP calling for full development of nuclear power, including breeder reactors, to enhance economic opportunities for minorities. *(Breeder reactors, box, p. 111)*

Carter promised in his April 1977 energy message to send Congress legislation designed to cut red tape then entangling the licensing of nuclear power plants. That tangle added three years and millions of dollars to plant construction, the industry said.

"I know how bad things are," conceded George L. Gleason, executive vice president of the American Nuclear Energy Council — the industry's lobbying arm — during an interview. "It's going to get worse before it gets better.

"Some days I question whether we can sustain this thing as a viable industry," Gleason said.

What Went Wrong

After World War II, America's booming economy triggered an energy growth binge. For almost 30 years, electricity consumption grew at a profitable, predictable average rate of seven to eight percent per year. Utility expansion plans were based directly on that predictable future demand for more power.

Then in October 1973, the Arab oil embargo and the resultant two-year recession slammed the brakes on electric utility expansion. In 1974 and 1975 there was virtually no growth in demand for electric power.

Many utilities were caught with their financial pants down. In the late 1960s and early 1970s, the push for clean air had driven many of them to shift their power plants from coal to oil, which caused less pollution. The conversion to oil required large capital outlays. When oil prices quadrupled in 1973-74, "the utilities were put into a very difficult financial bind," explained Eric S. Beckjord, acting director of the Department of Energy's nuclear power division, in remarks Dec. 13, 1977, at a department briefing.

"In fact, there was a period in 1974 where a number of utilities were financially very much on the edge," Beckjord said. "So they did what they had to do. They stopped all new construction projects, or almost all."

September 1974 was the high point for America's nuclear power industry. At that time there were 239 reactors totaling more than 237,000 megawatts (MWe) capacity either operating, under construction, or on order. *(For 1978 figures, see map p. 107)*

Downhill Slide

Between June 30, 1974, and April 30, 1976, utilities cancelled 23 orders for nuclear reactors, according to the Nuclear Regulatory Commission. In the same period utilities deferred plans for building another 143 reactors previously announced, citing lack of funds, reduced needs for the extra power, construction delays, and — in a few cases — governmental red tape as the cause.

In 1976, the two-year absence of growth in consumer demand for power lifted; electricity production was up 5.5 percent. In 1977, it rose again, up about 5 percent. And a 1975 study by the Edison Electric Institute, the trade association for private utilities, projected a continued electrical demand growth rate of about 5 percent annually through the year 2000.

But the rise in demand did not signal a turn in the fortunes of nuclear power. According to the Atomic Industrial Forum, the nuclear industry's trade association, utilities canceled orders for two nuclear reactors in 1976 and six more in 1977. They also deferred seven nuclear reactor orders in 1976, and another 43 in 1977.

Between October 1977 and the end of January 1978, according to the Nuclear Regulatory Commission, utilities

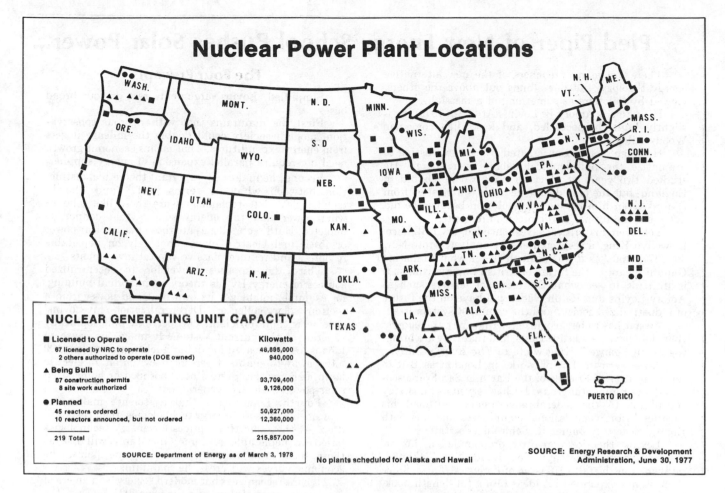

Nuclear Power Plant Locations

NUCLEAR GENERATING UNIT CAPACITY

	Kilowatts
■ **Licensed to Operate**	
67 licensed by NRC to operate	48,895,000
2 others authorized to operate (DOE owned)	940,000
▲ **Being Built**	
87 construction permits	93,709,400
8 site work authorized	9,126,000
● **Planned**	
45 reactors ordered	50,927,000
10 reactors announced, but not ordered	12,360,000
219 Total	**215,857,000**

SOURCE: Department of Energy as of March 3, 1978

No plants scheduled for Alaska and Hawaii

SOURCE: Energy Research & Development Administration, June 30, 1977

cancelled nine reactor orders and deferred three more. Of the cancellations, seven explained only that they had changed their long-range plans, one switched its order from a nuclear to a fossil fuel plant and one did not list a cause.

New orders for nuclear reactors hardly balanced that trend. Utilities placed only five new reactor orders in 1975; only three in 1976; and only four in 1977, according to the Atomic Industrial Forum.

Vendors' Slump

Four American firms make nuclear reactors: General Electric, Westinghouse, Babcock & Wilcox and Combustion Engineering Inc. As of early 1979, they could live off of filling back orders. But without new orders, the $10 billion a year industry soon would be in serious trouble. Together, the four reactor "vendors" were geared to deliver about 30 plants annually; delivering 20 a year would sustain a "viable industry" according to *Business Week*.

But to meet the Carter administration's projection of 380,000 MWe of nuclear power by the year 2000 meant only about 11 new plants needed to be ordered each year, according to Carl Walske, president of the Atomic Industrial Forum Inc. And, Walske added, through 1980 the prospects were that new orders would be scarcely half that much.

As Walske noted, to meet the 380,000 MWe target by the year 2000, only about 164,000 MWe in new orders must be added to existing orders and capacity of roughly 216,000 MWe. If the administration and the industry were success-

ful in their drive to reduce the lead time for a plant to eight years from the existing 10 to 12, Walske reasoned, the administration's projection of 380,000 MWe could be met with new orders averaging 11 plants a year through 1992. But a 1977 industry survey led Walske to conclude that nationally, utilities would order no more than 15 new reactors through 1979.

"[F]or the manufacturers to continue in business," Walske wrote in the November 1977 *Nuclear Engineering International* magazine, "they will eventually have to receive more orders."

But there was no certainty those orders would be for nuclear plants. In a July 1977 speech, Walske said: "In the past, we advocates of nuclear power have had one outstanding asset, namely the sincere belief of most utility executives that nuclear was the best way for them to go.

"They felt it produced the lowest cost power, was environmentally attractive and was very safe. But utility executives have been through a lot in the past four years. They stopped ordering new generating capacity — of all kinds.

"We know that electric load growth resumed last year [1976] and continues this year [1977]," Walske said. "New plant orders must come in the future. When? And for what type of units? These are our questions."

Nuclear Economics

The situation posed complex problems and challenges, both economic and political.

Pied Piper of New Energy School Pushes Solar Power...

There are many preachers of the new alternative energy theology, but one stands out above the others, viewed by followers as something of a messiah.

His name is Amory B. Lovins. At 30 (in 1979), he is slightly built, bespectacled, and looks like comedian Woody Allen.

He might have been created by central casting to dramatize the philosophical debate over energy. He studied two years at Harvard and two at Oxford in England, but the only degree he holds is a masters from Oxford given him by special resolution because he did not meet the formal academic requirements.

Yet even his critics have conceded his brilliance. Llewellyn King, a respected energy analyst, wrote Nov. 30, 1977, that "as it was difficult to see what Mahatma Gandhi meant to the future of British imperialism, so it is difficult to see what the effect of leaders such as Amory Lovins and Ralph Nader will have on the future of industrialized society and the capitalist system itself.

"What has to be recognized is that they are leaders: that they have persuasive views, and that they are bringing about change," King wrote in *The Energy Daily*.

An American, Lovins works in London as British representative of Friends of the Earth, a San Francisco-based environmental group. He has served as an energy consultant to the federal government, outlined his theories before congressional committees and met with Energy Secretary James R. Schlesinger's staff.

Lovins' theories were first propounded in his article "Energy Strategy: The Road Not Taken?", published in the fall 1976 issue of *Foreign Affairs.* Since then he has expanded his ideas into a full-length book, "Soft Energy Paths: Toward a Durable Peace."

The Four Precepts

Simplified, Lovins' arguments rest on four broad bases.

First, he maintains that with rigorous conservation, modern society could double the mileage it gets from energy expenditures. That means economic growth need not require parallel expansion of energy supplies.

Second, he makes an important theoretical distinction between what he terms "soft" and "hard" technologies. Soft technologies are those like solar or wind power that tap energy sources that cannot be depleted. Hard technologies are those like nuclear power or fossil fuel electric plants that rely on depletable resources and require massive capital investments.

Third, he espouses conversion to decentralized sources of energy. By his theory an individual building, for example, might get its own heat and power from a rooftop solar collector. Decentralization in Lovins' scheme is more efficient, cheaper and philosophically superior to the current system. It makes no sense to Lovins to require a billion dollar nuclear power plant 100 miles away to enable a person to switch on an electric lamp at home. He prefers neighborhood or home-sized solar-powered electric generators.

Fourth, Lovins says that as science makes improvements in "soft" energy technologies, their costs will drop. At the same time, prices for energy technologies based on depletable resources inevitably will rise as those fuels grow more scarce. At some point, the economic curves will cross, he maintains.

Lovins recognizes that modern society is in an era of energy transition. By around the year 2025, he says, the

On pure economics, energy experts said there was a good case to be made for nuclear power." ...[W]e conclude that the trade-off between coal and nuclear on direct economic grounds is a close one, with many uncertainties, and will vary with local conditions and expectations in each case," stated an authoritative and influential assessment of nuclear power issued in spring 1977 by the Ford Foundation and the Mitre Corp.

"...[D]espite large uncertainties, nuclear power will on the average probably be somewhat less costly than coal-generated power in most of the United States, or, to be more precise, in areas that contain most of the country's population.

"The advantage is likely to be largest in New England and in parts of the South. In large areas of the West, containing a small fraction of the country's population, coal-generated power is likely to be less costly than nuclear power," the report said. "In some areas, the costs are expected to be very similar."

Construction costs, the Ford Foundation study observed, dominated nuclear power plant expenses, not labor, fuel or maintenance charges. "The actual cost of constructing nuclear power plants has greatly exceeded original estimates," the study noted.

"The cost per kilowatt for plants becoming operational in 1976 is double those that became operational in 1970," it said. Such factors may "cast grave doubt on the ability of

the industry to predict or control costs for future plants."

Despite variations and uncertainties, the report concluded that on the average it would cost about $1,000 per kilowatt for large units going into operation in 1985.

Rating Plant Efficiency

That estimate, the authors warned, was dependent on the operating efficiency of the plant concerned. That measure, known as the capacity factor or plant reliability, has been notoriously low for nuclear plants.

The efficiency rate is derived by taking the total amount of electricity produced annually by a unit and dividing into that figure the amount of electricity the unit theoretically could produce if it ran constantly for a year.

According to the Department of Energy, the nation's 65 nuclear reactors operating during 1977 attained 62.8 percent efficiency, significantly higher than the 1976 rating of 57.4 percent.

The Ford Foundation report warned that such measures can be misleading, depending upon what technical data are used. They also warned that most new nuclear plants are large, averaging 1,000 MWe, and that such large plants have not been operating long enough for adequate measurement. "Several analyses suggest that performance is poorer for large units," the report stated. It said an averaging of large units' efficiency ratings for 1975 produced a low figure of only 51.1 percent.

...Establishment Finds His Ideas Heretical and Unworkable

"soft" technologies can be firmly in place if society's managers begin to implement them now. In the meantime, he insists, nuclear power can be avoided altogether.

Not All Agree

Others have espoused similar conceptual arguments but not so persuasively. One measure of Lovins' impact has been the reaction to him by opponents.

Industry's Reaction

The Edison Electric Institute, the trade association for the nation's privately owned utilities, devoted an entire issue of its bimonthly magazine to refutations of Lovins' analyses.

Ten critical essays attacking Lovins' views were published in June 1977, as a book: "Soft vs. Hard Energy Paths," by Charles Yulish, a consultant to the nuclear industry.

"The fact that Pied Piper Amory Lovins was welcomed into the Oval Office by the President to spread his anti-energy heresies ought to shiver the establishment's timbers— but it didn't seem to," fumed Craig Hosmer, president of the American Nuclear Energy Council in a speech Nov. 28, 1977, to a nuclear industry audience.

The Administration's Thoughts

John F. O'Leary, deputy secretary of the Department of Energy and the federal government's number two energy authority, said in an interview with Congressional Quarterly he has "great respect for Lovins as a thinker."

However, O'Leary said, he thought Lovins "is looking upon energy as a vehicle for social change.... I think he doesn't like the kind of world we find here."

O'Leary said Lovins and consumer advocate Ralph Nader "have certain similarities in their lifestyle—relatively spartan. There is a very telling reference in that book of his, the one that caused all the stir, where he describes the society that he would like as 'living in frugal elegance.' "

O'Leary said that Lovins explained that such a lifestyle would be rich in cultivation of the mind and short on material goods. And that is not the way a majority of Americans, rightly or wrongly, have chosen to live, O'Leary said.

He also observed that Lovins travels by transAtlantic jet many times annually, "so he's a big energy consumer. His lifestyle is made possible, despite the 'elegant frugality,' by a surplus of energy...."

Fifty Years To Solar

O'Leary flatly maintained that Lovins' vision of energy economics does not work.

"It is not a feasible option now. We just don't have the economics," he said. "You can go out and find half a dozen good hard analyses that just simply destroy his economics."

But if energy costs continue to go up and work continues in soft technologies to bring their costs down, then Lovins' theory might be feasible, O'Leary said.

"I'd like to see it. If the economics get there, that's great. And indeed, let me tell you, in my judgment we must go to solar.... [But] I think we've got 50 years before we have to get there."

Nevertheless, the Ford Foundation study said, large reactors should in time prove as reliable as small ones. Therefore energy planners realistically could count on new large nuclear units attaining an average efficiency rating of 60 percent.

New large coal plants by comparison would attain exactly the same rating — 60 percent — on average, if equipped with scrubbers to control pollution, the report said.

The Department of Energy agreed at a Dec. 13, 1977, briefing that nuclear power would be cheaper on the average than coal-generated power. Beckjord, head of the nuclear division, said that for plants going into service in 1985, a nuclear unit would cost about three cents per kilowatt hour. That would be 10 percent less than a coal-powered plant and "of course, it is far less than it would be from an oil-fired station," he said.

Beckjord cautioned however, that his estimates presumed an efficiency rating of 65 percent. "Clearly, if the capacity factor should be less than that, then the margin favoring nuclear would be less and eventually would disappear," he conceded.

Coal vs. Nuclear

The case for using both fuels was highlighted by the 1977-78 coal strike. The United Mine Workers walked off their jobs on Dec. 6, 1977. By mid-February 1978 the

Midwest was experiencing serious power shortages. By early March, the situation clearly was growing into a national crisis. From it, the nuclear industry drew some hope.

On Feb. 15, Gleason of the American Nuclear Energy Council testified before the House Interior Committee on the role nuclear power was playing during the coal strike. His message was that utilities with nuclear reactors were safe from the strike and producing electricity. Nuclear power in 1977 replaced the equivalent of 100 million tons of coal, he said, or about one-sixth of the total coal produced.

In a Feb. 28 interview, the coal strike was one of the first things Gleason mentioned in discussing nuclear power's future. Of coal, Gleason said: "Do you think you'd want to put all of your eggs in that basket?" And except for nuclear power, he said, "there is no other basket around."

"Clearly, there is an increasing awareness on the part of Congress, if not the administration, that you've got to have a diversified fuel supply."

The "awareness" apparently was increasing in the administration as well. President Carter told a delegation of the nation's governors Feb. 27 that nuclear power plants had been "extremely reliable" during the strike and had served as "sort of a mainstay" according to O'Leary.

And Energy Secretary Schlesinger, in a March 5, 1978, appearance on CBS television's "Face the Nation," commented that "I think the events in the Midwest in recent weeks, have underscored the desirability of a greater degree of diversity. . . ." Utilities there, he said, have been "overly dependent on coal, obviously."

Testifying the next day before the Senate Energy Committee, Schlesinger said "the United States must move more aggressively in developing not just coal, but nuclear power, solar power . . . geothermal energy, and a multitude of other renewable resources."

Such words must have pleased the nuclear industry. Since Carter became president, it had cried repeatedly for help from an administration it admittedly was unsure of.

Administration Divided

The industry was not alone in its inability to pin down where the Carter White House stood on nuclear power. Critics of "the nuclear option" expressed bafflement as well.

When Carter was campaigning, nuclear power, he often said, was to be embraced only as "a last resort." On the other hand, he named Schlesinger as his energy adviser. That upset many environmentalists, who viewed Schlesinger as pro-nuclear. It also disturbed many in the indus-

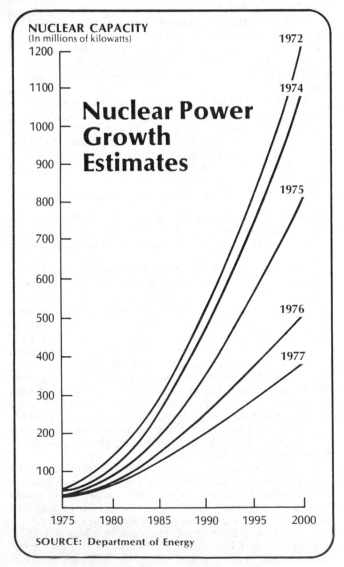

NUCLEAR CAPACITY
(In millions of kilowatts)

Nuclear Power Growth Estimates

1972
1974
1975
1976
1977

SOURCE: Department of Energy

try: "Schlesinger is well-remembered for his tough, arms-length relationship with industry when he headed the old Atomic Energy Commission," observed a 1976 year-in-review analysis by the Atomic Industrial Forum. *(Schlesinger profile, p. 47)*

On April 7, 1977, Carter launched his campaign against the use of plutonium, an active ingredient in nuclear weapons, as a nuclear fuel. He ordered a halt to the Clinch River, Tenn., breeder reactor project, a move that incensed the nuclear industry. *(Box, p. 113)*

The industry considered reprocessing fuel essential to the nuclear process, and the Clinch River breeder was to be the prototype for the next generation of nuclear reactor technology. Environmentalists supported Carter.

Then as part of his comprehensive energy policy, Carter called April 20, 1977, for streamlining the licensing process of nuclear plants. The industry welcomed the call; environmentalists grew uneasy.

And on June 7, 1977, Schlesinger told a House committee that conventional nuclear power — Carter's "last resort" for energy during the campaign — would expand sevenfold by the year 2000 to 380,000 MWe. To the industry, the figure provided a glimmer of hope; to nuclear critics, it sounded like betrayal.

The industry's frustration with the Carter White House was vented Nov. 28, 1977, in a stormy speech to the Atomic Industrial Forum by Craig Hosmer, then president of the American Nuclear Energy Council.

"There are two White Houses instead of one," Hosmer proclaimed. "There is the White House symbolized by Schlesinger & Co., where a courageous effort goes on. . . . And then there is that other White House, populated by no-growth, counter-culture activists. . . ." The latter group, Hosmer said, were "bad guys" whose aim was to "convert the country into a drab, energyless, no-growth sleeping bag society. That is their goddamned transcendental notion of a great future for the U.S.A.

"We pray of course," Hosmer said, ". . . the President . . . decisively takes charge of the United States government, grasps its reins, decides where he wants to go, and shuts up or fires any s.o.b. that gets out of line. . . .

"If Harry Truman could fire the great Douglas MacArthur," Hosmer said, "there is no reason why Jimmy Carter can't torpedo a few rebellious, anti-nuclear pipsqueaks. . . ."

Anthony Z. Roisman of the National Resources Defense Council, used a less strident tone in an interview describing the inner administration turmoil.

"I think there is a split, if you will, between the president on the one hand — in terms of his articulated policies — and his Department of Energy on the other," Roisman said. "I don't understand it," he added. "I don't pretend to understand it. . . ."

"It is at best unclear" exactly what Carter's nuclear policies are, concluded Mark Reis of Friends of the Earth.

O'Leary's Defense

But O'Leary of the Energy Department showed little sympathy with the argument that the administration's nuclear policies seemed schizophrenic.

"There is more than one school of thought within the administration," he said, "and I regard that as healthy. . . ." The only time you do not find debate in governments over controversial issues, he said, is when the governments are totalitarian.

The 380,000 MWe estimate of nuclear power's role in the year 2000 was "a projection, not a goal," O'Leary said. And rather than a sevenfold increase in existing installed nuclear power, he argued, it was only double the amount of nuclear capacity currently operating, under construction or on order.

As for where the administration truly stood, he said, "You find out where the administration is when the administration speaks."

One clear-cut stand on nuclear power came in Carter's Feb. 18, 1978, remarks at a forum in Nashua, N.H. "I think there is a legitimate place in our country for nuclear power," Carter said. He went on to say he considered it a safe technology, and one which was needed.

The Energy Council's Gleason handed out copies of Carter's remarks at Nashua to office visitors. "...Here he was speaking extemporaneously, not filtered through six layers of staff, right?" Gleason said.

Licensing Bill

But the facts were that there was a structural tension in the Carter administration on nuclear power questions, and the built-in conflict interfered visibly with decision-making. Nowhere was that more evident than in the politics behind the drafting of legislation to streamline licensing of nuclear power plants.

Such a measure was by far the industry's highest priority — "the most singularly critical and pressing item," in Hosmer's words. The industry maintained that delays in the governmental process were why American nuclear reactors took 10 to 12 years to build.

President Carter was sympathetic. "[E]ven with the most thorough safeguards, it should not take ten years to license a plant," he said April 20, 1977.

Schlesinger pledged in early August 1977, that such legislation soon would be sent to Capitol Hill. The first target date was to be Sept. 7. But that date passed with no bill submitted.

Throughout the fall and into the winter, there were reports at least monthly that the licensing reform bill would be submitted imminently, always "next week." But as next weeks came and went, the phrase became something of a not-so-funny joke to the nuclear industry.

Draft Bill

In August 1977, there was an original draft bill prepared by the Energy Department. It was, according to nuclear industry sources, "pro-industry."

That draft included two basic and non-controversial reforms. First, it would have authorized and encouraged utilities to work with state and federal authorities in designating "site banks" or land areas which would receive prior approval for future use as power plant sites.

And second, it would have authorized and encouraged utilities, reactor vendors and state and federal regulators to agree on standardized plant designs, which would receive near-automatic governmental approval upon submission for a license.

But the Energy Department draft also included a number of controversial proposals. It would have imposed limits on public participation in licensing proceedings. It would have restructured the hearing process, making it more informal and less like an adversary courtroom proceeding as was the existing process. It would have shifted

Breeder Reactors

Though licensing reform appeared likely to be the big nuclear issue in 1979, the long-term future of the industry could hang equally on whether a workable breeder reactor program could be developed.

Breeder reactors long have been awaited as the full flowering of the nuclear power industry. Conventional nuclear reactors burn scarce uranium so inefficiently that it will not be feasible to rely on them much beyond the year 2000, energy planners say.

Breeder reactors, on the other hand, are many times more efficient fuel users and "breed" more fuel than they consume.

The problem is that most research on breeders to date has centered on those which would use plutonium as their base fuel. President Carter rejected development of plutonium-based breeders in 1977 because of the threat they would add to the spread of nuclear weapons.

In a highly controversial battle with Congress, the outcome of which was still uncertain as of early 1979, he committed the executive branch to shutting down the plutonium-fueled Clinch River, Tenn., trial breeder reactor project. Congress insisted on keeping it going.

His stand against plutonium-based breeder reactors notwithstanding, the Carter administration remained commited to developing breeder nuclear reactors.

On Feb. 27, 1978, the Electric Power Research Institute announced it had solved the plutonium problem. It had devised a process, it said, to reprocess nuclear fuel without separating or allowing the separation of plutonium from spent nuclear fuel.

Under its process, the institute said, plutonium could not be obtained for nuclear weapons development, and besides, it added, the plutonium itself would have such a low concentration, it could not be used in weapons.

The institute, the electric utility industry's research arm, contended its new process separated concerns over nuclear weapons proliferation from decisions over breeder reactor development.

But John F. O'Leary, deputy secretary of the Department of Energy, was very skeptical. "It is a very expensive proposition to prove this concept out," he said. He noted that the Energy Department's breeder effort was based on a similar aim — developing a breeder that would not use plutonium. Thorium was the proposed substitute.

A thorium blend fuel, O'Leary said, would make separation of plutonium from power plant fuel two to three times more expensive and difficult than it is with conventional nuclear fuels.

"We've got a lot of paper on this," O'Leary said, but "we don't have any hardware on it. ...I think a lot of our investment over the next 10 years should be in the thorium cycle."

much of the burden for governmental oversight to states from the Nuclear Regulatory Commission, and it would have given Schlesinger's Energy Department a strong coordinating role among federal agencies' involvement, where the department had no role at all under existing practice.

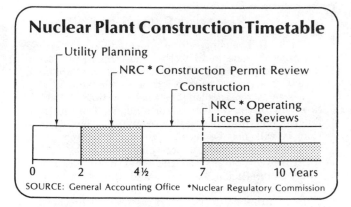

Nuclear Plant Construction Timetable

- Utility Planning
- NRC * Construction Permit Review
- Construction
- NRC * Operating License Reviews

0   2   4½   7   10 Years

SOURCE: General Accounting Office *Nuclear Regulatory Commission

The Energy Department bill was circulated for comment to state governors, relevant interest groups and federal agencies like the Nuclear Regulatory Commission, the Department of the Interior and the Council on Environmental Quality. It then was redrafted.

Reaction

The Nuclear Regulatory Commission objected strongly to the proposed cutback in its role, the restructuring of its proceedings and Schlesinger's proposed intrusion into its turf. The Council on Environmental Quality pushed many amendments. Foremost among them a suggested policy requiring the government to solve the problem of how to dispose of deadly nuclear wastes before any new nuclear plants could be licensed. *(Nuclear waste, p. 115)*

Public interest groups objected to restraints on citizen involvement and pressed for inclusion within the bill of a guarantee of government funding for citizen expenses from intervention in licensing proceedings.

"Democracy is not the most efficient system in the world," O'Leary observed.

In sending the final version of the bill to Congress in March 1978, Schlesinger said the measure was designed to cut total time in the process to perhaps as little as six years.

The measure would give states primary responsibility for deciding environmental issues and approving plant sites, Schlesinger said. It also would enable the Nuclear Regulatory Commission to give fast approval to plants conforming to standardized designs.

Proposed Provisions

As introduced, the bill:

● Authorized the Nuclear Regulatory Commission (NRC) to approve sites for nuclear plants prior to the filing of a construction permit. The site approval would be valid for 10 years and could be renewed for 10 year periods.

● Authorized the NRC to approve standard nuclear reactor designs prior to the filing of a construction permit and independent of where the plant would be located. The approval would be valid for five years and renewable for periods of three years.

● Authorized the NRC to grant construction permits and operating licenses jointly, avoiding the existing system providing opportunities for two sets of hearings.

● Required states rather than the NRC to determine whether applicants needed the extra power that a proposed plant would provide.

● Allowed states, or voluntary regional groups of states,

to assume some or all responsibility for assuring that proposed nuclear power plants met environmental impact standards set forth under the National Environmental Policy Act of 1969, a duty of the NRC under existing law.

● Specified that when states chose to administer environmental assessments, their findings would not be subject to challenge by the NRC or by a federal court review of NRC action.

● Reserved to NRC all authority to assess radiological health and safety questions.

● Permitted the NRC to issue interim operating licenses, valid for up to one year, before the completion of a hearing if there were an urgent public need or emergency and all matters concerning health and safety were resolved first.

● Cut back public hearings by mandating that if an opportunity once existed in any hearing for discussion of an issue, that issue could not be raised at later hearings unless significant new information had surfaced in the interim.

● Required the NRC to hold a formal hearing before granting a site permit, approving a standard design or issuing a joint construction/operation license.

● Required NRC to hold courtroom-style hearings for all health and safety issues, but required less formal legislative-style hearings for environmental challenges.

● Provided government funding for a five-year pilot program to cover costs of citizen intervenors.

Would It Help?

There has been substantial debate over whether reforming the licensing process would make any difference.

The long lead times require utilities to forecast up to a dozen years in advance that they will need that much extra power in the future. With the obvious uncertainties of forecasting so far ahead, utilities hesitate to commit themselves to such costly and controversial projects. Streamline the licensing process, reduce the uncertainty, and nuclear plant production will begin moving again, the industry has argued.

But a controversial study by the Congressional Research Service, issued Oct. 20, 1977, reached a different conclusion.

"[T]he major causes of delay in bringing nuclear plants on line since the 1973 oil embargo have been the difficulty utilities have had in obtaining capital to finance construction of plants and reduction in projected growth of future electric demand," the study said. "These factors are extraneous to the licensing process."

Licensing reform would make no difference between 1977 and 1985, the report continued. But better coordination between state and federal regulators "could have a positive effect on schedules in the post-1985 period," it concluded.

Why So Long?

A March 2, 1977, report by the General Accounting Office (GAO) explained why construction of a nuclear plant takes 10 years or more. Two years are consumed on average in a utility planning stage. That phase begins with a utility decision to build a power plant and ends with submission to the Nuclear Regulatory Commission of an application to build.

In that time the utility must choose a site, prepare an extensive environmental impact statement and fill out detailed reports for the commission on the plant's design.

Controversy Over Clinch River Breeder Reactor

The Carter administration's proposals for fiscal 1980 spending on nuclear breeder reactors appeared to carry out a controversial agreement made in August 1978 with Sen. James A. McClure, R-Idaho.

If the pact between McClure and Carter held, the president had a better chance of finally winning congressional approval to end construction of the $2 billion breeder reactor at Clinch River, Tenn.

But McClure challenged the administration's commitment to the agreement, complaining that the budget did not include funding for an Idaho project on breeder safety that the senator said was promised by Carter.

The dispute over Clinch River would come up during congressional action on appropriations and also during debate on the annual Energy Department authorization bill.

Background

Though Carter announced his opposition to the demonstration plant in 1977, the administration was forced to spend $15 million a month on the project because Congress refused to kill it. Carter argued that the project was uneconomical, its design was obsolete and the fuel it produces could be used to make atomic bombs. *(Details, appendix, p. 106-A)*

McClure, an ardent support of Clinch River, agreed in August 1978 to cool his enthusiasm in return for a commitment from Carter to spend roughly $1 billion in fiscal 1981 to develop breeder technology, including another demonstration plant to replace Clinch River.

Then in May 1981, Carter would decide whether to continue Clinch River, build another demonstration plant or not build any plant.

The agreement also had "something to do with the national energy plan," as McClure described it in a Jan. 23, 1979, statement. Just as the breeder agreement was reached, McClure provided a crucial signature needed to get the conference report on natural gas pricing, which he had originally opposed, out of committee and to the floor. The agreement brought cries of "deal" from other senators and almost backfired on the fragile compromise. *(Natural gas pricing, energy bill chapter, p. 5)*

Though the budget called for spending $462 million on liquid metal fast breeder reactors in fiscal 1980 instead of the $504 million promised McClure, Energy Secretary James R. Schlesinger attributed the reduction to general budget-cutting and not to any "reneging" on the agreement.

"We are still prepared to fulfill those arrangements" made with McClure, Schlesinger told the Joint Economic Committee Jan. 23, 1979.

The fiscal 1980 budget included $55 million in budget authority for conceptual design of a breeder demonstration plant and $142 million for basic breeder research.

But McClure zeroed in on the budget's treatment of an Idaho project that he said was to receive $27 million in fiscal 1980 under the agreement. Budget authority for the Idaho Safety Research Experimental Facility (SAREF) was proposed at $3 million by the administration, rounding out funding of roughly $27 million for Phase I of the project.

But McClure wanted another $27 million for Phase II of the project, which would eventually cost $417 million to complete. As a member of the Senate Energy Committee, McClure was expected to push for the Phase II funding.

Then follows a period averaging between two and two-and-one-half years while the government reviews whether to grant a construction permit. Public hearings are held; challenges by anti-nuclear activists bring delays.

Once authorized to build, actual construction takes about six years, the GAO said. In the final two years of the construction process, the utility seeks permission from the Nuclear Regulatory Commission to start operating the plant, which requires a second license. Hearings must be held on that license as well, and challengers at that stage can bring further delays.

While endorsing use of pre-approved sites and reactor designs, the GAO concluded: "Prospects are not good for reducing leadtimes in the future...."

That conclusion, GAO said, was based upon many factors, including growing state and local review requirements, swelling public concern about nuclear power and the need for maintaining thorough safety reviews.

Industry's Response

On behalf of the nuclear industry, Gleason, in testimony Feb. 15, 1978, before the House Commerce Subcommittee on Energy and Power, blasted the Congressional Research Service report as being based on inadequate data.

"...[T]he true cause of delay is often masked by what is known as the 'ripple effect,'" Gleason said. "For example, a change in [Nuclear Regulatory Commission] regulatory criteria will necessitate a design change which will require an equipment change which in turn will result in a construction delay. More often than not, the equipment change will be labeled by [the Nuclear Regulatory Commission] as the cause of delay. ...Architect and engineering firms have estimated that the actual time required to construct a facility is about 60 months," Gleason said, which he noted, corresponded to foreign experience. "This means that the licensing process adds approximately 37 months to time required to build a nuclear facility," Gleason said.

A delay that long, he said, could add $200 million to total plant construction expenses, which already required about $1.2 billion per plant. That "greatly diminishes the utility's ability to attract investment capital," Gleason observed.

And, he warned, without reform, the system would get worse. He cited regulatory commission reports that estimated that the average length of construction reviews would increase by 34 months, or 37 percent, by 1990 if the system were unchanged. "Licensing reform is needed now to avoid this actually happening," Gleason said.

At the same hearing, Roisman of the Natural Resources Defense Council objected that the only value being discussed was how to build reactors faster.

"...[T]he licensing process is designed to decide *whether* to build and operate nuclear reactors, not how quickly...," he said.

Solar Alternative

An alternative to nuclear power has been pushed by those who believe in conscientious conservation. Its proponents argued that through more efficient use of energy and through increased reliance on "soft" or "renewable" energy sources, like solar power, modern societies can have all the power they need. Needs can be met economically without relying on nuclear power, a technology they regarded not only as inherently unsafe but also inherently unwise economically. *(Lovins box, p. 108)*

"I think the nuclear industry is pretty much dead or dying," commented Reis of Friends of the Earth in an interview. Asked why, he said simply: "We don't need it and it's too expensive."

The energy establishment has disagreed with such reasoning on timing more than anything else. "...[I]n my judgement we must go to solar," said the Energy Department's O'Leary. "But I think we've got 50 years before we have to get there."

The transition to solar will have to come then, he said, because continued reliance on conventional and nuclear fuels would produce so much heat that the earth's environmental balance would be threatened.

Impact of Reactor Incident

The Three Mile Island accident, the worst nuclear reactor accident in the nation's history, touched off what portended to be a major public policy debate that could determine the future of the nuclear industry. The events at the facility could be an exceptionally serious blow for an industry already reeling from financial troubles and widely publicized federal government actions that left doubts about nuclear power safety. Moreover, the accident appeared to give industry critics more leverage to turn congressional attention toward a greater emphasis on safety in the debates over licensing speedups and waste disposal. *(See next chapter)*

Industry spokesmen all agreed that nuclear energy would have no future unless the technology has public support. But events unfolding in the first months of 1979 greatly undermined the industry's credibility.

In January the NRC repudiated sections of a 1975 study done by Dr. Norman Rasmussen, a Massachusetts Institute of Technology physicist. The Rasmussen report, which estimated the chances of various types of nuclear accidents, had been used by the industry to support its contention that the technology was safe.

Later the same month, the Union of Concerned Scientists, the most highly respected of the groups criticizing the industry, called on the government to shut down 16 U.S. reactors because of safety problems. On March 13, shortly before the Three Mile Island accident, the NRC ordered the shutdown of five nuclear plants after it determined that a computer model used to determine their ability to resist earthquakes had been faulty. The same day a special 14-agency governmental review unit raised questions about the scientific and technical feasibility of safely disposing of radioactive wastes created by commercial reactors. The report called into question a matter the industry had long argued it would have no problem resolving.

As events at Three Mile Island unfolded, the General Accounting Office March 30 released a report that said local and state authorities in areas surrounding nuclear facilities — including those in Pennsylvania — were unprepared for a mass evacuation in the event of a serious accident.

Both the nuclear industry and its critics were looking to the 96th Congress to resolve some of the fundamental controversies about nuclear power. Until the Three Mile Island accident, it appeared that the industry viewpoint was receiving more attention. Industry officials had hoped for legislation on temporary storage of spent fuel and permanent storage of nuclear waste, a commitment from Congress to development of the fast breeder reactor and regulatory changes to speed the licensing process. Anti-nuclear groups were considering a similar list of legislative priorities, but from a different perspective. A well-organized coalition of environmental and solar energy advocates along with anti-nuclear critics were preparing to dispute the industry's case for speeded up licensing. The two sides were also preparing for a fight over the waste issue, which many industry spokesmen viewed as even more important to the industry's future than the licensing issue.

In his nationally televised speech on energy April 5, President Carter said he would appoint an independent commission of experts to investigate the Three Mile Island accident and make recommendations on how to improve safety at nuclear plants. But the president gave no indication that the administration was backing off from its support of nuclear power. Prior to Carter's speech, Energy Secretary Schlesinger April 2 said he would continue to push for legislation to speed up the licensing process, which he said would "not reduce any consideration by the Nuclear Regulatory Commission of safety issues." And Senate Energy Committee Chairman Henry M. Jackson, D-Wash., said he planned to move ahead with hearings on a bill (S 685) to speed licensing and force early storage of nuclear waste.

However, in a letter to the White House April 4, six senior members of the Senate Environment and Public Works Committee asked Carter to withhold the licensing bill. "Transmittal of such a bill at this time would be ill-advised, pending resolution of the safety issues" raised by the Pennsylvania accident and other events, said the letter from committee Chairman Jennings Randolph, D-W.Va., ranking Republican Robert T. Stafford, Vt., Gary Hart, D-Colo., and others.

The real measure of whether the traditional congressional support for nuclear power had changed would be among those members who had not been firmly set in the pro- or anti-nuclear column. And their decision would be influenced by the way their constituents reacted — or did not react — to the Three Mile Island incident and investigations. "The aura of confidence in nuclear energy has been shattered," predicted Udall. But Rep. Robert S. Walker, R-Pa., whose district abutted that of the Three Mile Island plant, said, "Hopefully I'll still come out an advocate of nuclear power. But I want the facts first — then I'll make judgments."

The Problem of Nuclear Waste Disposal

The swimming pools in the backyards of the nation's nuclear reactors have been filling up with used fuel, but despite growing awareness of the problem, as of early 1979 there was no firm plan to dispose of the deadly radioactive waste.

During his first year in office, President Carter Oct. 18, 1977, proposed that the government accept responsibility for the spent fuel once the utilities paid a storage fee. The nuclear industry welcomed the proposal because the plan they had developed to get rid of the wastes — reprocessing to extract still usable uranium and plutonium — had been thwarted by Carter's indefinite postponement of reprocessing in April 1977.

But the welcome mat was only cautiously extended even though the industry found waste disposal one of its most visible problems, a solution to which was a key to its survival.

Congress, environmentalists, state governments and even foreign countries were waiting for details of the Carter plan because they were skeptical that — 30 years into the nuclear age — an easy answer to waste disposal was just around the corner. Indeed, an October 1978 federal inter-agency task force report concluded that although the problem of disposing of nuclear wastes could be solved, the solution could take as long as 17 years.

The nuclear industry has been hampered by public doubt about the government's ability to store safely the toxic wastes created by nuclear weapons development and by private nuclear power plants. The government has repeatedly missed its deadlines for storing the wastes, and as a result no permanent disposal site was in operation in early 1979.

"We are not going to have nuclear power if people are not sure the nuclear system and all its components are reasonably safe," House Interior Chairman Morris K. Udall, D-Ariz., said during hearings he held on the waste problem.

The Carter administration had made waste disposal one of its top priorities. The budget for fiscal 1980 increased federal spending for nuclear waste by 30 percent — and by 91 percent if $300 million to be repaid by industry is included.

But many members of Congress have wanted to give states a larger role in deciding where the wastes will go. Worry about states becoming "dumping grounds" for the nation prompted many to support giving a state the right to veto any waste site within its borders. The administration, while agreeing to seek a state's "concurrence," opposed giving states the right of veto.

There were also disputes in 1979 over a Waste Isolation Pilot Plant planned for an abandoned salt mine outside Carlsbad, N.M.; the future of an unfinished private plant in Barnwell, S.C., designed to reprocess spent fuel; the amount government should charge industry for storing spent fuel from reactors; the type of storage to be provided for the spent fuel and the direction of research on waste storage methods.

In addition to the administration's interagency study, Congress in 1978 included in the Energy Department authorization bill additional funds to pay for a study of and to select sites for the temporary storage of spent fuel from nuclear power. However, the bill died at the end of the session. Another bill authorizing $333 million for the Nuclear Regulatory Commission in fiscal 1979 (S 2584 — PL 95-601) directed the NRC to undertake major studies on the adequacy of safeguards at nuclear power plants and of the role to be played by states in the storage of nuclear wastes. *(DOE authorization, appendix p. 99-A; NRC authorization, appendix, p. 107-A)*

Background

Spent fuel from commercial light water reactors has been around since 1960, when Commonwealth Edison's Dresden 1 plant in Morris, Ill., began operating.

The spent fuel, which contains fission products with a life of less than a century, also contains new, man-made byproducts such as plutonium, which must be isolated from the environment for thousands of years before the radioactivity decays to a harmless level. Genetic disorders, cancer and other illnesses are the results of contact with minute particles of this most toxic of substances.

A reactor runs on uranium pellets, which are housed in thin, 15-foot long fuel rods. Within each rod, atomic reactions are taking place, with atoms splitting and releasing energy in the form of heat. Water circulating among the rods to cool them also carries the heat to the other parts of the reactor where steam is generated. The steam turns a turbine that generates electricity.

Because radioactive byproducts from the atomic reactions, including plutonium, begin to build up in the fuel rods, not all the uranium housed in the rods can be used, or "burned up." The byproducts begin to interfere with the nuclear reactions.

The situation can be loosely compared to that of oil getting dirty in a gasoline engine. Every 12 to 18 months, about a third of the rods are removed from the reactor and replaced with fresh ones filled with uranium.

Utility companies with reactors have been storing the spent fuel rods on a temporary basis at plant sites in large concrete pools of water. The water acts as a shield for the radioactivity and aids cooling of the rods.

The storage has been temporary because the utilities hoped to sell the spent fuel to commercial reprocessors who would melt down the rods and their contents and then extract the usable uranium and plutonium. Disposal of the wastes remaining after reprocessing would be the responsibility of the federal government, although the reprocessor would first have to convert the liquid wastes into solid form and then pay the government some sort of fee.

However, reprocessing was ruled out as a way to get rid of spent fuel when Carter in April 1977 deferred it indefinitely as part of efforts to curb international proliferation of nuclear weapons. The plutonium extracted from the spent fuel during reprocessing can be fashioned into bombs, while the spent fuel, still a mixture of many different elements in metal rods, cannot.

India and the Bomb

The role that nuclear energy can play in the spread of atomic weapons was made evident when India detonated a plutonium-powered atomic device in 1974. The United States and Canada had donated fuel, technology and expertise to help India build nuclear reactors, with the bomb an unexpected result.

Until proliferation of nuclear weapons through nuclear energy byproducts such as plutonium was recognized as a threat, the future of nuclear energy was thought to be plutonium, the fuel used by breeder reactors, which then "breed" even more plutonium. Fuel shortages, such as those predicted for oil and uranium, would not threaten the plutonium-powered breeder, reasoned its supporters. As part of the deferral of the use of plutonium, Carter had sought to end funding for the demonstration Clinch River, Tenn., breeder reactor. However, Congress voted to continue the plant in an energy research bill (S 1811) that Carter vetoed Nov. 5, 1977. *(Details, p. 93-A)*

Even before Carter postponed reprocessing, it was on shaky ground as a viable commercial venture. A Nuclear Fuel Services Inc. plant in West Valley, N.Y., operating since 1966, was closed in 1972 for repairs because of leaking radioactivity; by the end of 1978, it had not reopened.

Because of financial and technical difficulties, two other plants in Morris, Ill. (General Electric), and Barnwell, S.C. (Allied General), had not opened. A factor in the failures was the lack of a government proposal for permanent disposal of the wastes from reprocessing.

Spent Fuel Policy

The Department of Energy (DOE) statement Oct. 18, 1977, on the administration's spent fuel policy called it a "logical extension, given the indefinite deferral of reprocessing, of the long-established federal responsibility for permanent disposal of high-level wastes."

The administration proposed to take title to the spent fuel for a one-time storage fee that would cover costs of keeping the fuel rods in an interim site, probably a water-filled pool, transporting the fuel to a permanent geologic site and then housing the rods in the geologic site, once it has been located. No interim or geologic sites have been definitely named, and the fee to be charged the utilities was still being worked out, as of early 1979. As part of the policy, the administration also offered to take spent fuel from other countries "when this action would contribute to meeting non-proliferation goals," the statement said.

Storage Fee

The one-time storage fee was designed to remove the uncertainties about the cost of waste disposal that have made economic calculations difficult for utilities. The spent fuel policy "should once and for all establish a fee, a cap for the cost question," said Mike Lawrence, acting assistant director for spent fuel at DOE.

However, Lawrence emphasized that the fee would change in coming years to reflect actual costs, whether they are lower or higher than the original estimate. Although the fee set in a contract for a batch of fuel would not change,

the fee could be different the next time the utility and the government signed a contract, Lawrence said. "A utility doesn't send fuel once," he said, but many, many times, allowing the fee to be changed.

Critics of the nuclear industry were worried that the fee would be too low and would not reflect the cost of containing the radioactivity for thousands of years.

Taxpayers, instead of the utilities, would absorb any additional costs, thus giving nuclear energy an unfair advantage over other forms of energy, such as solar, argued Robert D. Pollard of the Union of Concerned Scientists. Pollard was a former staff member of the old Atomic Energy Commission who resigned because of his concerns about plant safety.

"If the industry had to stand on its own economic feet, without government doing the research, taking the waste and limiting liability for insurance claims, the industry would fail," said Pollard, a physicist based in Washington, D.C.

Anticipating criticism of the one-time fee, the DOE statement noted, "It is important . . . that the utilities pay the full costs of nuclear waste storage and ultimate disposal."

Even Carter acknowledged the concern about hidden costs of nuclear energy, such as waste disposal, when he told an international conference on the fuel cycle Oct. 19, 1977: "All the costs of the nuclear fuel cycle should be accurately known, as well as possible. And there should be an open-minded approach to this very controversial and very difficult subject."

To those who doubted the feasibility of fixing a fee for a cemetery that must last half a million years, Lawrence replied, "We feel we can give a reasonably good cost estimate." There was even a chance the fee would go down, he said, because "we want to be conservative; we are using high numbers."

Some utilities were asking how much of the fee would go for interim storage and transportation, with the idea that they could perhaps save money by holding the spent fuel themselves until the geologic site was ready, Lawrence said.

Early DOE estimates of the storage fee were that it would cost a utility 1 mill per kilowatt hour. With 40 mills the typical cost of a nuclear-generated kilowatt hour, that meant a 25 percent increase in the cost of electricity if waste disposal costs had not already been factored in.

A rough translation of that estimate into the cost per kilogram of spent fuel would be $225, Lawrence said, depending on the "burn up rate" in the reactor. Because a typical reactor discharged 30 metric tons of spent fuel a year, or 30,000 kilograms, the annual cost of waste disposal for a reactor would be about $6.8 million. However, DOE officials cautioned that these were only rough estimates.

General Electric, which was storing some spent fuel at the defunct Morris reprocessing plant for those utilities that had reprocessing contracts, charged about $10 to $17 per kilogram per year for storage.

In fixing the fee, DOE would assume the value of the uranium and plutonium in the rods at zero, but some rebate was possible to industry if reprocessing became acceptable in the future.

Interim Storage

The interim storage was needed because many utilities would run out of room in their on-site storage pools before

Possible Disposal Sites for Nuclear Wastes

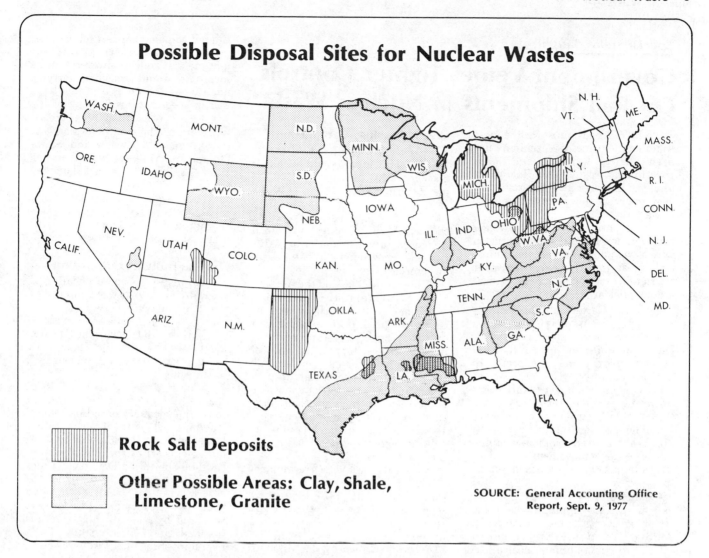

Rock Salt Deposits

Other Possible Areas: Clay, Shale, Limestone, Granite

SOURCE: General Accounting Office Report, Sept. 9, 1977

1988, when the Department of Energy planned at the earliest to have a geologic site ready to accept waste. Without adequate storage, the plants would be forced to shut down.

The adminstration also wanted the fuel rods to be retrievable for several years or possibly longer because it was unwilling to throw away the energy resources left in the rods. Many DOE officials thought reprocessing would be acceptable in the near future.

However, finding a geologic site that allowed the rods to be removed might be difficult, which meant interim storage might be needed beyond 1988.

Before the government builds a water basin for the spent fuel, DOE planned to ask the utilities and potential reprocessors, such as General Electric, if they would provide the interim storage.

Because of the need for retrievability, some environmental groups and administration officials were worried that DOE would resurrect an old idea of housing the spent fuel above ground in huge, concrete, mausoleum-like structures the size of football fields.

The Environmental Protection Agency in 1974 rejected an environmental impact statement on the idea as "inadequate" and unsafe. As a result, the plan was dropped.

EPA, the White House Council on Environmental Quality and environmental groups feared that the concrete storage facility, which could last 100 years, would ease pressure on the federal government to find a permanent geologic site.

Fred Weinhold, director of technical programs evaluation at DOE and an author of the spent fuel policy, said, "I share the concern of the environmental people about the interim facilities. We've got to demonstrate a permanent solution," not just postpone it.

Permanent Disposal

The federal government has been responsible for permanent disposal of all commercial and military waste since the Atomic Energy Act of 1954 allowed private industry to enter the military-dominated field of atomic energy.

Finding a geologic storage site has been difficult. Government efforts have recently been concentrated on salt deposits. If salt is fissured by earthquakes or other shifts in the earth, it seals itself, thus keeping the nuclear waste surrounded. The very existence of salt also indicates a lack of water, which reduces the problem of radioactivity leaking out of a storage site in groundwater.

Government Vetoes Tighter Controls On Rail Shipments of Nuclear Waste

The railroad industry, like most American businesses, seldom has been one to welcome additional government regulation. Traditionally, the industry has been reluctant even to accept new safety rules without a fight.

In a curious reversal of roles, however, the federal government in 1978 turned down the railroad industry's pleas for stronger government restrictions on the shipment of hazardous nuclear wastes.

If the Carter administration's goal of increasing the nation's reliance on nuclear power is realized, the amount of spent nuclear fuel and other nuclear wastes is expected to increase rapidly in coming years as more and more nuclear plants begin operating. Most of these wastes are transported by train.

The problem of nuclear waste disposal has been a major stumbling block to the achievement of the Carter administration's nuclear energy program.

Nuclear wastes are shipped by rail in special shipping casks, some weighing over 92 tons. Because the radioactive wastes represent a special hazard to human health, the casks must meet safety requirements established by the federal government's Nuclear Regulatory Commission (NRC) to assure that the public is not exposed to radiation in case of an accident.

In 1974, however, a nuclear study task force established by the railroad industry concluded that "train accidents produce forces and thermal exposures far in excess of the NRC's...certification requirements" for casks used to ship nuclear wastes. As a result, the Association of American Railroads (AAR), the industry trade association, recommended to its members that they take special precautions in shipping nuclear materials. When the railroads attempted to implement its proposals, however, they were prevented from doing so by the Interstate Commerce Commission (ICC).

Special Nuclear Cargo Trains

"When the AAR looked at the NRC's certification requirements for nuclear casks, it suggested to its member railroads that the casks be carried in a controlled environment to reduce the likelihood of exceeding the certification limits," explained Conan P. Furber, manager of AAR's Office of Environmental Studies, in an interview.

Specifically, he said the Association of American Railroads recommended that the casks be carried at speeds of 35 miles per hour or less; that if a train carrying nuclear wastes approached another train, one should stop completely so the maximum potential impact speed in case of an accident would not exceed 35 miles per hour; and that special trains be used, consisting solely of a locomotive, caboose and the cars bearing the nuclear materials.

Once the task force's recommendations were formulated, the railroads in late 1976 filed three separate requests with the ICC for special tariffs for transporting nuclear wastes.

The first, filed by the Missouri, Kansas and Texas Railroad, stated that, although the ICC normally considered railroads to be "common

---

According to the Energy Department, about 90 percent of spent nuclear fuel currently is shipped by train and 10 percent by truck.

---

carriers" and required by law to accept whatever cargo is given them, the railroad would refuse to carry nuclear waste materials under any condition.

The Eastern Roads Association, a trade group representing eastern railroads, argued in a separate filing that its members should not be con-

sidered common carriers for the purpose of transporting nuclear materials. It added, however, that its members would consider carrying nuclear wastes on a contract basis and in special trains.

The Western Railroad Association, the Southern Railway, the Atchison, Topeka and Santa Fe, and the Missouri Pacific, on the other hand, acknowledged that they were common carriers, but requested ICC approval of a supplementary tariff of $18 to $20 per mile to cover the additional costs of carrying the material in special trains.

Nuclear Industry Opposition

An investigation and hearing on the railroads' filings was approved by the ICC in March 1976. But the railroads soon found their position opposed by the NRC, the Department of Energy, and practically every major utility and nuclear firm in the country.

The ICC ruled March 13, 1978, that it did not have the power to judge the adequacy of railroad safety standards set by the Transportation Department or the shipping cask requirements set by the NRC. Because the Transportation Department and the NRC already found the standards acceptable, the ICC concluded that the additional precautions proposed by the railroads were unjustified and unreasonable. As a result, all three filings were rejected.

In interviews following the ICC's decision, Transportation and NRC officials said their agencies had no plans to review or upgrade the safety requirements for rail shipment of nuclear wastes. An NRC official, however, said the commission's Office of Nuclear Materials Safety and Safeguards recently had begun a three-year evaluation of whether tougher safety requirements should be set for shipment of nuclear materials by various modes of transportation. Existing rules apply equally to all transportation modes, the official said.

Rail Shipments Increasing

It was estimated that there would be 4,000 metric tons of spent reactor fuel accumulated by the end of 1978. The amount was expected to increase rapidly as more and more nuclear plants are licensed. In addition to power plants, a variety of military projects also create highly radioactive nuclear wastes.

Most spent fuel from power plants has been stored at the reactor sites, but rail shipments of spent fuel were expected to skyrocket as these sites filled up. When that happens, the utilities would have to shift the wastes from site to site or to permanent government disposal sites as they become available.

According to the Energy Department, about 90 percent of spent fuel has been shipped by train and 10 percent by truck. All high-level waste from military applications has been shipped by rail. For security reasons, the railroads themselves often were not informed when government shipments contain nuclear materials.

Although as of early 1979 there had been no serious rail accidents that have involved the release of hazardous nuclear wastes, the possibility exists. According to a 1972 report by the Atomic Energy Commission, the probability of such an accident is "small," but if it were to occur, its "consequences could be serious."

The question of whether shipping cask standards are adequate was complicated by the fact that casks were not being manufactured. So eager was the government to transport wastes via these casks that, according to a February 1978 Energy Department report on nuclear waste management, "there is a need to provide incentives to expeditiously restore a national capability to fabricate large casks."

Shipment Standards

The NRC has established four standards for certifying the casks used to ship nuclear materials. In sequence, a cask must be able to withstand:

● A free-fall drop of 30 feet onto an "unyielding surface," entailing a speed at the moment of impact of about 30 miles per hour.

● A 40-inch drop onto a pin six inches in diameter.

● Thirty minutes in a fire of 1,475 degrees Fahrenheit.

● Eight hours' immersion in three feet of water.

Under NRC requirements, a cask design could be certified without actual field tests.

According to Furber, the cask design requirements would not offer sufficient protection in case of certain types of railroad accident. "A supermarket tomato can pass the 40-inch drop test," Furber said in an interview. Another test that concerned AAR, he added, is the heat test.

Casks use lead in their linings to prevent radiation from leaking out, he explained. In a railroad accident in which there is a fire, he said, the 30-minute requirement "isn't long enough. We have many fires that burn for hours, and some that burn for days. Government tests showed the lead became molten in less than two hours. After the lead melts, it slumps. Even if the cask isn't broken or punctured, radiation will leak out."

Finally, Furber said a cask that did not break at an impact of 30 miles per hour still was not sufficient protection. "Puncture or breaking apart of the cask would definitely be possible in a railroad accident," he said. "What if the cask hits the side of a tunnel at 60 miles per hour, or falls off a rail car on a bridge higher than 30 feet?"

Risks Denied

The railroads' fears were dismissed by William A. Brobst, chief of the Energy Department's Transportation Branch. "Our position before the ICC was that our shipments are much safer than the things they're hauling already," he said.

Besides, he added, the railroad tariffs, if approved, would have cost the nuclear industry up to $20 million annually in shipping costs, and the Energy Department—which ships military nuclear materials—an additional $5 million - $7 million annually.

Government tests, he said, "proved that they [the railroads] were wrong." In five tests held in Albuquerque in 1977, he explained, the casks were crashed into concrete walls on a rocket sled, a truck and a rail car at speeds up to 84 miles per hour. In each test, little or no damage resulted, he said.

Another cask was placed on a rail car in a pool of jet fuel, and the fuel ignited. "It burned for two hours," Brobst said. "The rail car melted. The cask was undamaged by the fire."

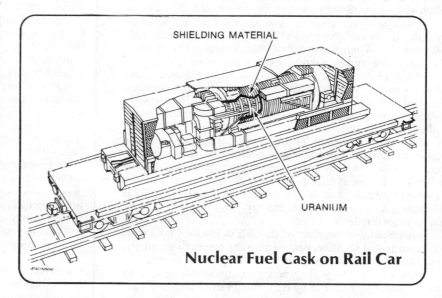

SHIELDING MATERIAL

URANIUM

Nuclear Fuel Cask on Rail Car

As for the lead, he said that "just because the lead melts it does not decrease its protection. If the lead melted, radiation would only be able to escape in an upward direction. This would pose a danger only to a helicopter flying over the cask at a height of three feet."

The department's tests, Brobst said, "were close enough to the laboratory predictions.... This gives me great confidence that we can predict with great accuracy what's going to happen in transportation accidents. These containers will withstand the impact of a serious transportation accident."

However, salt deposits are not considered suitable if the waste is to be retrieved because it is so flexible, or, the term used in physics, plastic. The salt would seal in the nuclear waste and could even slowly shift it away from its original location, making it difficult to retrieve. The salt would also corrode the storage tanks.

Other possible geologic sites being studied were deposits of shale, granite and limestone. *(See map.)*

The General Accounting Office (GAO), in a study of nuclear waste management dated Sept. 7, 1977, said the DOE goal of having a geologic site by 1985 was overly optimistic. The geology was complicated, but the biggest problem, GAO noted, would be "opposition of public and some political leaders."

"It is reasonable to anticipate that the public hearings (on proposed sites) may be hotly contested and could last for years," the GAO report said.

Past efforts to find geologic sites have pointed up the problems in tucking away radioactive wastes for centuries. In Lyons, Kan., a salt deposit thought to be suitable turned out to be marred by holes drilled nearby during oil and gas exploration. GAO reported that the government thought it could overcome these problems, but not the local political opposition.

Another stab was made at salt deposits in northern Michigan. Again, political opposition caused the government to abandon the sites. The agency had neglected to inform the state government that its surveys were only preliminary. When state officials found safety criteria inadequate, the governor asked federal officials to leave.

Another possible conflict touched on in Michigan, and at other sites, was that of waste disposal versus exploration for and extraction of oil, gas or minerals. States were reluctant to contaminate a possibly profitable area with radioactive wastes.

The administration, aware of the obstacles to geologic waste disposal and public concern about dangers of radioactive waste, said the waste disposal problem was a high priority. The spent fuel policy was simply "a step in the process of increased attention to waste disposal," said John Ahearne, a senior aide to Energy Secretary James R. Schlesinger, in 1977.

Gus Speth, a member of the White House Council on Environmental Quality, summed up the concerns about the government's track record in a well-publicized September 1977 speech: "Perhaps the waste problem is manageable in theory; perhaps not. I hope it is. But many things that are theoretically doable never get done. Certainly the sorry history of radioactive waste management in this country to date provides no basis for confidence that things will work out." Speth went on to suggest setting a near-term deadline for resolving the waste question; if the deadline were not met, no new licenses would be issued.

Industry Views

Because the Carter administration created the spent fuel disposal problem by deferring reprocessing, nuclear industry spokesmen thought it only logical that the government solve the problem by taking over the spent fuel. But the utilities and private companies, like environmentalists and others, wanted the government to finish planning and start implementing. "Anything DOE can do to lend certainty to the policy, by naming sites, fixing schedules or whatever, would help," said Edward A. Wiggin of the Atomic Industrial Forum Inc., an industry association.

Supreme Court Ruling

The lack of a disposal site has been used to raise questions about the legality of Nuclear Regulatory Commission licensing. The Supreme Court April 3, 1978, unanimously overturned two appellate court decisions which had backed environmentalists' challenges to nuclear power plants in Michigan and Vermont.

The court reversed the rulings of the District of Columbia Circuit Court of Appeals, which required the Nuclear Regulatory Commission to reconsider its decision to grant an operating license for a new power plant in Vermont, to formulate a new rule concerning the environmental impact of fuel reprocessing and waste disposal, and to consider those issues — and energy conservation alternatives — in reviewing the application of a Michigan power company for approval of its plans to build two nuclear reactors in Midland, Mich. In both cases, the court of appeals had found that the Nuclear Regulatory Commission — and its predecessor, the Atomic Energy Commission — had not sufficiently considered these issues in reviewing the applications from the power companies for approval of their plans.

Federal judges are not authorized to intervene so far into agency decisions, wrote Justice William H. Rehnquist for the majority. "Absent constitutional constraints or extremely compelling circumstances 'the administrative agencies "should be free to fashion their own rules of procedure and to pursue method of inquiry capable of permitting them to discharge their multitudinous duties." ' "

"Nuclear energy may some day be a cheap, safe source of power or it may not," wrote Justice Rehnquist.

"But Congress has made a choice to at least try nuclear energy, establishing a reasonable review process in which courts are to play only a limited role. The fundamental policy questions appropriately resolved in Congress and in the state legislatures are *not* subject to re-examination in the federal courts under the guise of judicial review of agency action. Time may prove wrong the decision to develop nuclear energy, but it is Congress or the states within their appropriate agencies which must eventually make that judgment.... Administrative decisions should be set aside in this context, as in every other, only for substantial procedural or substantive reasons as mandated by statute ... not simply because the court is unhappy with the result reached." *(Vermont Yankee Nuclear Power Corp. v. Natural Resources Defense Council, Consumers Power Co. v. Aeschliman)*

As long as the government did not have temporary and geologic disposal sites, Wiggin and others have said, the public concern about radioactive wastes would hinder the growth of the nuclear industry.

Environmental Concerns

Environmental groups wanted the storage fee to reflect actual disposal costs so the nuclear industry would be forced to factor those costs into its economic calculations.

The Natural Resources Defense Council (NRDC), a non-profit, public interest law firm active in nuclear-related lawsuits, wrote a letter to DOE Secretary Schlesinger in November 1977 that criticized the spent fuel policy. The government plan would "essentially insulate the nuclear industry from any economic risks associated with the handling and disposal of nuclear wastes," said NRDC attorney Anthony Roisman in the letter. Cost overruns, which NRDC expected because of the many unanswered questions about waste disposal, would be absorbed by the government and the taxpayer, not the nuclear industry, NRDC argued.

NRDC's Thomas Cochran was worried about more than the fee and cost overruns. Just as the utilities were running out of storage room, and they and the public were forced to face up to the waste problem, the government was going to take it away, Cochran said, "out of sight, out of mind," so utilities no longer would have to deal with it.

Cochran also pointed to the moral questions raised by the inter-generational transfer of the risks of nuclear power. The benefit of the energy from nuclear plants was going to the people alive today, but all the risks of containing the radioactivity for centuries would go to future generations, Cochran said. That made traditional cost-benefit analysis invalid, he said.

Though the government has focused its attention on the need for geologic disposal, the buildup of spent fuel at reactor sites also posed environmental and safety problems, the 1977 GAO report said. Utilities have been expanding the storage capacity of the water basins by stacking the spent fuel rods more compactly.

The 1977 GAO report suggested that NRC not allow additional expansion of storage capacity until more safety and environmental studies had been done. NRDC said adding more fuel rods could "increase the risk of unintended criticality," or, in other words, cause an atomic reaction that could blow up the basin and areas around it.

International Aspects

As part of the nuclear spent fuel policy, the Carter administration also offered to take spent fuel from other countries. Carter described the proposal Oct. 19, 1977, in his speech to the plenary session of the International Nuclear Fuel Cycle Evaluation in Washington, D.C. "We are very eager also to help solve the problem of the disposal of spent nuclear fuel itself. We cannot provide storage for the major portion of the world's spent fuel, but we are willing to cooperate. And when a nation demonstrates to us your need for spent nuclear fuel storage, we hope to be prepared to accept that responsibility," he said.

The DOE policy statement said the spent fuel from foreign countries would be accepted "when this would contribute to meeting nonproliferation goals."

Though there has been some support for taking fuel from a country with an unstable political situation where misuse of plutonium was more likely, critics were worried that the United States could end up taking fuel from other developed countries "simply because we have more land mass than they have," as one Senate committee aide put it.

Congress in 1977 indicated its concern by adding a provision to an energy research bill (S 1811) that gave Congress veto power over any shipment of foreign fuel to the United States. S 1811 was vetoed by Carter.

The DOE policy statement said the administration would continue to encourage other countries to expand their own storage capacity and would work for regional or international storage sites.

1978 DOE, Task Force Reports

A Department of Energy Report released March 15, 1978, admitted it would be 1988 or even 1993 before the federal government could store nuclear wastes underground.

Though the report generally was optimistic that the government could handle waste disposal, it pointed out political and institutional obstacles in what was perhaps the most candid government assessment thus far of waste disposal problems.

"There's not a lot of rhetoric [in the report] saying it's all rosy," said Cochran of the Natural Resources Defense Council. But Cochran said the report did not go far enough in recognizing the magnitude of the problems of safe waste disposal.

The report's recommendations were sent to a new interagency task force set up by President Carter March 15. That group submitted its final recommendations in October.

Political Problems

The importance of public participation in decisions about waste management was a theme running throughout the report. In the past, the report said, waste disposal programs were "too ambitious," and "public concerns were aggravated rather than resolved."

John M. Deutch, Energy Department director of research and head of the study group that prepared the DOE report, said he thought the government could convince people near a waste disposal site that it would be safe by opening up the decision process, following licensing procedures scrupulously and discussing concerns with interested citizen groups.

Public resistance to waste disposal thwarted government study of possible sites in Michigan and Kansas. Louisiana and New Mexico also raised questions about potential sites there.

California passed a moratorium on construction of new nuclear plants until the federal government provided permanent disposal of wastes. Moreover, as of mid-1978, 11 states banned a nuclear waste repository within their borders, and at least 15 more were considering such a ban.

Several members of Congress have said they supported legislation that would require state legislatures, through a vote, statewide referendum or other method, to okay a waste disposal site before it could be licensed by the Nuclear Regulatory Commission.

Asked what would happen if no state wanted the waste, Deutch replied: "I worry about that. I don't know."

Costs

Deutch said the costs of permanent waste disposal would be $13 billion to $23 billion, depending on the amount of waste generated.

Those figures did not reflect the fees the government planned to charge utilities for storing the waste. Deutch said those fees would result in a 4 to 5 percent increase for ratepayers using nuclear-generated electricity.

For fiscal 1979, the Carter administration had requested $186.8 million for commercial waste management; $3 million for domestic spent fuel programs; $3 million for international spent fuel programs and $350 million for defense waste management.

Recommendations

The DOE report recommended that the federal government:

● Require licensing of all disposal sites — temporary and permanent — by the Nuclear Regulatory Commission, a change that would require legislation.

● Demonstrate by 1985, using a pilot program, the geologic disposal in salt deposits of a limited amount of spent fuel in a retrievable manner. The report suggested that plans to store low-level defense waste in Carlsbad, N.M., be expanded to include the pilot project.

● Retain the concept of a one-time charge to industry for storing and disposing of wastes, but make sure the charge equaled expected costs.

● Take over operations of the six privately owned, low-level waste storage sites regulated by states or the federal government. Low-level waste is equipment, clothing or other materials contaminated with radioactivity.

● Provide by 1983 interim storage for spent fuel from commercial reactors. On March 16, Sen. James A. McClure, R-Idaho, used staff projections to question the Energy Department's ability to meet that deadline.

● Consider environmental impacts of waste programs and require the Energy Department to strengthen its efforts to follow requirements for environmental impact statements.

● Identify and solve various problems associated with transporting waste.

The report also said reprocessing of spent fuel to extract still usable uranium and plutonium was "not required for safe disposal of commercial spent fuel."

Interagency Report

Plans for disposal of nuclear waste were further postponed on Oct. 19, 1978, when the administration's interagency task force issued a two-volume report recommending more study before making a decision on permanent sites or methods of disposal. The report said that work should begin "at once" only on the siting and construction of "one or more" medium-size burial vaults for the short-term storage of the most poisonous radioactive wastes. The report did not identify states or regions where these intermediate-scale facilities should be located.

The report said the first permanent "repository" could not be selected before 1984 and construction of the first repository could not be completed before 1992. "Prudent planning suggests anticipating initial operation during the period 1992 to 1995," the report said.

The task force said waste burial in salt still seemed the best solution to the disposal problem, but it did not rule out burial in other deep rock formations.

Other recommendations included:

● A greater role for states and regions in making decisions on nuclear waste;

● Extending the NCR's authority to license waste sites to cover new facilities for disposal of medium-level and low-level waste from both civilian and military uses;

● Legislation setting the terms under which utilities could pay a one-time fee for disposal.

In releasing the task force report, Deutsch said it was his hope that "as many as 1,000" spent fuel assemblies or waste canisters could be stored at the first burial vault.

On Nov. 14, 1978, Deutsch announced plans to press ahead with a pilot project to bury radioactive wastes in a salt bed near Carlsbad. "We hope to submit a license application by 1981, defend it and then submit the license to environmental review," he said in a speech before the American Nuclear Society. "I'm optimistic that we can bury our first nuclear wastes in New Mexico by 1985 or 1986."

"One problem we've had with the Carlsbad plan is the credibility of the federal government," said Nick Franklin, secretary of the New Mexico Energy and Minerals Department. "It's very important to us that the federal government reestablish its credibility on this plan." Franklin and Deutch said public hearings would be held on the proposal and that New Mexico would have the right to veto the plan. ∎

Controlling Uranium Mill Wastes

Mesa County, Colo., has an acute leukemia rate that is twice the state average, according to preliminary studies by the state health office.

Mesa County also is the site of an inactive mill where uranium ore was processed between 1951 and 1970.

Sen. Jake Garn, R-Utah, has a friend named Dick Wells whose right eye was surgically removed because of a malignant tumor. Wells owned property in Salt Lake City next to an inactive mill site where uranium was processed between 1951 and 1968. Wells was in that area every day from 1970-78, Garn said.

There is no proven, definite scientific cause and effect relationship between high cancer rates and proximity to uranium mill sites, scientists have said. But the implications are clear, and many are convinced the linkage exists.

The mills leave behind piles of sand-like "tailings," radioactive bits of uranium ore. The tailings' radioactivity level is low compared to wastes from nuclear power plants. For years such low-level radioactivity was believed to be safe.

Indeed, in Mesa County, in western Colorado, and in Salt Lake City, the mill tailings were considered so harmless that they were used as construction material. Hundreds of homes, businesses, schools, churches, roads and other structures were built with materials that included the possible cancer-causing agent, according to congressional testimony.

But in 1978, William D. Rowe, deputy assistant administrator for radiation programs at the Environmental Protection Agency, (EPA), said scientists no longer think uranium wastes are harmless. In fact, Rowe testified, EPA has concluded that mill tailings "may constitute one of the most severe radiation problems in the nation, both as to its individual exposure and the number of people exposed."

Grand Junction, a community of about 20,000 in Mesa County, and Salt Lake City, with about 460,000 residents, are the tailings sites that pose the greatest threat because they are densely populated areas, experts have said.

All told, in 1978 there were 22 abandoned mills in eight western states where uranium ore was processed for nuclear power plants and nuclear weapons. Those 22 sites, which operated between the 1940s and early 1970s, left behind about 25 million tons of largely unattended waste "tailings" in piles and ponds, according to a June 20, 1978, report from the General Accounting Office (GAO).

Those tailings plus the residue from 16 operating plants have produced a total of 140 million tons of uranium mill tailings accumulated at all U.S. mill sites, according to testimony by Joseph M. Hendrie, chairman of the Nuclear Regulatory Commission (NRC). And the NRC estimated that as many as 109 mills would be necessary for U.S. uranium needs by the year 2000, the GAO report said.

In 1977, those 16 operating plants added 10.3 million tons of tailings to the national supply. The amount of waste generated could be expected to grow as the nation's reliance on nuclear power increases, according to an Energy Department spokesman.

Processing mills and waste dumping sites were located in Colorado, Arizona, Idaho, New Mexico, Oregon, Pennsylvania, Texas, Utah and Wyoming.

1978 Legislation

Responding to these concerns, the Carter administration and several members of Congress from western states proposed legislation to clean up the abandoned mill sites. In mid-1978, it looked as though time was running out on the possibility of enactment, since the legislation was stuck in committees in both House and Senate.

There was a general consensus that the sites probably were dangerous and needed to be cleaned up. But there was disagreement among the states and the federal government over how to split the cleanup costs. And there were other conflicts over how to administer the program and whether remedial action for abandoned sites should be tied to a program regulating mills still in operation.

Despite these difficulties, Congress managed to clear a uranium mill waste control bill on the final day of the session. The bill (HR 13650 — PL 95-604) mandating the cleanup also provided for stricter controls on future handling and disposal of wastes from the processing of uranium.

Background: Radiation Threat

About 85 percent of the radioactivity occurring naturally in uranium remains in the tailings after mill processing. Two uranium components, radium and thorium, are the principal sources of the radioactivity.

Radium takes thousands of years to decay enough to lose its radioactivity, according to the GAO. As it decays, it gives off two hazardous substances — gamma radiation and radon gas.

Exposure to enough gamma radiation can cause cancer, the GAO report said. Radon gas diffuses into surrounding air and as a result exposes people to radiation who may not be in the immediate vicinity of tailings piles, according to NRC Chairman Hendrie.

Production of radon from mill tailings "continues for times on the order of a hundred thousand years. . . . The health effects of this radon production are tiny as applied to any one generation, but the sum of these exposures can be made large by counting far into the future," Hendrie testified.

As many as 339 cases of cancer could be avoided over a period of 100 years if the 22 inactive tailings sites were cleaned up, according to a study commissioned by the Energy Department. And the study cautioned that as many as three or four times that many cases actually might be spawned by the tailings piles.

Prior to 1978, no federal agency had explicit authority to regulate or dispose of wastes at abandoned uranium mills. The Environmental Protection Agency (EPA) had some jurisdiction over the tailings. But Sen. Pete V.

Domenici, R-N.M., told the Senate that EPA would not be able to issue regulations governing the wastes for several years, possibly not before 1984.

Cleanup Methods

Possible cleanup remedies have ranged from putting a fence around inactive mill sites to physically moving the tailings to isolated spots where they would be carefully and expensively shielded, according to the Western Governors' Conference.

But the GAO noted that the "technology to stabilize the mill tailings has not been fully developed."

Precautions ideally should be taken against erosion of the piles by wind or water, chemical compound formation through inadvertent mixing with other substances and possible contamination of grazing lands, which could lead the radioactive material into the human food chain, expert testimony indicated.

At least one firm, Ranchers Exploration and Development Corp. of Albuquerque, N.M., has been making money from the tailings. In July 21, 1978, testimony before the House Commerce Subcommittee on Energy and Power, the firm's president, Maxie L. Anderson, described how his business works.

Milling processes today are more efficient than those used by the now-abandoned mills, he said. Consequently, tailings from the old mills often contain significant quantities of uranium and vanadium, an element used in nuclear processes and in steel production. Anderson said his firm bought 600,000 tons of tailings, which covered about 20 acres at the Naturita, Colo., site of a former mill on the San Miguel River.

The firm trucks the tailings 3.5 miles to three large rectangular tanks lined with clay where they are mixed with acid. The solution that is produced is run through a plant that extracts the uranium and vanadium.

The operation cost about $8 million, Anderson said, and yielded about 1,000 pounds of uranium and 4,000 pounds of vanadium a day. The operation was expected to be finished by mid-1979, Anderson said.

Covering tailings with a foot of compacted clay blocks out the gamma radiation, Anderson maintained, and putting them into clay-lined tanks covered with two feet of compacted shale cuts radon gas emanations to naturally occurring levels.

Anderson said his firm also had acquired a 35-acre tailings site on the banks of the Animas River near Durango, Colo., and planned a similar operation there.

Sharing Cleanup Costs

While there was general consensus that the cleanup work needed to be done, there was disagreement about how the program should operate.

The Carter administration proposed legislation April 27, 1978, that would allow the Department of Energy to enter into cooperative agreements with states to clean up inactive mill tailings sites.

Under the administration bill, the Energy Department would pay 75 percent of the cleanup costs and states would pay 25 percent. The Energy Department, after consulting with states, the EPA and the NRC, would determine whether cleanup efforts were needed and would choose appropriate remedies.

The administration argued that states should pay part of the costs because they would benefit from the cleanup,

would have a voice in selecting cleanup options and gained employment and tax benefits from the mills when they were operating.

But the states saw it differently. They argued that the nation's uranium procurement program mounted after World War II was undertaken in the national interest for national projects. The uranium was used for weapons, power development and research.

Also, state spokesmen pointed out, the federal government ran the whole show. The old Atomic Energy Commission chose contractors, provided them with technology, regulated ore production, set ore prices and was the exclusive purchaser of the processed uranium, states argued.

The states, speaking through the Western Governors' Conference, therefore concluded that the federal government should pay full cleanup costs.

Legally, there was no clear obligation on anyone to pay, according to the GAO. The problem was not anticipated and laws and contracts did not assign responsibility for cleaning up mills and tailings.

But the GAO argued that the federal government had a moral obligation to pay at least part of the costs, although it warned that a precedent could be set that might obligate the government to clean up other radioactive sites. The costs could run into the billions of dollars because nuclear facilities, including power plants, become contaminated with radioactivity after a few decades and so far the procedures and liabilities for "decommissioning" those facilities have received little attention.

Another slant in the who-should-pay debate was provided by the Environmental Policy Center, a private organization. That group argued in testimony that though contracts did not require mill owners to provide future cleanup costs, the owners had ample reason to realize the need would occur and, therefore, ought to be sued by the Justice Department to recover costs and damages.

There were other controversies. Some objected to the provision in the administration bill waiving federal liability for injuries or illness resulting from work with radioactive materials. The provision meant that if members of federal cleanup crews got cancer, they could not sue the government.

There also were disputes over whether the NRC or the EPA should have primary jurisdiction over regulating the tailings, and how the dividing lines between them should be drawn.

Many of these controversies were reflected in the differing versions of legislation reported by House and Senate committees.

House, Senate Action

The Senate Energy and Natural Resources Committee ordered reported its uranium wastes cleanup bill (S 3078) Oct. 3. On Sept. 26, the House Commerce Committee ordered reported the House bill (HR 13650), which had been stalled for more than a month. The House Interior Committee, which shared jurisdiction on the issue with Commerce, had reported its version of HR 13650 Aug. 11.

The major difference among the three cleanup bills concerned how much of the cost was to be shouldered by the federal government.

The Carter administration originally called for the federal government to pay 75 percent of the cost, with the remaining 25 percent paid by states where abandoned mills were located.

Inactive Uranium Mills

Site	Tons of Tailings	Current Owner	Mid-1978 Estimated Cleanup Cost		
Arizona					
Monument	1,200,000	Navajo Nation	$ 585,000	to	$ 1,165,000
Tuba City	800,000	Navajo Nation	671,000	to	2,904,000
Colorado					
Durango	1,555,000	Ranchers Exploration and Development Corp. of Albuquerque, N.M.	4,300,000	to	13,600,000
Grand Junction	1,900,000	Shumway, Inc.	470,000	to	18,000,000
Gunnison	540,000	Three individuals in partnership: Clarence A. Decker, N. Marcus Bishop, and Roger L. McEachren	480,000	to	5,900,000
Maybell	2,600,000	Union Carbide Corp.	250,000	to	4,500,000
Nuturita	704,000	Rangers Exploration and Development Corp. of Albuquerque, N.M.	270,000	to	950,000
New Rifle and Old Rifle (two sites)	3,050,000	Union Carbide Corp.	224,000	to	20,300,000
Slick Rock-North Continent	37,000	Union Carbide Corp.			
Slick Rock-Union Carbide	350,000	Union Carbide Corp.	370,000	to	1,100,000*
Idaho					
Lowman	90,000	Nelsicol Chemical Corp.	393,000	to	590,000
New Mexico					
Ambrosia Lake	2,600,000	United Nuclear Co.	920,000	to	2,230,000
Shiprock	1,650,000	Navajo Nation	540,000	to	12,500,000
Oregon					
Lakeview	130,000	Precision Pine (partnership)	40,000	to	290,000
Texas					
Falls City	2,500,000	Solution Engineering Co.	1,840,000	to	2,450,000
Ray Point	490,000	Exxon Co.	[Exxon is providing funding]		
Utah					
Green River	123,000	Union Carbide Corp.	700,000	to	926,000
Mexican Hat	2,200,000	Navajo Nation	370,000	to	4,390,000
Salt Lake City	1,700,000	Salt Lake County Suburban Sanitary District; two individuals: D. Eugene Moenich and David K. Richards	550,000	to	39,400,000
Wyoming					
Converse County	187,000	Wyoming Mining and Milling Co.	81,000	to	142,000
Riverton	900,000	Solution Engineering Co.	460,000	to	1,140,000
TOTAL	25,306,000		$13,514,000	to	$132,477,000

* Two Slick Rock, Colo. sites have combined cost estimates.

SOURCE: General Accounting Office; Cost projections from Western Governors' Conference

The House Interior Committee raised the federal share to 90 percent, but said that no state would be required to pay more than one-fourth of 1 percent of its general revenues. If the state's 10 percent share exceeded that level, the federal government would make up the difference. Colorado, Utah and Pennsylvania were the only states that would be affected by the ceiling.

The House Commerce Committee went along with the 90 percent federal share, but refused to back the provision for higher shares in Colorado, Utah and Pennsylvania. Rep. Clarence J. Brown, R-Ohio, said the 10 percent state share "is not unreasonable."

Rep. John D. Dingell, D-Mich., argued that increasing the federal share "could conceivably serve as a pattern for future legislation of this type. It would be extremely dangerous and a bad precedent."

The Senate Energy Committee was more receptive to the pleadings of the governors of those states. The panel

Uranium mill in the Gas Hills of Wyoming

adopted an amendment by Sen. Pete V. Domenici, R-N.M., requiring the federal government to pay 100 percent of the cleanup costs.

"Why shouldn't the federal government pay for the whole thing?" Domenici asked fellow committee members. "This was the federal government's responsibility in the first place." Four of the mill sites were in New Mexico.

In its version, the House Interior Committee authorized $180 million for fiscal 1979. That was in addition to the $3 million for cleanup included in the Department of Energy authorization bill (HR 11329).

The Commerce Committee bill provided for the cleanup funds to come out of the annual Energy Department authorization, but did not specify an amount.

The Senate Energy bill authorized $3 million for fiscal 1979, with the stipulation that future funds be authorized each year.

All three versions:
• Required federal ownership of uranium mill sites, although the Senate bill allowed states to take over sites after they were cleaned up.
• Required the federal government to pay 100 percent of the cleanup costs for wastes sites on Indian lands.

• Gave states the authority to concur in the type of cleanup activity and the location of disposal sites for tailings.

The Senate Energy and House Commerce bills directed the attorney general to study whether private corporations owning uranium waste sites could be held liable for environmental damage. The attorney general could then file suit to recover damages, which would be used to help pay the cleanup costs.

The House passed its version of the bill on Oct. 3. When the bill reached the Senate Oct. 13, the 90-10 split was adopted, along with the provision that money for the cleanup would have to be provided each year in the Energy Department authorization bill.

Final Provisions

As cleared by Congress, HR 13650:
• Gave the Nuclear Regulatory Commission, in cooperation with the Environmental Protection Agency, authority to develop standards for the safe disposal of wastes from uranium processing mills.
• Directed the Energy Department to enter into agreements to clean up 22 abandoned disposal sites with states where the uranium wastes were located.
• Provided that the federal government would pay 90 percent of the cleanup costs, with the remaining 10 percent paid by the states, but specified that the federal government would pay 100 percent of the cleanup costs at two sites located on Indian lands.
• Gave states the right to "participate fully" in the selection and implementation of procedures to clean up the wastes.
• Required that the uranium wastes be turned over to the federal government or to the states where they were located.
• Required that waste disposal sites be turned over to the state or federal government, unless the NRC determined that such a turnover was unnecessary.
• Directed the NRC to conduct a study to determine if it had the authority to compel the owners of two active processing mills in New Mexico to clean up abandoned uranium wastes on their property. If the NRC determined that it did not have that authority, the commission could enter into an agreement with the state of New Mexico for a government-run cleanup program.
• Directed the attorney general to conduct a study to determine if the private companies owning uranium waste disposal sites could be held liable for damages caused by the wastes. Any damages collected from the companies would be used to help pay the cleanup costs. ▮

Congress Looks to Gasohol As Energy Source

On May 9, 1978, several members of Congress urged their colleagues to drive their cars up to a tank truck on Capitol Hill and fill up their tanks with a free sample of gasohol, a blend of gasoline and alcohol.

Their publicity stunt was designed to focus attention on what they believed was one way of battling dwindling energy supplies — making fuel from resources America has in abundance, such as grain, garbage, wood and coal.

Those ingredients can be used to make alcohol. By itself or in a gasohol blend — 10 to 15 percent alcohol and the rest gasoline — it has proved to be an effective motor fuel.

Proponents have said that replacing all gasoline with gasohol nationwide could cut this country's annual consumption of 103 billion gallons of gasoline by 10 percent. It also could reduce dependence on foreign oil by 20 percent. They noted that alcohol comes from inexhaustible raw materials — basically anything that grows. And they claimed it makes engines burn cleaner and more efficiently so it could cut pollution levels and increase gas mileage.

New Crop Market

Those who favored a blend using ethyl alcohol, which is made from farm products, have said this kind of gasohol's greatest advantage would be to open a new market for America's farmers in addition to decreasing dependence on foreign oil.

Production of ethyl alcohol, known as ethanol, would allow farmers to plant their land fence post to fence post, its proponents said, utilizing even "set-aside" land they were required to take out of production in order to participate in federal crop subsidy programs. A provision allowing this was included in the 1978 emergency farm bill *(See next page)*

But gasohol has its problems, too. Alcohol generally is more expensive to manufacture than gasoline at 1978 prices, and it takes more energy to produce a gallon of alcohol than the alcohol produces when burned.

The Energy Department has asserted that alcohol fuels could not be competitive commercially before 1985 without a federal subsidy. The oil industry also contended that alcohol fuels are not economically competitive with gasoline. But they have said alcohol should be considered as one of a number of energy alternatives, including synthetic gasoline from shale and oil.

Some members of Congress, anxious to spur interest in alcohol fuels, have pushed for greater federal involvement in their development. Seventy-three senators and representatives wrote to Agriculture Secretary Bob Bergland and Energy Secretary James R. Schlesinger in October 1977 asking for a "major national commitment" to develop fuels from agricultural and forest products.

And a number of farm state members sponsored bills intended to promote alcohol fuels. Most of the measures would provide tax breaks for plants that would produce alcohol and gasohol.

Background

There are two types of alcohol fuel — ethanol and methanol. Ethanol is produced from growing plants; plant waste, like husks and stalks; whole grain; solid waste; food waste, like potato peelings, and petroleum. Methanol, or wood alcohol, can be made from wood, sewage, garbage, coal, natural gas, peat, shale, tar or petroleum. Because it could help bail out the troubled agriculture industry, ethanol has received more of the attention in proposed state and federal alcohol fuels legislation.

But methanol is cheaper. The reason, according to ethanol proponents, is because the technology required to produce methanol is more advanced as a result of government funded research on coal gasification and liquefaction, one step of which yields methanol. Methanol costs 30 to 50 cents a gallon to produce compared to about $1 to $1.30 for ethanol and about 40 cents for a gallon of gasoline.

New Ideas, Old Fuel

Alcohol has been in use as a motor fuel in various parts of the world for more than 60 years, generally in a blend with gasoline. The first modern combustion engine, the Otto cycle, developed in 1876, ran on alcohol as well as gasoline.

Advocates of alcohol fuels have included Alexander Graham Bell, who, in 1922, called it "a beautifully clean and efficient fuel which can be produced from vegetable matter . . . waste products of our farms and even the garbage of our cities."

Henry Ford favored it and designed the Model T automobile with an adjustable carburetor so it could use alcohol, gasoline or any mixture between.

Despite the fact that production and retail costs of alcohol fuels have consistently exceeded those of petroleum, alcohol has come into use periodically in response to oil shortages, agricultural surpluses and drives for national independence from foreign fuel.

In the 1930s most European countries raised farm crops specifically for alcohol to supplement fossil fuels and stabilize farm production. During World War II, Germany fueled its vehicles on alcohol made from potatoes and the United States operated an ethanol plant in Omaha to produce motor fuel for the Army.

During the same period, service stations in Kansas, Nebraska and Illinois sold an alcohol-gasoline blend called Agrol. But Agrol producers eventually went out of business because gasoline was cheaper.

A 1936 Department of Agriculture study predicted that fossil fuel supplies would be exhausted eventually but concluded that their replacement by alcohol fuels would not be economically feasible without government subsidy.

Oil Embargo

The alcohol fuel idea got a boost in 1973, the year the Arab oil embargo led to a fourfold increase in the interna-

127

tional standard price of crude oil. During that embargo, Sun Oil Co. used methyl alcohol as a gasoline extender.

After the embargo, the Energy Research and Development Administration (ERDA) — which became part of the Department of Energy in 1977 — spent about $2 million to $3 million a year on alcohol fuels research, according to Eugene Ecklund, chief of the department's Alternative Fuels Branch. That amount increased to $6.8 million in fiscal 1978.

The president's fiscal 1979 budget recommended $18.6 million for alcohol fuels research. Of that, $12.1 million was designated for research on alcohol from biomass (vegetable or waste material), including $3.5 million for research on alcohol from fermentation of grain. A total of $3 million was designated for research on methanol from coal.

Alcohol fuels in 1978 accounted for 1.33 percent of the fuel used in highway vehicles in this country. The majority of the 1.1 billion gallons of methanol and 100 million gallons of non-beverage ethanol produced annually goes for industrial uses such as cleaning solvents and chemical processing. Traditionally, both types of alcohol have been produced almost totally from petroleum or natural gas.

Other countries also were looking to alcohol fuels. In Brazil, for example, fuel of up to 30 percent alcohol, made from sugar or manioc root, has been in use since 1968, and construction was under way in 1978 on 15 alcohol distilleries as part of a drive to replace 20 percent of the country's gasoline with alcohol by 1980.

Gasohol Commission

To promote the use of alcohol as an alternative fuel, representatives of agriculture, business and state and local governments of 13 western and midwestern states met in Lincoln, Neb., in January 1977 to form the National Gasohol Commission, a non-profit corporation aimed at promoting the passage of state and federal laws to encourage the use of gasohol. Member states were Nebraska, North Dakota, Oklahoma, Montana, Minnesota, Washington, Kansas, Idaho, Iowa, Colorado, Indiana, Wyoming and Kentucky.

At least ten states have introduced or passed legislation endorsing gasohol, exempting it from state gasoline taxes or anti-pollution regulations or funding alcohol fuels research.

Nebraska's Plan

In 1971, the Nebraska legislature established a program to promote a 10 percent ethanol blend the state officially titled "Gasohol."

With funds from a committee set up to monitor the gasohol program, University of Nebraska Professor William A. Scheller conducted a two-million-mile road test using 45 state vehicles operated on gasohol. The results were encouraging to proponents of the alternative fuel. Gasohol powered vehicles had 5.3 percent better mileage than those run on gasoline. In addition, carbon monoxide and nitrous oxide emissions were down about 10 percent.

Volkswagen has run similar test fleets on methanol blend gasohol in Germany. The vehicles showed fewer pollutant emissions and no significant mechanical problems. And the German government was sharing half of the cost of a joint study with automobile and fuel producers to develop a 15 percent alcohol fuel.

Gasohol also has received the endorsement of such diverse groups as the Republican Conference of the Senate,

the Democratic National Committee, the American Automobile Association and the American Agricultural Movement.

In October 1977, gasohol backers, including a group of farm wives from Montana, drove gasohol powered vehicles to a rally on the Capitol steps in an effort to spur congressional action.

Congress' Role

The first major congressional endorsement of alcohol fuels came with the Food and Agriculture Act of 1977 (PL 95-113). The measure authorized a 5-year, $24 million research program to be carried out by the Department of Agriculture through grants to colleges and universities. It also authorized the department to extend up to $15 million in loan guarantees for each of four pilot plants to produce alcohol and industrial hydrocarbons, such as asphalts, adhesives and solvents.

Congressional interest in alcohol fuels was further demonstrated by a provision in the 1978 energy bill that exempted from the federal excise tax on motor fuel, gasohol sold after Dec. 31, 1978, and before Oct. 1, 1984, if the gasohol was at least 10 percent alcohol. The exemption would apply only if the alcohol was made from products — such as grain or solid waste — other than petroleum, natural gas or coal. The bill also directed the treasury secretary to expedite applications for permits to distill ethanol for use in the production of gasohol. The energy secretary was directed to make annual reports to Congress on the use of alcohol in fuels from 1980 through 1984.

A provision relating to alcohol fuels was contained in the 1978 emergency farm bill (PL 95-279) as well. The bill, which cleared Congress May 2, authorized the agriculture secretary to permit farmers to produce crops on set-aside land for production of gasohol. In years with no set-aside, the secretary could provide incentive payments to encourage gasohol production.

Of the more than 20 alcohol measures introduced in the 95th Congress, the majority involved general endorsement of the alcohol fuels concept, provided tax exemptions for gasohol, allowed rapid amortization of facilities producing alcohol fuels or exempted gasohol from certain portions of the Clean Air Act (PL 91-604).

Among those pressing for congressional action on gasohol was Sen. Birch Bayh, D-Ind., who proposed to amend the Department of Energy fiscal 1979 authorization bill (S 2692) by doubling funds for research on fuels from biomass. Congressional committees approved the measure, which would bring the authorization for biomass fuels research to $52.1 million, but the bill died in the final days of the 1978 session. However, the president's fiscal 1980 budget contained a request for $54.5 million for biomass research.

Bayh's Bill

Bayh also proposed legislation to create a National Alcohol Fuels Commission composed of six senators, six representatives and seven presidential appointees from industry, labor, agriculture and consumer groups. The commission would report to the president by the end of 1980 on the potential of alcohol fuel and make recommendations about its future use.

Bayh generally has been displeased with what he considered the Energy Department's lack of action on alcohol fuels. A position paper the department issued on the subject March 16, 1978, "reflects a lack of effort,

More Mileage, Less Pollution in Findley Gasohol Test

It was October 1977, the price of grain had fallen as the cost of producing it continued to rise, and Congress had just passed the controversial 1977 farm bill.

In Montana, farm wives fueled their cars with gasohol — gasoline plus alcohol made from grain — and began the long trek across country to protest on the steps of the Capitol in Washington.

In Pittsfield, Ill., Rep. Paul Findley, R-Ill., did some serious thinking about gasohol. Then he put it in his 1973 Malibu station wagon and spent three weeks driving around his district testing emissions, mileage and performance.

The test revealed a small increase in gas mileage, a substantial drop in pollution emissions and little change in performance.

"It was a period of low grain prices," said Findley. "I had had several constituents who for years had been convinced that alcohol should be mixed with gas and that farm land provides a source of fuel for the nation. There was a lot of talk in the press and controversy about gasohol, so I decided to try it."

He and staff aide Don Norton each used a mixture of nine gallons of unleaded gasoline to one gallon of 200 proof ethyl alcohol, called ethanol, in Findley's station wagon and in Norton's three-quarter ton 1977 GMC pickup truck.

At that time the only service stations selling gasohol from the pump were in Nebraska, so the pair bought their ethanol in 55-gallon drums from a local chemical company at a cost of $1.85 per gallon. It would have been cheaper in larger quantities.

They carried cans of the ethanol in the backs of the vehicles and mixed it with gasoline every time they stopped to refuel.

A mixture of unleaded gasoline averaging 66 cents per gallon and the ethanol, costing $1.85, produced their 10 percent gasohol mixture for about $1.25 cents per gallon.

Pollution Tests

Findley said the most dramatic result of the test was the drop in the vehicles' emission of pollutants.

Carbon monoxide emissions from the Malibu dropped by 36 percent with gasohol and hydrocarbon emissions down by 31 percent. Norton achieved similar results with his pickup.

Emissions dropped even further — by about 85 percent for carbon monoxide and 60 percent for hydrocarbons — when Findley tried a 35 percent alcohol blend of gasohol.

Mileage

The gasohol also boosted mileage, Findley's test found. Mileage in his Malibu went from 16.4 miles per gallon (mpg) on gasoline to 16.7 mpg with the 10 percent gasohol blend, a 2 percent increase. The mileage of Norton's pickup truck went from 12.4 to 12.5 mpg with the same fuel. They did not test mileage on the 35 percent blend.

"It was not an auspicious gain in mileage," Norton noted, "but there were some people who claimed that with gasohol your mileage went down. So we disproved that. Of course, that depends a lot on the age of your

Rep. Paul Findley, R-Ill., (right) discusses his gasohol-powered car with corn farmers in his district.

car. Older models tend to get more mileage from gasohol because of its higher octane level."

Both vehicles were equipped with a one gallon auxiliary tank mounted on the hood to allow rapid switches from one type of fuel to the other and testing of both fuels under the same driving conditions in the same vehicles.

Findley said he observed "no noticeable difference" in the way his car operated whether it was running on gasoline or gasohol.

"We experienced no driveability problems such as stalling, hesitation, cold starts or separation of the alcohol from the gasoline," he said.

Norton reported a few side effects from the gasohol. He said it had a slightly more pungent exhaust odor than gasoline, slightly faster idling and a sensation of quicker acceleration.

commitment and foresight with respect to this energy source . . . which I find disturbing," Bayh said.

"I am confident that a national alcohol fuels program can draw very broad based support from the American people, the business, farm and scientific communities. . .," he added.

Bayh and Sen. Frank Church, D-Idaho, said they would not hesitate to seek federally mandated targets for production and use of alcohol fuel.

Church's Targets

Church sponsored a bill that would set such goals. It would require the secretary of energy to establish a program to replace gasoline with gasohol from renewable resources and mandates that 1 percent of all U.S. motor fuel production consist of gasohol by 1981. The required percentage would increase to 5 percent in 1985 and to 10 percent in 1990.

It provided for a $1 per gallon maximum penalty for all fuel sold by refiners that was not in compliance with the established gasohol consumption goal and required any facility constructed to distill alcohol motor fuel to use renewable raw materials, such as grain or forest products.

Some energy experts have said the Church deadlines were too ambitious because they could not be met with existing technology and supplies of raw materials.

But a Church aide said the deadlines were included to ensure a market for alcohol. "Without a sure market, we believe financiers would not be willing to loan the money to construct alcohol . . . production facilities," the aide said.

Administration Initiatives

Charges against the administration of footdragging on alcohol fuels dated from President Carter's April 20, 1977, energy message. It devoted only one sentence to the subject.

Gasohol backers said the creation in December 1977 of a Department of Energy task force on alcohol fuels was the bureaucracy's first serious recognition of their potential. The move came in response to the letters from the 73 lawmakers who had called for the national commitment to develop alcohol fuels.

The department position paper on alcohol fuels said they were too expensive for commercial use in the near term but pledged that the department would include the fuels in the phase two energy plan.

Gasohol's Potential

Gasohol proponents have said that its problems in 1978, such as its high price, were only short term.

The 1978 pump price of 69 cents to 76 cents for a 10 percent ethanol blend — available to motorists in Nebraska and Illinois — will not look so high when gasoline prices rise to predicted levels of $1.25 to $1.50 a gallon in the mid-1980s, they argued.

The Energy Department has predicted that because of the high cost of alcohol fuels, they could not be commercially competitive before 1985 without federal help. The department also has asserted that there were not enough production facilities for widespread commercialization of alcohol fuels and that there was no ready market for them.

Grain for ethanol production is more expensive and less abundant than coal, which can go into methanol. As a result, "methanol at this time appears to be the most economical of the alcohol fuel substitutes," according to Leslie Goldman, deputy assistant energy secretary for policy development and competition. But he suggested that ethanol could play a major role in regional markets.

Gasohol backers have argued that infusions of federal money for research could produce the technology needed to make gasohol commercially feasible. And, they said, federally mandated production and consumption goals would force the fuel industry to develop technology and would ensure financing and markets for alcohol fuels.

Richard Merritt, lobbyist for Nebraska's Gasohol Committee, suggested that alcohol fuel made from renewable sources, like crops, was not too popular with the Energy Department because it contradicted President Carters' emphasis on conserving rather than developing fuel sources.

New Process

Ethanol proponents also said they have developed a new, cheaper process to make ethanol out of plant leaves,

stalks and husks. The process, developed by Dr. George Tsao of Purdue University, would cut production costs by reducing the time required for fermentation and would ensure an inexhaustible supply of raw materials that would not diminish world food supplies.

In testimony before the Senate Appropriations Committee Jan. 31, 1978, Tsao said that with his process he could produce twice the ethanol using half the energy of a process using whole grain. The alcohol produced would cost about 74 cents a gallon.

Supporters of ethanol noted that its cost could be reduced still further if the energy value of fermentation byproducts, such as distiller's grain for cattle or cereal-like products for human consumption, were considered.

The Department of Agriculture released a report in February 1978 entitled, "Gasohol from Grain — The Economic Issues." It said a program to replace gasoline with ethanol gasohol made from whole corn would require a federal subsidy of 10.4 cents per gallon — $10 billion a year — to bring it down to 67 cents per gallon, the average national cost for unleaded gasoline.

Ethanol supporters protested that the study unfairly compared the cost of gasohol to less expensive domestic gasoline rather than the 73 cents per gallon average cost of gasoline from imported oil.

Dr. Thomas Reed of the Solar Energy Research Institute in Golden, Colo., told the Appropriations Committee that comparisons with alcohol fuel prices should take into account government subsidies of petroleum, such as depletion allowances, that cut the real cost of producing gasoline from 80 cents to less than 40 cents per gallon.

Ethanol vs. Methanol

Ethanol supporters have argued that large oil companies opposed alcohol fuels in general because potentially they could replace gasoline as the nation's main motor fuel. They noted that nearly anyone, from a small farmer to the City of New York, could supply cheap raw materials. They also claimed that oil companies, as owners of large coal reserves, favored methanol, which can be made from coal.

However, Ellis G. Campbell, crude oil supply manager for Mobil Oil Co., said the company supported balanced consideration of all synthetic fuels. He said Mobil had developed a process to convert methanol from coal into high octane gasoline from a ton of bituminous coal. The gasoline produced cost 40 to 50 cents more than a gallon of petroleum-based gasoline.

"Ethanol worked better in the catalyst we have developed for converting alcohol into synthetic gasoline," he said. "But we favor methanol because of the volume of the raw material, coal, and because it is cheaper. It is more cost effective."

Basically, said Ecklund of the Energy Department, "[it] comes down to the fact that ethanol is easier to use and more expensive while methanol is less expensive but creates more problems. Which one you favor depends on where you put your emphasis."

Octane Levels

Finally, alcohol fuel supporters pointed out, mixing alcohol, which has a high octane level, with cheaper, lower octane gasoline forms gasohol with a price closer to that of premium gasoline. (The higher a fuel's octane level, the more efficiently it performs.)

That price reduction, Sen. Carl T. Curtis, R-Neb., argued before the Appropriations Committee, combined

A program to replace gasoline with ethanol gasohol made from corn would require a $10 billion a year federal subsidy, the government says

with an exemption from the federal four-cent-a-gallon excise tax on gasoline could bring the price of gasohol down to about 64 cents a gallon.

Mixing 5 percent ethanol and 5 percent of cheaper methanol to form a 10 percent alcohol blend with gasoline also could reduce gasohol prices, advocates contended.

Energy Balance

One of the major arguments against alcohol fuels is that they take more energy to produce than they yield and that they produce energy poorly compared with petroleum.

Ethanol yields two-thirds and methanol yields one-half the energy of gasoline when burned. In terms of overall fuel efficiency, ethanol yields about 35 percent of the energy needed to produce it, and methanol yields 45 percent. That compares with about 90 percent yielded by gasoline.

But gasohol advocates claimed that improving technology would narrow the energy deficit. Ethanol, for example, would become more efficient to produce if fermentation time were cut. They added that the gap also could be narrowed by using renewable sources, such as plant wastes, husks, wood or power plant exhaust heat, instead of petroleum products to fuel the plants producing the alcohol.

Driving Performance

Experts from Ford Motor Co. and General Motors Corp. said in congressional testimony that most engines can operate on gasohol blends of up to about 15 percent alcohol without modification.

Beyond that point, however, carburetor adjustments would be needed to fight the potential problems of poor cold weather starting and vapor lock, a warm weather condition where bubbles of vaporized fuel block the flow of fuel in the gas line. Air and gasoline are mixed in the carburetor.

Although the Nebraska test fleet showed a decrease in emissions of air pollutants when they ran on a 10 percent ethanol blend, Dr. Serge Gratch of Ford said the company's tests indicated increased emissions of aldehydes (dehydrated alcohol) and oxides of nitrogen with gasohol powered vehicles.

As for the gasohol claims of better gas mileage, Ford and General Motors representatives testified that mileage probably would depend on the age of the vehicle involved. Older, high performance engines would get better mileage on gasohol because alcohol contains more oxygen than gasoline. Up to a point, the more oxygen added to gasoline, the better the mileage.

Most new car engines, however, have been designed to burn the maximum amount of oxygen and still run smoothly. So the infusion of extra oxygen from alcohol could hinder new car performance and decrease mileage.

The automotive experts testified that auto makers expected to be able to design new engines to handle any future gasohol blends well in advance of the time they were marketed.

Industry's Position

Oil producers cited the expense of producing alcohol, the problems of transporting it and the difficulties it causes for motorists as obstacles to its immediate use on a large scale.

The American Petroleum Institute (API) said that a new distribution system would be needed to handle the problem of alcohol separating from gasoline during transport because of water seeping into container trucks. API also cited potential driving problems, such as stalling, vapor lock and cold weather starting and noted that alcohol causes increased corrosion in some engine metals.

A policy statement approved April 6, 1978, by API concluded that research on alcohol as fuels, converting them to gasoline and using them to power land-based turbine engines, such as those that power electrical generators, should be encouraged. But, it added, "there should be no governmental mandating of the sale or use of alcohols as fuels. Under current conditions, mandating would force the product on consumers at a price higher than they would otherwise have to pay and would force consumers to subsidize alcohol producers."

Appendix

CQ

Energy Legislation: 1973-76

In December 1773, American colonists dumped British tea into Boston Harbor, willing to do without this popular drink rather than acquiesce in British efforts to monopolize its sale.

Two hundred years later, American motorists sat in mile-long lines for hours to fill the tanks of their automobiles with ever more expensive gasoline, a fuel made suddenly scarce by the decision of Arab nations to halt shipments of oil to the United States.

Somewhere between the War for Independence and Project Independence, Americans came to accept their dependence on other nations for certain essential goods. With that dependence, they surrendered a measure of control over their everyday lives. America's increasing energy dependence gave the federal government major new problems to solve during the 1973-76 period, but few solutions were forthcoming.

The Embargo

The Arab oil embargo was the central energy event of the period. The embargo was imposed Oct. 18, 1973, by the Organization of Petroleum Exporting Countries (OPEC), who were displeased with the pro-Israeli policy of the United States and certain European countries during the October Middle East war. It remained in effect until March 18, 1974.

The most visible effects of the embargo were the long lines at service stations. In addition, most service stations closed on Sundays, sharply curtailing weekend driving and leaving many motels and ski resorts empty. Fear of running out of heating oil led office managers and homeowners to turn down thermostats, and many Americans donned extra sweaters for the 1973-74 winter.

But the more fundamental effect of the embargo was a hike of almost 400 per cent in the cost of foreign oil. From Oct. 1, 1973, to Jan. 1, 1974, the price of a barrel of oil imported into the United States went from $3.00 to $11.65.

Energy was no longer a bargain, as it had been for the entire post-World War II era. Consumer prices soon reflected this leap in the cost of imported oil; they jumped 33.5 per cent in 1974. Regular gasoline that cost 35 cents a gallon in mid-1973 cost 56 cents a gallon by August 1974. Along with the price of oil, the price of coal, natural gas, electricity and even firewood increased.

The economic impact was severe. Purchasing power dropped as utility bills climbed. Sen. Henry M. Jackson (D Wash.) estimated in 1974 that the year's energy price increases added almost $500 a year to the average American's gasoline, electricity and heating oil bills.

Industrial output dropped; unemployment rose. Prices continued to rise, accelerating inflation, and workers sought pay increases in order to cope with the higher bills.

Secretary of State Henry A. Kissinger said that the embargo "cost the United States 500,000 jobs, more than $10-billion in national production, and a rampant inflation."

The embargo did not create the energy crisis. It simply brought dramatically to world attention a fact that experts had been pointing out for some time: The United States was each year consuming more oil and producing less, therefore becoming ever more dependent on imported oil. Suddenly the meaning of this trend came home to the average American as fuel supplies dwindled and prices climbed.

The Response

"We have an energy crisis," said President Nixon late in 1973, "but there is no crisis of the American spirit."

Hoping to mobilize the national determination that had supported efforts to harness the power of the atom and to place a man on the moon, Nixon announced Project Independence in November 1973. The goal of this, the U.S. response to the embargo, was self-sufficiency in energy by 1980.

Among the emergency steps proposed by the president were: a return to year-round daylight savings time; a reduction of speed limits to 50 miles per hour; congressional funding for research and development; and authority to implement gas rationing and emergency conservation measures as well as to relax environmental regulations (particularly clean air standards for coal conversion) where necessary. Nixon also called for passage of bills to authorize construction of the trans-Alaska pipeline, to deregulate natural gas prices, to establish federal standards for strip-mining of coal and to reorganize the energy bureaucracy.

Energy experts descried Nixon's goal as an impossible timetable, and by 1974 the goal was quietly redefined as independence from insecure foreign sources of oil. The timetable was also quietly shifted back five years, to 1985. Soon after taking office, President Ford said that "no nation has or can have within its borders everything necessary for a full and rich life for all its people. Independence cannot mean isolation. The aim of Project Independence is not to set the United States apart from the rest of the world; it is to enable the United States to do its part more effectively in the world's effort to provide more energy."

This point was echoed by the Project Independence report issued late in 1974 that disclaimed the goal of reducing oil imports to zero: "While zero imports is achievable, it is simply not warranted economically or politically.... Some imports are from secure sources. Others are from insecure sources, but they can be insured against through emergency demand-curtailment measures or standby storage."

The embargo and Nixon's call for action came late in the first session of the 93rd Congress. Congress had already been working on energy problems and it quickly sent Nixon

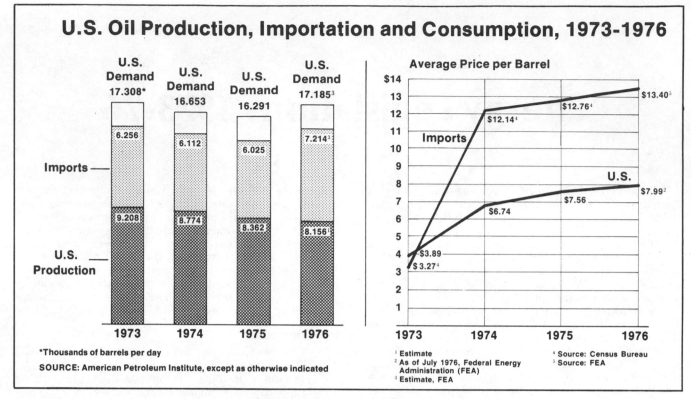

U.S. Oil Production, Importation and Consumption, 1973-1976

U.S. Demand 17.308*
U.S. Demand 16.653
U.S. Demand 16.291
U.S. Demand 17.185[3]

Imports: 6.256 / 6.112 / 6.025 / 7.214[3]

U.S. Production: 9.208 / 8.774 / 8.362 / 8.156[5]

1973   1974   1975   1976

*Thousands of barrels per day

SOURCE: American Petroleum Institute, except as otherwise indicated

Average Price per Barrel

Imports: $3.27[4] ... $12.14[4] ... $12.76[4] ... $13.40[5]

U.S.: $3.89 ... $6.74 ... $7.56 ... $7.99[2]

1973   1974   1975   1976

[1] Estimate
[2] As of July 1976, Federal Energy Administration (FEA)
[3] Estimate, FEA
[4] Source: Census Bureau
[5] Source: FEA

two major energy measures—one authorizing a fuel allocation and price control system, the other clearing the way for construction of the Alaska pipeline. The pipeline was to carry up to two million barrels of oil a day from the frozen northern oil fields to a southern port for distribution to the lower 48 states beginning in mid-1977.

Early in 1974 the embargo was lifted, and the problem of energy began to recede from national attention. But Congress responded to presidential requests to reorganize the federal agencies to deal with energy matters. It approved creation of a "temporary" energy crisis manager—the Federal Energy Administration (FEA)—and a new Energy Research and Development Administration (ERDA), which took over much of the work of the old Atomic Energy Commission.

Congressional Complications

As the memory of the long gasoline lines faded, however, partisan and regional interests came into play to complicate the efforts of the Ford administration and the heavily Democratic 94th Congress to write a national energy policy.

President Ford in January 1975 offered a plan to cut energy consumption and stimulate domestic energy production by relying on higher fuel prices. Prices would have been allowed to rise through a combination of import fees and a lifting of federal controls.

Sensitized by rising unemployment and seemingly uncontrollable inflation, Democratic leaders were wary of any plan to raise prices or cut back energy use, fearing such moves would further slow the already sluggish economy. They instead advocated a tax-based approach that involved increasing gasoline taxes to encourage conservation and providing tax incentives to spur energy production.

Congress rejected both the Ford and Democratic leadership approaches, coming up instead with the moderate "Energy Policy and Conservation Act" whose provisions fell far short of the goals implied by its title. Congressional leaders of both parties ended 1975 with a sense of frustration and weariness born of the long wrangle over energy matters.

"It is extremely difficult to write an energy bill," commented House Majority Leader Thomas P. O'Neill Jr. (D Mass.) in December. "This, perhaps, has been the most parochial issue that could ever hit the floor," he added.

"I have come to feel like the mythological Greek, Sisyphus, who was condemned to rolling the great rock up the hill in Hades, only to have it slip when he got it close to the top and roll to the bottom again where he had to start over," said Rep. Clarence J. Brown (R Ohio).

"In total candor, I must say...that what began as a thrilling and dramatic enterprise has degenerated at times into a farcical comedy of frustrations," said Jim Wright (D Texas), head of the House Democratic task force that developed the Democrat's alternative energy plan early in 1975. "Too often the Congress has been simply unwilling to make the hard decisions and take the difficult steps necessary to achieve energy sufficiency for the United States," he continued.

A year later, Wright was even more critical of Congress' record on energy: "Since the Arab oil embargo three years ago, we have tried to do a few timid things to reduce consumption, but they have not been very successful, because total domestic consumption has risen.... We have dabbled with oil and gas pricing. We have made more money available for long-range research, for things like solar energy, that may help us 30 or 40 years from now. But as far as doing anything practical to increase the supply of energy and reduce our dependence upon foreign sources in the foreseeable future, we have done nothing."

Strong regional and political differences, compounded by the splintering of energy issues among different committees and the lack of forceful leadership, diluted the leverage the numerically strong Democrats had been expected to have in determining national energy policy.

Congress reorganized the federal energy bureaucracy, but it did not reorganize its own structure to deal with energy matters, and so one energy measure might be referred to as many as four different committees in one chamber before reaching the floor—sometimes in four different versions.

Suspicion of Industry

Not only was congressional energy policymaking complicated by concern for the economy and the hard-pressed consumer but it was also affected by reluctance on the part of many members to enlarge the federal role in energy matters and a deep suspicion on the part of others of the oil and gas industry and the extent to which it had created and would profit from the energy crisis.

The oil industry reported record profits for 1973, up an average of 48 per cent over 1972. Angry consumers termed such profit levels "obscene," a characterization not modified when profits continued to rise with prices. Profits for the first six months of 1974 were up 82 per cent over the first six months of 1973.

It was in this atmosphere that Congress early in 1975 moved to revoke the tax depletion allowance for major oil and gas producers, retaining it only for small producers. This tax advantage, enjoyed since 1926, allowed them to reduce the amount of their income subject to federal taxes by a percentage intended to represent the extent to which their oil and gas wells had been depleted through production in that year.

But a direct attack on the structure of the industry—which critics charged was concentrated in too few hands—was beaten back later in 1975 when the Senate refused to require energy companies to divest themselves of all but one aspect of the business production, transportation, refining or marketing. The narrowness of the margin of defeat, nine votes, was a surprise to both sides, encouraging advocates of divestiture proposals to redouble their efforts and setting off a massive anti-divestiture public relations campaign by the industry. In 1976 a divestiture measure was reported to the Senate by the Senate Judiciary Committee, but the leadership did not want to wrestle with the tricky issue in an election year. The bill went no farther and died with adjournment.

Elsewhere in the 94th Congress, similar distrust of industry could be heard through the rhetoric of oil price control debates, in the rejection of administration-backed proposals for aid to industry for commercial production of synthetic fuels and for turning over to private industry the business of enriching uranium, and in the chilly welcome Ford's proposed Energy Independence Authority received on Capitol Hill.

In these last matters—the synthetic fuel loan guarantee battle, uranium enrichment and Energy Independence Authority proposals—liberals and conservatives found themselves in an unexpected alliance in opposition to the administration. For the most part, the liberal opposition arose from an unwillingness to approve federal largesse to the industry, and the conservative hostility sprang from a distaste for increased federal involvement in the affairs of private industry.

But industry chalked up some victories on Capitol Hill during this period—sweeping away environmental challenges to the Alaskan pipeline, repeatedly blocking enactment of a federal strip mining regulation measure, killing a measure that would have stiffened requirements and procedures for leasing and development of federal offshore oil and gas resources, winning extension of the federal insurance program for nuclear power plants, and providing continued funding for nuclear power development.

Consumption - Production = Imports

The goal of Project Independence was a substantial reduction in the number of barrels of oil the United States needed to import each day. The equation was a simple one: Oil imports were necessary to supply the difference between the amount of oil the United States consumed and produced.

The energy independence push had two prongs: to reduce consumption of oil and to increase domestic energy production.

The conservation effort had not succeeded by the end of the third year after the embargo. Neither Congress nor the executive had been willing to demand or impose stiff conservation measures on the American voters. In 1976 consumption edged back up to its 1973 level of more than 17 million barrels a day.

And as consumption rose, domestic oil production dropped. By 1976 it was down one million barrels a day from 1973—to 8.2 million barrels, despite the fact that the average wellhead price of domestic oil doubled during this same period—to $7.99 per barrel from $3.89.

By the end of 1976 the United States was not only more dependent on imported oil than in 1973; it was more dependent on expensive Arab oil. The United States was importing more than seven million barrels each day, one million more than in 1973, at a price ($13.40) quadruple that paid for each barrel in 1973 ($3.27). At the end of 1976 OPEC nations agreed again to raise their oil prices; the action seemed unlikely to affect U.S. demand.

And the percentage of U.S. oil imports coming from Arab countries doubled over this period. In 1973, almost one of every three barrels of oil imported into the United States came from Canada. Concerned about its own supply situation, however, Canada began to cut back on oil exports, announcing in 1975 that it would cease entirely to export oil to the United States by 1981. Canadian oil imports to the United States fell from 365 million barrels in 1973 to 219 million barrels in 1975, and Canada said it was reducing that amount by one-third in 1976. Meanwhile the amount imported from Saudi Arabia rose steadily, from 168.5 million barrels in 1973 to 256 million in 1975.

In March 1976, the Federal Energy Administration revised its Project Independence forecast of oil imports for the next decade. In 1974, it had projected that oil imports could be reduced to between three million and five million barrels a day by 1985 (compared to seven million barrels per day in 1976). The revised estimate projected that imports would fall only to 5.9 million barrels per day by that time.

In 1973 President Nixon had asked Congress to provide for the building of deepwater ports off the U.S. coasts to receive and off-load new supertankers bringing oil into the

United States. In 1974 Congress approved this legislation, tacit admission of the long-term dependence of the nation on oil imports. Late in 1976, Secretary of Transportation William T. Coleman announced that he would approve licenses for the construction of two such ports in the Gulf of Mexico, which together could receive seven million barrels of oil a day.

Energy Sources

At the end of the nation's bicentennial year, hopes for progress toward greater energy independence were pinned, for the short-term, on a revitalized conservation effort, Alaskan and offshore oil and gas, and increased coal production. But in each instance, serious questions dimmed the promise of these energy sources.

For the longer-term, nuclear power was still the cornerstone of federal energy policy planning, despite an increasing chorus of criticism. Solar energy had developed a broad and vigorous constituency, although convincing demonstration of its widespread applicability was yet to come. And Congress, hoping to weaken the individual's attachment to his gasoline-guzzling automobile, gave the go-ahead in 1976 to a large-scale federal demonstration of the usefulness of electric automobiles.

Alaskan Oil

The first major energy crisis measure enacted was the Trans-Alaska Pipeline Authorization Act, which cleared away environmental and procedural obstacles for the building of the 789-mile-long pipeline from the oil fields of Alaska's frozen north.

Late in 1976, the pipeline was 95 per cent complete and the Alyeska Pipeline Service Co. promised that 1.2 million barrels of oil a day would begin to flow through the pipeline in mid-1977. But doubts about the reliability of this estimate were raised by reports of sloppy workmanship on the pipeline, evidenced in faulty welds of pipeline seams, and an unexpected pipeline rupture during pressure testing.

Still another problem, foreshadowed earlier, appeared in more definite form late in the year. When the project was approved, plans called for Alaska's oil to be used by western states, where the oil was to be shipped. In September, however, FEA officials announced that the West Coast had no need for Alaskan oil. They predicted that up to 600,000 barrels of oil might pile up unused on western shores each day by 1978 if some alternate final destination were not selected. The government had not decided what to do with the excess oil as of late 1976. Proposals ranged from piping it to oil-starved eastern states, which would require expensive new pipelines, to selling it to Japan, a politically explosive alternative.

Hoping to speed a decision on the proper pipeline route to distribute the natural gas produced in Alaska to markets where it was needed, Congress—in one of its last actions of 1976—enacted legislation calling for executive branch resolution of this question by late 1977.

Offshore Oil

In 1975 and 1976, the federal government granted the first leases of offshore lands in heretofore untapped "frontier" areas, for development of oil and gas resources found there. But environmental challenges, economic risks and general uncertainty about the nation's energy policy all worked to slow progress during the 1973-76 period toward the development and production of the billions of barrels of oil thought to lie on the Outer Continental Shelf (OCS).

And even before the first frontier lease sale was held, the promise of the underwater riches on the OCS began to dim.

In 1975 the Interior Department quietly abandoned the goal of leasing 10 million acres offshore in that and succeeding years. President Nixon had in 1973 set a goal of three million acres a year, three times the highest acreage leased in any previous year; in 1974, he increased the goal again to 10 million.

Also in 1975 estimates of the size of the energy resources on the OCS lands were reduced. Oil companies were noticeably less enthusiastic about undertaking the risky and expensive business of underwater exploration and production. When the first set of frontier leases was offered for bidding in December 1975, the response was disappointing. Although the 1.3 million acres offered off Southern California were estimated to contain billions of barrels of oil—and bids were expected to total more than $1-billion—bids were actually submitted for fewer than one-third of the sites offered and totalled less than $500-million.

Hopes rose again in August 1976, however, when oil companies entered unexpectedly high bids totalling more than $1.1-billion for leasing the tracts in the Atlantic off New Jersey and Delaware.

Congress in 1976 had approved a billion-dollar aid program for coastal states coping with the environmental and economic effects of OCS development. But the House at the last minute killed a measure that would have stiffened federal requirements for leaseholders, given states a stronger voice in leasing and development decisions, and set up a new structure for cleaning up and compensating for damages from oil spills offshore. A rash of large spills from tankers late in 1976 and early in 1977 aroused new environmental protests and rekindled hostility to OCS development.

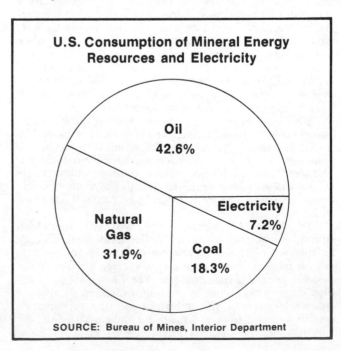

U.S. Consumption of Mineral Energy Resources and Electricity

Oil 42.6%
Electricity 7.2%
Natural Gas 31.9%
Coal 18.3%

SOURCE: Bureau of Mines, Interior Department

Coal Production

The nation's coal production grew slowly over the 1973-76 period. Environmental restrictions on the use of high-sulphur coal, plus controversy over the human risks of deep mining and the environmental damage caused by strip mining, worked together to prevent any strong spurt in the demand for coal. In 1973, the nation's total production of bituminous and lignite coal was 591.7 million tons; in 1976 it was projected to reach 665 million tons.

Development of almost half of the recoverable coal in the United States—that which lies on and below federal lands—remained at a standstill during this period as a result of a moratorium on new coal leases. Congress in 1976 approved, over presidential veto and industry opposition, changes in the federal laws governing coal leasing.

Even if the moratorium on federal leasing came to an end, the pace and extent of future federal coal development was made uncertain by continuing controversies over strip mining, the building of coal slurry pipelines, and the impact of the development of this coal—much of it in the western plains—on the environment and the economy of that area. "We're not interested in being a colony for the rest of the country," commented New Mexico Gov. Jerry Apodaca.

Nuclear Power

Despite concern about its safety and economic feasibility, nuclear power—in particular the development of a commercially useful liquid metal fast breeder reactor—remained the nation's top priority energy development program throughout this period. The breeder uses the fission process to produce energy, and additional fuel (uranium and plutonium) for subsequent fission reactions. Government and industry continued work on a demonstration plant for the liquid metal fast breeder program, to be located on the Clinch River in Tennessee.

Delays due in part to the reorganization of the federal energy structure and the shift in responsibility for the program to ERDA from the old Atomic Energy Commission—and to changes in the management structure of the demonstration project—resulted in postponement of the plant's start-up date for operations from 1980 until 1983.

Attempts in the House and Senate to halt funding and work on the plant to enable Congress to reassess the program as a whole were soundly rejected although cost estimates on the demonstration plant rose steadily from the original $700-million to more than $1.9-billion by early 1976.

Debates over the hazards of plutonium, the problem of storing radioactive nuclear waste, and the reality of the need for vastly expanded electric generating capability continued into 1977. But advocates of nuclear power won a 10-year extension by the 94th Congress of the federal insurance program that protected the industry against claims for damages inflicted by a nuclear accident. In both chambers, the nuclear power industry demonstrated its muscle, beating back efforts to eliminate the $560-million limit on the industry's liability to such damage claims despite general agreement that such a limit was unrealistically low.

Although reports persisted that plans for building more nuclear power plants were being curtailed as a result of uncertainty and criticism, by mid-1976 more than 200 plants were operating, under construction or planned. Sixty were operable; another 93 were either under construction or in the site preparation stage.

Concern about the safety of these plants was dramatized in 1976 when several Nuclear Regulatory Commission (NRC) engineers resigned, protesting that the NRC was failing to do its job of ensuring that safety problems were dealt with. Early in the year three engineers from the nuclear reactor division of General Electric expressed similar concern when they resigned their posts to go to work for the movement to halt the spread of nuclear power.

But Congress and the majority of the voters expressing their opinions on nuclear power continued to trust in its promise of clean, abundant energy. In June 1976, Californians rejected, by more than 2-1, a referendum initiative that would have severely limited existing and future nuclear plant construction and operation. Both the pro-nuclear power and the anti-nuclear power forces mounted tremendous public relations campaigns before the vote. In November voters in six other states rejected similar referenda proposals.

Solar Energy

The power of the sun—free as well as abundant and clean—was espoused by many persons skeptical of nuclear energy as the best hope for the nation's future fuel supply. To counter the pro-nuclear energy orientation of much of the federal energy structure, Congress in 1974 called for a 10-year $20-billion investment of federal funds in non-nuclear power development, and underscored the role it intended for solar power by passing two separate measures setting up specific solar energy programs.

The Solar Energy Research, Development and Demonstration Act of 1974 authorized the Energy Research and Development Administration (ERDA) to devote substantial manpower and funds to develop various solar technologies. A second measure directed the government to demonstrate the use of solar energy for heating and cooling buildings.

And those who backed solar energy development did not remain satisfied with the legislation enacted in 1974, but continued to press ERDA to push on in the solar field. They increased the funds available for those programs far beyond the Ford administration requests and even beyond the level requested by ERDA itself.

For fiscal 1976 Congress added $100-million to the administration request for solar programs, authorizing $173-million. For fiscal 1977 the administration requested $160-million, considerably less than the $255-million that ERDA had asked for and less than half the $358-million that ERDA's solar division had requested. Congress restored both the funds cut from the ERDA request and some of those deleted within ERDA itself, including $320-million for solar programs in the ERDA authorization measure that died at the end of the 1976 session. Congress appropriated $290-million for those programs to spend in 1977.

Carter and Conservation

During his campaign, Jimmy Carter emphasized the need for conservation as the foundation of the nation's effort to move into a stronger energy posture. Critical of the failure of the nation's leaders to convince the American people of the urgency of the energy problem, he promised to institute a comprehensive conservation program to cut back on energy waste. "Americans are willing to make sacrifices," he said, "if they understand the reason for them and if they believe the sacrifices are fairly distributed." Only the future would prove, however, whether Carter could be sufficiently convincing to the American people to overcome the inertia that had frustrated earlier conservation efforts.

Chronology

of Action

on Energy

1973

Initially, the congressional response to the energy crisis appeared impressive. Three weeks after the Arab oil producers imposed their boycott, two major energy measures arrived at the White House for the President's signature.

President Nixon signed both. One—clearing the way for construction of the Alaska oil pipeline—he had sought. The other—directing him to impose a mandatory fuel allocation system on the nation—he had opposed and signed reluctantly.

This running start for Congress was deceptive. Both measure were already in the final stages of the legislative process when the embargo was imposed. The only other energy bills cleared by Congress in 1973 were two conservation measures requested by Nixon in his Nov. 7 address announcing Project Independence. One of these lowered the speed limit nationwide to 55 miles per hour; the other instituted daylight saving time year-round.

Both the House and the Senate did pass a number of other energy measures in December but none were enacted. They reorganized the federal energy structure, provided the President with special emergency powers to deal with an energy crisis, urged energy conservation, and accelerated energy research efforts. The lack of coordination between the two chambers produced a confusing criss-cross of similar provisions in differing bills, and Congress adjourned without clearing any.

An early indication of the problems that would continue to impede the congressional effort to formulate an energy policy was provided by the fate of the bill granting the President emergency powers to control the production and use of energy. Both chambers approved versions in December—the House including a windfall profits restriction not part of the Senate bill. Conferees worked feverishly to compromise the differences; congressional leaders prolonged the session, hoping to complete work on the bill.

On Dec. 21, the Senate moved to consider the conference report, only to have it blocked by oil-producing state senators filibustering against the windfall profits

provision. Finally, Senate leaders dropped the provision and won approval of a compromise.

Late in the evening the House received the revised version of the conference bill. Outraged by what they considered a high-handed Senate move, the House voted resoundingly three times to insist on the windfall profits provision and to reject any compromise. Tired and angry, members of Congress gave up their effort for this session and adjourned Dec. 22.

Alaska Pipeline

In the first major energy legislation enacted after the imposition of the Arab oil embargo, Congress overrode environmental challenges blocking construction of a huge oil pipeline to carry two million barrels of crude oil a day from Alaska's frozen north to the rest of the United States.

As signed by President Nixon Nov. 16, 1973, the Trans-Alaska Pipeline Authorization Act (S 1081—PL 93-153) directed the Secretary of the Interior to move immediately to authorize construction of the 789-mile pipeline connecting the oil-rich North Slope with the ice-free port of Valdez. Tankers were to carry the oil from Valdez to the other parts of the United States.

PL 93-153 disarmed pipeline opponents of their most effective weapons—the National Environmental Policy Act of 1969 and the Mineral Leasing Act of 1920.

Alarmed by the potential danger that the pipeline posed to the Alaskan tundra and wildlife, and by the increased possibility of oil spills from the tankers it fueled, environmental groups sought to block federal approval of its construction.

Their initial challenges were based on the 1969 law, which required thorough examination of the environmental impact of all major federal actions. But the ruling that had stymied construction was based on the older law, which limited to 50 feet in width the rights-of-way that could be issued across federal lands. The oil companies planning to build the pipelines had requested widths up to three times that size.

PL 93-153 removed the 50-foot limit and barred any future challenges to the pipeline based on the 1969 law. It provided expedited procedures for consideration of any other court challenges to construction of the pipeline.

Congress moved actively into the pipeline dispute early in 1973, after the Nixon administration asked for legislation overturning the court ruling by waiving the 50-foot limit. The pace of congressional activity quickened in April after the Supreme Court turned down the government's request that it overrule the lower court.

The Senate approved its version of the bill in July; the House, in August. Conferees finished work in mid-October, just as the Organization of Petroleum Exporting Countries (OPEC) moved to impose the embargo.

President Nixon prodded Congress to complete action on the bill when he addressed the nation Nov. 7 to announce Project Independence. Alaskan oil was a major component of the nation's effort to attain energy independence. Within a week of Nixon's speech, the pipeline bill was on his desk for his signature.

Background

Atlantic Richfield Company struck oil on the North Slope of Alaska in the summer of 1968. Subsequent explora-

Nixon Outlines 'Project Independence'

"We must...face up to a very stark fact: We are heading toward the most acute shortages of energy since World War II," President Nixon warned the nation in a televised address on Nov. 7, 1973, two weeks after the imposition of the Arab oil embargo. "In the short run, this course means that we must use less energy.... In the long run, it means that we must develop new sources of energy which will give us the capacity to meet our needs without relying on any foreign nation," Nixon continued.

"Let us unite in committing the resources of this nation to a major new endeavor, an endeavor that in this bicentennial era we can appropriately call 'Project Independence,' " the President said. "Let us set as our national goal, in the spirit of Apollo, with the determination of the Manhattan Project, that by the end of this decade we will have developed the potential to meet our own energy needs without depending on any foreign energy sources.... We have an energy crisis, but there is no crisis of the American spirit."

The following day, President Nixon sent a message to Congress announcing the administrative actions he had taken to deal with the crisis and asking Congress to:

● Authorize restrictions on public and private consumption of energy;
● Authorize a national 50-mile-per-hour speed limit *(Story p. 13-A)*
● Provide that steps taken under energy emergency authorities be exempted from the requirements of the National Environmental Policy Act;
● Give federal regulatory agencies emergency powers to adjust the operations of transport carriers to conserve fuel;
● Empower the Atomic Energy Commission to grant nuclear power plants temporary operating licenses for up to 18 months;

● Authorize full production from the Elk Hills Naval Petroleum Reserve and exploration and development of the other reserves, including the Alaskan reserve *(Story, p. 18-A)*;
● Permit year-round establishment of daylight saving time *(Story p. 13-A)*
● Authorize the President to order power plants and other installations to switch from using oil to using coal;
● Authorize the President to allocate and ration energy supplies;
● Provide additional authority for using funds from the federal highway program for mass transit capital improvements;
● Authorize the Federal Power Commission to suspend the wellhead price regulation of new natural gas during the energy emergency;
● Empower the President to exercise any authority contained in the Defense Production Act, the Economic Stabilization Act and the Export Administration Act, even though those acts may have otherwise expired.

To move toward the long-term goal of energy independence, Nixon requested congressional action to:
● Authorize construction of the Alaskan pipeline. *(Story p. 8-A)*
● Permit the competitive pricing of new natural gas. *(Story p. 16-A)*
● Set reasonable standards for the surface mining of coal. *(Story p. 17-A)*
● Set up a Department of Energy and Natural Resources. *(Story p. 14-A)*
● Simplify procedures for siting and approving electric energy facilities.
● Set up procedures for approving construction and operation of deepwater ports. *(Story p. 17-A)*
● Create an Energy Research and Development Administration to direct the $10-billion program aimed at energy self-sufficiency by 1980. *(Story p. 14-A)*

---

tion located billions of barrels of proved reserves of oil, and estimates of the potential there ran higher than 100 billion barrels, more than all other known U.S. oil reserves combined. The major obstacle to development of this oil was its location: how could it be transported to its markets, all far to the south?

The oil industry went to work on the problem. A consortium of oil companies was formed, first known as the Trans-Alaska Pipeline System and later as Alyeska Pipeline Service Company. The companies, involved directly or through subsidiaries, were Atlantic Richfield, Amerada Hess Corporation, Standard Oil Company (New Jersey), British Petroleum, Mobil Oil Company, Phillips Petroleum Company, Union Oil Company of California, and Home Oil Company of Canada, which later withdrew from the group.

The consortium applied for permits from the Interior Department to build an access road and the pipeline to Valdez, much of which would run across federal lands.

Environmental groups wasted little time. In April 1970, three of them—the Wilderness Society, Friends of the Earth, and the Environmental Defense Fund—-won a federal district court order forbidding the Secretary of

Interior to issue the permits until a full environmental impact statement had been prepared on the pipeline and alternative methods of transporting the oil.

It was two years before such a statement was completed and released. When made public in March 1972, it filled nine volumes. In May of that year Interior Secretary Rogers C. B. Morton said he intended to issue the permits. In August, the federal court lifted its order forbidding him to issue the permits. The environmentalists appealed.

The result of their appeal was a February 1973 decision by the court of appeals, District of Columbia circuit, forbidding Morton to issue the permit. The basis for the prohibition was the 1920 Mineral Leasing Act, which limited rights-of-way across public lands to 50 feet in width.

Morton said the Nixon administration would appeal to Congress to amend that requirement and to the Supreme Court to overturn the court of appeals. On April 2, the Supreme Court upheld the court of appeals' order.

Senate Action

The Senate Interior and Insular Affairs Committee reported the bill (S 1081—S Rept 93-207) June 12. As reported, its major provisions authorized the Secretary of Interior to grant rights-of-way across public lands without restriction as to their width and requested the President to begin negotiations with Canada to determine the feasibility of a trans-Canada pipeline.

Floor Action. The Senate approved the bill July 17 by a vote of 77-20, after adding language immunizing all future federal actions regarding the construction of the pipeline from further court challenge under the National Environmental Policy Act of 1969 (NEPA). This amendment, proposed by the two senators from Alaska, Mike Gravel (D) and Ted Stevens (R), was adopted by a vote of 49-48. Its addition to S 1081 was a victory for the oil companies and the Nixon administration, ensuring that the pipeline would be delayed no longer by litigation or court orders resulting from such challenges.

By approving this amendment, the Senate declared all actions taken by the Secretary of Interior and other federal agencies regarding the pipeline, related highways and airports to be in compliance with the 1969 Act. Gravel said that Congress, in approving this language, was simply stating that the environmental impact statement filed on the pipeline was sufficient to fulfill the requirements of the law. Interior Committee Chairman Henry M. Jackson (D Wash.) disagreed and argued against the amendment, saying that it was beyond the power of Congress to foreclose further judicial review of such matters.

After the Senate voted to adopt the amendment, Gravel routinely moved for reconsideration of the vote and, as was customary, a move was made to table that motion and thus close the matter. The vote to table was a tie, 49-49. In the case of a tie, a motion fails. But Vice President Spiro T. Agnew, who was presiding over the Senate, broke the tie, voting for the motion and thus confirming Senate adoption of the amendment.

The other major point of controversy during Senate consideration of S 1081 was an effort by environmentalists and midwestern senators to delay construction of any pipeline across Alaska for at least a year during which an alternative pipeline route across Canada would be studied. Sens. Walter F. Mondale (D Minn.) and Birch Bayh (D Ind.) introduced such an amendment. They argued that the Alaska pipeline would bring the oil to the West Coast, from which much of it would be exported to Japan, instead of supplying the rest of the United States. The Canadian route would link up with two pipelines, one to the West Coast and one to New York, thus delivering the Alaskan oil nationwide. Opponents argued that consideration of a trans-Canada pipeline would result in a prolonged delay in shipment of North Slope oil, and that such a pipeline was risky because it would not be under sole U.S. control. The Senate rejected this amendment on a key vote of 29-61 (R 5-34; D 24-27).

House Action

The House Interior and Insular Affairs Committee reported its Alaska pipeline bill (HR 9130—H Rept 93-414) July 28, less than two weeks after Senate passage of S 1081. As reported, HR 9130 amended the 1920 Mineral Leasing Act to allow grants of rights-of-way wider than 50 feet, directed the Secretary of Interior to grant the rights-of-way for the Alaska pipeline, and declared the pipeline to be in compliance with NEPA.

Floor Action. The House approved HR 9130 Aug. 2, by a vote of 356-60, after rejecting an effort to remove the

provision immunizing the pipeline against further NEPA challenges. The amendment deleting that section, proposed by John Dellenback (R Ore.) and Wayne Owens (D Utah), was rejected on a close key vote of 198-221 (R 65-120; D 133-101).

By voice vote, the House also rejected an amendment to delay the Alaska pipeline until the Canadian alternative had been more fully studied.

Final Action

The conference report (H Rept 94-624) declared that Congress had determined that the trans-Alaska pipeline should be built without further delay and intended to leave federal officials no discretion to postpone it.

The conferees retained several Senate amendments to S 1081 that were strongly opposed by the business community and the administration, even producing veto threats late in October. The problem provisions gave the Federal Trade Commission more authority to take its antitrust efforts to court, required confirmation of persons named to certain energy-related posts, and transferred to the General Accounting Office from the Office of Management and Budget the authority to screen requests from federal agencies for information from the business community.

After refusing, 162-213, to strike out these administration-opposed provisions, the House adopted the conference report Nov. 12 by a 361-14 vote.

The Senate adopted the conference report, 80-5, on Nov. 13, clearing the bill for the White House.

President Nixon signed the measure Nov. 16.

Provisions

As signed into law, PL 93-153 contained major provisions which:

Trans-Alaskan Pipeline

- Required the Secretary of Interior to authorize construction of the trans-Alaskan pipeline.
- Provided that all actions necessary for completion of the pipeline be taken without further delay under the National Environmental Policy Act of 1969.

● Restricted judicial review 1) to the constitutionality of the act, 2) to actions taken under the act which violated constitutional rights, and 3) to actions which went beyond the authority granted by the act.

● Provided expedited procedures for consideration of such challenges to the pipelines and the law.

● Provided liability of up to $50,000 for each incident for damages resulting from pipeline construction or operations which affected the subsistence or income of Alaskan natives.

● Held the pipeline owners liable for the full costs of controlling and removing any pollution caused by the pipeline.

● Established liability without regard to fault of up to $100-million for each incident of oil spills from vessels carrying oil from the pipeline unless the oil spills were caused by acts of war or actions of the United States.

● Limited liability for oil spills to $14-million for owners of vessels transporting crude oil.

● Established a Trans-Alaskan Pipeline Liability Fund to meet claims of more than $14-million.

● Provided that oil companies using the pipeline pay into the fund five cents for each barrel loaded on vessels until the fund reached $100-million.

● Directed the President to ensure the equitable allocation of Alaskan North Slope crude oil among all regions of the United States.

● Authorized semi-annual advance payments of $5-million starting in fiscal 1976 for the Alaska Native Fund, pending delivery of North Slope oil to the pipeline, and limited total payments to $500-million.

● Authorized the President to negotiate with Canada concerning an alternative pipeline to carry North Slope oil across Canada to the midwestern United States.

Rights-of-Way

● Permitted the Secretary to authorize rights-of-way wider than 50 feet, in addition to the ground occupied by pipelines and related facilities, if necessary.

● Provided that no domestically produced crude oil transported through any pipeline authorized under the act could be exported unless the President found and reported to Congress that such exports 1) would not diminish oil supplies in the United States and 2) would be in the national interest.

● Provided that such exports would be prohibited if Congress disapproved the President's findings by concurrent resolution within 60 days after receiving the report.

Miscellaneous Provisions

● Required Senate confirmation of the director of the White House Energy Policy Office and the head of the Interior Department's Mining Enforcement and Safety Administration, including the incumbents.

● Permitted the Federal Trade Commission (FTC) to go to court to enforce its own subpoenas and to seek temporary injunctions to avoid unfair competitive practices.

● Permitted the FTC to prosecute cases under its jurisdiction after consulting with the U.S. Attorney General and giving him 10 days in which to take the action proposed by the FTC.

● Transferred from the Office of Management and Budget to the General Accounting Office the authority to review regulatory agency requests for information from businesses and corporations.

● Exempted from price controls under the Economic Stabilization Act of 1970 and from subsequent fuel allocation programs the sale of oil and natural gas liquids from wells producing no more than 10 barrels daily.

● Advanced the effective date of the Ports and Waterways Safety Act of 1972 (PL 92-340) with respect to U.S. vessels engaged in coastal trade to June 30, 1974, from Jan. 1, 1976. (The 1972 act established construction standards for tankers to prevent pollution.)

● Specified that the rest of the act would not be affected if any provision were held invalid.

Fuel Allocation

To spread scarce fuel supplies evenly, Congress in 1973 insisted that the President impose mandatory controls allocating oil and oil products among different regions of the nation and sectors of the petroleum industry.

The Nixon administration first opposed this legislation, but its objections weakened as the failure of voluntary allocation efforts became obvious. By the time Congress cleared the Emergency Petroleum Allocation Act (S 1570—PL 93-159) for the White House in mid-November, President Nixon had already announced mandatory allocation systems for propane, heating oil, jet fuel and diesel fuel. Earlier in 1973, Congress had given the President discretionary power to set up such systems (S 398—PL 93-28).

PL 93-159 required the President to set up a comprehensive allocation program for oil and oil products within 30 days. Additional time was granted for allocation of gasoline and the products already covered by the Nixon plan.

In provisions which would become increasingly controversial as the price of foreign oil rose precipitously over the following months, PL 93-159 also directed the President to set prices—or to set out a formula by which they should be determined—for crude oil, residual fuel oil and refined petroleum products. Retailers could pass on to consumers increases in wholesale prices. Most oil exports were banned.

PL 93-159 also offered protection for independent retailers and refiners by requiring that they receive as much oil or oil product as they had in 1972—or a proportional amount, if supplies were lower than in 1972. Independent marketers supported a mandatory allocation system, saying that many of them were forced out of business when suppliers cut off oil deliveries altogether. The major oil companies opposed any mandatory allocation systems.

The Senate approved S 1570 in June—and, to emphasize the need for such a measure, attached a stripped-down version of the bill to a minor House measure in August. The House passed its version of the bill Oct. 17—the day that Arab nations announced their plans to curtail oil production and exports to the United States.

Conferees filed their report on the bill Nov. 10. The final version of S 1570 stated that shortages of oil, caused by inadequate domestic production, environmental constraints and insufficient imports, were imminent, and would create severe economic hardships constituting a national energy crisis. The purpose of the mandatory allocation system, S 1570 stated, was to minimize the adverse impact of these shortages on the American people and their economy. The House adopted the conference report Nov. 13; the Senate Nov. 14. President Nixon signed the bill Nov. 27.

Background

Demands for a mandatory allocation program for oil and oil products escalated in 1973 as mid-winter fuel shortages were succeeded by summer gasoline shortages and finally by the Arab embargo on oil shipments to the United States following the Middle East war in October.

Congress included in the Economic Stabilization Act Amendments of 1973 (S 398—PL 93-28), which was cleared April 30, a Senate amendment giving the President discretionary authority to allocate petroleum products. Under PL 93-28 the President was also empowered to control prices — including oil prices — until April 30, 1974.

The administration May 10 announced "voluntary" guidelines to assure that independent gasoline stations and other oil product purchasers would not suffer a cutoff in their supplies. Under the plan suppliers were urged to sell to their customers the same percentage of refinery output and crude oil supplies that they sold in 1972. An administration spokesman said that if the voluntary guidelines were not effective, "more stringent measures" would be applied.

The administration resisted imposition of a mandatory allocation program, but by autumn it was clear that the voluntary program had failed.

On Oct. 2 the administration announced a mandatory allocation program for propane gas, followed Oct. 12 by a similar program — effective Nov. 1 — for heating oil, kerosene and jet and diesel fuels.

Senate Action

The Senate Interior and Insular Affairs Committee reported S 1570 (S Rept 93-159) May 17, stating that something more than the discretionary authority provided by PL 93-28 was necessary. The fuel shortage, stated the committee report, was "so imminent that executive discretion as to whether or not to implement mandatory allocation measures is no longer warranted." The bill directed the President to draw up a plan for a mandatory fuel allocation system within 60 days of its enactment. The authority granted by S 1570 would expire Sept. 1, 1974.

Floor Action. The Senate June 5 passed S 1570, 85-10. The bill required the President to submit to Congress within 30 days a plan for a mandatory fuels allocation system, giving priority to supplying public health facilities, public utilities and agricultural production and distribution systems.

During debate on S 1570, the Senate adopted amendments guaranteeing small independent oil companies continuing supplies of fuel, reducing to 30 days the time for preparation of the President's plan, and changing the act's expiration date to March 1, 1975. The Senate rejected amendments that would have excluded independent oil producers from the allocation formulas and that would have allowed oil companies to sell fuel at free market prices, free of price controls. Both amendments were proposed by Dewey F. Bartlett (R Okla.). The first was rejected 42-51, after Senate Interior Committee Chairman Henry M. Jackson (D Wash.) warned that one-third of all petroleum producers could slip through the loophole it created. The second was rejected, 21-71.

House Action

The House Interstate and Foreign Commerce Committee reported its allocation bill (HR 9681—H Rept 93-531) Sept. 29. As reported, the House bill required the President to submit plans for an allocation system within 10 days of enactment and implement them 15 days later. The system set up under the bill was to be effective through Feb. 28, 1975.

Floor Action. The House Oct. 17, by a 337-72 vote, passed HR 9681, over objections from the Nixon administration that it did not give the President sufficient flexibility to administer an effective allocation program.

During consideration of the bill, the House rejected several amendments backed by the oil industry, which generally opposed a mandatory allocation system. The first, proposed by J. J. Pickle (D Texas), would have prohibited the allocation of crude oil at the producer level unless it was necessary to assure the maintenance of public services, agricultural operations and competition in the oil industry. The Pickle amendment was rejected, 136-245.

The House subsequently rejected, 152-256, an amendment proposed by John M. Ashbrook (R Ohio) that would have made the General Accounting Office, rather than the Federal Trade Commission, the monitor of the allocation program. It also rejected, by voice vote, an amendment moving the program's expiration date up to April 30, 1974.

Final Action

Conferees filed their report on S 1570 (H Rept 93-628) Nov. 10, agreeing that it was imperative for the federal government to intervene in the marketplace to preserve competition and to ensure an equitable distribution of scarce supplies of oil and oil products.

The House Nov. 13 adopted the conference report, 348-46. The Senate Nov. 14 cleared the measure for the White House, adopting the report, 80-3.

Provisions

As signed into law, PL 93-159, the Emergency Petroleum Allocation Act of 1973:

● Directed the President to issue regulations for the allocation and pricing of crude oil and oil products within 15 days of enactment and to put the regulations into effect 15 days after they were issued.

● Gave the President an additional 15 days to put into effect allocation regulations covering gasoline and products covered by the allocation program established by the President under the Economic Stabilization Act of 1970 (PL 91-379). The President's allocation program covered propane, home heating oil and jet and diesel fuels only.

● Established as objectives which were to be considered in issuing the regulations the following: maintenance of all public services, agricultural operations and public health, safety and welfare, preservation of competition in the oil industry, equitable allocation and pricing of oil and oil products, and allocation of enough oil to ensure the exploration, production and transportation of new fuel supplies.

● Permitted retailers to pass on to their customers increases in the wholesale price of oil and oil products.

● Required the same base period to be used to compute all price markups.

● Required that oil and oil products be allocated to each user in an amount not less than that supplied to them during the corresponding period of 1972.

● Provided for proportional reductions of supplies to each user if the total supply of oil was less than that for a corresponding period of 1972.

● Required the President to give special consideration in allocating oil and oil products to anyone whose use of other fuels had been curtailed or terminated in compliance with an order of a federal or state agency.

● Directed the President to make equitable adjustments in the program to account for any increases in total supply or for the entry into the market of new users.

● Directed the President to the extent practicable and necessary to allocate propane in a way which did not deny supplies to industrial users which had no alternative supply of fuel.

● Required that all oil and oil products produced or refined within the United States be totally allocated within the United States to the extent practicable and necessary to carry out the act.

● Exempted from price and allocation regulations oil from wells which produced 10 barrels or less of oil daily. *(Similar provision, Alaskan pipeline bill, this chapter)*

● Permitted the President to exclude from the allocation program crude oil at the producer level if he found such allocation was unnecessary to meet the objectives of the act.

● Permitted the President to exempt from the allocation program for a period of 90 days oil and oil products for which he found no shortages and where such an exemption would not reduce the supply of other oil products.

● Provided that either the House or the Senate could disapprove such an exemption from the allocation program by a simple resolution of disapproval passed within five days of receiving notice from the President of the proposed exemption.

● Provided for the same fines and injunctive relief as were authorized under the Economic Stabilization Act of 1970: a fine of up to $5,000 for each willful violation, and a fine up to $2,500 for civil penalties, for each violation; the Attorney General could seek injunctions to prevent violations of the act.

● Made compliance with regulations issued under the act a defense in breach of contract and federal antitrust cases.

● Directed the Federal Trade Commission to monitor the allocation program during the first 45 days that it was in effect, and to report to Congress and the President within 60 days on the effectiveness of the act and the actions taken under it.

● Terminated the act at midnight, Feb. 28, 1975.

Daylight Saving Time

Congress in December approved an administration request to institute year-round daylight saving time (HR 11324—PL 93-182). President Nixon included this proposal in his Nov. 7 energy message. Officials estimated that the time change could save 2 to 3 per cent in fuel consumption a year. PL 93-182 provided for year-round daylight saving time through the winters of 1973-74 and 1974-75. *(Nixon message, p. 9-A)*

Highway Speed Limit

Congress late in December gave final approval to a measure (HR 11372—PL 93-239) lowering the maximum speed limit on the nation's highways to 55 miles per hour until June 30, 1975. President Nixon Nov. 7 had asked Congress to empower him to set a nationwide speed limit of 50 miles per hour. After protests by truckers that their vehicles would operate less efficiently at the lower speed, Nixon amended his request to allow truckers to operate at 55-miles per hour. As approved by Congress, PL 93-239 used the leverage of federal highway funds to persuade states to lower their speed limits to 55 miles per hour for all vehicles. Advocates of the measure said it would save 130,000 to 165,000 barrels of gasoline each day.

Energy Emergency Act

Strenuous efforts to pass a bill (S 2589) giving the President broad emergency powers to control the production and consumption of energy failed in 1973. The refusal of oil-state senators to accept a provision restricting windfall profits for fuel companies and the refusal of the House to approve the bill without that provision prevented final action on the measure during the last days of the first session of the 93rd Congress.

The Energy Emergency Act, introduced the day after Arab leaders indicated their intention to cut off exports of oil to the United States, incorporated a number of the special powers that President Nixon had requested in his Project Independence Address. Among them were the power to reduce speed limits, restrict the non-essential outdoor use of fuel, restrict energy-use advertising, require lower indoor temperatures, limit fuel consumption by public and commercial establishments, order industries and utilities to change types of fuel, and require refineries to adjust the mix of products they manufactured. But—in a provision opposed by the administration—Congress retained for itself the power to block the implementation of such measures.

Senate Action

Senate Interior Committee Chairman Henry M. Jackson (D Wash.) introduced S 2589 Oct. 18. After two closed-door sessions with White House Energy Policy Office Director John A. Love, a one-day, 11-hour hearing on the day after Nixon's Nov. 7 address, and two open mark-up sessions, the bill was amended and reported by the Interior Committee (S Rept 93-489) Nov. 13.

As reported, S 2589 required the President to issue regulations within 15 days for rationing fuel supplies. It required that energy consumption be reduced 10 per cent through rationing and conservation within 10 days and 25 per cent within four weeks. The bill granted the President most of the emergency authority he had requested in his speech, including the power to authorize production of oil from the naval petroleum reserves. The bill gave Congress 15 days to disapprove the exercise of these powers.

The Senate passed S 2589 Nov. 19 by a 78-6 vote. The Senate rejected, on a key vote of 40-48 (D 38-12, R 2-36), an amendment proposed by Floyd K. Haskell (D Colo.) requiring that gasoline rationing be put into effect by Jan. 15,

1974. The Nixon administration opposed the provision, maintaining that rationing should be implemented only as a last resort.

Before passing the bill, the Senate did make several major changes in the measure. Among them were amendments allowing the relaxation of clean air standards during the energy emergency, deleting the authorization for producing oil from the naval reserves, providing unemployment benefits for persons laid off because of fuel shortages, and providing some defense against charges of antitrust violations by persons or companies working together to comply with the emergency energy program.

House Action

The House Interstate and Foreign Commerce Committee Dec. 7 reported its version of the energy emergency measure (HR 11450—H Rept 93-710), making clear its intent to preserve a strong congressional role in the exercise of these emergency powers.

As reported, the House bill set up a Federal Energy Administration to administer the fuel allocation program and other federal energy programs. The agency was directed to submit energy conservation plans to Congress within 30 days for its approval. The House bill also allowed some easing of clean air standards during the emergency, prohibited any major fuel-burning installation from using oil or natural gas if it could use coal, and restricted windfall profits by fuel sellers by providing for hearings by the Renegotiation Board on suspected excess profits.

After three days of debate, the House passed the Energy Emergency Act Dec. 15, 265-112. Sixty-four amendments were considered during debate on the measure; 37 were adopted. Some members criticized the bill for giving the President too much power; others for giving him too little. Since there was no national energy policy, said Richard T. Hanna (D Calif.), House members working on this bill were "like a bunch of blind men trying to put together a jigsaw puzzle in the bottom of a sack in the middle of the night."

The House rejected an amendment that would have converted the congressional approval requirement for energy plans into a congressional veto, to be cast within 15 days of the President's proposing a conservation plan. It also adopted an amendment requiring the President to submit any rationing proposals to Congress for final approval.

The excess profits provision of the bill was the target of a number of amendment efforts. In the major vote on this issue, the House rejected, 188-213, an amendment that would have permitted the President to define reasonable profits, to propose regulation of excess profits and to give industry incentives to reinvest profits in research and exploration. The amendment would have eliminated the role of the Renegotiation Board.

Proposals to suspend environmental protection standards during the energy crisis—in particular those controlling auto emissions—provoked some of the hottest debate on the bill. The House refused to suspend clean air requirements altogether during the emergency, but did agree to postpone the effective date for some of them. On a key vote of 180-210 (D 78-137; R 102-73) the House Dec. 14 rejected an amendment proposed by Louis C. Wyman (R N.H.) to suspend auto emission controls until Jan. 1, 1977, or whenever the President said the fuel shortages were over. This was the most far-reaching of proposals to relax these standards.

Conference Action

Conferees reached agreement Dec. 20 after a week of intense negotiations; the conference report (S Rept 93-663) was not available as the House and Senate attempted to complete action on the bill before adjournment. On the major point of controversy, conferees retained the House windfall profits provisions and added language directing the President to set prices for crude oil and oil products which would avoid windfall profits. The conference version of the bill gave Congress a veto over energy conservation plans proposed before July 1, 1974, and required its affirmative approval of plans proposed after that date.

Senate Debate. Oil state senators, led by Russell B. Long (D La.) and Paul J. Fannin (R Ariz.), expressed their opposition to the windfall profits language by a filibuster against the conference version of S 2589, when Senate leaders attempted to bring it up for consideration Dec. 21. Long argued that the Finance Committee, of which he was chairman, should have held hearings on the provision. Fannin argued that the language would inhibit the industry's search for new sources of oil.

While the Senate voted three times to reject a motion to recommit the bill with instructions to add language barring shipments of oil for military operations in Southeast Asia, Senate leaders met in the cloakroom and drafted a compromise version of S 2589, omitting the windfall profits section. The Senate then agreed to tack this compromise on to S 921, a non-controversial wild and scenic rivers bill already approved by the House. The compromise was approved Dec. 21, 52-8.

House Debate. A confused and angry House took up the compromise measure late on Dec. 21. Commerce Committee Chairman Harley O. Staggers (D W.Va.) expressed outrage at the Senate action on windfall profits: "The Senate considers the House...its doormat." Instead of considering the compromise attached to S 921, Staggers first offered a substitute bill which consisted of the conference version of S 2589 with a modified windfall profits provision. He moved that the House suspend the rules and approve the substitute bill. The motion failed, by seven votes, to obtain the two-thirds majority needed for approval. The vote was 169-95; 176 votes were needed. The House then defeated, 22-240, a Staggers motion that it approve the conference version without a windfall profits section.

The final vote came early on Saturday morning, Dec. 22, the last day of the 1973 session. Staggers moved that the House suspend its rules and accept the Senate compromise, an action which would have sent S 921 to the White House. The motion failed utterly on a key vote of 36-228 (R 28-79; D 8-149). Congress then adjourned without further efforts to pass the energy emergency bill. The bill was eventually cleared in 1974 and then vetoed by President Nixon. *(Story p. 24-A)*

Energy Reorganization

President Nixon in 1973 proposed comprehensive reorganization of executive branch energy functions, but Congress did not give a final stamp of approval to the restructuring during the year.

Nixon's proposal had three parts:

● To administer federal efforts to cope with energy shortages, he asked Congress to create a Federal Energy Administration empowered to take all actions its chief deemed necessary to meet the nation's energy requirements. Both chambers approved language (HR 11450, S 2776) setting up a less powerful Federal Energy Administration, but neither measure cleared Congress by the session's end.

● To spearhead the federal energy research effort, Nixon asked Congress to unify the energy research and development units of the Atomic Energy Commission (AEC), the Interior Department, the Environmental Protection Agency (EPA) and the National Science Foundation (NSF) in an Energy Research and Development Administration (ERDA). The House approved this proposal; the Senate voted approval of a similar entity called the Energy Research Management Project, but neither chamber acted on the other's bill (HR 11510, S 1283) in 1973.

● To unify the other federal energy and resource units scattered throughout the government, Nixon revived his proposed Department of Natural Resources—which had received scant attention when first proposed in 1971—and asked Congress to create a cabinet Department of Energy and Natural Resources, replacing the Interior Department. This proposal was the subject of subcommittee hearings in both chambers, but received no further attention during 1973.

FEA

Three separate measures containing language authorizing a Federal Energy Administration (FEA) were receiving congressional attention late in the 1973 session. The House Dec. 15 approved its emergency energy bill (HR 11450—H Rept 93-710), which provided for the creation of such an agency—but House-Senate disagreement over windfall profit provisions stymied final action in 1973. *(Story p. 13-A)*

After the end of the session, the House Government Operations Committee Dec. 28 reported a bill (HR 11793—H Rept 93-748) setting up an FEA with a wide range of enumerated powers—to stimulate energy development, to control excess profits, to impose energy conservation plans.

The Senate Dec. 19, by a 86-2 vote, passed a bill (S 2776—S Rept 93-634) setting up a Federal Energy Emergency Administration less powerful than Nixon had proposed. S 2776 limited the new agency's powers to those specifically granted it by the President or by Congress.

To provide a data base for energy policy decisions, S 2776 directed the FEA to undertake a massive energy information-gathering effort. The bill provided for public disclosure of much of this information, and directed the General Accounting Office to monitor the new agency's operations. S 2776 also mandated creation of a White House Council on Energy Policy, a directive opposed by the White House. *(Story below)*

Most controversial of the amendments proposed to S 2776 from the Senate floor were two dealing with the price of fuel. The Senate narrowly rejected an effort to place a ceiling on the cost of oil and petroleum products to consumers, and on the oil industry's profits during the energy emergency. Walter F. Mondale (D Minn.) proposed an amendment limiting price increases for oil and oil products to actual increases in the costs of producing them. This amendment was tabled on a key vote of 47-44 (R 28-10; D 19-34). A second amendment, proposed by James L. Buckley (Cons-R N.Y.), would have approved the administration plan for lifting federal price ceilings on the

---

White House Energy Advisers, 1973

The White House post of chief presidential adviser on energy had three different occupants and almost as many different names in 1973, reflecting some of the uncertainty of the nation's effort to come to grips with its energy problems.

In February, Nixon named Charles J. DiBona his special consultant on energy.

In June, DiBona became the deputy director of a new Energy Policy Office in the White House. John A. Love, Republican governor of Colorado, resigned that post to become the director of the new White House office. Love found himself ignored by the President and at odds with the Treasury Department, which also had definite ideas on how to deal with the energy crisis.

And so in December, Love and DiBona resigned. The following day—Dec. 4—President Nixon asked Congress to create a separate energy agency—a Federal Energy Administration. In the interim, he reorganized the White House Energy Policy Office into a Federal Energy Office, and named William E. Simon, deputy secretary of the Treasury, to head it. John C. Sawhill, an associate director of the Office of Management and Budget, was made Simon's deputy.

---

cost of new natural gas. This amendment was also tabled, by an even closer margin, 45-43. *(Story on natural gas deregulation, p. 16-A)*

ERDA

The same day that the Senate passed its FEA bill, the House approved the Energy Reorganization Act of 1973 (HR 11510—H Rept 93-707), consolidating federal energy research programs in an independent Energy Research and Development Administration.

As approved by the House Dec. 19, by a 355-25 vote, HR 11510 followed the lines of Nixon's proposal, giving ERDA all AEC functions except licensing and regulating nuclear power plants (responsibilities that would remain with the AEC, renamed the Nuclear Energy Commission), plus energy research units from Interior, the NSF and EPA. The House adopted a floor amendment emphasizing the role that ERDA should play in encouraging energy conservation, but rejected amendments intended to direct the new agency's attention to future energy sources other than nuclear power and to ensure its independence of the industry as well as of the executive.

The Senate Dec. 7 had approved its energy research bill (S 1283—S Rept 93-589) setting up an Energy Research Management Project to direct federal energy research and development. The House did not act on the bill. *(Story p. 17-A)*

Both the FEA and ERDA were created in 1974.

Energy Policy Council

Intent upon creating a body of energy advisers in the White House comparable to the Council of Economic Advisers, the Senate three times in 1973 approved language mandating creation of a permanent White House Council on Energy Policy. The House did not give final approval to creation of this council.

The Senate May 10 approved a bill (S 70—S Rept 93-114) requiring the creation of the White House Council on Energy Policy. The vote was 79-12. S 70 provided for a three-person council, responsible for centralizing the collection and analysis of energy information, coordinating the energy activities of the government and preparing a comprehensive long-range energy development and conservation plan. The House did not act on S 70.

Emphasizing its determination on this matter, the Senate included language similar to that of S 70 in two other energy bills passed late in the year, the energy conservation bill (S 2176) and the federal energy emergency administration act (S 2776). Neither measure was enacted in 1973. *(Story pp. 17-A, 14-A)*

Natural Gas Deregulation

Despite the boost of administration support, the oil and gas industry push for an end to federal regulation of natural gas prices did not move past the hearing stage in Congress in 1973.

The Senate Commerce Committee held hearings in October and November on the Nixon administration proposal (S 2408, HR 7507) to end price regulation for all "new" natural gas, and several alternative measures, including one (S 2506) to exempt small producers from this regulation but increase this authority over large producers.

Administration and industry officials argued that deregulation would give the industry new incentive to explore and develop new sources of natural gas. They warned that the nation's reserves of this fuel were shrinking and that a shortage was likely.

Consumer-oriented witnesses expressed skepticism about the validity of any shortage, questioning the industry-supplied estimates of natural gas reserves, and the effectiveness of price increases as a spur to exploration.

During consideration of two other energy measures by the Senate, gas deregulation amendments were debated, but neither were adopted.

Background

Since 1954, the Federal Power Commission (FPC) had regulated the wellhead price of natural gas sold outside the state in which it is produced. In that year the Supreme Court ruled, to the dismay of gas producers, that Congress had granted the FPC this price control authority as part of the Natural Gas Act of 1938 *(Phillips Petroleum Co. v. Wisconsin.)*

Gas sold within the state of its production was not subject to federal regulation and could be sold at whatever price the market would bear.

Just two years after the Supreme Court decision, oil and gas producers won passage of a bill ending this regulation.

But after Sen. Francis R. Case (R S.D. 1951-1962) disclosed that he had been offered campaign funds — an offer he regarded as a bribe in return for a vote for deregulation — by an oil company attorney, President Eisenhower vetoed the bill, which he otherwise approved.

This scandal caused Congress to shy away from deregulation measures in later years.

Natural gas is the cleanest of the nation's fossil fuels and, due to federal regulation, it was the cheapest as well through the 1960s and early 1970s.

Not surprisingly, consumption of natural gas increased steadily, particularly in the industrial sector, as environmental awareness enhanced the attractiveness of this cheap, pollution-free fuel.

By 1973, natural gas accounted for 32 percent of the energy consumed in the United States. But five years earlier, in 1968, the rate at which new reserves of natural gas were discovered had begun to fall behind the rate of their consumption. From 1966 to 1973, the nation's reserves of natural gas decreased by 20 per cent.

In 1972, the FPC moved to encourage exploration, adopting an optional pricing procedure that allowed certain gas to be sold at more than the regulated price. Gas drilling began to increase.

In April 1973, President Nixon asked Congress to end FPC control over the price of natural gas from new wells, gas newly dedicated to interstate sales, and gas from old wells, once the existing contract for its sale expired. Nixon re-emphasized this request in his Project Independence Message to Congress later in the year.

Hearings. Interior Secretary Rogers C. B. Morton, White House Energy Office Chief John A. Love, and FPC Chairman John N. Nassikas testified in favor of the administration proposal at the Commerce Committee hearings. Love pointed out that the low price for natural gas—22 cents as compared to 72 cents for an equivalent amount of domestic oil—was contributing to its increasingly inefficient use by industry. Morton noted that the administration bill would retain for the Interior Department the power to set price ceilings to keep the natural gas prices from rising too sharply.

Testifying in favor of immediate deregulation, rather than the gradual process envisioned by the administration plan, were five Republican oil-state senators—John G. Tower (Texas), Paul J. Fannin (Ariz.), Clifford P. Hansen (Wyo.), Dewey F. Bartlett (Okla.) and Henry Bellmon (Okla.)—and Rush Moody Jr., FPC vice-chairman.

David S. Schwartz, assistant chief of the FPC office of economics, and James T. Halverson, director of the Federal Trade Commission's (FTC) bureau of competition, cast doubt on the assumptions underlying the deregulation proposals. Schwartz said that the oil and gas industry was insufficiently competitive to keep prices down to a reasonable level, without continued regulation. He warned that deregulation in a time of shortages would result in skyrocketing prices for gas and other fuels. Halverson said that the FTC was investigating the accuracy of reports from the gas industry of reserve figures, saying that it appeared that there had been serious under-reporting of reserves—a factor that could contribute to the reported shortage of gas supplies.

Amendments. During Senate debate on its energy research bill (S 1283) Dec. 7, Sen. James L. Buckley (Cons.-R N.Y.) proposed the administration deregulation plan as an amendment to S 1283. After the amendment was discussed, Buckley withdrew it because 10 senators who supported it were absent.

Later in December, during Senate consideration of the bill (S 2776) to set up a Federal Energy Emergency Administration, Buckley again offered his amendment. After some debate, the Senate tabled the amendment by a vote of 45-43. *(Story, p. 14-A)*

Energy Research

The Senate in 1973 approved a bill (S 1283) calling for a 10-year, $20-billion federal energy research, development and demonstration program focused on coal and other non-nuclear energy sources. The House held hearings on similar legislation but did not take any further action on the matter in 1973. The Nixon administration opposed the bill as unnecessary.

The Senate Interior and Insular Affairs Committee reported S 1283 (S Rept 93-589) Dec. 1. As reported, the bill set up an Energy Research Management Project to direct energy research and development. It set out a plan under which coal and oil shale would provide the basis for short-term energy solutions (by 1980), geothermal and solar energy for mid-term solutions (through the year 2000), and these plus nuclear fusion and hydrogen fuels for long-range solutions. The bill authorized a wide range of federal aid for research, development and demonstration projects, including contracts, federal guarantees, loans and creation of a government-industry corporation.

The Senate approved S 1283 Dec. 7 by an 82-0 vote. During three days of debate on the measure, the Senate tabled a substitute version of the bill proposed by Henry Bellmon (R Okla.) that would have provided that revenues from leasing areas on the Outer Continental Shelf for gas and oil development be used to subsidize energy demonstration projects. The amendment was tabled, 70-17. During debate on S 1283, the Senate also discussed a natural gas deregulation amendment proposed, and subsequently withdrawn, by James L. Buckley (Cons.-R N.Y.). *(See natural gas story, p. 16-A)*

Strip Mining Control

Congress confronted conflicting energy and environmental needs head-on in dealing with measures to impose federal regulation on the strip mining of coal. Far safer to the men working to extract the coal, strip mining methods had left much of the Appalachian coal fields a wasteland. The prospect of similar environmental damage in the Western Great Plains—as the vast coal deposits there were unearthed—and the hope of reclaiming already damaged lands moved the Senate in 1973 to pass a strip mining bill (S 425). The bill set minimum federal standards for reclaiming strip mined lands and regulated new and ongoing strip mining. The House did not act on the matter in 1973.

Energy Conservation Policy

The Senate in 1973 approved a bill to establish a national energy and fuel conservation program, but the House did not act on similar legislation.

The Senate bill (S 2176) was designed to encourage energy conservation in the use of automobiles and major household appliances. It required a 50 per cent increase in the average new car mileage by 1984, to more than 20 miles per gallon. It required all major appliances and automobiles to be labeled to indicate their annual operating costs. And it authorized federal grants and loans for the development of a low-polluting, energy-efficient automobile engine and for mass transit demonstration projects. Some of the provisions were eventually included in the broad energy policy act (PL 94-163) enacted in 1975. *(Story p. 37-A)*

Legislative History

The Senate Interior and Insular Affairs Committee Sept. 27 reported S 2176 (S Rept 93-409), stating that its purpose was to make energy conservation a national imperative. The Interior Committee bill created an office of energy conservation in the Interior Department to oversee a coordinated federal energy policy; it required every federal agency to adopt energy conservation measures. The bill provided for development of auto labeling standards and imposition of mandatory energy labeling requirements for major appliances.

The Senate Commerce Committee, to which S 2176 was subsequently referred, reported out Nov. 14 a much broadened version that included provisions of an earlier Senate-passed bill (S 70) creating a White House Council on Energy Policy as the coordinating point for federal energy programs. In addition, the Commerce Committee, which did not file a written report with the revised bill, provided for fuel economy standards for new automobiles, federal aid for research on improved auto engines and for mass transit projects, and required the energy efficiency labeling of appliances.

The Senate Dec. 10 adopted a substitute version of S 2176 that amalgamated the provisions recommended by the two committees, and passed the substitute measure 75-15. Before final passage, the Senate rejected amendments requiring the 50 per cent improvement in gasoline mileage to come by 1980 rather than 1984, and curbing the use of fuel for busing school children.

Energy Conservation in Buildings

The House in 1973 considered, but failed to approve, a measure (HR 11714—H Rept 93-732) directing the General Services Administration (GSA) to take the lead in developing design, lighting, insulation and architectural guidelines for the efficient use of energy in new buildings. In December, the House refused, by a vote of 230-160, to suspend the rules and approve the bill. Thirty more votes were needed for the two-thirds majority required to approve the bill under the suspension of the rules procedure.

Both chambers approved, but Congress did not complete action on, another measure (HR 11565) to promote energy conservation in federal buildings. The House version of the bill (H Rept 93-678), approved by voice vote Dec. 3, directed the GSA to develop ways of reducing energy use in new and existing federal buildings. The Senate version (S Rept 93-654) incorporated provisions of the larger energy conservation bill (S 2176) requiring federal agencies to use energy conservation policies in designing and operating federal buildings. It was passed by voice vote Dec. 20.

Deepwater Ports

Conflicting measures to permit construction of deepwater ports off U.S. coasts where supertankers could offload imported oil were reported by two House committees late in 1973. No further action occurred on the measures during the year but a version was enacted in 1974. *(Story p. 31-A)*

Small tankers—of an average size of 30,000 dead weight tons—brought most imported oil to the United States. Larger tankers—from 100,000 to 300,000 dead weight tons—were in use elsewhere, but no ports on the U.S. East or Gulf Coast were deep enough to receive them.

Conceding that "in the foreseeable future we will have to import oil in large quantities," President Nixon in April asked Congress to authorize construction of these ports to enable the United States to be served by the more economical large tankers. Existing law did not provide authority for licensing such ports, which would be more than three miles offshore, in international waters outside U.S. territorial limits.

The House Merchant Marine and Fisheries Committee Dec. 3 reported a bill (HR 5898—H Rept 93-692) similar to the Nixon proposal. It gave the Secretary of the Interior the authority to issue licenses for the construction and operation of the deepwater ports, giving consideration to the land and water use laws and other requirements of states which would be directly affected by the port.

Several days earlier, the House Public Works Committee Nov. 28 had reported its bill (HR 10701—H Rept 93-668), giving affected states a larger role in deepwater port decisions. HR 10701 gave the licensing authority to a special federal commission, and gave states a veto over the construction of a port inconsistent with its environmental program. The administration opposed this and other state-oriented provisions of HR 10701.

Naval Petroleum Reserves

Hoping to reduce the demand that the military would make on the nation's dwindling oil supplies, the Senate late in 1973 approved a measure (S J Res 176) authorizing production of oil from the Elk Hills naval petroleum reserve in California, at a daily rate of 160,000 barrels.

The House did not act on the bill. Provisions authorizing Elk Hills production were included in the Energy Emergency Act (S 2589) but were removed from the bill on the Senate floor.

Oil from the naval petroleum reserves, set aside early in the twentieth century for exclusive military use, could only be produced when the President and Congress agree that production is necessary for the national defense.

To secure necessary supplies, the Pentagon Nov. 1 invoked the Defense Production Act—a 1950 statute designed to assure the military a sufficient supply of national resources—to acquire 300,000 barrels of oil per day otherwise available to civilian consumers. On Nov. 7 President Nixon asked Congress to authorize Elk Hills production of 160,000 barrels per day. *(Nixon Nov. 7 message, p. 9-A)*

Background

It was not the energy crisis that first brought the Elk Hills naval petroleum reserve to public attention.

In 1922, Interior Secretary Albert B. Fall leased the Elk Hills oil reserve to Edward L. Doheny of the Pan American Petroleum and Transport Co. and the Teapot Dome reserve in Wyoming to Harry F. Sinclair's Mammoth Oil Co. The leases were granted without public notice or competitive bidding and led to the Teapot Dome scandal of the Warren G. Harding administration.

Elk Hills was established in 1912 and Congress in 1920 authorized in the General Leasing Act the leasing of oil reserves on public lands to private oil operators. Of the seven existing oil reserves (four petroleum and three oil shale reserves) all managed by the Navy, only one was producing oil in 1973.

Much of the oil in the reserves was not currently accessible. The vast bulk was either in Reserve No. 4 on the North Slope of Alaska or was locked in oil shale.

Only Reserve No. 2—Buena Vista—was currently producing oil. Most of the field was leased by private companies and oil was being produced from the field with royalties going to the Navy.

All of the reserves were established by executive orders, starting with Elk Hills in 1912. Oil for national security purposes previously had been produced from all the petroleum reserves except the one in Alaska during World War II.

Elk Hills. Reserve No. 1: 46,000 acres in Kern County, Calif., near Taft, containing known reserves of more than one billion barrels. Twenty per cent of the land in Elk Hills was owned by Standard Oil of California, but the Navy had complete control over production and exploration.

Buena Vista. Reserve No. 2: 30,000 acres adjacent to Elk Hills, also established in 1912 and largely depleted.

Teapot Dome. Reserve No. 3: 9,500 acres located 30 miles north of Casper, Wyo. Established in 1916, it was also largely depleted, containing only about 50 million barrels.

North Slope. Reserve No. 4: 23.7 million acres near Barrow, Alaska, containing 100 million barrels in proved reserves and 10-30 billion barrels in estimated new reserves.

Legislative History

The Senate Armed Services Committee reported S J Res 176 (S Rept 93-635) Dec. 17. S J Res 176 authorized production for one year from Elk Hills at a rate of 160,000 barrels per day. Income from this production was to be used to finance further exploration at Elk Hills and on the North Slope.

The Senate Dec. 19 approved S J Res 176 by a vote of 67-10.

Congress in 1976 finally cleared legislation (HR 49) to open up production from the first three reserves and encourage exploration of the Alaskan reserve. *(Story, p. 74-A)*

Atomic Energy Commission

Congress in 1973 authorized almost $2.5-billion for use by the Atomic Energy Commission (AEC) in fiscal 1974 and appropriated $2.38-billion for the agency.

In both measures, Congress expressed its concern about the nation's energy posture, bolstering funds for civilian nuclear programs while reducing funds for the weapons programs run by the AEC.

Congress June 25 cleared the authorization bill (S 1994—PL 93-60), providing $2,429,055,000 for the agency. The bill was approved overwhelmingly by the Senate June 22 (S Rept 93-224), and was cleared by House passage June 25 (H Rept 93-280). In November, a supplemental authorization of $40.7-million (S Rept 93-487, H Rept 93-619) was quickly approved by voice vote in both chambers, clearing Nov. 13 (S 2645—PL 93-158).

The fiscal 1974 appropriations bill (HR 8947—PL 93-97) provided $2,336,538,000 for the AEC, $93-million less than requested. The House approved it June 28 (H Rept 93-327) and the Senate July 23 (S Rept 93-338). Both chambers adopted the conference report (H Rept 93-409) July 30.

On Dec. 21 the Senate cleared for the White House a supplemental appropriations bill (HR 11576—PL 93-245) containing an additional $41.3-million for the AEC.

Energy Leadership

Nixon administration spokesmen on energy matters in 1973 were headed by Interior Secretary Rogers C. B. Morton and White House Energy Policy Office John A. Love. Preceding Love as the chief White House energy official was Charles J. DiBona, serving in that post from February to June; and succeeding Love and DiBona, both of whom resigned in December, were William C. Simon, deputy Treasury secretary, and John C. Sawhill, an associate director of the Office of Management and Budget in charge of energy matters. Simon and Sawhill Dec. 4 were named by President Nixon as the director and deputy director of a new White House Federal Energy Office. *(See box, energy reorganization story, p. 15-A)*

The energy crisis turned public attention to two regulatory agencies responsible for dealing with important segments of the energy sector—the Federal Power Commission (FPC) and the Atomic Energy Commission (AEC).

President Nixon filled two seats on the FPC during 1973, but in the process suffered the first rejection of a regulatory agency nominee since 1950. In May the Senate confirmed Nixon's choice of former Rep. William L. Springer (R Ill. 1951-73) to the FPC. But on June 13, by a vote of 51-42, the Senate killed the nomination of Robert H. Morris to the FPC. Morris, a Democrat and a California attorney, had represented Standard Oil of California for 15 years and opponents of his nomination argued that he was likely to favor the interests of the power industry over consumers. The Senate recommitted the nomination on a key vote of 51-42 (R 9-30; D 42-12). This rejection was the first for a nominee to a major independent regulatory agency since Martin A. Hutcheson was rejected as a nominee to the Federal Trade Commission in 1950. The Senate in November confirmed the nomination of Don S. Smith, a member of the Arkansas Public Service Commission, to the vacant seat.

The other FPC members were Chairman John N. Nassikas, appointed in 1969; Rush Moody, appointed in 1971; and Albert B. Brook, appointed in 1968.

Nixon also named two new members of the AEC—former astronaut William A. Anders, confirmed in August, and William E. Kriegsman, confirmed in May. The other members of the AEC were Clarence E. Larson, appointed in 1969; William Offutt Doub, appointed in 1971; and Chairman Dixy Lee Ray, appointed in 1972.

1974

Reorganization of the federal energy bureaucracy was the major accomplishment of the second session of the 93rd Congress in energy affairs.

By mid-1974, Congress had approved a Federal Energy Administration, a temporary agency replacing the Federal Energy Office, to be responsible for managing federal efforts to cope with fuel shortages. Congress later in the year endorsed the unification of many federal energy research programs in a new Energy Research and Development Administration (ERDA) that took over most of the functions of the Atomic Energy Commission (AEC) as well as non-nuclear research programs scattered through other parts of the government. The AEC was abolished and its regulatory functions given to a new body, the Nuclear Regulatory Commission. At the year's end the transition from the old to the new agencies was underway; it did not become official until January 1975.

To counterbalance the nuclear emphasis that ERDA would reflect by virtue of receiving the bulk of its funds and personnel from the AEC, Congress in 1974 declared that the federal government should plan to invest $20-billion over the next decade to develop new non-nuclear sources of energy. Congress did not authorize specific programs—other than several to speed the commercial use of solar and geothermal power—but directed ERDA to formulate plans for such an investment.

The Arab oil embargo was lifted in March 1974 and, with its end, the sense of crisis vanished. The Energy Emergency Act, left dangling at the end of the 1973 session, was finally cleared in February, only to die of a veto in March. Efforts to revive it failed. Congress did extend several other measures initially adopted during the embargo—among them the 55-mile-per-hour speed limit and the emergency fuel allocation system. And it cleared a measure authorizing the construction of deepwater ports to receive the supertankers loaded with imported oil for the United States.

Energy Reorganization

Congress in 1974 approved two-thirds of President Nixon's plan for reorganizing the federal energy structure.

In May the President signed a measure (HR 11793—PL 93-275) creating a temporary Federal Energy Administration (FEA) to manage federal efforts to deal with fuel shortages. The FEA replaced the Federal Energy Office, which Nixon had created late in 1973. Its first administrator was John C. Sawhill, deputy head of the Federal Energy Office. William E. Simon, head of the predecessor office, became Secretary of the Treasury the same month.

And in October President Ford signed a second reorganization measure (HR 11510—PL 93-438) creating a new Energy Research and Development Administration (ERDA) to direct federal research into the better use of existing fuels and the development of new sources of energy. ERDA took over most of the functions of the old Atomic Energy Commission, which was abolished by PL 93-438, plus programs from the Interior Department, the National Science Foundation, and the Environmental Protection Agency. Robert C. Seamans Jr., a former Secretary of the Air Force, was named to head the new agency.

Congress did not move in 1974 to approve creation of a Department of Energy and Natural Resources, the other portion of Nixon's reorganization plan.

FEA

The Federal Energy Administration created by PL 93-275 was less powerful than Nixon had proposed. Rather

Early Message Outlined Nixon's 1974 Energy Program

In an effort to spur Congress to deal with the energy crisis, President Nixon broke tradition to send his 1974 energy message to Congress Jan. 23, 1974, even before the State of the Union Message. "No single legislative area is more critical or more challenging to us as a people," the President said.

Nixon set out a long list of measures he requested Congress to approve. Among them were:

● A special energy emergency act permitting restrictions on public and private consumption of energy and temporary relaxation of Clean Air Act requirements for power plants and automobile emissions.

● A windfall profits tax to prevent private profiteering from raising fuel prices.

● Unemployment insurance to help persons losing jobs because of the energy crisis.

[These requests were all involved in the Energy Emergency Act (S 2589). *(Story pp. 13-A, 24-A)*

● Establishment of a Federal Energy Administration. *(Story, p. 19-A)*

● A requirement that major energy producers provide a full and constant account to the government of their inventories, production and reserves.

In addition to these short-term measures, Nixon asked Congress to approve:

● Deregulation of the price of new natural gas. *(Story p. 27-A)*

● Temporary production of oil from the Elk Hills reserve. *(Story p. 18-A)*

● Legislation permitting coal surface mining in an environmentally safe manner. *(Story p. 28-A)*

● Legislation allowing construction and operation of deepwater ports. *(Story p. 31-A)*

● Expansion of the investment tax credit for all exploratory oil and gas drilling.

● Revision and consolidation of federal mineral leasing laws.

● Establishment of an Energy Research and Development Administration and a Department of Energy and Natural Resources. *(Story p. 19-A)*

● Elimination of the tax depletion allowance for foreign oil and gas resources developed by U.S. companies, but retention of the allowance for domestic oil and gas resources. *(Story p. 34-A)*

● Acceleration of the procedure for licensing and building nuclear power plants.

● A requirement for energy efficiency labeling of products.

● Streamlining of site selection procedures for energy facilities.

Nixon said he had ordered acceleration of federal leasing of Outer Continental Shelf oil and gas resources, to lease 10 million acres in 1975. He reported that the administration would act quickly on proposals to build the Alaska pipeline, would study what incentives might be needed to encourage domestic production of synthetic fuels, and would propose increased federal aid for mass transit and energy research.

In his September 1974 legislative priorities message to Congress, President Ford endorsed Nixon's proposals for creation of the Energy Research and Development Administration, deregulation of new natural gas, authorization of deepwater port construction, passage of energy tax changes in the windfall profits, tax depletion and foreign tax credit provisions affecting oil companies, and approval of production of oil from Elk Hills.

than giving it broad authority to deal with the problems of energy shortages, Congress limited FEA powers to those specifically granted by law.

In December 1973, the Senate had approved an even more restrictive measure (S 2776). Later, between the 1973 and 1974 sessions, the House Government Operations Committee reported HR 11793 (H Rept 93-748) on Dec. 28. *(Background, p. 14-A)*

The House passed HR 11793 March 7, 353-29, after refusing to attach to it the controversial provisions of the vetoed Energy Emergency Act (S 2589) that rolled back the price of domestic oil. The Senate approved the bill March 13 after amending it to substitute the text of S 2776. *(Energy Emergency Act, pp. 13-A, 24-A)*

House Action

Debate on HR 11793 was dominated by the effort to salvage the oil price control language of the Energy Emergency Act. The proposed amendment to HR 11793 would have rolled back the price of most domestic oil to $5.25 per barrel. It was proposed by John Dingell (D Mich.) on March 6—the day President Nixon vetoed the Energy Emergency Act and the Senate sustained his veto. Dingell was frank about his reasons for proposing this addition to HR 11793, and scathing in his criticism of the "scandalous level" to which oil prices had risen and the "grotesque and

outrageous profits" thus generated for the oil industry. Opponents of the amendment said it would guarantee a presidential veto for HR 11793.

The Dingell amendment was modified by Bob Eckhardt (D Texas), to exempt from price controls producers of new oil amounting to no more than 30,000 barrels per day. Eckhardt said that this would encourage small independent oil producers to continue searching for and developing new sources.

The House approved the amendment March 6, 218-175 (R 61-115; D 157-60), but reversed itself the following day, rejecting the amendment, 163-216 (R 34-136; D 129-80). Fifty members evenly divided between the two parties switched from support to opposition, including a sizable number of freshmen and southern Democrats.

The House by voice vote approved an amendment limiting the number of energy-related offices transferred to FEA to those mentioned in the bill, and deleting authority for the President to make additional transfers in the first three months of FEA's life. The House also added language limiting the price increase that producers of propane gas could charge consumers to actual production-related costs incurred after May 15, 1973.

Final Action

Conferees filed their report on HR 11793 (H Rept 93-999) April 23, emphasizing the short-term nature of the new agency and the circumscribed nature of its powers. The life of the agency was scheduled to end June 30, 1976.

The House adopted the report April 29, 356-9. The Senate adopted it by voice vote May 2, clearing the bill for President Nixon who signed it May 7.

Provisions

As signed into law, the major provisions of PL 93-275:

● Established a Federal Energy Administration (FEA) to manage short-term fuel shortages.

● Made the agency's administrator, two deputy administrators, six assistant administrators and general counsel subject to Senate confirmation.

● Granted the administrator authority to take actions delegated to him by Congress or the President under specific laws. HR 11793 also granted specific powers, including authority to develop plans for dealing with energy shortages, to prevent unreasonable profits in the energy industry, and to impose mandatory energy saving measures.

● Transferred to the new agency from the Interior Department the offices of petroleum allocation, energy conservation, energy data and analysis, and oil and gas. The energy division of the Cost of Living Council also was transferred to the new agency.

● Gave the Cost of Living Council five days to approve or disapprove proposed actions dealing with energy prices.

● Gave the Environmental Protection Agency five days to comment on, but not veto, energy policies which could affect environmental quality.

● Provided for judicial review of agency actions.

● Gave the agency's administrator and the General Accounting Office (GAO) authority to compel energy suppliers or major energy consumers to produce information.

● Directed the GAO to monitor and evaluate the agency's actions.

● Directed the administrator to provide access for the public to all information except that which could be excluded from public reports to the Securities and Exchange Commission.

● Directed the President to report to Congress six months before the act expired on 1) his recommendations for a permanent federal energy organization, and 2) whether the FEA should be continued, terminated or reorganized.

● Directed the FEA administrator to report within one year of enactment on the nation's oil and gas reserves and annually on the FEA's activities and on estimates of the nation's future energy supplies.

● Directed the administrator to submit a comprehensive energy plan within six months of enactment.

● Required the administrator to conduct a comprehensive review of foreign ownership of domestic energy sources and supplies.

● Authorized appropriation of $75-million for fiscal 1974 and $200-million for each of fiscal 1975-76.

● Provided that the act would expire June 30, 1976.

ERDA

Congress in 1974 created a new billion-dollar agency to take the lead in research and development of new energy sources. President Ford Oct. 11 signed a measure (HR 11510—PL 93-438) creating an Energy Research and Development Administration (ERDA) expected to have a budget of $2.6-billion in 1975 and a staff of more than 7,000 employees.

Ford had labeled the bill his top-priority energy measure; he signed it the day after Congress completed work on it.

ERDA took over the nuclear power development functions of the Atomic Energy Commission (AEC), which was abolished by PL 93-438. A new Nuclear Regulatory Commission was created by the bill to take over AEC's safety and regulatory responsibilities. The bulk of ERDA's budget ($2.2-billion) and staff (6,000) was to come from the AEC.

Yet as enacted, PL 93-438 established an agency oriented more toward energy conservation, environmental protection and nuclear safety than President Nixon had initially proposed. When the House considered the bill in December 1973, it rejected all but one of a series of amendments attempting to broaden the agency's focus beyond nuclear power, but the Senate and conferees included language designed to encourage such a shift in emphasis. In addition to the AEC programs, ERDA acquired fossil fuel energy research programs from the Interior Department and geothermal and solar energy development programs from the National Science Foundation. *(1973 action, story p. 14-A)*

Senate Action

The Senate passed its version of the ERDA bill (S 2774—S Rept 93-980) by voice vote Aug. 15 after unanimously agreeing to incorporate in the bill the bulk of another bill (S 1283) calling for a 10 year, $20-billion nonnuclear energy research and development program. The Senate had passed S 1283 in December 1973. *(Story p. 17-A)*

A number of provisions designed to ensure fair representation of and funding for non-nuclear energy programs were inserted in the bill by the Senate Government Operations Committee which reported it June 27. These included the requirements that the ERDA administrators be generalists, that separate energy conservation and safety programs be set up, and that no energy program receive less than 7 per cent of ERDA's annual funds.

In addition to the inclusion of language calling for the massive non-nuclear energy research program to balance the AEC's nuclear programs that ERDA would receive, the Senate bill differed from the House measure in abolishing the AEC, rather than simply renaming it, and in creating a new regulatory body called the Nuclear Safety and Licensing Commission. The Senate bill did not transfer to ERDA Environmental Protection Agency (EPA) programs to develop a low-pollution automobile engine and technology to control pollution from power and industrial plants. But it did create a Council on Energy Policy in the White House, an administration-opposed step that the Senate had approved three times in 1973. *(Story p. 15-A)*

The Senate also amended its ERDA bill to provide that the nation would return to standard time, from daylight saving time, for the period from late October 1974 through February 1975. Congress in 1973 had provided that the nation would be on daylight saving time year-round until April 1975. Only a small amount of energy had been saved by this move, said Robert Taft Jr. (R Ohio), the sponsor of the amendment, while the lives of small children were endangered as they walked to school in the dark.

Final Action

Conferees filed their report on the bill (H Rept 93-1445) Oct. 8.

They dropped from the final version the non-nuclear research programs added on the Senate floor, explaining that legislation containing such provisions (S 1283) was already in conference with a similar House bill (HR 13565). *(Story, this page)*

Otherwise, the conference version of the bill resembled that approved by the Senate. Conferees compromised by agreeing to language abolishing the AEC and creating a new structure for a new Nuclear Regulatory Commission, and by transferring part of the EPA automobile engine research program to ERDA.

Conferees dropped the Senate provision for a White House Council on Energy Policy, the Senate language requiring a basic 7 per cent share of ERDA funds for each energy program, and the daylight saving time repeal. Congress Sept. 30 had cleared legislation (HR 16102—PL 93-434) returning the nation to standard time for the four winter months. *(Story, p. 33-A)*

The House adopted the conference report on HR 11510 Oct. 9 by a vote of 372-1. The Senate cleared the bill Oct. 10 by voice vote.

Provisions

As signed into law, the major provisions of PL 93-438:

ERDA Establishment

● Established an Energy Research and Development Administration (ERDA) within 120 days of enactment of PL 93-438.

● Provided that the ERDA administrator, deputy administrator and six assistant administrators be appointed by the President and confirmed by the Senate.

● Established six program areas, one under each of the assistant administrators, for fossil energy, nuclear energy, environment and safety, energy conservation, solar, geothermal and advanced energy systems, and nuclear weapons programs.

● Required the administrator and his deputy to be specifically qualified to manage the full range of energy research and development programs; prohibited appointment of military officers to either position until two years after retirement.

Program Transfers

● Abolished the Atomic Energy Commission (AEC) and transferred all of its functions, except licensing, regulation and safety, to ERDA. Regulatory functions were transferred to the Nuclear Regulatory Commission.

● Transferred to ERDA from the Interior Department the programs of the Office of Coal Research, the fossil fuel research of the Bureau of Mines and underground electric transmission research.

● Transferred to ERDA from the National Science Foundation (NSF) the geothermal and solar heating and cooling development programs. NSF retained control of basic research on the conversion of solar energy for generating electricity from central power stations.

● Transferred to ERDA from the Environmental Protection Agency (EPA) authority for research and development of an alternative automobile power system. EPA would retain research authority related to monitoring and control of air pollution from automobiles.

Energy Policy Coordination

● Established in the White House a temporary Energy Resources Council to ensure coordination among federal energy agencies and to advise the President and Congress.

● Directed that the council be composed of the Secretary of Interior, the federal energy administrator, the ERDA administrator, the Secretary of State, the director of the Office of Management and Budget and other federal officials.

● Provided that the council would terminate upon creation of a permanent department for energy or natural resources or within two years, whichever occurred sooner.

Nuclear Safety

● Established a five-member Nuclear Regulatory Commission, appointed by the President, to take over the AEC's safety, licensing and regulatory powers.

● Created an Office of Nuclear Reactor Regulation and an Office of Nuclear Regulatory Research.

● Upgraded the AEC's regulatory division into an Office of Nuclear Material Safety and Safeguards.

● Made the safety office responsible for protecting commercial facilities against threats, sabotage or theft of nuclear materials.

● Directed the office's director to make a study and report on whether the office should establish a security force to protect facilities and fuels.

● Required employees of firms regulated by the commission to report immediately to the commission any violation of the Atomic Energy Act or any cases of facilities having a safety defect that could create a substantial safety hazard.

● Directed the commission to report quarterly to Congress on any abnormal occurrences at licensed nuclear facilities; such incidents would have to be reported to the public within 15 days of an occurrence.

Future Energy Reorganization

● Directed the President to report to Congress by June 30, 1975, his recommendations for further reorganization of federal energy activities.

Non-Nuclear Energy Research

To bring federal support of research and development of non-nuclear energy sources into better balance with aid for work on nuclear energy, Congress in 1974 approved legislation (S 1283—PL 93-577) calling for a 10-year program of non-nuclear energy research and development.

PL 93-577 established broad policy guidelines for research and development in non-nuclear energy to parallel nuclear energy policy established by the Atomic Energy Act of 1954 (PL 84-141). The law declared that the nation's energy problems required federal investment of $20-billion over a 10-year period to develop non-nuclear energy sources. It contained no specific program authorizations, however.

The administrator of the new Energy Research and Development Administration (ERDA) was directed by PL 93-577 to send Congress by mid-1975 a comprehensive plan for meeting the nation's short-term (through the early 1980s), middle-term (through the year 2000) and long-term (beyond the year 2000) energy problems. PL 93-577 specified that this plan should focus on use of non-nuclear energy.

PL 93-577 was opposed by the Nixon administration as unnecessary, but the executive branch reversed its position under President Ford. The Senate approved S 1283 in December 1973; the House approved its version in September 1974; the bill was cleared for the President Dec. 17, 1974.

Senate Action

Intended to provide unified management and adequate funding for non-nuclear energy programs, S 1283 was unanimously approved by the Senate Dec. 7, 1973. As approved by the Senate, the measure focused the nation's immediate efforts to cope with the energy crisis on coal, its most abundant fossil fuel. S 1283 called for federal research on improving methods for mining coal and for turning coal into gas-like and oil-like "synthetic" fuels. It placed heavy emphasis on government-industry cooperation to demonstrate the commercial feasibility of new energy sources, such as underground heat, oil shale, and gas and oil synthesized from coal. *(Story p. 17-A)*

In August 1974 the Senate, frustrated by the lack of House action on S 1283, inserted its provisions in the measure (S 2744—HR 11510) creating the new Energy Research and Development Administration (ERDA). Conferees dropped these provisions from the ERDA bill after House passage of S 1283. *(Story p. 21-A)*

House Action

The House Sept. 11 approved its version of the non-nuclear energy research bill (HR 13565) by a 327-7 vote. The bill, as reported June 26 by the House Interior and Insular Affairs Committee (H Rept 93-1157), authorized a total of $3.1-billion over fiscal 1975-76 in federal aid to such research.

The major change made by the full House in the bill was the removal of these specific authorizations and their replacement with a statement of congressional finding that $20-billion should be invested in these non-nuclear programs over the next decade. The change resolved a jurisdictional conflict between the Interior Committee and the House Science and Astronautics Committee, which contended that it had jurisdiction over some of the specific programs involved.

Before passing the bill, the House rejected more than a dozen amendments proposed by Craig Hosmer (R Calif.), the ranking Republican member of the Interior Committee; most of the amendments were designed to reduce the energy conservation and environmental factors to be considered in energy planning and to give the ERDA administrator more flexibility in administering the program.

The House agreed to an amendment striking out the patent provisions of the bill as reported, which provided that the federal government would retain the rights to patents developed under these programs. In place of that language, the House authorized a report on the adequacy of existing patent law. This amendment was adopted, 182-142.

Conference Action

Conferees filed their report (H Rept 93-1563) Dec. 11. The most difficult issue facing them had been the patent policy to cover the technologies developed under S 1283. The administration objected to Senate language requiring the federal government to retain the rights to all the

Energy Research Funds

Reorganizing its appropriations procedure for energy programs even before energy reorganization legislation had cleared, Congress in 1974 lifted appropriations for energy-related programs out of seven different regular appropriations measures and dealt with them as a package.

On June 24, Congress cleared a bill (HR 14434—PL 93-322), appropriating $2,236,089,000 only for energy research and development programs in fiscal 1975. In subsequent years Congress returned to the practice of funding those programs in regular appropriations bills.

The bill had been approved by the House Appropriations Committee April 25 (H Rept 93-1010), and approved by the House April 30, 392-4. The Senate Appropriations Committee reported the measure June 5 (S Rept 93-903) and the Senate passed the bill June 12, 92-0. Conferees filed their report June 19 (H Rept 93-1123), and both chambers adopted the report June 24 by voice vote.

The components of the $2.2-billion measure included:

● Environmental Protection Agency (EPA) research to control pollutants associated with energy extraction, transmission and use—$54-million.

● National Aeronautics and Space Administration (NASA)—$4.4-million.

● National Science Foundation (NSF) research, particularly into solar and geothermal energy—$101.8-million.

● Interior Department—a total of $557.2-million, including $43.1-million for the Geological Survey, $142.3-million for the Bureau of Mines, $261.3-million for the office of coal research, $69.6-million for fuel allocation, oil and gas, $26.9-million for conservation, data and analysis, and $8.5-million for underground electric transmission research.

● Atomic Energy Commission—$1.5-billion, the largest single component of the total.

● National Oceanic and Atmospheric Administration (NOAA) for assessing the environmental impact of developing oil and gas resources on the Outer Continental Shelf—$6.6-million.

● Transportation Department research to improve the energy efficiency of cars and trucks—$6.4-million.

● Federal Energy Office—$19-million.

The energy reorganization measures approved by Congress in 1974 provided new homes for some of these programs. The new Energy Research and Development Administration (ERDA) received some of the NSF programs, the office of coal research, the fossil fuel programs of the Bureau of Mines, the Interior Department's work on underground electric transmission lines, and most of the AEC programs. The Federal Energy Administration provided a place for the fuel allocation, oil and gas, conservation, data and analysis programs from the Interior Department. *(Details, story pp. 21-A, 19-A)* technologies and to license them on a non-exclusive basis. The House bill called for a study and report on the adequacy of existing patent law. Conferees modeled the final patent provisions on policy governing work done for the National Aeronautics and Space Administration, similar to the Senate language but less restrictive.

Final Action

The House Dec. 16 adopted the conference report by a 378-5 vote. The Senate cleared the bill for the President Dec. 17, adopting the conference report by a vote of 91-1.

Provisions

As signed into law, the major provisions of PL 93-577:

● Declared that the nation's energy problems required a 10-year federal investment of $20-billion for non-nuclear energy research and development.

● Made it the policy of Congress to develop on an urgent basis the technological capability to support the broadest range of energy policy choices through conservation and the use of domestic energy resources in socially and environmentally acceptable ways.

● Emphasized that the research and development programs should give primary consideration to energy conservation, environmental protection, development of renewable resources and water requirements of new technologies.

● Directed that the program should 1) facilitate the commercial development of adequate energy supplies for all regions of the United States; 2) consider the urgency of the public need for the technologies supported; 3) ensure that the problems treated had national significance; and 4) direct federal support to areas which might not attract private capital.

Planning and Programming

● Directed the ERDA administrator to send to Congress by June 30, 1975, a comprehensive plan and program designed to solve short-term energy problems through the early 1980s; middle-term problems through the year 2000; and long-range problems beyond the year 2000.

● Specified that the energy program should focus on 1) agricultural and other wastes; 2) the reuse and recycling of materials; 3) improved efficiency of automobile engines; and 4) improvement in the design of homes and buildings.

● Directed that the research program also stress the development of low-sulfur fuels; improved methods of producing and delivering electrical energy; the development of synthetic fuels from coal and oil shale; and improved methods for recovering petroleum.

Forms of Federal Assistance

● Authorized federal assistance in the form of joint federal-industry corporations, contracts, federal purchases or price guarantees of products from demonstration plants, loans to non-federal entities and incentives for inventors.

● Provided that joint government-industry corporations or price supports could not be implemented unless authorized by an act of Congress.

● Authorized the administrator to provide assistance for projects to demonstrate the commercial feasibility of new energy technologies.

● Limited to $50-million the amount of federal assistance that could be appropriated for any project without a specific authorization by Congress.

● Directed the administrator to report to Congress on any project for which the federal contribution exceeded $25-million.

Patent Policy

● Required that the federal government retain the rights to any technologies developed under the act and directed the government to grant licenses for use of technologies on a non-exclusive basis.

● Permitted a waiver of federal rights if such waiver would make the benefits of the technology quickly and widely available to the public; would promote the commercial use of the technology; would encourage participation of private persons in the energy research program; and would foster competition.

● Permitted the administrator to grant exclusive licenses for a technology if it promoted the interests of the general public; if the desired use of the technology had not occurred under a non-exclusive contract; or if an exclusive license was needed to encourage the investment of private risk capital in development of the technology.

● Prohibited the granting of an exclusive license if the grant tended to substantially lessen competition.

Environmental Evaluation

● Directed the Council on Environmental Quality to evaluate the application of non-nuclear energy technologies supported under the act for their adequacy of attention to energy conservation and environmental protection.

● Directed the Water Resources Council, at the request of the ERDA administrator, to assess the water resource requirements and the availability of water for energy technologies which were supported under the act.

Reports to Congress

● Directed the administrator to send to Congress each year at the time the President's budget was submitted a report on the activities supported during the previous fiscal year and a detailed description of the nuclear and non-nuclear energy plan then in effect.

Authorizations

● Authorized annual appropriations of $500,000 for the environmental evaluation and $1,000,000 for the water resource evaluation.

Energy Emergency Act

The ill-fated Energy Emergency Act (S 2589) died a slow death in the first months of the 1974 session. The immediate cause of death was a presidential veto, complicated by a fading sense of crisis after the end of the Arab oil embargo in March.

In 1973, the measure—which gave the President special powers he had requested to use to control the production and consumption of energy in an emergency—had been approved by both chambers and a conference committee. But final action on the bill was stalled on the next-to-the-last day of the session when oil state senators filibustered in opposition to language in S 2589 which would have limited the windfall profits made by oil companies. *(Story p. 13-A)*

In addition to the energy emergency powers and the windfall profits provisions, S 2589 also permitted a temporary loosening of clean air standards. When Congress reconvened in 1974, an unusual coalition formed in the Senate—oil-state senators and conservation-minded senators—to send the measure back to conference.

In February the Senate approved the second conference version, which substituted a ceiling on oil prices for the windfall profits provision. Both the Nixon administration and the oil industry opposed the price ceiling provisions. The House then cleared this version of S 2589 for the White House after forestalling a move to send the bill back for a third conference.

President Nixon vetoed the bill March 6, citing as particularly objectionable the price ceiling provisions and those providing unemployment benefits for workers losing their jobs because of energy shortages. The Senate sustained the veto, 58-40, the same day.

Revised versions of the energy emergency bill (HR 13834, S 3267) reached the House and Senate floors in May. But after the House refused to pass the bill, the effort to revive the measure died. The clean air provisions and those granting new powers to the Federal Energy Administration were enacted as separate legislation (HR 14368—PL 93-319. *(Story, p. 26-A)*

Senate Recommittal

The Senate Jan. 29, by a 57-37 roll-call vote (R 32-7; D 25-30), recommitted S 2589 to a Senate-House conference committee. Because the Senate had voted on a compromise rather than the report in the final days of the 1973 session, it was able to take the bill up again when Congress reconvened.

Supporters of the bill said "an unholy alliance" of senators was responsible for recommitting S 2589. Offered by Gaylord Nelson (D Wis.), the recommittal motion brought together some conservation-minded senators—mostly northern Democrats—who wanted less stringent modifications in the 1970 Clean Air Act's standards, oil state senators who wanted the windfall profits limitations expunged, and backers of President Nixon, who wanted everything dropped from the bill except the basic authority to impose rationing and conservation programs and provisions easing the federal clean air regulations.

Henry M. Jackson (D Wash.), floor manager of the conference report, declared that the 57-37 vote was "a victory for the oil industry."

Nelson, a member of the Finance Committee, asserted that enactment of the windfall profits section would play "a gigantic con game on the American people."

Nelson argued that the provision, as written into S 2589, was not a tax but rather a method to limit prices and provide for consumer appeals through the Renegotiation Board, which was created during the Korean War to recapture excess profits from the defense industry. Consumers could petition the board for a roll-back of prices and rebates of excessive profits, Nelson said. He contended that any of the nation's 220,000 service station operators could be hauled before the board if a customer complained.

Jackson defended the windfall profits provision, saying that it would serve as "a burr under the saddle" to get Congress to pass legislation dealing more effectively with excess profits in the oil industry.

Nelson criticized S 2589 for allowing a five-year delay in meeting air pollution standards. But Edmund S. Muskie (D Maine), chairman of the Senate Public Works Subcommittee on Air and Water Pollution, argued that the conference provisions modifying the Clean Air Act were superior to those originally approved by the Senate.

Second Conference Action

Conferees filed their second report on S 2589 (S Rept 93-681) Feb. 6. Junking the windfall profits restriction, they replaced it with language setting the price of all domestic crude oil at $5.25 per barrel. "Meteoric increases" in oil prices had become "one of the most serious...aspects of the energy emergency," conferees asserted, pointing to the 150 per cent increase from October to December 1973 in the price of the fuel oil used by electric utilities.

The price ceiling adopted by conferees was that already imposed on 71 per cent of all domestic crude oil by the Cost of Living Council, acting under the authority of the Economic Stabilization Act. Crude oil exempt from this ceiling—oil from new wells and oil from low-producing wells—was selling for about $10.35 per barrel, conferees said. It was the price of this exempt oil that would have to be rolled back. Conferees also included language in the bill allowing the President to increase the price of oil that was costly to produce—up to about $7.09 per barrel.

Conferees expanded the unemployment benefits provision to cover all workers losing their jobs because of energy shortages, not only those losing their jobs because of actions taken under S 2589.

The Senate Feb. 19 by a 67-32 vote—just one more than a two-thirds majority—approved the second conference report on S 2589. Before adopting the report, the Senate by votes of 38-60, 37-62 and 37-62 rejected efforts to send the bill back to conference to remove the price ceiling requirements.

The House Feb. 27 adopted the conference report by a 258-151 vote—15 short of a two-thirds majority. Earlier, the House had forestalled the possible death of the bill—or a third conference—by amending the rule for consideration of the report to allow the House to vote separately on three controversial provisions. The key vote came when the House, 144-259, refused to adopt the rule without amendment. Without a change in the rule, any objection raised to the conference report and sustained would have killed the bill unless the House asked for another conference.

In subsequent votes, the House refused, 173-238, to delete the oil price ceiling from the bill. It refused, 66-343, to delete language allowing Congress to veto presidential plans to conserve energy, and it refused, 199-211, to strike out language authorizing the President to impose rationing. On this last vote, and on final passage, the margin of victory was provided by Republicans, preserving the conference language despite administration and oil industry opposition.

Provisions

As sent to the President, key provisions of S 2589, the Energy Emergency Act:

● Authorized the President to draft a rationing plan for oil and oil products, but provided that rationing be used to limit energy demands only if all other means failed.

● Set up a Federal Energy Emergency Administration, whose head was authorized to implement energy conservation plans, to require power plants to use coal rather than oil or natural gas, to propose a means of allocating energy-related materials and to require maximum production from public and private oil fields.

● Provided Congress with the power to veto energy conservation plans proposed before Sept. 1, 1974, and required that subsequent conservation plans be approved by Congress.

● Directed the President to reduce to $5.25 per barrel the price of domestic crude oil presently exempt from price controls, allowing increases to $7.09 per barrel for domestic crude oil that cost more to produce.

● Authorized $500-million for grants to states to pay unemployment benefits to people losing their jobs due to fuel shortages.

● Postponed until 1977 the 1976 final standards for automobile emissions of hydrocarbons and carbon monoxide mandated by the Clean Air Act; permitted the Environmental Protection Agency (EPA) to grant another year's delay; delayed to 1978 the standard for nitrogen oxide; authorized EPA to suspend until Nov. 1, 1974, fuel and emission standards for industrial and electrical facilities; waived those standards through Jan. 1, 1979, for facilities ordered to convert to use of coal.

● Exempted for one year actions taken under the act from the environmental impact statement requirement of the National Environmental Policy Act.

● Provided for expiration of these authorities and for termination of the Federal Energy Emergency Administration on May 15, 1975.

Veto

Nixon March 6 vetoed the bill, saying that "after all the hearings and speeches, all the investigations, accusations and recriminations, the Congress has succeeded only in producing legislation which solves none of the problems, threatens to undo the progress we have already made, and creates a host of new problems." Nixon said that the price ceiling was so low that the oil industry would be unable to sustain its present level of production. Furthermore, the unemployment provisions were unworkable and inequitable, Nixon said.

Senate Action. The Senate that day sustained the veto, 58-40. On the vote, six senators who had voted to adopt the conference report two weeks earlier supported the veto: Democrats John Sparkman (Ala.), J. Bennett Johnston Jr. (La.), Russell B. Long (La.), John L. McClellan (Ark.) and Republicans Hugh Scott (Pa.) and James B. Pearson (Kan.).

In the debate preceding the vote, Jackson challenged the assumption that price and production were linked so closely. "In February 1973," he said, "the domestic oil industry was producing 9.4 million barrels of crude oil per day at an average price of $3.40. In February 1974 it produced 9.2 million barrels a day at an average price of $6.95.... Crude oil prices have doubled and crude oil production has not increased one whit."

Defenders of the veto argued that the price rollback would increase U.S. reliance on oil imports. "Every barrel of domestic oil that the industry cannot afford to produce at $5.25...a barrel will be imported," said Paul J. Fannin (R Ariz.). A vote to override the veto, said Dewey F. Bartlett (R Okla.) would be a vote "for continued long lines at the filling stations...for more unemployment...for less productivity."

FEA Powers

Energy Emergency Act provisions granting the Federal Energy Administration (FEA) authority to order the increased use of coal, to conduct energy studies, and to gather energy data were enacted in 1974 as part of a bill (HR 14368—PL 93-319) delaying clean air standards. PL 93-319 was entitled the Energy Supply and Environmental Coordination Act.

PL 93-319 authorized FEA to prohibit the use of oil or natural gas by facilities able to use coal, to require that new power plants be designed to burn coal, and to allocate coal to facilities receiving such orders. This authority was to expire June 30, 1975.

The measure also directed FEA to report to Congress within six months on the potential for energy conservation; it directed the Secretary of Transportation to recommend within 90 days a plan for saving energy by improving public transportation; and it ordered the FEA administrator and the Transportation Secretary to report within 120 days on the feasibility of requiring a 20 per cent improvement in new car mileage by 1980. It directed FEA to gather and make public information necessary to make energy policy decisions and gave it subpoena power to obtain that information.

Revival Efforts

A final effort to enact an energy emergency bill collapsed May 21, when the House by the key vote of 191-207 (R 30-147; D 161-60) refused to approve a revised version of the bill (HR 13834).

William E. Simon, head of the Federal Energy Office, had told the House Interstate and Foreign Commerce Committee early in April that the nation no longer needed the measure because the Arab oil embargo was over.

But the Senate Interior and Insular Affairs Committee reported out its revised bill (S 3267—S Rept 93-785) April 19, without the oil price ceiling provision; and the House Committee reported a similar bill, with the oil price provision, April 29 (HR 13834—H Rept 93-1014). HR 13834 also contained language requiring the President to set a ceiling price for imported oil. The Commerce Committee late in April reported a separate bill (HR 14368) containing the clean air, coal conversion and energy data provisions of S 2589. That bill was enacted in June. *(Box on new FEA powers, this page)*

The House bill (HR 13834) was brought to the floor May 21 under suspension of the rules. A two-thirds majority was needed to pass the bill; it did not obtain a simple majority.

The fading of the crisis atmosphere after the end of the winter and the embargo contributed to its defeat, as did the fact that the House Ways and Means Committee was working on a tax bill—not enacted in 1974—imposing new taxes on the oil industry. James T. Broyhill (R N.C.), who had earlier supported the price provisions of S 2589, explained his vote against HR 13834, saying that the price provisions of S 2589 were written "in a different year and a different time and under different circumstances than exist today."

The Senate had begun debate on S 3267 May 8 and 13, expecting to resume the week of May 20. After the House vote rejecting the companion measure, the Senate indefinitely suspended consideration of its bill.

Natural Gas Deregulation

Again in 1974, administration urging did not propel natural gas deregulation measures (S 2408, HR 7507) beyond the committee hearing stage. But reports of a worsening shortage of this fuel kept the matter alive. And the Federal Power Commission (FPC) moved boldly to revise and increase the price ceilings that the administration and industry sought to scrap. *(Background, p. 16-A)*

President Ford told Congress Oct. 8 that deregulation to increase domestic energy supplies was his number-one energy priority. The Senate Commerce Committee, which began hearings on the issue in 1973, continued them early in 1974. Hearings resumed again in December after their staff had drafted a new bill that directed the FPC to set a flat and final price between 40 and 60 cents per thousand cubic feet (mcf) for new natural gas.

Interior Secretary Rogers C. B. Morton opposed the new bill as inadequate, saying that it "tries to regulate our way out of something we've regulated our way into." FPC Chairman John N. Nassikas agreed with Morton that deregulation would provide the necessary incentive to spur increased production, but he urged that the FPC be given authority to reimpose price ceilings if new gas supplies did not result from higher prices.

FPC Actions

Under Nassikas, selected by President Nixon in 1969 to head the FPC, that agency had already allowed prices to rise in the various areas, granting exemptions from price ceilings for small producers, for emergency sales, and for producers who chose to use certain optional pricing alternatives.

On June 21, 1974, the FPC took its boldest step, abolishing the area rates and replacing them with a single nationwide rate of 42 cents per mcf for new gas. This was nearly double the maximum price allowed before 1969. The new rate had a built-in escalator of 1 per cent per year. It applied to all gas sold from wells going into production after Jan. 1, 1973, and all gas contracted for interstate sales after that date. The new rate applied to onshore and offshore gas, and to oil-well as well as gas-well gas.

Six months later, in December, the FPC again raised the rate—to 50 cents per mcf—squarely in the middle of the range which the Commerce Committee draft measure prescribed.

The Intrastate Problem

But even this new higher price, argued proponents of deregulation, was not enough. Interstate gas purchasers still could not effectively compete with those in the unregulated intrastate market. A Library of Congress report issued in November bore out this fact. The percentage of gas production sold interstate had slipped from 55 per cent in 1972 to 53.5 per cent in 1973. Intrastate gas prices ranged between $1.00 and $1.25 per mcf and even as high as $2.00 per mcf.

"The fact is," concluded the study, "that the interstate market is losing out to the unregulated intrastate market. Notwithstanding, gas production as a whole has virtually not grown at all since 1969."

But the study was skeptical about the argument that deregulation and resulting price increases would spur production: "Our recent experience with oil may serve as a guide here. The price of new oil, that is, the incentive price for generating new production, has increased three-fold in the past year. Nevertheless, production continues to decline. Indeed, it is 700,000 barrels per day lower than it was a year ago."

Nuclear Accident Insurance

President Ford in 1974 vetoed a bill (HR 15323) extending for five years the federal program insuring the public and the nuclear power industry against a nuclear power accident.

Ford favored the extension, but vetoed the measure because of a provision which usurped, he said, his constitutional power to give the final stamp of approval to legislation with his signature. Concerned about the safety of expanding the use of nuclear power, Congress had inserted in HR 15323 language giving it the opportunity—after the President signed the measure—to disapprove the extension, if warranted by the results of a study on nuclear safety due to be completed in late 1974.

The existing nuclear insurance program, created by the Price-Anderson Act of 1957 (PL 85-256), did not expire until Aug. 1, 1977. Early extension of the program was intended to encourage investments in nuclear power plants.

Background. The Price-Anderson Act was enacted to reassure the public that there would be compensation for any damage resulting from a nuclear power plant accident and to limit the liability of the industry for any one accident. Such reassurance was needed in 1957 to encourage the development of the infant nuclear power industry. The law was named for Rep. Melvin Price (D Ill.) and Sen. Clinton P. Anderson (D N.M. 1949-1973).

PL 85-256 required all nuclear power plants to obtain the maximum coverage private insurance companies would provide—in 1957, about $60-million. It limited the industry's liability for any one accident to $560-million—and the government assumed responsibility for paying the $500-million difference.

As the amount of insurance obtainable from private sources increased (to $110-million by 1974), the government's liability decreased, but the $560-million limit on the industry's liability remained in place. The federal government had never paid any claims under the act, because there had been no accidents. Thus the system had actually produced revenue for the government, because the power plants paid a fee for the government's backing. From 1957 to 1975, these fees totaled $5.6-million.

Spurred by the increasing reliance of government officials on nuclear power as the prime energy source of the future, environmentalists and consumer spokesmen began in the early 1970s to question the safety of expanding nuclear power production. (By 1973, some three dozen nuclear power plants were in operation, producing electricity, and another 200 were in various stages of development.) This concern was enhanced in 1973 by the leak of 115,000 gallons of liquid radioactive nuclear waste from an Atomic Energy Commission (AEC) facility at Hanford, Wash.

The Joint Atomic Energy Committee began hearings in 1973 on the safety issue. AEC officials testified that nuclear reactors were safer than other means of generating energy. They expressed confidence that this assessment would be supported by the results of a new study of reactor risks, directed by Norman C. Rasmussen of the Massachusetts Institute of Technology, due for completion in 1974.

When the Joint Committee resumed hearings early in 1974, critics of nuclear power appeared to rebut the AEC position. Consumer advocate Ralph Nader testified, calling nuclear power a form of "technological suicide." Henry W. Kendall, a nuclear physicist speaking for the Union of Concerned Scientists, cited the Hanford leak and other recent accidents as illustrative of the need to halt construction of new nuclear plants. Joint Committee member Rep. Mike McCormack (D Wash.), a nuclear research chemist associated with the Hanford project for 20 years before his election to Congress in 1970, took issue with Kendall's statements as "reckless and irresponsible."

House Action

The House July 10 approved a 10-year extension of the federal nuclear insurance program (HR 15323) by a vote of 360-43. The measure had been reported by the Joint Committee June 18 (H Rept 93-1115) after the committee reduced the extension to 10 years, from 20 years.

As approved by the House, HR 15323 provided for an eventual increase in the $560-million liability ceiling and the phasing out of the government's role in the program as more nuclear power plants went into operation. In the event of an accident, each plant would have to pay between $2-million and $5-million in "retrospective premiums" into a pool to cover damages. When enough plants were participating, the pool would rise to the $560-million level and above, allowing the government to bow out.

Before passing the bill, the House easily rejected, 138-267, an amendment limiting the extension to two years. It adopted, however, an amendment delaying the effective date of the bill until the Joint Committee evaluated the Rasmussen report.

Committee Action

The Joint Committee took the unusual step of reviewing the House-passed version of the bill and then reporting it July 23 (S Rept 93-1027) to the Senate. The committee usually reported identical bills simultaneously to both chambers. The Joint Committee eliminated from the bill a House-added provision barring coverage, by the Price-Anderson Act, of nuclear accidents occurring in other countries. This was unnecessary, the committee said, because the act did not cover reactors owned by foreign countries.

Senate Action

The Senate approved HR 15323 by voice vote Aug. 8, after amending it to reduce the extension to five, rather than ten years, and to prohibit its taking effect if Congress by concurrent resolution disapproved the extension after review of the Rasmussen report.

Both amendments were proposed by Gaylord Nelson (D Wis.). The Senate also adopted by voice vote language expanding the insurance program to cover nuclear thefts as well as nuclear accidents.

Conference Action

Conferees reported the final version of the bill (H Rept 93-1306) Aug. 20, agreeing to the five-year extension and the provision allowing Congress to disapprove the extension after enactment of HR 15323. They dropped the Senate extension of coverage to accidents involving nuclear theft and the House language barring coverage of accidents outside the United States.

Final Action, Veto

The House Sept. 24 adopted the conference report, 376-10. The Senate adopted the report Sept. 30 by voice vote, clearing the measure for the President.

President Ford vetoed the bill Oct. 12, objecting to the provision allowing Congress later to nullify the extension. "Congress, in effect, requests my approval," he said, "before it has given its own," disturbing the proper sequence of legislative enactment set out in the Constitution.

A new version of the bill, without the offending provision, was enacted in 1975. *(Story, p. 49-A)*

Strip Mining Control

A measure setting minimum environmental standards to be observed in strip mining of coal (S 425) was pocket vetoed by President Ford late in 1974. Passed by overwhelming majorities in the House and the Senate, S 425 was opposed by the coal industry and the Ford administration, which argued that the new regulatory scheme would reduce the nation's coal production and undercut the national push for energy independence.

Solar Energy

To speed the harnessing of energy from the sun, Congress in 1974 approved two new solar energy programs. In August, Congress sent President Ford legislation (HR 11864—PL 93-409) authorizing a program to demonstrate the commercial feasibility of heating and cooling buildings with solar energy. President Ford signed the measure Sept. 3.

And in October, on the day President Ford signed the bill creating the Energy Research and Development Administration (PL 93-438), Congress cleared a second solar energy bill, authorizing a broad federal program to speed the development and commercial use of advanced solar energy technology (S 3234—PL 93-473).

Solar Heat

A five-year, $60-million demonstration program to build public confidence that solar energy could be used to heat and cool homes and other buildings was authorized by HR 11864. Rep. Mike McCormack (D Wash.), sponsor of the legislation, said that although the cost of equipping a home with the necessary solar energy equipment ranged between $2,000 and $5,000, the cost would be recaptured in subsequent fuel savings. If just 5 per cent of the nation's buildings obtained 80 per cent of their energy needs from solar energy, he said, it would save 600,000 barrels of oil a day.

The demonstration program, to be run by the National Aeronautics and Space Administration (NASA) in cooperation with the National Science Foundation and the Department of Housing and Urban Development (HUD), involved the development, installation and monitoring of solar heating and cooling units in residential and commercial buildings in different locations and climates across the country.

NASA was directed to contract with private firms to develop the units; HUD was to oversee their installation and performance; the National Science Foundation was to provide research support. The program was eventually to be transferred to the new Energy Research and Development Administration (ERDA).

In fiscal 1975, $5-million was authorized for NASA and the same amount for HUD; for fiscal years 1976-1979, a total of $50-million was authorized for the program.

Legislative History

The House Feb. 13 passed HR 11864 by a vote of 253-2. The House Science and Astronautics Committee had reported the bill (H Rept 93-769) Jan. 28. After consideration by five committees, the Senate passed its version of the bill by voice vote May 21. The bill was reported (S Rept 93-734) March 13 by the Aeronautical and Space Sciences Committee, which scaled down the House-passed provisions, and was subsequently reported May 14 by the Committees on Labor and Public Welfare and on Banking, Housing and Urban Development (S Rept 93-847) in a form similar to the House-approved version. It was also considered by the Senate Commerce and Interior and Insular Affairs Committees. The Senate approved the bill as reported by the Labor and Banking Committees.

Conferees filed their report (H Rept 93-1083) Aug. 12, and the Senate adopted the report by voice vote the same day. The House adopted the report Aug. 21 by a vote of 402-4, clearing the measure for the President.

Solar Research

Congress in 1974 laid what it intended to be the foundation for a billion-dollar federal solar energy research, development and demonstration program. It approved, as the initial step, a $75-million research and development program in fiscal 1976, and formulation, in 1975, of a comprehensive program definition to guide future authorizations.

The Solar Energy Research, Development and Demonstration Act (PL 93-473) directed a national appraisal of solar energy resources, to identify promising areas for commercial exploitation and development. It authorized a broad federal research and development program, including specific technologies—direct solar heat for industrial use, thermal energy conversion, conversion of organic materials to fuel, photovoltaic and other direct conversion processes, ocean thermal power conversion, wind power conversion, solar heating and cooling and energy storage.

PL 93-473 authorized demonstration projects to show the technical and economic feasibility of solar energy, requiring congressional authorization for any particular project estimated to cost more than $20-million. It set up a

Solar Energy Information Data Bank and established a Solar Energy Research Institute. The National Science Foundation was directed to prepare the comprehensive program definition, and $2-million was authorized for that purpose.

Interim responsibility for these programs was given to an inter-agency Solar Energy Coordination and Management Project, and was to be transferred to the Energy Research and Development Administration once that agency was in operation.

Legislative History

The Senate approved S 3234 by voice vote Sept. 17, after adopting an amendment by the bill's sponsor, Hubert H. Humphrey (D Minn.), to establish the Solar Energy Research Institute. The bill had been reported Sept. 12 by the Interior and Insular Affairs Committee (S Rept 93-1151).

The House approved a companion bill (HR 16371) Sept. 19 by a 383-3 vote. The Science and Astronautics Committee had reported the bill Sept. 10 (H Rept 93-1346).

Conferees filed their report (H Rept 93-1428) Oct. 4. The House adopted the report by voice vote Oct. 9; the Senate adopted it by voice vote Oct. 11, completing congressional action.

Geothermal Energy

Hoping to tap the potential of the energy locked below the earth's surface, Congress in 1974 authorized a coordinated federal effort to locate prime sources of geothermal energy, solve the technological problems of getting to it, and demonstrate its commercial use in generating electric power.

President Ford Sept. 3 signed legislation (HR 14920—PL 93-410) that authorized federal loan guarantees of up to $50-million to encourage private industry, utilities and municipal power companies to acquire geothermal resources and use them to produce energy. Efforts were expected to focus on hot dry rock, geopressurized zones and hot water resources. Technology already existed to produce electricity from underground steam.

PL 93-410 set up a Geothermal Energy Coordination and Management Project to coordinate the work of the federal agencies carrying out the directives of the new program. The Interior Department was directed to conduct an evaluation of the nation's geothermal resources, through the U.S. Geological Survey. The National Aeronautics and Space Administration (NASA) was to draw up a comprehensive definition of the effort needed to develop those resources and work on developing the technology needed to tap this energy. The Atomic Energy Commission and the National Science Foundation were to cooperate with NASA on the research and development to resolve the major technical problems hindering commercial development of the geothermal resources, and on the design of demonstration plants.

The chairman of the management project was authorized to make cooperative agreements with utilities and municipalities to build geothermal facilities to produce energy commercially and to enter into similar agreements with federal agencies to produce energy for federal consumption. Congress would have to give specific approval to any federal contribution of more than $10-million for a demonstration project. PL 93-410 authorized $50-million for loan guarantees to back these programs and set up a Geothermal Resources Development Fund in the Treasury Department to guarantee the loans.

All these research, development and demonstration functions were to be transferred to the Energy Research and Development Administration, once it was created.

Legislative History

The House approved HR 14920 July 10 by a vote of 404-3. It had been reported June 17 (H Rept 93-1112) by the House Science and Astronautics Committee, which stated as the goal of the legislation commercial demonstration of the use of geothermal power by six to 10 geothermal power plants by the end of fiscal 1980.

The Senate approved a companion bill (S 2465) by voice vote July 11, and then approved HR 14920 after amending it to contain the provisions of the Senate bill. The Senate Interior and Insular Affairs Committee had reported S 2465 (S Rept 93-849) May 15. As reported, S 2465 contained the geothermal energy provisions of the Senate's comprehensive non-nuclear energy research bill (S 1283). The Senate had passed S 1283 in December 1973, but the House Interior and Insular Affairs Committee had stalled further action on the measure. *(Story, p. 17-A)*

Conferees filed their report on the bill (H Rept 93-1301) Aug. 19. The Senate adopted the report by voice vote Aug. 20, and the House by voice vote cleared the measure Aug.

Outer Continental Shelf

Overriding administration opposition, the Senate in 1974 approved legislation (S 3221) intended to assure maximum development of the energy resources of the outer continental shelf without undue environmental risk. The House did not act on the bill.

Major controversy focused on provisions that would have established a special fund to provide federal grants to coastal states to help them deal with the environmental, economic and social effects of offshore oil and gas development. By a 61-29 vote, the Senate killed an amendment to delete the grant provisions, which opponents described as "unconscionable bribery" to keep coastal states from resisting the offshore leasing programs to be established under the bill.

The administration contended that the legislation was not needed and would seriously disrupt current development efforts. President Nixon, in a Jan. 23 energy message, had announced plans to triple outer continental shelf leasing to 10 million acres by 1975. A letter from Interior Secretary Rogers C. B. Morton, read during Senate debate, said the administration was "firmly opposed to passage of this bill at this time." During committee hearings, oil industry witnesses also opposed the bill.

Background

The outer continental shelf (OCS) was defined legally as the land beneath the ocean from the end of state jurisdiction—3 to 10½ miles from shore—to the edge of the shelf—up to 200 miles from shore. State jurisdiction was defined as the states' historical boundaries under the Submerged Lands Act of 1953 (PL 83-31). OCS lands have been managed by the Interior Department, primarily for leasing purposes, under the Outer Continental Shelf Act of 1953 (PL 83-212).

The first offshore oil well was drilled in 1896, when the Summerfield, Calif., field was extended into the Pacific Ocean by drilling from a wooden pier. The first undersea well completed from a mobile platform was drilled in the Gulf of Mexico in 1947.

About 1,081,000 barrels of oil per day were produced by U.S. offshore wells in 1973—1,029,000 barrels from the Gulf of Mexico and 52,000 barrels from southern California fields. Offshore gas production was 8.9 billion cubic feet per day in 1973.

Environmental Impact. Noting the increasing U.S. reliance on foreign oil supplies, the President in his 1973 energy message directed the Council on Environmental Quality to study the environmental impact of oil and gas production on the Atlantic outer continental shelf and in the Gulf of Alaska.

In that speech, Nixon announced that the pace of leasing offshore lands would be tripled from 1 million acres per year to 3 million acres. He again tripled the rate to 10 million acres in his 1974 energy message.

The council made its report, "OCS Oil and Gas—an Environmental Assessment," on April 18, 1974, exactly one year from the day the President called for the study.

Energy Benefits. The U.S. Geological Survey estimated that there were 10 billion to 20 billion barrels of oil and 55 trillion to 110 trillion cubic feet of natural gas beneath the Atlantic. The estimated reserves for the Gulf of Alaska were 3 billion to 6 billion barrels of oil and 15 trillion to 30 trillion cubic feet of gas. The United States in 1973 consumed about 6 billion barrels of oil and 23 trillion cubic feet of gas.

Nobody knew for sure, however, if oil and gas would be found in commercial quantities until exploratory holes were actually drilled in the seabed. Estimates were based on geological and geophysical evidence.

But the Atlantic and Gulf of Alaska, the undeveloped and largely unexplored "frontier" areas, represented only a fraction of the nation's potential off-shore resources. Total reserves on the U.S. continental margin, including all of Alaska's, were estimated by the Geological Survey at 80 billion to 150 billion barrels of oil and 490 trillion to 900 trillion cubic feet of gas. It would be enough oil to last 15 to 25 years and enough gas to last 17 to 40 years at existing rates of production.

Environmental Risks. The environmental stakes of OCS development were also high. The potential fields in the frontier areas lie off some of the most valuable, and often the most fragile, real estate in the nation.

An oil spill from an Atlantic field could heavily damage the lucrative tourist industry that relies on beaches that extend from Cape Cod to Florida. Many species of fish, birds and mammals—some of them endangered and some commercially valuable—could be threatened by a spill in the Gulf of Alaska.

Offshore development in the new areas would be subject to all the normal environmental hazards of offshore drilling plus some new ones.

The Council on Environmental Quality (CEQ) report said the oil industry would face harsher conditions in the Atlantic and Gulf of Alaska than any it had encountered in nearly 30 years of offshore operations around the world.

Both areas were subject to severe storms and massive waves. The gulf had special problems. The CEQ report said a major earthquake could be expected in the gulf every three to five years. The gulf also was subject to tsunamis—tidal waves that traveled at great speeds and resulted in waves of up to 100 feet as they approached shore.

Also of concern to environmentalists was the onshore impact of OCS activity, the development of refineries, storage areas and petrochemical plants that would be built in the coastal zone to process the offshore oil.

Senate Action

The Senate Interior and Insular Affairs Committee reported S 3221 (S Rept 93-1140) Sept. 9, amending the Outer Continental Shelf Lands Act of 1953 to set new guidelines for the orderly and environmentally safe development of the oil and natural gas resources on the outer continental shelf. For the next decade, the committee asserted, these resources represented the best source of large increases in domestic energy supplies. They could be developed with less cost to the consumer and less risk to the environment than any other large-scale potential energy supply, it said.

As reported, S 3221 required the Secretary of the Interior to develop a 10-year leasing program for these areas, and to survey them to determine the probable site and characteristics of energy resources there. A leaseholder would be liable regardless of fault for any oil spill damages; an offshore oil pollution settlements fund was set up, financed by a 2.5 cents per barrel fee on offshore oil.

S 3221 set up a coastal states fund for grants to states to help them deal with the onshore consequences of offshore development, and provided that up to 10 per cent of the federal revenues from these offshore lands—to a maximum of $200-million a year—could be used for these grants. S 3221 also revised the way these resources were leased, eliminating royalty bids and authorizing several alternative bidding systems.

Five of the committee's six Republican members filed views critical of the measure.

Floor Action. The Senate Sept. 18 approved S 3221 by a vote of 64-23. Before passage, the Senate adopted, 54-39, an amendment proposed by Charles McC. Mathias (R Md.) establishing procedures through which a governor could delay—for up to three years—the issuance of offshore leases which would have an adverse environmental, economic, or other impact on his state. The Senate refused, 61-29, to consider an amendment which would have struck out of the measure the language setting up the coastal states fund. That move was made by Dewey F. Bartlett (R Okla.), who argued against giving this "windfall" to coastal states out of the federal Treasury.

Legislation containing some elements of S 3221 was enacted in 1976. *(Story, p. 79-A)*

Deepwater Ports

Congress in 1974 cleared the way for construction and operation of deepwater ports in international waters off U.S. coasts to receive huge oil tankers too large for all but two existing U.S. ports. The new large tankers cut oil transportation costs because of the large volume they carry, and advocates of their use said that the new ports would reduce the risk of oil spills as well.

The Deepwater Port Act of 1974 (HR 10701—PL 93-627) authorized the Secretary of Transportation to issue licenses for the construction and operation of these ports, if the particular port would meet environmental specifications and if adjacent coastal states did not object. The legislation, requested by President Nixon, was supported by the Ford administration.

HR 10701 had a complicated legislative history. As a result of a jurisdictional dispute, it was reported by two committees in the House in 1973, the Public Works Committee and the Merchant Marine and Fisheries Committee. The more restrictive Public Works version would have required that a state whose waters adjoined a proposed port had to specifically authorize construction of such a port. The version passed by the House in June did not give adjacent states that power, which in effect permitted a veto, but it did require that a proposed port had to be in line with state land- and water-use plans.

The Senate bill (S 4076) was jointly reported by three committees and then passed Oct. 9. S 4076 gave adjacent coastal states outright power to veto the issuance of licenses for deepwater port development off their shores.

The final version, cleared Dec. 17, was very close to the Senate-passed bill. Conferees accepted the Senate provision giving adjacent states veto power, but narrowed it to preclude the possibility that remote states might be able to veto port development. Charging that House conferees made "no effort whatever" to support the House-passed version of the bill, Merchant Marine and Fisheries Committee Chairman Leonor K. Sullivan (D Mo.) refused to sign the conference report.

House Action

The House Public Works Committee reported its bill Nov. 28, 1973 (HR 10701—H Rept 93-668). Its key provisions gave adjacent coastal states a veto over construction of deepwater ports and set up a special commission to license them.

The House Merchant Marine and Fisheries Committee Dec. 3 reported its bill (HR 5898—H Rept 93-692). It required consideration of and cooperation with states in construction and operation of the ports, but did not give states the power to block the construction of ports off their shores. It authorized the Secretary of the Interior to issue the licenses for construction of the ports and the Secretary of Transportation to issue the licenses for their operation. *(Background, story p. 17-A)*

Early in 1974 both committees revised their bills in response to Rules Committee concern, adding language to assure domestic control of the ports and to limit their use to imported crude oil and refined products. As a result of these changes, the Merchant Marine measure was given a new identifying number, HR 11951; the Public Works bill remained HR 10701.

Floor Action. The House June 6 chose the less state-oriented measure of the Merchant Marine Committee over the Public Works bill by a vote of 178-154. The House substituted the language of HR 11951 for that of HR 10701 so that the bill contained the Merchant Marine provisions under the number of the Public Works bill. Debate on the alternatives made clear that supporters of the Public Works bill saw its strongest point to be the state veto provisions, while critics of the bill saw that as the measure's most objectionable feature. By a margin of 24 votes, the critics prevailed.

Before passing HR 10701 by a vote of 318-9, the House adopted an amendment that added language creating a high seas oil port liability fund, financed from 2-cents-a-barrel user charges, to pay for damages to property from an oil spill connected with deepwater port operations.

Senate Action

The Senate Commerce, Interior and Insular Affairs, and Public Works Committees jointly reported the Senate deepwater ports bill (S 4076—S Rept 93-1217) Oct. 2.

In an unusual legislative action, the committees agreed to report the bill as drafted by their Special Joint Subcommittee on Deepwater Ports, but each committee included in the report amendments it planned to offer during Senate consideration of the bill.

As reported, S 4076 authorized the Secretary of the department in which the Coast Guard operated (currently the Transportation Department) to issue the licenses for the deepwater ports. It gave the head of the Environmental Protection Agency (EPA) the power to veto issuance of a license if it would violate federal clean air, clean water or marine protection laws.

S 4076 also gave adjacent coastal states the power to veto the issuance of licenses for construction of deepwater ports off their shores. The bill provided unlimited recovery for damages from spills associated with a deepwater port, with the cost of these damages borne first by the responsible port or vessel operator and then by a Deepwater Port Liability Fund financed by user charges.

Floor Action. After making some minor changes in the bill as reported, the Senate Oct. 9 approved S 4076 by a vote of 78-2. It then substituted its language for that of the House version of HR 10701 and approved its version of that bill by voice vote.

Before passage of the bill, the Senate killed an amendment offered by the Commerce Committee that would have barred oil companies from owning deepwater ports. This amendment was tabled, 48-34.

Final Action

Conferees filed their report (H Rept 93-1605) on HR 10701 Dec. 16, accepting the Senate version of the bill with a few significant changes. They adopted a modified state veto provision; they gave the Secretary of Transportation responsibility for the ports; and they accepted modified liability provisions approved by the Senate.

Both the Senate and House adopted the report by voice votes Dec. 17, clearing the measure for the President.

Provisions

As signed into law, the major provisions of PL 93-627, the Deepwater Port Act of 1974:

Licensing

• Authorized the Secretary of Transportation to issue licenses to own, construct and operate deepwater ports to be used for the transfer of oil to the United States; barred most other uses of the facilities.

• Required the Secretary, before issuing a license, to determine that construction and operation of the deepwater port were in the national interest, would not unreasonably interfere with other uses of the high seas and would involve use of the best available technology.

• Required him further to consult with other interested federal agencies and to receive the opinions of the Federal Trade Commission (FTC) and the Attorney General as to the antitrust implications of a license.

• Stipulated that a license could not be issued if the Environmental Protection Agency (EPA) found that the deepwater port would not conform to the provisions of the Clean Air Act, the Federal Water Pollution Control Act or the Marine Protection, Research and Sanctuaries Act.

• Prohibited the Secretary from granting a license unless each adjacent coastal state approved or, by its failure to act, was "presumed to approve" it; defined an adjacent coastal state as any state that would be connected by a pipeline to or located within 15 miles of a deepwater port, or one that the Secretary determined would be as vulnerable to environmental damage from the deepwater port as the state to which the port was directly linked by pipeline.

• Barred issuance of a license unless the state that would be directly connected by pipeline to the deepwater port had made "reasonable progress" toward developing an approved coastal zone management program under the Coastal Zone Management Act of 1972.

• Directed the Secretary, upon request, to compare the economic, social and environmental effects of a proposed deepwater port with plans to dredge an existing inshore port to superport depths; the Secretary could determine which project best served the national interest or that both developments were warranted.

• Made any citizen of the United States who otherwise qualified eligible for a deepwater port license.

• Limited the duration of licenses to 20 years; provided that licenses could be renewed, transferred, suspended or revoked under certain conditions.

• Provided for public hearings on license applications, to be followed by approval or denial of a license within 90 days.

• Required the Secretary, in considering relatively equal competing license applications within a geographic area, to give preference 1) to an application from a state or local government unit; 2) to an applicant who was independent of the petroleum producing, refining or marketing industry; or 3) to any other person.

Administration

• Directed the Secretary to establish environmental review criteria to evaluate deepwater ports, in accordance with the recommendations of the administrators of EPA and the National Oceanic and Atmospheric Administration (NOAA) and after consultation with other federal agencies.

• Made deepwater ports and related storage facilities subject to regulation as common carriers under the Interstate Commerce Act and barred discrimination in accepting, transporting or conveying oil.

• Directed the Secretary to issue and enforce regulations for marine environmental protection and navigational safety.

• Provided for public access to information, except in the case of trade secrets, which could only be disclosed under limited circumstances and in a manner designed to maintain confidentiality.

• Directed the Secretary of State, in consultation with the Transportation Secretary, to work with international organizations to develop appropriate international regulations for deepwater ports; requested the President to undertake regional negotiations with Canada and Mexico.

● Set maximum penalties for violation of the act at $25,-000 for each day of violation and/or one year's imprisonment.

● Provided for citizen civil actions for alleged violations of the act and for judicial review of licensing decisions.

Liability

● Made the owner and operator of a vessel that discharged oil while operating in a safety zone around a deepwater port or after leaving a deepwater port where it received oil from another vessel liable, without regard to fault, to cleanup costs and damages up to $150 per gross ton of the vessel or $20-million, whichever was less.

● Made the licensee of a deepwater port liable, without regard to fault, for cleanup costs and damages up to $50-million for discharges that emanated from a deepwater port or a vessel moored to a deepwater port.

● Provided maximum penalties of $10,000 in fines and/or one year's imprisonment for failure to report oil spills.

● Established a $100-million Deepwater Port Liability Fund, to be financed by user charges of 2 cents a barrel, to pay cleanup costs and damages in excess of the liability limits.

● Permitted the Attorney General to bring class action suits for damages and permitted private parties to institute class actions if the Attorney General failed to act.

● Stipulated that the act did not pre-empt state law in the field of liability, but precluded double recovery of damages.

● Directed the Attorney General to study and report to Congress on ways to implement a uniform liability system.

Other Provisions

● Made the laws of the nearest adjacent coastal state applicable to any deepwater port.

● Prohibited a foreign-flag vessel from calling at a deepwater port unless it recognized the jurisdiction of the United States over the vessel while at port.

● Required annual reports to Congress on implementation of the act.

● Required the Secretary of Transportation, in cooperation with the Secretary of Interior, to establish and enforce safety standards for pipelines on the outer continental shelf.

● Authorized appropriations of $2.5-million annually in fiscal 1975-77 for administration of the act.

Highway Speed Limit

Congress in 1974 made permanent the nationwide speed limit of 55 miles-per-hour, first enacted late in 1973. A provision establishing this limit was included in legislation (S 3934—PL 93-643) extending the Federal-Aid Highway Act of 1973.

Daylight Saving Time

Congress in 1974 responded to public complaints about its decision to institute year-round daylight saving time in 1973 and approved legislation (HR 16102—PL 93-434) to restore standard time for the months of November, December, January and February. .

Fuel Allocation

Congress in 1974 extended the Emergency Petroleum Allocation Act of 1973 (PL 93-159) for six months, from Feb. 28 to Aug. 31, 1975. PL 93-159 authorized the President to control the allocation and the price of oil and refined petroleum products. *(Story, p. 11-A)*

The Senate approved a four-month extension (S 3717—S Rept 93-1082) Aug. 12 by voice vote. The House Nov. 19 approved a different measure (HR 16757—H Rept 93-1443), providing for the six-month extension, by a vote of 335-55. The Senate approved the House bill Nov. 21, clearing the measure (PL 93-511).

Atomic Energy Commission

Congress authorized $3.7-billion and appropriated $3.3-billion for the Atomic Energy Commission in fiscal 1975, the last year of its life. The AEC was abolished by the energy reorganization plan (PL 93-438) which divided its functions between the new Energy Research and Development Administration and the new Nuclear Regulatory Commission. *(Story, p. 19-A)*

Congress authorized $3,677,433,000 for the AEC in its regular authorization measure (S 3292—PL 93-276), an increase of $77-million over the administration request. The Senate approved the bill (S Rept 93-773) April 11 and the House April 23, both by voice votes. The Senate April 24 cleared the measure, agreeing to a House amendment.

In December, Congress approved a supplemental authorization of $45.25-million (HR 16609—PL 93-576) for the AEC weapons testing and nuclear materials safeguards programs, after cutting the amount provided for the testing program in half and boosting the amount for the safeguards program.

Appropriations for the AEC came in three separate bills:

● The Public Works-AEC appropriations measure (HR 15155—PL 93-393) included $1,742,665,000 for the AEC, primarily its weapons and military programs.

● The energy research appropriations bill (HR 14434—PL 93-322) included an additional $1,486,660,000 for the AEC, funding its nuclear reactor research, nuclear fuel processing, biomedical and environmental research, thermonuclear fusion research and reactor safety research programs.

● The fiscal 1975-76 supplemental appropriations bill (HR 16900, H Rept 93-1503, S Rept 93-1255—PL 93-554) contained an additional $34,650,000 for the AEC weapons testing and nuclear safeguards programs.

Bonneville Power Administration

To encourage expansion of regional electric generating capability, Congress in 1974 revised the financing policy for the Bonneville Power Administration to make it less dependent on congressional appropriations. Passage of this measure (S 3362—PL 93-454) was intended to give the administration more flexibility in building new transmission lines.

Bonneville provided about 80 per cent of the power transmission capability of the Pacific Northwest. Uncertainty about the size of its annual appropriations, and its new construction plans, had hampered local utilities in their decisions to expand their generating capacity.

PL 93-454 set up a fund in the Treasury to receive appropriations and revenues from bond sales and from the Columbia River Power System, whose power Bonneville marketed and transmitted. PL 93-454 also authorized the head of Bonneville to sell up to $1.25-billion in revenue bonds to finance construction of new transmission facilities.

The Senate approved S 3362 by voice vote July 30; it was reported July 25 by the Senate Interior and Insular Affairs Committee (S Rept 93-1030). The House cleared the bill by voice vote Oct. 7; it was reported Sept. 25 by the House Interior and Insular Affairs Committee (H Rept 93-1375).

Commission on Shortages

In an effort to end the "crash-planning" approach to dealing with the nation's energy problems, Congress in 1974 created an independent National Commission on Supplies and Shortages to monitor supplies of fuel and other resources.

The 13-member commission was given a budget of $500,000 and an expiration date of June 30, 1975. It was to gather and analyze information about shortages of energy resources and other needed materials, to suggest to Congress and the executive ways of dealing with the shortages, and to recommend a permanent body to carry out these functions.

The measure creating the commission (S 3270—PL 93-426) also extended until June 30, 1975, the Defense Production Act of 1950 (PL 81-774), which authorized the President to act to allocate and guarantee supplies needed for the national defense. PL 93-426 amended the 1950 act to change the method of financing the stockpiles of material assembled for emergency situations. No longer would these materials be bought with Treasury loans; PL 93-426 provided that Congress would appropriate money to pay for them. Sponsors of the change said that the stockpiles were threatened with depletion as a result of the high interest rates.

Legislative History

The Senate June 12 by voice vote approved a bill (S 3523) setting up a national commission on shortages. The Senate amended the measure, which had been reported June 5 by the Senate Commerce Committee (S Rept 93-904), to reduce the life of the commission to one year from three.

The following day, June 13, the Senate by voice vote approved S 3270, extending the Defense Production Act. S 3270 had been reported by the Senate Banking, Housing and Urban Affairs Committee June 12 (S Rept 93-922).

The House Aug. 1 approved its version of S 3270, after substituting for the Senate provisions those of a similar House bill (HR 13044) that had been reported June 19 (H Rept 93-1121) by the House Banking and Currency Committee.

When the House version of the Defense Production Act extension (S 3270) returned to the Senate Aug. 20, the Senate by voice vote amended it to include the substance of S 3523, creating the shortages commission. The House accepted the Senate changes by voice vote Sept. 17 and the Senate cleared the consolidated bill for the President the same day.

Pipeline Safety

Congress authorized $9.15-million in fiscal 1975-76 funds (HR 15205—PL 93-403) for programs authorized by the Natural Gas Pipeline Safety Act of 1968. Of the total, $4.3-million was provided for grants to aid states in instituting a pipeline safety program; $4.85-million was provided for administrative costs.

The 1968 Act set minimum safety standards for natural gas pipelines, establishing federal jurisdiction over regulation of pipeline systems.

The Nixon administration in 1974 asked for a one-year $3.2-million authorization. The Senate Aug. 19 by voice vote approved a bill granting the administration request (S 3620—S Rept 93-1087).

The House Aug. 19 by voice vote approved the two-year $9.15-million authorization (HR 15205—H Rept 93-1296).

The Senate Aug. 21 by voice vote approved the House bill, clearing the measure for the President. President Ford signed the measure Aug. 30.

Two days earlier the President had signed a transportation appropriations bill (HR 15405 — PL 93-391) providing $1.158-million in fiscal 1975 grants to states under the pipeline safety act.

Tennessee Valley Authority

President Ford Dec. 23 pocket vetoed a bill (HR 11929) that would have permitted the Tennessee Valley Authority (TVA) to defer or offset its repayment obligations to the federal Treasury for five years by crediting the cost of pollution control facilities against those obligations. This would allow TVA to avoid rate increases that would otherwise be required as a result of the pollution control outlays.

Ford said that it was inequitable to give TVA this special treatment; its rates should reflect the cost of power production, including pollution control, he said.

The House approved HR 11929 (H Rept 93-891) March 20, 209-193. The Senate approved its version of the bill (S 3057—S Rept 93-1247) by voice vote Nov. 19. The conference report (H Rept 93-1512) was filed Dec. 3. The Senate agreed to it Dec. 4; the House Dec. 9.

The Oil Industry and Taxes

As energy prices rose, and reports of oil industry profits further aggravated consumers, Congress gave serious consideration to proposals to increase the taxes paid by the oil and gas industry, primarily by repealing the percentage depletion allowance.

Oil-industry lobbyists were successful in delaying action on these measures for the 93rd Congress by dividing the House Ways and Means Committee on the issue. The committee approved two separate oil tax measures (HR 14462, HR 17488) during the year, but failed to push either of them to the floor.

Independent Refineries

The Senate in 1974 approved a measure (S 2743) designed to encourage independent oil refiners to build and expand their refinery capacity; the House did not act.

Originally proposed as an amendment to the ill-fated Energy Emergency Act (S 2589), S 2743 set up an independent refinery financing fund to guarantee federal loans for up to 75 per cent of the construction costs of independent oil refineries. Independent refiners were defined as those who produced less than 100,000 barrels of crude oil a day or had direct or indirect control of less than 30 per cent of their crude oil production a day, so long as that production did not exceed 500,000 barrels a day.

The Senate Interior and Insular Affairs Committee reported S 2743 (S Rept 93-1293) Nov. 21. The Senate approved it by voice vote Nov. 26.

Gasoline Retailers

The Senate approved a measure (S 1694) designed to protect independent retailers of petroleum products from arbitrary termination of their franchises by petroleum distributors and refiners. The House did not act on the measure.

The language of S 1694 was added as an amendment to the Emergency Petroleum Allocation Act of 1973 (PL 93-159) but was dropped in conference. The same language was included in the Energy Emergency Act, which died after President Nixon vetoed it. *(Story, p. 24-A)*

As approved by the Senate, S 1694 forbade arbitrary termination of a retail franchise except under certain stated conditions, and required 90-day notice in any case. Franchisees could challenge termination in federal court. About 90 per cent of the nation's service stations were operated independently, the Senate Commerce Committee said, reporting the bill Aug. 5 (S Rept 93-1071). The Senate approved the bill Aug. 7 by voice vote.

Coal Slurry Pipelines

The Senate, but not the House, approved in 1974 a measure (S 3879) to clear the way for construction of coal slurry pipelines. The bill, an amendment to the Trans-Alaska Pipeline Act of 1973 (PL 93-153), would have permitted the Secretary of the Interior to grant rights-of-way across federal lands for coal pipelines.

It would also have permitted coal pipeline companies to acquire land for the pipelines through eminent domain proceedings.

Energy Leadership

Interior Secretary Rogers C. B. Morton remained one of the chief administration voices on energy matters in 1974. In October President Ford named Morton as coordinator of his national energy policy.

Federal Energy Office Chief William E. Simon, who held that post simultaneously with that of deputy treasury secretary, become Treasury Secretary late in the spring. His deputy at the FEO, John C. Sawhill, became head of the new Federal Energy Administration. Sawhill, an outspoken advocate of such unpopular measures as higher gasoline taxes, was fired by President Ford Oct. 29.

Ford first named Andrew E. Gibson, a former assistant secretary of commerce, to succeed Sawhill. He withdrew the Gibson nomination, however, after *The New York Times*

disclosed that Gibson was to receive $880,000 over a 10-year period under a settlement with his former employer, an oil shipping firm. Ford then named Frank G. Zarb to head FEA; Zarb had succeeded Sawhill as associate director of the Office of Management and Budget in charge of energy matters.

Abolition of the Atomic Energy Commission (AEC) at the year's end gave President Ford the opportunity to name the entire membership of its successor, the Nuclear Regulatory Commission. As its chairman, he selected former astronaut William A. Anders, a Nixon-nominated member of the AEC. Dixy Lee Ray, who had been AEC chairman, became assistant secretary of state for oceans and international, environmental and scientific affairs. As the other members of the Nuclear Regulatory Commission, Ford selected Victor Gilinsky from the Rand Corporation, Richard T. Kennedy from the National Security Council staff, Edward A. Mason from the Massachusetts Institute of Technology, and Marcus A. Rowden, former general counsel to the AEC. They were all confirmed by the Senate in December.

And to head the new Energy Research and Development Administration, Ford selected Robert C. Seamans Jr., former secretary of the Air Force (1969-1973) and at the time of his selection, president of the National Academy of Engineering. His nomination was confirmed by the Senate in December.

1975

Congress in 1975 came face-to-face with the full difficulty of writing a national energy policy. After a year of sustained effort, the 94th Congress passed a mammoth energy policy bill of uncertain effect. It also cleared the first authorization legislation for the new Energy Research and Development Administration (ERDA), and a bill extending the federal program of insurance for the nuclear power industry.

President Ford seized the initiative early in the year, sending a multi-part energy package to the new Congress in January. Ford's conservation strategy was based on still higher energy prices: He proposed to tack on an additional $3 in import fees to every barrel of imported oil and to lift federal controls holding down the price of domestic oil. If energy were more expensive, his reasoning ran, production would be encouraged—and so would conservation.

Caught off guard, Congress tried to buy time. It quickly moved to suspend the President's power to raise the oil import fee and urged Ford to delay his planned oil decontrol proposal. Democratic leaders huddled to formulate an alternative energy plan less damaging to the already weak economy and less painful for the already pressed consumer.

The heavily Democratic Congress seemed ready to move boldly: In March it sent the White House a tax bill that, among other provisions, repealed for major oil producers the long-cherished depletion allowance for oil and gas, thereby increasing the oil companies' federal taxes by an estimated $2-billion in 1975. When Ford compromised on further import fee increases and decontrol moves in March, agreeing to delay them, Sen. John O. Pastore (D R.I.), head of the Senate energy task force, spoke optimistically of congressional ability to come to grips with the energy problem:

Ford Proposed 13-Part Energy Independence Act in 1975

Moving quickly to present the 94th Congress with his energy program, President Ford Jan. 31 sent to Capitol Hill a 13-part Energy Independence Act. He urged its quick approval. Without these measures, he warned, "we face a future of shortages and dependency which the nation cannot tolerate and the American people will not accept."

Taken together with other administrative actions—such as his proposed $3-per-barrel increase in the import fee on foreign oil and decontrol of the price of domestic oil—these proposals would reduce oil imports by one million barrels per day by the end of 1975 and by two million barrels per day by the end of 1977, he said.

As proposed, the Energy Independence Act would have:

● Authorized full development and production of oil from the Elk Hills, Buena Vista and Teapot Dome naval reserves—up to 300,000 barrels per day by 1977; and authorized exploration and development of the Alaskan oil reserve. *(Story, p. 53-A)*

● Provided for creation of a military strategic petroleum reserve of 300 million barrels and a civilian strategic petroleum reserve of up to one billion barrels of oil. *(Story, p. 53-A)*

● Deregulated the price of new natural gas and imposed an excise tax of 37 cents per thousand cubic feet on natural gas. *(Story, p. 51-A)*

● Amended the 1974 Energy Supply and Environmental Coordination Act to extend federal authority to require power plants to use coal rather than oil or natural gas. *(Story, p. 37-A)*

● Delayed deadlines for compliance with clean air requirements until 1985 for industrial emissions and until 1982 for automobile emissions. *(Story, p. 56-A)*

● Deleted from the Clean Air Act the language requiring disapproval of any clean air plan allowing any significant deterioration of air quality, regardless of the original air quality level.

● Allowed utilities to pass through higher costs to their customers and limit the period of time for which proposed rate increases could be delayed.

● Approved development of a national plan for siting and building needed energy facilities and provide $100-million in federal grants to states for implementing this plan.

● Authorized development of mandatory thermal efficiency standards for all new homes and commercial buildings. *(Story, p. 57-A)*

● Approved a three-year, $165-million program of federal aid to encourage low-income families to insulate their dwellings. *(Story, p. 57-A)*

● Required energy efficiency labeling of all major appliances and automobiles. *(Story, p. 37-A)*

● Granted the President standby powers to control supplies, production, allocation and consumption of energy and energy-related materials. *(Story, p. 37-A)*

● Authorized the President to impose tariffs, quotas or variable import fees on imported oil when there was a drop in foreign oil prices that threatened to undercut domestic oil prices. *(Story, this page)*

"If we can't resolve this in 30 days, we can't resolve it at all."

In June, however, the House dealt such enthusiasm a body blow, overwhelmingly rejecting any increase in gasoline taxes, the cornerstone of an energy tax bill that had been heralded as the basis for the Democratic energy policy. When finally passed by the House, the measure received little attention in the Senate.

The focus of congressional energy activity shifted to an energy policy measure, which moved to the House floor in July and immediately bogged down in a dispute over whether to extend, expand or end the existing system of federal controls on the price of domestic oil. The authority for these controls was to expire Aug. 31. Eventually cleared and reluctantly signed by Ford in December, the bill was an amalgam of energy measures; it extended oil price controls until early 1979.

Congress also approved the first authorization bill for ERDA after weathering storms over the wisdom of proceeding with the premier nuclear energy project—the Clinch River Breeder Reactor—and over giving government aid to industry to encourage development of synthetic fuels. And, despite the vigorous opposition of the critics of nuclear power, it granted a 10-year extension of the existing federal program of insuring industry against a nuclear accident.

Congress passed, Ford again vetoed, and the House sustained the veto of a bill to regulate strip mining. And Congress took the first full step in almost 20 years toward deregulation of natural gas with Senate passage of such a measure. Also in the legislative pipeline at the end of the 1975 session were bills to unlock the naval petroleum reserves for production, to set new standards for leasing federal resources offshore and in the West for development, and to modify clean air requirements.

Oil Import Fees

The fate of the first energy measure sent to the White House by Congress in 1975 foreshadowed the stalemate that would prevail between Congress and the President during much of the year.

In January, Ford told Congress, in his State of the Union message, that he intended to encourage conservation of oil by raising the fees paid on imported oil and petroleum products. The fee on crude oil would increase $3 in three steps—Feb. 1, March 1 and April 1—Ford said. This action was taken under the power of the President to adjust imports of any product affecting national security.

In February, Congress cleared for the White House HR 1767, suspending the import adjustment authority for 90 days—and nullifying the announced $1 increase.

Early in March, Ford vetoed the bill, agreeing to defer the second and third $1 increases until May 1 to give Congress more time to come up with its energy program.

Congressional leaders postponed indefinitely a vote on a motion to override the veto.

The first $1 increase in the import fee took effect Feb. 1. Ford—irritated by the lack of congressional action on energy—imposed the second $1 increase June 1. Congress made no attempt to undo this second fee increase.

In mid-August, a federal court of appeals declared the import fees illegal, saying that President Ford had overstepped his legal authority in imposing these tariffs. Ford appealed this ruling to the Supreme Court to clarify the question of presidential power.

But Ford also offered to drop the $2 fee increase early in September if Congress sustained his veto of an extension of oil price controls. Decontrol of oil prices was expected to raise the price of oil and petroleum products about the same amount as the $2 increase. Thus, dropping the increase would offset the higher cost of decontrolled oil prices. *(Story, p. 44-A)*

But Congress refused to sustain Ford's veto, and the $2 import fee remained in place.

Later in the year, during final negotiations on the omnibus energy policy bill (S 622) which he signed into law Dec. 22, Ford agreed to lift the $2 import fee. A formal proclamation was issued Jan. 3, 1976, lifting the fee as of Dec. 22, 1975. *(Story, this page)*

Suspension Legislation

President Ford officially ordered into effect the first $1-increase in oil import fees on Jan. 23, telling reporters that he felt it was time for decisive action: "We've diddled and dawdled long enough."

The next day, the House Ways and Means Committee moved to suspend Ford's power to take such action, power granted by the Trade Expansion Act of 1962 to adjust imports that were posing a threat to the national security. The committee Jan. 24 voted, 19-15, to report HR 1767, suspending for 90 days the President's authority to adjust imports of petroleum and petroleum products. HR 1767, which was reported (H Rept 94-1) Jan. 30, also negated any action taken by the President to adjust petroleum imports after Jan. 15, 1975, the date of the State of the Union message.

Anticipating that Ford would veto such a measure, the Ways and Means Committee coupled it with provisions increasing the temporary federal debt limit to $531-billion.

The debt limit provision was considered essential legislation that the President would be reluctant to veto because the federal debt was expected to exceed the existing $495-billion limit on Feb. 18.

The committee report tacitly acknowledged that HR 1767 was intended to suspend the first steps of Ford's energy program in order to give Congress time to formulate an alternative.

The House passed HR 1767 Feb. 5 by a 309-114 vote, after acquiescing in a decision by the House Rules Committee to separate the import fee and debt limit provisions.

The Senate Finance Committee Feb. 17 reported HR 1767 without amendment (S Rept 94-11).

The Senate cleared the measure Feb. 19, approving it, 66-28. Ford immediately announced that he would veto the bill.

President Ford March 4 sent the measure back to Congress without his signature, but in his veto message he accepted the suggestion of congressional leaders that he defer the second and third $1 increases, originally set for March 1 and April 1, until May 1. During this period, Ford said, he hoped that Congress would agree to workable and comprehensive energy legislation. He also postponed until May 1 at the earliest his plan to lift price controls on domestic oil.

"This is quite a concession," said Sen. John O. Pastore, (D R.I.), head of a Senate task force working to develop a congressional energy plan. "I think it behooves the Congress to respond in kind," he continued. "If we can't resolve this in 30 days, we can't resolve it at all." House and Senate leaders postponed indefinitely any attempt to override the veto.

Court Challenge

Soon after President Ford announced his plan to increase the oil import fees, the governors of eight northeastern states (Massachusetts, New York, New Jersey, Connecticut, Rhode Island, Pennsylvania, Vermont and Maine), a group of 10 utilities and Rep. Robert F. Drinan (D Mass.) filed suit, challenging the fees as unauthorized by Congress. The Northeast was heavily dependent on imported oil, and thus would be first to feel the bite of the cost increases generated by the import fee rise.

In August, the court of appeals, District of Columbia circuit, ruled for the challengers, finding the fees imposed by Ford—and earlier ones ordered by President Nixon — illegal.

Presidential Powers

Congress had given the President the power to adjust imports of any product in the interest of national security, first in the Trade Agreements Extension Act of 1955 and later in the Trade Expansion Act of 1962.

In 1959 President Eisenhower had exercised this power to impose a system of oil import quotas; in 1973, President Nixon had replaced that system with import fees. But the court held that Congress had not authorized the use of such indirect methods as import tariffs, that tariffs were an exercise of the taxing power, which Congress had not delegated to the President.

President Ford said he would ask the Supreme Court to reverse this ruling. The Court in 1976, upheld the President's power to use export fees to control imports.

Energy Policy Act

"This legislation...puts into place the first elements of a comprehensive national energy policy," said President Ford Dec. 22, announcing his decision to sign S 622 (PL 94-163), the Energy Policy and Conservation Act. Congress cleared the omnibus energy bill for the White House Dec. 17.

"The time has come to end the long debate over national energy policy," Ford said, explaining why he opted for signing the bill in the face of intense opposition from conservative Republicans, oil-state representatives and the oil industry. The bill was "by no means perfect," Ford conceded, but it "provides a foundation upon which we can build a more comprehensive program."

Most controversial of the provisions of S 622 were those that required Ford to continue federal controls on the price of domestic oil. In addition, the bill required an extension of those controls to "new" oil, which was previously not subject to federal price controls. This extension was required by

Sources of Energy

The figures below show trends in energy production in the United States from the mineral energy fuels, water power and nuclear power. For purposes of comparison, the energy produced from these sources in the selected years is expressed in terms of heat units—British thermal units. The figures reveal the decline of coal as a source of energy, the increasing share of production enjoyed by oil and natural gas until the 1970s, and the relative stability of water power, whose share of total production remained relatively constant for some time. Figures for energy produced are shown in terms of trillion British thermal units. Each fuel's percentage of total production is also shown.

Fuel	1900	1945	1962	1969	1975*
Bituminous & Lignite Coal					
Trillion BTUs	5,563	15,134	11,034	13,957	15,187
Per cent	70.5%	46.8%	25.1%	23.5%	25.2%
Anthracite Coal					
Trillion BTUs	1,457	1,395	429	266	157
Per cent	18.4%	4.3%	1.0%	0.4%	0.3%
Crude Petroleum					
Trillion BTUs	369	9,939	15,522	19,556	17,202
Per cent	4.7%	30.7%	35.3%	32.9%	29.4%
Natural Gas					
Trillion BTUs	254	4,423	15,004	22,838	22,186
Per cent	3.2%	13.7%	34.2%	38.5%	36.9%
Water Power					
Trillion BTUs	250	1,442	1,937	2,648	3,150
Per cent	3.2%	4.5%	4.4%	4.5%	5.2%
Nuclear Power					
Trillion BTUs	___	___	___	146	1,827
Per cent				0.2%	3.0%
TOTAL					
Trillion BTUs	7,893	32,333	43,926	59,411	60,209
Per cent	100%	100%	100%	100%	100%

Projected figures.

Source: Bureau of Mines, Mineral Industry Surveys.

language setting $7.66 as the average maximum per-barrel price for domestic oil, $1.09 below the present average. Administration officials indicated that this average would be attained initially by retaining the $5.25-per-barrel price ceiling for "old" oil—about two-thirds of the oil produced in the United States—and by holding the price of "new" oil to $11.28 per barrel. "New" oil sold at up to $14 per barrel at the time PL 93-163 was enacted.

By signing the bill, President Ford acknowledged defeat—at least for the short term—of his effort to reduce consumption of oil and increase domestic production by allowing the price of this fuel to rise. This "conservation-by-price" philosophy had marked the major difference between the administration approach to the energy problem and that taken by congressional Democrats. Ford also said that he was removing effective Dec. 22, the $2-per-barrel oil import fee which he had imposed in two stages earlier in the year to make imported oil more expensive and thereby to reduce its volume and spur Congress into action. *(Story, p. 36-A)*

Legislative History

In addition to the oil pricing provisions, S 622 dealt with a wide variety of topics. *(Major provisions box, next page)*

The measure was a composite of five bills:

● S 622, the Standby Energy Authorities Act, approved by the Senate April 10.

● S 1883, the Automobile Fuel Economy Act of 1975, approved by the Senate July 15.

● S 349, the Energy Labeling and Disclosure Act, approved by the Senate July 11.

● S 677, the Strategic Energy Reserves Act, approved by the Senate July 8.

● HR 7014, the Energy Conservation and Oil Policy Act of 1975, approved by the House Sept. 23. HR 7014 was much more comprehensive than any of the Senate bills.

The bill went to conference Sept. 25. Conferees reached agreement in mid-November, but then took nearly a month to draft the conference report, in part because of disagreements about what had been agreed upon verbally. In the end, Republican conferees refused to sign the report because of dissatisfaction with the price control provisions.

Final action came when the Senate Dec. 17, by a vote of 58-40, concurred in the House changes in the final version of the bill. The House Dec. 15 had made two revisions in the conference version before sending it to the Senate by a vote of 236-160. The key House vote on the final version came when the House agreed, 215-179, to allow no further changes in the measure.

In neither chamber did these final votes demonstrate sufficient strength to override a presidential veto, should one have been cast. Federal Energy Administrator Frank G. Zarb Dec. 18 said he still did not know if the President would sign the bill.

Zarb had had a hand in developing the conference version and had urged the President to sign the bill. Ending weeks of suspense about his decision, Ford did so Dec. 22.

The provisions contained in S 622 had originally been envisaged as companion to an energy tax bill (HR 6860) that would have increased gasoline taxes, placed an excise tax on industrial use of oil and natural gas and provided for flexible use of quotas and import fees to curtail petroleum imports. But in passing the tax bill June 19, the House knocked out its key provisions and the Senate Finance Committee did not act on the measure. *(Story, p. 45-A)*

Senate Action

S 622 - Standby Energy Authorities

The Senate April 10 approved S 622 by a vote of 60-25. The Senate Interior and Insular Affairs Committee had reported the bill (S Rept 94-26) March 5. S 622 equipped the President with a variety of powers for use in an energy emergency, including the power to ration gasoline, to restrict fuel exports and otherwise to control the nation's production and use of energy.

Title I of S 622 was similar to portions of the Emergency Energy Act (S 2589), which President Nixon had vetoed early in 1974. *(Story, p. 24-A)*

In part S 622 met President Ford's early 1975 request for authority for such standby powers from Congress, but it restricted the President's exercise of those powers by requiring congressional review of plans for their exercise and in some cases, of the decision to put them to use.

As approved in April by the Senate, S 622 also extended the Emergency Petroleum Allocation Act of 1973 until March 1,1976, from its existing expiration date of Aug. 31, 1975. The bill further directed the President to impose a price ceiling on all domestic oil, "new" oil as well as "old" oil. Affirming their determination to retain oil price controls, authorized under the 1973 Allocation Act, the senators voted four times during debate on S 622 to reject—by margins of almost 3-1—efforts to allow the price control authority to expire and the price of "old" oil to rise. The Senate did, however, approve an amendment to S 622 that allowed an increase in the price of some "old" oil—from $5.25 per barrel to $7.50 per barrel—for that produced from existing wells by secondary and tertiary recovery methods.

Title II of S 622 directed the President and the Federal Energy Administration to set energy conservation goals and adopt programs to reduce domestic energy consumption by at least 4 per cent a year, an amount equal to 800,000 barrels

Major Provisions

The key elements of the congressional energy program contained in PL 94-163 included:

● Expanded authority for the Federal Energy Administration (FEA) to order major power plants and fuel burning installations to switch to using coal in place of oil or natural gas, and a new program of loan guarantees to encourage development of new underground mines producing less-polluting forms of coal. (Title I)

● Increased presidential authority to control the flow of energy supplies and energy-related materials. This included the power to restrict exports of these items; to allocate scarce supplies; to require increased oil and gas production; to require refineries to adjust the relative proportions of fuel oil or refined products they produce; and to order companies engaged in the oil business to accumulate, maintain or distribute certain levels of oil and petroleum product inventories. (Titles II, IV)

● A new measure of insulation for the United States in the event of another oil embargo or unexpected interruption of foreign energy supplies, provided through creation of a national strategic petroleum reserve of 1 billion barrels of oil and petroleum products, sufficient to replace three months' oil imports. (Title II)

● An arsenal of standby powers for use by the President under congressional review in case of an energy emergency or if needed to fulfill U.S. obligations under the international energy agreement, including the power to order national energy conservation measures and gasoline rationing. (Title II)

● Mandatory federal fuel economy standards for new automobiles manufactured or imported in any model year after 1977, targeted to reach an average fuel economy level of at least 26 miles per gallon by 1985. (Title III)

● A federal energy testing and labeling program for major consumer products from refrigerators to television sets. (Title III)

● Continued federal price controls on domestic oil into 1979, eventual conversion of the price control authority into a standby power, and an immediate rollback of domestic oil prices to an average per-barrel price of no more than $7.66. (Title IV)

● Authorization for federal audits of all persons and companies required to submit energy information to the federal government (except the Internal Revenue Service) and of all vertically integrated oil companies, to verify the information they report. (Title V)

of oil per day. A White House-backed effort to strike this title from the bill failed, 25-60.

S 1883—Fuel Efficiency

The Senate July 15, by a 63-21 vote, approved mandatory fuel efficiency standards, requiring American automobile manufacturers to double the fuel efficiency of their average new car by 1985, to 28 miles per gallon from the 1974 average of 14 miles per gallon. The fuel efficiency measure (S 1883—S Rept 94-179) had been reported by the Senate Commerce Committee June 5.

By passing S 1883, the Senate rejected the auto industry's bid to improve fuel efficiency voluntarily in exchange for a five-year delay in the final auto emission standards, currently scheduled to take effect in 1978. President Ford asked Congress in January for this delay, saying he had accepted the promise of General Motors, Ford and Chrysler to improve their average fuel efficiency by 80 per cent by 1980—to 18.7 miles per gallon. Under S 1883, the average fuel efficiency of all new cars had to be at least 21 miles per gallon by 1980.

S 1883 also authorized a research and development program in the Department of Transportation to develop a prototype gasoline-powered car that was fuel-efficient, non-polluting, safe and feasible for mass production.

S 349—Energy Labeling

The Senate July 11 approved a measure (S 349—S Rept 94-253) requiring manufacturers to label large household appliances and automobiles to indicate the cost of the energy needed to run them. The vote was 77-0.

President Ford had requested efficiency labeling requirements as part of his comprehensive energy plan. They were intended to give consumers the information needed to compare the energy cost of different products.

S 677—Strategic Oil Reserves

The Senate July 8 approved a measure (S 677—S Rept 94-260) authorizing creation of a strategic reserve of oil to cushion the nation against the impact of future interruptions or reductions in oil imports. The vote was 91-0.

President Ford had proposed creation of such a reserve as part of his energy program.

As approved by the Senate, S 677 authorized the creation of a stockpile of crude oil sufficient to replace oil imports for a period of 90 days. This amount was to be accumulated by the Federal Energy Administration (FEA) over a period of seven years from oil wells on federal lands, from the naval petroleum reserves (if production there were authorized), as royalties from future production from federal lands, including the Outer Continental Shelf, and from purchases or exchanges of oil. The bill also authorized creation of regional reserves of petroleum products.

Later in July, the Senate also added the provisions of S 677 as a second title to its version of HR 49, the bill to open up production from the naval petroleum reserves. *(Story, p. 53-A)*

House Action

The House Sept. 23 approved an omnibus energy policy bill (HR 7014) by a vote of 255-148. A motion to recommit the bill was rejected, 171-232.

The House Interstate and Foreign Commerce Committee reported HR 7014 July 9 (H Rept 94-340).

"This bill represents an almost perfect example of how not to legislate in the best interest of the people," said James C. Cleveland (R N.H.) Sept. 23. "The House began consideration of HR 7014 on July 17; we continued our deliberations on July 18, 22, 23; interrupted our proceedings until July 30; continued on July 30 and 31 and Aug. 1; recessed for the month of August and resumed debate on Sept. 17 and 18. Today, Sept. 23, we have finally reached the end of our initial deliberations. In the midst of this scenario, we debated other important but unrelated legislation and at one point simultaneously considered legislation

relating to oil pricing authority which was contradictory to the language contained in this bill."

As passed by the House the bill contained provisions:

● Granting the President standby energy emergency powers to be exercised with congressional consent, including the power to impose gasoline rationing and to prescribe energy conservation plans.

● Authorizing creation of a national civilian strategic petroleum reserve of up to 1 billion barrels of oil and petroleum products.

● Extending oil price controls on domestic crude oil indefinitely, setting up a four-tier system of oil price ceilings. Ceilings would range from $5.25 per barrel for oil which was subject to controls until Aug. 31 to $11.50 per barrel for some of the new oil produced by independent producers.

● Establishing a mandatory gasoline allocation program requiring the President to hold down the domestic supply consumption over the next three years.

● Setting fuel economy standards for domestic passenger cars, ranging up to 28 miles per gallon by 1985, and establishing an energy labeling and energy standards program for major household appliances.

● Extending the coal conversion authority of the Federal Energy Administration (FEA) until June 1977, and authorizing FEA to prohibit the use of natural gas as boiler fuel for generating power.

● Prohibiting the use of any gasoline or diesel-powered vehicle for busing school children to schools beyond their neighborhood school.

● Authorizing the General Accounting Office to verify through audits of the books of oil producers any reports those producers were required to submit to the government and directing the Securities and Exchange Commission to set out uniform accounting standards for oil and gas producers to use in reporting their energy data.

● Barring joint ventures by major oil companies to develop oil, gas, coal or oil shale resources on federal lands.

Oil Price Controls. The controversy over oil price controls—authority for which was to expire Aug. 31, 1975—dominated debate on HR 7014.

The Energy and Power Subcommittee, which drafted HR 7014, approved a gradual phasing out of oil price controls, but the full Commerce Committee—by a one-vote margin—discarded the decontrol language and instead approved an extension of price controls and mandated a rollback on the price of new oil to $7.50 per barrel. [The day the House began debating HR 7014, July 17, it cleared for Ford a measure setting $11.28 as the per barrel ceiling price for new oil. The bill was vetoed. *(Story, p. 44-A)*

An effort on the floor July 23 to restore the subcommittee decontrol language failed by 18 votes, 202-220. But later that afternoon, the House decided, on a key vote of 215-199 (R 125-15; D 90-184), to take all the oil pricing provisions out of the bill. (The day before, July 22, the House had rejected President Ford's 30-month decontrol proposal 262-167. A week later, on July 30, it rejected a second Ford decontrol plan by a narrower margin, 228-189.)

And then in August, the House reversed itself again, voting 218-207, to set up a three-tiered oil price control system: $5.25 per barrel for old oil, $7.50 per barrel for new oil and up to $10.00 per panel for hard-to-produce oil. Later in action on HR 7014, the House added still another tier, allowing some oil produced by independent companies to sell for up to $11.50 per barrel.

Other Changes. Defending other portions of the committee bill against Republican efforts to weaken or delete them, the House refused to strike out the provision requiring a 2-per cent reduction in gasoline consumption over a three-year period. Its critics called this the "long lines" provision, charging that it would cause the long lines at gasoline stations during the Arab oil embargo to reoccur. The vote was 150-239.

The House also refused, 146-254, to delete provisions authorizing the President to act as the exclusive agent for the nation's purchases of foreign oil in certain circumstances.

The House refused, 117-284, to strike out the 28-miles-per-gallon auto efficiency goal for 1985, but did adopt an amendment lowering the mileage loss due to auto emission controls that would trigger revision of the fuel economy standards. The House then refused, 146-243, to delete language calling for energy efficiency standards for certain consumer products.

Supporters of the bill also deflected an effort to kill the so-called "super-snoop" title, the portion of HR 7014 authorizing the General Accounting Office (GAO) to collect energy data and to audit the records of oil and gas producers. By adopting, 233-162, amendments modifying the committee language to authorize audits only of oil and gas producers already required to submit energy data to various federal agencies, the House rejected a motion to delete these provisions altogether.

The House also adopted an anti-busing amendment, phrased in terms of conserving fuel by prohibiting its use to transport children to public schools other than the closest appropriate school to their home. First adopted by voice vote, the House reaffirmed its addition to the bill by a three-vote margin, 204-201, Sept. 23.

And the House before passing HR 7014 Sept. 23 reversed its earlier one-vote rejection of an amendment prohibiting major oil companies from engaging in joint ventures to develop energy resources on federal lands. It also adopted language adding a fourth tier of prices to the three-tier oil price provision adopted in August; the new language allowed independent oil and gas producers to charge up to $11.50 per barrel for the first 3,000 barrels of oil they produced each day.

Conference Action

Immediately after passing HR 7014 the House by voice vote substituted its provisions for those of S 622, and asked for a conference.

The Senate concurred in the House amendment with an amendment substituting the text of its version of S 622, S 1883, S 349, and S 677, and asked for conference.

"We have a big problem on our hands," said Interior Committee Chairman Henry M. Jackson (D Wash.), after the Senate completed this maneuver. "That is the understatement of the closing day of the week. But...we have brought together all of the problems, except a few remaining, into one forum."

The House disagreed to the Senate amendments Oct. 1, sending the bill to conference. Conferees reached agreement in mid-November, but the work of drafting the language of the final provisions and writing the conference report consumed almost a month. The conference report was filed Dec. 9 (H Rept 94-700, S Rept 94-516); none of the Republican conferees signed it—nor did three of the Democratic senators, J. Bennett Johnston Jr. (D La.), James Abourezk (D S.D.) and Ernest F. Hollings (D S.C.).

On the chief controversy—oil pricing—conferees scrapped both the House and Senate provisions setting up tiers of prices, and substituted a system giving the President the flexibility to adjust prices for various categories of oil to optimize production, so long as the average per barrel price for domestic oil did not exceed $7.66. This average could be adjusted for inflation and to encourage production from certain areas, but the combined increase in any one year could be no more than 10 per cent. Conferees agreed to extend price controls for 39 months, into early 1979.

Among other actions, conferees dropped from the bill the House-approved gasoline allocation program requiring a 2-per cent reduction in consumption of gasoline from the volume used in 1973-74. They also discarded the House anti-busing provision, and narrowed the House ban on joint ventures to develop federal resources, applying that ban only to leases on the Outer Continental Shelf for gas or oil development.

Final Action

The final House and Senate votes on S 622 were relatively close, reflecting the disagreements and divisions which continued to plague Congress as it attempted to deal with this difficult issue. "This, perhaps, has been the most parochial issue that could ever hit the floor," said House Majority Leader Thomas P. O'Neill Jr. (D Mass.) Dec. 15. "It is extremely difficult to write an energy bill. We in New England...who depend upon so much Arab and Venezuelan oil, feel differently about the legislation from those members from Texas, or Oklahoma, or California, or Louisiana, or from the Tennessee Valley Authority section. We feel differently from those in the Northwest where there is an abundance of natural gas."

House Approval. Before the House approved the final version of S 622 Dec. 15, it made two changes in the measure as agreed upon by conferees.

First, the House struck out of the conference version language—originally part of the Senate fuel efficiency measure (S 1883)—providing loans and grants to encourage the development of advanced automotive technology. The vote was 300-103. Rep. Olin E. Teague (D Texas), chairman of the House Science and Technology Committee, had objected to their inclusion in the conference bill because they fell within his committee's jurisdiction and it had not considered them. By making this change in the bill, the House rejected the conference report.

It then blocked an effort to make further changes in the oil price provisions, 215-179, and by a vote of 236-160, adopted a motion approving and returning to the Senate a clean bill (S 622) containing all the language approved by conferees except the automotive technology program and language expanding a loan guarantee program for coal mines.

Senate Action. The Senate cleared S 622 for the President Dec. 17 on a key vote of 58-40 (R 8-30; D 50-10), concurring in the House changes in the conference bill. But final approval came only after a considerable amount of criticism.

"Since January, the President and the Congress have been deadlocked over national energy policy," said Henry M. Jackson (D Wash.), leading off discussion of S 622 Dec. 16. "This deadlock...has resulted in a dangerous game of 'economic brinksmanship.' For the third time in four months, as of midnight last night, all petroleum price control and allocation authority has expired," he said referring to the Dec. 15 expiration of the Emergency Petroleum Allocation Act of 1973. *(Box, p. 44-A)*

"For the third time in four months, the nation's economy is threatened by a sharp and sudden surge in energy prices and all goods and services in which energy is a component.

"The debate on energy policy can continue; the deadlock cannot."

But despite Jackson's urging, opponents of the bill—particularly its oil pricing system—did delay Senate action sending the bill to the President until Dec. 17. Efforts to have the bill read in its entirety and to block setting a definite time for a vote hampered efforts by the leadership to move to a vote on Jackson's motion that the Senate concur in the changes which the House had made in the conference version of S 622.

"When we needed a national energy policy, we got a political energy cop-out," said Lowell P. Weicker (R Conn.) criticizing the final version of the bill. "It is not so that this is better than nothing. It is far worse than nothing.... The first goal of this bill was supposed to have been maximizing domestic production. Congress decided upon the carrot-and-the-stick approach. It decided to clobber the oil companies with the carrot, and after 1976, stick it to the unsuspecting citizen."

When the Senate reconvened on the morning of Dec. 17, opponents of the bill said they would not delay final approval any longer and after more rhetoric it was sent to the White House.

Provisions

PL 94-163, the Energy Policy and Conservation Act, established a national energy policy designed to 1) maximize domestic production of energy and provide for strategic storage reserves of oil and petroleum products; 2) minimize the impact of disruptions in energy supplies by providing for emergency standby measures; 3) provide for a level of domestic oil prices which would both encourage production and not impede economic recovery; and 4) reduce domestic energy consumption through voluntary and mandatory energy conservation programs.

The bill's short-term objectives were protective: to reduce the economic and social impact of higher foreign oil prices and any accompanying shortages. Its long-term aims were more positive: to increase available domestic energy supplies and the efficiency with which they were used.

To achieve these goals, PL 94-163 contained the following major sections and provisions:

Title I—Domestic Energy Supplies

To encourage increased use of coal, Title I:

● Extended to June 30, 1977, from June 30, 1975, the authority of the Federal Energy Administration (FEA) to order power plants and other major fuel-burning plants to convert from use of oil or natural gas to use of coal.

● Authorized loan guarantees to small coal operators opening up new underground coal mines.

To ensure domestic energy supplies, Title I:

● Authorized the President to restrict exports of coal, crude oil, natural gas, residual fuel oil, any refined petroleum product, any petrochemical feed stock, equip-

ment or material necessary for domestic energy production or domestic consumption.

● Required the President to bar the export of crude oil or natural gas produced in the United States but allowed him to permit exemptions in the national interest.

● Amended the Defense Production Act (PL 81-774) to authorize the President to allocate supplies of materials and equipment essential for domestic energy needs; this authority would expire Dec. 31, 1984.

● Required the Secretary of Interior to ban joint bidding for rights to develop oil or natural gas on the Outer Continental Shelf by any joint venture in which two or more major oil companies or their affiliates participate.

● Authorized the President to require production from domestic oil and gas fields at the maximum efficient rate or at a temporary emergency rate above that maximum during an energy supply emergency.

● Authorized creation of a strategic petroleum reserve of 1 billion barrels of oil and petroleum products within seven years of enactment of PL 94-163, including an early storage reserve of 150 million barrels accumulated within three years after enactment; directed FEA to submit to Congress, by Dec. 15, 1976, a plan for development of the strategic reserve, which could be vetoed by either chamber of Congress within 45 days.

● Granted the FEA administrator a wide range of powers including that of condemnation, to use in implementing the reserve plan; authorized use of supplies from the reserve in a severe energy supply interruption or when required by international obligations; authorized necessary appropriations for creation of the early storage reserve, and $1.1-billion for the strategic reserve.

Title II—Standby Authorities

Title II equipped the President with standby authority to deal with future energy supply emergencies through provisions which:

● Authorized the President to prescribe national energy conservation and gasoline rationing plans; required the President to submit to Congress contingency plans for exercising these powers within 180 days of enactment of S 622; provided that the plans had to be approved by both chambers within 60 days in order to become potentially effective.

● Allowed Congress to block implementation of a rationing plan if, when the President sent Congress a finding that it was necessary to put the plan to use, one chamber disapproved that finding within 15 days; limited the effective period of a plan to nine months.

● Authorized the President to take or order such actions necessary to fulfill U.S. obligations in international oil allocation under the international energy programs.

Title III—Energy Efficiency

To improve the efficiency with which U.S. automobiles consume fuel, Title III amended the Motor Vehicle Information and Cost Savings Act to add provisions that:

● Required that the average fuel economy for passenger cars manufactured or imported by any one manufacturer in any model year after 1977 be no less than:

18 miles per gallon in 1978
19 miles per gallon in 1979
20 miles per gallon in 1980
27.5 miles per gallon in 1985 and succeeding years.

● Directed the Secretary of Transportation to set standards for the interim, 1981-1984, at the maximum feasible average fuel economy level which would result in progress toward the 1985 standard, which the Secretary could adjust downward to 26 miles per gallon if necessary.

● Authorized the Secretary to adjust the average fuel economy downward as it applies to a certain manufacturer if he finds that other federal standards—such as clean air requirements—reduce the fuel economy of the cars produced by that manufacturer despite the application of a reasonably selected technology to prevent such a fuel economy reduction.

● Required labeling of cars manufactured or imported in any year after model year 1976 to indicate fuel economy performance.

● Set penalties at $5 per 0.1 miles per gallon for every 0.1 miles by which a manufacturer's average failed to meet the standard, multiplied by the number of cars produced by that company; gave a credit in the same amount to any manufacturer for any year in which his average fuel economy exceeded the standard.

Consumer Product Efficiency

Title III also:

● Authorized FEA to set up an energy testing, labeling, and standards program for other major consumer products.

● Directed FEA to set energy efficiency targets for these products, designed to achieve an aggregate improvement of at least 20 per cent in efficiency by 1980 over similar products manufactured in 1972; required FEA to set enforceable energy efficiency standards for products which failed to meet those targets.

Conservation Programs

To encourage conservation on other fronts, Title III:

● Authorized a three-year, $150-million program of federal grants to assist states in developing and carrying out energy conservation programs to reduce their consumption by 5 per cent below the expected level for 1980; required certain elements in any state plan in order for the state to receive federal funds, which included establishing building efficiency standards and allowing right turns after a stop at a red light.

● Directed FEA to set voluntary energy efficiency improvement targets for the 10 most energy-consumptive industries in the country.

● Directed the President to develop and implement a 10-year energy conservation plan for the federal government.

Title IV—Oil Pricing

Title IV amended the Emergency Petroleum Allocation Act of 1974 (PL 93-159) with new provisions which:

● Required the President, within two months of enactment, to set a ceiling price for the first sale of domestic oil which would keep the average per-barrel price for all domestic oil at $7.66 or less for 39 months.

● Allowed the President, within that required average price, to allow the price of "old crude oil production" to increase if such would result in increased production or was needed because of declining production. ("Old oil" was defined as the amount of oil produced from a well or field equal to the volume produced from that source in 1972. "Old crude oil production" was defined by PL 94-163 as the volume of oil produced from a well or field in a month, equal to or less than the volume of "old oil" produced and sold from that source in September, October and November 1975, divided by three.)

● Granted the President authority to set particular ceiling prices for certain categories of domestic oil.

● Allowed the President to adjust the ceiling price for domestic oil to: 1) take inflation into account, and 2) to encourage production either from high-cost, high-risk properties, through the use of enhanced recovery techniques, or from marginal properties, including stripper wells, through sustaining production; limited any adjustment for encouraging production to that permitting an increase of no more than 3 per cent per year in the average first-sale, per-barrel price of domestic oil; provided that the total increase in the average ceiling price in any one year resulting from the inflation adjustment and the production incentive adjustment could be no more than 10 per cent; allowed the President to propose that the 3 per cent and the 10 per cent limit be raised, and provided that either house of Congress could disapprove such a proposal within 15 days.

● Required the President to report to Congress by Feb. 15, 1977, on the impact of these price ceilings and changes on the economy and the nation's fuel supply; specified that at that time the President could also propose to continue or modify the incentive adjustment factor or the limits placed on it, a proposal which could be vetoed by either chamber within 15 days; if such a proposal did not take effect then, the power to adjust the ceiling price to encourage production would expire.

● Required the President, by April 15, 1977, to report to Congress on the adequacy of the incentive provided under existing price ceilings for development of Alaskan oil; directed the President—if he found the ceilings inadequate—to propose exemption of up to 2 million barrels per day of Alaskan oil from those price ceilings and from the calculation of the average domestic oil price and to propose another ceiling price for this exempted oil no higher than the highest average price allowed for any other class of domestic oil; either chamber could veto such a proposal within 15 days.

● Repealed language requiring allocation of all domestic oil production for domestic use and exempting low-producing stripper wells from price controls.

● Required that all decreases in oil costs be passed through to the consumer at the retail level on a dollar-for-dollar basis; limited to 60 days the period during which oil producers could "bank" increased crude oil prices before passing them on to the consumer.

● Required an equitable distribution, across the range of oil products, of the costs of crude oil.

● Forbade the President from using any authority under the Emergency Petroleum Allocation Act or the Energy Policy and Conservation Act to set minimum prices for crude oil or petroleum products.

● Exempted from the entitlements program—for the first 50,000 barrels per day of their production—small refiners who on and after Jan. 1, 1975, had refining capacity of no more than 100,000 barrels per day.

● Set penalties for violations of the pricing sections of the Emergency Petroleum Allocation Act: for non-willful violations, civil fines of up to $20,000 per day for producers and refiners, up to $10,000 per day for wholesale distributors, and up to $2,500 per day for retail distributors; for willful violations, up to one year in prison or fines of up to $40,000 per day, $20,000 per day and $10,000 per day respectively.

Extending Oil Price Controls: A Long Story

Enactment of S 622 ended a year-long debate on the question of extending federal controls holding down the price of domestic oil.

As signed by President Ford, S 622 set $7.66 as the average maximum per-barrel price for domestic oil, more than $1.00 below the current average per-barrel price of $8.75. The President could adjust prices for various categories of oil so long as the average price was not exceeded. S 622 continued mandatory federal oil price controls for 40 months, into early 1979.

President Nixon imposed price controls on domestic oil in 1971, under authority granted him by the Economic Stabilization Act. In 1973, Congress shifted authority for these controls from the original act, which expired in 1974, to the Emergency Petroleum Allocation Act. Authority for the controls was extended in 1974 until Aug. 31, 1975. *(Story, pp. 11-A, 33-A)*

Under the price control system, most domestic oil was classified as "old"—that produced from wells existing in 1973 at a rate equal to 1972 production—or "new"—that produced from newly drilled wells or from old wells in excess of the 1972 volume. Old oil was subject to a price ceiling of $5.25 per barrel in 1975; new oil was not subject to any price ceiling. Old oil accounted for about 60 per cent of all domestic oil production in 1975.

Administration Proposals

President Ford announced his intention, in his 1975 State of the Union message, to remove all controls on the price of domestic oil April 1. Congress, under the 1973 law, could block such a move if either chamber approved—within five days of the President's formal proposal—a resolution disapproving that plan.

The rationale for decontrol, explained administration officials, was that higher prices for domestic oil would spur increased domestic production at the same time that the higher consumer costs would work to reduce energy consumption.

But the concept of decontrol met substantial opposition among congressional Democrats who worried that it would boost inflation, weaken the already sagging economy, and burden the American consumer in order to enlarge the already considerable profits of the nation's oil companies which they felt were large enough to spur increased exploration and production.

As negotiations with Congress began over an energy policy for the nation, Ford delayed and modified his plans for decontrolling oil prices. On April 30, he said he would propose a 24-month phase-out of controls, to begin in June. But a formal decontrol proposal was not sent to Capitol Hill from the White House until mid-July, and it provided for a 30-month phase-out period, and a price ceiling of $13.50 on all domestic oil.

Congressional Response

The tug-of-war on oil price controls then proceeded along these lines:

● Congress July 17 sent Ford a bill (HR 4035) which:
1) Extended oil price controls to Dec. 31, 1975.
2) Extended the congressional review period to 20 days.
3) Directed Ford to set a ceiling of no more than $11.28 per barrel for new oil.

The Senate had approved its version of the bill, 47-36, May 1 (S 621—S Rept 94-32); the House approved HR 4035 (H Rept 94-65) June 5, 230-151. Conferees filed their reports on the measure July 14 without the signature of any of the Republican conferees on the bill (H Rept 94-356, S Rept 94-282). The Senate adopted the conference report July 16, 57-40; the House July 17, 239-172.

● Ford vetoed HR 4035 July 21, as allowing "a drift into greater energy dependence." Congressional leaders, lacking the votes to override the veto, shelved the measure.

● Responding with a veto of its own, the House July 22 voted 262-167 to adopt a resolution (H Res 605) to block Ford's 30-month oil decontrol plan.

● Ford July 25 proposed still another decontrol plan, under which oil price controls would be phased out over a 39-month period during which a gradually rising price ceiling would be imposed on all domestic oil.

● The House July 30 vetoed this second plan, adopting a resolution of disapproval (H Res 641) by a vote of 228-189.

● Congress July 31 completed action on another price control extension measure (S 1849), simply extending until March 1, 1976, the price control authority under the Emergency Petroleum Allocation Act which would otherwise expire Aug. 31. The bill was not sent to the White House until Aug. 28, in order to prevent a pocket veto during the summer recess. The Senate had approved the bill (S Rept 94-220), July 15, 62-29; the House approved it, 303-117, July 31, without change.

● Ford vetoed S 1849 Sept. 9, but said that if his veto were sustained he would agree to a temporary 45-day extension of controls. The Senate Sept. 10 sustained the veto by six votes, 61-39.

● Congress Sept. 26 sent Ford a bill extending oil price control authority until Nov. 15 and providing that controls would be retroactively effective for the period since Aug. 31. Ford signed the bill (HR 9524—PL 94-99) Sept. 29. The House had approved it by voice vote Sept. 11; the Senate approved it with amendments 72-5, Sept. 26; the House accepted the Senate changes the same day, 342-16.

● To give conferees on S 622 more time to work out differences among themselves and with the administration on the oil price control issue, Congress and Ford agreed in November on one last temporary extension of oil price controls. Congress Nov. 14 sent Ford a bill (S 2667) extending those controls to Dec. 15; Ford immediately signed the bill (PL 94-133). Both chambers approved the bill by voice vote Nov. 14.

• Authorized the President to submit to Congress a plan granting the federal government the exclusive right to purchase foreign oil and petroleum products for import into the United States; the plan would take effect if not disapproved by either house within 15 days.

• Authorized the President to require adjustments in the operations of domestic refineries with respect to the relative proportions of residual fuel oil or other refined products produced, and to require adjustments in the amounts of oil or petroleum products held in inventory by any persons engaged in importing, producing, refining, marketing or distributing such products, including direction that inventories be distributed to certain persons at specified rates or that inventories be accumulated to certain levels and at certain rates.

• Prohibited the willful hoarding of petroleum products during a severe supply interruption by any person engaged in any aspect of petroleum production or distribution, except as required by the strategic petroleum reserve provisions of Title I.

• Provided for conversion of the mandatory pricing requirements of the Emergency Petroleum Allocation Act to discretionary authority 40 months after the new ceiling price provisions took effect; provided for expiration of these standby powers of the Allocation Act on Sept. 30, 1981.

Title V—General Provisions

Energy Data

To provide data upon which energy policy decisions could be made, Title V:

• Authorized the General Accounting Office, headed by the Comptroller General, to conduct verification audits of the records of 1) any person required to submit energy information to the FEA, the Interior Department or the Federal Power Commission (FPC); 2) any person engaged in production or distribution of energy (except at the retail level) who has furnished energy information to a federal agency, with the exception of the Internal Revenue Service (IRS), which that agency is using; 3) any vertically integrated oil company.

• Authorized such audits if requested by any congressional committee with legislative or oversight responsibilities in the energy field or with regard to laws administered by the Interior Department, the FEA or FPC; the report on such an audit would be committee property.

• Granted the Comptroller General the power of subpoena, access to energy information possessed by any federal agency except the IRS and other related powers for use in the audits; provided civil penalties of up to $10,000 per day for failure to provide information sought in such an audit.

• Stated that any information obtained through these audits and related to geological matters, disclosure of which would result in significant competitive disadvantage to the owner, could be given only to a congressional committee; unauthorized disclosure could be subject to the penalties specified for violations of the Emergency Petroleum Allocation Act.

• Directed the Securities and Exchange Commission (SEC) to prescribe rules to assure development and observance of uniform accounting practices for persons engaged in domestic oil or gas production.

• Extended to Dec. 31, 1979, from June 30, 1975, the provision of the 1974 Energy Supply and Environmental Coordination Act (PL 93-319) which required energy-

Oil Companies and Taxes

The oil industry's campaign to preserve its 22 per cent depletion allowance for oil and gas production ended in failure early in 1975 when Congress repealed that allowance for the major oil companies retroactive to Jan. 1, 1975. This allowance was retained for most natural gas producers and for the first 2,000 barrels of oil or equivalent amount of gas pumped each day by an independent producer who owned no retail outlets or major refineries. The change raised industry taxes an estimated $2-billion a year.

These changes were part of tax cut legislation (HR 2166—PL 94-12) enacted early in the 1975 session. The oil and gas industry during consideration of that bill did succeed in blocking other proposed revisions that would have increased the tax paid on oil-related foreign income.

producing companies to supply production and reserve data to FEA.

In other administrative provisions, Title V:

• Required all FEA or Interior Department employees to disclose, by Feb. 1, 1977, any financial interest in coal, natural gas or oil production or property.

• Set penalties for violations of Title I, Title II, the oil recycling provision of Title III, Title V and for failure to comply with an energy conservation plan at up to $5,000 for a non-willful violation; up to $10,000 for a willful violation; and up to $50,000 and/or six months in prison for a willful violation following a penalty for a non-willful violation.

• Provided that Titles I and II, with certain exceptions noted in individual provisions, would expire June 30, 1985.

Energy Taxes

An omnibus energy tax bill (HR 6860), once expected to be a major vehicle for congressional energy policy, languished in the Senate Finance Committee at the end of the 1975 session. Even before it reached the Senate, it had been severely weakened. First, Ways and Means Committee Democrats, who had initially appeared able to produce a strong bill, were forced to settle for a lot less than they had hoped. Then, when that bill reached the floor, the House voted overwhelmingly to delete the toughest proposal, a 23-cent gasoline tax. The stripped down bill was then passed and sent to the Senate Finance Committee. The committee held a few hearings on the proposal, but took no further action.

Committee Action

The Ways and Means plan was one of several competitive Democratic alternatives to President Ford's proposals to curb U.S. dependence on foreign crude oil by raising the cost of energy consumption through import fees and domestic oil and gas excise taxes. Ford's program, which included other controversial measures such as natural gas price deregulation, called for offsetting the $30-billion energy tax drain on the economy through permanent individual income tax cuts, direct payments to the poor, more revenue sharing with state and local governments and a 6-per cent cut in the corporate tax rate.

Democrats' Plan. Working separately from House and Senate leadership task forces that were preparing energy proposals, the Ways and Means Democrats March 2 outlined a comprehensive energy policy designed to reduce oil imports without undercutting economic recovery.

The plan, drawn up by eight task forces on the basis of initial proposals by Ways and Means Chairman Al Ullman (D Ore.), selected a phased-in approach that would have deferred the full impact of energy use restraints until economic recovery was well under way. Key components included quotas to gradually cut back oil imports, step-by-step gasoline tax increases if gasoline consumption rose, a trust fund to finance energy supply and conservation development, taxes on cars that failed to meet fuel consumption standards, tax incentives for energy-saving investments and a windfall profits tax tied to gradual removal of federal oil and gas price controls.

Although Ways and Means Republicans had been excluded from the task force studies, administration officials and committee Republicans welcomed the Democrats' suggestions as a good start toward compromise with the administration on energy policy. But Republicans thereafter consistently opposed the Democrats' key proposals, particularly the gasoline tax and import quotas, and administration officials were not satisfied by concessions that Ullman made when the committee started marking up a bill.

Nor did the committee Democrats rally behind Ullman's efforts. At the end of a month and one-half mark-up process, the committee majority was badly divided, with oil-state conservatives joining all twelve Republicans in opposition and liberals calling for a tougher auto fuel consumption tax.

In the end, some Ways and Means Democrats evidently supported the final committee bill (HR 6860) mainly to keep from embarrassing the panel and its new chairman. The measure was reported by a 19-16 vote on May 12 (H Rept 94-221) with one Democratic opponent not participating.

Committee Bill. As sent to the floor, HR 6860 was expected to cut U.S. oil consumption by about 2.1 million barrels a day in 1985, with roughly half of those savings resulting from a 23-cents per gallon gasoline tax increase that the bill would trigger automatically as consumption rose. In its final form, the measure imposed an additional 3 cents per gallon tax in 1976 to finance a trust fund and set in place a standby additional tax of up to 20 cents per gallon that almost inevitably would go into effect in stages as gasoline use climbed back above its pre-recession 1973 high.

The measure also established yearly quotas that would have cut oil imports to 5.5 million barrels a day by 1979, replaced the President's already imposed $1 per barrel oil import fee with percentage duties, set up a ten-year energy conservation and conversion trust fund, imposed excise taxes on business use of oil and gas for fuel, and granted various tax incentives for energy-saving investments by business and homeowners.

HR 6860 also imposed graduated taxes on 1978-80 model automobiles that failed to meet fuel efficiency standards. But the committee, after intense lobbying by auto manufacturers and their employees' union, reduced the standards and curtailed application of the tax.

Floor Disaster

When it reached the floor on June 10, the energy tax bill already was in deep trouble. The Ways and Means Committee had asked and been granted an open rule for the measure, and House leaders had postponed floor debate until after the Memorial Day recess after a deluge of proposed amendments underscored opposition to its provisions.

But the decisive defeats that the House inflicted on the Ways and Means recommendations still were unexpected. In a stunning key vote of 345-72 (R 134-5; D 211-67), the House June 11 stripped out the standby 20 cents per gallon gasoline tax, then went on to kill the milder 3 cents per gallon trust-fund tax. The House also defeated Ways and Means' liberal efforts to strengthen the auto efficiency tax on the floor, finally dropping even the committee's less stringent tax and substituting an Interstate and Foreign Commerce subcommittee's alternative proposal for standards enforced by fines instead of taxes.

The House upheld the committee's import quota system but raised the limit to 6.5-million barrels a day in 1980 and thereafter. After making several other minor changes, the House passed HR 6860 by a 291-130 recorded vote divided largely along party lines.

Ullman insisted that the bill still would set "the basic foundation for an energy policy," but he later acknowledged that much stronger measures would be required to meet the oil import quotas. For its part, the Finance Committee held hearings and conducted a few tentative mark-up sessions on HR 6860, but took no further 1975 action on energy taxes.

In 1976, the Finance Committee wrote several energy conservation tax incentives based on parts of HR 6860 into its version of massive tax revision legislation (HR 10612). But House-Senate conferees dropped the revenue-losing energy provisions to help meet congressional budget goals for revenue gains by the bill.

Energy Research Authorization

The continuing heavy nuclear emphasis of federal energy research was again confirmed as Congress approved the first authorization bill for the new Energy Research and Development Administration (ERDA), which formally came into being Jan. 19, 1975. The bill (HR 3474—PL 94-187) authorized $5-billion for fiscal 1976 and a proportional amount, $1.27-billion, for the transition quarter. Of the total, approximately $4-billion was for nuclear programs.

In both the House and the Senate, advocates of nuclear power and the top-priority nuclear demonstration project—the liquid metal fast breeder reactor—defeated efforts to slow work on that program. *(History of action on breeder reactor, p. 64-A)*

ERDA was created as part of the general reorganization of the executive branch energy structure directed by Congress in PL 93-438. The Atomic Energy Commission (AEC) was abolished and most of its functions transferred to ERDA. AEC regulatory functions were moved to a new Nuclear Regulatory Commission.

Also transferred to ERDA were the Interior Department programs of coal research, fossil fuel research and work on underground transmission of electric energy; the geothermal and solar heating and cooling development programs of the National Science Foundation, and the authority of the Environmental Protection Agency for research and development of an alternative automobile power system. *(Story, p. 19-A)*

Jurisdictional and policy elements complicated the legislative history of ERDA's first authorization bill. Responsibility for the bill was divided among three congressional committees: the Joint Committee on Atomic Energy dealt with the nuclear portions of the bill while the Senate Interior and the House Science and Technology Committees dealt with the non-nuclear portions. Several areas—physical research, environmental and safety matters—were considered by all three committees.

In addition to the controversy over the liquid metal fast breeder reactor, the path of the ERDA measure was further complicated by disagreement over Senate language providing up to $6-billion in federal loan guarantees for private industry willing to undertake commercial-scale production of synthetic fuels—oil and gas-like fuels produced from other substances such as coal. In an unusual last-minute maneuver, the House struck this language out of the final version of the bill after the Senate had adopted the conference report.

House Action

The Joint Committee on Atomic Energy and the House Committee on Science and Technology June 13 reported HR 3474 (H Rept 94-294) to authorize $4,642,156,000 in fiscal 1976 funds for ERDA, and $1,216,140,000 for the transition period from July through September 1976.

The amounts recommended increased the fiscal 1976 total by $354.7-million over the budget request. The major increases recommended were $20,000,000 for the nuclear fusion research program, $30,250,000 for plant and capital equipment expenses for nuclear programs, $70,400,000 for solar energy development, $30,500,000 for geothermal programs, and $84,760,000 for energy conservation.

The joint referral of HR 3474 to the two committees was required under the new House rules adopted in 1974. The rules change left nuclear legislative jurisdiction with the Joint Committee on Atomic Energy, and gave jurisdiction over all other energy research and development programs to the Committee on Science and Technology.

Although HR 3474 as introduced did not separate the non-nuclear from the nuclear matters, the committees limited their consideration to aspects within their respective jurisdictions.

Comparison of the amounts provided for nuclear and non-nuclear matters and for items considered in part by both committees was complicated by the fact that the two committees dealt with different budgetary categories in making their recommendations. The Science and Technology Committee approved new budget (obligational) authority for the items under its jurisdiction. The Joint Committee approved requests based on costs (approximate budget outlays) rather than budget authority.

The Joint Atomic Energy Committee continued the national emphasis on development of the liquid metal fast breeder reactor, approving the full ERDA request for $211,700,000 for operating expenses for the program in fiscal 1976.

The joint committee also approved the full ERDA request of $168,500,000 for 1976 for government assistance in work on the liquid metal fast breeder reactor demonstration plant to be located on the Clinch River in Tennessee.

The House Science and Technology Committee insisted again that a stronger commitment be made to

Synthetic Fuel Debate

Should U.S. taxpayers guarantee billions of dollars in loans to encourage development of new fuels to substitute for natural gas and oil—"synthetic" fuels made from coal, oil shale, wood and other natural resources?

Congress in 1975 answered "no" to this question, rejecting a Senate-approved and Ford administration-backed provision in the energy research authorization bill (HR 3474) which would have authorized federal guarantees for up to $6-billion in loans to private companies willing to undertake the commercial production of synthetic fuels.

As part of the nation's push for energy independence, President Ford in his 1975 State of the Union message urged Congress to provide new incentives for the commercial production of 1 million barrels per day of synthetic fuel by 1985, a goal which would require construction of at least 20 major synthetic fuel plants.

Synthetic fuels are liquid or gaseous fuels created by treating or processing other natural resources. Most synthetic fuels could be used as substitutes for natural gas, oil or other petroleum products. Among the fuels in this group were:

● Oil extracted from shale.

● Gas of pipeline and lesser quality produced from coal through processes described as gasification.

● Oil produced from coal through liquefaction processes.

● Gas or liquid fuel produced from waste products, often referred to as biomass: this category includes methanol, which can be produced from coal, wood wastes, farm or municipal wastes.

The Ford administration was also urging Congress to approve other economic incentives, to convince American industry that production of these fuels is economically feasible. By 1995, administration planners estimated the United States would need to produce at least 5 million barrels per day of synthetic fuels. In order to develop that capability, the administration proposed a commercialization program for the 1970s and the 1980s to lay to rest industry's doubts about the economic, regulatory, environmental and technological difficulties of producing synthetic fuels.

Most of the technology for producing synthetic oil and gas from coal, oil shale or other natural resources already existed. But the federal government needed to act to convince industry to undertake large-scale production of synthetic fuels, advocates of the loan guarantee program argued. Chief among them was Sen. Jennings Randolph (D W.Va.), author of the Senate's loan guarantee language, who described that program as "the single most important action that can be taken by the federal government to expedite the commercial development of a domestic synthetic fuels industry." On the other hand, Ken Hechler (D W.Va.) opposed the proposed program as "sort of like attaching a big platinum-plated caboose to the end of the ERDA train.... It is very heavy. It is very well-appointed. It is like a private car. It is very difficult for the rest of the taxpayers of this nation to pull it along."

development of new non-nuclear sources of energy. In line with this intent, the committee doubled the amounts requested by the administration for solar and geothermal energy and tripled the amount requested for energy conservation.

Floor Action. After approving a further increase in funding for solar energy research and development, the House June 20 passed HR 3474, 317-9. As approved, HR 3474 authorized $4,696,256,000 in fiscal 1976 funds for ERDA and $1,226,040,000 for the transition quarter.

Earlier the House added $65-million to the amount recommended by the Science Committee for solar energy, increasing that item to $194,800,000 from the $140,700,000 recommended and the $70,400,000 requested.

The major controversy during debate on the bill focused on the development of the liquid metal fast breeder reactor—which would produce more nuclear fuel than it consumed—and the proposed demonstration plant to be located on the Clinch River in Tennessee. The House June 20 rejected an amendment barring the use of funds authorized by the bill for on-site construction of the demonstration plant or for procurement of any component for the plant. The amendment was rejected, 136-227; it was proposed by R. Lawrence Coughlin (R Pa.).

"This is a major crossroad in the program which, if we take it now, will irretrievably commit us to this program in the long run," argued Coughlin. To date, he said, the demonstration project had been "a disaster in terms of cost overruns...schedule delays...and maladministration."

"This is the time to look at this program, which has been billed as our No. 1 energy priority," Coughlin continued, "to make sure that we are really on the right track."

"This program is an essential research and development program," responded John B. Anderson (R Ill.), opposing the amendment.

"We have all responsible officials of the government supporting this project," added John Young (D Texas). "We have industry supporting it. We have the labor organizations supporting it.... I have never seen such an array of responsible people asking us to do our responsible duty."

After rejecting the Coughlin amendment, the House by voice vote approved an administration amendment reducing by $71.2-million the funds allocated to the liquid metal fast breeder reactor program in 1976. The reduction was a result of delays in the program, due to the energy reorganization of the federal bureaucracy and the restructuring of the management of the demonstration project.

Senate Action

The Senate Interior and Insular Affairs Committee reported S 598, a companion bill to HR 3474, July 24 (S Rept 94-332). As reported the bill authorized $4,736,107,000 for ERDA in fiscal 1976 and $1,242,312,000 for the transition quarter. The Joint Atomic Energy Committee had reported identical sections of S 598 and HR 3474, filing its Senate report (S Rept 94-104) May 6.

The Interior Committee increased non-nuclear authorizations by $448.6-million over the budget request, boosting funding for energy conservation, advanced energy systems research, solar energy, fossil fuels and biomedical and environmental research.

In addition, the committee added language authorizing federal guarantees of up to $6-billion in loans to private companies willing to undertake the commercial production of synthetic fuels. It also added a provision allowing ERDA to work with private industry on a large-scale demonstration of the feasibility of developing oil shale on federal land *in situ,* by working to release the oil from the shale underground, rather than mining the shale first and processing it later.

Floor Action. The Senate July 31 passed its version of HR 3474 July 31, by a 92-2 vote. As sent to conference, the Senate version authorized $4,832,292,000 for ERDA in fiscal 1976 and $1,261,288,000 for the transition quarter.

The Senate refused to make any major changes in the bill as reported except to approve a committee-recommended set of administration amendments submitted after the bill was reported. These amendments increased funding in several areas and reduced the allocation to the breeder reactor program, as the House had approved.

Again, debate focused on the development of the Clinch River breeder reactor demonstration plant. John V. Tunney (D Calif.) offered an amendment prohibiting the procurement of long-lead items for the demonstration plant in fiscal 1976. "We simply do not know what is right and what is wrong or whether our present schedule for breeder development is rational or not," argued Tunney. "Yet we are preparing to make a major commitment to the breeder by authorizing long-term commitments for the Clinch River plant."

Opposing the amendment, Joseph M. Montoya (D N.M.) argued that adoption of the Tunney prohibition would destroy the momentum of the program. The Senate, 66-30, adopted a Montoya motion to table the Tunney amendment.

The Senate adopted several other amendments, including one limiting the air shipment of plutonium until ERDA certified the existence of a container for the material that would not rupture even in the event of a crash. It rejected a series of amendments which would have adjusted various program authorizations, including one to increase solar energy funds.

Conference Action

Conferees were appointed in September, but concern among House members over the Senate loan guarantee and oil shale provisions delayed sessions until November. In the interim, hearings on the two controversial provisions were held by two subcommittees of the House Science and Technology Committee.

Conferees filed their report on HR 3474 Dec. 8 (H Rept 94-696). The final version of the bill authorized $4,992,483,-000 for ERDA in fiscal 1976 and $1,270,983,000 for the transition quarter. The total was $473-million more than requested, with most of the increase coming in the non-nuclear side of the bill—$102-million more for solar energy, $105-million more for fossil fuels, $115-million more for conservation.

Conferees resolved the major differences between the two versions by accepting the Senate amendments concerning plutonium shipments, loan guarantees and oil shale development, and splitting the difference between amounts authorized for the non-nuclear programs.

Final Action

The Senate adopted the conference report Dec. 9, 80-10.

In an unusual move, the House Rules Committee granted a rule for consideration of the conference report that allowed the House to vote separately on motions to strike the loan guarantee and oil shale provisions out of the bill. This rule (H Res 919) was adopted by voice vote Dec. 11.

Proponents of retaining the two sections argued that government encouragement of synthetic fuel development was needed to spur investment by private industry. "We are simply at the point now where development of synthetic fuels will either go the way of the Roman steam engine—a device for toys only—or will become a valuable addition to our national energy supplies," said J. J. Pickle (D Texas). President Ford backed both provisions, and urged their adoption Dec. 10.

But its opponents objected to them as windfalls for the large oil, gas and coal companies and as unnecessary federal interference in the free market system. Some saw it as a first step toward the proposed Energy Independence Authority. An unusual coalition of liberals and conservatives opposed the provisions. The House voted, 263-140, to strike out the loan guarantee provisions, and 288-117, to strike out the oil shale demonstration provisions. Both motions were offered by Ken Hechler (D W.Va.). *(Energy Independence Authority proposal, p. 57-A)*

The House then approved the revised version of the conference bill by voice vote, sending it back to the Senate. The Senate accepted the House changes Dec. 18, clearing the measure for the President.

Provisions

As signed by the President, PL 94-187 authorized the following amounts for major energy research and development programs in fiscal 1976:
- $498-million for fossil fuel research and development.
- $173-million for solar energy research and development.
- $56-million for geothermal energy research and development.
- $156-million for energy conservation research.
- $158-million for fusion energy research and development operating expenses.
- $506-million for fission energy research and development operating expenses, of which up to $123-million could be spent on the proposed Clinch River demonstration plant in the liquid metal fast breeder reactor program.
- $222-million for the operating expenses of the naval reactor research and development program.
- $1-billion for the operating expenses of the nuclear materials research and development program.
- $985-million for national security programs operating expenses, including $897-million for weapons systems.

In addition, PL 94-187:
- Amended the Federal Non-Nuclear Energy Research and Development Act of 1974 to direct ERDA to set up a central source of information on all non-nuclear energy resources and technology.
- Forbade the air transport of plutonium by ERDA—except as required for medical application, national security, public health and safety or emergency maintenance, or to preserve the chemical, physical or isotopic properties of the material—until ERDA certified to Congress that a safe container had been developed and tested that would not rupture if the airplane crashed and exploded.

ERDA Appropriations

Congress in 1975 appropriated a total of $4,493,176,000 for the Energy Research and Development Administration in fiscal 1976, the first full budget year of its existence. The lion's share of this total—$4,038,407,000—came in the Energy-Public Works appropriations bill (HR 8122—PL 94-180). The remainder was provided in the Interior appropriations bill (HR 8773—PL 94-165) that funded most fossil fuel and some conservation research programs in ERDA at a level of $454,669,000.

Specific programs funded by PL 94-180 and the funding levels included:
- Solar energy—$82.7-million.
- Geothermal energy—$31.2-million.
- Conservation—$25.8-million.
- Nuclear energy—$1.7-billion, including $120-million for fusion power research, $404-million for fission research including the liquid metal fast breeder reactor program, and $958.5-million for nuclear materials.
- National security—$920.6-million, including $849-million for weapons systems.

Nuclear Regulatory Funds

Congress in 1975 authorized $222,935,000 for the new Nuclear Regulatory Commission in fiscal 1976, the first full fiscal year of its life. The authorization measure (S 1716—PL 94-79) also authorized $52,750,000 for the transition quarter between fiscal 1976 and 1977.

Major components of the budget for the NRC, which took over the regulatory functions of the Atomic Energy Commission Jan. 19, 1975, were:
- Nuclear regulatory research—$97-million.
- Nuclear reactor regulation, licensing, inspection, enforcement—$66-million.
- Nuclear materials safety and safeguards—$11-million.

S 1716 was reported by the Joint Committee on Atomic Energy June 4 (H Rept 94-260, S Rept 94-174). It was approved by the Senate June 17 by voice vote, and by the House June 20 by a vote of 233-2. The Senate July 31 accepted the House amendments, clearing the bill for the White House.

Congress appropriated $215,423,000 for the NRC, including this amount in the energy/public works appropriations bill (HR 8122—PL 94-180) cleared Dec. 12.

Nuclear Accident Insurance

Congress in 1975 approved a 10-year extension (HR 8631—PL 94-197) of the program of federal insurance against a nuclear power accident. PL 94-197 extended the program until Aug. 1, 1987, and provided for phasing out the government's role as insuror as the amount of available private insurance and the number of operative nuclear power plants increased.

The insurance program, created by the Price-Anderson Act, was set up in 1957 as an amendment to the Atomic Energy Act of 1954. It was designed to assure the public of compensation for any damages resulting from a nuclear power accident and to limit the liability of the industry for damages from a single accident. It required nuclear power plants to obtain the maximum private insurance coverage available. It limited the industry's liability to $560-million for a single accident; the government agreed to pay the difference in damages between the amount covered by private insurors and that limit.

During consideration of measures extending the insurance program in 1974 and 1975, the liability limit came under attack by critics who argued that it was unnecessary if nuclear power was as safe as the industry claimed, and that it prevented adequate recovery for damages if a severe nuclear accident did occur.

But both the House and the Senate rejected efforts in 1975 to eliminate or increase this liability limit; PL 94-197 provided for this ceiling to rise gradually as the number of nuclear power plants increased.

Background

President Ford vetoed a five-year extension of this insurance program in 1974. His veto came, not because of disagreement with the extension, but because of concern over the inclusion of a provision that allowed Congress to nullify the extension legislation later, if it felt that such action was warranted by a nuclear reactor safety study due for release late in 1974. *(Story, p. 27-A)*

The study, headed by Norman C. Rasmussen of the Massachusetts Institute of Technology, was released in October 1975. It found that the likelihood of a serious nuclear accident with severe consequences for the public was quite small. The 1975 bill therefore did not contain the provisions to which President Ford had objected in 1974.

Joint Committee Action

The Joint Committee on Atomic Energy reported HR 8631 (H Rept 94-648) to the House Nov. 10. An identical measure was reported to the Senate (S 2568—S Rept 94-454) Nov. 13. The committee report said that early extension of the program was necessary to avoid uncertainty and a slowdown in the long planning process for new nuclear power plants. In 1975 there were 56 such plants in operation in the United States; the Ford administration hoped to quadruple that number—to 200—by 1985. The report cited the Rasmussen study as support for its earlier findings that a serious nuclear accident was extremely unlikely, and pointed out that the study concluded that the $560-million coverage provided by Price-Anderson was adequate to cover "any credible accident which might occur."

House Action

The House approved HR 8631 Dec. 8 by a vote of 329-61.

The $560-million liability limit was the target of two unsuccessful floor amendments designed to reduce the amount of protection afforded the industry while increasing that provided for the general public.

The first amendment, proposed by Jonathan B. Bingham (D N.Y.) with the backing of labor, environmental groups and consumer advocate Ralph Nader, would have eliminated the liability limit. "These are big boys in the industry now," argued Bingham, "and they should be able to stand on their own feet and not say that if the damages from an accident exceed a certain amount, they will only be liable for a set figure so that the people who might be outside the limit...would have no remedy."

The Ford administration and the nuclear power and insurance industries, opposing the amendment, argued that if

an accident did cause more than $560-million in damages, Congress would act to compensate the injured persons. HR 8631 did provide for a gradual increase in the liability limit as the number of operating nuclear plants rose, argued Melvin Price (D Ill.), its floor manager and one of the key figures in the 1957 measure. Removal of the liability limit, warned John B. Anderson (R Ill.), floor manager for the bill, would mean "that we are not going to get the financing we need to continue this viable industry in this country."

The Bingham amendment was rejected, 176-217.

The second key amendment, proposed by Bob Eckhardt (D Texas), would have allowed citizens 90 days after HR 8631 became effective to go into federal court and to challenge the liability limitation as unconstitutional. This amendment was also rejected, 161-225.

Senate Action

The Senate approved its version of HR 8631 Dec. 16 by a vote of 76-18. Again, debate on the measure centered on the liability limit.

The Senate rejected an amendment to increase the potential liability of the industry by allowing victims of a nuclear accident who were not sufficiently compensated under conceivable occurred, said Mike Gravel (D Alaska), the amendment's sponsor, damages of as much as $15-billion could result. Under the $560-million limit, a victim of that accident "could probably get a return of three cents on the dollar for what he has lost."

Opposing the Gravel amendment, John O. Pastore (D R.I.) argued that it effectively meant that "the sky is the limit" on damage suits. "The minute we do that, no insurance company will underwrite it," he continued. "So if one cannot buy insurance we do not build a reactor. If we do not build the reactor, we do not achieve energy independence. We begin to put sections of the country in the dark."

The Senate rejected the Gravel amendment, 34-62.

The Senate subsequently rejected, 46-47, an amendment similar to the Eckhardt amendment rejected by the House, providing for a court test of the constitutionality of the liability limit. By wider margins, it also rejected two other Gravel amendments—one extending the insurance program for only five years, and the other accelerating the pace at which the government would phase out its role as insuror of the industry.

Final Action

The House cleared HR 8631 for the President Dec. 17, agreeing by voice vote to the Senate changes.

Provisions

As signed into law, PL 94-197 amended the Atomic Energy Act of 1954 to:

● Extend coverage of the insurance system set up by the Price-Anderson Act to nuclear plants licensed before Aug. 1, 1987. Existing law allowed coverage only for plants licensed before Aug. 1, 1977.

● Phase out the government's role as insuror by requiring all licensed nuclear power plants to pay, in the event of a nuclear accident resulting in damages exceeding the amount of available private insurance, a "deferred premium" between $2-million and $5-million per plant in order to provide funds to pay the damages up to $560-million. The government would continue to pay damages in excess of the combined total of private insurance and deferred premiums until that total reached the $560-million limit.

● Allow the liability limit to increase, once the private insurance/deferred premium total reached $560-million. The limit would increase as the total of private and industry commitments increased.

● Extend Price-Anderson insurance coverage to ocean shipment of fuel between licensed nuclear plants outside the territorial limits of the United States and to nuclear facilities licensed by the government but located outside those territorial limits.

● Extend to 20 years from 10 years the statute of limitations applying to damage suits resulting from nuclear accidents.

● Require the Nuclear Regulatory Commission to report to the Joint Atomic Energy Committee, senators and representatives from affected states and districts on the causes and extent of any damages resulting from a serious nuclear accident, and to make public such findings except for information damaging to the national defense.

Strip Mining Control

For the second time within a year, President Ford in May vetoed a bill (HR 25) setting minimum federal standards for control of strip mining of coal and reclamation of strip-mined lands. Ford had pocket vetoed a similar bill in December 1974. The House in June sustained the second veto by three-vote margin on a key vote of 278-143 (R 56-86; D 222-57). In this case, 281 votes were needed to override the veto.

Economic and energy considerations outweighed the environmental benefits of such a measure in the eyes of the Ford administration. Ford said that imposition of the new standards and related costs on the coal mining industry would exact too much in lost jobs, lost coal production and higher electric bills.

Natural Gas Deregulation

Congress moved in 1975 toward ending more than 20 years of federal controls on the price of natural gas sold interstate. For the first time since 1956, the Senate approved a bill (S 2310) that gradually removed federal price ceilings for new natural gas. *(Background, story pp. 16-A, 27-A)*

Congressional action in 1975 was spurred by awareness that the nation's reserves of natural gas were dwindling and by predictions of severe shortages of the supplies of that fuel available in interstate commerce during the winters of 1975-76 and 1976-77. Drastic curtailment of the supplies of this fuel available to interstate pipelines would result in many lost jobs, as plants closed down for lack of fuel, and in many cold homes.

Advocates of deregulation, including President Ford, argued that the resulting higher prices were needed to encourage increased exploration and development of domestic natural gas reserves and to channel more natural gas into interstate sales from the intrastate market where federal price controls did not apply. When natural gas was sold within the state where it was produced, it sold, in 1975, for prices as

high as three or four times the top regulated interstate price of 51 cents per thousand cubic feet.

In June a badly divided Senate Commerce Committee rejected the administration plan and voted out a bill of its own (S 692) that continued price controls while allowing higher prices for new natural gas. Handicapped by a lack of enthusiastic support and blocked by opposition from advocates of deregulation, S 692 never came to the Senate floor.

Alarmed by predictions of a severe natural gas shortage in the coming winter, the Senate late in September took up an emergency natural gas bill (S 2310) that had been introduced earlier in the month and placed directly on the calendar without going to committee. The Senate Democratic leadership planned to consider the short-term measure first and then to move on to consider S 692 and the more controversial long-range issues.

But with administration and industry support, this plan was overridden and the Senate voted, 50-41, to add a gradual deregulation plan to the emergency provisions of S 2310. The deregulation proposal was sponsored by Sens. James B. Pearson (R Kan.) and Lloyd Bentsen (D Texas). The combination bill was then approved, 58-32, and sent to the House.

The House did not approve a natural gas bill before the end of the year, but at the close of the 1975 session the stage was set for floor consideration of the issue in 1976. Although the impetus for consideration of a natural gas bill had been weakened by the fact that the predicted shortages for the winter of 1975-76 had not materialized, the House Interstate and Foreign Commerce Committee did report an emergency measure (HR 9464). A rule was granted for its consideration by the full House, which would allow consideration of a substitute combining long-term deregulation with the short-term provisions.

Senate Committee Action

The Senate Commerce Committee June 12 reported a "re-regulation" bill (S 692—S Rept 94-191) intended to provide an alternative to the Ford administration plan for complete deregulation.

The committee bill was approved by the narrow margin of two votes within the committee, and was opposed by all six Republican members. It retained the existing system of price controls for "old" natural gas—gas from identified wells already committed to interstate sale. For "new" natural gas, S 692 sought to encourage exploration and production by allowing higher prices. "New" natural gas produced by independent producers from onshore gas wells, not as a byproduct of oil production, was to be exempt from price controls and could rise as high in price as the equivalent amount of new domestic crude oil (to almost $2 per thousand cubic feet at 1975 oil prices). The price of other "new" gas—that produced by major oil companies onshore or produced offshore—could rise as high as 75 cents per thousand cubic feet, at the discretion of the Federal Power Commission.

Natural gas is "the dominant energy source for U.S. industry and it provides heat for 55 per cent of the nation's homes," stated the report. It pointed out that natural gas accounted for 40 per cent of the domestic energy produced in the United States—more than that supplied by crude oil.

"The shortage of natural gas will continue and become more acute in the years ahead, no matter what action is taken with respect to price controls at the wellhead," the committee conceded. "This bill will, however, facilitate discovery and production of what is available."

Senate Floor Action

After delaying action on S 692 for four months, the Senate approved a different measure (S 2310) providing for the eventual deregulation of all "new" natural gas. The Senate Oct. 22 approved S 2310 by a vote of 58-32.

Introduced in early September as an emergency measure providing some temporary relief from price controls on natural gas during the expected shortages of the coming winter, S 2310 was placed directly on the Senate calendar.

Democratic leaders planned to have the Senate consider S 2310 first, and, after disposing of it, to move on to consider S 692, keeping the short-term and long-range measures separate.

But soon after debate began on S 2310 Sept. 29, the Senate overrode its leaders' plans, moving to combine the emergency measure with deregulation language. On Oct. 2, on a key vote of 45-50 (R 5-33; D 40-17), deregulation advocates demonstrated that they had the votes to pass a measure providing for an eventual end to price controls on natural gas. By that 45-50 vote, the Senate refused to kill a substitute measure that linked language providing for eventual deregulation to the emergency provisions of S 2310. This combination measure was proposed by James B. Pearson (R Kan.) and Lloyd Bentsen (D Texas), with the backing of the oil and gas industry and the Ford administration. Earlier, an immediate deregulation proposal had been soundly rejected, 57-31.

The majority in favor of the Pearson-Bentsen measure was further confirmed Oct. 8 when the Senate rejected, 45-55, a substitute which would have imposed ceilings on all domestic oil as well as on natural gas, allowing the price of gas to rise while bringing down the price of oil. This substitute was proposed by Adlai E. Stevenson III (D Ill.).

Now convinced that the Pearson-Bentsen measure would win Senate approval, its opponents set out to amend it to tighten the definition of the gas to be freed from price controls and thereby to minimize the price impact of deregulation on consumers and the economy. The Senate adopted amendments to channel the higher-priced new gas to large customers, rather than residential and small users; to impose a ceiling on the price at which gas could be sold during the period before April 4, 1976, when the emergency provisions were in effect; to continue price regulation of all old natural gas presently under contract (instead of allowing it to become exempt from price controls once the existing contract expired); and to prevent the deregulation of natural gas produced from new wells in old fields.

The Senate Oct. 22 adopted the Pearson-Bentsen language with these modifications, 50-41, and then passed the amended version of S 2310, 58-32.

Provisions

As passed by the Senate, S 2310:

Title I - Emergency Natural Gas Authority

● Authorized the Federal Power Commission (FPC) to exempt from regulation and price controls for 180 days interstate natural gas suppliers whose supplies of natural gas were insufficient to supply high-priority customers. This exemption would allow those suppliers to buy natural gas from intrastate sources not subject to federal regulation.

● Defined high-priority customers as those with no reasonably available alternative fuel whose supply requirements must be met to avoid substantial unemployment, impairment of food production or the public welfare or safety. (Residential consumers are generally given first priority in allocation of scarce supplies.)

● Limited the wellhead price that could be charged for natural gas sold for the first time interstate under this exemption; set a price ceiling equal to the highest wellhead price at which natural gas was sold in that state from June 1 to Aug. 1, 1975.

● Provided that natural gas sold for the first time interstate under the emergency exemption did not thereby become forever subject to federal regulation.

● Forbade natural gas suppliers from passing through the higher costs of natural gas purchased under this exemption to residential customers and small users.

● Authorized the Federal Energy Administration (FEA) to ban the use of natural gas as boiler fuel for generation of electricity.

● Extended for one year, to June 30, 1976, the power of the FEA—under the Energy Supply and Environmental Coordination Act of 1974—to order plants to convert from use of natural gas and other petroleum products to coal. *(Story, p. 26-A)*

● Extended until April 4, 1976, the authority of the President under the Emergency Petroleum Allocation Act of 1973 to allocate and control the price of propane and butane. *(Story, p. 11-A)*

● Authorized high-priority consumers of natural gas that were unable to obtain sufficient supplies of the fuel from interstate pipelines to purchase natural gas directly from intrastate suppliers and to arrange for the delivery of that gas through interstate pipelines.

● Provided for the expiration of the emergency provisions at midnight April 4, 1976.

Title II—Natural Gas Act Amendments

● Deregulated the price of new onshore natural gas as of midnight, April 4, 1976.

● Defined new natural gas as that committed to interstate commerce for the first time on or after Jan. 1, 1975, or produced from wells discovered on or after that date, or from wells begun in extensions of old reservoirs on or after that date.

● Deregulated the price of new offshore natural gas as of Jan. 1, 1981.

● Authorized the FPC to set a national ceiling for the price of new offshore natural gas during the 1975-1980 phase-out period, taking into account several specific factors, including the prospective cost of producing the gas; allowed higher prices for new offshore natural gas from high-cost production areas.

● Set an interim price ceiling for new offshore natural gas equivalent to the average price of a barrel of oil produced on federal land, divided by 5.8. A barrel of oil provides 5.8 times the energy of a thousand cubic feet of natural gas, expressed in British thermal units.

● Directed the FPC to conduct its own study of natural gas supplies, facilities and reserves in the United States and to complete, within 90 days of enactment of S 2310, an initial study of total estimated natural gas reserves.

● Directed the FPC to give priority, in assuring sufficient supplies of natural gas, to essential agricultural and industrial users, except as those supplies were necessary for

Divestiture or Dismemberment?

Three times during debate on the 1975 natural gas bill (S 2310), efforts to "break up" the nation's major oil and gas companies came surprisingly close to success.

By a key vote of 45-54 (R 6-31; D 39-23), the Senate Oct. 8 rejected an amendment requiring oil and gas companies to divest themselves of all but one phase—exploration, production, refining, marketing—of their business within five years. By a vote of 40-49, the Senate Oct. 22 refused to require the largest oil companies to divest themselves by 1981 of any oil refining, transporting or marketing operation. And later the same day, by a vote of 39-53, the Senate rejected an amendment requiring the major oil companies to divest themselves within three years of any interests in alternative forms of energy, such as coal, uranium, solar or geothermal resources.

Already stung by the loss, early in the year, of their oil depletion allowance, the major oil companies were shocked by the narrow margin of their victory against these amendments, and set out on an intensive public relations campaign urging the public to reject such "dismemberment" of their business.

residential and small users, hospitals and other essential public services.

● Extended FPC jurisdiction over synthetic natural gas production, transportation and sales.

● Directed the FPC to ban most use of natural gas as boiler fuel.

● Directed pipelines to sell the less expensive old natural gas to residential and small users.

● Directed the FPC to set and modify every two years a national ceiling price for old natural gas—including gas presently flowing in interstate commerce under contracts, when those contracts expire; specified factors to be considered in setting the national price, including the prospective cost of producing the gas.

● Authorized the Secretary of Interior to require production of oil or natural gas on federal lands up to the maximum efficient rate in order to deal with emergency shortages.

● Directed the Secretary of Interior to sell to the public natural gas produced from leased federal lands and due the United States as royalty natural gas; provided for channeling of such natural gas to regions threatened by emergency shortages of natural gas.

House Committee Action

The House Interstate and Foreign Commerce Committee Dec. 15 reported its emergency natural gas measure (HR 9464—H Rept 94-732), allowing suspension of natural gas price ceilings for distressed interstate pipelines, so that they could purchase new natural gas wherever they could find it and at whatever price. This special exemption would expire by April 15, 1977.

The Commerce Committee chose to send only the emergency measure to the House floor, separate from any long-term deregulation proposal, but the House Rules Committee Dec. 16 granted a rule that allowed the House to con-

sider a substitute for HR 9464 combining the long-term and short-term measures.

The full House did not take up the issue in 1975, however, in part because as of mid-December the predicted shortages of natural gas during the winter had simply not materialized.

Naval Petroleum Reserves

Military and domestic energy interests deadlocked in 1975 over varying versions of a bill (HR 49) granting President Ford's request to authorize production of oil from the naval petroleum reserves. The reserves had long been set aside for exclusive military use.

Both the House and Senate approved HR 49 in 1975, but by the year's end conferees had not worked out a compromise version. The chief differences between the two chambers' bills were that the House bill allowed unlimited production from three of the four reserves, transferring jurisdiction over them to the Secretary of the Interior from the Secretary of the Navy, while the Senate bill restricted production to 350,000 barrels a day from each reserve, limited the production period to five years, and left jurisdiction over the reserves with the military. A bill was enacted in 1976. *(See p. 74-A)*

The reserves were located at Elk Hills and Buena Vista, Calif., at Teapot Dome, Wyo., and on the North Slope of Alaska. The Buena Vista and Teapot Dome reserves were largely depleted.

The debate over HR 49 aroused ghosts of Teapot Dome, the worst U.S. government scandal prior to Watergate. Early in the 1920s, President Warren G. Harding granted authority over the reserves to the Secretary of Interior. Subsequently, Secretary of the Interior Albert B. Fall was convicted of taking bribes from the oil companies to whom he leased the reserves for development. Authority over the reserves was transferred back to the military. Opponents of HR 49 hinted that the bill, by transferring authority back to the Secretary of Interior, might result in similar corruption. But the House rejected such implications, handing the House Armed Services Committee a major defeat when it rejected its proposal to retain military control of the reserves, 102-305.

Background. During the Arab oil embargo, President Nixon asked Congress late in 1973 to authorize production of 160,000 barrels of oil per day from the Elk Hills reserve. The Senate quickly approved this request, but the measure died in the House Armed Services Committee. *(Story, p. 18-A)*

President Ford again brought the matter to the attention of Congress early in 1975, asking for authority to produce oil from all four reserves, including the vast Alaska reserve, as part of his comprehensive energy plan. Both versions of HR 49 authorized production from the California and Wyoming reserves, but not from the one in Alaska.

House Action

Committee. The House Interior Committee March 18 reported HR 49 (H Rept 94-81, Part I), authorizing the Interior Secretary to set up national petroleum reserves on public lands that could include the naval petroleum reserves. The Interior Committee bill authorized the Secretary to plan for the development and production of oil from the national reserves, except for the Alaskan reserve, which he was authorized only to explore. These development and production plans would take effect within 60 days unless either chamber of Congress vetoed them.

At the request of Melvin Price (D Ill.), Armed Services Committee Chairman, the Speaker then referred HR 49 to the Armed Services Committee. Price had protested that the Interior Committee was encroaching on his committee's jurisdiction by including the naval reserves in its bill.

The Armed Services Committee April 18 reported both its own bill (HR 5919—H Rept 94-156) and an identical bill as an amended version of HR 49 (H Rept 94-81, Part II). The real purpose of the Interior Committee bill, the committee report said, was to open the naval reserves for commercial exploitation with no concern for national security considerations. To forestall this, the Armed Services version of HR 49 left control over them with the military and authorized only limited production—200,000 barrels per day for three years—for exclusive military use.

Floor Action. The House July 8 rejected the Armed Services Committee version of the bill, 102-305, despite the arguments of F. Edward Hebert (D La.), former chairman of that committee, that the Interior Committee bill gave the Interior Department a "blank check" while the Armed Services version provided "an orderly blueprint" for use of the reserves.

The House then approved the Interior Committee version of HR 49, 391-20, after adopting an administration-backed amendment to set up a special fund within the Treasury to receive the proceeds from sale of the oil produced from the national petroleum reserves. Congress could appropriate money from this fund to purchase oil for storage in a national strategic reserve or to develop and produce the oil and gas in the naval reserves.

Senate Action

Committee. The Senate Armed Services Committee July 24 reported S 2173 (S Rept 94-327), authorizing production of up to 350,000 barrels of oil per day for up to five years from the three reserves, under the supervision of the Secretary of the Navy. S 2173 set up a separate Treasury account for revenues from this oil production and authorized its use to offset production costs. The bill also allowed the President to place oil from the reserves in a strategic reserve.

Floor Action. The Senate July 29 approved S 2173, 93-2, and then substituted the provisions of its bill for those of the House version of HR 49. The Senate rejected an amendment which would have transferred jurisdiction over the Alaskan reserve to the Interior Department, 13-81, but adopted an amendment directing the Federal Energy Administration (FEA), rather than the Secretary of the Navy, to recommend plans for developing that fourth reserve.

Three weeks earlier, the Senate had approved a bill (S 677) authorizing creation of a national strategic reserve of crude oil. By voice vote, the Senate added the provisions of S 677 to its version of HR 49, but S 677 later became part of the final version of the omnibus energy policy bill (S 622—PL 94-163), making its addition to the final version of HR 49 unnecessary. *(Story p. 37-A)*

Outer Continental Shelf

Spurred into action by Ford administration plans to accelerate the development of oil and gas resources on the

---

OCS: Federal Property

Unpersuaded by state claims founded on their original royal charters, the Supreme Court March 17 unanimously reaffirmed federal ownership of the oil and gas resources of the Outer Continental Shelf.

In 1947 the court had ruled in the case of *U.S. v. California,* rejecting that state's claim to ownership of the Pacific seabed. Protection and control of this marginal sea area, held the court, was "a function of national external sovereignty...."

Three years later, the court rejected Louisiana's claim of sovereignty over 27 miles of seabed and a companion claim from Texas.

Despite these earlier denials of similar state claims, the state of Maine moved in 1969 to lease lands off its shore on the Outer Continental Shelf for private development. In response, the United States brought a complaint in the Supreme Court against the thirteen states with Atlantic coastlines—Maine, New Hampshire, Massachusetts, Rhode Island, New York, New Jersey, Delaware, Maryland, Virginia, North Carolina, South Carolina, Georgia and Florida. The United States asked for a declaration of its ownership of the seabed and subsoil under the Atlantic from a point beyond the statutory three-mile limit—to which state ownership extended—to the outer edge of the continental shelf. *(U.S. v. Maine)*

Twelve of the 13 states—Florida excepted—responded with a claim to that same area as successor to the colonies established by grants from the kings of England and Holland. Florida filed a separate claim based on an 1868 federal law approving the boundary of the state.

Detailing the history of earlier disputes, Justice Byron R. White wrote for the unanimous court: "Under our constitutional arrangement paramount rights to the lands underlying the marginal sea are an incident to national sovereignty and...their control and disposition in the first instance are the business of the federal government." Any prior ownership of such areas during the colonial period "did not survive becoming a member of the Union," he added.

"We are convinced," continued White, that the position announced in the *California* ruling "has peculiar force and relevance in the present context. It is apparent that in the almost 30 years since *California,* a great deal of public and private business has been transacted in accordance with those decisions....

"Since 1953...33 lease sales have been held in which 1,940 leases, embracing over eight million acres, have been issued. The Outer Continental Shelf, since 1953, has yielded over three billion barrels of oil, 19 trillion mcf of natural gas, 13 million long tons of sulfur and over four million long tons of salt. In 1973 alone, 1,081,000 barrels of oil and 8.9-billion cubic feet of natural gas were extracted daily from the Outer Continental Shelf.... We are quite sure that it would be inappropriate to disturb our prior cases, major legislation, and many years of commercial activity, by calling into question, at this date, the constitutional premise of prior decisions."

Outer Continental Shelf (OCS), the Senate in 1975 approved two measures designed to guide that development and cushion its impact.

The House, because of the jurisdictional conflicts raised by the OCS issue, created a new ad hoc select committee to consider OCS development, but did not act on either Senate measure during 1975.

The Ford administration took the position that legislation was unnecessary, that the existing statute authorizing OCS leasing—the Outer Continental Shelf Lands Act of 1953—was sufficient.

The first bill approved by the Senate (S 586) provided three forms of federal aid to states adversely impacted by OCS development: automatic grants of up to $100-million a year for fiscal years 1976-1978, facility grants or loans of up to $200-million a year, for fiscal years 1976-1978, and authority for the federal government to guarantee state or local bond issues to finance public facilities needed as a result of OCS development.

Framed as an amendment to the Coastal Zone Management Act of 1972, S 586 was reported by the Senate Commerce Committee and was approved by the Senate July 16, 73-15.

The second measure (S 521) amended the OCS Lands Act of 1953 to spell out in more detail guidelines for leasing OCS areas for development, requiring, for example, a five-year plan for leasing, and to enlarge the role which coastal states might play in federal OCS decisions through the establishment of regional OCS advisory boards. S 521 also authorized federal aid to coastal states.

The Senate had approved a similar bill (S 3221) in 1974. *(Story p. 30-A)*

S 521 was reported by the Senate Interior Committee and was passed July 30, 67-19.

In order to avoid conflict between the coastal state aid programs authorized by the two measures, both were amended on the Senate floor with compromise language worked out between sponsors of the two bills. (S 586 was enacted in 1976. *(Story p. 77-A)*

Coastal Zone Management Amendments

After a debate marked by critical comments from inland senators, the Senate approved S 586 July 16, 73-15. The Commerce Committee had reported it July 11 (S Rept 94-277).

As reported, S 586 authorized a $50-million automatic grant program and $250-million per year in discretionary grants and loans to affected states. The Senate by voice vote agreed to revise the allocation of these funds to provide $100-million in automatic grants and $200-million in the other grants and loans.

"What this looks like to me," said Henry Bellmon (R Okla.), "is a bribe to get these states to do the things they ought to do anyway."

"It is not a bribe at all," responded J. Bennett Johnston Jr. (D La.), comparing the aid to that provided to school districts crowded with children from military bases or other federal installations.

The Senate rejected two efforts to narrow the use to which coastal states could put these aid funds, to ensure they were used to soften the impact of OCS energy development in particular, not energy development in general. But later, the Senate adopted an amendment providing some aid to certain inland states by revising the 1920 Mineral Leasing Act to increase the state share of royalties paid to

the federal government by companies mining public lands within the state to 60 per cent from 37.5 per cent. This amendment, proposed by Clifford P. Hansen (R Wyo.), was adopted by voice vote.

OCS Lands Act Amendments

After adding a highly controversial amendment authorizing experimental federal exploration of the OCS, the Senate July 30 approved S 521, 67-19. The Interior Committee had reported it July 17 (S Rept 94-284).

S 521 was also amended by voice vote to conform its grant and loan provisions to the compromise version already contained in S 586.

The federal exploration amendment, proposed by Interior Committee Chairman Henry M. Jackson (D Wash.), and adopted by a vote of 46-41, directed the Interior Secretary to contract for exploratory work in order to obtain better information about the value of OCS resources before putting them up for leasing. The exploratory work would include drilling, but that was simply an experiment, Jackson said.

"For the federal government to start drilling the wells on an exploratory basis is the first step to...a federal oil and gas corporation," said Russell B. Long (D La.). "This is a first step to nationalization," said Paul J. Fannin (R Ariz.).

The Senate rejected an amendment to the Jackson amendment striking out the language allowing exploratory drilling, but adopted an amendment limiting spending for this program to $500-million.

The Senate also adopted an amendment increasing to 60 per cent the state share of federal revenues from mining on federal lands in the state. Proposed by Hansen, this amendment was similar to that added to S 586 and was adopted by a vote of 46-40.

An effort to strike out the coastal state aid program was rejected, 12-80.

Coal Leasing

The Senate in 1975 approved revised procedures for the leasing of federal coal deposits for development by private industry (S 391). A similar coal leasing measure (HR 6721) was reported in the House late in the year, but did not come to the floor before the end of the session. (A version was enacted over a presidential veto in 1976. *Story, p. 75-A)*

The Interior Department did not endorse the Senate bill, preferring a comprehensive revision of all mineral leasing laws rather than separate revision of the coal leasing procedures.

Reviving the controversial issue of strip mining, the Senate included a second title in S 391, setting up strip mining standards for federal coal leases. In June, the House had sustained President Ford's second veto of a strip mining control measure (HR 25). Later in the year, however, the House Interior and Insular Affairs Committee rejected efforts to add provisions similar to those of HR 25 to its coal leasing bill.

Background

Coal accounts for almost 75 per cent of the fossil fuel reserves of the United States. Federal coal lands are located primarily in Alaska, Colorado, Montana, New Mexico, North Dakota, Oklahoma, Utah and Wyoming.

Only a small amount of the coal located on federal lands has been produced. In 1974, coal production from these lands amounted to only 3 per cent of the nation's coal production. In 1974 the Department of Interior predicted that the increasing need for coal should result in production of seventeen times as much coal in the year 2000 as in 1972. It noted that much of the federally owned coal was low in sulfur content and could be strip mined.

The Mineral Leasing Act of 1920 authorized the Secretary of Interior to grant leases on federal coal lands to companies wishing to develop them. This process was left almost entirely to the discretion of the Secretary. The leasing company pays the government a royalty plus an annual amount of rent for the lease.

Outstanding coal leases covered over 780,000 acres of federal land.

In 1971 the Interior Department halted issuance of new coal leases to reassess its coal leasing policy. This decision followed a department study in 1970 which showed that the acreage of coal under lease on public lands had increased almost tenfold from 1945 to 1970 but that production of coal from these leases had declined from 10 million tons in 1945 to 7.2 million tons in 1970.

Senate Action

The Senate July 31 approved S 391 by a vote of 84-12. The Senate Interior and Insular Affairs Committee had reported the measure July 23 (S Rept 94-296).

The full Senate made only minor changes in the provisions of S 391 as reported. As passed, the measure amended the Mineral Leasing Act of 1920 to require preparation of a five-year plan for federal coal leasing and to require that no federal coal leases be granted unless they were consistent with that plan. S 391 required that leases be issued only by competitive bidding, that they be for a term of 20 years, and that the minimum annual rental be increased to at least $1 per acre. The bill provided for termination of leases for failure to develop them with due diligence. And it increased to 60 per cent from 37.5 per cent the state share in revenues from leases within the state, expanding the permissible use of these funds. Title II of the measure applied to federal lands and federal coal the basic surface coal mining standards and reclamation standards of the strip mining measure (HR 25) vetoed by President Ford earlier in the year.

House Action

The House Interior and Insular Affairs Committee reported its coal leasing bill (HR 6721 - H Rept 94-681) Nov. 21. Before ordering the bill reported, the committee refused by voice vote to add the provisions of the vetoed strip mining bill to the coal leasing measure.

As reported HR 6721 made many of the same changes in the Mineral Leasing Act of 1920 as did S 391. Explaining the need for these changes, the committee report pointed out that of the 533 active federal coal leases covering more than 782,000 acres and including reserves of over 16 billion tons, only 59 leases were currently producing coal. In 1974, these leases produced only 20.6 million tons of coal, slightly more than 3 per cent of the national total. (The moratorium on granting additional federal coal leases had been in effect since 1971.)

Speculation—obtaining the lease and holding it without producing until the price of coal rises—was one major problem in the existing system, said the report. HR 6721 addressed this problem by requiring termination of non-producing leases, barring granting new leases to those holding old nonproducing leases, and eliminating preference right prospecting permits which allowed the prospector to obtain a lease without competitive bidding.

To deal with the concentration of lease-holdings, HR 6721 set a national limit on the amount of acreage one entity could lease. It required that half of all acreage leased in a year be leased on a deferred bonus bid system; this required less capital for the initial investment and thus should allow smaller companies to compete for the leases. Fifteen companies control 66 per cent of all federal and Indian lands leased for coal development, noted the report. The top five leaseholders in terms of acreage are Kennecott Copper Company, Continental Oil, Utah International, Pacific Power & Light, and El Paso Natural Gas.

"The public is being paid a pittance for its coal resources," stated the report, criticizing the lack of competition in most leasing of federal coal deposits through the use of prospecting permits and preference leases and the low royalty and rental fees set by law for these lands. To remedy this situation, HR 6721 required that all leases be awarded by competitive bids which must be as high as the fair market value of the coal.

Clean Air

As part of his omnibus energy package sent to Congress early in 1975, President Ford proposed a series of amendments to the Clean Air Act of 1970, modifying the clean air standards to reduce the burden they placed on industry in a time of energy shortages and economic difficulties. The administration-proposed amendments would delay imposition of final auto emission standards for five years (until 1982), give industrial plants in remote areas until 1985 to meet final emission requirements, and postpone the clean-up schedule for traffic-congested cities until as late as 1987.

Environmental groups contested the assumption that such relaxation of clean air standards was necessary, arguing that new evidence of the effects of air pollution on human health made strict enforcement of the law even more important. Subcommittees in both chambers labored through the year on resolving these arguments and producing the first comprehensive overhaul of the 1970 law. The draft bills which emerged late in the year from the subcommittees did not go as far as the administration proposed, but did recommend postponements in auto tailpipe controls and more flexibility in timetables for reducing smokestack pollution.

Electric Automobiles

With the hope of promoting use of electric cars as a practical alternative to gasoline-powered cars for short-range driving, the House in 1975 approved a five-year, $160-million research and demonstration project of the feasibility of these cars. The Senate did not act on the bill (HR 8800) in 1975. The Ford administration opposed the bill. It was enacted over a veto in 1976. *(Story p. 82-A)*

Background. Cars powered by electrically charged batteries were popular in the early 1900s, but by the 1930s were almost completely superseded by autos with internal-combustion engines. The need to conserve fuel and reduce tailpipe pollution inspired new interest in electric cars in 1975.

Electrically powered cars would not be potential competitors for highway driving in the near future, however, since they could travel an average of only 50 miles before requiring a recharge. But that range was considered more than adequate for use as a second or third car for city driving.

Of all car trips taken nationwide, half are less than five miles in total distance traveled—well within the range of existing electric cars, which could go from 30 to 70 miles at speeds of up to 50 mph without recharging.

Electric cars are quieter than gasoline-powered cars and do not emit tailpipe exhaust. The generation of electric power to charge the cars' batteries does cause air pollution, but the House committee report on HR 8800 said it can be "more reliably and effectively controlled at central electric generating plants than at the exhaust pipes of thousands of vehicles in a city."

As for fuel consumption, the report maintained that electric cars use less energy than gasoline-powered cars in heavy traffic and stop-and-go driving because they do not use energy when not in motion. And, the report pointed out, electric car batteries could be recharged during the "off-peak" hours of generating plants, another energy savings.

Legislative History. The House Science and Technology Committee reported HR 8800 (H Rept 94-439) July 31, authorizing $93-million for research to advance the technology of electric cars in fiscal years 1976-1980, and $67-million for the production, distribution and use of about 8,000 demonstration models. HR 8800 also allowed the federal government to guarantee up to $60-million in private loans to companies participating in the project and provide for government planning grants to small businesses that otherwise could not participate.

The House passed HR 8800 Sept. 5 by a vote of 308-60.

Energy Independence Authority

President Ford's proposal that Congress create a $100-billion government corporation to stimulate commercial development of new energy sources met with a resounding lack of enthusiasm on Capitol Hill.

Announcing his plan in San Francisco Sept. 22, Ford said it would help the nation achieve energy independence, stimulate the economy, create jobs and "supplement" the private enterprise system.

But even before the draft bill reached Congress, many doubts had been raised. Liberal Democrats expressed concern that the corporation would not be accountable to Congress and would subsidize one segment of the economy, particularly the major oil companies, at the expense of others. And conservatives were not eager to endorse creation of a new layer of federal bureaucracy—especially one with so much money to dispense.

"It is almost incredible that President Ford, supposedly a fiscal conservative, would propose that we set up an independent agency, with far less of the usual executive and congressional review than other agencies, to allocate $100-billion of our gross national product during the next 10 years," said Rep. John J. LaFalce (D N.Y.) Oct. 9.

As outlined in a White House fact sheet, the proposed Energy Independence Authority (EIA) would be a govern-ment corporation programmed to self-destruct in 10 years. It was designed to boost commercial development of domestic energy resources by making loans, guaranteeing private loans, investing or otherwise financing operations that "will contribute directly and significantly to energy independence," and "would not be financed without government assistance."

The corporation was to have $25-billion in equity, to be appropriated by Congress gradually, and $75-billion in government-backed borrowing authority, to be raised through the public sale of bonds and other obligations. "Because the Authority is to be self-liquidating and its investments repaid, its outlays will not be included in the budget of the United States," the fact sheet said. "However, the Authority's losses or gains from its operations will be included in the federal budget."

The types of projects to be financed, the White House said, would include commercialization of technologies for extracting synthetic fuels such as oil from shale and liquefied coal; other emerging technologies such as production of solar and geothermal energy; and conventional operations like electric utilities and uranium enrichment plants. "Projects of unusual size or scope could include new energy parks or major new pipelines for transportation of oil and gas."

The Authority was to be run by a five-member board of directors to be appointed by the President with Senate confirmation. No more than three members could be from the same political party. It was to be required to report to Congress each year and submit to audits by the General Accounting Office (GAO).

To expedite high-priority projects, the Federal Energy Administration (FEA) was to be authorized to issue certificates that would entitle applicants to speedy action by federal agencies in granting licenses or other permits needed to proceed. Agencies were to be asked to complete action on such cases within 18 months.

The energy corporation idea was developed by the staff of Vice President Nelson A. Rockefeller. Ford's decision to endorse it was viewed as an internal victory for Rockefeller over other administration advisers—notably Treasury Secretary William E. Simon and Alan Greenspan, chairman of the Council of Economic Advisers—who reportedly had serious reservations about the proposed corporation's scope and powers.

Energy Conservation in Buildings

At different times in different bills, the House and Senate in 1975 endorsed development of energy conservation standards for new buildings and aid for the insulation of dwellings occupied by low-income persons, but neither proposal was enacted by the session's end.

President Ford asked Congress early in 1975 to approve development of mandatory thermal efficiency standards and aid for insulation of the dwellings of low-income persons as part of his comprehensive energy program.

The Senate included the mandatory efficiency standards language in the Emergency Housing Act of 1975 (S 1483), but that provision was dropped in conference and the bill was subsequently vetoed.

The House Sept. 8 approved the Energy Conservation in Buildings Act (HR 8650) by a vote of 258-130. HR 8650, reported by the House Banking, Currency and Housing

Committee July 22 (H Rept 94-377), simply encouraged—and did not mandate—the development of building energy standards. Yet those opposing it argued that even this language was too strong and foreshadowed the imposition of a federal building code.

The Senate passed HR 8650 in 1976 but the bill became stalled in conference. Similar provisions were included in legislation extending the Federal Energy Administration. *(p. 60-A)*

Gasoline Retailers

Trying again to protect the independent gas station dealer against arbitrary termination of his franchise by the major oil companies, the Senate in 1975 approved a bill (S 323) setting out the conditions under which terminations were acceptable. The House did not act on the bill in 1975.

The Senate had added similar provisions to the Emergency Petroleum Allocation Act of 1973, but they were deleted in conference. Again, these provisions were added to the Energy Emergency Act of 1974, but that bill was vetoed. In August 1974, the Senate passed a bill similar to S 323, but the House did not act and the measure died with the 93rd Congress. *(Story p. 35-A)*

The Senate approved S 323 (S Rept 94-120) by voice vote June 20. As passed, the bill required written notice from the oil company of intent to terminate the franchise at least 90 days before the termination became effective. It provided that the termination was justified only if the supplier withdrew entirely from selling refined petroleum products or if the franchise holder had failed to comply substantially with some essential reasonable requirement of the franchise.

Commission on Shortages

Congress in 1975 extended the life of the National Commission on Supplies and Shortages through March 31, 1977. As established in 1974, the commission was to issue its final report June 30, 1975. *(Story p. 34-A)*

Due to difficulties in selection of its members, the commission was unable to meet the original deadline for its report to Congress. In July, Congress cleared a measure (H J Res 560—PL 94-72) extending the commission through Oct. 1, 1976.

Later in the year, Congress granted a further extension, until March 31, 1977. This provision was part of a measure (S 1537 - PL 94-152) extending the Defense Production Act of 1950 through Sept. 30, 1977.

Tennessee Valley Authority

Congress in 1975 approved an increase to $15-billion from $5-billion in the amount of outstanding revenue bonds which the Tennessee Valley Authority (TVA) could issue to finance expansion of its power system.

Created by Congress in 1933, by 1975 TVA supplied electric power to an area of 80,000 square miles, containing 7 million people, 50 industries and 11 federal installations.

Congress in 1959 authorized TVA to issue up to $750-million in bonds to finance power plants; in 1966, this ceil-

ing was raised to $1.75-billion; in 1970 it was increased again to $5-billion. By Dec. 31, 1975, TVA bonds and notes outstanding were expected to exceed $4-billion, and other commitments were anticipated to have consumed the remaining unobligated borrowing authority.

Without the increase in the bond ceiling, only the most critical construction and procurement would continue, TVA officials said.

The $10-billion increase in bonding authority would allow the generation of funds to complete building of six power plants already underway—including four nuclear plants—and would allow the construction of three other nuclear plants. Because the TVA paid the principal and interest on these bonds from its revenues from sale of electric power, the increase in bonding authority had no effect on the federal government's debt.

The House approved the TVA bonding increase measure (HR 9472—H Rept 94-510) by voice vote Oct. 23. The Senate cleared the measure (S Rept 94-461) Nov. 20 by voice vote (PL 94-139).

Energy Leadership

Interior Secretary Rogers C. B. Morton, named energy policy coordinator for the Ford administration late in 1974, moved to head the Commerce Department in April 1975, taking with him the hat of energy czar.

However, the most visible administration energy policymaker during 1975 was Frank G. Zarb, who continued as head of the Federal Energy Administration (FEA) during the year. Zarb was credited with winning Ford's signature for the omnibus energy bill (S 622—PL 94-163) at year's end.

Named to succeed Morton at the Interior Department was former Wyoming Governor Stanley K. Hathaway. Opposed by environmental groups for his conservation actions—or lack thereof—as governor, Hathaway underwent unusually close scrutiny by the Senate Interior Committee during hearings in April and May. The Senate confirmed him June 11 by a vote of 60-36. But after only six weeks in office, Hathaway resigned July 25, citing fatigue and depression as the reasons for his departure.

In September President Ford nominated Thomas S. Kleppe, since 1971 head of the Small Business Administration (SBA) and a former member of the House (R N.D. 1967-1971), to the post of Secretary of Interior. Despite a lack of background or experience in dealing with environmental matters and questions raised by charges of undue political influence and loan mismanagement in the SBA during his tenure, Kleppe was quickly confirmed. The Senate Interior Committee approved his nomination unanimously Oct. 7 after Kleppe told the panel he would, within nine months, divest himself of all stock holdings which might constitute a conflict of interest. The Senate approved his nomination by voice vote Oct. 9.

The membership of the new Nuclear Regulatory Commission remained unchanged through 1975, the first year of its operation, but President Ford named three new members of the five-member Federal Power Commission: Richard L. Dunham, deputy director of the White House Domestic Council, as chairman, confirmed in October; John H. Holloman III, a Mississippi attorney, confirmed in July; and James G. Watt, an Interior Department official, confirmed in November.

1976

In the presidential election year of 1976, Congress continued half-heartedly to seek answers to the nation's continuing, but less visible, energy problems. Early in the year, Ford asked Congress to act on 16 energy proposals; by the session's end, only four were enacted.

Congressional ambivalence and unwillingness to make difficult decisions led to oddly unequal treatment for several pairs of measures. A year-and-a-half extension for the Federal Energy Administration—the government's "temporary" energy crisis management agency—was easily approved, but Congress adjourned without completing action on the billion-dollar measure authorizing federal energy research and development programs. Congress approved a billion-dollar program of aid to coastal states affected by development of oil and gas resources on the Outer Continental Shelf, but killed a related bill that would have modernized the procedures for leasing those federally-owned resources for development.

Congress overrode one presidential veto to enact a measure authorizing government efforts to promote the development of electric cars, but sustained a veto of a related bill to put federal money behind efforts to develop advanced automobile engines.

And after insisting on retaining oil price controls in 1975, Congress acquiesced in Ford administration proposals to lift those controls on a variety of petroleum products.

Congress did enact changes in federal procedures for leasing its coal deposits (over a presidential veto); it approved opening of the naval oil reserves for production; and it set deadlines to spur a decision on transporting Alaskan natural gas to the other United States. It killed, or left dangling, Ford proposals to deregulate the price of natural gas, to allow private industry to get into the uranium enrichment business, to provide federal backing for commercial production of synthetic fuels, and to relax clean air deadlines for auto and industrial emissions.

FEA Extension

Congress in 1976 extended the life of the Federal Energy Administration (FEA) for 18 months, until Dec. 31, 1977. The law creating FEA as a temporary agency to cope with the fuel shortages of 1974-75 (PL 93-275) had provided that it would go out of existence June 30, 1976. President Ford had requested a 39-month extension, through Sept. 30, 1979. *(PL 93-275, p. 19-A)*

The FEA extension measure (HR 12169—PL 94-385) was transformed by the Senate into a full-fledged energy policy measure. As enacted it also authorized the President to submit to Congress late in the year plans for a general reorganization of federal energy policy machinery. PL 94-385 also put new weight behind federal efforts to spur reform of electric rate structures and to encourage energy conservation.

The House version of HR 12169, approved June 1, simply extended the life of FEA for 18 months, half the period recommended by the Interstate and Foreign Commerce Committee.

But the Senate, while recommending only a 15-month extension for FEA, laid the groundwork for a complete restructuring of federal energy efforts and expansion of FEA involvement in reform of electric rate structures, a subject also dealt with by the House bill. On the Senate floor, still more policy provisions were added, authorizing new federal financial incentives for energy-efficient buildings, expanding FEA's mandate to collect financial date from oil companies, and lifting price controls on certain categories of domestic oil.

Conferees adopted the House's 18-month extension for FEA and most of the House authorization levels for FEA activities. They retained most of the provisions of both versions after softening some of the more controversial aspects of the Senate building conservation and energy data provisions, and dropping from the final version of the bill House language providing a congressional veto over FEA regulations.

Conferees were unable to work out a final version of the bill between Senate passage June 16 and FEA's June 30 expiration date. The agency was therefore extended for one month by passage of a stopgap extension bill (S 3625—PL 94-332). When that expired before the conference agreement on HR 12169 was completed, President Ford July 30 signed an executive order creating for the interim a Federal Energy Office to perform the functions of FEA.

House Committee Action

Despite congressional criticism of FEA's handling of federal programs to deal with fuel shortages the House Interstate and Foreign Commerce Committee recommended three more years of life for the agency, reporting HR 12169 May 10 (H Rept 94-1113) to extend the authorization for FEA through June 30, 1979.

Reflecting congressional intent to keep more control over the agency's activities, HR 12169 set specific budget ceilings for FEA's operating divisions, cutting $1.3-million from the request for the agency's public affairs office and denying a request for funds to set up a proposed office of nuclear affairs.

As reported HR 12169 authorized $212.4-million for FEA in fiscal 1977, a small increase over the $200 million authorized for both fiscal 1975 and 1976. This total included $40.7-million added by the committee to the amounts requested for conservation, environmental and solar energy programs, plus funds for encouraging electric utilities to reform their load management practices and rate structures.

House Floor Action

The House June 1 approved HR 12169 by a vote of 270-94 after cutting in half the extension of FEA's life—to 18 months, through Dec. 31, 1977—and reducing the authorization for fiscal 1977 to $172.8-million.

The reduced extension was approved as the House, by a 194-172 vote, adopted an amendment proposed by Floyd Fithian (D Ind.) extending the agency's life for only 18 months. The House had earlier rejected by voice vote an amendment allowing FEA to expire June 30, 1976.

Fithian argued that the three-year extension provided by the committee bill left "little if any hope that we might ever limit that agency or that we might ever make it tractable." John D. Dingell (D Mich.), chairman of the Commerce Subcommittee on Energy and Power, responded that the three years was "about long enough to allow FEA to conclude its statutory authority."

The House also adopted amendments stripping away the funds which the committee had added for FEA solar energy and conservation programs.

The House approved several amendments restricting FEA's use of its powers, including a proposal by Energy and Power Subcommittee Democrat Bob Eckhardt (Texas) to prohibit FEA from packaging its decisions to decontrol oil prices and end mandatory supply allocations.

Accepted by a 200-175 margin, Eckhardt's amendment required separate FEA pronouncements to free crude oil or any petroleum product from federal price and allocation controls, giving Congress a chance to veto one or both actions. *(Box next page)*

Senate Committee Action

In proposing a 15-month FEA extension, the Senate Government Operations Committee laid the legislative groundwork for a general reorganization of federal energy policy machinery.

Approved unanimously and reported May 13 (S 2872—S Rept 94-874), the Senate committee's measure directed the President to submit by the end of 1976 a plan for restructuring federal government programs and agencies that deal with energy and natural resource issues.

The panel wrote into S 2872 other provisions for transferring FEA's multi-faceted programs to other federal departments and agencies when its extended authority expired after Sept. 30, 1977.

A 15-month FEA extension "allows ample time for the planning and implementation of the reorganization plan," the committee contended in its report.

The Senate committee recommended fiscal 1977 authorizations of $183.3-million for FEA activities.

Like the House measure, S 2872 denied funds sought to set up an FEA Office of Nuclear Affairs and set a $2.3-million ceiling on funds which could be allocated to the agency's controversial communications and public affairs operation.

The Senate committee tacked onto S 2872 a second title containing a set of provisions to expand and strengthen FEA's support for revision of state electric utility rate structures by authorizing FEA to develop guidelines for such reform, to aid state commissions in rate revision, and to encourage consumer representation in utility regulatory proceedings.

Senate Floor Action

The Senate June 16 passed HR 12169 by an 81-12 roll-call vote after substituting the provisions of S 2872. Before passing the 15-month extension, it adopted a number of major amendments providing financial incentives for energy-saving investments, expanding FEA's power to collect data from energy-producing companies and lifting federal price controls on oil pumped from partly depleted marginal wells.

By a 57-37 roll call, the Senate June 15 adopted an extensive amendment by Ernest F. Hollings (D S.C.) and Edward M. Kennedy (D Mass.) setting federal energy conservation standards for new buildings, and providing grants and loan guarantees to assist conservation efforts by states, small businesses, low-income persons, homeowners and industry.

The amendment in part revived Senate-passed legislation (HR 8650) imposing mandatory efficiency standards for new buildings. The bill had been stalled in conference

Presidential Requests: 1976

"We must regain our energy independence," President Ford again asserted to Congress in his 1976 energy message, delivered Feb. 26. "During the past year, we have made some progress toward achieving our energy independence goals, but the fact remains that we have a long way to go...."

"Thus far, the Congress has completed action on only one major piece of energy legislation—the Energy Policy and Conservation Act—which I signed into law on Dec. 22, 1975...."

Ford then asked Congress to:

● Deregulate the price of new natural gas. This, Ford said, was "the most important action that can be taken by the Congress to improve our future gas supply situation." *(Story p. 70-A)*

● Provide additional short-term authority needed to deal with severe winter shortages of natural gas.

● Expedite selection of a route and construction of a transportation system to bring Alaskan natural gas to the lower 48 states. *(Story p. 84-A)*

● Streamline licensing procedures for the construction of new powerplants.

● Approve the Nuclear Assurance Act to provide the basis for transition from a government monopoly to a private competitive uranium enrichment industry. *(Story p. 72-A)*

● Approve proposed Clean Air Amendments to permit greater use of coal and to delay auto emission standards deadlines. *(Story p. 69-A)*

● Allow production from the Naval Petroleum Reserves. *(Story p. 74-A)*

● Approve creation of an Energy Independence Authority, to assist private sector financing of new energy facilities. *(Story p. 57-A)*

● Authorize loan guarantees to aid in the construction of commercial facilities to produce synthetic fuels. *(Story p. 67-A)*

● Approve energy facilities siting legislation.

● Approve utility rate reform legislation.

● Approve the Electric Utilities Construction Incentives Act.

● Approve the Federal Energy Impact Assistance Act to set up a $1-billion program of aid to areas affected by new federal energy resource development.

● Set up a $55-million weatherization assistance program for low-income and elderly persons. *(Story p. 63-A)*

● Provide for thermal efficiency standards for new buildings. *(Story p. 62-A)*

● Provide a 15 per cent tax credit for energy conservation improvements in existing residential buildings.

At the end of the 94th Congress, legislation had been enacted to grant Ford's requests concerning Alaskan natural gas, the naval petroleum reserves, weatherization assistance and thermal building standards, but the other requests had either failed to win final approval or had been ignored by Congress altogether.

'Energy Actions' Allow End To Some Price Controls

The second session of the 94th Congress passed up opportunities to block Ford administration proposals lifting price and allocation controls on various types of fuel and eliminating an exemption for small oil refiners from the oil entitlements program.

In its omnibus 1975 energy bill (PL 94-163), Congress gave the Federal Energy Administration authority to modify price and allocation controls and the entitlements program, subject to congressional veto. FEA was to send such proposed changes to Congress as "energy actions"; if neither chamber disapproved the change in 15 days, the change could take effect. *(Story p. 37-A)*

In April the House refused to consider a resolution disapproving the first "energy action"—lifting of price and allocation controls on residual fuel oil, the least refined product derived from processing crude oil. In May the House and Senate both refused to block a second "energy action" eliminating an exemption from the entitlements program for small refiners.

On June 15, FEA sent to Congress its third and fourth "energy actions," proposing to end the price and allocation controls for the next level of refined products, home heating oil, diesel fuel, and all other middle-distillate refined petroleum products. Again, the House and Senate rejected efforts to take up resolutions disapproving those actions.

On Sept. 15 FEA sent Congress proposals to exempt naphtha jet fuel from federal controls. Congress made no effort to disapprove them and they took effect Oct. 1. Aviation gasoline and kerosene fuel remained under controls.

As a result of the "energy actions," more than half of the products of a barrel of crude oil were exempted from controls, but no significant price increases or shortages developed, reported FEA.

The Ford administration in November unveiled a plan to propose to Congress an end to controls on the price of gasoline, but no proposal was formally submitted until the 95th Congress.

Residual Fuel Oil

The House April 13 turned down an effort to block President Ford's plan to end federal controls on residual fuel oil prices on June 1.

By a 109-272 recorded vote, the House defeated an attempt by Interstate and Foreign Commerce Committee Democrats to push to the floor a resolution (H Res 1135) that would have vetoed the administration's initial proposal for phasing out federal price and allocation controls over petroleum products.

The Federal Energy Administration (FEA) March 29 had announced its intention to terminate the existing price and allocation system for residual fuel oil, the heavy, least refined product derived in processing crude oil. Eastern coastal states, particularly New England, rely heavily on imported residual oil for electrical generation and other large-scale uses.

In lifting price and allocation controls under authority conferred by 1975 omnibus energy legislation,

FEA concluded that the existing system actually was holding residual prices up by restraining competitive market forces.

The Senate made no move to disapprove the plan.

Small Refiner Exemption

Congress May 27 turned down efforts to keep the Federal Energy Administration's second "energy action" of 1976 from taking effect.

The second energy action eliminated the 1975 exemption for small oil refiners from the oil entitlements program. The Senate refused to act to discharge a resolution of disapproval from committee on a 28-57 roll-call vote. The House followed suit by a standing vote of 15-34. Congress had had 15 days to disapprove the proposal; the deadline was May 27.

Background. The entitlements program was set up in November 1974 to equalize the cost of a barrel of crude oil to refiners, by requiring refiners with sources of cheaper 'old' oil to pay a certain amount to those who had to buy 'new' oil at as much as $8 per barrel more.

Concerned that the program worked to the disadvantage of small refiners because of the high per barrel cost of small-scale operations, Congress in 1975 exempted refiners whose capacity was less than 100,000 barrels per day from having to buy entitlements for the first 50,000 barrels of oil they processed. That law also authorized the Federal Energy Administration (FEA) to modify the exemption if it resulted in further inequities. *(Story p. 43-A)*

The exemption took effect Dec. 31, 1975; FEA moved Feb. 28 to revoke it. On May 12, FEA officially notified Congress of the proposal to eliminate the exemption and to increase the bias in the entitlement regulations favoring small refiners over the major oil companies. FEA explained that the exemption was giving small refiners who would otherwise have had to buy entitlements an unfair advantage over other small refiners who were sellers of entitlements.

Middle Distillate Fuels

Congress June 30 refused to block a Ford administration proposal to end controls on the price and allocation of diesel fuel, home heating oil, and other middle distillate refined petroleum products

The House voted 194-208 to reject a motion to discharge the House Interstate and Foreign Commerce Committee from consideration of resolutions disapproving these changes. The Senate voted 52-32 to table a motion to take up similar resolutions.

As a result those controls were lifted July 1.

According to the Senate Interior and Insular Affairs Committee reports (S Rept 94-1000, 94-1001) on the resolutions (S Res 469, S Res 470) disapproving these actions, these products accounted for 17 per cent of the domestic demand for petroleum products—about three million barrels per day of middle distillates. Half of these three million barrels were used for residential and commercial heating, a highly seasonal demand, and another third were used for transportation.

by House conferees' objections to provisions that would cut off most mortgage credit for new homes in areas that failed to comply with federal insulation requirements. Those controversial provisions were strongly backed by the Ford administration.

The provisions were added by the Senate Banking, Housing and Urban Affairs Committee after the House had passed the bill in 1975. The Senate passed its amended version March 9, 52-35. Before accepting the Kennedy-Hollings proposal, the Senate by a 45-49 recorded vote defeated Jake Garn's (R Utah) attempt to strip out the compliance provisions. *(Story p. 57-A)*

The Kennedy-Hollings amendment coupled those provisions of HR 8650 with federal financial incentives for improving the efficiency of existing buildings provided by separate legislation drafted by Kennedy. That measure (S 3424) was reported by the Senate Commerce Committee on May 13 but then stalled in the Senate Interior and Insular Affairs Committee.

Going off in another direction, the Senate adopted two separate amendments that lifted federal price controls on oil produced from slow-flowing wells that had been partly depleted.

By allowing the price for such hard-to-pump crude oil to rise, industry allies argued, the amendments would encourage producers to use more expensive techniques required to keep marginal wells in production.

By a 61-29 roll call, the Senate adopted an amendment to exempt from federal price controls all oil produced from "stripper" wells producing 10 barrels or less a day. Congress reapplied price controls to stripper well oil in 1975 omnibus energy legislation, ending an exemption provided in 1973. *(Story p. 37-A)*

By a 58-35 roll call, the Senate subsequently approved a proposal to end price controls on the additional oil produced after Feb. 1, 1976, as the result of using secondary and tertiary techniques. Such methods, including the injection of water or gases, were used to bring to the surface crude oil that cannot be produced by normal well pumping operations.

By a narrow 46-45 roll call, the Senate adopted an amendment to create within FEA an independent office for gathering and analyzing information on the nation's supply and consumption of energy.

The amendment empowered the office to collect financial data from major energy producing companies and compile statistical profiles of the separate energy activities of the industry. The amendment specifically made that information available to Congress in an attempt to redress continued frustration among members and committee staffs about the lack of independent energy statistics.

Conference Action

House and Senate conferees filed their reports on the bill Aug. 4 (H Rept 94-1392) and Aug. 5 (S Rept 94-1119). Because few of the provisions of the two versions of the bill collided head-on, conferees were able to adopt most of both measures.

Conferees, however, delayed a final decision on the most controversial aspect of the Senate federal energy efficiency standards for new buildings—the sanctions by which they were to be enforced. The final version of HR 12169 provided for Congress to decide, after the performance standards were formulated, whether it was necessary to ensure their application through the sanction

of denying all federal financial assistance for construction to an area of a state not adopting these standards.

Final Action

Final action came when the House Aug. 10, by a vote of 293-88, adopted the conference report on the bill. It had earlier adopted the rule for consideration of the conference report, 267-117.

The Senate had adopted the report Aug. 5 by voice vote.

Provisions

The major provisions of PL 94-385:

● Extended the life of the Federal Energy Administration (FEA) for 18 months, to Dec. 31, 1977, from July 1, 1976.

● Authorized appropriations of $189.9-million for existing FEA programs in fiscal 1977, and $41.3-million for the transition quarter between fiscal 1976 and 1977. (The bill set a ceiling of $2.036-million for FEA's controversial communications and public affairs office; it also specifically denied funds for setting up an office of nuclear affairs within FEA.)

● Created an office of energy information and analysis within FEA, to establish and maintain a national energy information system to describe and facilitate analysis of energy supply and consumption as a basis for the work of FEA, Congress and other energy-policy-making officials.

● Directed the President, by Dec. 31, 1976, to submit to Congress a plan for the reorganization of the federal government's activities in energy and natural resources.

● Extended the life of the Energy Resources Council to Sept. 30, 1977.

● Exempted oil produced from stripper wells, which produce an average of 10 barrels or less per day, from federal price controls, but required that its price continue to be factored into the composite price for domestic oil, which the President was required, by the 1975 Energy Policy and Conservation Act, to maintain at a certain gradually rising level. *(Story, p. 37-A)*

● Lifted the 3 per cent limitation on the overall price increase for domestic oil which the President could allow in order to stimulate domestic production.

● Directed FEA to develop proposals for improving electric utility rate design and to submit them to Congress within six months of enactment.

● Directed FEA to fund demonstration projects to improve electric utility load management procedures and to fund regulatory rate reform initiatives; authorized FEA intervention and participation in state utility regulatory commission proceedings upon the request of a participant in those proceedings.

● Authorized FEA grants to states for setting up offices of consumer services to aid consumer representation in utility regulatory proceedings.

● Directed the Department of Housing and Urban Development (HUD) to develop within three years of enactment federal performance standards for energy efficiency in all new commercial and residential buildings.

● Denied federal financial assistance—including mortgage loans from federally regulated institutions—for construction of any new commercial or residential buildings in any part of any state which did not certify its adoption of and the building's compliance with the new performance standards; conditioned the use of this sanction upon passage of a concurrent resolution by Congress finding this sanction necessary and appropriate to assure application of these standards.

• Authorized FEA grants to states and Indian tribes, and to city governments and community action agencies in a non-participating state, for insulation and other weatherization investments (of up to $400 in materials per unit) in dwellings occupied by low-income persons; authorized $55-million for fiscal 1977, $65-million for fiscal 1978 and $80-million for fiscal 1979.

• Directed FEA to develop guidelines for supplemental state energy conservation plans; authorized FEA grants to states for implementing these plans; authorized $25-million for fiscal 1977, $40-million for 1978, $40-million for 1979.

• Directed the Department of Housing and Urban Development to undertake a national demonstration program to test the feasibility and effectiveness of aid to encourage energy conservation and adoption of renewable-resource measures in existing dwellings; authorized HUD to use grants, loans, loan subsidies and guarantees to encourage this use of these conservation measures; limited the subsidies to $400 or 20 per cent of a loan for conventional energy devices and to $2,000 or 25 per cent of loans for solar, wind or other renewable resource devices; authorized $200-million for this aid.

• Provided authority for FEA to guarantee loans to corporations, institutions, governments and other eligible borrowers for financing energy conservation or renewable resource measures for industrial goals or otherwise to improve the efficiency of the large-scale use of energy; set a ceiling of $2-billion upon aggregate commitments under this program.

ERDA Authorization

Three years after the Arab oil embargo jolted the United States into its energy crisis, the 94th Congress adjourned without completing action on the major energy funding measure of 1976. Dead at adjournment was the bill (HR 13350) authorizing almost $8-billion in fiscal 1977 energy research programs administered by the Energy Research and Development Administration (ERDA).

HR 13350 was approved by overwhelming votes in the House in May and the Senate in June, after nuclear power supporters beat back efforts to slow funding for the liquid metal fast breeder reactor demonstration plant and advocates of solar energy and conservation measures won additional funding.

But conferees were not appointed until late in September, a delay that Senate aides attributed to House Science Committee Chairman Olin E. Teague (D Texas), who was trying to win House approval of a related bill (HR 12112) providing federal loan guarantees for synthetic fuels projects. *(Story 67-A)*

In late 1975, the House had struck from that year's ERDA authorization measure Senate language authorizing such loan guarantees. The Senate version of HR 13350 authorized $900-million in such guarantees for production of synthetic fuels from biomass, and gave ERDA the option of broadening this program to include other types of synthetic fuels, with congressional approval. *(Story p. 46-A)*

But the House Sept. 23 refused to consider Teague's bill; the same day, the House formally asked for a conference on HR 13350. Conferees on HR 13350 filed their reports (H Rept 94-1718, S Rept 94-1327) Sept. 28. The House adopted the conference report—which included substantially narrowed synthetic fuel loan guarantee provisions—by voice vote Sept. 30.

Delayed by a last-minute State Department objection to nuclear export sections of the measure, HR 13350 did not arrive on the Senate floor for consideration until after two o'clock in the morning on Saturday, Oct. 2. When Sen. Henry M. Jackson (D Wash.) moved for consideration of the conference report, Sen. Mike Gravel (D Alaska) blocked that move, asking that the report be read in full. Gravel was angered by Jackson's refusal to back his bid for a seat on the Joint Atomic Energy Committee, a refusal which Gravel attributed to his criticisms of nuclear power.

After a sharp exchange, Jackson withdrew his request and the bill died. The Senate then adjourned.

Under the continuing resolution (H J Res 1105), most of the ERDA programs would be funded through March 1977. The bill appropriating ERDA funds had been enacted earlier in 1976. *(Story p. 65-A)*

The conference version of the ERDA authorization bill provided almost $6-billion for nuclear programs and almost $2-billion for non-nuclear programs. The non-nuclear total was approximately $400-million more than the administration requested, with the bulk of the increases coming in solar and conservation programs.

The nuclear and non-nuclear portions of the bill were reported by separate committees and then considered in both chambers as one bill.

House Committee Action

Reporting their respective portions of the measure, two congressional committees in May recommended that the House boost Energy Research and Development Administration (ERDA) funding requests by $614.2-million in fiscal 1977 to $7.2-billion.

In projecting a total 47.7 per cent increase above fiscal 1976 funding levels, the panels' combined proposal (HR 13350) authorized fiscal 1977 funding of $5.9-billion for nuclear energy development and $1.4-billion for fossil fuels, solar power and other alternative energy technologies.

Congressional jurisdiction over energy funding was divided along nuclear and non-nuclear lines. With the weighing of priorities thus restricted, the House received separate judgments from the Joint Atomic Energy and Science and Technology Committees on the merits of the programs with which they were most familiar.

Both committees provided substantial increases for some programs while making no cuts in fund requests for the rest. Both panels followed the general congressional pattern in handling energy funding by restoring many Office of Management and Budget (OMB) cuts in ERDA's own budget proposals.

The committees followed different formats in setting out their proposals in their two-part joint report (H Rept 94-1081). The Science and Technology Committee followed conventional congressional practice of authorizing funding levels in terms of budget authority. After programs are authorized, Congress usually confers budget authority—the power to spend federal funds on programs—to federal agencies through annual appropriations bills.

The Joint Atomic Energy Committee, on the other hand, broke its authorization recommendations down in terms of estimated costs. For ERDA operating expenses,

The Nuclear Breeder Reactor: Hope of the Seventies

Expanded use of nuclear power to generate electricity was a cornerstone of the nation's plans in the 1970s for future energy self-sufficiency. To counter the fact that supplies of nuclear fuel, usually uranium, were finite, energy planners looked with hope to the expanded use of "breeder" reactors, which create more nuclear fuel than they consume, thereby ensuring an almost inexhaustible supply of fuel. In these reactors, the fission produces heat that is converted to steam to drive turbines that generate electricity.

For two decades the United States had been involved in research and development of breeder reactors. In the 1960s, the liquid metal cooled fast breeder reactor (LMFBR) was selected as the focus for an intensified federal push. Its fuel was regular uranium (U-238), rather than the enriched uranium (U-235) used by other types of reactors. A product of its fission was plutonium, which also served as nuclear fuel. By the early 1970s several LMFBRs had been built and successfully operated in the United States, demonstrating their basic technological feasibility.

To demonstrate that the LMFBR was practical for use by electric utilities and to begin the development of an industrial base to supply parts and equipment for commercial scale plants, Congress in 1970 authorized initial work toward a demonstration project, to be administered jointly by the Atomic Energy Commission (later the Energy Research and Development Administration, ERDA) and private industry. This go-ahead was included in the fiscal 1971 authorization measure for the AEC (PL 91-273). By fiscal 1973, Congress had provided $100-million for the project, all the direct government funding originally estimated as needed for the plant itself—engineering, hardware, construction and its operation for five years. This figure did not include supporting development for the project, an element of about $350-million.

In July 1973, the AEC signed a contract with the Tennessee Valley Authority and Commonwealth Edison and the Project Management Corporation representing the utility industry to build the plant near the Clinch River near Oak Ridge, Tenn. The project was entitled the Clinch River Breeder Reactor Plant. Its estimated cost at that time was $700-million, of which utilities were to pay $250-million, and the government the rest.

In fiscal 1974 and 1975, Congress provided $73.8-million more for applied development efforts required for the Clinch River plant. In fiscal 1975 the first equipment was ordered for the project.

By 1974, it had become obvious that the cost of the project had more than doubled, in part because the date at which the plant would go into operation had been delayed from 1980 to 1982. The cost was re-estimated at $1.736-billion (of which the government share was $1.468-billion). Based on this revised cost estimate, Congress in 1975 reauthorized the project and provided that ERDA should assume complete responsibility for its management. This was part of the fiscal 1976 ERDA authorization bill (PL 94-187).

Early in 1976 the plant operational ("criticality") date was delayed further—to late 1983—and the cost estimate rose again—to $1.95-billion. The amount paid by private industry—$258-million by the utilities and $10-million by reactor manufacturers—remained the same.

As of late 1976, the amounts authorized, appropriated and spent for the federal share in building the Clinch River plant were:

Fiscal Year	Authorization	Appropriations
	(amounts in millions of dollars)	
1970	$ 7.0	$ 4.0
1971	43.0	10.0
1972	50.0	36.0
1973	—	50.0
1974	11.0	11.0
1975	62.8	62.8
1976[1]	131.1	131.1
1977	—[2]	171.0

1 Including transition quarter.
2 Congress did not complete action on the 1977 ERDA authorization bill in 1976.

Source: Energy Research and Development Administration

As the Clinch River project moved toward the construction phase, controversy over nuclear power and the fast breeder reactor project escalated.

Concern about public safety was central to unsuccessful efforts in Congress in 1975 and 1976 to slow work on the project and to force a re-examination of its desirability. *(Story, pp. 46-A, 63-A)*

Environmental groups argued that the LMFBR program, by enlarging the supply of plutonium, would establish the preconditions for a major new threat to public health. Microgram quantities of this element—termed "fiendishly toxic" by its discoverer—regularly produced cancer in the lungs of experimental animals. They said a safe, leak-proof means of storing the radioactive wastes which are produced by nuclear reactors had not been developed.

Critics also argued that by increasing the amount of plutonium available, LMFBR development would multiply the chances that terrorists would steal plutonium to make "home-made" bombs.

In support of the Clinch River project, the breeder reactor concept and nuclear power in general, ERDA officials pointed to estimates that U.S. demand for electrical energy would double between 1970 and 1985 and would double again by the year 2000. They expected the percentage of U.S. electric generating capacity provided by nuclear power to rise from 6 per cent in 1975 to 60 per cent by the year 2000.

The nation's need for the breeder reactors outweighed the risks of nuclear power, supporters of the project argued. Nuclear power could assure the nation a continuing supply of energy at relatively stable prices with little environmental impact, they said.

An increased supply and use of plutonium did not inevitably mean that more people would be exposed to its hazards, ERDA officials said, emphasizing the elaborate safety and safeguards systems developed to isolate the material and ensure that it was not stolen or otherwise diverted from its proper use. A safe way could be found to store radioactive wastes, they added, and the risk of a nuclear accident was very small.

those figures were equivalent to the related appropriations requests.

The two committees' different budgeting methods complicated comparisons between their nuclear and non-nuclear proposals.

Nuclear Energy. Reporting its proposals May 1, the Joint Atomic Energy Committee recommended total increases of $145,280,000 in ERDA's nuclear program operating funds. It also approved a $265,232,000 increase in plant and capital equipment authorizations, primarily for expansion of the federal government's own uranium enrichment capacity.

The joint committee continued its support for nuclear breeder reactors, approving the full request of $455.2-million for the liquid metal fast breeder reactor program, a $151-million increase over authorized fiscal 1976 costs. The fiscal 1977 figure included $171-million for the Clinch River breeder reactor demonstration project.

In addition, the joint committee approved an increase of $46.5-million in the administration request for fusion power research and development operating expenses, bringing the total for that category to $271.8-million. And the committee approved $1.4-billion in operating expenses for weapons development and weapons material production, plus $202.6-million for naval reactor development.

The committee added to HR 13350 a $230-million authorization to start construction of additional uranium enrichment capacity at the federal government's Portsmouth, Ohio, plant.

ERDA had made no formal request for the Portsmouth add-on authorization, although it was starting planning for the expansion as a hedge against failure of the Ford administration's plan to turn the processing of uranium into fissionable form over to private companies. *(Story, p. 72-A)*

The committee approved the full $873.1-million request for operating the government's three existing uranium enrichment plants.

Non-nuclear Energy. In reworking ERDA's non-nuclear budget, the House Science and Technology Committee increased the President's budget proposals by $289,832,000.

Those increases, many restoring funds cut from ERDA's requests by OMB, included $55.4-million for fossil fuels, $66.7-million for solar energy and $82.5-million for conservation research and development.

In all, the panel approved more than $1.4-billion for non-nuclear programs, roughly $400-million more than for fiscal 1976. The committee reported HR 13350 May 3.

The committee increased coal research and development authorizations to $354.5-million, and solar energy requests to $229.2-million, nearly double the fiscal 1976 estimate of $114.7-million. The recommended total for solar programs included $85.6-million for direct thermal applications and $78.9-million for solar heating and cooling research and demonstrations.

The $82.5-million boost in conservation program funds approved by the committee was spread across five of the conservation programs in ERDA—energy storage, buildings conservation, industrial conservation, transportation, and improved conversion efficiency. The committee also authorized $10-million for a proposed federal energy extension service to help channel new conservation techniques to consumers.

Energy Funds

Despite the lack of a fiscal 1977 authorization measure, Congress in 1976 appropriated $6.3-billion for the Energy Research and Development Administration in fiscal 1977. The bulk of these funds was contained in the Energy/Public Works appropriations bill (HR 14236—PL 94-355), which cleared Congress June 29. This measure contained $5,749,973,000 for ERDA programs, including the following amounts in operating expenses for certain specific categorical programs:

- Solar energy—$258.5-million
- Nuclear fusion—$275-million
- Nuclear fission reactors—$630.3-million
- Nuclear weapons—$1.36-billion
- Uranium enrichment—$925.2-million

Additional funds for ERDA—$583,995,000 for fossil fuel research and some conservation programs—were included in the Interior Department appropriations bill (HR 14231—PL 94-373). HR 14231 also appropriated $598,069,000 for the Federal Energy Administration (FEA) in fiscal 1977. This amount was $152.8-million less than requested by the Ford administration but included about $450-million for the purchase of oil to place in the strategic reserves authorized by Congress in the omnibus energy policy measure enacted in 1975 (PL 94-163). In addition, HR 14231 provided $406-million to finance production of oil from the naval petroleum reserves. *(Story on PL 94-163, p. 37-A; on naval petroleum reserves, p. 74-A)*

House Floor Action

The House passed HR 13350 May 20 by an overwhelming 316-26 vote, recommending a total authorization of $7.4-billion.

Before passage the House rejected tight safety and financing restrictions on the Clinch River breeder reactor. It adopted floor amendments boosting solar power funding another $116-million. That action brought the increase in budget requests for solar energy to $182.7-million.

No challenge was made during floor debate to the Joint Atomic Energy Committee's proposal to grant ERDA's full $455.2-million request for the liquid metal fast breeder reactor program.

Initially estimated at $699-million in 1972, the projected cost of the Clinch River plant had escalated to $1.95-billion by 1976. And amid general public uneasiness about nuclear power plant safety, environmentalists were charging that breeder reactors and their plutonium products posed unacceptable safety and health risks. *(Box on breeder reactors, p. 64-A)*

The House defeated proposed financing restrictions on the demonstration plant, rejecting by a 173-209 recorded vote an amendment by R. Lawrence Coughlin (R Pa.) to require private utilities to share the burden of additional Clinch River cost overruns with the federal government.

Under Coughlin's amendment, the utility companies that were participating in the breeder project would be responsible for a percentage of any cost increases that raised the total Clinch River estimate above $2-billion. Private utilities were sharing in the Clinch River project, but their total financing contributions amount to only $258-million of the nearly $2-billion estimated cost.

Coughlin's proposal would limit federal contributions toward paying costs above $2-billion to 70 per cent of the first additional $250-million, 60 per cent of the next $250-million and to 50 per cent of any cost above $2.5-billion.

Coughlin, who had offered an unsuccessful 1975 amendment to defer construction of the Clinch River plant, argued that his cost-sharing proposal would hold down further overruns by giving private participants a greater stake in efficiency. *(1975 action, p. 46-A)*

Joint Atomic Energy Committee members defended the breeder project management, pointing out that ERDA had renegotiated its contract with private participants to give the federal government full management responsibility.

The House subsequently sidetracked breeder critics' attempt to force federal officials to make a definitive safety ruling before building the Clinch River plant.

The House instead adopted, by a 238-140 recorded vote, Joint Atomic Energy Committee member John B. Anderson's (R Ill.) substitute proposal requiring only "reasonable assurance" that the breeder would be safe before construction got underway.

By adding $116-million to the Science and Technology Committee's $229.2-million proposal, the House May 19 lifted ERDA solar development authorizations to the $345.2-million level proposed by solar power advocates.

The House restructured the $116-million increase, however, by allocating half to solar heating and cooling projects and dropping specific line-item project authorizations that backers of the spending boost had written into their floor amendment.

As proposed by James M. Jeffords (R Vt.), the initial amendment provided no additional solar heating and cooling funds and allocated the entire $116-million increase among solar electric, wind, ocean thermal and other solar energy technologies. Their proposal was designed to boost funding for those technologies, which generally were less advanced than heating and cooling projects, back toward levels that ERDA officials had sought during Ford administration budget deliberations.

But by a 265-127 recorded vote, the House accepted a substitute that kept the $116-million total increase but assigned $58-million to ERDA's solar heating and cooling program. It then adopted the Jeffords amendment as amended by the substitute, 321-68.

The House turned down other major changes in the two committee's recommendations, defeating by a 97-286 recorded vote Bella S. Abzug's (D N.Y.) proposal to strip from the bill $1.2-billion in nuclear weapons authorizations. Abzug argued that ERDA's weapons programs should be funded through separate legislation.

The House by voice vote accepted Anderson's amendment offered on behalf of the joint committee to require congressional review of any U.S. agreements to export nuclear fuel and technology to nations that had not ratified the Nuclear Non-proliferation Treaty.

Senate Committee Action

The nuclear ERDA funds recommended to the Senate April 23 by the Joint Atomic Energy Committee (S 3105—S Rept 94-762) were identical to the $5.9-billion recommendation it made to the House.

But the Interior and Insular Affairs Committee, which handles ERDA's non-nuclear budget for the Senate, drew up substantially different funding proposals than the House Science Committee for ERDA's smaller but fast-growing efforts to develop fossil fuels, solar energy and other more exotic alternatives and to encourage conservation to slow energy demand. Its report on the non-nuclear funds was filed May 14 (S 3105—S Rept 94-879).

Like the House measure, the Interior Committee's non-nuclear recommendations spread proposed increases above President Ford's budget proposals across the range of energy programs and technologies. The Senate panel distributed its increases differently, however, and more specifically targeted funds on particular energy projects.

In all, the Senate committee increased the administration's total $1,424,958,000 non-nuclear budget request to $1,803,493,000. The comparable House-passed figure, including authorizations for program management and staffing, was $1,835,990,000, roughly $32.5-million more than the Senate committee's proposal.

The Senate committee actually cut authorizations for running fossil fuel programs by roughly $7-million, but more than offset that reduction by boosting construction funding by $62.3-million.

That increase included funds for two additional ERDA demonstration plants for turning coal into synthetic gas for pipelines and for generating electricity. Altogether, the committee provided $535.2-million for fossil fuel development.

The committee proposed fiscal 1977 authorizations of $278.3-million for solar energy development, a $115.8-million increase in the President's budget proposal.

The panel more than doubled the administration's request for conservation program funding, increasing the total to $252.1-million, spread across the range of ERDA's conservation efforts, and including authorization of $25-million for the proposed energy extension service.

The committee also authorized $900-million in federal loan guarantees for industry to make synthetic fuels from various organic materials or societal wastes: the "biomass" component of its 1975 proposal for $6-billion in federal loan guarantees to encourage development of a U.S. synthetic fuels industry. S 3105 limited federal guarantees for each project to 75 per cent of its total cost. The guarantees would cover loans for construction and start-up costs only.

Senate Floor Action

The Senate June 25 passed HR 13350 by a 77-0 vote after substituting the provisions of S 3105.

By substantial margins, the Senate defeated two floor amendments that were similar to breeder reactor restrictions that the House had turned down in its consideration of ERDA funding.

Those proposals, both offered by Sen. Floyd K. Haskell (D Colo.), were designed to slow or kill the Clinch River project by imposing safety and financing requirements.

By a 31-50 key vote (R 6-22; D 25-28), the Senate rejected Haskell's amendment to force the private utilities participating in the government-financed Clinch River project to assume half of any further overruns that raised the plant's cost above $2-billion.

With adoption of the amendment, "the breeder reactor will go out the window, purely and simply," joint committee Chairman John O. Pastore (D R.I.) argued, because utilities would be unwilling to comply with the requirement.

By a 30-53 roll call, the Senate also turned down an anti-breeder amendment that Haskell offered on behalf of absent joint committee member John V. Tunney (D Calif.). Tunney's proposal would have required the Nuclear Regulatory Commission (NRC) to declare the Clinch River breeder safe to operate before granting a permit for construction to start.

The Senate adopted by voice vote John Glenn's (D Ohio) amendment to require congressional review of the next license for export of nuclear fuel to a country that had not ratified the nuclear non-proliferation treaty. Glenn's amendment applied congressional review requirements of 1974 law to nations that had been exempted because their nuclear export agreements with the United States had been reached before the law went into effect.

The Senate approved several amendments to the Interior Committee's non-nuclear program proposals, including a proposal by Jennings Randolph (D W.Va.) to give ERDA the option of broadening the proposed "biomass" synthetic fuel loan guarantee program to include other synthetic energy projects.

Adopted by a 65-15 roll call, Randolph's amendment gave ERDA authority to ask Congress to expand the $900-million biomass program to make loan guarantees available for specific oil shale, coal gasification or other synthetic fuel commercialization demonstration plants.

Conference Action

Conferees filed their reports (H Rept 94-1718, S Rept 94-1327) Sept. 28.

Concerned about undue delay caused by congressional review of nuclear export decisions, conferees adopted substitute language for provisions added by the House and Senate requiring such review of exports to nations that had not ratified the nuclear non-proliferation treaty. The substitute language required this review only if the export was found inconsistent with the national interest or if the recipient country was found unlikely to deal with the export in a manner consistent with the principles of non-proliferation.

Conferees split the difference between the two chambers' allocations for solar energy, settling on $319.7-million, and geothermal energy, $68-million. Most of the Senate increase for conservation work was accepted, for a total of $241.5-million.

Conferees trimmed back the Senate language allowing loan guarantees for biomass synthetic fuel projects, reducing the amount of such guarantees to $300-million from $900-million.

Conferees retained Senate language creating an energy extension service and authorizing $25-million for initial programs. The House Aug. 2 had approved such a service in a separate bill (HR 13676—H Rept 94-1348) by a vote of 323-55. That measure had been sent to conference with HR 13350.

As reported by conferees, the totals for non-nuclear programs were:

● Fossil fuel development—$541.4-million; the administration requested $480-million.

● Solar energy—$319.7-million; the administration requested $162.5-million.

● Geothermal energy—$68-million; the administration requested $50.1-million.

● Conservation—$241.5-million; the administration request was $120-million.

Final Action

The House Sept. 30 approved the conference version of HR 13350 by voice vote after several colloquies establishing the narrow focus of the synthetic fuel loan guarantee provisions.

After the end of the filibuster on the Clean Air Act Amendments late Friday afternoon, Oct. 1, the ERDA conference report was to come up for Senate approval, just ahead of the omnibus rivers and harbors bill (S 3823), of which Mike Gravel (D Alaska) was floor manager.

But a last-minute administration objection to the revised wording of the nuclear exports section of HR 13350 was raised. Republicans objected to consideration of the ERDA bill at that point, knocking it out of its protected place ahead of the politically potent water projects measure. Later that evening the administration objection was lifted.

But it was well after midnight before the ERDA measure was back in line for consideration, as the last order of business of the Senate during the 94th Congress. Jackson, Senate Interior Committee chairman, asked for its consideration. Gravel responded with a request that the clerk read the entire document—which was more than 150 pages in length.

"I certainly do not understand this kind of a move after a year's effort...to get a bill that will place some guidelines on ERDA," said Jackson. "What the Senator from Alaska will do is give ERDA a blank check. They can do what they want within the appropriations areas...."

"There is no apparent rational reason" for Gravel's action, Jackson continued. "I know the real reason.... You want to be on the [Joint] Atomic Energy Committee."

"That is right," Gravel responded. "I was prepared to make a deal with you."

"Imagine," responded Jackson, "a senator of the United States. I am one who will not be blackmailed. I will tell you right now."

Jackson said that Gravel had come to him, saying that he would not block the ERDA conference report if Jackson, a member of the steering committee and in line to be the ranking Senate Democrat on the joint committee, would help Gravel obtain a joint committee seat.

Gravel confirmed Jackson's statement, saying that he had tried to get on the Atomic Energy Committee for eight years and charging that some of the Senate leaders had blocked that effort "for the very simple reason that I was not part of the establishment with respect to the nuclear situation."

As a result of Gravel's action, Jackson withdrew the request for consideration of HR 13350.

Synthetic Fuels

Legislation (HR 12112) authorizing federal loan guarantees and price supports for development of synthetic fuels was killed by the House late in the 1976 session when it voted 192-193 on Sept. 23 to defeat the rule for floor consideration. This echoed a 1975 House action knocking synthetic fuels authorizations out of a broader bill.

Opponents of the bill argued that the measure was too new, too complex and too unstudied to be considered responsibly before the scheduled Oct. 2 adjournment. Different versions of HR 12112 had been reported by four committees and a new substitute had been slated for consideration on the House floor.

An unusual coalition of fiscal conservatives and environmentally sensitive liberals combined to reject the measure, which was supported by the Ford administration, the AFL-CIO, the U.S. Chamber of Commerce, the National Association of Manufacturers, the American Gas Association and the oil shale industry. Allied against the bill were the United Auto Workers, the Environmental Policy Center, the Sierra Club, Friends of the Earth and Congress Watch, among others.

In mid-1975, the Senate inserted language authorizing $6-billion in federal loan guarantees for synthetic fuel commercialization in the fiscal 1976 authorization bill for the Energy Research and Development Administration (ERDA). The Ford administration threw its support behind such aid, proposing additional forms of assistance for synthetic fuel development, including construction grants and price subsidies. But the House, which had not addressed this issue before the final version of the ERDA authorization bill arrived on the floor late in the year, killed the loan guarantee provision before approving the ERDA bill. *(Story p. 46-A)*

House Committee Action

The House Science and Technology Committee May 15, 1976, reported HR 12112. The bill provided up to $4-billion in federal loan guarantees for programs to demonstrate the feasibility, and the costs and benefits, of synthetic fuel technologies and of new methods for conserving energy, converting urban waste to fuel and for using solar energy and other renewable sources. It also provided various forms of aid to communities impacted by the development of these new energy technologies, particularly by synthetic fuel plants (H Rept 94-1170).

After being reported, HR 12112 was referred to three other House committees. Each reported the bill in June with proposed amendments. The House Banking, Currency and Housing Committee reported the bill June 18, proposing to amend the bill to authorize slightly less—$3.5-billion—in loan guarantees plus $500-million in price supports (H Rept 94-1170, Part 2). The House Ways and Means Committee reported the bill June 21 and suggested amendments to some of the tax-related provisions of its community assistance sections allowing ERDA to guarantee municipal or local bonds (H Rept 94-1170, Part 3).

And the House Interstate and Foreign Commerce Committee proposed a complete substitute for the Science Committee bill, cutting back the loan guarantee program to a $2-billion program, available only to projects demonstrating synthetic fuel production from biomass (various forms of waste) and oil shale, demonstrating energy-saving techniques and using renewable resources. In new separate programs, the Commerce Committee bill provided regulatory support and up to $500-million in price guarantees for synthetic fuels produced from coal (H Rept 94-1170, Part 4).

The leadership did not move to bring the bill to the floor and new questions about the wisdom of providing such aid to the embryonic synthetic fuels industry were raised by a Government Accounting Office (GAO) study released Aug. 24.

"Synthetic fuels production is not cost effective in that the total cost of output is not price competitive with foreign oil," the report stated.

"In the present circumstances, GAO believes government financial assistance for commercial development of synthetic fuels should not be provided at this time. Full priority should be directed to development of improved synthetic fuels technologies; however, it appears possible to gain adequate information of an environmental and regulatory nature from smaller plants under government control. When commercialization of the technology becomes a prime objective, consideration also should be given to approaches other than loan guarantees for gaining private industry interest."

But Science and Technology Committee Chairman Olin E. Teague (D Texas) Sept. 1 wrote House Speaker Carl Albert (D Okla.) threatening to tie up the House during its final weeks through parliamentary obstruction unless the Rules Committee acted on the bill. As a result the panel added HR 12112 to its agenda and Sept. 15 granted a rule by voice vote. The rule would have allowed for consideration of a Teague substitute which had not been reported from any committee authorizing $3.5-billion in federal loan guarantees and $500-million in price supports. It was that rule which was defeated Sept. 23.

Senate provisions authorizing $900-million in loan guarantees for production of synthetic fuels from biomass were included in the conference version of the fiscal 1977 ERDA authorization bill (HR 13350), but the bill died at the end of the session. *(Story p. 63-A)*

House Floor Action

The House Sept. 23 rejected, by the key vote of 192-193 (R 82-42; D 110-151), the rule (H Res 1545) which would have allowed four hours of debate on the comprehensive substitute for HR 12112 drawn up by Science Committee Chairman Teague.

Key provisions of the Teague substitute:

● Authorized $3.5-billion in loan guarantees to be administered by the Energy Research and Development Administration (ERDA) over the next nine years for development of synthetic fuel technologies.

● Permitted up to 50 per cent of the guarantees to be used for high-Btu coal gasification; up to 30 per cent for fossil-based synthetic fuels, including oil shale; and up to 50 per cent for such renewable energy sources as solar, geothermal and biomass.

● Authorized $500-million in price supports for synthetic fuels beginning in fiscal 1978.

Proponents of the measure, led by Teague and Rep. John B. Anderson (R Ill.), argued that the legislation's merits had long been studied and that the question deserved to be decided on the House floor. Teague said Senate Interior and Insular Affairs Committee Chairman Henry M. Jackson (D Wash.) had assured him the Senate would pass the measure this session if it passed the House.

Opponents saw the question differently. "I think it is an absolute outrage that we are asked to consider this important legislation with just five legislative days left," commented Rep. Richard L. Ottinger (D N.Y.).

Resentful of Teague's threat of parliamentary obstruction, the 80-year-old chairman of the Rules Committee, Ray J. Madden (D Ind.), said the measure was expected to draw up to 50 amendments and would tie up the House for days. He termed the legislation "too complicated, too controversial and too long delayed" to be considered. "This is not only a turkey, it's a gobbler," he said.

Nuclear Regulatory Funds

Congress in 1976 authorized $274.3-million for the operations of the Nuclear Regultory Commission (NRC) in fiscal 1977, and appropriated $244.4-million.

In approving the authorization measure (S 3107—PL 94-291), Congress restored the full amount initially requested by the NRC for supervising the U.S. nuclear power industry, rejecting a reduction of $24.9-million exacted by the Office of Management and Budget.

The Joint Atomic Energy Committee had endorsed the full NRC request for funding its fiscal 1977 salaries and expenses, arguing that the newly created agency "should receive the resources it needs to get the job done" in controlling the risks of nuclear power development.

Despite continuing concern over nuclear plant safety and nuclear material hazards, neither the House nor the Senate spent much time debating the NRC request. Both gave quick approval to authorizing legislation (S 3107) that the joint committee had reported May 3 (S Rept 94-772).

The joint panel's proposal included a $20.9-million authorization increase for nuclear regulatory research, primarily for development of ways to verify reactor safety. On top of the administration's $122.4-million proposal, which contemplated doubling research efforts on nuclear safeguards, the committee's amendment brought the research authorization up to the NRC's $143.3-million request.

The Senate May 5 passed S 3107 by voice vote without debate. The House May 10 by a 356-5 recorded vote passed an identical bill (HR 12387) that the joint committee had reported separately (H Rept 94-1079).

The House then took up the Senate version (S 3107) and passed it by voice vote, clearing the measure.

Congress appropriated $244,430,000 for the NRC in fiscal 1977, including that amount in the Energy-Public Works appropriations bill (HR 14236—PL 94-355). The amount appropriated was $5-million less than requested.

Clean Air

A last-minute Senate filibuster killed a complex measure amending the Clean Air Act of 1970 (PL 91-604). The bill (S 3219), killed Oct. 1, included provisions extending deadlines for compliance with auto emission standards until 1979, except for a less stringent nitrogen oxide limit effective in 1981. Defeat of the bill left the auto industry under the timetable in existing law, imposing strict emission limits for tailpipe pollutants on 1978 model cars.

Vertical Divestiture

The explosive oil divestiture issue, long buried in committee, was reported to the Senate floor for the first time in 1976. But the Senate leadership was reluctant to take the controversial, time-consuming issue to the floor in an elec-

tion year—especially when the bill faced a certain veto—and it was never brought up for debate.

The proposal approved by the Senate Judiciary Committee June 15 by an 8-7 vote (S 2387) would have forced the breakup of the nation's 18 largest oil companies. It required companies engaged in production, marketing, refining and transportation to divest themselves of all but one phase of the business within five years, a procedure known as vertical divestiture. Under the existing system most major companies operated in all four areas and achieved substantial economies—and, critics said, market domination—by being able to supply their own needs with their own resources. The bill would have forced the companies to compete with each other in buying and selling the resources.

The first signs of growing support for oil company divestiture appeared in October 1975 when the Senate rejected by only nine votes, 45-54, a divestiture measure offered by Philip A. Hart (D Mich.) and James Abourezk (D S.D.) as an amendment to a natural gas deregulation bill (S 2310). Related divestiture amendments to the same bill were rejected by subsequent votes of 40-49 and 39-53. *(Story p. 53-A)*

The oil industry, which had been caught off guard by the 1975 divestiture votes on the Senate floor, mobilized a heavy lobbying campaign against the proposal. Birch Bayh (D Ind.) called it "the most sophisticated, elaborate and expensive lobby effort I've ever seen."

Before the 1975 Senate votes, the major congressional action on divestiture had been 10 years of hearings on the issue by the Senate Judiciary Subcommittee on Antitrust and Monopoly. Subcommittee Chairman Hart had nursed the bill through the hearings but avoided a subcommittee vote because he did not have the support to free the bill.

That situation changed at the beginning of the 94th Congress with the replacement on the subcommittee of conservative retirees with more liberal members. The reconstituted subcommittee April 1 approved S 2387 and sent it to the full committee by a vote of 4-3.

Provisions

S 2387 was formally reported (S Rept 94-1005) June 28. Major provisions of the bill:

● Defined a major marketer as one that markets or distributes 100 million barrels of refined petroleum products in a calendar year; a major producer as one that produces 36.5 million barrels of crude oil in a calendar year; a major refiner as one that refines 100 million barrels of oil in a calendar year.

● Made it illegal, five years after enactment, for any major producer to own or control any marketing, refining or transportation asset; for any petroleum transporter, including crude oil and refined product pipelines without regard to size, to own or control any production, refining or marketing asset; for any major refiner or major marketer to own or control any production or transportation asset; for anyone owning a refining, production or marketing asset to transport oil by a transportation asset in which he has an interest.

● Upon enactment, barred major refiners from owning or operating any marketing asset not operated before Jan. 1, 1976.

● Allowed the Federal Trade Commission (FTC) to exempt from the provisions of the act a transportation asset upon finding that the asset is so integral to the operations of the firm that no public purpose would be served by divestiture and that retention of the asset would not injure competition.

● Allowed the FTC to grant exemptions of up to one year from existing laws prohibiting interlocking relationships, in order to facilitate divestiture.

● Required firms affected by divestiture to provide the FTC with information it requests within 120 days.

● Gave the FTC jurisdiction over proxy solicitations by those affected by divestiture until divestiture is completed.

● Empowered the FTC to require submission of divestiture plans within 18 months of enactment; gave the FTC authority to approve, modify and enforce the plans.

● Directed the FTC to sue companies if necessary to assure compliance with the act.

● Provided civil penalties of $100,000 for an individual and $1-million for a corporation for violation of the act.

● Provided civil penalties of $100,000 for persons who violate orders issued by the FTC under the act, or $100,000 per day in cases of continuing noncompliance.

● Established a special Temporary Petroleum Industry Divestiture Court, consisting of at least three judges appointed by the Chief Justice of the United States from U.S. district court and courts of appeal judges.

● Empowered the U.S. Chief Justice to designate one of the judges as chief justice of the court.

● Gave the court the powers of a U.S. district court.

● Gave the court exclusive jurisdiction over matters arising from the act.

● Gave the U.S. Supreme Court sole jurisdiction over appeals arising from the temporary court; required any appeal petitions to be made to the Supreme Court within 30 days of an order or judgment by the temporary court; and instructed the Supreme Court to expedite action on matters arising from the act.

Energy Taxes

Some provisions of the energy tax bill approved by the House in 1975 (HR 6860) were included by the Senate Finance Committee in the tax revision bill (HR 10612) it reported in June 1976 and were approved by the Senate in August. But conferees on the measure deleted the energy-related provisions, which the Senate Finance Committee immediately ordered reported as an amended version of HR 6860 on Aug. 27 (S Rept 94-1181).

No further action was taken on the measure by the 94th Congress.

Natural Gas Deregulation

The continuing effort by the Ford administration and the energy industry to win enactment of legislation deregulating the price of natural gas was again unsuccessful in 1976. The primary reason was a July 27 decision by the Federal Power Commission (FPC) to substantially raise the price ceiling on natural gas sold in interstate commerce. That action reduced the pressure for deregulation. *(Box, next page)*

But even before the FPC move, enactment of a natural gas deregulation bill in the 94th Congress had become unlikely due to a complicated legislative situation. The Senate and House had passed legislation so different that a

compromise appeared impossible, and a new "compromise" bill subsequently reported to the Senate became unpopular even with its supporters.

Early in the 94th Congress it had appeared that some sort of legislative natural gas deregulation was likely. Advocates of deregulation, including President Ford, argued that the higher prices which would result from deregulation were needed to encourage increased exploration and development of domestic natural gas reserves and to channel more natural gas into interstate sales from the intrastate market where federal price controls did not apply. (When natural gas was sold within the state where it was produced, it sold, in 1975, for prices as high as three or four times the top regulated interstate price of 52 cents per thousand cubic feet.)

The Senate Oct. 22, 1975, passed a bill (S 2310) providing for gradual long-term price deregulation. S 2310 would have ended controls on "new" gas from onshore reserves immediately and terminated offshore gas regulation after five years. The House did not pass the bill before adjourning the first session, but the House Interstate and Foreign Commerce Committee did report an emergency short-term bill (HR 9464) before adjournment. *(p. 51-A)*

When the second session convened, HR 9464 was one of the early orders of business. When the bill reached the floor Feb. 3, the prospects for long-term deregulation looked good after the House voted 230-184 to adopt the rule granted by the Rules Committee that provided for consideration of a permanent deregulation alternative offered by Robert Krueger (D Texas). But then, in a surprise upset, the House voted 205-201 to adopt a substitute ending price controls over small gas producers but enlarging regulation of major companies and then went on to pass the bill.

The House-passed bill was so different from the 1975 Senate-passed measure that Senate supporters of deregulation chose not to take the bills to conference. Instead, they worked out a new bill (S 3422) to retain price controls but allow all prices to rise substantially above the existing 52 cents per thousand cubic feet limit set by the FPC. S 3422, which was reported May 19, was first hailed as a major compromise. But as it came under more scrutiny, industry opposed it, calling for a full lifting of controls. Consumer and labor groups objected that it was too costly to consumers. The measure never came up on the Senate floor.

House Action

With a vote that signaled victory to some proponents of deregulation, the House brought the natural gas issue to the floor Feb. 3, adopting the rule that allowed for consideration of deregulation along with the emergency short-term bill (HR 9464) approved by the Commerce Committee late in 1975. The vote was 230-184. Although a majority of Democrats (175) opposed the rule, 102 supported it.

The rule allowed for floor consideration of a long-term deregulation substitute by Robert Krueger (D Texas) that was similar to the terms of the 1975 Senate-passed bill. The substitute was opposed by a majority of Commerce Committee members, including Chairman Harley O. Staggers (D W.Va.) and Energy and Power Subcommittee Chairman John D. Dingell (D Mich.) who had succeeded in blocking its consideration by the committee.

Adoption of the rule outflanked the Commerce Committee leaders by bringing the Krueger proposal before the House. Once on the defensive, Dingell, Staggers, Rep. Bob Eckhardt (D Texas) and other hard-line deregulation opponents began a delaying action while preparing a compromise measure.

As the House neared adjournment on Feb. 4, deregulation foes brought up the compromise amendment that Commerce Committee staff members had been preparing while debate dragged on.

The compromise, offered by Neal Smith (D Iowa), deregulated prices of new natural gas sold by independent producers with sales of less than 100 billion cubic feet a year. The plan defined new gas as gas that was not dedicated to interstate commerce before Jan. 1, 1976.

While thus deregulating prices for 5,000 to 7,000 independent producers, supporters of Smith's amendment said it would keep controls in place on 25 to 30 major gas producers. The proposal actually enlarged controls over the major companies, moreover, by extending federal regulations to gas sold by those producers in intrastate markets not subject to the existing regulatory system.

The compromise proposal, a substitute for Krueger's own substitute amendment, authorized the FPC to set a national average price for that interstate and intrastate gas using flexible procedures more favorable to the producers than existing regulations, and considering future costs of production and the need for a reasonable rate of return.

Coming to a vote on the proposal with unexpected suddenness, the House Feb. 5 approved the Smith proposal by the key vote of 205-201 (R 13-117; D 192-84), thus replacing Krueger's long-term deregulation language with Smith's compromise provisons. The House then voted to replace the provisions of HR 9464 as approved by committee with the provisions of the Smith measure. The vote was 219-184. As written into the bill, Smith's amendment dropped the committee's initial recommendation for emergency sales of intrastate gas to interstate pipelines. Those provisions had been aimed at meeting a gas shortage which had not developed.

In a 198-204 recorded vote, the House then defeated a last-ditch attempt to revive the deregulation proposal, rejecting a motion by top-ranking Energy and Power Subcommittee Republican Clarence J. Brown (Ohio) to send HR 9464 back to committee with instructions to resubstitute Krueger's amendment.

The House then passed the amended bill by a 205-194 recorded vote.

Provisions

As passed by the House, major provisions of HR 9464:

Independent Producers

● Deregulated the price of new natural gas sold by an independent producer whose total marketed natural gas production during the previous year was 100 billion cubic feet or less.

● Defined new natural gas as that committed to interstate commerce for the first time after Jan. 1, 1976, pumped from a reservoir discovered after that date or produced from wells started and completed after that date in a previously discovered reservoir.

● Excluded from that definition natural gas produced from offshore federal lands under contracts for less than 15 years or less than the life of the reservoir.

● Included in that definition intrastate gas that had been sold in interstate commerce before the effective date of the bill under temporary contracts to meet emergency shortages.

The Regulators Deregulate

The Federal Power Commission further lessened the impetus for legislative action to deregulate natural gas prices by administrative action taken July 27, 1976. The FPC announced that it was increasing the nationwide price ceiling for 'new' interstate natural gas produced or contracted for after 1974 from the existing rate of 52 cents per thousand cubic feet of gas to $1.42 per thousand cubic feet. For gas produced in 1973-74, the ceiling was raised to $1.01. The increases brought the price of interstate gas closer in line with that of unregulated intrastate gas, which had been selling at $1.50 to $2.00 per thousand cubic feet.

The FPC justified its decision on grounds that both drilling costs and taxes had gone up for gas producers. Opposing groups, led by Energy Action, argued that the agency did not consider the issue fully before acting.

In announcing the increase, the FPC estimated that it would cost consumers $1.5-billion in the first year. The House Commerce Subcommittee on Oversight and Investigations Oct. 16, however, said preliminary data from interstate pipelines showed the cost would be at least $2.25-billion a year. The report said the decision defined new gas so loosely as to give producers an "overwhelming incentive...to convert 'old gas' into 'new gas' by drilling shallow and probably unnecessary wells in known fields."

The FPC Oct. 20 responded that producers had filed for rate increases totaling about $2-billion. Acknowledging that it had originally underestimated the impact of the increase, the FPC Nov. 5 revised the price ceiling for 1973-74 gas down to $.93 from $1.01. Further revisions were considered possible.

● Continued regulation of gas produced by an independent producer if that producer or an affiliate earned more than 10 per cent of its annual gross revenues by operating an interstate gas pipeline.

● Continued regulation of gas sold by an independent producer if major producers had direct interests in the proceeds or profits or held more than 20 per cent of royalty interests in the proceeds.

Major Producers

● Directed the Federal Power Commission (FPC) to set a national ceiling price for new natural gas sold in both interstate and intrastate commerce by a natural gas producer whose total marketed production during the previous year had exceeded 100 billion cubic feet.

● Applied that ceiling to gas sold in intrastate markets under contracts signed after the FPC established the ceiling.

● Directed the FPC, in setting the national ceiling price, to take account of the prospective costs of producing gas and a reasonable rate of return required to provide adequate incentives to attract capital investments and encourage exploration and development of new natural gas resources.

● Allowed the FPC to set price limits higher than the national ceiling if necessary to take account of extraordinary costs incurred in drilling deep wells or undertaking other high-cost, high-risk projects.

Natural Gas Conservation

● Directed the FPC to prohibit boiler-fuel use of natural gas not contracted for before Jan. 1, 1976. The commission could waive that prohibition if it found that no alternative fuels were available.

● Directed the FPC to prohibit boiler-fuel use of natural gas sold under existing contracts when the contracts expire.

● Allowed the FPC to exempt the burning of natural gas to operate pollution abatement systems from the prohibition on boiler-fuel use.

● Forbade the FPC to prohibit boiler-fuel use of natural gas to alleviate short-term air quality emergencies or other public dangers.

● Directed the FPC to assure continued natural gas supplies to agricultural and food-processing users in drawing plans for curtailing less essential uses if shortages occur.

Senate Action

Senate deregulation proponents resisted a conference on the 1975 Senate gas bill and 1976 House bill, worrying that Senate Democratic conferees opposed to deregulation would go along with the House approach. That left deregulation legislation in limbo until six Senate supporters and opponents of deregulation came up with a new compromise bill. The bill (S 3422—S Rept 94-907) was reported May 19 by the Senate Commerce Committee.

S 3422 followed the general format of the Senate's 1975 deregulation legislation, drawing distinctions between existing and "new" natural gas production and between onshore and offshore gas fields.

The compromise measure, while allowing new gas prices to rise, kept onshore production under congressionally dictated price limits for seven years. And it left offshore gas from federal lands subject to permanent FPC regulations at higher prices keyed to domestic oil prices.

For new onshore gas, the bill set a $1.60 per thousand cubic feet ceiling price substantially above the average unregulated intrastate price of $1.29. During the seven years after enactment, interstate pipelines would be prohibited from paying higher prices for new onshore gas.

The measure directed the FPC to adjust the new onshore gas ceiling price at three-month intervals to offset the general inflation rate. The FPC also could authorize higher prices for gas from high-cost production areas or deep wells.

For new offshore gas, S 3422 set a base price tied to federally regulated oil prices at the time of enactment. That base price, which was expected to work out to about $1.35 per thousand cubic feet, would stay in effect through the end of 1980 again with quarterly inflation rate adjustments.

After reviewing the 1976-80 base price, the FPC would set offshore gas price limits for the following five years.

While prospects for S 3422 originally appeared good, supporters and opponents of deregulation later spoke out against the bill and it was never brought up on the Senate floor.

Uranium Enrichment

President Ford's plan to open up the uranium enrichment industry to private enterprise died in the Senate in 1976. The proposal (HR 8401) was passed by the House after a series of close votes. But opponents kept it off the Senate floor until late in the session when a motion to bring it up was rejected.

HR 8401 would have permitted private industry to begin production of enriched uranium, ending 30 years of government monopoly over the technology. Uranium must be enriched to serve as fuel in nuclear power plants. The private nuclear power industry had been seeking such authority since 1969 with the support of the Nixon and Ford administrations.

As passed by the House Aug. 4, the bill authorized the Energy Research and Development Administration (ERDA) to make tentative contract agreements with private firms to produce enriched uranium. Such tentative contracts would be submitted to Congress, which would have to approve any contract within 60 days in order for it to take effect.

ERDA would have been authorized under HR 8401 to guarantee domestic investors that the government would assume all assets and liabilities, including debt, if a private uranium enrichment venture failed prior to the end of approximately one year of commercial operation. Foreign investment would not be protected under the guarantee.

ERDA would have been limited to $8-billion in contract authority, a figure estimated by the administration to be the maximum potential cost to the government if up to four private ventures covered by cooperative agreements with the government failed. The money was to cover costs of assuming assets and liabilities of the ventures, including taking over the plants.

HR 8401 also directed ERDA to expand the federally-owned enrichment facility at Portsmouth, Ohio, and authorized $255-million in fiscal 1977 for that project.

The controversial nature of HR 8401 was reflected by House floor votes on an amendment by Jonathan B. Bingham (D N.Y.) which would have dropped all of the bill's provisions except expansion of the federal facility at Portsmouth. The amendment was originally accepted 170-168, but then rejected by a key vote, 192-193. The Senate's Sept. 29 vote against bringing the bill to the floor was also close—33-30.

Background

Conventional nuclear reactors generate power by tapping the energy released as the nuclei of uranium isotope atoms are split when bombarded with neutrons. That fissioning can be achieved, however, only in the lighter of the two uranium isotopes, U-235, that makes up the element in its natural state.

U-235 makes up only about 0.7 per cent of raw uranium, with the rest consisting of the heavier U-238 isotope, which has three additional neutrons in its atomic nucleus. But a larger U-235 concentration is required to make a fission reaction possible by ensuring that nuclei released from each split atom find another fissionable atom of U-235. So natural uranium must be enriched, increasing the proportion of U-235, to allow its use in nuclear reactions.

Since building the atomic bomb during World War II, the federal government has developed and operated the uranium enrichment processes required to produce sufficient quantities of U-235, both for U.S. nuclear weapons and for sale to domestic and foreign commercial power reactors.

For that purpose, the government between 1945 and 1956 built three enrichment plants—at Oak Ridge, Tenn.;

Paducah, Ky.; and Portsmouth, Ohio—using gaseous diffusion technology developed during the World War II nuclear bomb project.

Operated by private companies under contracts with the government, those plants provide enrichment services to both foreign and domestic customers.

Even with completion of $1-billion in improvements to expand output of the existing plants, their entire productive capacity has been fully obligated since 1974 for supplying about 300 existing and planned electric generating plants in the United States and overseas.

With the existing plants fully committed, "the next increment of enrichment capacity must be ready by 1983-84...," Robert C. Seamans Jr., ERDA administrator, contended in December testimony. "Beyond that, it is estimated that the United States will need three to five full-size enrichment facilities to supply fuel for the domestic nuclear powerplants expected to be completed in the 1984-2000 period."

And to keep U.S. control over nuclear fuel supplies to foreign nations, Seamans added, "another five to seven plants will be needed in the same time frame to meet the foreign market that we can and should supply."

With the federal budget already stretched tight, the Ford administration urged that private industry be allowed to build and operate all the additional enrichment capacity that U.S. nuclear fuel needs require.

Continuing a commercialization policy adopted by the Nixon administration in 1969, President Ford on June 26, 1975, sent Congress legislation to authorize ERDA to reach agreements with private companies that wanted to enter the enrichment business.

The proposed measure, termed the Nuclear Fuel Assurance Act (S 2035 and HR 8401), gave ERDA power to provide various technical assistance and government controlled technology that private companies would need to build and operate enrichment facilities.

The bill also gave ERDA authority to acquire a private enrichment project, and assume its liabilities, if the firm could not finish building the plant or bring the plant into operation.

To back up that commitment, the measure provided ERDA with contract authority of up to $8-billion, the estimated potential cost to the government if all projected private enrichment ventures failed.

UEA Plan

Ford's proposal envisioned several separate enrichment projects, including some that would use advanced technology being developed to enrich uranium by gas centrifuge and laser beam methods. But debate on commercialization centered on a proposal by a San Francisco-based consortium to build the first increment in enrichment capacity using the well-established gaseous diffusion technology that the three government plants perfected.

That group, known as Uranium Enrichment Associates (UEA), proposed to build a $3.5-billion gaseous diffusion plant near Dothan, Ala., that could supply about 90 large nuclear power plants.

Bechtel Corp., a San Francisco architect-engineering and construction company, has been the prime UEA participant. Other U.S. companies were expected to join UEA. The domestic partners were expected to put up about $1.4-billion of the project's cost, under tentative plans, with foreign participants supplying another $2.1-billion.

The domestic partners would control UEA operations, as required by the Atomic Energy Act of 1954, although foreign interests would contribute 60 per cent of the financing and contract for a proportional share of the plant's output. Major potential foreign participants included Iran and Japan, each with a 20 per cent interest, as well as France and West Germany.

The UEA plant was scheduled to start operations in 1981 and reach full production in 1983, a timetable that assumed federal government approval in 1976.

While private investors would supply the financing for the Alabama plant, the UEA proposal asked for several types of guarantees from the federal government. Those included both technical assurances and financial guarantees.

The proposed contract still was the subject of negotiations between ERDA and UEA officials. Under the agreement proposed by UEA in 1975, the federal government would:

● Supply essential enrichment machinery.
● Assure that the plant will work.
● Give UEA access to ERDA's stockpile of enriched uranium to meet its contracts.
● Buy up to two-thirds of the plant's output during the first five years if the nuclear powerplants expected to use the enriched uranium had not reached full operation.
● Agree to buy the domestic owners' interests in the plant and assume all domestic liabilities if the project failed before reaching full operation for one year.

Joint Committee Action

The Joint Atomic Energy Committee May 14 reported an amended version of HR 8401 (H Rept 94-1151). The bill had been approved May 11 by a 15-0 vote. The committee insisted on several changes in the administration plan that limited federal guarantees for private projects and required congressional scrutiny of the government's final contract for supplying assistance.

The key provisions of HR 8401 as reported and subsequently passed by the House authorized ERDA to contract with private industry to produce enriched uranium, guaranteeing that the government-supplied enrichment technology would work.

These contracts would be submitted to Congress, which would have 60 days to approve or disapprove a proposed contract.

The contract could be executed only if Congress approved a favorable concurrent resolution, and then the government liability under that contract could not exceed the amount approved previously for that purpose in an appropriations bill.

House Floor Action

The House passed HR 8401 Aug. 4 by a 222-168 vote.

Passage of the bill was not as easy as the final tally indicated. The key votes came by seesawing one- and two-vote margins on an amendment sponsored by Rep. Jonathan B. Bingham (D N.Y.) that would have eliminated from the bill all the provisions except those authorizing expansion of the government's Portsmouth, Ohio, enrichment facility, thereby maintaining the federal monopoly.

On Friday, July 30, the Bingham amendment was adopted 170-168.

On Aug. 4, the following Wednesday, the House reversed itself and by a key vote of 192-193 (R 18-117; D 174-76) rejected Bingham's proposal. On this vote, a 192-192 tie was broken when Speaker Carl Albert (D Okla.) voted against the amendment.

HR 8401 was the subject of three days of debate in the House—July 29, 30 and Aug. 4. The leading opponents of the legislation were unaccustomed allies—Reps. Joe Skubitz, a Kansas Republican, Joe L. Evins, a Tennessee Democrat, and Bingham, a New York Democrat. The spokesmen defending the bill were members of the Joint Atomic Energy Committee, primarily John B. Anderson (R Ill.) and Melvin Price (D Ill.).

Bingham charged that the bill "was tailored for one contract. It was tailored from the beginning to suit the needs of the combine known as UEA."

Bingham's attack on the measure was assisted by Skubitz, who expressed skepticism about ERDA's advocacy of the bill: "[I]n my role as a congressman, I have experienced the skullduggery, the half truths, and the demagoguery of the AEC when it attempted to make my state the atomic slop jar for the nation. In part because of that experience, I find it difficult to accept at face value the word of ERDA, the son of the old AEC. The same gang who set up business at AEC and discredited that agency is now operating within ERDA." Skubitz had opposed proposals to store nuclear waste materials in Kansas salt mines.

Anderson defended the bill by repeatedly saying it did not commit Congress to approval of any contract or construction of any private plant, but simply established a framework for prior congressional review of any cooperative effort between ERDA and private industry.

Bingham responded by arguing that UEA was trying to "get Congress to pass an innocuous-seeming bill and then come back later on and say, 'Well, you have agreed in principle. Now you are letting us down if you do not approve the contract.' "

A roll-call vote on the Bingham amendment on July 30 wound up at the end of the 15-minute voting period in a 168-168 tie. Reps. James H. Scheuer (D N.Y.) and Thomas L. Ashley (D Ohio) changed their votes from "no" to "aye," providing the margin of victory for the Bingham amendment despite the late "nay" votes of Reps. Olin E. Teague (D Texas) and Speaker Albert.

The House Aug. 4 proceeded to a second roll-call vote on the Bingham amendment with little further substantive debate. At the end of the 15-minute voting period, the Bingham forces were ahead 193-190. The switches from "yea" to "nay" of Majority Whip John J. McFall (D Calif.) and Robert W. Kasten Jr. (R Wis.) led to a tie at 192-192, which was broken when Speaker Albert voted against the amendment, killing it amid cheers from the Republican side of the aisle and boos and hisses from the Democrats. The House then approved the bill.

Senate Consideration Blocked

A late session attempt to bring HR 8401 to the Senate floor was blocked Sept. 29 on a 33-30 vote.

The Senate did not reject the measure on its merits. Rather, the vote was on a procedural motion to block consideration of the bill, and it was approved in part because full debate would have taken too much time. Congress was scheduled to adjourn three days later, and the Senate leadership hoped to push through several important bills prior to adjournment. Acting Majority Leader Robert C. Byrd (D W.Va.) made the motion to table the legislation.

Naval Petroleum Reserves

Congress in 1976 approved the Naval Petroleum Reserves Production Act (HR 49), granting President Ford's request to allow production of oil from reserves heretofore set aside for the exclusive use of the Navy. President Ford signed it into law (PL 94-258) April 5.

Without passage of such a measure, petroleum could be produced from these reserves only when Congress and the President agreed it was necessary for the national defense.

As sent to the President, HR 49 directed the Secretary of the Navy to begin production of oil from three of the four reserves within 90 days of enactment. Production would continue at the maximum efficient rate for no more than six years, unless the President and Congress approved a three-year extension. The President was given authority to store the oil in a strategic petroleum reserve for use in national emergencies such as another oil embargo. Congress subsequently appropriated $406,116,000 for the production of oil from these reserves. That sum was included in the fiscal 1977 appropriations bill for the Interior Department (HR 14231—PL 94-355).

HR 49 transferred to the jurisdiction of the Interior Department the fourth reserve, the largest and richest, which was located in Alaska. It designated it a national reserve to be explored and studied. The bill barred production of oil from the Alaskan reserve until Congress explicitly approved it.

Final action came when the House, by a 390-5 vote, adopted the conference report on the bill. The Senate had adopted the report by voice vote March 24. The original bills had been very different. The final bill, which was completely rewritten, represented a compromise between the two versions.

Debate over the wisdom of tapping these reserves as part of the national effort toward energy self-sufficiency was compounded by several nonenergy-related factors. Among them was suspicion of the major oil companies—Standard Oil of California owned 20 per cent of one reserve (at Elk Hills, Calif.) and the only pipeline out of that reserve—and the extent to which they would benefit from production of these reserves. Other factors included environmental concern about military supervision of the development of the Alaskan reserve, memories of the Teapot Dome scandal, and jurisdictional conflicts between those who wished the Navy (and the House and Senate Armed Services Committees) to retain control over the reserves and those who wished the Interior Department (and the House and Senate Interior Committees) to have that supervisory responsibility.

The bill was passed by both chambers in 1975, with the House taking the approach favoring Interior and the Senate taking the approach favored by the military. *(See p. 53-A)*

Conference Action

House and Senate conferees, after seven meetings and many hours of informal negotiations, announced agreement March 4 on the final version of the bill. Their report (H Rept 94-942, S Rept 94-708) was filed March 23.

The report said that the differences between the two versions were so great that any side-by-side comparison was impractical. However, the major differences were resolved by:

• Dividing the reserves between the Navy, which would continue to supervise Elk Hills, Buena Vista and Teapot Dome, and the Interior Department, which would administer the Alaskan reserve, redesignated a national reserve. The Senate bill would have left all the reserves with the Navy; the House would have transferred them all to Interior. Congressional oversight responsibilities would likewise be divided between the Armed Services and Interior Committees.

• Retained the Senate limit on the period of production from the naval reserves, lengthening it to six from five years and providing for three-year extensions.

• Retained House language barring production from the Alaskan reserve without further explicit authorization from Congress.

• Deleted as unnecessary in light of passage of PL 94-163 Senate language authorizing creation of the strategic petroleum reserves, but authorized use of oil from the naval reserves to fill the strategic reserves.

Final Action

The House March 31 cleared HR 49 for the President, adopting the conference report by an overwhelming 390-5 recorded vote. The Senate had approved it by voice vote March 24.

Provisions

The major provisions of PL 94-258:

• Directed the transfer by June 1, 1977, of jurisdiction over the Naval Petroleum Reserve #4 to the Secretary of Interior, and redesignated that area as the National Petroleum Reserve in Alaska.

• Specified that the Secretary of the Interior would assume full responsibility for the protection of environmental, fish and wildlife, and historical or scenic values in this area; excluded these lands from coverage by the Mineral Leasing Act of 1920.

• Prohibited production of petroleum from the reserve, and any development leading to production until such activity was authorized by Congress.

• Provided for continuation of the ongoing petroleum exploration program in the reserve by the Secretary of the Navy until the transfer to Interior; provided for further exploration after the transfer to Interior.

• Directed an executive branch study to determine the best procedure for development, production, transportation and distribution of the petroleum resources in the reserve, giving consideration to the economic and environmental consequences of that production.

• Authorized whatever appropriations were necessary to carry out the provisions relating to the Alaskan reserve.

• Directed the Secretary of the Navy to commence production of petroleum from Naval Petroleum Reserves #1 (Elk Hills), #2 (Buena Vista) and #3 (Teapot Dome) within 90 days of enactment of HR 49, and to continue production at the maximum efficient rate for a period of six years.

• Provided that the President could, at the end of the six-year period, extend the period of production for any of the naval reserves by up to three years after an investigation finding such continued production necessary, and after submitting the report of that investigation to Congress and certifying that such production was in the national interest.

• Gave either chamber of Congress 90 days after receiving this report to veto the extension of the production period.

• Conditioned authorization for production from the Elk Hills reserve upon agreement by the private owner of any interest in that reserve to continue operating the reserve as a unit in a manner adequately protecting the public interest; empowered the Secretary, if agreement was not reached in 90 days of enactment of HR 49, to exercise condemnation authority to acquire that interest. (Standard Oil of California owned 20 per cent of the Elk Hills reserve.)

• Authorized the use, storage, or sale to the highest bidder, of the petroleum produced from the reserves; stated that no contract could be awarded allowing any person to control more than 20 per cent of the estimated annual U.S. share of oil produced from Elk Hills.

• Directed the Secretary of the Navy to consult with the Attorney General on matters relating to the development and production of this oil that might affect competition; gave the Attorney General veto power over any contract or operating agreement that could create or maintain a situation inconsistent with antitrust laws.

• Redefined the term "national defense" in the law dealing with the naval petroleum reserves to allow production from them to meet economic emergencies such as that resulting from the 1973 Arab oil embargo.

• Stated that any pipeline which carried oil produced from Elk Hills or Teapot Dome should do so without discrimination and at reasonable rates as a common carrier.

• Directed that any new pipeline for the Elk Hills reserve should have the capacity to carry at least 350,000 barrels of oil a day within three years after enactment of PL 94-258.

• Gave the President authority to place any or all of the U.S. share of petroleum produced from the naval petroleum reserves in the national strategic petroleum reserve set up by the Energy Policy and Conservation Act (PL 94-163)—or be exchanged for oil of equal value to be placed in that reserve.

• Set up in the Treasury Department a "Naval Petroleum Reserves Special Account" to receive all proceeds from sale of the U.S. share of the oil produced from the reserves, any related royalties or other revenues from the operation of the reserves and any additional sums appropriated for the maintenance, operation or development of the reserves; specified that these funds could be used for 1) further exploration and development of the reserves; 2) production from the reserves; 3) the construction of facilities related to the production and delivery of the petroleum, and their operation; 4) the procurement of oil for and the construction and operation of facilities for the strategic petroleum reserve; and 5) exploration and study of the national petroleum reserve in Alaska.

Coal Leasing

Congress in 1976 overrode President Ford's veto—and coal industry opposition—to enact S 391, the Federal Coal Leasing Amendments Act, which revised the procedures for leasing and development of federal coal deposits (PL 94-377).

President Ford vetoed the bill July 3, saying it would cause unnecessary delay in coal production from federal lands and increase coal prices.

Rebutting Ford's objections, the Senate Aug. 3 overrode the veto by a 76-17 vote. The House Aug. 4 completed the override by a 316-85 vote. Both votes were well over the required two-thirds majority.

Ford's veto was his 24th during the 94th Congress, and his 51st since taking office in August 1974. It was only the sixth Ford veto to be overridden by the 94th Congress.

The Senate had approved S 391 in July 1975, after attaching provisions to regulate strip mining of coal on public lands. The House passed its version, without any strip mining provisions in January 1976. The bill had never gone to conference, in part because key House members refused to attach any strip mining provisions to the bill unless they applied to private as well as public lands. In June, giving up the effort to link the two issues, the Senate by voice vote adopted the House version of the bill. *(1975 action, p. 55-A)*

Coal accounts for almost 75 per cent of the nation's recoverable reserves of fossil fuels. It is estimated that the coal deposits on federal lands amount to half the national total of reserves, but in 1974 production from these leases amounted to only 3 per cent of national production. A primary purpose of PL 94-377 was to spur the efficient development of these national resources.

House Action

The House Jan. 21 passed HR 6721, revising procedures governing the leasing and development of coal deposits on federal lands. The vote was 344-51. The House then substituted the provisions of the companion Senate-passed measure (S 391) by voice vote.

The full House went along with its Interior and Insular Affairs Committee, which reported the bill Nov. 21, 1975 (H Rept 94-681), in refusing to add strip mining regulations to the measure.

The strip mining controversy was mentioned several times during House debate on HR 6721, but the House rejected the only amendment proposed to link the two. It would have barred new coal strip mines on federal lands until such time as Congress approved a strip mining bill. *(1976 action on strip mining, p. 77-A)*

Also soundly rejected were a set of amendments proposed by Philip E. Ruppe (R Mich.) and backed by the Ford administration. The administration had indicated late in 1975 that it would oppose the bill unless these amendments were adopted. The effect of most of them would have been to preserve existing procedures and requirements for the coal leasing program.

The House adopted other amendments that:

● Reduced to 10 years from 15 the period for which a lease could be held without development.

● Allowed a governor to delay for six months issuance of a lease to allow strip mining within a national forest in his state.

Bill Cleared

There was no further action on S 391 for months after House passage because the Senate refused to consider clearing the bill without strip mining provisions for federal lands and the House held out for separate legislation providing for strip mining controls on private as well as federal lands.

Concluding that "prospects for timely enactment of strip mine legislation in this Congress are not bright," Interior Subcommittee on Minerals, Materials and Fuels Chairman Lee Metcalf (D Mont.) finally brought the House version of S 391 directly to the Senate floor June 21. With conference action unlikely, Metcalf urged that the Senate accept the House changes as the only way to send a bill to the President in 1976.

After brief debate, the Senate cleared the bill by voice vote.

Veto

President Ford July 3 vetoed S 391, objecting that its requirements "would inhibit coal production on federal lands, probably raise prices for consumers and ultimately delay our achievement of energy independence."

While calling for revised coal leasing provisions, the President embraced amendments that Congress wrote into S 391 to boost state federal leasing revenues to help state and local governments cope with federal energy development. Those provisions increased state shares of federal mineral leasing revenues to 50 per cent from 37½ per cent.

The Office of Management and Budget (OMB) had opposed the 50 per cent mineral leasing revenue formula, contending that energy impact aid instead should be conferred through the President's own $1-billion proposal for planning grants, loans and loan guarantees for both coastal and inland western states.

Ford nonetheless accepted the approach of S 391 as the form of impact assistance for western states chosen by Congress. "If S 391 were limited to that provision, I would sign it," he declared. But Ford objected to the "rigidities, complications and burdensome regulations" that the measure's coal leasing provisions imposed. Following Interior Department objections, he protested provisions setting 12½ per cent minimum royalties and requiring production of federal leases within 10 years.

The Senate Aug. 3 overrode the veto by a 76-17 vote. The House followed suit Aug. 4, 316-85, enacting the measure into law.

Provisions

As enacted, major provisions of PL 94-377 amended the Mineral Leasing Act of 1920 to:

● Require that coal leases be issued only by competitive bidding and that at least 50 per cent of all lands leased in any year be leased on the basis of a deferred bonus bidding system.

● Forbid issuance of new leases to any leaseholder who has not produced any coal on a lease for 15 years—beginning to count only from the date of enactment of PL 94-377.

● Require inclusion of federally owned coal leases in a comprehensive land use plan before any of that land was leased for coal development and allow leasing only if compatible with that plan.

● Require disapproval of any mining plan or lease which will not achieve the maximum economic recovery of coal.

● Eliminate use of coal prospecting permits and preference right leases, replacing them with a system of non-exclusive exploratory licenses; make unlicensed exploration subject to a fine of up to $1,000 per day.

● Authorized the Interior Secretary to consolidate, or require leaseholders to consolidate, several mining tracts into one logical mining unit (LMU) not to exceed 25,000 acres in order to foster the most economically efficient mining; require all reserves within the unit to be mined within 40 years.

● Provide that coal leases would be for a term of 20 years and so long afterwards as coal is being produced in commercial quantities; require termination of any lease not producing in such quantity after 10 years.

● Increase the minimum royalty from $.05 per ton to 12.5 per cent of the value of the coal, except for underground coal for which the Secretary could set a lower royalty.

● Permit the Secretary to waive the requirement that a lease be continuously operated, if the leaseholder paid an advance royalty for each year of non-production no less than that which would have been paid in a producing year.

● Require federal exploration of lands to be offered for leasing, with publication of all resulting data.

● Increase to 50 per cent from 37.5 per cent the state share in revenues from leases within the state; allow use of the additional 12.5 per cent for planning, construction and maintenance of public facilities; provide that all revenues from geothermal leasing be divided between state and federal treasuries in the same manner as those from coal leasing.

● Limit to 100,000 acres the amount of federal coal lands which any corporation, person, association, subsidiary or affiliate could control at one time.

● Give a governor a chance to delay for six months proposed leases for surface mining in national forests within his state. The Interior Secretary was required to reconsider the proposed lease during that six-month period in light of the governor's objections.

Strip Mining Control

The House Rules Committee twice in 1976 blocked revival of federal strip mining legislation (HR 9725, HR 13950), sparing members a tough election year energy vs. environment vote in a veto showdown with President Ford.

The Rules Committee's refusal to clear the bills for floor action doomed Democratic efforts to resurrect in 1976 a proposal that Ford had vetoed twice before. House Democrats had lost an epic veto battle with the administration over a similar 1975 bill and the President had pocket-vetoed an earlier version after the session ended in 1974.

The first 1976 version was approved by the Interior and Insular Affairs Committee, 28-11. It included some modifications of the earlier legislation that had been aimed at objections raised during intensive administration, coal company and electric utility lobbying against the 1975 measure.

Despite the modifications, the administration continued to oppose the bill.

Advocates of the legislation mounted a new push for passage late in the summer, after Congress passed, over presidential veto, a measure (S 391) revising the procedures for leasing federal coal deposits for development. Most of this coal, located in the western states, would be strip-mined, and environmentalists expressed concern that federal leasing should not resume without passage of some strip mining standards. *(Story p. 75-A)*

The House Interior Committee Aug. 9 began marking up a slightly revised strip mining bill (HR 13950) which it reported Aug. 31. HR 13950 came before the Rules Committee Sept. 15. The panel tabled it on a 9-6 vote, ending once and for all its chance for enactment by the 94th Congress.

Coastal States Aid

Congress in 1976 amended the Coastal Zone Management Act of 1972 to authorize a $1.2-billion program of federal aid to coastal states, to assist them in dealing with the effects of offshore gas and oil development (S 586—PL 94-370).

The new aid program consisted of $800-million in loan and bond guarantee authority to be used over a 10-year period and $400-million authorized for direct grants to coastal states, for use over an eight-year period ending in fiscal 1984. Sponsors of the program hoped that the aid would moderate fears in those states of social, environmental and economic disruption resulting from the development of resources on the Outer Continental Shelf (OCS). By relating the amount available to each state to the volume of oil and gas produced off its shores and the level of new energy activity in the state, members of Congress hoped also to speed up OCS development.

S 586, approved by the Senate in July 1975 and by the House in March 1976, was the only OCS measure enacted by the 94th Congress. Its passage, and that of related measures, was complicated both by overlapping jurisdictions within the House and Senate and by conflicting views on the need for the legislation.

Neither the oil industry nor the Ford administration displayed any enthusiasm for proposed changes in the way offshore development was currently administered, questioning the need for new procedures or requirements, but President Ford signed S 586 July 26. In his 1976 energy message, Ford had proposed creation of a $1-billion program of federal aid to areas affected by federal energy resource development. Congress did not act on that proposal in 1976.

As it moved to the White House, S 586 was criticized by some members who had worked hard for the measure earlier in the process. To escape an administration veto, conferees on the bill inserted new language—in neither the House nor Senate version of the measure—to make federal grants a last resort for states and cities seeking aid for building or expanding public facilities and services made necessary by coastal energy development. By making this use of these funds contingent upon a finding that loans or bond guarantees were unavailable for that purpose, the new provision reduced the probable level of federal spending under the grant program.

Members of Congress from Louisiana, a state already substantially impacted by offshore oil and gas development, protested this change as severely reducing the assistance which that state would obtain under the new billion-dollar program. Proponents of the measure responded with figures estimating that of the $400-million in grant funds, $188-million would go to Gulf states, $112-million to Alaska, $56-million to Atlantic Coast states and $43-million to Pacific Coast states.

At one point, provisions of S 586 were included in a bill (S 521) revising OCS leasing procedures. Enactment of S 586 removed the impetus for action on the more controversial leasing bill and it died when the House recommitted the conference report. *(Story, p. 79-A)*

Senate Action

As approved by the Senate July 16, 1975, by a vote of 73-15, S 586 authorized automatic grants of up to $100-million a year for fiscal years 1976-78, facility grants or loans of up to $200-million a year for fiscal years 1976-78, and federal guarantees of state or local bond issues needed to finance OCS-related public facilities.

House Committee Action

The House Merchant Marine and Fisheries Committee March 4 reported a companion to S 586 (HR 3981—H Rept 94-878) authorizing $1.45-billion in new impact aid to coastal states over five years. The bill also provided federal guarantees for up to $200-million in state and local government bonds for public facilities and services required by offshore energy development.

The complex measure also liberalized federal aid to help 34 states and territories develop coastal management plans.

All in all, the committee contended in its report, those measures were needed to help coastal states step up their planning to protect their coastlines. Since Congress first set up federal machinery to encourage state coastal management policies in 1972, the committee pointed out, the nation's need for petroleum imports and domestic offshore reserves "has dramatically added to the great stresses which already exist in our coastal areas."

In recommending that the House follow the multi-faceted approach to coastline development aid that the Senate approved in 1975, the committee dismissed President Ford's proposal for a $1-billion impact loan program to help both coastal and interior states deal with energy development.

Following the Senate bill's format, the House committee recommended a two-part impact aid program for coastal states, automatic federal payments and discretionary federal grants.

States were directed to use the funds for the following purposes, in order of priority: retiring federally guaranteed bonds issued under the bill's provisions, planning and carrying out additional public facilities and services, and mitigating the loss of ecological or recreational resources.

In a significant change from the Senate bill, the panel restricted use of grants under the companion discretionary impact assistance program to public projects prompted by facilities that could only be built along coastlines.

The Senate's approach, which made grants available for coping with a broader range of energy developments, "runs the risk...of providing inducement to locate such facilities on the coasts," the committee argued. Environmentalists supported the change.

House Floor Action

The House March 11 passed HR 3981 by a 370-14 vote, making only minor changes in the committee bill. It then substituted the provisions of HR 3981 for those of S 586, and approved its version of the Senate bill.

Conference Action

Conferees filed their report (H Rept 94-1298) June 24. Major differences between the two versions of the bill were resolved by:

● Broadening the Senate formula for calculating a state's share of the automatic grant monies to give more weight to indicators of new energy activity within the state.

● Adopting Senate provisions providing that this aid would be administered through loans, as well as grants and guarantees.

● Providing for an $800-million ceiling on bond and loan guarantees instead of the $200-million ceiling set by the House.

● Authorizing the House amount, $400-million over eight years, for the automatic grants, rather than the Senate amount, $300-million over three years.

In a controversial last-minute change justified by conferees as necessary to avoid a veto of the bill, the conference committee inserted a new provision allowing states to use grant funds for new public services and facilities only if they were not able to obtain the funds for these services and facilities through federal loans or bond guarantees.

Final Action

The Senate adopted the conference report by voice vote June 29.

"The primary assistance offered by the [new aid] program...for financing public facilities and services made necessary by any coastal energy activity," explained Ernest F. Hollings (D S.C.) June 29, "are federal loans and bond guarantees, not grants. Initial assistance...is in the form of credit rather than grants because in many cases the adverse fiscal impacts experienced by a coastal state or local government will only be temporary and will be offset later on by increased tax revenues from the coastal energy activity involved" which would allow repayment of the loan or retirement of the bonds.

The House June 30 approved the conference report by a 391-14 vote.

The condition placed on the use of grants for public facilities and services, said Pierre S. (Pete) du Pont (R Del.), was approved by the House conferees by a vote of 4-3. "This change had the effect of inserting a major discretionary element into an otherwise straightforward and uncomplicated grant provision," he said. "I feel that we have, in effect, robbed the coastal states of the one previously attractive feature which they overwhelmingly supported."

Provisions

As signed into law, the major provisions of PL 94-370 amended the 1972 Coastal Zone Management Act to authorize a coastal energy impact program to provide federal aid to help coastal states deal with the impact of offshore oil and gas development. Aid would be provided through:

● Planning grants for up to 80 per cent of the cost of studying and planning for any economic, social or environmental consequence of coastal energy development.

● Loans to coastal states and local government units to aid in providing new or improved public facilities or services needed as a result of coastal energy activity.

● Guarantees of bonds issued by coastal states or local governments for the purpose of providing new or improved public facilities or public services required as a result of coastal energy activity.

● Automatic annual grants to states. Each state's share would be calculated on the basis of four factors:

(1) the volume of oil and gas produced from OCS acreage adjacent to the state during the preceding year;

(2) the volume of oil and gas produced from OCS acreage leased by the federal government which was first landed in that state during the preceding year;

(3) the amount of OCS acreage adjacent to the state and newly leased in the preceding year, and

(4) the number of persons residing in that state who obtain new jobs in that year as a result of new or expanded OCS energy activities.

The grant funds could be used for three purposes:

(1) to retire state and local bonds which had been federally guaranteed under this aid program;

(2) to prevent or ameliorate any unavoidable loss, as a result of coastal energy activity, of valuable environmental or recreational resources in the coastal zone;

(3) to provide new or improved public facilities and services required as a direct result of new or expanded OCS energy activity and approved as eligible by the Secretary—but funds could be used for this purpose *only if* aid for these programs was unavailable under the loan or bond guarantee provisions.

To finance this aid, the bill set up a Coastal Energy Impact Fund in the Treasury, a revolving fund based on appropriations.

PL 94-370 authorized $50-million for automatic grants for each fiscal year from 1977 through 1984; and $800-million for other forms of aid under the new program through fiscal 1986.

PL 94-370 further amended the 1972 Act to:

● Increase to 80 per cent the federal share of costs of completion and initial implementation of state coastal zone management plans, authorizing $20-million per year for development grants and $50-million a year for implementation grants for fiscal years 1977, 1978 and 1979.

● Require every federal lease for exploration, development or production of OCS energy resources that affects the coastal zone of a state to be certified by the state as consistent with its coastal zone management program before any license or permit could be issued for such OCS activity.

Outer Continental Shelf

The efforts of the 94th Congress to revise the procedures guiding development of federal offshore oil and gas resources ended in failure late in September 1976. The House Sept. 28, by a 198-194 vote, recommitted the Outer Continental Shelf Lands Act Amendments (S 521) to conference with instructions that two controversial provisions of the bill be modified.

The chief sponsors of the bill—Rep. John M. Murphy (D N.Y.) and Sen. Henry M. Jackson (D Wash.)—decided that it would be futile to reconvene the conferees for further action so late in the session.

The vote to recommit the bill was a victory for the oil and gas industry and the Ford administration which had opposed the measure as creating unnecessary delays in the process of leasing and developing Outer Continental Shelf (OCS) oil and gas. They contended that the existing framework for leasing and development, which left considerable discretion to the Secretary of the Interior, was sufficient. If the bill had reached the President, a veto was probable.

The Senate had approved its version of S 521 in July 1975, by a vote of 67-19. A year later, in July 1976, the House had approved its version (HR 6218), 247-140. *(1975 action, p. 54-A)*

Conferees filed their report (H Rept 94-1632) Sept. 20. The final version of the bill was similar to the House measure. Conferees had rejected a list of more than 50 administration-proposed changes in the measure.

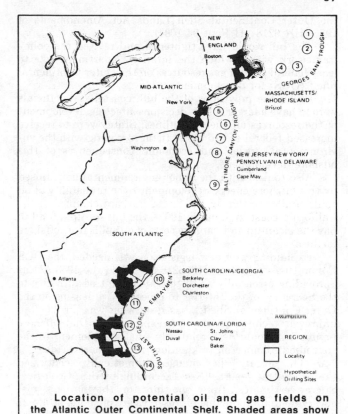

Location of potential oil and gas fields on the Atlantic Outer Continental Shelf. Shaded areas show onshore regions which would be affected economically by offshore operations.

The major provisions of S 521 required the Interior Secretary to develop a five-year leasing plan for frontier OCS areas. All subsequent lease sales would have to be consistent with that plan.

The bill gave the states affected by OCS development a larger voice in federal OCS decisions, requiring the Interior Secretary to accept the recommendations of governors or regional advisory boards on leasing decisions, unless they were inconsistent with the national interest. It also attempted to open OCS bidding to more oil and gas companies other than the majors.

The two controversial provisions that conferees were directed to reconsider by the recommittal motion were Senate language authorizing the federal government to contract for exploratory drilling on the OCS—to obtain an independent evaluation of the resources there before putting them up for bid—and the provisions revamping the existing structure for formulating safety regulations for the OCS operations.

Although S 521 died, the 94th Congress did clear a related bill (S 586—PL 94-370), some of whose provisions had once been part of S 521, expanding federal aid to coastal states that would feel the populations, economic and environmental impact of offshore oil development. Enactment of S 586 as a separate bill in July diminished pressure for Congress to clear the less popular leasing bill. *(Story p. 77-A)*

House Committee Action

The Ad Hoc Select Committee on the Outer Continental Shelf May 4 reported the bill it was created to consider, the Outer Continental Shelf Lands Act Amendments of 1976 (HR 6218—H Rept 94-1084).

The bill would have tightened and revised the policy framework within which the Interior Department acts to lease federal oil and gas resources on the Outer Continental Shelf (OCS) for development.

Under the provisions of the bill, coastal state officials were to have a larger role in decisions affecting development of the resources off their coastlines. States were to receive increased federal aid to assist them in coping with the environmental, social and economic consequences of this offshore development.

Also to deal with the major environmental issue raised by this offshore energy development—the probability of oil spills similar to that in the Santa Barbara channel off the California coast in January 1969—the bill set up a fund to pay the clean-up and damage costs of oil spills from offshore facilities.

Explaining why new legislation was needed, the OCS Committee's report on HR 6218 described the 1953 Act as "providing essentially an open-ended grant of authority to the Secretary of the Interior to proceed with leasing on the Outer Continental Shelf,...based on what was, in 1954, an unproven technology, and on expectations that offshore production would be a relatively small supplement to the continued reliance on production from onshore fields.

"This situation has changed dramatically," continued the committee report. "Now, according to U.S. Geological Survey estimates, fully one-third of the nation's discoverable and producible oil reserves are offshore, as are 22 per cent of our natural gas deposits.... It is today's reliance on Outer Continental Shelf resources, given conclusively demonstrated proof by the since-modified but still accelerated, plan to lease millions of acres in the next few years—that has spurred the move to reform OCS procedures and to provide new protections."

All six Republican members of the ad hoc committee joined in a statement of their views criticizing the bill for creating a "bureaucratic nightmare" that would "frustrate the very purposes" it was intended to achieve. The six were Hamilton Fish Jr. (N.Y.), Edwin B. Forsythe (N.J.), Pierre S. (Pete) du Pont (Del.), Donald E. Young (Alaska), Robert E. Bauman (Md.) and Charles E. Wiggins (Calif.).

"The administrative delays built into the committee bill must be eliminated, if it is to serve both our energy and our environmental needs," they wrote, promising to propose, as a floor amendment, a substitute for Title II of the bill as reported.

House Floor Action

After the committee had completed work on the bill, the Ford administration proposed more than 30 changes to the bill. Negotiations began on those points. The House began general debate on HR 6218 June 4. Consideration of amendments began June 11 and 14 before the bill was laid aside as the House moved on to consider the various authorization and appropriations bills to be dealt with in June.

When debate resumed July 21, the House disposed of more than 50 amendments to HR 6218, many of them compromises on relatively noncontroversial points worked out in an effort to ease administration opposition to the bill. It passed the bill that day by a 247-140 vote and then substituted the provisions for those of S 521.

Before passage, Fish offered a motion to recommit the bill with instructions to amend it on several major points. The House rejected the motion, 151-235.

Among the major changes made through House adoption of amendments to the committee-approved provisions were:

● An increase to 33 1/3 per cent from 10 per cent in the portion of total frontier area leases which must be leased under bidding systems other than the cash bonus system currently in use. This amendment was intended to increase competition in lease sales by allowing smaller companies with a smaller amount of ready cash to bid on the leases.

● Revision of the grounds and procedures for cancellation of OCS leases only if there is actual demonstration of serious harm or damage which would not decrease over a reasonable period and which results from activity on the lease—and entitling the leaseholder to compensation.

● Deletion by voice vote of Title IV of HR 6218 as reported, which had authorized impact aid to coastal states, provisions made unnecessary by enactment of S 586.

● A grant to Congress of the right to review and veto all rules and regulations promulgated under the amended OCS Lands Act.

The liveliest debate on the bill came as the House refused to adopt amendments that were designed to cure what the administration considered to be major defects in the bill. Among these were a comprehensive amendment in the form of a minority-sponsored substitute for Title II of HR 6218, the portion amending the OCS Lands Act. This substitute title, proposed July 11 by Fish, contained a number of changes responsive to administration objections, including 1) provisions allowing 10-year (not five-year) leases, 2) elimination of the percentage requirement for use of new bidding systems in lease sales, 3) retention of responsibility for environmental baseline studies of OCS areas with the Interior Department (not the Commerce Department), 4) elimination of the pre-lease exploratory drilling requirement and 5) modification of the language requiring the Interior Secretary to accept all recommendations of states or regional advisory boards on OCS leasing matters unless they were inconsistent with national security or the overriding national interest. The House rejected this amendment June 14, 139-209.

The House also refused to delete the pre-lease drilling requirement. This change was proposed July 21 by Alphonzo Bell (R Calif.) who argued that drilling one well in an area often produced ambiguous results and that this requirement would discourage, rather than encourage exploration and development on the OCS. "By the explore-first-lease-later approach what we are doing is shifting some of the responsibility and the gamble for this highly risky exploratory activity from the oil company to the federal government and the taxpayer," he continued. The House rejected the Bell amendment July 21 by a 17-23 standing vote.

The House rejected a proposal to modify the "veto" power given states and regional advisory boards. Proposed July 21 by Edwin B. Forsythe (R N.J.), this amendment would have required the Interior Secretary to consider state and regional recommendations, but would have allowed him to reject them so long as he explained his reasons in writing. The language in the bill as reported, said Forsythe, "does not balance state and national interest, but gives state interests the upper hand. The present language assumes that, except in the case of those specified conflicts of national security or overriding national interest, whenever there is a disagreement between a Governor and the Secretary over the size, timing or location of a lease sale or over a development plan, the Governor is always right and the Secretary is always wrong. This is a fundamentally dangerous assumption for development decisions regarding a federally owned resource."

John M. Murphy (D N.Y.) responded by saying that the areas in which most such state and regional recommendations would come would be ones involving the safety, environmental and onshore implications of OCS leasing and development. "The states are not given an absolute veto power," he continued, but to require a finding of national interest or security to override their recommendations "seems the most effective way of insuring that the Secretary actually will consider recommendations from the states seriously...." The House rejected the Forsythe amendment by voice vote.

Conference Action

Conferees filed their report (H Rept 94-1632) Sept. 20. The reported version of the bill generally followed the outline of the House version of S 521. As approved by conferees, the major provisions of the bill amended the Outer Continental Shelf Lands Act of 1953 to add provisions that:

● Required the Secretary of Interior to prepare a comprehensive five-year plan for leasing areas of the Outer Continental Shelf.

● Required all leaseholders, including those already awarded leases, to submit an exploration plan to the Secretary for approval before undertaking further exploration of a leased area.

● Required a leaseholder to submit a development and production plan to the Secretary for approval before beginning this phase of the operation.

● Authorized establishment, by the governors of states affected by OCS development, of regional OCS advisory boards to counsel the Secretary on all matters relating to OCS oil and gas development.

● Required the Secretary to accept specific recommendations of a regional board or an affected state's governor regarding the size, timing or location of a proposed lease sale or regarding a proposed development and production plan—unless the Secretary determined that the recommendation was not consistent with the national security or the overriding national interest.

● In addition, S 521 amended existing provisions of the 1953 Outer Continental Shelf Lands Act to:

● Authorize the leasing of OCS lands by the Secretary of Interior after competitive bidding on the basis of:

1) cash bonus bids with a royalty of at least 12.5 per cent;

2) variable royalty bids with a cash bonus determined by the Secretary;

3) cash bonus bids with diminishing or sliding royalties which initially were at least 12.5 per cent of the production from the lease;

4) cash bonus bids with a fixed share of the net profits which was at least 30 per cent of that derived from production from the lease;

5) fixed cash bonuses with the net profit share reserved as the bid variable;

6) cash bonus bids with a royalty of at least 12.5 per cent and a per cent share of net profits of at least 30 per cent;

7) cash bonus bids for 1 per cent shares of a working interest in the area, with shares awarded on the basis of the bid per share, with a fixed share of the net profits;

8) cash bonus bids for 1 per cent shares of a working interest in the area, with shares awarded on the basis of the bid per share, and with a fixed or diminishing royalty.

● Required the Secretary to use bidding systems other than the first—the cash bonus with fixed royalty—for at least 33 1/3 per cent of the total frontier OCS area offered for lease in each of the five years after enactment of S 521; allowed the Secretary to lease more than 66 2/3 per cent of the area in the first year under the cash bonus/fixed royalty bidding system if necessary to avoid undue delay in OCS oil and gas development; allowed the Secretary to exceed that limit in subsequent years only if he notified Congress of his reasons for doing so, and if his action was approved within 30 days by either the House or the Senate.

● Forbid joint bidding for an OCS lease by any two companies which both directly or indirectly controlled average daily production of oil, or its equivalent, of 1.6 million barrels or more.

● Provide that leases should be granted for an initial five-year term, or for 10 years if the longer term was necessary to encourage exploration and production under unusual circumstances.

● Prohibit awarding or extending a lease for any leaseholder found not to be exploiting the resources on all the leases he holds with due diligence.

● Provide for the suspension, by the Secretary of Interior, of activity on an OCS lease and for the cancellation of a lease (after a period of suspension and a hearing) if it is found that continued activity would cause serious harm or damage, not decreasing over a reasonable period of time, to life, property, mineral deposits, the national security or defense or the marine, coastal or human environment; provide for compensation to the holder of a canceled lease.

● Require the Secretary of Interior to have geological exploration drilling take place at least once in each frontier area—in the area most likely to contain oil and gas; authorize the Secretary to contract for such exploratory drilling on structures which he determined should be explored by the federal government for national security or environmental reasons or to expedite development in frontier areas; state that such exploratory drilling should not be done in areas included in the five-year leasing program prepared under the Act.

To deal with oil spills from any OCS facility or any vessel or other transportation device carrying oil and gas from the offshore facility, S 521:

● Established an offshore oil pollution compensation fund to receive appropriations and the revenues from a three-cent-per-barrel fee levied on oil produced on the OCS.

● Provided that the owner and operator of an offshore facility or vessel which spilled oil were liable, regardless of fault, for the full cleanup costs and for damages from such a spill without regard to fault unless they proved the spill to result from an act of war or the negligent and intentional act of a third party.

● Set limits on that liability of $35-million for the offshore facility owner and operator and $150 per gross registered ton for the vessel owner and operator—but specified that these limits did not apply—and their liability was unlimited—if the spill resulted from gross negligence, willful misconduct or violation of applicable regulations.

● Provided that the oil spill fund could be used to pay administrative expenses, public clean-up costs, private cleanup costs of an owner or operator when the discharge was caused by an act of war or negligence on the part of the federal government, and all damages not paid by the owner or operator of the responsible facility or vessel.

Report Recommitted

After brief debate, the House Sept. 28 voted to kill the bill, recommitting it by a vote of 198-194 to conference. The motion, offered by Fish, directed conferees to delete provisions authorizing federal exploration and to revise the bill's safety provisions to leave responsibility in that area where it was currently located.

Conference managers refused to reconvene sessions so close to adjournment; thus the recommittal motion killed the bill.

Electric Cars

In a notable election-year setback to the President, Congress Sept. 17, 1976, overrode Ford's veto of a bill (HR 8800) to promote development of electric-powered cars. The bill became PL 94-413.

It was only the 11th override by Congress out of 56 vetoes by Ford during his two years in the White House.

The House voted to override first on Sept. 16, by a 307-101 vote, 35 more than the necessary two-thirds majority.

The Senate followed suit the next day, 53-20, exceeding the two-thirds mark by four votes.

In vetoing the $160-million bill on Sept. 13, Ford had characterized it as an expensive and unnecessary congressional spending scheme. "I am not prepared to commit the federal government to this type of massive spending program which I believe private industry is best able to undertake," he said.

But supporters of the bill contended it was necessary precisely because the automobile industry had failed to meet the need. They said the President had vetoed the bill on "very bad advice," since it had support from Republicans and had been worked out with the administration in advance.

HR 8800 authorized $160-million, plus $60-million in loan guarantees, for a six-year program to develop and demonstrate electric cars suitable for mass production. Over the period, the government would procure some 7,500 such vehicles and distribute them for use by government, business and private motorists. The aim of the program, sponsors said, was at the second-car market that accounts for about 40 per cent of the automobiles on the road.

A companion bill (HR 13655) did not fare so well. HR 13655 authorized a five-year federal program to develop propulsion systems, such as the steam engine, that would provide an alternative to the gasoline-dependent internal combustion engine. President Ford vetoed it Sept. 24. The House also overrode that veto, but the Senate voted to sustain it. *(Story, p. 83-A)*

House Action

The House Science and Technology Committee reported HR 8600 July 31, 1975 (H Rept 94-439). The committee bill authorized $93-million in fiscal 1976-80 for research to advance the technology of electric cars and $67-million for production, distribution and use of demonstra-

tion models. The House passed the bill with minor changes Sept. 5, 1975, 308-60. *(Details, p. 56-A)*

Senate Action

The Senate Commerce Committee reported a similar bill (S 1632—S Rept 94-836) May 13.

The Senate June 14 passed HR 8800 by a vote of 72-16 after substituting the provisions of S 1632.

Both versions of HR 8800 had two elements: a research and development program in ERDA concentrating on battery technology, and a three-stage demonstration program.

Sponsors characterized the demonstration program as the heart of the bill. In specific stages over the five-year period, ERDA would 1) gather basic data on the existing state of the art of electric car technology; 2) using that data, develop standards for some 2,500 cars to be purchased by the government for demonstration purposes; and 3) using newly developed information, issue standards for 5,000 advanced-state cars also to be purchased by the government.

Conference Action

Conferees filed the conference report on HR 8800 in the House (H Rept 94-1363) on July 22 and in the Senate (S Rept 94-1048) on July 23.

The demonstration projects provided for in the House and Senate versions were similar in overall framework but different in detail. Where the two bills differed, essentially, involved the duration of the program and the degree of flexibility within it. The House program was both shorter and more rigid than the Senate's. It set up a four-and-one-half year demonstration schedule, with specific deadlines for completion of each stage and specific numbers of demonstration cars to be built for procurement.

The Senate bill, by contrast, established a five-year production schedule, with provision for extension of up to two additional years—a maximum of seven in all—for final production and procurement. Like the House bill, it set production targets of 2,500 second-stage vehicles and 5,000 third-stage vehicles, but it allowed the ERDA administrator to change those numbers to "whatever is appropriate for the adequate demonstration of the vehicles."

Conferees agreed to a six-year program phased over three stages, as follows:

1) Within one year of enactment, ERDA would develop "baseline data" on the state of the art of electric cars through the purchase and lease of "a reasonable number" of electric and hybrid—combination electric and other engine—vehicles.

2) Within 15 months of enactment, ERDA would issue performance standards for existing electric vehicles, and, within another six months, would contract for procurement of 2,500 vehicles, to be delivered within 39 months of enactment. If that number were unavailable for procurement, ERDA would notify Congress to that effect and then contract for the maximum available.

3) Within four years of enactment, ERDA would issue revised performance standards for advanced vehicles—electric and hybrid cars that represent a "significant improvement" over the earlier cars. Within six months more, ERDA would contract for 5,000 advanced cars for delivery within a year and a half—a total of six years after enactment. If fewer cars were available, the agency would notify Congress and contract for the maximum possible.

And the final deadline of six years could be extended another six months if it would permit procurement of more cars, up to the maximum 5,000.

Final Action

The Senate adopted the conference report Aug. 26 by voice vote; the House cleared the measure by voice vote Aug. 31.

President Ford vetoed HR 8800 Sept. 13, saying that electric car development should be left to the auto industry.

The President's veto appeared to take a number of Republicans by surprise and it was overridden in both houses after brief debate. The House voted to override Sept. 16, 307-101. The margin was 35 more than the necessary two-thirds majority. The Senate followed suit Sept. 17, by a four-vote margin, 53-20.

Provisions

As enacted into law, PL 94-413:

● Defined electric and hybrid vehicles as those powered by battery or other sources of electric current or by combinations of an electric motor and other engines, including internal combustion engines.

● Established a research, development and demonstration project in ERDA; provided specifically for research and development into 1) energy storage systems; 2) vehicle control systems, including regenerative braking; 3) urban design and traffic management to promote energy conservation and protection of the environment; and 4) vehicle design that emphasized durability, lifetime, ease of repair, and interchangeability of parts.

● Required ERDA, within 12 months of enactment, to develop data on the state of the art of electric car technology.

● Required ERDA, within another three months, to issue performance standards for existing vehicles and, within an additional six months, to purchase or lease 2,500 vehicles, or the maximum number available up to 2,500, for demonstration by government, business and private entities.

● Required ERDA, within four years of enactment, to issue performance standards for advanced electric and hybrid vehicles and, within another six months, to purchase or lease 5,000 such vehicles, or the maximum available up to 5,000 for demonstration purposes.

● Provided for federal guarantees of up to $60-million in loans for research and development, prototype development, capital construction and initial operating expenses of participants in the program; provided further that a loan could not exceed 90 per cent of the cost of a project, and that no loan to a borrower could exceed $3-million, except in specified circumstances.

● Required the U.S. Postal Service, the General Services Administration, the Defense Department and other federal agencies to study and arrange for use of electrical vehicles; permitted ERDA, if an agency determined vehicles to be uneconomical, to pay an agency for the extra cost of operating electric vehicles.

● Provided that the patent provisions of the Federal Non-nuclear Energy Research and Development Act of 1974 (PL 93-577) would apply to contracts under the program. *(Story p. 22-A)*

● Authorized $160-million, spread over fiscal 1977-81, for the program, and directed that $10-million be used for battery research in fiscal 1977.

Automotive Research

Two weeks after it rejected President Ford's veto of a bill to promote electric car development, Congress Sept. 29, 1976, backed down and sustained Ford's veto of companion legislation (HR 13655) that would have pumped federal money into development of advanced automobile engines.

The vote to sustain came late the afternoon of Sept. 29 when the Senate failed, 41-35, to override the veto of HR 13655. That was 10 short of the two-thirds required to override. Earlier in the day, the House had overridden the veto by a vote of 293-102, 29 more than the two-thirds required.

The Senate action killed a program that would have provided $100-million for the first two years of a five-year effort to find alternatives to the gasoline-consuming internal combustion engine. The program would have been a joint industry/government effort, with funding for later years to come in future authorizations for the Energy Research and Development Administration (ERDA)

In vetoing the bill Sept. 24, Ford objected that HR 13655 would: 1) duplicate existing ERDA programs, 2) invade "areas private industry is best equipped to pursue" and 3) be only the first step in "a massive spending program" that would require considerably more than the $100-million start-up funds.

But sponsors of the bill, arguing for an override, contended the extra program was necessary to spark what had previously been sluggish efforts by both ERDA and private industry. They stressed that the project was essentially a research and development program that would build on the existing ERDA work and would "supplement but not supplant" the automobile industry effort.

The Senate action was a reversal of its stand on the companion electric car bill (HR 8800). On Sept. 17 it overrode Ford's veto of HR 8800 by a 53-20 vote, four more than the two-thirds necessary. *(Story p. 82-A)*

Background

HR 13655 had a tangled legislative history. Its genesis was in a sweeping energy conservation bill (S 2176) that passed the Senate in late 1973 during the energy crisis precipitated by the Arab oil embargo. The bill was never acted on by the House. *(Story p. 17-A)*

In the 94th Congress, an automobile research program was included in a fuel economy bill (S 1883) passed by the Senate July 15, 1975. The entire bill subsequently was incorporated into a broader energy measure (S 622) that went before House and Senate conferees in September. Conferees approved a compromise version of the bill that included the automobile development provisions and on Dec. 9 sent it back to the House and Senate floors for final action, but the House voted 300-103 to strike the language from the conference bill. *(Story p. 37-A)*

Although the House and Senate committee bills shared the goal of developing fuel-efficient automobiles to reduce U.S. dependence on imported oil, they took widely divergent paths to that goal. The Senate bill supplied the Secretary of Transportation with hefty financing—$155-million, plus $175-million in loan guarantees—and instructed him to come up with a "car of the future" within four years.

The House committee bill was less ambitious, emphasizing technological advancement rather than actual prototype production. Accordingly, HR 13655 placed the administrative responsibility in a research agency, the Energy Research and Development Administration (ERDA), and directed it to concentrate on propulsion systems rather than whole cars. The funding was less too—$20-million in the first year with annual authorizations required thereafter.

The House passed HR 13655 June 3 without change. The Senate bill was passed June 14 after sponsors agreed to narrow the scope of the program and place it in ERDA instead of the Department of Transportation. Even so, the Senate-passed bill was much more ambitious than the House measure. The conference bill was scaled down considerably from the Senate version, but some Republicans warned that it still was too expensive for the administration—a prediction that turned out to be correct.

House Action

The House passed HR 13655 June 3 with relative ease, despite the opposition of the Ford administration which contended that the legislation was unnecessary because ERDA already had the authority to conduct such research. The vote on passage was 296-86.

The House Science and Technology Committee had reported the bill May 15 (H Rept 94-1169), authorizing a five-year research and development program administered by ERDA, conducted jointly by government and private industry, with initial funding authorized at $20-million for 1977. The objective of the program was the generation of knowledge and technology on advanced propulsion systems for automobiles.

Senate Action

The Senate passed its automotive technology measure (S 3267) June 14, 63-27, and then substituted its provisions for those of HR 13655.

The Senate Commerce Committee had reported S 3267 (S Rept 94-835) May 13, directing the Department of Transportation to develop production prototypes of advanced automobiles within four years of enactment. The bill authorized $155-million for in-house programs, grants and contracts and $175-million in guaranteed loans.

The Senate amended the Commerce Committee bill to narrow the focus of the program, to emphasize propulsion systems and to give ERDA, rather than the Department of Transportation, responsibility for administering the program. This amendment was adopted by voice vote, replacing another amendment even closer to the House-passed bill, which the Senate had first adopted, 46-43.

Conference Action

The conference report on HR 13655 was filed July 21 in the House (H Rept 94-1351) and the Senate (S Rept 94-1043).

The major issue before conferees was the scope of the federal program. The House had taken a very narrow approach, authorizing a modestly funded five-year program to boost private industry efforts to develop advanced propulsion systems.

The Senate bill was much broader. It authorized a major federal research and development program and provided considerable federal money, including loan guarantees, for a joint government-industry effort to develop entire cars, not only engines. The bill set timetables, stretched over a four-year period, for development of a fleet of advanced cars, numbering in the hundreds, that eventually would be procured by the government for use by such agencies as the Postal Service.

Although their report said they had settled on a "middle ground" between the two versions, conferees chose a plan much closer to the House bill. This authorized a five-year program for development of "advance automobile propulsion systems, advance automobile subsystems and integrated test vehicles." Emphasis would be on the propulsion systems, with lower priority given to subsystems, such as exhaust and braking, and prototype production.

Final Action

Final action on HR 13655 came Sept. 13 when the Senate voted 58-19 to adopt the conference report on the bill. The House had approved the conference report on Aug. 31 by voice vote.

Although HR 13655 had been scaled down considerably in conference from the $155-million bill passed June 14 by the Senate, Senate Republicans warned on the floor that the conference product still was too expensive for the administration. "It is a ridiculous, wasteful expenditure of the taxpayers' money," said Minority Whip Robert P. Griffin (R Mich.).

By involving the government in car development, Griffin argued, the bill would displace and discourage automobile development in the automobile industry.

President Ford vetoed HR 13655 Sept. 24. He said ERDA and the Transportation Department already had sufficient authority to accomplish the objectives of the bill.

The House Sept. 29 overrode the veto by a vote of 293-102, 29 over the two-thirds required. But the Senate later the same day sustained the veto, 41-35, falling 10 short of the two-thirds required.

Coal Slurry Pipelines

Coal slurry pipeline proponents failed in an effort to convince the 94th Congress to pass legislation to enable them to put their technology to use on a large scale.

Before they could begin to lay pipe, pipeline developers had to acquire from public and private landowners hundreds of miles of right-of-way from the mines to the markets. Among the major landholders were the railroads. They were counting on capturing a large share of the growing coal transport industry to revive their financially troubled industry and they refused to let the pipelines through.

In order to bypass the railroads and other recalcitrant landowners, the pipeline developers asked Congress to grant them the right of eminent domain—the power to take private land in the public interest—when they cannot purchase land through private negotiation.

The eminent domain legislation was at the center of a lobbying storm in the 94th Congress that was settled temporarily in favor of the railroads.

After postponing a decision for months, the House Interior and Insular Affairs Committee June 30, 1976, voted to table a pending eminent domain bill (HR 1863), thus killing it for the year.

Alaskan Gas

Hoping to expedite delivery of natural gas from Alaska to the lower 48 states, Congress in 1976 approved a measure

(S 3521—PL 94-586) setting deadlines for federal decisions on how to transport that fuel. President Ford signed it despite administration reservations about certain provisions.

PL 94-586 directed the President to tell Congress by Sept. 1, 1977, whether he recommended construction of a transport system to deliver Alaska's gas, and if so, directed him to specify the delivery system he preferred. For the decision to become effective, Congress would have to approve the choice by joint resolution within 60 days.

The measure provided for a steamlined decision process within the executive branch. Once a final decision was approved, the measure authorized federal officials to waive normal procedural restrictions in issuing permits to hasten construction and operation of the transport system.

The legislation also restricted judicial review of its provisions in an effort to avoid lengthy delays in construction of the system due to court challenges.

Congress declared in the legislation that "a natural gas supply shortage exists" and that expediting access to the gas reserves in Alaska could help ease the problem. Proponents of the bill argued that unless it was enacted a pipeline decision could be tied up in litigation for years.

Three proposals were pending before the Federal Power Commission (FPC) when the measure passed. One, submitted by the El Paso Alaska Company, sought permission to build an 800-mile pipeline parallel to the Alaskan oil pipeline from the North Slope to Southern Alaska. Gas would then be liquefied and shipped 1,900 nautical miles to Southern California and distributed from there, primarily through existing pipelines.

A second proposal from the Alaskan Arctic Gas Pipeline Co., a consortium of American and Canadian companies, called for construction of a 3,700-mile-long pipeline from the North Slope to the Mackenzie Delta area of Canada's northwest territories, where other gas reserves lay, then south to Alberta. From there the line would divide into two legs to serve markets in the American West and Midwest. Canadian pipeline customers would be served under that proposal as well as Americans. (In late 1976 the FPC staff recommended this plan.)

A third proposal pending before the FPC was submitted by the Northwest Pipeline Corporation. It called for a new pipeline parallel to the Alaskan oil pipeline to Delta Junction, where the new line would follow the Alcan Highway to the Alaska Yukon border. Canadian companies would sponsor a pipeline from the Yukon border to Fort Nelson, British Columbia and Zema Lake, Alberta, to connect with existing systems bringing the gas to the lower 48 states. The proposal would require construction of 1,700 new miles of pipeline.

At least one other proposal pending before Canadian authorities called for an all-Canada pipeline from the Mackenzie Delta. Also, the Westinghouse Oceanic Division and the U.S. Maritime Administration were studying prospects of bringing Alaska's natural gas to the contiguous 48 states in the form of methanol.

There were an estimated 26 trillion cubic feet of proved reserves of natural gas beneath Alaska's Prudhoe Bay, with more at Canada's Mackenzie Delta and Beaufort Sea. Current estimates concluded that the Prudhoe Bay reserves could supply 2 to 6 per cent of the United States total natural gas requirements.

Legislative History

The Senate approved S 3521 by voice vote July 1. The bill was jointly reported (S Rept 94-1020) June 30 by the Senate Commerce and Interior and Insular Affairs Committees.

The House by voice vote approved its version of S 3521 Sept. 30. The House Interstate and Foreign Commerce Committee had reported the bill Sept. 22 (H Rept 94-1658).

The Senate Oct. 1 cleared the measure by voice vote, approving it as amended by the House.

Provisions

As signed into law, the major provisions of PL 94-586:

● Required the FPC to recommend to the President by May 1, 1977, whether to proceed with a natural gas transportation system from Alaska, and if so, what kind.

● Required that the FPC recommendation "include provision for new facilities to the extent necessary to assure direct pipeline delivery of Alaska natural gas contemporaneously to points both east and west of the Rocky Mountains in the lower continental United States."

● Specified information which the FPC report must contain, including estimates of the annual gas volume expected from Alaska for 20 years, environmental and competitive impacts, and costs.

● Directed the President to report his recommendation to Congress by Sept. 1, 1977, although he could delay up to 90 days longer.

● Gave Congress 60 days to approve the President's recommendation by joint resolution. If not approved, the President was allowed 30 more days to offer a second and final recommendation.

● Limited judicial review of the legislation to challenges to the act's overall validity or allegations that action under the measure denied constitutional rights.

● Required that challenges to the act's constitutionality be filed within 60 days after its enactment.

● Required that challenges to federal actions under the measure be filed within 60 days of the action.

● Declared that congressional and presidential acceptance of submitted environmental impact statements would satisfy terms of the National Environmental Policy Act of 1969 and prohibited courts from considering that such accepted statements might be unsatisfactory.

● Required that the President report to Congress within six months on what procedures would be necessary to ensure fair allocation of Alaskan oil to the states of Washington, Oregon, Idaho, Montana, North Dakota, Minnesota, Michigan, Wisconsin, Illinois, Indiana and Ohio.

● Directed the Attorney General to study antitrust issues and problems relating to production and transport of Alaskan natural gas and report to Congress within six months.

Pipeline Safety

Congress in 1976 amended the Natural Gas Pipeline Safety Act of 1968 (PL 90-481) to increase authorized funds for the safety program, to allow citizen suits against violators of the law and to encourage consumer education.

The measure (HR 12168—PL 94-477) authorized $7.16-million for implementing the 1968 Act in fiscal 1977 and $9.5-million for fiscal 1978. PL 94-477 also authorized federal payment of up to the full cost to each state of employing three full-time pipeline safety inspectors, required all pipeline companies to conduct consumer education programs on gas leaks, and authorized citizen suits in federal court against persons not in compliance with the law. *(Background, earlier amendments, p. 34-A)*

Legislative History

HR 12168 had been approved by the House May 3; the Senate had approved a companion measure (S 2042) May 28. Conferees filed their report (H Rept 94-1660) Sept. 22. The House cleared the report Sept. 27 and the Senate followed suit Sept. 28.

Gasoline Retailers

A bill (HR 13000) restricting oil companies' authority to terminate the leases of gas station dealers and requiring public display of gasoline octane ratings was reported Sept. 18 by the House Interstate and Foreign Commerce Committee (H Rept 94-1615), but was never brought up on the House floor.

The legislation prohibited franchisors of motor fuels from cancelling a gas station owner's contract or failing to renew it, unless the contract termination met certain tests of "reasonableness" as detailed in the bill. Further, a legal lease cancellation under the bill could not be completed unless the franchisor notified the station operator in writing at least 90 days in advance of the termination, unless "reasonable circumstances" intervened.

Title II of the bill required the testing and certification of the octane ratings of gasoline, and public display of the ratings by gasoline retailers. The bill also required

automobile manufacturers to display proper octane requirements on the dashboards or fuel gauges of new vehicles.

The Senate in 1975 passed a bill (S 323) placing restrictions on the right of oil companies' to disenfranchise gas station operators. By voice vote on July 30, 1976, the Senate passed a measure (S 1508) requiring public display of gasoline octane ratings. *(Story p. 58-A)*

Energy Leadership

There was little change in the top energy-related posts in the Ford Administration in 1976. Frank G. Zarb, head of the Federal Energy Administration, remained the chief energy spokesman for the administration. Thomas S. Kleppe continued as Secretary of the Interior.

At the end of the year vacancies existed on the Nuclear Regulatory Commission (NRC) and the Federal Power Commission (FPC). Marcus Rowden, one of the original members of the NRC, became chairman when William Anders resigned, but the Senate did not confirm Ford's nomination of Joint Atomic Energy Committee executive director George F. Murphy Jr. to fill the fifth commission seat. Confirmation of Murphy's nomination was blocked by a threatened filibuster during the waning hours of the 94th Congress. Also dead at the end of the Congress was Ford's nomination of Barbara Ann Simpson to fill the vacant seat on the FPC; earlier in the year, Ford had reappointed John H. Holloman to his seat on the FPC.

Energy Legislation: 1977

Energy was the major issue for Carter and Congress in 1977 and the major one left unfinished.

The administration unveiled a massive plan in April designed to save energy by raising the price of fuel through taxes on crude oil, gas guzzling cars and business and industrial users of oil and natural gas.

Other proposals included switching industrial oil or natural gas users to coal, raising federal price controls on natural gas and extending controls to intrastate gas.

The omnibus energy program as submitted by the President included 113 separate proposals. The House passed the plan largely intact Aug. 5 as one omnibus bill (HR 8444).

The Senate took a different approach, breaking the package into six separate bills. The Senate eventually passed each bill, the last on Oct. 31, but the Senate-passed legislation differed drastically from Carter's proposals and the House-passed measure.

House and Senate conferees had reached compromise agreements on three of the five basic sections of the Carter energy plan by mid-December. But the remaining two portions, on natural gas pricing and on energy taxes, were still tied up in conference when Congress adjourned. *(Energy bill, 1977 action, p. 33)*

In contrast to the comprehensive energy bill, Carter's proposal to set up a Cabinet-level Department of Energy passed Congress by August. *(See DOE chapter, p. 45)*

With support from the White House, Congress July 21 cleared for President Carter's signature the Surface Mining Control and Reclamation Act of 1977 (HR 2). The action ended a five-year effort to regulate the strip mining of coal nationwide. Similar legislation was vetoed by President Ford in 1974 and 1975. *(See chapter on strip mining, p. 79)*

In other actions on energy Congress:
● Passed legislation providing funds for the development of a plutonium-producing nuclear breeder reactor at Clinch River, Tenn., despite Carter's request to terminate the project. Carter vetoed the bill Nov. 5.
● Cleared legislation giving Carter powers he sought to combat a natural gas shortage. The measure gave the President temporary authority to order transfers of interstate natural gas to areas where a merciless cold wave had so depleted fuel supplies that even homes and hospitals were in danger of having no heat. The legislation also gave the President authority through July 31 to approve sales of gas to interstate buyers at unregulated prices, a deviation from federal policies regulating gas sales first set in 1938.

The Senate passed legislation tightening federal regulation of offshore oil and gas development, but the bill never reached the House floor in 1977. (The measure cleared in 1978, however.)

Emergency Gas Bill

In their first major test, the new Democratic President and Congress proved they could work together smoothly—and quickly.

Six days after an unrelenting winter forced President Carter to request unprecedented powers to meet the nation's latest energy crisis, he had the powers he sought. Congress passed the Emergency Natural Gas Act of 1977 in less than a week.

The measure (S 474—PL 95-2) gave the President temporary authority to order transfers of interstate natural gas to areas where a merciless cold wave in the East had so depleted fuel supplies that even homes and hospitals were in danger of having no heat. The legislation also gave the President authority through July 31 to approve sales of gas to interstate buyers at unregulated prices, a deviation from federal policies first set in 1938.

"Our people are suffering," Carter said in requesting the powers. Congress could hardly have been unaware. The headlines and newscasts for weeks had told how record low temperatures and punishing blizzards had swept over the entire nation east of the Rocky Mountains, transforming already depleted fuel supplies into a crisis. Millions of workers were jobless, children were unable to attend schools, goods could not be transported and there was no early end in sight.

Despite muttered gripes that the administration had not consulted them early enough, the Democratic congressional leaders moved fast to give the President what he requested to meet the crisis.

The House held brief hearings on a Friday, marked the bill up in committee the following Monday, and voted the committee's bill through on Tuesday, Feb. 1, 367-52. The legislation contained only one major provision unsought by Carter.

The Senate hopped even quicker under the lash of Majority Leader Robert C. Byrd (D W.Va.). Ignoring the usual committee process, Byrd took Carter's bill straight to the floor. After two days debate, the Senate approved the bill without substantive amendment, 91-2.

Reaching a compromise took less than a day; the House amendment was dropped. On Feb. 2, the Senate approved the conference version by voice vote and the House cleared the measure, 336-82. Carter signed the bill that evening shortly before sitting down in the White House library, clad in a sweater, to deliver his first "fireside chat" via television to the American people.

Although Congress moved swiftly, few of its members were pleased with the legislation. It was designed only to ensure that homes not go heatless. It did nothing to generate more gas or to send workers back to their jobs. It did not cure the situation, but was intended only to help people live through it.

Provisions

As signed into law, PL 95-2:

● Gave the President authority to declare a natural gas emergency if he found a severe shortage endangering the supply for high priority use.

● Defined high-priority use as use in a residence, use in a commercial establishment in amounts of less than 50 mcf (thousand cubic feet) on a peak day, or use necessary to protect life and health or maintain physical property.

● Empowered the President to require any interstate or intrastate pipeline to transport emergency supplies of inter-state gas where directed through April 30, 1977.

● Empowered him to require pipelines to construct or operate facilities necessary for such emergency transpor-tation.

● Granted the President power to subpoena information to carry out his authority under the act and to require written interrogatories under oath.

● Provided antitrust protections for actions taken to com-ply with the act.

● Authorized through July 31, 1977, emergency purchases of gas from intrastate markets by interstate buyers at un-regulated prices as approved by the President.

● Established penalties of $25,000 a day for violations of orders to transport emergency supplies of gas and $50,000 a day for willful violations of such orders.

● Directed the President to require weekly reports on prices and volume of gas transported under the act and to report to Congress Oct. 1, 1977, on the operation of the act.

Background

The 1938 Natural Gas Act gave the Federal Power Commission (FPC) broad powers to regulate transportation and wholesale sales of natural gas in interstate commerce. Sales of gas within the state in which it was produced—intrastate—were not made subject to federal control.

The FPC's powers under the act were intended to benefit consumers. There usually are three sales transac-tions between the tapping of a gas reserve and its ultimate use by consumers, however, and the 1938 act limited the FPC's powers to govern them. The first step occurs when gas producers sell gas "at the wellhead" to a pipeline company. The pipeline company then sells the gas to local dis-tributors, such as gas companies or utilities. The local dis-tributor then sells the gas to consumers.

The 1938 act specifically authorized the FPC to regulate gas sales at only the second stage. Sales "at the wellhead" were unregulated initially. And sales from local distributors to customers were left to be regulated by state utility commissions. High prices charged "at the wellhead" frustrated the FPC's ability to hold down consumer prices because those initially high prices would force gas prices up at each subsequent stage of the sales chain.

The FPC's authority to set gas prices was given teeth June 7, 1954. The Supreme Court ruled 5-3 that day in the Phillips Petroleum case that the FPC could regulate inter-state gas sales "at the wellhead." Since that decision, the FPC's regulatory powers have been a burr in the seat of the

gas industry. Annual battles to cut back the authority were waged in Congress throughout the 1950s, but always failed.

Natural gas prices were held low throughout the 1950s and 1960s by strict FPC regulation. The cheap, clean-burning gas became increasingly attractive as a fuel source, until by the mid-1970s roughly 30 per cent of America's energy was fueled by natural gas.

The turning point for natural gas came in 1968. As that year started, there were 292.9 tcf (trillion cubic feet) of gas in domestic reserves. But finding new gas reserves had grown increasingly difficult and more expensive. The industry con-tended that new exploration and production was hardly worthwhile when its returns on such risky investments were held down by FPC regulation.

Domestic natural gas production peaked in 1973 at 22.6 tcf (trillion cubic feet), according to FPC sources. It fell 6 per cent in 1974 and another 7.5 per cent in 1975. During the first seven months of 1976, according to the Federal Energy Administration, production fell about 2 per cent more below 1975 levels.

To meet America's energy appetite, however, the known reserves continued to be tapped even while new discoveries failed to replace the gas used. At the end of 1975, the most recent year for which figures are available, total domestic gas reserves were 228 tcf.

What all that meant, according to Ray Sauve, special assistant to the FPC's Bureau of Natural Gas, was that, "In the past eight years, proved reserves in the lower 48 states have shrunk 42 per cent. During this time, we have con-sumed twice as much gas as we have found."

Price Hikes. For years the gas industry and the Nixon and Ford administrations pushed Congress to deregulate natural gas prices. Deregulation would drive prices up, bringing more money to the industry to finance increased exploration and production while encouraging consumers to use less gas, they reasoned. But the Democratic Congress refused, fearful of the impact of deregulation on the weak economy and on consumers' pocketbooks, and possibly on election returns as well.

But while prices remained regulated, the Republican-dominated FPC saw to it that those regulated prices went up.

Energy Action Committee, a consumer group, challenged the FPC price hikes in federal court. On Nov. 9, 1976, a federal appeals court ruled that the prices could go into effect provided that the increased costs to consumers were rebated later if the ceilings were ruled invalid. The case was still pending when S 474 was enacted.

While the industry did not oppose the increase, it still insisted that only decontrol would solve the problem. An in-dustry lobbying group, the Natural Gas Supply Committee, noted that the higher rates applied only to gas brought into production since 1973. Almost 87 per cent of the total gas being produced was on line before that, the industry group said, and therefore remained subject to the 52-cent rate. That meant the price hikes were bringing less money to the industry for exploration expenses than might otherwise be assumed, the group said.

Emergency Powers. Even before the passage of the emergency bill sought by Carter, the FPC was approving sales of large volumes of gas to interstate pipelines at un-regulated rates far above the regulated limits.

The commission claimed for itself authority to allow such emergency sales by adopting rules permitting such sales for up to 60 days. Section 7(c) of the 1938 Natural Gas

Act provided that the FPC could temporarily alter its regulations during emergencies.

A federal court in 1975 slapped down the commission's self-delegated authority to approve unregulated emergency gas sales for up to 180 days. But the 60-day emergency sales rule was not challenged in court.

With the worsening of the gas crisis, the FPC pushed its authority one step further Jan. 13 by approving a new to-day emergency sale at unregulated prices to two interstate pipelines already buying gas under a previous 60-day emergency sale permit. In effect, the commission approved back-to-back two-month periods of unregulated purchases by those companies, although the legal technicalities of the second order were juggled to distinguish the sale from the first.

Besides buying gas at unregulated prices through the emergency sales provision, some interstate companies had arranged to purchase gas from Canada. The Canadian National Energy Board in January approved several emergency shipments of gas to the United States to help meet the crisis there. In other cases, natural gas supplies had to be supplemented by synthetic gas, priced at $3.50 to $4.00 per mcf.

Senate Action

From the beginning, the Senate Democratic leadership worked closely with the Carter administration to pass the bill in the form requested by the new President.

Senate Majority Leader Robert C. Byrd (D W.Va.) introduced the measure (S 474) Jan. 26, the same day it was drafted. It went straight to the floor, bypassing committee review. After one day of debate Jan. 28, apparently designed to get positions on the record, the Senate convened Monday, Jan. 31, with Byrd warning repeatedly that there would be no recess until the measure was passed. He also stressed that the leadership would oppose all substantive amendments to avoid opening the measure to time-killing debate.

"It is imperative that we act upon this bill," Byrd stressed. Later there would be time for lengthy thrashing out of long-range solutions to the energy crisis, he advised, noting the administration had promised to deliver a comprehensive energy program to Capitol Hill by April 20.

His position made clear, Byrd and the bill's floor manager, Sen. Adlai E. Stevenson III (D Ill.), spent the next 10 hours batting down proposed amendments.

Except for the first two, which were purely technical amendments by Stevenson accepted without objection, no amendments were adopted. The Senate passed S 474, 91-2, on Jan. 31.

House Action

As in the Senate, the House Democratic leadership was committed to pushing the legislation through quickly. One day of hearings before an ad hoc subcommittee of the House Interstate and Foreign Commerce Committee was held Jan. 28, and the full committee marked up the bill Jan. 31. It was brought to the floor without a formal report and the next day the House passed it, 367-52.

Basically, the committee bill (HR 2500) was the same as that requested by Carter and passed by the Senate, with one important difference—an amendment by Rep. Bob Eckhardt (D Texas) that set a price ceiling on emergency gas sales. The Eckhardt amendment put a lid of $2.02 per thousand cubic feet of gas sold to interstate purchasers by

intrastate producers, and $2.22 for sales by intrastate pipelines and distributors.

Eckhardt argued that a ceiling would prevent a bidding war between purchasers for interstate customers and intrastate consumers. He said it was necessary to protect consumers in gas producing states such as Texas who had already been paying very high intrastate prices for years. The committee voted to include his amendment in the bill, 23-17.

The House version came to the floor with the Senate bill number under suspension of the rules, which meant that a tight time limit was imposed on debate, no amendments were allowed, and passage required a two-thirds majority.

The Eckhardt amendment drew fire from Rep. Clarence J. Brown (R Ohio) on the floor. The Eckhardt terms would limit interstate purchasers to paying only about the same price that producers already get from intrastate buyers, Brown said. That meant, he said, that "the prospect for sales to the desperately needy interstate market is unlikely."

But Majority Leader Jim Wright (D Texas) noted the measure had only limited intent. "When people are drowning, there is not time to build a better ship.... In the crisis at the moment, there is time only to throw out a lifeline."

Final Action

Resolution of the differences between the House and Senate versions of S 474 came quickly but with some confusion.

Following initial House passage, leaders from both chambers met informally Feb. 1 to work out a compromise. Once they did, the formal conference committee reached agreement in about 10 minutes. Their report (H Rept 95-7) was filed Feb. 2.

Conferees agreed to drop the Eckhardt amendment. The Carter administration preferred the Senate version, despite reports that Carter congressional liaison Frank Moore told House leaders, "We can live with it." Moore's position reportedly miffed Byrd, for it left him in an uncomfortable position. He could not easily return to the Senate and ask acceptance of any amendment after his unyielding efforts to block all amendments Jan. 31. So the Eckhardt amendment was dropped.

The Senate adopted the conference version of S 474 by voice vote with little debate Feb. 2. Stevenson assured the Senate that the bill was virtually the same as the one it approved two days before, except for clarifying language that did not alter the substance or intent of the legislation.

House leaders the same day made the same assurances but were met with obstinate skepticism. Rep. Joe D. Waggonner Jr. (D La.) insisted that the clarifying language added by conferees would result in opening all intrastate gas supplies to presidential allocation authority, and perhaps make it subject to FPC regulation in the future.

Reps. Harley O. Staggers (D W.Va.), John D. Dingell (D Mich.) and Brown all insisted that was neither the intent nor the case.

The House then cleared the conference version of S 474 Feb. 2, 336-82.

President Carter signed it into law (PL 95-2) the same day.

In a televised fireside chat that evening, Carter congratulated Congress "for its quick action." He designated FPC Chairman Richard L. Dunham to administer the new emergency powers.

The next day Dunham issued his first order, requiring daily transfers of 150 million cubic feet of gas from the West to the East.

Coal Slurry

The House Interior Committee late in the session agreed that in 1978 it would mark up a bill (HR 1609) to permit development of coal slurry pipelines.

Earlier in the year a joint session of two Interior subcommittees had voted to delay consideration of the measure. The Interior Committee's later action had the effect of recalling HR 1609 from those subcommittees and ensuring that it would not be buried there.

Background

Coal slurry technology involves crushing coal at the mine, mixing the powder with water and pumping the resultant mixture—slurry—through underground pipelines to distant utilities. The coal would be filtered and dried at the utility and burned to generate electricity.

But before they could begin to lay pipe, pipeline developers would have to acquire from public and private landowners hundreds of miles of right-of-way from the mines to the markets. Among the major landholders were the railroads. They were counting on capturing a large share of the growing coal transport industry to revive their financially troubled industry and they refused to let the pipelines through.

In order to bypass the railroads and other recalcitrant landowners, the pipeline developers asked Congress to grant them the right of eminent domain—the power to take private land in the public interest—when they cannot purchase land through private negotiation.

The eminent domain legislation was at the center of a lobbying storm in the 94th Congress that was settled temporarily in favor of the railroads. After postponing a decision for months, the House Interior and Insular Affairs Committee June 30, 1976, voted 21-19 to table a pending eminent domain bill (HR 1863), thus killing it for the year.

1977 Committee Action

In the 95th Congress new eminent domain legislation (HR 1609) was referred jointly to two subcommittees—Mines and Mining, and Indian Affairs and Public Lands.

In 1977, the two subcommittees teamed up to hold three days of hearings on HR 1609 in April and June. The testimony reiterated past arguments for and against the bill. Railroads said that the pipelines would rob their economically-troubled industry of a big share of the western coal boom. Environmentalists argued that the technology would use large quantities of water in water-short states like Wyoming. In addition, they said that since the technology has only been tried in a couple of places in the United States, its environmental effects were largely unknown.

Pipeline advocates repeated their arguments that they needed the right of eminent domain because railroads were blocking them from running pipelines across their lands. Railroads would not be able to deliver all the western coal needed in coal-short states, they said. They also said slurry pipelines would be cheaper and cleaner than rail delivery of coal.

On June 27 the combined membership of the two sub-

committees voted 13-12 to delay consideration of HR 1609 until 1978.

The full Interior Committee Oct. 12 voted 21-16 to recall HR 1609 from the subcommittees. But in a concession to opponents, it agreed not to mark up the bill until 1978.

The hour's debate before the vote was contentious. Opponents argued that it was unorthodox to recall a bill from subcommittee and said action should be postponed until the OTA study was completed.

Atomic Energy Committee

The Joint Atomic Energy Committee, once termed by scholars "the most powerful congressional committee in the history of the nation," went out of existence in 1977. The proposal was included in a package of House rules changes approved on opening day and an extensive Senate committee reorganization passed Feb. 4. Subsequently a bill (S 1153—PL 95-110) officially abolishing the committee was enacted routinely.

Background

The Atomic Energy Act of 1946 (PL 79-585) created the Atomic Energy Commission (AEC) and the Joint Committee to foster development of the new power of atomic energy.

It was the only permanent joint committee ever created that received continuing authority to report legislation. Granted unique oversight powers in its chartering act, the committee soon dominated policy formation to an extent unprecedented for a legislative panel. Sen. Henry M. Jackson (D Wash.), a long-time committee member, asserted as far back as 1953 that "the committee made the decisions, with the advice and consent of the executive branch," instead of the reverse, as was more usual.

A 1967 Brookings Institution study said the committee's philosophy toward nuclear power was best expressed by its own declaration in 1951: "Greater boldness...should be brought to bear upon the program."

For most of its life, the Joint Committee functioned almost as a unicameral legislature within the bicameral Congress. It usually reported identical bills simultaneously to each chamber, and when presented with floor amendments, resolved differences between House and Senate versions by functioning as its own conference committee.

Opponents' Campaign

In 1976, opponents of the Joint Committee began to flex their muscles and, unlike previous years, to win.

A Joint Committee proposal to open the uranium enrichment process to private investment was killed in the Senate. *(1976 action, p. 72-A)* A committee authorization measure funding the Energy Research and Development Administration (ERDA) was blocked in the Senate. *(1976 action, p. 63-A)* The appointment of a veteran Joint Committee staffer to the Nuclear Regulatory Commission (NRC) also was blocked.

There also was an increasing tendency for other committees to infringe upon the once exclusive jurisdiction of the Joint Committee. On Sept. 22, for example, the House voted 313-82 to allow another committee's bill on a nuclear question to come to the floor, despite howls of outrage from Joint Committee members.

Retirements and electoral defeats in November left six vacancies among the panel's 18 members. These trends indicated that the time was ripe to move against the Joint Committee.

Bingham Proposal. Rep. Jonathan B. Bingham (D N.Y.) led the charge. The key battle was fought Dec. 8 when the caucus of House Democrats voted to back Bingham's proposal to emasculate the Joint Committee.

Bingham proposed changing the House rules to strip the Joint Committee of all legislative powers except for an empty "oversight" authority.

With the Dec. 8 endorsement of the Bingham proposal by the Democratic Caucus, formal adoption by the full House came with ease Jan. 4. The proposal was included in a package of House reforms (H Res 5) that the Democrats muscled through, 256-142, on the 95th Congress' opening day.

· Specifically, the Bingham proposal:
● Assigned military nuclear concerns to the Committee on Armed Services;
● Assigned general regulation of the nuclear industry to the Committee on Interior and Insular Affairs;
● Assigned nuclear export questions to the Committee on International Relations;
● Assigned research and development questions to the Committee on Science and Technology;
● Assigned jurisdiction over facilities regulation and oversight to the Committee on Interstate and Foreign Commerce.

Opponents of nuclear power hailed the reform as providing nuclear power critics with access to policy questions from the subcommittee stage on up for the first time. Also, they welcomed the entry of the Interior Committee, headed by liberal environmentalist Morris K. Udall (D Ariz.), into direct nuclear power policy-making. Finally, the reforms seemed to put nuclear power on an equal footing with other energy technologies.

Senate Action. The Senate Feb. 4 passed, 89-1, a resolution providing for a major overhaul of the Senate committee structure. Among its elements was abolition of the Atomic Energy Committee. It shifted the Joint Committee's authority over military matters to the Senate Armed Services Committee; placed its authority over non-military development of nuclear energy in a new Committee on Energy and Natural Resources; and placed non-military environmental nuclear regulation in a new Committee on Environment and Public Works. Many aspects of the committee reform proposal were controversial, but there was no visible effort to block the changes that related to atomic energy.

Action on S 1153. The Senate March 31 passed by voice vote S 1153 amending the Atomic Energy Act (PL 83-703) to abolish the Joint Committee. The Senate-passed bill also contained provisions establishing a Senate Office of Classified National Security Information to provide a centralized office to safeguard classified data. It was to be used "under the policy direction" of the majority leader, minority leader and chairman of the Rules and Administration Committee.

The House passed S 1153 by voice vote Aug. 5 after removing the provisions that related only to the Senate. The Senate cleared it the same day by voice vote. It transferred the provisions dropped by the House to a resolution (S Res 252), which it also adopted by voice vote that day, completing action on the proposal.

Energy Extensions

A bill (S 1468) extending the life of the Federal Energy Administration (FEA) through fiscal 1978 and stepping up the schedule to fill the strategic oil reserves was cleared for the President by unanimous consent of the House June 30. The bill authorized $1.44-billion for FEA, of which $1.21-billion was for the oil reserves. President Carter signed S 1468 (PL 95-70) July 21.

The measure also extended through Dec. 31, 1978, the FEA's authority to order certain utility and industrial facilities to convert to coal. That authority was to expire after June 30; it was granted by section two of the Energy Supply and Environmental Coordination Act of 1974 (HR 14368 — PL 93-319). *(1974 action, p. 26-A)*

S 1468 (S Rept 95-123) first passed the Senate by voice vote May 11 providing only for a six-month extension of the FEA's authority to order conversion to coal.

On June 6, the House passed, 272-111, a bill (HR 6794) which extended the coal conversion authority through 1978, and the life of the FEA for that long as well. The FEA was set to expire Dec. 31, 1977, under existing law.

In addition, HR 6794 authorized $221-million for FEA operating funds in fiscal 1978, and $500-million for fiscal 1978 acquisition and storage of oil for the nation's strategic petroleum reserves. All those terms were included in the measure as reported May 16 by the House Interstate and Foreign Commerce Committee (H Rept 95-323).

On May 26, however, the administration had sent to Congress Energy Action Number 12, which would speed the schedule for the oil storage program so that 500 million barrels would be in place by the end of 1980, instead of 1982 as mandated by the Energy Policy and Conservation Act of 1975 (S 622 — PL 94-163). *(Details, p. 37-A)*

In line with the administration's request, the bill's sponsors in the House attempted to amend HR 6794 by unanimous consent June 6 to boost the oil storage program's funding level to $1.21-billion for fiscal 1978. But because the bill was considered under suspension of the rules, an objection by Rep. Steven D. Symms (R Idaho) blocked that move and the bill was passed with the lower amount. The House then substituted the terms of HR 6794 for S 1468, and returned it to the Senate.

The Senate June 8 approved S 1468 as amended by the House after accepting an amendment by Henry M. Jackson (D Wash.) adding the extra $710-million for the strategic oil program sought by the administration.

On June 30, the House approved S 1468 as amended by the Senate, clearing the measure for the President.

Though the FEA was extended by S 1468 through 1978 the agency was abolished Oct. 1 and its functions merged with the new Cabinet-level Department of Energy created by enactment of S 826 — PL 95-91 Aug. 4. *(Details, p. 45)*

Alaska Gas Route

Congress gave the go-ahead to one of the largest construction projects ever conceived. But doubts remained about who would put up the money.

The House and Senate Nov. 2 approved by voice votes H J Res 621 (PL 95-158), approving President Carter's choice of a pipeline route to carry natural gas from Alaska. The Senate the same day had passed S J Res 82, an identical resolution, by an 87-2 vote.

Presidential Decision

President Carter and Canadian Prime Minister Pierre Elliott Trudeau announced in Washington Sept. 8 their agreement in principle on a plan to build a pipeline from Alaska's North Slope through western Canada to transport natural gas to the American Midwest and West Coast. Eventually the pipeline would also move Canadian gas to Canadian markets.

The privately-financed pipeline, scheduled for completion by early 1983, was estimated to cost between $10- and $15-billion. About 3,600 miles long, it would be the longest natural gas pipeline ever built and the largest single private energy project.

Carter considered three major pipeline proposals before choosing the Canadian route. Called the Alcan-Foothills pipeline, it would follow the route of the new oil pipeline from Prudhoe Bay past Fairbanks, then approximately parallel the Alaska Highway through Canada and on to Calgary, Alberta. Existing pipelines branch southward from there to Canadian and American markets. The new pipeline would be built by subsidiaries of Northwest Pipeline Corp. of Salt Lake City and Foothills Pipe Lines Ltd. of Calgary.

Proposed Gas Routes

Alcan Route Selected

Carter rejected a plan by the El Paso Alaska Company to build an 800-mile gas pipeline to parallel the oil pipeline from Prudhoe Bay to Valdez, Alaska. Gas then would have been liquefied and shipped to Southern California. There had been considerable congressional support for the El Paso proposal.

A third proposal by Canadian and American companies (Arctic Gas) for a 3,700-mile pipeline that would have passed through the Mackenzie Delta in Canada was rejected by Canada for environmental and social reasons. Its backers then supported the Alcan-Foothills route.

In their joint statement Sept. 8, Carter and Trudeau said the Alcan-Foothills plan would save American consumers $6-billion more than the El Paso plan over the life of the project. Carter said the recommended proposal was cheaper, faster, safer, caused less damage to the environment and provided a more direct route to the Midwest. When completed, the project was to transport 3.5 billion cubic feet of natural gas daily to the United States and Canada.

Congressional Concerns

Congress' action Nov. 2 endorsing the decision was made in accordance with the terms of a 1976 law (PL 94-586). *(1976 action, p. 84-A)*

Endorsement was made easy by the fact that the El Paso Company had withdrawn its plan after Carter announced his support for Alcan. But during consideration of the pipeline resolution members of Congress expressed concern about various aspects of the proposal.

A key question was whether the project could be completed without federal financial help. Congressional suspicions that some form of federal loan guarantees might eventually become necessary remained strong. During House debate Clarence J. Brown (R Ohio) said, "All of you should know that by voting for this resolution, you may be faced later with a vote on whether or not to guarantee the financing of this project."

The presidential decision assumed that the state of Alaska and the gas producers would help out, either with direct loans or guarantees. But both the state and the three major producers—Exxon, Arco and Sohio, had indicated reluctance to participate, although the producers stood to gain up to $25-billion in profits if the line were opened.

The Carter plan ruled out an "all-events" tariff to make financing easier to obtain. Such a tariff would require consumers to pay for the project even if it is not completed.

During Senate debate, Mike Gravel (D Alaska) argued that federal guarantees would not be so bad anyway, since they could help cut the cost of the project by enabling the pipeline companies to get lower interest rates on loans. But John A. Durkin (D N.H.) vowed that it would be a "cold day in hell" before he could support guarantees or an all-events tariff.

Complicating the financing question was the uncertainty surrounding the price of the natural gas to be transported. While the price of gas was still undecided, the producers were unwilling to negotiate sales contracts. Without sales contracts, the pipeline companies would have trouble obtaining financing.

Under the presidential energy program, gas from Alaska would be classified as "old gas under a new contract," costing $1.45 per thousand cubic feet. Supporters of natural gas deregulation argued that continued price controls would make federal loan guarantees inevitable.

Opponents of the Alcan route raised the specter of another Panama Canal situation, with a vital transportation route passing through foreign territory. They argued in favor of the El Paso proposal, which had called for a pipeline entirely within the United States.

The administration rejected the El Paso plan in part because it would have led to significantly higher prices to consumers. Supporters of El Paso argued back that their proposal would have substantial economic benefits, in the form of over 700,000 new jobs per year.

The El Paso company had promised to use only American-made steel in the pipeline. Representatives of steel-producing areas suggested that further efforts were needed to ensure that the U.S. steel companies got a big enough share of the Alcan pipeline business. Canadian law required that domestic companies be given the exclusive right to bid on a percentage of materials used in construction.

National Security Energy

Congress in 1977 authorized $2.6-billion for the national security programs of the new Department of Energy. Until October 1977, these programs were administered by the Energy Research and Development Administration (ERDA). The authorizing legislation (S 1339—PL 95-183) was signed into law Nov. 15.

Half of the $2,607,100,000 authorized by the bill was for the development and production of nuclear weapons. The total authorized for that category was $1,390,050,000. Since 1953, this responsibility has been shared by the Department of Defense, first with the Atomic Energy Commission, then with ERDA and most recently with the newly-created Department of Energy.

House debate on S 1339 was devoted almost entirely to discussion of the so-called "neutron bomb"—an enhanced radiation warhead—which causes less physical destruction but more lethal radiation than other nuclear warheads. The issue was not discussed in the Senate because at the time of debate most members were not aware that the warhead was involved in the bill. A portion of the $1.4-billion authorized by S 1339 would be devoted to work on the warhead. The exact amount, like the amount for most of the items within S 1339, was classified information. A House effort to limit the use of the funds authorized by S 1339 for the "neutron bomb" failed.

In addition to the funds authorized by S 1339 for weapons programs, the bill contained $585.7-million for production of special materials for use in the weapons projects, $137.4-million for laser fusion programs and $231.9-million for the naval reactor program. The total provided by S 1339 was within $56-million of the Carter administration's request. Congress trimmed some of the authority requested for construction programs, especially in the weapons category, and added funds for laser fusion development.

Energy Research Funds

As 1977 ended, a bill authorizing the Department of Energy to devote as much as $6.2-billion to civilian energy research and development in fiscal 1978 was left for dead on Capitol Hill. The bill was a victim of the ongoing dispute between President Carter and Congress over the future of the not-yet-built Clinch River Breeder Reactor Plant, once the nation's number-one nuclear power project.

The energy research bill passed the Senate in July and the House in September. It was cleared for the White House Oct. 20. President Carter vetoed it Nov. 5, casting the first veto of his administration. The veto came primarily because buried deep within the $6,161,445,000 authorized by the bill was an $80-million item for continued work on the controversial breeder plant.

No attempt was made during the remaining weeks of the 1977 session to override the veto. In December the House approved another bill (S 1340) which was identical to S 1811 but from which had been deleted the Clinch River provisions and one other set of provisions to which Carter had objected. The Senate, however, did not act on the revised bill before adjournment.

Consideration of S 1811 in both chambers was dominated by debate over President Carter's proposal to terminate the Clinch River plant, which was to be built on the Clinch River in Tennessee near Oak Ridge to show that plutonium-fueled and plutonium-producing "breeder" reactors were a feasible source of electricity and nuclear fuel.

The original budget request for the plant for fiscal 1978 was $150-million. After Carter decided to terminate the project—because of his concern that increasing the use of plutonium would enlarge the risk of nuclear proliferation—he asked Congress to provide only $33-million in termination costs. Congress eventually decided on $80-million, enough to keep the project going in fiscal 1978 while it studied his proposal to end it.

Neither the veto of S 1811 nor congressional inaction spelled final doom for the plant. The fiscal 1978 supplemental appropriations bill (HR 9375) left pending at the end of

the 1977 session contained $80-million appropriated for the plant, which could be spent even without enactment of the authorizing legislation. Further action was expected on HR 9375 in January 1978.

The total authorized in S 1811 included about $3.2-billion for nuclear power projects and $1.8-billion for non-nuclear programs. They were to be administered by the research division of the Department of Energy, formerly the Energy Research and Development Administration (ERDA).

Earlier Controversies

Since the creation of ERDA in 1974, every one of its authorization measures had found the path through Congress a difficult one.

The first ERDA authorization bill, passed in 1975, authorized $5-billion. Its passage was marked by controversy over the Clinch River demonstration plant—increasingly more expensive than originally estimated—and over Senate-added language authorizing federal loan guarantees to encourage industry to get into the business of synthesizing oil and gas-like fuels from more plentiful natural resources, like coal. *(1975 action, p. 46-A)*

The second ERDA authorization bill was never enacted. Reported by conferees late in the 94th Congress, it was blocked from final passage by a senator frustrated in his effort to become a member of the Joint Committee on Atomic Energy. The fiscal 1977 bill, which died at the end of the 94th Congress, would have authorized almost $8-billion. *(1976 action, p. 63-A)*

Both of these measures contained authority for ERDA's military research programs as well as its civilian ones. In 1977, the military programs were separated out into another measure (S 1339) which was considered apart from the civilian research and development programs.

Fiscal 1977 Funding

The fiscal 1977 appropriations bill for ERDA included provisos forbidding release of the ERDA funds until authorizing legislation was enacted. After the authorizing bill was blocked, a continuing resolution was approved that allowed release of these appropriations until March 31, 1977. It was expected that the new Congress would quickly approve the 1977 authorization bill.

But such was not the case. In part due to the Senate committee reorganization, the 95th Congress was slow in acting. Congress abolished the Joint Committee on Atomic Energy, which had held responsibility for ERDA's nuclear programs. Jurisdiction over the civilian nuclear programs of ERDA then moved to the new Energy and Natural Resources Committee in the Senate and to the Science and Technology Committee in the House. *(Atomic Energy Committee, p. 90-A)*

Congress Feb. 7, 1977, removed the need for enactment of the 1977 ERDA authorization bill, repealing the provisos conditioning further release of the appropriations on enactment of the authorization measure. The House Appropriations Committee added this repeal to H J Res 227 (H Rept 95-8, S Rept 95-7), which provided emergency funds for the Southwestern Power Administration. The House approved the measure Feb. 7 by a vote of 341-5; the Senate approved the measure by voice vote the same day.

Nevertheless, Congress did enact a bill (S 36—PL 95-39) authorizing funds for ERDA's non-nuclear programs in fiscal 1977. The provisions of the measure were virtually identical to those contained in the bill that died at the end of the 94th Congress.

S 36 was reported by the Senate Energy Committee March 28 (S Rept 95-69) and was approved by the Senate by voice vote April 4. Reported from the House Science Committee April 27 (H Rept 95-224), it was passed by the House May 2 under suspension of the rules. The Senate agreed to the House version with amendments May 13; the House accepted the Senate amendments May 18, clearing the bill for the President.

1978 Veto Strategy

Well aware of the possibility that S 1811 would be vetoed, Congress sought to make such a veto ineffective by requiring that the $80-million appropriated for the Clinch River project be spent even if S 1811 was vetoed. Language allowing expenditure of the appropriated funds, even without authorizing statutes, was included in the supplemental appropriations bill moving through the House at the time S 1811 was sent to President Carter.

Because the regular ERDA appropriations bill (HR 7553—PL 95-96) had moved through Congress ahead of the authorizing legislation, similar language was included in that bill. The presidential veto therefore had no effect on spending for any ongoing ERDA programs, including the Clinch River demonstration project. Only programs for which the initial authority was included in or revised by S 1811 were affected.

Synthetic Fuels Aid

The debate over the future of the Clinch River project so dominated discussion of the fiscal 1978 energy research authorization bill that provisions authorizing federal aid for a synthetic fuels industry slipped through the House and Senate with relatively little notice.

Such legislation had been the subject of intense disagreement between the Senate and the House for two years. In 1975 the Senate approved, as part of the ERDA authorization bill, language authorizing guarantees of up to $6-billion in loans to companies willing to undertake synthetic fuels demonstration projects. The House killed the loan guarantee language before passing the bill. *(1975 action, p. 46-A)*

In 1976, the House voted, 193-192, not to consider a synthetic fuels loan guarantee measure that would have authorized up to $4-billion in aid. Also in 1976, the never-enacted ERDA authorization bill contained language allowing ERDA to guarantee up to $300-million in loans for plants that could convert biomass into fuel. *(1976 action, p. 63-A)*

As sent to the President, S 1811 authorized the Department of Energy to guarantee loans to private industry for building plants to demonstrate the possibility of commercial production of synthetic fuels from coal, wood, oil shale, biomass, municipal wastes and other plentiful natural resources.

Final Provisions

As vetoed, S 1811 authorized a grand total of $6,161,-445,000 for civilian research and development programs in fiscal 1978.

Of that total, just over half—$3.2-billion—was for nuclear programs, while $1.8-billion would fund non-

nuclear research and development. The remaining funds would be devoted to environmental and safety research, basic research and program management. (Authorization totals include *both* operating expenses *and* plant and capital equipment.)

Offsetting the grant total were expected revenues of $947-million, primarily from sales of enriched uranium. These reduced the net total authorized by the bill to $5,214,904,000.

NRC Authorization

Congress in 1977 authorized $297,740,000 in fiscal 1978 funds for the Nuclear Regulatory Commission (NRC).

The final bill (S 1131—PL 95-209) dodged involvement in the struggle over the Clinch River breeder reactor. At the time it was cleared President Carter had vetoed funds for the Clinch River program but members of Congress were trying to ensure that they would be spent anyway. S 1131 authorized $2.7-million for the NRC to cover expenses relating to the project, but also included a contingency provision that the authorization total would be reduced by that amount if the project were canceled. *(Clinch River debate, p. 64-A)*

The conferees split the difference between House and Senate figures in reaching a total amount of $297.74-million. Originally, the House had authorized $301.95-million. The Senate's initial total had been between $292.84-million and $299.64-million, with the variance due to flexible authorizations for the Clinch River project and an equally controversial nuclear fuel reprocessing plant under construction at Barnwell, S.C. Conferees provided $2.1-million for NRC activities at the Barnwell plant, and also added a contingency clause specifying that if that project also were canceled, NRC's total authorization would be reduced by that amount.

The original Senate bill authorized a single lump sum authorization to the NRC, but the House bill authorized specific sums for each of the commission's seven major programs. The conference committee followed the House approach.

S 1131 was originally reported (S Rept 95-196) May 16 by the Senate Environment and Public Works Committee and passed by voice vote May 25. The companion House bill (HR 3455—H Rept 95-289) was reported by the Interior and Insular Affairs Committee May 11 and passed by a 396-2 vote Sept. 12. The conference report (H Rept 95-788) was filed Nov. 1. The House adopted it by voice vote Nov. 3 and the Senate cleared it by voice vote Nov. 29.

'Energy Actions'

By not taking action to block them, Congress in 1977 let two Federal Energy Administration (FEA) "energy actions" take effect.

Under the 1975 Energy Policy and Conservation Act (PL 94-163), the FEA can modify fuel price and allocation programs, subject to veto by either house of Congress within set time limits. *(1975 act, 1975 chronology, p. 37-A)* Those proposed FEA modifications are called "energy actions." Seven energy actions were submitted in 1976. *(1976 chronology, p. 61-A)* President Ford Jan. 19, 1977, submitted energy actions, providing for gasoline price decontrol, but President Carter rescinded them. Carter was expected to resubmit his own gas decontrol proposal in early 1978.

Energy Action 10. This FEA proposal took effect April 18; neither house had moved to veto it during a 45-day review. It detailed a program to stockpile 500 million barrels of crude oil by the end of 1980 as insurance against a future supply crisis like the 1973-74 Arab oil embargo. The program had been authorized by PL 94-163.

The FEA first proposed the "strategic petroleum reserve" program under the Ford administration on Dec. 14, 1976. Ford's version targeted a 1982 completion date.

The Carter administration resubmitted the plan Feb. 16, and on Feb. 22 announced through its proposed fiscal 1978 budget revisions that it would speed completion of the program by year-end 1980.

Energy Action 11. This FEA proposal took effect March 15. It continued authorization of a 10 per cent annual increase in the average price of a barrel of domestic oil.

The 1975 Energy Policy and Conservation Act set an average price of $7.66 per barrel of domestic oil, and allowed that price to increase by up to 10 per cent per year to offset inflation and provide an incentive for production.

On July 1, 1976, the FEA ordered the price of domestic oil frozen for one year at June 1976 price levels. This was done because under initial operation of the price control system, oil producers earned excess profits when real-world sales did not correspond to FEA projections.

The freeze was designed to eliminate excess profits by holding prices back.

In testimony before the House Commerce Subcommittee on Energy and Power, Federal Energy Administrator John F. O'Leary said the price freeze would have achieved its goals by June 1977. He added that if Congress blocked energy action 11, "crude oil production can be expected to decline in response to the decline in real prices.... The inevitable result...will be an increase in imports."

Energy Legislation: 1978

Congress wrestled with energy policy for two years and, just before adjournment, cleared legislation to raise the price of natural gas gradually until 1985, when price controls were to be lifted altogether, and to provide tax incentives for fuel conservation.

Carter claimed success for his energy plan, but it was easy to lose sight of the fact that the broad national energy policy he put forth at the outset of his presidency had largely been abandoned.

Congress refused to go along with the centerpiece of that initial proposal, a tax on domestic crude oil to raise its price to the world level, and declined to approve a tax on business use of oil and gas, as Carter had asked. Moreover, the natural gas pricing legislation that was adopted was a far cry from Carter's plan to expand price controls.

The attention paid the energy bill left Congress little time for other energy-related measures. For example, the fiscal 1979 authorization for the Department of Energy was not passed because of the threat of lengthy haggling over amendments, which congressional leaders feared would distract from work on the energy bill.

Other energy highlights of 1978 were:

● The first overhaul of offshore oil and gas leasing laws in 25 years. The new act, four years in the making, was expected to end uncertainty that had slowed development of frontier areas on the federally owned Outer Continental Shelf off the Atlantic coast. *(Details, p. 73)*

● Defeat of efforts to spur construction of special pipelines to carry coal slurry — pulverized coal mixed with water. The railroad industry, joined by westerners concerned about depletion of scarce water supplies, got the credit for defeating the administration-backed bill.

● The first full year of operation of the Department of Energy, during which it spent more than $10 billion. *(DOE establishment, p. 45)*

● Continued difficulties for the nuclear industry. Public concern about safe disposal of radioactive nuclear waste was one of the central problems plaguing the industry, but government in 1978 provided only studies of the waste, not solutions. Congress did not complete action on a bill supported by the industry that would have shortened the time it takes to get a nuclear plant licensed by the government. *(Nuclear power, p. 105; nuclear wastes, p. 115)*

● Writing of regulations to implement the strip mining law of 1977, which required coal miners to restore strip-mined land. But the regulations were criticized by industry and even by some within the Carter administration, who considered them inflationary. *(Strip mining, p. 79)*

● No resolution of the long-running dispute between Carter and Congress over the plutonium-powered nuclear breeder reactor at Clinch River, Tenn. Carter continued his attempts to terminate the project, which he said was obsolete and over-priced. *(Clinch River, p. 64-A)*

Coal Slurry Bill

An intense lobbying campaign by the nation's railroads led to the stunning defeat July 19 of a bill to promote development of coal slurry pipelines. The measure was rejected 161-246.

HR 1609 was debated on the House floor July 17 and 18 and votes on amendments began July 19.

Proponents — led by Bob Eckhardt, D-Texas, the measure's sponsor, and Morris K. Udall, D-Ariz., chairman of the Interior Committee — argued the bill was necessary to provide another means of moving the increased loads of needed coal and would benefit consumers by providing competition to the railroads. Bringing coal to gas- and oil-producing states like Texas, would free those fuels for other uses elsewhere. Lastly, they argued the pipelines were less harmful to the environment than the trains used by railroads.

Opponents of the measure — led by Fred B. Rooney, D-Pa., chairman of the Commerce Subcommittee on Surface Transportation, and Joe Skubitz, R-Kan., ranking minority member of the Interior Committee and of Rooney's subcommittee — argued it would deprive railroads of vitally needed future income, would drain scarce western water and would give an unwarranted grant of federal power to private developers.

In defeating the bill, the House took the unusual step of turning its back on the judgment of two House committees — Interior and Public Works — that had urged passage of the measure.

Coal slurry pipelines would pump a mixture of pulverized coal and water from mines to coal users like utilities. Five major pipelines had been on the drawing boards for years, but they would cross lands owned by railroads. The railroads, anxious to block competition in the lucrative coal hauling business, had thwarted pipeline development by refusing to grant rights of way.

HR 1609 would have given the Department of the Interior authority to grant pipeline developers federal powers of eminent domain — the power to take private lands in the public interest — subject to certain restrictions.

Railroad Opposition

The railroad industry, led by the Association of American Railroads and rail-affiliated unions, spearheaded opposition to the bill. As the measure neared a floor vote, the group called in members from all over the country to press their regional congressmen to defeat it.

The railroads were aided by some farmers and landowners concerned about the impact of slurry pipelines on their property and by some environmentalists and western state House members fearful that the pipelines would deplete scarce western water supplies.

But only one environmental group, the Environmental Policy Center, ever testified against the bill. And western state members voted for the measure by a nearly two-to-one margin.

Although the Carter administration had announced in January that it would back HR 1609, with amendments, it ultimately took no position on the bill as reported.

The Senate Energy Subcommittee on Public Lands and Resources, chaired by Dale Bumpers, D-Ark., completed three days of hearings June 19 on two coal slurry pipeline measures (S 707, S 3046) but took no further action.

Background

A similar bill was rushed through the Senate in 1974, but never got out of committee in the House. Further hearings stalled action in 1975. In 1976, the Office of Technology Assessment (OTA), a congressional research agency, began a comprehensive study of coal slurry pipeline issues, and the controversy largely lay dormant while Congress awaited the report, which was issued Jan. 19. *(Background, appendix, p. 35-A)*

The 190-page OTA report, released 18 months after the congressional agency's board decided to analyze the slurry pipeline controversy, concluded that both pipelines and railroads had some advantages and some disadvantages as methods for hauling coal.

In major conclusions, the OTA report said that:

● In some circumstances, slurry pipelines could haul coal more cheaply than railroads, but each case varied.
● There was enough western water for such pipelines to be viable, but such use could deprive future needs.
● Given eminent domain powers, pipelines would enjoy significant regulatory advantages over railroads.
● Without federal or state eminent domain powers, pipelines would have a hard time competing, but that the pipeline industry could develop without federally given powers of eminent domain.
● Growth of a slurry pipeline industry would cut future railroad profits.
● Coal development would not be significantly boosted nationally by the use of slurry pipelines.
● Both posed differing threats to the environment.

House Interior Action

HR 1609 was ordered reported by the House Interior Committee Feb. 22 on a 30-13 vote (H Rept 95-924, Part I)

The surprisingly lopsided committee vote was a defeat for a coalition of railroads, environmentalists and rail-dependent unions which had opposed the measure vigorously. Credit for the victory was shared by a variety of business groups, utilities, construction trade unions and the coal industry.

Whether the Carter administration could claim victory was difficult to say. It supported the bill to complement its energy program. But it conditioned its support upon the adoption of several major changes in the legislation. Yet the administration never submitted formal amendments to the Interior Committee embodying the changes it testified it wanted.

House Public Works

The House Committee on Public Works and Transportation, which shared original jurisdiction with the Interior Committee, voted 23-20 May 16 to report the bill. The report (H Rept 95-924, Part 2) was filed May 25.

Public Works made only four significant changes, otherwise accepting the bill as reported from Interior.

First, the panel broadened the role played in the eminent domain licensing process by the Department of Transportation and by the Interstate Commerce Commission. The report stressed that as amended HR 1609 would ensure that the commission would have full regulatory authority over rates charged by slurry pipelines licensed under the act. "Lack of such control might place the railroads at a regulatory disadvantage," the report said.

The panel also loosened Interior's controls on ownership of licensed pipelines. The Interior Committee language was aimed at promoting competition in the fuel and fuel transport industry. Public Works said Interior's definition of pipeline ownership control was too strict and might limit investment in slurry pipelines. The two committees reached agreement on a compromise definition.

Third, Public Works required that the U.S. Geological Survey study the likely water table impact of a slurry pipeline project anywhere in the United States, not just in the West, as the Interior version provided.

And fourth, Public Works added language requiring congressional approval of rules or regulations put forward under the act by the interior secretary.

House Commerce Action

Amid charges of foul play and deception, the House Interstate and Foreign Commerce Committee voted 19-9 July 11 to urge the House to kill HR 1609.

Rep. Bob Eckhardt, D-Texas, sponsor of the measure and a Commerce Committee member, hotly accused opponents of the legislation of trying to trick him into being absent from the meeting so they could more easily turn the vote against his bill.

The committee had before it a report from the Subcommittee on Transportation and Commerce, chaired by Rooney, Commerce's leading opponent of HR 1609.

The subcommittee held two hearings on coal slurry pipelines in early February. Three substitutes to HR 1609 were put forward by panel members but were abandoned by the subcommittee in late June. Instead, the panel drafted the report, which attacked HR 1609.

The report (committee print 95-96) argued at length that:

● The bill provided unprecedented, extraordinary and unfair federal powers of eminent domain to private carriers.
● Sufficient rail capacity to haul coal already existed.
● Pipelines were expensive and could burden consumers.
● Railroads would be denied a chance to compete with pipelines because the lines would be committed to long-term supply contracts up to 30 years.
● The railroad industry would be hurt because it needed the increased capital that future coal traffic would bring.
● As many as 16,000 railroad jobs could be lost if slurry pipelines were fully deployed.
● Slurry pipelines used too much water and HR 1609 failed to provide adequate protection of state water allocation rights.
● Water discharged at the end of slurry lines could damage the environment.

House Floor Action

The House defeated HR 1609 July 19 by a 161-246 vote.
Of 75 voting House members from 13 western states,

including Alaska and Hawaii, 47 voted for passage compared to 28 against.

Defeat of HR 1609 killed the legislation for the 95th Congress. However, Robert B. McNeil, spokesman for the Slurry Transport Association, the pro-pipeline lobby group, said it would press the fight again in 1979. The group included contractors, utilities and pipeline suppliers.

McNeil noted that proponents had convinced a majority of two House committees that the bill was needed and had won about 40 percent support on the House floor. With that much success, he said, "You just don't walk away and forget it."

Asked what the pipeline backers could do next time to win, McNeil said, "You have to translate this some way into how it can affect every congressional district ... I think not only we have that problem, I think the president has that problem," he added, referring to President Carter's frequent inability to pass energy legislation.

The administration supported the principle of developing slurry pipelines, but insisted the bureaucratic procedures for issuing grants of eminent domain should differ from those set out in HR 1609. Consequently, the administration had no position on the bill and did not lobby for its passage.

The administration proposal, McNeil said, "was an unworkable, cumbersome kind of thing. I think they're going to have to rethink that."

DOE Authorization

Legislation to authorize programs for the Department of Energy for fiscal 1979 failed to clear in 1978, leaving in limbo the future of the controversial breeder reactor at Clinch River, Tenn.

Three authorization bills (S 2692, HR 12163, HR 11392) were reported by committees. Two of them, S 2692 and HR 11392, never reached a floor vote. The third measure, HR 12163, was passed by the House July 17 but was not taken up by the Senate.

The legislation languished when the Democratic leadership in both houses refused to bring it up for fear it would become the vehicle for several controversial attempts to remove or modify price controls on oil.

The leaders wanted to avoid a major floor fight on energy until after Congress had completed action on President Carter's energy package. But the energy bill did not clear until the final day of the session, which did not leave enough time before adjournment for action on the Energy Department authorization. *(Energy bill, p. 5)*

Clinch River Reactor

Because Congress failed to act, spending for the Clinch River reactor project — which was opposed by the administration — continued at the rate of about $15 million a month.

Without a new bill providing authority to modify or terminate the plutonium breeder, the Energy Department had to continue to operate under existing authority, which required construction. The $172 million appropriated for the project in fiscal 1979 in the public works appropriations bill (HR 12928 — H J Res 1139) had to be spent on new parts, engineering, design and other scheduled work on the $2.56 billion reactor.

Carter wanted the project killed because he said it was too expensive, its design was obsolete and it would lead to the spread of nuclear weapons. The reactor would produce plutonium, a nuclear fuel that could be used to make bombs.

Throughout the year, the administration attempted to work out some sort of compromise that would end the project.

But in July, the House voted twice to refuse to allow the administration to terminate the breeder. The two votes were on amendments to HR 12163.

But the Senate Energy Committee, in its bill (S 2692) reported July 5, gave Carter authority to end the Clinch River project. The committee bill required the administration to develop another breeder reactor demonstration project instead.

Still another alternative was presented in August when Carter — trying to round up votes for his beleaguered energy package — reached an agreement involving Clinch River with Sen. James A. McClure, R-Idaho.

Unlike the 1978 Senate committee bill, the McClure compromise did not require a commitment from Carter to construct another breeder, according to Michael D. Hathaway, legislative assistant to McClure.

The agreement would postpone the decision to terminate or construct Clinch River until March, 1981. In the meantime, work would continue on design of Clinch River, and components for the project would continue to be purchased. At the same time, government researchers would try to come up with another, more modern type of breeder reactor that would not use plutonium or, if plutonium were the fuel, would be designed to prevent its diversion to nuclear weapons.

Then, according to Hathaway, one of four options would be chosen in 1981: construction of Clinch River; cancellation of Clinch River and construction of the more modern breeder; construction of both projects or construction of neither.

The agreement also reportedly included support by the administration for a $417 million energy research project in Idaho that Carter previously had opposed.

The agreement was never put to a Senate vote because the bill did not come to the floor.

Background

For decades, energy planners had looked to "breeder" reactors as the future source of electric power. Conventional nuclear power reactors used only one to two percent of the potential energy in the scarce uranium they used as fuel, according to a study by the General Accounting Office (GAO). "Breeder" reactors, however, would extract more than 60 percent of the potential energy in uranium and would "breed" more fuel than they consumed.

But breeder reactors also produce plutonium, a byproduct of nuclear fission that does not occur in nature. Breeder reactors would run on a fuel blend of uranium and plutonium and would produce a great deal more plutonium than conventional reactors, providing an endless supply of breeder fuel.

Plutonium, however, can be used to make nuclear bombs. It also is highly poisonous and can cause cancer if inhaled or exposed to an open wound. It remains radioactive for thousands of years and thus presents storage problems once it is spent as fuel.

Since 1970, American development of a commercially viable breeder reactor technology was keyed to a project to build a trial demonstration plant at Clinch River near Oak Ridge, Tenn.

The Clinch River reactor was designed to have a 380 megawatt capacity at a cost of about $2.5 billion.

Original plans called for site preparation to begin by October 1977 and construction to start one year later, with plant operation to begin in mid-1984.

President Carter on April 7, 1977, announced plans to turn away from use of plutonium as a nuclear fuel because of the dangers of nuclear weapons proliferation.

As part of that policy, he later asked Congress to cut funding for the Clinch River project from $150 million to $33 million in fiscal 1978, enough to cover termination costs.

Congress refused to go along. The House insisted on providing the full $150 million while the Senate authorized $80 million to sustain the project through fiscal 1978. Conferees agreed on $80 million, accompanied by language asserting the will of Congress that the project continue.

Casting his first veto, Carter killed the authorization bill (S 1811) Nov. 5. *(1977 background, p. 93-A)*

1978 Action

The Clinch River project remained alive, however, because Congress also included the $80 million in a fiscal 1978 supplemental appropriations bill (HR 9375).

The $7.3 million bill included funds for several projects which Carter could not afford to sacrifice. He signed it on March 7 but said he would spend the $80 million to kill the Clinch River breeder.

But Comptroller General Elmer B. Staats ruled March 10 that if the president did that he would be breaking the law. In a letter hand-delivered to the White House, he said funds for the project were authorized to be spent only on its construction, not its termination. Administration officials ordering funds spent to kill the project would be held personally liable for the money, he said.

But there was one way the president could legally end the project. Staats explained it in a March 6 letter to Sens. Henry M. Jackson, D-Wash., and Clifford P. Hansen, R-Wyo., chairman and ranking minority member respectively of the Senate Energy Committee.

The original contract between the government and private utilities to build the project allowed any party to begin contract termination under specific conditions. One eligible criterion was if any necessary government license were delayed six months or more, Staats noted. He pointed out that the Clinch River schedule already had slipped 18 months and said that delay would qualify as grounds for the government to kill the contract.

But if Carter pursued that strategy, some observers noted, the issue probably would end up in the courts and take so long to resolve that the project would effectively be killed anyway.

Administration Compromise Offer

In his fiscal 1979 budget request Jan. 23, President Carter asked for only $13 million for the Clinch River project to cover final termination costs.

But in late February the House Science Subcommittee on Nuclear Energy voted 17-6 to boost the authorization level another $159 million to continue the project.

To avoid further fighting, the administration led the effort to compromise. In a March 17 letter to Science Committee Chairman Olin E. Teague, D-Texas, Energy Secretary James R. Schlesinger explained his proposal to

"redirect the nation's breeder program...(which) would in our view strengthen the breeder...program."

Under the compromise, the Clinch River plant would be shelved. In its place the Department of Energy would undertake a 30-month study of alternate breeder technologies feasible for a plant two to three times as big as the one planned. The compromise made no firm commitment to actually build any breeder reactor; however, it did not rule out construction later.

The Clinch River project would be stopped short of construction work upon completion of systems design and component testing, Schlesinger said. The overall government breeder research program then would focus on study of "a larger, advanced fission facility" which administration spokesmen said would have a capacity of up to 900 megawatts.

The study would examine alternate fuel options aimed at minimizing plutonium availability, Schlesinger said. The administration proposed spending $33 million in fiscal 1979. Also, he added, 90 percent of the design crew working on Clinch River — 850 professional employees — would be kept together as a team and transferred to the new project.

House Action

Action on the Energy authorization bills was held up by a months-long turf fight among three House committees for jurisdiction over the Energy Department budget.

The squabble pitted the Science Committee against the combined team of Commerce and Interior. The origins of the dispute lay in the formation of the Energy Department in 1977. The new Cabinet-level department was created by combining many independent federal agencies and sub-units of other departments. *(Energy Department, p. 45)*

Dispersed, they fell naturally under the jurisdictions of several House committees. Energy Research and Development Administration (ERDA) programs, for example, were under the control of the House Science and Technology Committee. Similarly, energy regulatory programs were administered by the Federal Energy Administration (FEA), and House oversight of that agency was the duty of the Commerce Committee. Interior's jurisdictional claims stemmed from its oversight responsibilities for environmental programs. The departmental fiscal 1979 budget request was the first one presented since the department was created.

The dispute raised many important questions.

The most immediate ones were what to do about two competing versions of the department's fiscal 1979 authorization, which in some cases contained conflicting policy initiatives and funding levels for the same programs.

One measure (HR 12163) was primarily the product of the Science Committee and ostensibly confined itself only to authorizations for research and development programs. As reported by the Science Committee, that bill authorized $5.87 billion for civilian energy research programs. But both Commerce and Interior won referral of certain sections of that bill to their panels and adopted many amendments to it.

In addition, Commerce and Interior jointly produced their own version of a fiscal 1979 authorization bill (HR 11392). That measure dealt primarily with departmental regulatory and administrative programs, and authorized a total of $7.121 billion as reported by Commerce, with $2.6 billion the figure approved by Interior for the programs in that bill over which it claimed jurisdiction. The Science Committee voted 32-2 June 6 to report that version to the House with the recommendation that the measure "not pass."

Also at stake was whether Science or Commerce and Interior would increase their respective roles overseeing the Energy Department. If any panel were to gain power at the expense of the others, there could be far-reaching implications for congressional relations with the Energy Department.

The Science Committee typically backed high-cost, high technology solutions to policy problems. An example was its stand on Clinch River.

Commerce, on the other hand, had established a history of strict and at times hostile oversight over energy programs and officials subject to its jurisdiction. Generally considered more sympathetic to consumer and environmental activists than Science, an increased oversight role by either Commerce or Interior at Science's expense likely would influence energy policy formation.

Legislative History

On Feb. 16, Energy Secretary Schlesinger submitted a bill proposing fiscal 1979 authorizations for the Energy Department. That measure (HR 11137) was introduced by request by Science Chairman Teague.

But the day before Teague had introduced HR 10969, the fiscal 1979 authorization for department programs that the Science Committee believed fell under its jurisdiction.

On March 8, Commerce Chairman Harley O. Staggers, D-W.Va., and Interior Chairman Morris K. Udall, D-Ariz., introduced HR 11392, covering fiscal 1979 authorizations for the department programs they believed fell under the jurisdiction of their committees. Some items overlapped and conflicted with the Science bill.

On April 18, the Science Committee by voice vote ordered its version reported as a "clean bill", which was filed April 20 as HR 12163 (H Rept 95-1078, Part 1). Two days later, Speaker Thomas P. O'Neill Jr., D-Mass., ordered HR 12163 referred to Interior and Commerce as a result of a March 10 Staggers and Udall request. After amending it, Interior ordered the bill reported by voice vote May 15 (H Rept 95-1078, Part 2). Commerce ordered it reported May 15 by voice vote and filed its report May 19 (H Rept 95-1078, Part 3)

The Commerce and Interior amendments to HR 12163 were the same as their decisions in their own version of the authorization bill, HR 11392. Interior ordered that bill reported by voice vote May 15 and filed its report (H Rept 95-1166, Part 1). Commerce ordered the bill reported May 15 by a 25-16 vote and filed its report (H Rept 95-1166, Part 2) May 19.

Speaker O'Neill insisted that the Science Committee mark up the Commerce/Interior bill, and on June 6, without discussion of the specific provisions in the measure, the panel voted 32-2 to report HR 11392 to the House with the recommendation that it not pass.

House Floor Action

On July 17, the House voted 325-67 to pass HR 12163, which authorized $4.5 billion in fiscal 1979 funds for civilian research and development programs in the Department of Energy. The measure also contained full funding for the Clinch River breeder reactor.

Clinch River

The arguments on Clinch River echoed those of past years.

Debate centered around the administration "compromise" amendment, offered by Science Committee Chairman Walter Flowers, D-Ala. It was the same proposal Flowers had submitted earlier to the Science Committee.

The amendment authorized $55 million and directed the secretary of energy to finish only the design work on the Clinch River project. The Energy Department would be required to study advanced breeder reactor concepts and recommend to Congress by March 31, 1981, how to proceed toward development. But the amendment contained no commitment to ever build anything.

Proponents of the compromise, including Science Committee Chairman Teague, argued that Carter was determined to kill Clinch River, that the president held enough votes to make a veto stick, and, therefore, that the project was as good as dead.

But Clinch River defenders could not be convinced.

Citing unanimous support for the project from the nuclear power and utility industries, they argued the project was essential for development of nuclear-generated electricity in the United States. The nation would fall hopelessly behind Western Europe and Japan in developing nuclear technology if it were scrapped, the defenders asserted.

On Friday, July 1, the House rejected the Flowers amendment, 142-187.

However, administration sympathizers tried again Monday, July 17. Hamilton Fish, R-N.Y., moved to recommit the bill to the Science Committee with instructions that the panel add the language contained in the Flowers amendment.

"[I]f we are to have a bill then this compromise is an essential part of it," Fish said, observing the high absentee rate for the first vote. "I happen to have several things that I want very dearly in this measure and I would hate to see it vetoed," Fish explained.

Debate was short and repetitious, and the House rejected Fish's motion, 157-238.

Coal Plant

Flowers was more successful in pushing an amendment to add $75 million to cover initial construction costs for a plant to make liquid fuel from coal using a process called SRC-II (solvent refined coal). Only Gulf Oil Corp. was ready to demonstrate the process in a commercial-sized plant.

Flowers argued that the nation's need for new energy supplies was so pressing that the time was at hand for Congress to authorize public funding to demonstrate the process. His amendment was adopted 165-132.

Oil Pricing Controversy

The second authorization bill, HR 11392, had been expected to come to the floor shortly after approval of HR 12163. But it was yanked from the schedule, and eventually died, because of a controversial amendment that would have decontrolled the price of about half the oil produced in the United States.

Majority Leader Jim Wright, D-Texas, said he intended to offer the amendment to HR 11392, which would have provided $6.2 billion in fiscal 1979 authorizations for non-research civilian Energy Department programs.

But the House Democratic leadership held up consideration of the bill when informed by Henry M. Jackson, D-Wash., chairman of the Senate Energy Committee, that if Wright's amendment passed the House, several Senate conferees would retract their approval of the natural gas pricing compromise. Those members objected to the amendment, they said, because together the oil and gas proposals would give exorbitant profits to the oil and gas industry. At that point, the gas pricing compromise was threatening to fall apart at any moment, and leaders in both houses did not want to risk alienating any of the compromise's supporters.

Senate Action

The controversy over oil pricing also held up action on the Senate version of the Energy authorization bill (S 2692). Senators from oil-producing states were expected to press to end federal price controls on some domestically produced oil.

As a result, the leadership did not bring the bill to the floor, because they feared such an amendment would turn votes away from the delicate compromise on natural gas pricing that was the joint leadership's primary energy priority.

The two issues were closely related because both the gas compromise and any oil plan would raise the prices consumers paid for oil and natural gas while handing oil and gas producers billions in new profits. On the other hand, proponents of both proposals said they would increase energy supplies.

S 2692 was introduced March 8 at the administration's request by Energy Committee Chairman Jackson. Nineteen days of hearings were held by the panel and its subcommittees before markup began May 3 for 15 sessions. On June 20, the committee voted 15-0 to report the bill. The 307-page report (S Rept 95-967) was filed July 5.

As reported, S 2692 authorized $10.3 billion in fiscal 1979 for civilian programs in the Department of Energy, $420.7 million more than the administration sought.

The committee noted that $646.8 million in authorizations under S 2692 duplicated decisions approved by conferees on various portions of Carter's energy program. The report explained that the duplications were intended to continue existing programs that might otherwise be cancelled if the Carter energy program were not enacted.

Nuclear Licensing Reform

The Carter administration's nuclear licensing reform plan, designed to aid the ailing nuclear industry by speeding plant licensing, failed to clear Congress in 1978.

The last hope for even limited action by the 95th Congress was in a House Energy panel chaired by Morris K. Udall, D-Ariz. But Udall abandoned his plan for an "informal" markup Aug. 14 when he ran into resistance from members of his Interior Subcommittee on Energy.

Neither the House Commerce Committee, which shared jurisdiction, nor the Senate Environment Committee reported a licensing reform bill in 1978.

"We should give guidance [to the Carter administration] before we fold our tents for the year," Udall told the panel. The Department of Energy proposed a reform bill (HR 11704) in March that was attacked both by industry and environmentalists.

But James Weaver, D-Ore., who opposed the administration bill, said it would be "going into the snake pit for no purpose" to hold a markup where there was no hope of further action.

Bob Carr, D-Mich., agreed with Weaver. He complained that the administration had devised changes to end delays in nuclear licensing without first pinpointing what caused the delays.

Jonathan B. Bingham, D-N.Y., argued that a markup would be useful because the panel could "crystallize" its thinking and "be further along when we come back next year."

When a motion by Carr to end the markup appeared about to fail, Carr noted the absence of a quorum. The eight members present were one shy of the required number.

At that point, after a brief attempt to find another member, Udall gave up trying to meet on licensing reform in 1978. *(See chapter on nuclear power, p. 105)*

Solar Satellite Research

The drive by the nation's aerospace industry to increase federal support for construction in space of giant solar power satellites received a boost June 22, when the House passed legislation authorizing research funds. However, the measure never got to the Senate floor.

By the one-sided vote of 267-96, the House approved a bill (HR 12505) providing $25 million in fiscal 1979 funds for stepped-up research on the satellites' feasibility. The bill called for studies "leading to a solar power satellite ... and the placing of a demonstration satellite unit or units into orbit...."

Backers of the idea — including such firms as Grumman Aerospace Corp., Boeing Aerospace Corp., Lockheed Missile and Space Co., McDonnell Douglas Corp., and others — said the satellites could be the answer to projected future energy supply shortages.

Opponents said the satellites would cost too much, would be environmentally dangerous and were designed mainly to provide a federal bail-out for the moribund aerospace industry.

The satellites would weigh up to 20,000 tons, would stretch as much as 10 square miles and would have to be built in space. They would operate from a fixed orbital position 22,000 miles above Earth. The sunlight they collected would be converted to microwaves, which would be beamed to Earth-based antennae, turned into electricity and fed into conventional utility power grids.

After House passage of HR 12505, sponsored by Ronnie G. Flippo, D-Ala., the measure went to the Senate where it was referred to the Energy Subcommittee on Research and Development. The panel took no action on the bill.

In a related development, the Senate June 28 authorized $500,000 for the National Science Foundation (NSF) to study the feasibility of solar satellites. The provision was included in the fiscal 1979 NSF authorization bill (HR 11400).

House Committee Action

HR 12505 was ordered reported May 9 by the House Science and Technology Committee on a 30-1 vote. Richard L. Ottinger, D-N.Y., was the lone dissenter.

The panel's report (H Rept 95-1120) said the solar satellite technology was feasible and that economic studies projected it would be cost competitive with other power generation methods in the future. Aside from producing electricity, the report said, other possible benefits of such satellites included expansion of high technology industries, more jobs and possible U.S. export of energy and technology.

The report said the legislation would require the Department of Energy and the National Aeronautics and Space Administration (NASA) to prepare a comprehensive plan on how to develop the technology.

"The operation of the solar power satellites could produce environmental effects, several of which involve a large degree of uncertainty and will require much more understanding before their effects can be reliably quantified," the report said.

The committee estimated that continuation of the government research program would require $245 million through fiscal 1983 in addition to the $25 million authorized for fiscal 1979.

The report included position statements from the Department of Energy and NASA saying the legislation was not necessary and would prematurely push the existing research program.

Ottinger filed a dissent with the report detailing his views that the project would be expensive and dangerous.

Among Ottinger's charges were that microwave technology presented a broad range of possible threats to health and safety, that cost projections varied widely and that the bill explicitly committed the government to commercial demonstration of a solar satellite. He also said the satellites would have possible military applications and that the materials required to build them would increase American dependence on foreign minerals.

House Floor Action

Proponents of the measure gave repeated assurances on the House floor June 22 that HR 12505 did not commit the nation to construction of any satellite. They said it would only accelerate the research effort from "merely paper studies toward hardware verification," in the words of Mike McCormack, D-Wash.

Ottinger led the opposition. He persuaded the bill's proponents to strike language mandating a study of nuclear satellites. The motion to strike was agreed to by voice vote.

SBA Solar Loan Program

Legislation creating a $75 million loan program for small businesses involved in the solar energy, renewable energy and energy conservation fields was cleared by Congress June 19.

The bill (HR 11713 — PL 95-315) authorized $30 million in fiscal 1979 for the Small Business Administration (SBA) to make direct loans to eligible businesses. It also authorized $6.75 million in fiscal 1979 so SBA could insure $45 million in guaranteed bank loans for such companies.

The bill made loans available for plant start up, construction, conversion or expansion for firms producing solar, renewable source or energy conservation equipment. Engineering, architectural and consulting firms in those fields also were eligible.

Sponsors of the bill said it was needed to provide startup capital for untested new energy businesses that had had difficulty obtaining financing from commercial sources or through regular SBA loan programs.

House Action

The House Small Business Committee reported HR 11713 April 19 (H Rept 95-1071).

The committee said that small businesses had been unable to compete with large corporations in gas, oil, coal and nuclear energy. As a result they had concentrated their limited capital on developing new technologies, such as solar energy, energy from renewable sources and energy conservation devices, the report said.

In 1978, about 860 small firms were involved in manufacturing, servicing or distributing solar energy and energy conservation equipment, the committee estimated. But, the report noted, large corporations were producing a growing share of the nation's solar collectors. At the same time, small businesses had found it increasingly difficult to borrow capital for entering into or expanding in the field.

"Small business persons admit that private capital is available from very large corporations, especially major oil companies," said the committee report. "Invariably, however, a precondition to . . . such capital is the surrender of controlling interest in the small business concern."

The committee also quoted a report from the Department of Energy which determined that firms in the solar energy field had received "no effective assistance from SBA." The administration granted only three energy-related loans between October 1977 and March 1978, the committee said.

SBA, based on its own estimation of the state of the solar energy art, had "apparently determined that (loan) applicants did not demonstrate the required assurances of ability to repay loans," according to the committee.

"The committee is aware that loans made to businesses involved in these new and emerging energy fields may be associated with somewhat higher than normal risks," the report said. "Nevertheless, it intends, by the express language of this bill to signal clearly to SBA the committee's determination that (these) . . . loans . . . should be made."

Dissenting views were filed by M. Caldwell Butler, R-Va., and John J. LaFalce, D-N.Y. They said it was "unwise for Congress to single out one part of one industry and tell the SBA to throw out its well established standards in this instance."

The House passed the bill May 2, 375-17, under suspension of the rules, which meant no amendments were permitted.

Senate Action

The Senate Small Business Committee substituted its language for that of House-passed HR 11713 and reported the measure May 15 (S Rept 95-828).

The bill made loans available for plant start up, construction, conversion or expansion for firms producing solar, renewable resource or conservation energy equipment. It also added engineering, architectural and consulting firms in the energy field to the eligibility list.

The committee said the loan program was needed to provide capital for untested, new energy businesses that had had difficulty obtaining financing from commercial sources or through regular SBA loan plans.

It also expanded the definition of conservation equipment eligible for funding and, to provide flexibility for new developments in the field, left it to the SBA administrator to determine what new equipment could be come eligible.

The Senate passed HR 11713 May 24 by voice vote and without debate.

Final Action

When the bill was returned to the House June 16, members amended it further and prohibited loans from being used primarily for research and development. The House also stipulated that the $36.75 million authorized in the bill was for fiscal 1979.

The bill was then returned to the Senate, which cleared it by voice vote June 19.

Solar Energy Cell Program

An aggressive 10-year federal program for developing solar photovoltaic cells as a commercially competitive technology cleared Congress in the final days of the session. The cells convert sunlight directly into electricity.

As cleared by Congress, the bill (HR 12874 — PL 95-590) authorized $125 million in fiscal 1979 funds for research and development by the Department of Energy on solar photovoltaic technologies. The bill also established a statutory framework for the conduct of the Solar Photovoltaic Research, Development and Demonstration programs.

Legislative History

HR 12874 was ordered reported unanimously by the House Committee on Science and Technology. The report (H Rept 95-1285) was filed June 9.

In the report, the panel said solar photovoltaic cells were first developed in the early 1950's and were used extensively in the U.S. space program to provide electric power for spacecraft. But the high cost of the cells limited their widespread use on Earth.

"In order for the systems to compete with conventional energy systems and achieve broad commercial applications photovoltaic system costs will have to be reduced by a factor of 10-20 over the next 10 years," the report said.

The committee estimated that the program would require a total of $1.57 billion through fiscal 1987.

Under the bill, public and private entities could apply to the Energy Department for up to 75 per cent of the costs of purchasing and installing photovoltaic systems.

Administration Position

Mike McCormack, D-Wash., floor manager of the bill, said the Carter administration had taken no position on the measure. In its fiscal 1979 budget, the administration called for $76 million for solar photovoltaic research.

In mid-May the administration revised its request upward by adding $30 million to the $76 million, but that was less than the Science Committee had urged.

HR 12874 passed the House easily without opposition June 28 under suspension of the rules, a procedure that requires the approval of two-thirds of voting members and does not permit amendments. The vote was 385-14.

In the Senate, the Committee on Energy and Natural Resources Sept. 21 voted 17-0 to recommend passage of a similar bill. The bill passed the Senate Oct. 10 by voice vote, and the House agreed to the Senate version Oct. 13, clearing the measure for the president.

Coal Leasing Amendments

Congress Oct. 13 cleared a bill (S 3189 — PL 95-554) authorizing the interior secretary to exchange some leased federal coal lands in Utah and Wyoming for other lands where mining would have a less damaging effect on the environment.

But Congress put off a decision on the issue of giving the interior secretary general authority to swap federal coal leases in order to preserve environmentally valuable land.

The Senate version, passed by voice vote Sept. 20, gave the secretary authority to exchange or purchase leases to help resolve cases where there could be undesirable social or environmental damage from mining.

The bill was reported Aug. 25 by the Energy Committee (S Rept 95-1169). The measure was prompted by industry complaints about cumbersome requirements of the Federal Coal Leasing Amendments Act of 1975 (PL 94-377).

The House Interior Committee had debated giving the interior secretary broad authority to swap leases, but finally settled on a case-by-case approach (HR 13553). It voted to give the secretary authority to exchange the leases held by three companies, because they conflicted with a highway route in Wyoming and with potential wilderness areas in Utah. The measure was reported Sept. 27 (H Rept 95-1635).

HR 13553 was passed by voice vote under suspension of the rules Oct. 3. The House then substituted the language of its bill for S 3189, and the Senate accepted the amended version by voice vote Oct. 13, thus clearing it for the president.

Oil Shale Development

A bill requiring the government to test three methods of squeezing oil from shale rock was passed by the Senate June 27. The measure (S 419) required the Department of Energy to contract with private firms to run up to three federally-owned plants to do the testing. The House took no action on the bill, which passed the Senate 61-23.

Sponsored by Floyd Haskell, D-Colo., the measure authorized $1.4 million in fiscal 1979 funds. Of that, $1 million covered general start-up and administrative costs and the remaining $400,000 was for a program of special planning grants to state and local governments that suffered because of the bill.

In addition, the legislation authorized $40 million in loan guarantees in fiscal 1979-80 to cover state and local planning and development projects necessitated by the bill's passage.

The Senate Energy Committee estimated that if the plants actually were funded, they would cost from $275 million to $400 million to build and would have annual operating costs of $30 million to $40 million. Revenues from the oil produced would go to the federal treasury.

The only floor opposition to the measure was led by Clifford P. Hansen, R-Wyo., ranking minority member of the Senate Energy Committee. Hansen opposed having the federal government assume full financial responsibility for the projects. He proposed an amendment to require industrial participants to assume part of the financial risks or provide alternative incentives to oil shale production.

It was rejected 34-51.

Committee Action

The Senate Energy Committee voted 12-5 April 26 to report out S 419; all five opponents were Republicans. The report (S 95-802) was filed May 10.

"It is the judgment of the committee that the nation cannot afford to await, as has been the case for 20 years, the demonstration of the commercial viability of oil shale technologies by private industry and should begin now to test these technologies at public expense," the report said.

Oil shale, a sedimentary rock containing organic material called kerogen, can be converted to a liquid and recovered as oil. There are potentially up to two trillion barrels of shale oil in the United States, most of it within a 17,000 square mile area in western Colorado, eastern Utah and southwestern Wyoming, the report said. By comparison, there are only 657 billion barrels of oil in worldwide petroleum reserves. Almost 80 percent of the nation's oil shale is on publicly-owned lands, the report said.

There are various processes for deriving oil from shale. Most involve fracturing the rock and heating it to about 900 degrees Fahrenheit. This can be done either by mining the ore, cracking it and then processing it in above-ground plants or by any of several processes achieved below ground, known as "in-situ."

Although there have been attempts dating back to the 1860's to produce oil from shale, none has been commercially successful. Given the nation's pressing need to produce more fuel, the committee said, the government should step in to stimulate development of a workable process.

The report included written statements from the Department of the Interior and the Office of Management and Budget opposing the legislation as unnecessary and as likely to duplicate an Interior program begun in 1973. Under that program, choice federal shale-rich lands were leased for oil shale development. No oil had yet been produced as a result of the program.

Minority Views. In minority views filed with the report, Sens. Hansen and Dewey F. Bartlett, R-Okla., opposed the legislation as "wholly unnecessary and unjustified." It would cost too much and would not prove the commercial viability of any project because the government would swallow all economic risks, they said.

'Dealer Day in Court' Bill

The House June 6 cleared and sent to the president legislation to protect gas station owners from the arbitrary cancellation of their franchises. Final action came when the House approved Senate amendments to the bill (HR 130 — PL 95-297) by voice vote.

The measure also required refiners to determine gasoline octane ratings and post them on the pump.

A third section required the Energy Department to study the extent to which producers, refiners and other motor fuel suppliers subsidized retail and wholesale sales with profits from other operations.

The first two titles of the bill were basically uncontroversial. They were similar to HR 130 as passed by the House April 5, 1977.

The first title was designed to protect gasoline station franchise holders from arbitrary or discriminatory lease cancellation. Under the measure, franchise agreements could not be terminated or left to expire without renewal unless specific standards of reasonableness were satisfied, as spelled out in the bills. Contested franchise cancellations would be heard in federal court.

Title II required refiners to determine their gasoline octane ratings and to display the ratings at gasoline station pumps. It also required the Federal Trade Commission (FTC) to draft rules mandating motor vehicle manufacturers to display proper octane requirements on each new vehicle. Violations would be enforceable by the FTC.

But the Senate Energy Committee added a third title, which sparked controversy. It prohibited gas stations from being subsidized with funds or services derived from other operations performed by their parent companies.

". . .[F]ranchise termination or nonrenewal of a franchise relationship are not the only means at the disposal of a refiner or distributor supplier to exert pressure on a retailer or a distributor," the committee report explained. "The control of supply and the pricing of that supply provide powerful instruments for influencing profitability and, in many cases, the survival of a retail operation.

"Any refiner or distributor supplier who also operates his own outlets at the retail or wholesale level can, by subsidizing those outlets, place a sharp limit on the prices any independent competitor can afford to charge. . . . This flexibility can be used to eliminate independent buyers . . . ," the report said.

Senate Committee Action

The Senate Energy Committee voted 11-7 March 22 to report two identical bills (HR 130, S 743) to prevent unfair gas station franchise cancellation. The reports (HR 130 — S Rept 95-731, S 743 — S Rept 95-732) were filed April 10 and April 11 respectively.

An Energy Committee spokesman said the unusual step of filing separate reports on two identical bills was taken at the request of John A. Durkin, D-N.H., a panel member who sponsored S 743. Durkin wanted to have a Senate numbered bill on the floor to provide more tactical flexibility during debate and in conference, the spokesman said.

Eight committee members filed dissents to passage of Title III. They argued it would have an anti-competitive effect despite its intent, that there was insufficient evidence that it was needed, that the Justice Department and the Federal Trade Commission opposed it and that the remedy was unworkable.

Senate Floor Action

The Senate passed HR 130 May 9 on a 95-0 vote, after accepting a last-minute compromise amendment by Dale Bumpers, D-Ark., that provided for an Energy Department study of how oil refiners subsidize the sale of gasoline to stations.

The Bumpers amendment replaced the controversial Title III section of the measure reported by the Senate Energy Committee that prohibited refineries from subsidizing sales to gasoline stations they owned with funds or services derived from other operations of their company.

The National Congress of Petroleum Retailers, representing station owners, and the National Oil Jobbers Council, representing wholesalers, both favored outlawing subsidies from refiners. But while the jobbers supported the committee version of Title III, the retailers withheld their support from the controversial title in hopes of aiding passage of the rest of the bill.

Attempts to modify Title III dominated the debate on HR 130, which began May 5 and resumed May 9.

Bumper's amendment required the Energy Department to conduct a study of the extent to which producers, refiners and other motor fuel suppliers subsidize retail and wholesale sales with profits from other operations. The department also was required to make legislative recommendations to Congress within 18 months after the date of enactment. The amendment gave the president authority to develop interim methods for maintaining competition in gasoline sales. The amendment was adopted by voice vote.

Sen. Pete V. Domenici, R-N.M., author of Title III as reported by the Energy Committee, said the study called for in the amendment was like "prescribing aspirin for a severed jugular." But he conceded that the original Title III lacked sufficient votes for passage.

Sen. Edward M. Kennedy, D-Mass., then offered an amendment to make the findings of the Energy Department study available to the Federal Trade Commission (FTC) and the Justice Department.

The Energy Department should share its information with the agencies "that have the primary responsibility for protecting the little guy, the corner gas station," Kennedy argued in support of his proposal.

But the amendment was denounced by Bumpers, who warned that "the Secretary of Energy would not get into the front door," if the oil companies thought the Justice Department or the FTC would get the information.

Kennedy chided Bumpers for believing that "those nice, benevolent oil companies" would "give us all the information we want."

But Bumpers shot back that the Kennedy proposal provided no more clout for extracting information from the oil companies than his own amendment.

Members voted 55-38 to table the Kennedy amendment.

Final Action. The House accepted the Senate amendments to HR 130 by voice vote on June 6, clearing the bill for the president.

Strip Mining

Legislation authorizing $100 million in fiscal 1979-80 to carry out the 1977 strip mining control law (PL 95-87) was cleared by the Senate July 28 and sent to the president. *(Background, strip mining chapter)*

The bill (S 2463) increased the amounts originally provided under the Surface Mining Control and Reclamation Act for federal enforcement and state inspection programs and for aid to operators of small mines who were required to conduct various hydrologic and geologic tests.

The bill authorized $25 million each in fiscal 1979 and 1980 for state enforcement and federal inspection programs. Another $25 million in each of those years was authorized for the testing program. Under existing law, authorizations were pegged at a total of $30 million annually for the three programs.

The Senate Energy and Natural Resources Committee, which reported S 2463 May 9 (S Rept 95-788), recommended $25 million annually for fiscal 1979-80 for the

enforcement and test programs. An additional $15 million was authorized for the test program for each of the next 13 fiscal years.

The Senate approved S 2463 by voice vote May 16.

The House Interior and Insular Affairs Committee reported its version of the bill (HR 11827—H Rept 95-1143) May 12. The committee limited the authorization for the enforcement programs to $25 million for fiscal 1979, but provided such sums as necessary in fiscal 1980.

The House and Senate committee staffs worked out a compromise substitute bill. The bill retained the Senate-approved authorization of $25 million annually for fiscal 1979-80 for the enforcement programs, but eliminated the Senate's provision for 13-years of authorizations after fiscal 1980 for the small mine operators program.

The House approved the substitute version of HR 11827 July 11 by a 323-74 vote under suspension of the rules, a procedure that requires a two-thirds vote for passage and does not permit amendments.

The House then substituted the provisions of HR 11827 for those of S 2463 and returned the bill to the Senate, which passed it July 28 (PL 95-343).

Uranium Mill Waste Control

A program to clean up some 25 million tons of potentially hazardous uranium wastes was cleared by Congress Oct. 15.

The bill (HR 13650 — PL 95-604) mandating the cleanup also provided for stricter controls on future handling and disposal of wastes from the processing of uranium.

A substitute version of the bill was passed by the Senate Oct. 13. The House amended that substitute Oct. 14, and the Senate then accepted the final House version.

The major dispute between the two houses was resolved when the Senate agreed to accept House language calling for the federal government to pay 90 percent of the cleanup cost, with the remaining 10 percent to be paid by states where the wastes were located. The Senate had previously insisted that the federal government pay 100 percent of the cleanup costs.

Under existing law, no federal agency had explicit authority to regulate or dispose of wastes at abandoned uranium mills. *(Uranium wastes, p. 123)*

Energy Research

The Senate Feb. 8 by voice vote sent President Carter a new version of the energy research bill (S 1811) he vetoed Nov. 5, 1977. The new bill (S 1340 — PL 95-238) was identical to the earlier measure except that it dropped the two provisions opposed by the president: authorization of $80 million to continue work on the Clinch River breeder reactor and language revising uranium pricing arrangements. It had been passed by the House by voice vote Dec. 7, 1977. *(1977 action, p. 93-A)*

S 1340 provided $6,081,400,000 for energy research programs in fiscal 1978. During brief debate, senators stressed that passage of the authorization without Clinch River funds should not be construed as deauthorization of the project. Funding for the project in fiscal 1978 was contained in a supplemental appropriations bill (HR 9375).

Nuclear Agency Funds

Congress Oct. 15 cleared and sent to the president a bill authorizing $333 million for the Nuclear Regulatory Commission in fiscal 1979. That amount was $900,000 more than the House had voted and $3.4 million less than the Senate approved.

The bill (S 2584 — PL 95-601) directed the NRC to undertake major studies on the adequacy of safeguards at nuclear power plants and of the role to be played by states in the storage of nuclear wastes.

The Senate passed its version Sept. 18. The House adopted its bill (HR 12355) Oct. 4.

The energy and public works appropriations bill (HR 12928 — H J Res 1139) appropriated $322.3 million for the NRC in fiscal 1979.

Provisions

As cleared by Congress, S 2584:

● Authorized $333,007,000 for NRC operations in fiscal 1979, an increase of $35.3 million over fiscal 1978.

● Earmarked $1,152 million for studies of unresolved nuclear safety issues and to reduce a backlog of license applications.

● Earmarked $1 million for studies and evaluations of alternative fuel cycles.

● Required the NRC to prepare a report on ways in which states might participate in the siting, licensing and development of nuclear waste storage and disposal facilities.

● Earmarked $650,000 to develop a plan for a long-range study of the health effects of low-level radiation.

● Required the NRC to prepare an annual report on the adequacy of safeguards at facilities licensed and regulated by the commission.

● Tightened NRC internal operations by including new prohibitions on conflicts of interest involving contracts and requiring more careful commission scrutiny of its contracts.

Senate Action

In the Senate, the Committee on Environment and Public Works urged funding boosts totaling $5.725 million above the administration request (S 2584 — S Rept 95-848).

The committee also urged shifts totaling $8.1 million within the administration's request.

The Senate Sept. 18 by voice vote passed the bill making fiscal 1979 authorizations of $336.4 million for the Nuclear Regulatory Commission. Passage came after adoption of a floor amendment that provided for future NRC regulation of uranium wastes and mandated a study of which federal agencies should have jurisdiction over radioactive wastes of all kinds.

Calling for expanded NRC authority, Sen. Gary Hart, D-Colo., said the uranium wastes "are just as radioactive as the original uranium ore from which they came. In fact, if tailings are not properly controlled, they can be more dangerous than radioactive wastes generated by power plants and nuclear weapons programs."

Hart and Pete V. Domenici, R-N.M., sponsored the amendment giving NRC additional authority over uranium wastes. Hart was chairman of the Nuclear Regulation Subcommittee of the Environment and Public Works Committee.

As passed by the Senate, the amendment required the NRC and the EPA to develop standards for the storage of uranium mill tailings. After three years, the NRC would license and regulate all uranium tailing disposal sites, including previously abandoned sites. States would be allowed to maintain jurisdiction over mill sites if their standards were as rigid as the federal standards.

The amendment did not directly address the issue of immediately cleaning up uranium mill sites that were already abandoned.

The Senate amendment also required a study by March 1978 of the costs and benefits of expanding NRC regulations of all nuclear wastes, including those from nuclear power plants. The study would help Congress develop legislation in 1979.

Sponsors of the authorization bill avoided a potentially sticky floor fight over the issue of paying for citizen participation in NRC proceedings.

Sen. Patrick J. Leahy, D-Vt , proposed an amendment adding $500,000 to the NRC budget in fiscal 1979, and $3 million in fiscal 1980, for an "Office of Nuclear Energy Public Counsel." The counsel would represent communities and citizen groups before the NRC. But Leahy withdrew the amendment when Hart promised his subcommittee would hold hearings on the matter in 1979.

House Action

In its May 15 report, the House Interstate and Foreign Commerce Committee recommended additions totaling $3.43 million to the commission request (H Rept 95-1089, Part 2).

Of that, $2 million went for a program to pay the expenses of citizens who participated in proceedings before the NRC. Another $1.5 million went to the Office of Nuclear Reactor Regulation to beef up staff and programs for resolving safety issues and reducing the backlog of license applications. And the remaining $285,000 went for a program to insure the safety of nuclear exports.

As reported by the Commerce Committee, the $2 million would be used by the commission to establish a five-year program to help pay costs of eligible citizen intervenors.

The House Interior and Insular Affairs Committee reported its version of HR 12355 April 26 (H Rept 95-1089). The committee bill did not authorize funds for citizen intervenors, but in additional views filed with the committee report, seven Democrats, including panel chairman Morris K. Udall, D-Ariz., called for such a program and announced they would support the idea on the floor.

As reported by the Interior Committee, HR 12355 authorized $330.95 million in fiscal 1979 for the NRC, $285,000 more than the administration's $330.67 million request.

The House Oct. 4 approved the fiscal 1979 authorization for the Nuclear Regulatory Commission without having to deal with the controversial issue of providing federal money for citizen participation in NRC proceedings. The bill was passed by voice vote under suspension of the rules.

A House Commerce Committee amendment providing $2 million for citizen participation was withdrawn before the NRC authorization bill (HR 12355) came to the House floor.

House Republicans had promised to fight the citizen participation funding, and a protracted floor dispute on the issue could have tied up the entire NRC authorization bill.

The House bill authorized $332.1 million during fiscal 1979 for the NRC, an increase of $1.4 million over the NRC request.

Most of the difference — $1.2 million — came from a Commerce Committee amendment that authorized the commission to hire 35 additional employees to speed up the processing of nuclear power plant applications.

The citizen participation provision produced a strong reaction from Republicans who generally opposed federal funding for citizens' groups that intervened in regulatory actions.

Rep. Clarence J. Brown, R-Ohio, said it would be "a dangerous thing for the government to use tax revenues to finance one particular point of view before a regulatory commission."

One strong supporter of the citizen participation funding, Rep. Morris K. Udall, D-Ariz., said he would try in 1979 to get that provision added to Carter administration proposals to streamline the nuclear power plant licensing process. Those proposals were introduced earlier in 1978 but died in the 95th Congress.

In floor debate on the NRC bill, Udall said citizens who intervene in NRC cases should be reimbursed for their expenses because they "make important contributions to the regulatory process."

Conference, Final Action

Conferees filed their report on the bill Oct. 14 (S Rept 95-1796).

The conferees eliminated a provision that would have authorized the commission to regulate hazardous wastes from uranium processing mills. The provision had been attached by the Senate. But Oct. 14 Congress cleared HR 13650, which gave the commission the authority to regulate those wastes and which mandated a federal-state cleanup program. *(Uranium wastes, p. 123)*

Conferees adopted a Senate provision requiring the NRC to conduct a study by March 1979 of the costs and benefits of expanding NRC regulations to all nuclear wastes, including those from nuclear power plants. The study would help Congress develop legislation in 1979.

The House adopted the conference report Oct. 14 and the Senate followed suit Oct. 15.

Energy Boom Town Aid

Federal aid to energy boom towns died in the 95th Congress because of a disagreement in the Senate over whether to give grants as well as loans to affected communities.

A bill (S 1493), sponsored by Sen. Gary Hart, D-Colo., was aimed at helping communities whose services were overburdened by a sudden population explosion brought on by energy development, such as the opening of a coal field.

As reported by the Senate Environment Committee June 27, the bill provided $750 million in loans and grants to municipalities and Indian tribes over five years, with $150 million available annually. Each year, $15 million would go for grants; $15 million for emergency loans, loan guarantees or grants; and the remaining $120 million for a revolving loan fund run by state governments.

But the bill ran into trouble when it was referred to the Senate Governmental Affairs Committee. There, Energy Subcommittee Chairman John Glenn, D-Ohio, was skeptical about the need for grants. He reasoned that boom towns would develop local tax bases large enough to repay loans easily.

Advocates of grants replied that some communities would never realize sufficient tax revenue to build the hospitals, sewers and other facilities necessary to accommodate the increased population.

Glenn's subcommittee voted to knock out loans. But after negotiation with supporters of the Hart version, Glenn softened his position. At his behest, the full Governmental Affairs Committee Sept. 28 agreed to allow grants on a case-by-case basis if the secretary of commerce determined that there was "no practical alternative."

But backers of the Hart version were not satisfied with this either. They argued that the "no practical alternative" phrase did not adequately spell out the criteria.

"Some states prohibit going into debt," said a Hart staffer. "Does this mean that they have to try to change their constitutions to qualify?"

The staffs of the two committees tried to work out a compromise in the hectic closing days of the session, but failed.

A plan in the House to seek passage of a companion bill (HR 13559), which resembled the Hart version, also failed.

Observers said inland energy impact legislation likely would be enacted in 1979, when there would be time to fashion a compromise in the dispute over grants.

Liquefied Energy Gases

A bill to provide tougher federal regulation of the land transport and storage of highly explosive liquefied natural and petroleum gases passed the House in 1978, but the Senate took no action on the proposals.

The bill (HR 11622) was approved by the House Sept. 12 by voice vote and was substituted for the text of S 1895, a minor Senate-passed bill. There was no Senate companion to HR 11622, however, and the Senate declined to consider any of the House provisions on such topics as safety requirements for liquefied natural gas (LNG) storage facilities and reporting requirements for gas pipeline operators. Thus the bill died at adjournment.

Background

Liquefied petroleum gas (LPG) accidents in Spain and Mexico claimed about 200 lives, plus increasing publicity about the dangers of LNG had focused attention on the potential hazards of the fuels.

A report by the General Accounting Office (GAO), released July 31, detailed some of the dangers.

LNG. LNG is natural gas that has been reduced to −261 degrees Fahrenheit and the compressed 1/600th of its volume to make it easier to store and transport. The United States imported LNG from Algeria. Surplus domestic natural gas also was turned into LNG during slack periods so it could be stored for later use. Tank trucks sometimes carried LNG from storage facilities to terminals where it was distributed for home heating or industrial use. When the gas was needed, the LNG was regasified and fed through existing pipelines.

In 1978, LNG provided less than 1 percent of the nation's energy, but the Department of Energy predicted that by 1985 21 percent of the gas consumed in the United States would be imported.

There were two facilities receiving LNG ships from abroad — one at Everett, Mass., in the district of Edward J. Markey, D-Mass., cosponsor of the legislation, and the other at Cove Point, Md.

A typical tanker carried up to 125,000 cubic meters of LNG, and larger, 33-million-gallon ships were expected to be in service soon. There also were 121 "peak shaving" facilities — used to liquefy and store gas during slack periods — with a combined storage capacity of 2 million cubic meters. Nearly all of them were located in or near highly populated areas, according to the House Commerce Committee.

The committee estimated that if Energy Department estimates were true, three large LNG tankers would be entering U.S. waters on an average day and three to five new LNG storage facilities would have to be built. HR 11622 did not deal with LNG shipping.

LNG is heavier than air at -261 F, but becomes lighter than air when it warms to -160 F. "As it warms," the committee said, "LNG vaporizes and expands its volume significantly — eventually reaching 600 times its liquid volume — and moves with the prevailing winds. The drifting gas cloud that results could be ignited by any spark — even one as small as that caused by an auto horn."

The committee estimated that an accident involving release of 125,000 cubic meters of LNG from a typical tanker could produce a flaming cloud 20 miles long and five miles wide.

An LNG accident in Cleveland in 1944, caused when a storage tank gave way, killed 128 persons, injured 300 and caused $7 million in property damage.

A spokesman for the American Gas Association asserted that the structural problems that caused the 1944 accident had been corrected and that all plans for future LNG import facilities called for them to be located in remote areas. "The safety record speaks for itself," he said.

He said LNG facilities were reviewed by the Department of Energy. "We feel [the bill] is duplicative of regulations and authority already in current law," he said.

LPG. LPG is the name given to a whole category of fuels, including propane and butane, used for home heating, crop drying and other purposes. LPG normally was shipped by truck, rail or barge to one of the nation's 8,000 storage facilities where it was redistributed to consumers. LPG is heavier than air. If it were released, it would form a highly flammable cloud clinging to the ground and sinking into sewers and subway tunnels.

The committee said that 9,000 gallons of LNG or LPG, the amount carried by the average truck, could fill 110 miles of a 6-ft. sewer or 15 miles of a 16-ft. subway tunnel, "turning them into subterranean bombs of enormous destructive potential."

Some LPG explosions erupt "with enormous power creating a fireball and mushroom cloud which resembles that associated with nuclear explosions," the committee said. "The force of the explosion can propel a ruptured tank like a rocket, trailing liquid flame hundreds of feet."

The committee said the fact that LPG storage facilities often included more than one tank increased the danger.

In testimony before Congress, Francis H. McAdams, a member of the National Transportation Safety Board,

reported that although LPG was involved in only 9.7 percent of all reported liquid gas pipeline accidents in the previous nine years, it caused 65.5 percent of the reported deaths, 48 percent of the injuries and 30.5 percent of the property damage.

The committee said that there were 225,000 miles of pipe used to transport LPG.

Natural Gas. The Commerce Committee also addressed the hazards of natural gas, which was distributed to 44.6 million residential customers and accounted for more than 40 percent of domestic industrial energy consumption.

The committee said that about 750,000 natural gas leaks were reported each year. In 1976, 1,500 of those resulted in accidents that caused 63 deaths and 366 serious injuries.

Of the 1.4 million miles of natural gas lines in service, about 90 percent were built after 1971, the year the natural gas Pipeline Safety Act of 1968 (PL 90-481) went into effect. As a result, most lines were not covered by federal safety regulations, the committee said.

Information about pipelines built before 1971 was sketchy, but experts had speculated that some were built in the late 1840s, the report said, noting that one company was using pipe that it bought second-hand and installed 116 years before.

"Thus, the very pipeline which, due to age and less sophisticated technology at the time of installation, may be expected to present the greatest hazard, has not been subject to safety standards, and will not be required to be subject to such standards until an accident occurs," the report said.

The Gas Association spokesman said complying with the reporting requirements would be very expensive and that the cost would be passed on to consumers. He also questioned the value of the required data.

He said a committee provision requiring utilities to report all leaks they knew about or should have known about was ambiguous. "If they were known, they would have been reported," he said.

House Committee Action

The committee reported HR 11622 May 15 (H Rept 95-1167), and authorized $13.5 million for the bill in fiscal 1979.

The committee noted that the 1968 act gave the Transportation Department responsibility for setting standards for the safe design, construction, operation and maintenance of liquid and gas pipelines and related facilities. But the committee accused the department of failing to "forcefully and effectively" carry out the law.

The department's Office of Pipeline Safety Operation, designated to carry out the program, had not had a permanent director for seven of the previous 10 years.

"Lacking effective leadership," the report said, "the office has tended to follow the path of least resistance, adopting industry 'consensus' standards, delaying entry into controversial areas, and generally avoiding facing up to the hard issues of public safety by adopting the most conservative interpretation of its authorities and responsibility."

The committee chided the department for failing to adopt standards for the siting, design, operation and maintenance of LNG facilities.

To deal with the problem, the committee bill stipulated that no one could serve as acting director of the office for more than 180 days. If a permanent director were not appointed by then, the secretary of transportation had to personally administer the office. The panel said it would exercise "vigorous oversight" to assure the provision was met.

House Floor Action

The House passed HR 11622 Sept. 12 by voice vote. The bill had been slated to reach the floor July 26, but it was pulled off the schedule because its sponsors — John D. Dingell, D-Mich., chairman of the Commerce Subcommittee on Energy and Power, and Markey — objected to the Rules Committee's action on the bill.

The Rules Committee voted July 25 to bar a conference on HR 11622 and the minor Senate-passed bill (S 1895), but reversed itself Aug. 10 and approved a rule allowing the House to substitute the provisions of HR 11622 for those of S 1895, a routine reauthorization for the Department of Transportation's Office of Pipeline Safety. The House made the substitution after passing HR 11622.

As passed by the House, HR 11622 authorized the secretary of transportation to require natural gas pipeline operators to remove hazards in their lines and to provide information on line safety, such as location, age, type of material transported and geological conditions. The bill also required operators to report all pipeline leaks they knew about or should have known about.

Under the bill, the transportation secretary was authorized to approve construction of all new LNG facilities. However, the secretary was not given the authority to select sites. The secretary was also directed to establish standards for the location, construction operation and maintenance of new LNG facilities within six months after the date of enactment. The bill authorized $13.5 million in fiscal 1979 to carry out the program.

Supporters argued that the tougher safety regulations were needed to prevent catastrophic explosions and fires that could result from ignition of LNG or LPG truck or storage tank leaks.

They also argued that the poor condition of a large percentage of natural gas pipelines made the bill's pipeline leak reporting requirement necessary.

Opponents of the legislation countered that the natural gas industry has maintained an exemplary safety record. They argued that pipeline leaks were easy to spot and that the bill would force gas companies to pass on the cost of what they called the bill's onerous reporting requirements to consumers.

The House passed HR 11622 by voice vote after adopting an amendment by Robert W. Edgar, D-Pa. It required the transportation secretary to conduct a study to determine whether LPG storage and transportation facilities should be covered by the act. The amendment required the secretary to report to Congress within one year of enactment.

Selected Bibliography on Energy Policy

Books and Reports

Abrahamson, Bernhard, ed. *The Changing Economics of World Energy.* Boulder, Colo.: Westview Press, 1976.

Barzel, Yoram and Hall, Christopher D. *The Political Economy of the Oil Import Quota.* Stanford, Calif.: Hoover Institution Press, 1977.

Blair, John M. *The Control of Oil.* New York: Pantheon Books, 1977.

Bohi, Doughlas R. *U.S. Energy Policy: Alternatives for Security.* Baltimore: The Johns Hopkins University Press, 1975.

Brannon, Gerard M. *Energy Taxes and Subsidies: A Report to the Energy Policy Project of the Ford Foundation.* Cambridge, Mass.: Ballinger, 1974.

Breyer, Stephen. *Energy Regulation by the Federal Power Commission.* Washington: Brookings Institution, 1974.

Brown, William M. and Kahn, Herbert. *Suggestions for a Phase II National Energy Policy: Final Report for the Period March 1977-September 1977.* Prepared for the U.S. Energy Research and Development Administration. New York: Hudson Institute, 1977.

Carnesale, Albert et al. *Options for U.S. Energy Policy.* San Francisco: Institute for Contemporary Studies, 1977.

Cogan, John. *Energy and Jobs: A Long Run Analysis.* Ottawa, Ill.: Green Hill Publishers, 1976.

Commission on Critical Choices for Americans. *Vital Resources.* Lexington, Mass.: D. C. Heath, 1977.

Commoner, Barry, ed. *Energy and Human Welfare: A Critical Analysis.* 3 vols. New York: Macmillan, 1975.

Commoner, Barry. *The Poverty of Power: Energy and the Economic Crisis.* New York: Knopf; distributed by Random House, 1976.

Congressional Quarterly. *Continuing Energy Crisis in America.* Washington: Congressional Quarterly, 1975.

Cose, Ellis. *Energy and the Urban Crisis.* Washington: Joint Center for Political Studies, 1978.

_____, and Morris, Milton, eds. *Energy Policy and the Poor: A Roundtable Discussion.* Washington, D.C.: Joint Center for Political Studies, 1977.

Coyne, John R. and Coyne, Patricia. *The Big Breakup: Energy in Crisis.* Mission, Kan.: Sheed Andrews & McMeel Inc., 1977.

Darmstadter, Joel. *Energy in the World Economy: A Statistical Review of Trends in Output, Trade, and Consumption Since 1925.* Washington: Resources for the Future, 1972.

Doran, Charles F. *Myth, Oil, and Politics: Introduction to the Political Economy of Petroleum.* New York: The Free Press, 1977.

Editorial Research Reports. *Earth, Energy and Environment.* Washington: Congressional Quarterly, 1977.

Engler, Robert. *The Brotherhood of Oil: Energy Policy and the Public Interest.* Chicago: University of Chicago Press, 1977.

_____. *The Politics of Oil: A Study of Private Power and Democratic Directions.* Chicago: University of Chicago Press, 1961.

Eppen, Gary D., ed. *Energy: The Policy Issues.* Chicago: University of Chicago Press, 1977.

Institute for Electrical and Electronic Engineering. *Fuel for Electric Power to 1984.* New York: Institute for Electrical and Electronic Engineers, 1974.

Gordon, Richard L. *Coal and the Electric Power Industry.* Baltimore: Johns Hopkins University Press, 1975.

Hagel, John. *Alternative Energy Strategies: Constraints and Opportunities.* New York: Praeger, 1976.

Herman, Stewart H. et al. *Energy Futures: Industry and New Technologies.* Cambridge, Mass.: Ballinger, 1977.

Johnson, William et al. *Competition in the Oil Industry.* Washington: George Washington University Energy Policy Research Project, 1976.

Kalter, Robert J. and Vogely, William, eds. *Energy Supply and Government Policy.* Ithaca, N.Y.: Cornell University Press, 1976.

Krueger, Robert B., ed. *The United States and International Oil: A Report for the Federal Energy Administration on U.S. Firms and Government Policy.* New York: Praeger, 1975.

MacAvoy, Paul W. *Federal Energy Administration Regulation: Report of the Presidential Task Force.* Washington: American Enterprise Institute for Public Policy Research, 1977.

MacAvoy, Paul W., and Pindyck, Robert S. *Price Controls and the Natural Gas Shortage.* Washington: American Enterprise Institute for Public Policy Research, 1975.

McFarland, Andrew S. *Public Interest Lobbies: Decision Making on Energy.* Washington: American Enterprise Institute for Public Policy Research, 1977.

Mancke, Richard. *The Failure of U.S. Energy Policy.* New York: Columbia University Press, 1974.

_____. *Squeaking By: U.S. Energy Policy Since the Embargo.* New York: Columbia University Press, 1976.

Markham, Jesse et al. *Horizontal Divestiture and the Petroleum Industry.* Cambridge, Mass.: Ballinger, 1977.

Mitchell, Edward J. *Energy: Regional Goals and the National Interest.* Washington: American Enterprise Institute for Public Policy Research, 1976.

_____. *Perspective on U.S. Energy Policy: A Critique of Regulation.* New York: Praeger, 1976.

_____, ed. *The Question of Offshore Oil.* Washington: American Enterprise Institute for Public Policy Research, 1976.

Natural Gas Pricing Alternatives. A Report Prepared for Natural Gas Supply Committee. Washington: Foster Associates Inc., September 19, 1977.

Newman, Dorothy K. and Day, Dawn. *The American Energy Consumer.* Cambridge, Mass.: Ballinger, 1975.

Noreng, Oystein. *Oil Politics in the 1980s: Patterns of International Cooperation.* New York: McGraw-Hill, 1978.

Organization for Economic Cooperation and Development. *World Energy Outlook.* Paris: Organization for Economic Cooperation and Development, 1977.

O'Toole, James. *Energy and Social Change.* Cambridge, Mass.: M.I.T. Press, 1976.

Perlman, Robert and Warren, Roland L. *Families in the Energy Crisis: Impacts and Implications for Theory and Policy.* Cambridge, Mass.: Ballinger, 1977.

Phelps, Charles and Smith, Rodney T. *Petroleum Regulation: The False Dilemma of Decontrol.* Santa Monica, Calif.: Rand Corporation, 1977.

Phillips, Owen. *The Last Chance Energy Book.* Baltimore: The Johns Hopkins University Press, 1978.

Richardson, Harry W. *Economic Aspects of the Energy Crisis.* Lexington, Mass.: Lexington Books, 1975.

Russell, Milton. "Energy." In *Setting National Priorities: The 1978 Budget,* pp. 317-353. Edited by Joseph A. Pechman. Washington: Brookings Institution, 1977.

Sampson, Anthony. *The Seven Sisters: The Great Oil Companies and the World They Made.* New York: Viking Press, 1975.

Scheffer, Walter F., ed. *Energy Impacts on Public Policy and Administration.* Norman, Okla.: University of Oklahoma Press, 1976.

Schurr, Sam H. *Energy in the American Economy 1850-1975.* Baltimore: Johns Hopkins University Press, 1972.

Scott, David L. *Financing the Growth of Electric Utilities.* New York: Praeger, 1976.

Sunder, William. *Oil Industry Profits.* Washington: American Enterprise Institute for Public Policy Research, 1977.

Tietenberg, Thomas H. and Toureille, Pierre. *Energy Planning and Policy: The Political Economy of Project Independence.* Lexington, Mass.: Lexington Books, 1976.

Trager, Frank N., ed. *Oil, Divestiture and National Security.* New York: Crane, Russak & Company Inc., 1977.

Turner, Louis. *Oil Companies in the International System.* London: Institute of International Affairs. Boston: Allen & Unwin, 1978.

Twentieth Century Fund, Task Force on United States Energy Policy. *Providing for Energy.* New York: McGraw-Hill, 1977.

Vernon, Raymond. *The Oil Crisis.* New York: Norton, 1976.

Wildhorn, Sorrel. *How to Save Gasoline: Public Policy Alternatives for the Automobile.* Cambridge, Mass.: Ballinger, 1976.

Willrich, Mason. *Administration of Energy Shortages: Natural Gas and Petroleum.* Cambridge, Mass.: Ballinger, 1976.

Wilson, Carroll L., et al. *Energy: Global Prospects 1985-2000: A Report of the Workshop on Alternative Energy Strategies.* New York: McGraw-Hill, 1977.

Articles

"America's Energy Resources: An Overview." *Current History,* May/June 1978.

Boulding, Kenneth E. "Anxiety, Uncertainty, and Energy." *Society,* January 1978, pp. 28-33.

Browne, Lynn E., and Syron, Richard F. "The Deregulation of Natural Gas: Its Potential Impact on New England." *New England Economic Review,* September/October 1976, pp. 45-66.

Cambel, A. B. "Alternatives to the Energy Crisis." *Current History,* July 1978, pp. 16-18.

Campbell, Colin and Reese, Thomas. "The Energy Crisis and Tax Policy in Canada and the United States: Federal-Provincial Diplomacy vs. Congressional Lawmaking." *Social Science Journal,* January 1977, pp. 17-32.

Casper, B. M. "Congress and the Cozy Triangles: The Case of Energy." *Bulletin of the Atomic Scientists,* May 1977, pp. 33-35.

Church, Frank. "The Impotence of Oil Companies," *Foreign Policy,* Summer 1977, pp. 27-51.

Cohn, Herbert B. "The President's Energy Program and the Job that Needs to Be Done." *Public Utilities Fortnightly,* August 4, 1977, pp. 11-16.

Commoner, Barry. "For A New Energy Policy." *Current,* March 1977, pp. 17-22.

"Controversy Over U.S. Energy Policy: Pros and Cons." *Congressional Digest,* August/September 1978, pp. 193-224.

Corrigan, Richard. "The Energy Tax Bill's Long Road from the Senate to Conference." *National Journal,* Nov. 5, 1977, pp. 1716-1719.

"The Energy Crisis: Reality or Myth." *Annals of the American Academy of Political and Social Science,* November 1973.

Gibbons, John H. and Chandler, William U. "A National Energy Conservation Policy." *Current History,* July/August 1978, pp. 13-15.

Goldstein, Walter. "The Political Failure of U.S. Energy Policy." *Bulletin of the Atomic Scientists,* November 1978, pp. 17-19.

Greening, Timothy S. "Increasing Competition in the Oil Industry: Government Standards for Gasoline." *Harvard Journal on Legislation,* February 1977, pp. 193-224.

Hall, Robert E., and Pindyck, Robert S. "The Conflicting Goals of National Energy Policy." *Public Interest,* Spring 1977, pp. 3-15.

Hamer, John. "Oil Taxation." In *Editorial Research Reports,* Vol. I, pp. 203-220. Washington: Editorial Research Reports, 1974.

Heiman, Grover. "Energy: Searching for Substitutes." *Nation's Business,* September 1978, pp. 78-84.

Hohenemser, K. H. "Energy Efficiency vs. Energy Growth." *Environment,* June 1978, pp. 4-5.

Hyatt, Sherry V. "Thermal Efficiency and Taxes: The Residential Energy Conservation Tax Credit." *Harvard Journal on Legislation,* February 1977, pp. 281-326.

Louviere, Vernon. "Energy: Here Today, Gone Tomorrow." *Nation's Business,* December 1978, pp. 28-34.

Lovins, A. B. "Energy Strategy: The Road Not Taken?" *Foreign Affairs,* October 1976, pp. 65-96.

Manne, Alan S. "What Happens When Our Oil and Gas Runs Out?" *Harvard Business Review,* July/August 1975, pp. 123-137.

Moran, Theodore H. "Why Oil Prices Go Up — The Future: OPEC Wants Them." *Foreign Policy,* Winter 1976, pp. 58-77

Oppenheim, V. H. "Why Oil Prices Go Up — The Past: We Pushed Them." *Foreign Policy,* Winter 1976, pp. 24-57.

Phillips, Kevin P. "The Energy Battle: Why the White House Misfired." *Public Opinion,* May/June 1978, pp. 9-14.

Pindyck, Robert S. "OPEC's Threat to the West." *Foreign Policy,* Spring 1978, pp. 36-52.

Rasche, Robert H., and Tatom, John A. "Energy Resources and Potential GNP." *Federal Reserve St. Louis,* June 1977, pp. 10-24.

Rohatyn, F. G. "Energy Problems and Our Cities: Solving Two Problems Jointly." *Current,* October 1977, pp. 3-6.

Ronan, William J. "Transit and the Energy Crisis: Change Coming in City/Suburban Dynamics." *Journal of the Institute for Socioeconomic Studies,* Autumn 1977, pp. 9-16.

Rosa, Eugene. "The Public and the Energy Problem: Opinion Surveys Show a Minimal Level of Concern." *Bulletin of the Atomic Scientists,* April 1978, pp. 5-7.

Rosen, G. R. "Coal: Carter and Congress Hold the Key." *Dun's Review,* February 1977, pp. 56-60.

Rustow, Dankwart A. "U.S.-Saudi Relations and the Oil Crises of the 1980s." *Foreign Affairs,* April 1977, pp. 494-516.

Rycroft, Robert W. "U.S. Energy Demand and Supply." *Current History,* March 1978, pp. 100-103.

Sawhill, John. "A Gasoline Tax-Rebate: Needed Now." *The Journal of the Institute for Socioeconomic Studies,* Spring 1977, pp. 71-79.

Scandalls, Helen. "Coal — and Consequences." *Environmental Action.* Nov. 5, 1977, pp. 3-5.

Singer, S. Fred. "Limits to Arab Oil Power." *Foreign Policy,* Spring 1978, pp. 53-67.

Weinberg, Alvin M. "Reflections on the Energy Wars." *American Scientist,* March/April 1978, pp. 153-158.

Wirth, Timothy E. "Congressional Policy Making and the Politics of Energy." *Journal of Energy and Development,* Autumn 1975, pp. 93-104.

Yergin, Daniel. "The Real Meaning of the Energy Crunch." *New York Times Magazine,* June 4, 1978, pp. 32; 92-98.

Government Publications

Solar Energy and America's Future. Prepared by Stanford Research Institute for the Energy Research and Development Administration. Springfield, Va.: National Technical Information Service, 1977.

U.S. Congress. Congressional Budget Office. *Energy Policy Alternatives.* Washington: Government Printing Office, 1977.

U.S. Congress. Congressional Budget Office. *President Carter's Energy Proposals: A Perspective.* Washington: Government Printing Office, 1977.

U.S. Congress. House. Committee on Banking, Finance and Urban Affairs. *National Energy Act, Hearings May 23-26, June 1, 1977.* 95th Cong., 1st sess. Washington: Government Printing Office, 1977.

U.S. Congress. House. Committee on Banking, Finance and Urban Affairs. Subcommittee on the City. *Energy and the City, Hearings, September 14-16, 1977.* 95th Cong., 1st sess. Washington: Government Printing Office, 1977.

U.S. Congress. House. Committee on Interstate and Foreign Commerce, Subcommittee on Energy and Power. *Compilation of Energy Related Legislation — Vol. 1: Oil, Gas, and Electric Power; Vol. 2: Other Energy Legislation.* 95th Cong., 1st sess. Washington: Government Printing Office, 1977.

U.S. Congress. House. Committee on Interstate and Foreign Commerce, Subcommittee on Energy and Power. *Electric Utility Rate Reform and Regulatory Improvement, Hearings March 30, 31; April 1, 2, 5, 7-9, 1976.* 94th Cong., 2nd sess. Washington: Government Printing Office, 1976.

U.S. Congress. House. Committee on Interstate and Foreign Commerce, Subcommittee on Energy and Power. *Energy Information Handbook.* 95th Cong., 1st sess. Washington: Government Printing Office, 1977.

U.S. Congress. House. Committee on Interstate and Foreign Commerce, Subcommittee on Energy and Power. *Energy Information Digest: Basic Data on Energy Resources, Reserves, Production, Consumption and Prices.* 95th Cong., 1st sess. Washington: Government Printing Office, 1977.

U.S. Congress. House. Committee on Interstate and Foreign Commerce. Subcommittee on Energy and Power. *U.S. Energy Demand and Supply, 1976-1985: Limited Options, Unlimited Constraints; Final Report, March 1978.* 95th Cong., 2nd sess. Washington: Government Printing Office, 1978.

U.S. Congress. House Committee on Interstate and Foreign Commerce. Subcommittee on Oversight and Investigations. *Proposed National Energy Plan, Hearings, June 14, 1977.* 95th Cong., 1st sess. Washington: Government Printing Office, 1977.

U.S. Congress. Joint Economic Committee. *The Economics of the President's Proposed Energy Policies, Hearings May 20, 25, 1977.* 95th Cong., 1st sess. Washington: Government Printing Office, 1978.

U.S. Congress. Joint Economic Committee. *JEC Staff Analysis: Projected Taxes and Revenues Under President Carter's Energy Package.* 95th Cong., 1st sess. Washington: Government Printing Office, 1977.

U.S. Congress. Joint Economic Committee. *Economics of Solar Home Heating.* 95th Cong., 1st sess. Washington: Government Printing Office, 1977.

U.S. Congress. Joint Economic Committee. Subcommittee on Energy. *Energy In the Eighties: Can We Avoid Scarcity and Inflation? Hearings, March 8-21, 1978.* 95th Cong., 2nd sess. Washington: Government Printing Office, 1978.

U.S. Congress. Office of Technology Assessment. *Analysis of the Proposed National Energy Plan.* 95th Cong., 1st sess. Washington: Government Printing Office, 1977.

U.S. Congress. Senate. Committee on Energy and Natural Resources. *Authorizations for Department of Energy Civilian Programs, FY79.* Senate Report No. 95-967, July 5, 1978. 95th Cong., 2nd sess. Washington: Government Printing Office, 1978.

U.S. Congress. Senate. Committee on Energy and Natural Resources. *Economic Impact of President Carter's Energy Program, Hearings May 3, 1977.* 95th Cong., 1st sess. Washington: Government Printing Office, 1977.

U.S. Congress. Senate. Committee on Energy and Natural Resources. *Project Independence: U.S. and World Energy Outlook Through 1990.* 95th Cong., 1st sess. Washington: Government Printing Office, 1977.

U.S. Congress. Senate. Committee on Energy and Natural Resources. *Report of the Committee on Energy and Natural Resources to the Committee on the Budget FY79.* Committee Print No. 95-95, March 1978. 95th Cong., 2nd sess. Washington: Government Printing Office, 1978.

U.S. Congress. Senate. Committee on Finance. *Energy Tax Provisions: Summary and Section-by-Section Explanation of Title II of H.R. 8444 as Passed by the House.* 95th Cong., 1st sess. Washington: Government Printing Office, 1977.

U.S. Congress. Senate. Committee on Finance. Subcommittee on Energy and Foundations. *Incentives for Developing New Energy Sources, Hearings, June 20, 21, 1977.* 95th Cong., 1st sess. Washington: Government Printing Office, 1977.

U.S. Congress. Senate. Committee on Governmental Affairs, Subcommittee on Intergovernmental Relations. *Low-Income Family Assistance During Energy Emergency, Hearings February 3, 1977.* 95th Cong., 1st sess. Washington: Government Printing Office, 1977.

Index